A Practical English-Chinese
Pronouncing Dictionary

8C

By the same author

1. Christmas In The Market Place (Translation)

2. A Language Bridge For The Gospel of JoHn (In Mandarin)

3. Marriage and Divorce (Translation)

4. Perla in the Walled City (Translation)

5. Handbook of Doctrine in the Salvation Army (Translation)

6. Cantonese For Foreign Children

7. Conversation Drills in Everyday Cantonese

A Practical English–Chinese Pronouncing Dictionary

by Janey Chen

in collaboration with Ena G. Simms

English,
Chinese Characters,
Romanized Mandarin
and Cantonese

TUTTLE PUBLISHING
Boston, Rutland, Vermont, Tokyo

Published by Tuttle Publishing
an imprint of Periplus Editions (HK) Ltd.

LCC Card No. 78-77122
ISBN 0-8048-1877-0

First paperback edition, 1992
Seventh printing, 2001

Printed in Singapore

Distributed by:

North America
Tuttle Publishing
Distribution Center, Airport Industrial Park
364 Innovation Drive
North Clarendon, VT 05759-9436

Japan
Tuttle Publishing
RK Building, 2nd Floor, 2-13-10 Shimo-Meguro
Meguro-ku, Tokyo 153 0064

Southeast Asia
Berkeley Books Pte Ltd
5 Little Road, #08-01
Singapore 536983

CONTENTS

CONTENTS (Continued)

FOREWORD

I am pleased that Mrs. Janey Chen is publishing her new Pronouncing Dictionary which I am sure will be of great help to foreign students of the Chinese language.

Mrs. Chen is a most appropriate person to compile this dictionary. She has had ten years of teaching experience, seven years at the wellknown Taipei Language Institute in Taiwan and three years at this Center. In each assignment she proved a most competent and understanding teacher, as both institutions have testified. Her work, however, is not confined to teaching. She has devised new methods for teaching beginners of the Chinese language, and has written a number of textbooks for missionary students, prepared Sunday School material, and was one of those who helped revise "Speak Cantonese" Books I. II and III.

We feel grateful to Mrs. Chen for her present effort which is not only beneficial to the students of Chinese, but also to the Center.

B, P. Schoyer,
Chairman, Governing Committe of
the Chinese Language Center,
New Asia College,
The Chinese University of Hong Kong

PREFACE

Repeated entreaties from my students to help them by compiling a dictionary of this type has been my incentive to do so. Students of Chinese generally complain that, to date, there is no concise dictionary which gives both Mandarin and Cantonese pronunciations along with the Chinese characters. This dictionary has been designed to fill that need and to cover as far as possible in 15,000 words, a vocabulary which will be sufficient to cover everyday conversation and also be specialized enough to cover the words and phrases a missionary requires in his calling, or a member of the armed forces in his. Students at all levels should find much help in the various entries under the main heading of one word. The vocabulary of even English speaking students can be enlarged and better understood from these entries, This dictionary was, in fact, begun as a help to missionary students of Chinese. Their calling to spread the Gospel lies very close to my heart. I have, therefore, also put my best endeavours into compiling a religious appendix as comprehensive as possible in a dictionary of this size. May the Lord bless their work and endeavours and my humble efforts.

It is too much to hope that errors have been entirely avoided, I should, therefore, be grateful if users of this dictionary would bring to my notice any errors or important omissions.

Janey Chen

ACKNOWLEDGEMENTS

I am deeply endebted to many friends and students for research assistance, criticism, basic material, preparation of manuscript and help of various kinds. My gratitude goes especially to Mr. B. P. Schoyer, Chairman of the Governing Committee of the Chinese Language Center, New Asia College, the Chinese University of Hong Kong, for his much valued help and encouragement.

Heartfelt gratitude also to the Rev. C. M. Westergren, The China Alliance Press, whose enthusiasm and belief in the project and in my ability, kept me determined and resolute to continue this work.

I am also very grateful to the British Ministry of Defence (Army Department) for their permission to use their Military Service Terms Glossary.

Much credit is due to Mrs. Ena G. Simms for the months of work she has put into the editing of this dictionary. Her wealth of experience gained by years of teaching English as a second language has been invaluable, especially the knowledge gained during her ten years' experience on the staff of the BBC, London, in the English by Radio and Television Department. The lessons broadcast by this department are compiled by the leading experts on the subject who are carrying out research on teaching English as a second language in various universities in Great Britain, consequently Mrs. Simms was able to gain much knowledge and insight from this pioneer work.

I am glad to take this opportunity of showing my gratitude for all the help that has been so generously bestowed on this work and to offer my very sincere thanks.

Janey Chen

INTRODUCTION

The object of this dictionary is to bring under one cover, in a book of reasonable size, as much immediate information as possible about the word being sought and so to save valuable time and energy by avoiding cross reference. Consequently the dictionary has been arranged in four lists; the English word; the Chinese characters with the Chinese phonetics; the romanization in Mandarin with the tone signs; the romanization in Cantonese with tone signs, and where the spoken word differs from the written word, the spoken form is also given. Negative words have not been added where the negative form has been achieved by adding a prefix to a root word although these could have occurred frequently in the Appendix of Religious Terms; for these words reference can be made to the root word in the main dictionary.

Religious Terms In this section a separate page has been devoted to the Books of the Old and New Testaments. A list of the Christian Churches and Organizations in Hong Kong has been given to act as a focal point to those interested in Chinese Missionary work.

Access to Hong Kong is world. wide. A biography of Chinese religious notabilities has been given under the name in alphabetical order in the appendix.

Care has been taken to make the word entries as comprehensive as possible: under the entry "church" are all matters pertaining to the church-dedication, government, history, policy, ritual, etc.; under the entry "religion" the names of eleven world religions have been recorded: the entries of "Priest" and "Reverend" embrace the special terms used for Taoist and Buddhist as well as Protestant and Catholic.

Military Terms: These have been taken verbatim from the official glossary of Service Terms used in the Chinese Language School for the Army, Navy and Airforce personnel. The Mandarin and Cantonese romanizations as used in this dictionary have been added.

Sounds: The Yale system of romanization has been adopted in this dictionary but for those who have learnt the Wade-Giles ystem a comparative table of the two systems plus the phonetic symbols for Mandarin sounds will be found on page X For Cantonese sounds there is a comparative table of the Yale and Meyer-Wempe systems together with the IPA phonetic symbols on page XXvi

Tones: Many people have experimented and much hard work has gone into devising methods of romanization of the Chinese language and the very subtle tones required to give the correct meaning. A chart on page XXv shows the tones in Mandarin in the Yale system and compares it with the Wade-Giles and Pinyin system. For Cantonese, the tone method used in this dictionary is based on the Yale system with the modification that the"H" sign indicating a low tone has been written as a capital letter to make quite clear that it is merely a tone sign. It relieves the reader of the tedium of remembering why the "H" is there, namely, not as part of the pronuncialion of the word, bnt as a low-tone symbol only. The writer has tried various romanization and tone methods and has found that they all add greatly to the confusion of learning the language, whereas this method is so clear and simple that no extra brain agility is required to pronounce the words and phrases. The system can be learnt in half an hour and can be used with ease even by those who are used to another system. Those whe have studied and prefer to use a different system of Cantonese tones can easily add to the chart on page Xvii their own diacritics.

Simpified Chinese Characters: It has been found advisable to include an appendix which compares the simplified Chinese characters with the original characters. This has been done because newspapers and books in Mainland China are now written in these simplified characters. They have been placed in alphabetical order based on Mandarin.

Ena G. Simms

COMPARATIVE TABLES OF ROMANIZATION OF

MANDARIN SOUNDS

Yale	Wade-Giles	Pinyin	Chinese Phonetics
A	a	a	ㄚ
ai	ai	ai	ㄞ
an	an	an	ㄢ
ang	ang	ang	ㄤ
au	ao	ao	ㄠ
BA	pa	ba	ㄅㄚ
bai	pai	bai	ㄅㄞ
ban	pan	ban	ㄅㄢ
bang	pang	bang	ㄅㄤ
bau	pao	bao	ㄅㄠ
bei	pei	bei	ㄅㄟ
ben	pen	ben	ㄅㄣ
beng	peng	beng	ㄅㄥ
bi	pi	bi	ㄅㄧ
bin	pin	bin	ㄅㄧㄣ
bing	ping	bing	ㄅㄧㄥ
bou	pou	bou	ㄅㄡ
bu	pu	bu	ㄅㄨ
bwo	po	bo	ㄅㄛ
byan	pien	bian	ㄅㄧㄢ
byau	piao	biao	ㄅㄧㄠ
bye	pieh	bie	ㄅㄧㄝ

Yale	Wade-Giles	Pinyin	Chinese Phonetics
CHA	ch'a	cha	ㄔㄚ
chai	ch'ai	chai	ㄔㄞ
chan	ch'an	chan	ㄔㄢ
chang	ch'ang	chang	ㄔㄤ
chau	ch'ao	chao	ㄔㄠ
che	ch'e	che	ㄔㄜ
chen	ch'en	chen	ㄔㄣ
cheng	ch'eng	cheng	ㄔㄥ
chi	ch'i	qi	ㄑㄧ
chin	ch'in	qin	ㄑㄧㄣ
ching	ch'ing	qing	ㄑㄧㄥ
chou	ch'ou	chou	ㄔㄡ
chr	ch'ih	chi	ㄔ
chu	ch'u	chu	ㄔㄨ
chung	ch'ung	chong	ㄔㄨㄥ
chwa	ch'ua	chua	ㄔㄨㄚ
chwai	ch'uai	chuai	ㄔㄨㄞ
chwan	ch'uan	chuan	ㄔㄨㄢ
chwang	ch'uang	chuang	ㄔㄨㄤ
chwei	ch'ui	chui	ㄔㄨㄟ
chwo	ch'o	chuo	ㄔㄛ
chwun	ch'un	chun	ㄔㄨㄣ
chya	ch'ia	qia	ㄑㄧㄚ
chyan	ch'ien	qian	ㄑㄧㄢ
chyang	ch'ang	qiang	ㄑㄧㄤ
chyau	ch'iao	qiao	ㄑㄧㄠ
chye	ch'ieh	qie	ㄑㄧㄝ
chyou	ch'iu	qiu	ㄑㄧㄡ
chyu	ch'u	chu	ㄔㄨ
chyun	ch'un	qun	ㄔㄨㄣ

Yale	Wade-Giles	Pinyin	Chinese Phonetics
chyung	ch'iung	qiong	ㄑㄩㄥ
chywan	ch'uan	quan	ㄔㄨㄢ
chywe	ch'ueh	que	ㄑㄩㄝ
DA	ta	da	ㄉㄚ
dai	tai	dai	ㄉㄞ
dan	tan	dan	ㄉㄢ
dang	tang	dang	ㄉㄤ
dau	tao	dao	ㄉㄠ
de		de	ㄉㄜ
dei	tei	dei	ㄉㄟ
deng	teng	deng	ㄉㄥ
di	ti	di	ㄉㄧ
ding	ting	ding	ㄉㄧㄥ
dou	tou	dou	ㄉㄡ
du	tu	du	ㄉㄨ
dung	tung	dong	ㄉㄨㄥ
dwan	tuan	duan	ㄉㄨㄢ
dwei	tui	dui	ㄉㄨㄟ
dwun	tun	dun	ㄉㄨㄣ
dwo	to	duo	ㄉㄛ
dyan	tien	dian	ㄉㄧㄢ
dyau	tiao	diao	ㄉㄧㄠ
dye	tieh	die	ㄉㄧㄝ
dyou	tiu	diu	ㄉㄧㄡ
dz	tzu	zi	ㄗ
dza	tsa	za	ㄗㄚ
dzai	tsai	zai	ㄗㄞ
dzan	tsan	zan	ㄗㄢ
dzang	tsang	zang	ㄗㄤ

Yale	Wade-Giles	Pinyin	Chinese Phonetics
dzau	tsao	zao	ㄗㄠ
dze	tse	ze	ㄗㄜ
dzei	tsei	zei	ㄗㄟ
dzen	tsen	zen	ㄗㄣ
dzeng	tseng	zeng	ㄗㄥ
dzou	tsou	zou	ㄗㄡ
dzu	tsu	zu	ㄗㄨ
dzung	tsung	zong	ㄗㄤ
dzwan	tsuan	zuan	ㄗㄨㄢ
dzwei	tsui	zui	ㄗㄨㄟ
dzwo	tso	zuo	ㄗㄛ
dzwun	tsun	zun	ㄗㄨㄣ
E	o	e	ㄜ
en	en	en	ㄣ
eng	eng	eng	ㄥ
er	erh	er	ㄦ
FA	fa	fa	ㄈㄚ
fan	fan	fan	ㄈㄢ
fang	fang	fang	ㄈㄤ
fei	fei	fei	ㄈㄟ
fen	fen	fen	ㄈㄣ
feng	feng	feng	ㄈㄥ
fou	fou	fou	ㄈㄡ
fu	fu	fu	ㄈㄨ
fwo	fo	fo	ㄈㄛ
GA	ka	ga	ㄍㄚ
gai	kai	gai	ㄍㄞ

Yale	Wade-Giles	Pinyin	Chinese Phonetics
gan	kan	gan	ㄍㄢ
gang	kang	gang	ㄍㄤ
gau	kao	gao	ㄍㄠ
ge	ko	ge	ㄍㄜ
gei	kei	gei	ㄍㄟ
gen	ken	gen	ㄍㄣ
geng	keng	geng	ㄍㄥ
gou	kou	gou	ㄍㄡ
gu	ku	gu	ㄍㄨ
gung	kung	gong	ㄍㄨㄤ
gwa	kua	gua	ㄍㄨㄚ
gwai	kuai	guai	ㄍㄨㄞ
gwan	kuan	guan	ㄍㄨㄢ
gwang	kuang	guang	ㄍㄨㄤ
gwei	kuei	gui	ㄍㄨㄟ
gwo	kuo	guo	ㄍㄨㄛ
gwun	kun	gun	ㄍㄨㄣ
HA	ha	ha	ㄏㄚ
hai	hai	hai	ㄏㄞ
han	han	han	ㄏㄢ
hang	hang	hang	ㄏㄤ
hau	hao	hao	ㄏㄠ
he	ho	he	ㄏㄜ
hei	hei	hei	ㄏㄟ
hen	hen	hen	ㄏㄣ
heng	heng	heng	ㄏㄥ
hou	hou	hou	ㄏㄡ
hu	hu	hu	ㄏㄨ
hung	hung	hong	ㄏㄨㄤ

Yale	Wade-Giles	Pinyin	Chinese Phonetics
hwa	hua	hua	ㄏㄨㄚ
hwai	huai	huai	ㄏㄨㄞ
hwan	huan	huan	ㄏㄨㄢ
hwang	huang	huang	ㄏㄨㄤ
hwei	hui	hui	ㄏㄨㄟ
hwo	huo	huo	ㄏㄨㄛ
hwun	hun	hun	ㄏㄨㄣ
JA	cha	zha	ㄓㄚ
jai	chai	zhai	ㄓㄞ
jan	chan	zhan	ㄓㄢ
jang	chang	zhang	ㄓㄤ
jau	chao	zhao	ㄓㄠ
je	che	zhe	ㄓㄜ
jen	chen	zhen	ㄓㄣ
jeng	cheng	zheng	ㄓㄥ
ji	chi	ji	ㄐㄧ
jin	chin	jin	ㄐㄧㄣ
jing	ching	jing	ㄐㄧㄥ
jou	chou	zhou	ㄓㄡ
jr	chih	zhi	ㄓ
ju	chu	zhu	ㄓㄨ
jung	chung	zhong	ㄓㄨㄥ
jwa	chua	zhua	ㄓㄨㄚ
jwai	chuai	zhuai	ㄓㄨㄞ
jwan	chuan	zhuan	ㄓㄨㄢ
jwang	chuang	zhuang	ㄓㄨㄤ
jwei	chui	zhui	ㄓㄨㄟ
jwo	cho	zhuo	ㄓㄛ
jwun	chun	zhun	ㄓㄨㄣ

Yale	Wade-Giles	Pinyin	Chinese Phonetics
jya	chia	jia	ㄐㄧㄚ
jyan	chien	jian	ㄐㄧㄢ
jyang	chiang	jiang	ㄐㄧㄤ
jyau	chiao	jiao	ㄐㄧㄠ
jye	chieh	jie	ㄐㄧㄝ
jyou	chiu	jiu	ㄐㄧㄡ
jyu	chu	zhu	ㄓㄨ
jyun	chun	zhun	ㄓㄨㄣ
jyung	chiung	jiong	ㄓㄨㄥ
jywan	chuan	zhuan	ㄓㄨㄢ
jywe	chueh	jue	ㄐㄨㄝ
KA	k'a	ka	ㄎㄚ
kai	k'ai	kai	ㄎㄞ
kan	k'an	kan	ㄎㄢ
kang	k'ang	kang	ㄎㄤ
kau	k'ao	kao	ㄎㄠ
ke	k'o	ke	ㄎㄜ
ken	k'en	ken	ㄎㄣ
keng	k'eng	keng	ㄎㄥ
kou	k'ou	kou	ㄎㄡ
ku	k'u	ku	ㄎㄨ
kung	k'ung	kong	ㄎㄨㄥ
kwa	k'ua	kua	ㄎㄨㄚ
kwai	k'uai	kuai	ㄎㄨㄞ
kwan	k'uan	kuan	ㄎㄨㄢ
kwang	k'uang	kuang	ㄎㄨㄤ
kwei	k'uei	kui	ㄎㄨㄟ
kwo	k'uo	kuo	ㄎㄨㄛ
kwun	k'un	kun	ㄎㄨㄣ

Yale	Wade-Giles	Pinyin	Chinese Phonetics
LA	la	la	ㄌㄚ
lai	lai	lai	ㄌㄞ
lan	lan	lan	ㄌㄢ
lang	lang	lang	ㄌㄤ
lau	lao	lao	ㄌㄠ
le	le	le	ㄌㄜ
lei	lei	lei	ㄌㄟ
leng	leng	leng	ㄌㄥ
li	li	li	ㄌㄧ
lin	lin	lin	ㄌㄧㄣ
ling	ling	ling	ㄌㄧㄥ
lou	lou	lou	ㄌㄡ
lu	lu	lu	ㄌㄨ
lung	lung	long	ㄌㄨㄥ
lwan	luan	luan	ㄌㄨㄢ
lwo	lo	luo	ㄌㄛ
lwun	lun	lun	ㄌㄨㄣ
lya	lia	lia	ㄌㄧㄚ
lyan	lien	lian	ㄌㄧㄢ
lyang	lien	lian	ㄌㄧㄤ
lyau	liao	liao	ㄌㄧㄠ
lye	lieh	lie	ㄌㄧㄝ
lyou	liu	liu	ㄌㄧㄡ
lyu	lu	lu	ㄌㄨ
lywan	luan	luan	ㄌㄨㄢ
lywe	lueh	lue	ㄌㄩㄝ
MA	ma	ma	ㄇㄚ
mai	mai	mai	ㄇㄞ
man	man	man	ㄇㄢ

Yale	Wade-Giles	Pinyin	Chinese Phonetics
mang	mang	mang	ㄇㄤ
mau	mao	mao	ㄇㄠ
mei	mei	mei	ㄇㄟ
men	men	men	ㄇㄣ
meng	meng	meng	ㄇㄥ
mi	mi	mi	ㄇㄧ
min	min	min	ㄇㄧㄣ
ming	ming	ming	ㄇㄧㄥ
mou	mou	mou	ㄇㄡ
mu	mu	mu	ㄇㄨ
mwo	mo	mo	ㄇㄛ
myan	mien	mian	ㄇㄧㄢ
myau	miao	miao	ㄇㄧㄠ
mye	mieh	mie	ㄇㄧㄝ
myou	miu	miu	ㄇㄧㄡ
NA	na	na	ㄋㄚ
nai	nai	nai	ㄋㄞ
nan	nan	nan	ㄋㄢ
nang	nang	nang	ㄋㄤ
nau	nao	nao	ㄋㄠ
nei	nei	nei	ㄋㄟ
nen	nen	nen	ㄋㄣ
ni	ni	ni	ㄋㄧ
nin	nin	nin	ㄋㄧㄣ
ning	ning	ning	ㄋㄧㄥ
nou	nou	nou	ㄋㄡ
nu	nu	nu	ㄋㄨ
nung	nung	nong	ㄋㄨㄥ
nwan	nuan	nuan	ㄋㄨㄢ

Yale	Wade-Giles	Pinyin	Chinese Phonetics
nwo	no	no	ㄋㄛ
nwun	nun	nun	ㄋㄨㄣ
nyan	nien	nian	ㄋㄧㄢ
nyang	niang	niang	ㄋㄧㄤ
nyau	niao	niao	ㄋㄧㄠ
nye	nieh	nie	ㄋㄧㄝ
nyou	niu	niu	ㄋㄧㄡ
nyu	nu	nu	ㄋㄩ
nywe	nueh	nue	ㄋㄩㄝ
O U	ou	ou	ㄡ
P A	p'a	pa	ㄆㄚ
pai	p'ai	pai	ㄆㄞ
pan	p'an	pan	ㄆㄢ
pang	p'ang	pang	ㄆㄤ
pau	p'ao	pao	ㄆㄠ
pei	p'ei	pei	ㄆㄟ
pen	p'en	pen	ㄆㄣ
peng	p'eng	peng	ㄆㄥ
pi	p'i	pi	ㄆㄧ
pin	p'in	pin	ㄆㄧㄣ
ping	p'ing	ping	ㄆㄧㄥ
pou	p'ou	pou	ㄆㄡ
pu	p'u	pu	ㄆㄨ
pwo	p'o	po	ㄆㄛ
pyan	p'ien	pian	ㄆㄧㄢ
pyau	p'iao	piao	ㄆㄧㄠ
pye	p'ieh	pie	ㄆㄧㄝ
R	jih	ri	ㄖ

Yale	Wade-Giles	Pinyin	Chinese Phonetics
ran	jan	ran	日弓
rang	jang	rang	日尢
rau	jao	rao	日幺
re	je	re	日亡
ren	jen	ren	日ㄣ
reng	jeng	reng	日ㄥ
rou	jou	rou	日又
ru	ju	ru	日ㄨ
rung	jung	rong	日ㄨㄥ
rwan	juan	ruan	日ㄨㄢ
rwei	jui	rui	日ㄨㄟ
rwo	jo	ruo	日己
rwun	jun	run	日ㄨㄣ
SA	sa	sa	ㄙㄚ
sai	sai	sai	ㄙㄞ
san	san	san	ㄙㄢ
sang	sang	sang	ㄙㄤ
sau	sao	sao	ㄙㄠ
se	se	se	ㄙㄜ
sen	sen	sen	ㄙㄣ
seng	seng	seng	ㄙㄥ
sha	sha	sha	ㄕㄚ
shai	shai	shai	ㄕㄞ
shan	shan	shan	ㄕㄢ
shang	shang	shar.g	ㄕㄤ
shau	shao	shao	ㄕㄠ
she	she	she	ㄕㄜ
shei	shei	shei	ㄕㄟ
shen	shen	shen	ㄕㄣ

Yale	Wade-Giles	Pinyin	Chinese Phonetics
sheng	sheng	sheng	ㄕㄥ
shou	shou	shou	ㄕㄡ
shr	shih	shi	ㄕ
shu	shu	shu	ㄕㄨ
shwa	shua	shua	ㄕㄨㄚ
shwai	shuai	shuai	ㄕㄨㄞ
shwan	shuan	shuan	ㄕㄨㄢ
shwang	shuang	shuang	ㄕㄨㄤ
shwei	shui	shui	ㄕㄨㄟ
shwo	shuo	shuo	ㄕㄨㄛ
shwun	shun	shun	ㄕㄨㄣ
sou	sou	sou	ㄙㄡ
su	su	su	ㄙㄨ
sung	sung	song	ㄙㄨㄥ
swan	suan	suan	ㄙㄨㄢ
swei	sui	sui	ㄙㄨㄟ
swo	so	suo	ㄙㄛ
swun	sun	sun	ㄙㄨㄣ
sya	hsia	xia	ㄒㄧㄚ
syan	hsien	xian	ㄒㄧㄢ
syang	hsiang	xiang	ㄒㄧㄤ
syau	hsiao	xiao	ㄒㄧㄠ
sye	hsieh	xie	ㄒㄧㄝ
syi	hsi	xi	ㄒㄧ
syin	hsin	xin	ㄒㄧㄣ
sying	hsing	xing	ㄒㄧㄥ
syiu	hsiu	xiu	ㄒㄧㄡ
syu	hsu	xu	ㄒㄩ
syun	hsun	xun	ㄒㄩㄣ
syung	hsiung	xiong	ㄒㄩㄥ

Yale	Wade-Giles	Pinyin	Chinese Phonetics
sywan	hsuan	xuan	ㄒㄩㄢ
sywe	hsueh	xue	ㄒㄩㄝ
sz	szu	si	ㄙ
TA	t'a	ta	ㄊㄚ
tai	t'ai	tai	ㄊㄞ
tan	t'an	tan	ㄊㄢ
tang	t'ang	tang	ㄊㄤ
tau	t'ao	tao	ㄊㄠ
te	t'e	te	ㄊㄜ
teng	t'eng	teng	ㄊㄥ
ti	t'i	ti	ㄊㄧ
ting	t'ing	ting	ㄊㄧㄥ
tou	t'ou	tou	ㄊㄡ
tsa	ts'a	ca	ㄘㄚ
tsai	ts'ai	cai	ㄘㄞ
tsan	ts'an	can	ㄘㄢ
tsang	ts'ang	cang	ㄘㄤ
tsau	ts'ao	cao	ㄘㄠ
tse	ts'e	ce	ㄘㄜ
tsen	ts'en	cen	ㄘㄣ
tseng	ts'eng	ceng	ㄘㄥ
tsou	ts'ou	cou	ㄘㄡ
tsu	ts'u	cu	ㄘㄨ
tsung	ts'ung	cong	ㄘㄨㄥ
tswan	ts'uan	cuan	ㄘㄨㄢ
tswei	ts'ui	cui	ㄘㄨㄟ
tswo	ts'o	cuo	ㄘㄨㄛ
tswun	ts'un	cun	ㄘㄨㄣ
tsz	tz'u	ci	ㄘ

Yale	Wade-Giles	Pinyin	Chinese Phonetics
tu	t'u	tu	ㄊㄨ
tung	t'ung	tong	ㄊㄨㄥ
twan	t'uan	tuan	ㄊㄨㄢ
twei	t'ui	tui	ㄊㄨㄟ
two	t'o	tuo	ㄊㄛ
twun	t'un	tun	ㄊㄨㄣ
tyan	t'ien	tian	ㄊㄧㄢ
tyau	t'iao	tiao	ㄊㄧㄠ
tye	t'ieh	tie	ㄊㄧㄝ
WA	wa	wa	ㄨㄚ
wai	wai	wai	ㄨㄞ
wan	wan	wan	ㄨㄢ
wang	wang	wang	ㄨㄤ
wei	wei	wei	ㄨㄟ
wen	wen	wen	ㄨㄣ
weng	weng	weng	ㄨㄥ
wo	wo	wo	ㄨㄛ
wu	wu	wu	ㄨ
YA	ya	ya	ㄧㄚ
yai	yai	yai	ㄧㄞ
yan	yen	yan	ㄧㄢ
yang	yang	yang	ㄧㄤ
yau	yao	yau	ㄧㄠ
ye	yeh	ye	ㄧㄝ
yi	i	yi	ㄧ
yin	yin	yin	ㄧㄣ
ying	ying	ying	ㄧㄥ
you	yu	you	ㄩㄡ

Yale	Wade-Giles	Pinyin	Chinese Phonetics
yu	yu	yu	ㄩ
yun	yun	yun	ㄩㄣ
yung	yung	yong	ㄩㄥ
ywan	yuan	yuan	ㄩㄢ
ywe	yueh	yue	ㄩㄝ

發音機關圖

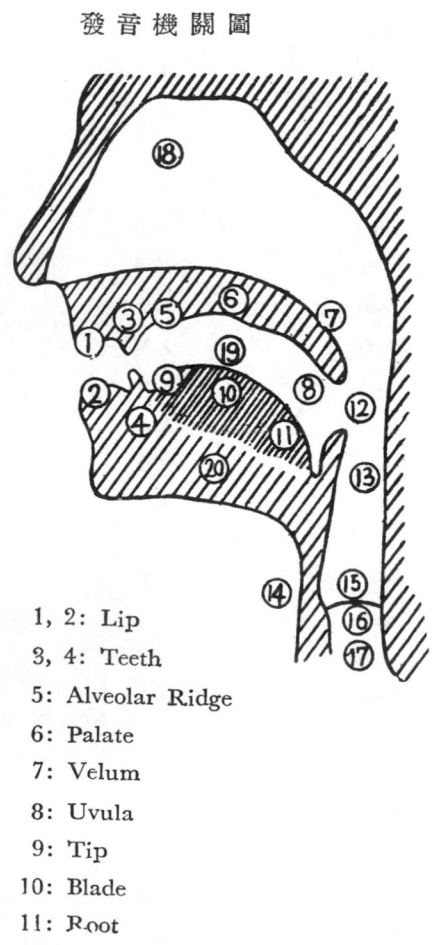

1. 上　唇
2. 下　唇
3. 上　齒
4. 下　齒
5. 上牙床
6. 硬口蓋
7. 軟口蓋
8. 小　舌
9. 舌　尖
10. 舌　前

11. 舌　根
12. 喉
13. 會厭軟骨
14. 喉　頭
15. 聲　門
16. 聲　帶
17. 氣　管
18. 鼻　腔
19. 口　腔
20. 下　顎

THE VOCAL ORGANS

1, 2: Lip
3, 4: Teeth
5: Alveolar Ridge
6: Palate
7: Velum
8: Uvula
9: Tip
10: Blade
11: Root

12: Pharyngeal
13: Epiglottis
14: Glottal
15: Vocal Gate
16: Vocal Cords
17: Trachea
18: Nasal Cavity
19: Cavity of Mouth
20: Lower Maxillary Bones

The Tones in Mandarin

The four tones in Mandarin are as follows:

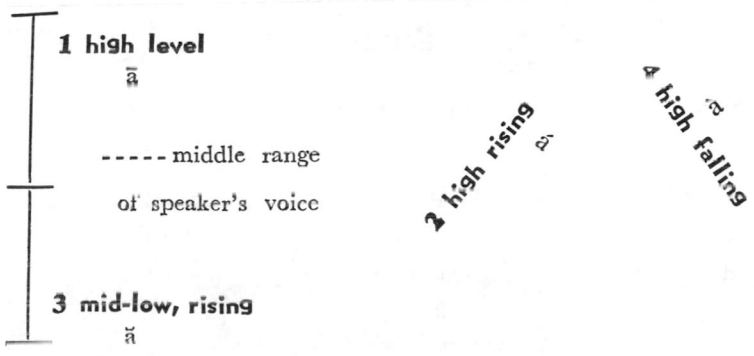

There is a modification of tone 3 when it precedes another tone 3, the first one is raised to tone 2

e. g. hěn hǎu becomes hén hǎu

Comparative Chart-Tones

Yale   Wade-Giles

Pinyin

Chinese Phonetics

1st Tone	—	1
2nd Tone	╱	2
3rd Tone	⌵	3
4th Tone	╲	4

COMPARATIVE TABLES OF ROMANIZATION OF

CANTONESE SOUNDS

Initials

Yale	Meyer-Wempe	IPA
p	p'	p'
b	p	p
t	t'	t'
d	t	t
k	k'	k'
g	k	k
ch	ch',ts'	t'ʃ'
j	ch,ts	tʃ
kw	k'w	k'w
gw	kw	kw
m	m	m
n	n	n
ng	ng	ŋ
f	f	f
l	l	l
h	h	h
s	s,sh	ʃ
y	i,y	j
w	oͻ,w	w

Finals

Yale	Meyer-Wempe	IPA	Yale	Meyer-Wempe	IPA
a	a	a:	i	i	i:
aai	aai	a:i	iu	iu	i:u
aau	aau	a:u	im	im	i:m
aam	aam	a:m	ip	ip	i:p
aap	aap	a:p	in	in	i:ŋ
aan	aan	a:n	it	it	i:t
aat	aat	a:t	ing	ing	iŋ
aang	aang	a:ŋ	ik	ik	ik
aak	aak	a:k			
ai	ai	ai	o	oh	ɔ
au	au	au	oi	oi	ɔ:i
am	am,om	am	on	on	ɔ:n
ap	ap,op	ap	ot	ot	ɔ:t
an	an	an	ong	ong	ɔ:ŋ
at	at	at	ok	ok	ɔ:k
ang	ang	aŋ	ou	o	ou
ak	ak	ak			
e	e	ɛ:	u	oo	u
eng	eng	ɛ:ŋ	ui	ooi	ui
ek	ek	ɛ:k	un	oon	u:n
ei	ei	ei	ut	oot	u:t
eu	oeh	œ:	ung	ung	u:ŋ
eung	eung	œ:ŋ	uk	uk	u:k
euk	euk	œ:k			
eui	ui	œi	yu	ue	y:u
eun	un	œn	yun	uen	y:n
eut	ut	œt	yut	uet	y:t

The Tones in Cantonese

Seven tone-signs have been used in this dictionary to distinguish the tones in Cantonese. The method has been kept very simple so that it can be learnt by any reader in half an hour. Those who have studied a different system of Cantonese tones can easily add to this chart their own diacritics.

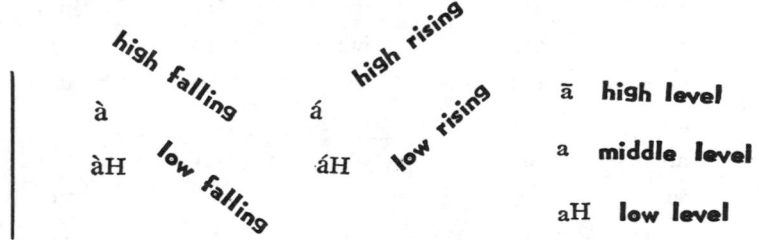

à   á   ā high level

àH   áH   a middle level

                   aH low level

The only exception is **higih falling** before another **high falling** or **high level** tone. Instead of falling during the first syllable, the pitch remains high throughout the first syllable.

e.g,   sìnsàang **becomes** sīnsàang

chànchĭk **becomes** chānchĭk

COMPARATIVE CHART-Tones

Yale			Meyer-Wempe
high falling	à	a	upper even
high rising	á	á	upper rising
middle level	a, at	à	upper going
		at	middle entering
high level	ā, āt	a	upper even
		at	upper entering
low falling	àH	ā	lower even
low rising	áH	ă	lower rising
low level	aH, aHt	ā	lower going
		āt	lower entering

The **capital letter** 'H' identifies the lower-tone initials from the upper-tone initials.

A Practical English-Chinese
Pronouncing Dictionary

abacus n.	算盤	swànpán	syunpùHn
abandon v. t.	放棄	fàngchì;	fonghei;
	棄絕	chìjyẃe	heijyuHt
abbreviate v. t.	縮短	swōdwǎn	sūkdyún
abdomen n.	腹部	fùbù	fūkbouH(tóuH)
ability n.	能力	nénglì;	nàHngliĭlk;
	才幹	tsáigàn	chòiHgon
able a.	能夠	nénggòu	nàHnggau
abnormal a.	變態	byàntài;	bintaai;
	反常	fǎncháng	fáansèuHng
aboard adv.	船上	chwánshàng	syùHnseuHng
abolish v. t.	廢止	fèijǐ;	faijí;
	廢除	fèichú	faichèuiH
aborigines n.	土人	tǔrén	tóuyàHn
abortion n.	墮胎	dwòtai	duHtòi
above a.	上面	shàngmyàn	seuHngmiHn
abroad adv.	海外	hǎiwài	hóingoiH
abrupt a.			
-curt	簡短	jyǎndwǎn;	gáandyún;
-sudden	倉猝	tsāngtsù	chòngchyut
abscess n.	膿瘡	núngchwāng	nùHngchòng
absence n.	缺席	chywēsyí	kyutjiHk
absent-minded a.	心不在焉	syìnbúdzàiyān	sàmbūtjoiHyìHn
absolute a.	絕對	jyẃédwèi	jyuHtdeui
absorb v. t.	吸收	syìshōu	kāpsàu
abstract a.	抽象	chōusyàng	chàujeuHng
absurd a.	荒謬	hwāngnyòu	fòngmauH
abuse n.			
-misuse	妄用	wàngyùng;	móHngyuHng
-injury	損傷	swǔnshāng;	syúnsèung;

-offence	侵犯	chīnfàn	chàmfaaHn
academic a.			
-scholarly	學風	sywéfēng	hoHkfùng
academy n.			
-a college	專門學校	jwānménsywésyàu	jyùnmùHnhoHkhaauH
accelerate v. t.	加速	jyāsù	gàchūk
accent			
-v. t. emphasize	重音	jùngyin	chúHngyām;
-n. tone	音調	yindyàu	yāmdiuH
accept v. t.	接受	jyēshòu;	jipsauH;
	領受	lǐngshòu	líHngsauH
accident n.	意外	yìwài	yingoiH
accommodate v. t.			
-find lodging for	收容	shōurúng;	sàuyùHng;
-oblige	通融	tūngrúng	tùngyùHng
accompany v. t.	作伴	dzwòbàn	jokbuHn (jouHpúHn)
accomplish v. t.	完成	wánchéng;	yùHnsìHng;
	實行	shŕsyíng	saHthàHng
according to adv.	按著	ànje	ngonjeuHk
account			
-v. i. give a reason	說明	shwōmíng;	syutmìHng;
-n. a calculation	賬簿	jàngbù	jeungbóu
accurate a.			
-correct	正確	jèngchywè;	jingkok;
-precise	精密	jingmì	jìngmaHt
accuse v. t.	控告	kùnggàu;	hunggou;
	控訴	kùngsù	hungsou
accustom v. t.	使慣於	shǐgwànyú	sigwaanyù (sáidou jaaHpgwaan)

ache n.	痛	téng or tùng	tung
achieve			
-v. t. accomplish	完成	wánchéng;	yùHnsiHng;
-v. t. gain	博得	bwódé;	bokdāk;
-v. i. reach	達到	dádàu	daaHtdou
acid a.	酸	swān	syùn
acknowledge v. t.	承認	chéngrèn	sìIIngyiHng
acoustics n.	音響學	yīnsyǎngsywé	yàmhéunghoHk
acquaintance n.	相識	syāngshì	sèungsik
acquit v. t.	付清	fùchǐng;	fuHchǐng;
-discharge	宣告無罪	sywāngàuwúdzwèi	syùngoumòuHjeuiH
across adv.	橫過	hénggwò;	wàaHnggwo;
-prep.	在那方面	dzài...nàfāngmyàn	joiH...náHfòngmiIIn
act n.	行動	syíngdùng;	hàIIngduHng;
-v. t. perform	演戲	yǎnsyì;	yìnhei (jouHhei);
-v. t. pretend	假裝	jyǎjwāng;	gájòng;
-v. i. behave	動作	dùngdzwò	duHngjok
action n.	行爲	syíngwéi	hàHngwàiH
add v. t.	加上	jyāshàng	gàséuHng
addict v. t.	慣於	gwànyú	gwaanyù
-drug addict	嗜好	shìhòu	sihou
address			
-n. of location	地址	dìjǐ;	deiHji;
-v t. speak	稱呼	chēnghū	chìngfù
adequate a.			
-proportionate	適當	shìdàng;	sikdong;
-sufficient	足夠	dzúgòu	jūkgau
adhesive a.	黏性	nyánsyìng	nìHmsing
adjective n.	形容詞	syíngrúngtsź	yìHngyùHngchìH

adjourn v. t.

  -disperse 　散會　sànhwèi;　saanwúi;

  -to another day 　改期　gǎichī　góikèiH

adjust v. t.

  -put in order 　整理　jěnglǐ;　jíngléiH;

  -set right 　調節　tyáujyé　tìuHjit

administration n.

  -government 　行政　syíngjèng;　hàHngjing;

  -of an enterprise 　經營　jīngyíng　gìngyìHng

admire v. t. & v. i.

  -fond of 　羨慕　syànmù;　siHnmouH;

  -with wonder 　佩服　pèifu　puifuHk

admit v. t.

  承認　chéngrèn;　sìHngyiHng;

  通入　tūngrù　tùngyaHp

adolescent n.

  青年　chīngnyán;　chìngnìHn;

  少年　shàunyán　siunìHn

adopt v. t.

  -use 　探用　tsǎiyùng;　chóiyuHng;

  -adopted son 　養子　yǎngdž　yéuHngjí

adult n.

  成人　chéngrén　sìHngyàHn
               (siHngnìHnyàHn)

adultery

  姦淫　jyānyín　gàanyàHm

advance

  -v. t. bring forward 　提前　tíchyán;　tàiHchìHn;

  -v. i. go forward 　前進　chyánjìn;　chìHnjeun;

  -n. early payment 　預付　yùfù　yuHfuH

adverb n.

  副詞　fùtsź　fuchìH

advertise v. t.

  廣告　gwǎnggàu　gwónggou

advice n.

  勸告　chywàngàu　hyungou

aeroplane n.

  飛機　fēiji　fèigèi

affairs n.

  事情　shìching　siHchìHng

affection n.	感情	gǎnchíng	gámchìHng
affidavit n.	宣誓書	sywēnshìshū	syùnsaiHsyù;
	供詞	gùngtsź	gùngchìH
affiliate v. t.			
-ally	聯合	lyánhé;	lyùHnhaHp;
-adopt	收養	shōuyǎng	sàuyéuHng
affirm v. t.	斷言	dwànyán;	dyunyìHn;
	肯定	kěngdìng	hángdiHng
affliction n.	痛苦	tùngkǔ;	tungfú;
	困苦	kwùnkǔ	kwanfú
affluence n.			
-wealth	富裕	fùyù;	fuyuH;
-flowing to	流向	lyóusyàng	làuHhoung
afford v. t.			
-provide	供給	gūngjǐ	gùngkàp
afraid a.	害怕	hàipà	hoiHpa (pa)
after adv.	之後	...jīhòu	...jìhauH
afternoon n.	下午	syàwǔ	haIInǵH
afterwards adv.	以後	yǐhoù;	yíHhauH;
	後來	hòulái	hauHlòiH
again adv.	再	dzài;	joi;
	又	yòu	yauH
against prep.			
-in opposition to	反對	fǎndwèi	fáandeui
age n.	年齡	nyánlíng;	nìHnlìHng;
	年紀	nyánjì	nìHngéi
agent n.	代理	dàilǐ;	doiHléiH;
	代辦	dàibàn	doiHbaaHn
ages n.	歷代	lìdài	liHkdoiH

agitate v. t.

-stir up	鼓動	gŭdùng;	gúduHng;
-debate	辯論	byànlwùn	biHnleuHn

agree v. t.

-consent	同意	túngyi;	tùHngyi;
-correspond	相符	syāngfú	seùngfùH

agriculture n.

農業	núngyè	nùHngyiHp

aid v. t.

幫助	bāngju	bòngjoH

aim

-n. purpose	宗旨	dzūngjĭr;	jùngjĭ;
-v. i. intend	指望	jĭwàng	jimoHng

air n.

空氣	kūngchì	hùnghei

aircraft n.

-balloon	氣球	chìchyóu;	heikàuH;
-aeroplane	飛機	fēijĭ	fèigèi

airmail n.

航空信	hángkūngsyìn	hòHnghùngseun

aisle n.

通路	tūnglù	tùnglouH

alarm

-v. t. fear	驚慌	jīnghwāng;	gìngfòng;
-n. warning	警告	jĭnggàu	gínggou

alas int.

哀哉	āidzāi	ōijòi

alcohol n.

酒精	jyŏujīng	jáujìng

alert

-a. watchful	留心	lyóusyìn;	làuHsàm;
-n. alarm	警備	jĭngbèi	gìngbeiH

alien a.

外國	wàigwó	ngoiHgwok

alike a.

	一樣	yíyàng;	yātyeuHng;
	相同	syāngtúng	sèungtùHng

alive a.	活的	hwóde	wuHtdìk
all a.	所有	swŏyŏu	sóyáuH
-all eternity	永世無盡	yŭngshìwújìn	wíHngsaimòuHjeuHn
-all nations	萬國	wàngwó	maaHngwok
-all people	萬民	wànmín	maaHnmàHn
-all things	萬物	wànwù	maaHnmaHt
alliance n.	聯盟	lyánmén	lyùHnmàHng
allowance n.	津貼	jīntyē	jèuntip
almost adv.	幾乎	jīhū;	gèifùH;
	差不多	chàbùdwō	chàbātdō
alms n.	賙濟	jōujì;	jàujai;
	施捨	shīshě	sìsé
alone adv.			
-single	單獨	dāndú	dàanduHk
-orphaned	孤獨	gūdú	gùduHk
aloud adv.	高聲	gōushēng	gòusìng (daaiIIsèng)
alphabet n.	字母	dzìmŭ	jiHmóuH
already adv.	巳經	yǐjīng	yíHgìng
also adv.	也	yě;	yáH;
	又	yòu;	yauH;
	都	dōu	dōu
altar n.	祭壇	jìtán	jaitàaHn
alter v. t.			
-change	改	gǎi;	gói;
	換	hwàn	wuHn
although conj.	雖然	swéirán	sèuiyìHn
always adv.			
-at all times	常常	chángcháng	sèuHngsèuHn (sìHsiH)
-without exception	總是	dzŭngshì	júngsiH (júnghaiH)
am v. i.	是	shì	siH (haiH)

amah n.	阿媽	àmā	àmàH
amaze v. t.	驚奇	jīngchí	gìngkèiH
ambassador n.	大使	dàshř	daaiHsi
ambition n.			
-good sense	志願	jìywàn;	jiyuHn;
-bad sense	野心	yěsyïn	yéHsàm
ambulance n.	救護車	jyòuhùchē	gauwuHchè
ambush			
-n.	伏兵	fúbǐng;	fuHkbìng;
-v. i.	埋伏	máifú	màaiHfuHk
amend v. t.			
-make better	改良	gǎilyáng;	góilèuHng;
-of a law or rule	修正	syōujèng	sàujing
American a.	美國	Měigwo	MéiHgwok
ammunition n.	軍火	jyūnhwǒ;	gwànfó;
	彈藥	dànyàu	dáanyeuHk
among prep.	在中間	dzài...jūngjyān	joiH...jùnggàan
amount			
-v. t. add up	一共	yigùng;	yātguHng;
-n. the total	總數	dzǔngshù	júngsou
amplifier n.	播音機	bwòyïnji	boyàmgèi
amputate v. t.			
-of arm or leg	鋸斷	jyùdwàn	geuityúHn
amuse v. t.			
-make happy	開心	kāisyïn;	hòisàm;
-for oneself	消遣	syāuchyǎn	sïuhín
amusement n.	娛樂	yúlè	yùHloHk
anaemia n.	貧血	pínsywě	pàHnhyut
anaesthetic n.	麻醉藥	mádzwèiyaù	màHjeuiyeuHk

English	Chinese		
analyse v. t.	分解	fēnjyĕ;	fàngáai;
	分析	fēnsyi	fànsïk
analysis n.	分析	fēnsyi	fànsïk
anarchy n.	無政府	wújèngfŭ	mòuHjingfú
ancestor n.	祖宗	dzŭdzūng	jóujùng
-a. ancestral worship	拜祖先	bàigdzŭsyān	baaijóusïn
anchor n.	錨	máu	màauH
ancient a.	古代	gŭdài	gúdoiH
and conj.	同	túng;	tùHng;
	和	hé;	wòH(tùHngmàaiH);
	跟	gēn	gàn(tùHng)
anger n.	怒氣	nùchì	nouHhei
angry a.	生氣	shēngchì	sàanghei (nàu)
animal n.	動物	dùngwù	duHngmaHt
ankle n.	脚脖子	jyăubwódz	geukbuHtjí (geukngáaHn)
annex v. t.	合併	hébìng	haHpbing
annihilate v. t'	消滅	syaumyè	sìumıHt
anniversary n.			
-yearly	週年	jōunyán;	jàunìHn;
-celebration	週年紀念日	jōunyánjìnyànì	jàunìHngéiniHmyaHt
announce v. t.	宣佈	sywānbù;	syùnbou;
	報告	bàugàu	bougou
annoy v. t.	討厭	tăuyàn	tóuyim
annual a.	每年	mĕinyán;	múiHnìHn;
	年年	nyánnyán	nìHnnìHn
another a.	第二	dìèr;	daiHyiH
	另外	lìngwài	liHngngoiH
answer			
-n.	回答	hwéidá;	wùiHdaap;

-v. t.	答應	dáyìng	daapying
ant n.	螞蟻	mǎyǐ	máHngáiH (ngáiH)
anthem (national) n.	國歌	gwógē	gwokgō
antique a.	古代	gǔdài	gúdoiH
anxious a.			
-worry	掛念	gwànyàn;	gwaniHm;
-troubled	煩惱	fánnǎu	fàaHnnóuH
any a.	任何	rènhé	yaHmhòH
anywhere adv.	何處	héchù	hòHchyu(bìnsyu)
apology n.	道歉	dàuchyàn	douHhip
appeal v. i.			
-ask earnestly	懇求	kěnchyóu;	hánkàuH;
-law	上訴	shàngsù	seuHngsou
appear v. i.			
-come into sight	現出	syànchū;	yiHnchēut;
-seem	好像	hǎusyàng	hóujeuHng
appearance n.			
-face	面貌	myànmàu;	miHnmaauH;
-aspect	現象	syànsyàng	yiHnjeuHng
appetite n.	胃口	wèikǒu	waiHháu
appetizer n.	開胃	kāiwèi	hòiwaiH
applause n.	喝采	hètsǎi	hotchói
apple n.	蘋菓	pínggwǒ	pìHnggwó
appliance n.	器具	chìjyù	heigeuiH
application n.			
-use	應用	yìngyùng;	yingyuHng;
-request	申請	shēnchǐng	sànching
apply v. t.			
-for	申請	shēnchǐng;	sànchíng;
-suit	適合	shìhé;	sìkhaHp;
-use	用	yùng	yuHng

appoint v. t.	選派 委任	sywǎnpài; wěirèn	syúnpaai; wáiyaHm
appointment n.			
-engagement	約定	ywēdìng;	yeukdìHng;
-position	職位	jŕwèi	jìkwaiH
appreciate v. t.			
-enjoy	欣賞	syìnshǎng;	yànséung;
-be grateful	感激	gǎnjí	gámgìk
apprehend v. t.	預料	yùlyàu	yuHliuH
approach v. t.			
-come near	臨近	línjìn;	làHmgaHn;
-move towards	接近	jyējìn	jìpgaHn
approve v. t.			
-satisfied with	合意	héyì;	haHpyi;
-sanction	批准	pijwǔn	pàijéun
are v. i.	是	shŕ	siH (haiH)
arch n.	弓形	gūngsyíng	gùngyìHng
architect n.	工程師	gūngchéngshŕ	gùngchìHngsi
argue v. i.	辯論	byànlwùn	biHnleuHn
arise v. i.	起立 起身	chǐlì; chǐshēn	héilaHp; héisàn
arithmetic n.	算術	swànshù	syunseuHt
arm n.	膀臂 手臂	bǎngbì; shǒubì	bóngbei; sáubei
army n.	陸軍	lùjyūn	luHkgwēn
armour n.	盔甲	kwēijyǎ	kwàigaap
arouse v. t.			
-from sleep	叫醒	jyàusyíng;	giuséng;
-sense of guilt	覺悟	jywéwù	gokngH

arrange v. t.			
-make plan	安排	ānpái;	ngònpàaiH;
-agreement	約定	ywēdìng	yeukdiHng
arrear adv.	在後	dzàihòu	joiHhauH
arrest v. t.			
-seize	捉	jwō;	jūk;
-catch attention of	引	yǐn	yáHn
arrival n.	到	dàu;	dou;
	到場	dàuchǎng	douchèuHng
art n.	美術	měishù;	méiHseuHt;
	藝術	yìshù	ngaiHseuHt
-n. arts and crafts	工藝	gūngyì	gùngngaiH
artificial a.			
-made by art	人工	réngūng;	yàHngùng;
-not real	假	jyǎ	gá
artist n.	畫家	hwàjyā;	wágā;
	美術家	mēishùjyā	méiHseuHtgā
ash n.			
-fine dust	灰	hwēi;	fùi;
one's ashes	骨灰	gǔhwēi	gwātfùi
ashamed a.	羞恥	syōuchř;	sàuchí;
	害羞	hàisyōu	hoiHsàu (pacháu)
Asia n.	亞洲	Yǎjōu	Ajàu
ask v. t.			
-inquire	問	wèn;	maHn;
-beg	求	chyóu	kàuH
aspirin n.	阿斯匹林	āsz̄pǐlín	asìpātlàHm
assemble v. t.			
-congregate	聚集	jyùjí;	jeuiHjaaHp
-collect	收集	shōují	sàujaaHp
assets n.	遺產	yíchǎn	wàiHcháan

assimilation n.	同化	túnghwà	tùHngfa
assist v. t.	幫助	bāngjù	bòngjoH
assistant n.			
-helper	助手	jùshŏu;	joHsáu;
-next in rank	副	fù	fʻı
associate v. i.	聯絡	lyánlwò;	lyùHnlok;
	交際	jyāujì	gàaujai
association n.	會	hwèi;	wúi;
	公會	gūnghwèi	gùngwúi
assurance	確據	chywèjyù;	kokgeui;
	保險	bǎusyǎn	bóuhìm
assure v. t.			
-make sure of	擔保	dānbǎu;	dàumbóu;
-insure	保險	bǎusyǎn	bóuhìm
asthma	哮喘病	syàuchwǎnbìng	hāauchyúnbeHng
astonish v. t.	驚奇	jīngchí	gìngkèiH
astrology n.	占星術	jānsyingshù	jìmsìngseuHt
astronomy	天文學	tyānwénsywé	tìnmàHnhoHk
asylum n.	救濟院	jyòujìywàn	gaujaiyún
atheism n.	無神論	wúshénlwùn	mòuHsàHnleuHn
athlete n.	運動員	yùndùngywán	waHnduHngyùHn
atmosphere n.	大氣	dàchì	daaiHhei
-absolute atmosphere	絕對氣壓	jywédwèichìyā	jyuHtdeuiheingaat
attach v. t.			
-as a label	貼	tyē;	tip;
-join	連	lyán;	lìHn;
-belong to	屬於	shǔyú	suHkyù
attack v. t.	攻擊	gūngji	gūnggìk

attempt v. t.	試	shr̀;	si;
	企 圖	chìtú	kéiHtòuH
attend v. t.			
-be present	出 席	chūsyí;	chēutjiHk;
-give care	照 顧	jàugù	jiugu
attention n.	注 意	jùyì;	jyuyi;
	留 心	lyóusyin	làuHsàm
attitude n.	態 度	tàidù	taaidouH
audit v. t.	查 賬	chájàng	chàHjeung
author n.	著 者	jùjĕ;	jyujé;
	作 者	dzwòjĕ	jokjé
authority n.			
-expert	權 威	chywánwēi;	kyùHnwài;
-power	權 力	chywánlì	kyùHnliHk
autobiography n.	自 傳	dz̀jwàn	jiHjyún
automatic a.	自 動	dz̀dùng	jiHduHng
automobile n.	汽 車	chìchē	heichè
autumn n.	秋 天	chiutyan	chāutin
auxiliary a.	補 助	bŭjù	bóujoH
available a.			
-of being used	可 以 用	kĕyĭyùng;	hóyíH yuHng;
-of being found	找 得 到	jăudédàu	jáaudākdou (wándākdóu)
aviation n.	航 空	hángkūng	hòHnghùng
avoid v. t.	避 免	bìmyăn;	beiHmíHn;
	逃 避	táubì	tòuHbèiH
awakened a.	儆 醒	jĭngsyĭng	gíngsíng
aware a.	覺 悟	jywéwù	gokngH
away a.			
-not in	不 在	búdzài;	bātjoiH (m̀háisyu)
-left	離 開	likāi	lèiHhòi
awful a.	可 怕	kĕpà	hópa

awkward a.

-clumsy	蠢笨	chwǔnbèn;	chéunbaHn;
-ungraceful	不嫻雅	bùsyányǎ;	bāthàaHnngáH (m̀màHnngáH)
-embarrassing	辣手	làshǒu	laaHtsáu

awning n.

-of a vessel	船篷	chwánpéng;	syùHnpàlIng,
of a window	遮篷	jēpéng	jèpàlIng

B

baby n.	嬰孩	yīnghái	yìnghòiH
bachelor n.	學士	sywéshì	hoHksiH
back n.	背部	bèibù;	buibouH;
-behind	背後	bèihòu	buihauH
backward a.	向後	syànghòu;	heunghauH;
-in civilization	落後	lwòhòu	loHkhauH
bacon n.	醃肉	yānròu	yìmyuHk
bad a.	壞	hwài	waaiH
badge n.	徽章	hwēijāng	fāijēung
bag n.	袋	dài	dói
bail			
-v. t. give security	擔保	dànbǎu;	dàambóu;
-n. security	保証金	bǎujèngjīn	bóujinggām
bake v. t.	烘	hūng;	huHng
	烤	kǎu	háau (hon)
bakery n.	麵包店	myànbāudyàn	miHnbāaudim
balance			
-v. t. counter poise	平衡	pínghéng;	pìHnghàHng;
-n. scales	天平	tyānpíng	tìnpìHng
balcony n.	陽臺	yángtái	yèuHngtòiH (kèHláu)
ball n.	球	chyóu	kàuH (bō)

ballast v. t.

-burden	負擔	fùdān;	fuHdàam;
-weigh down	壓下	yāsyà	ngaathaH
balloon n.	氣球	chìchyóu	heikàuH
ballot n.	選票	sywǎnpyàu	syúnpiu
bamboo n.	竹	jú	jūk
banana n.	香蕉	syāngjyāu	hēungjiu
bandage n.	綳帶	bēngdài	bāngdáai
bandits n.	土匪	tǔféi;	tóuféi;
	強盜	chyángdàu	kèuHngdouH
bang v. i.	打	dǎ	dá
bank n.			
-for money	銀行	yínháng;	ngàHnhòHng;
-of a river	河邊	hébyēn	hòHbīn
bankrupt n.	破產	pwòchǎn	pocháan
banner n.	旗	chí;	kèiH;
	旗幟	chíjř	kèiHjìk
banquet n.	筵席	yánsyí;	yìHnjiiHk;
	酒席	jyǒusyí	jáujiiHk
baptize v. t.	施洗	shřsyǐ;	sìsái;
	施浸	shřjìn	sìjam
barbarian n.	化外人	hwàwàirén;	fángoiHyàHn;
	野人	yěrén	yéHyàHn
barber n.	理髮師	lǐfǎshř	léiHfaatsì
bare a.	露體	lùtǐ	louHtái
bargain			
-n purchase	交易	jyāuyì;	gàauyiHk;
-v. i. about price	講價	jyǎngjyà	góngga
bark			
-n. of tree	樹皮	shùpí;	syuHpèiH
-v. i. of dog	犬叫	chywǎn jyàu	hún giu (gáu faiH)

barley n.	大麥	dàmài	daaiHmaHk
barn n.	穀倉	gŭtsāng	gūkchōng
barometer n.	風雨表	fēngyŭbyăo	fūngyúHbíu
barracks n.	兵營	bīngyíng	bìngyìHng
barrel n.			
-vessel	桶	tŭng;	túng;
-of gun	鎗身	chyāngshēn	chēungsan
base n.	基礎	jīchŭ	gèichó
basement n.	地下室	dìsyàshr̀	deiHhaHsāt
basic principles n.	大綱	dàgāng	daaiHgòng
basin n.	臉盆	lyănpén	líHmpùHn(miHnpún)
bass (music) n.	低音	dīyīn	dāiyām
bath n.	洗澡	syǐdzăo	sáichou (chùnglèuHng)
bathe v. t.	洗澡	syǐdzăo	sáichou (chùnglèuHng)
battalion n.	營	yíng	yìHng
battery n.	電池	dyànchŕ	diHuchìH(diHnsàm)
battle n.	戰爭	jànjēng	jinjàng
bay n.	海灣	hăiwān	hóiwāan
be v. i.	是	shr̀	siH (haiH)
beach n.	海邊	hăibyān	hóibīn
bean n.	豆	dòu	dáu
bear v. i.			
-on the back	負擔	fùdān;	fuHdàam;
-endure	忍耐	rěnnài;	yánnoiH;
-give birth to	生	shēng;	sāng (sàang);
-bear responsibility	負責	fùdzé;	fuHjaak;
-bear witness	作證	dzwòjèng;	jokjing;
-bear fruit	結果	jyégwŏ	gitgwó
beard n.	鬍子	húdz	wùHji (wùHsòu)
beast n.	走獸	dzŏushòu	jáusau
beat			
-v. t. hit	打	dă;	dá;

-v. i. of the heart	跳	tyàu;	tiu;
-n. music	拍子	pāidz	paakjí
beautiful a.	美麗	měili;	méiHlaiH;
	漂亮	pyàulyang	piuleuHng (leng)
become			
-v. t. suit	合適	héshì;	haHpsìk;
-v. i. come to be	成爲	chéngwéi	sìHngwàiH
becoming a.	合適	héshì	haHpsìk
because conj.	因爲	yīnwei	yànwaiH
bed n.	床	chwáng	chòHng
bedroom n.	寢室	chǐnshì	chámsāt (fanfóng)
bee n.	蜜蜂	mìfēng	maHtfūng
before Christ; B. C.	紀元前	jìywánchyán	géiyùHnchìHn
beg for food	討飯	tǎufàn	tóufaaHn (hātsiHk)
beggar n.	乞丐	chǐgài	hātkoi (hātyi)
begin v. t.	開始	kāishǐ;	hòichí;
	起	chǐ	héi
beginning n.	起頭	chǐtóu;	héitàuH;
	太初	tàichū	taaichò
behaviour n.	行爲	syíngwéi	hàHngwàiH
behind prep.	在後	dzàihòu	joiHhauH
belief n.	信仰	syìyǎng;	seunyéuHng;
	信心	syìnsyīn	seunsàm
believe v. t.	相信	syāngsyìn	sèungseun
bell n.			
-big	鐘	jūng;	jūng;
-small	鈴	líng	lìHng
belly n.	腹部	fùbù;	fūkbouH;
	肚子	dùdz	tòuHji (tóuH)
belong v. i.	屬於	shǔyú	suHkyù

below adv.	在下	dzài syà	joiH haH
belt n.	腰帶	yāudài;	yīudáai;
	皮帶	pídài	pèiHdáai
bench n.	長凳	cháugdèng	chèuHngdang
bend v. t.	彎曲	wānchyū	wāankuk
beneath prep.	在之下	dzài...jīsyà	joiH...jihaH
benefit m.			
-profit	利益	lìyì;	leiHyik;
-advantage	好處	hǎuchù	hóuchyu
benzine n.	汽油	chìyóu	heiyàuH
bequest n.	遺贈	yídzèng	wàiHjaHng
beseech v. t.	求告	chyóugàu;	kàuHgou;
	懇求	kěnchyóu	hánkàuH
best a.	最好	dzwèi hǎu	jeui hóu
bestow v. t.	賞給	shanggei;	sōungkāp
	贈送	dzèngsùng	jaHngsung
bet v. t.	賭注	dǔjù;	dóujyu;
	打賭	dǎdǔ	dádóu
betray v. t.			
-sell	出賣	chūmài;	chēutmaaiH;
-in violation of trust	背叛	bèipàn	bunpun
beware v. i.	防備	fángbèi	fòHngbeiH
bewilder v. t.	昏亂	hwūnlwàn	fànlyuHn
beyond			
-adv. besides	以外	yǐwài;	yíHngoiH;
-prep. on the further side of	在那邊	dzài...nàbyān	joiII...náIIbin (hái...góbiHn)
bicycle n.	脚踏車	jyǎutàche	geukdaaHpchè (dāanchē)
big a.	大	dà	daaiH
bigamy	重婚	chúnghwūn	chùHngfàn
bill n.			
-of thing bought	賬單	jàngdān;	jeungdāan;

English	Chinese		
-bank note	鈔票	chāupyàu	chàaupiu
billet n.	便條	byàntyáu	biHntìuH
billiards n.	撞球	chwàngchyóu	joHngkàuH
bind v. t.	捆綁	kwŭnbăng;	kwánbóng;
	包紮	bāujā	bàaujaat
biography n.	傳記	jwànjì;	jyuHngei;
	履歷	lyŭlì	léuiHliHk
biology n.	生物學	shēngwùsywé	sàngmaHthoHk
bird n.	鳥	nyău	níuH (jeukjái)
birth n.	誕生;	dànshēng;	daansàng;
	出生	chūshēng	chēutsàng
birthday n.	生日	shēngr̀	sàangyaHt
bishop n.	監督	jyāndū;	gāamdūk;
bite v. t.	咬	yău	ngáauH
bitterness n.	苦味;	kŭwèi;	fúmeiH;
	苦楚	kŭchŭ	fúchó
black a.	黑	hēi	hāak
blackboard n.	黑板	hēibăn	hāakbáan
blameless a.	無可指責	wúkějĭdzé	mòuHhójijaak
blanket n.	毯子	tăndz	jínji (jín)
blasphemy n.	褻瀆	syèdú	sitduHk
blemish n.	玷污;	dyànwū;	dinwù;
	瑕疵;	syátsz̄;	hàHchì;
	毛病	máubìng	mòuHbeHng
blessing n.	福氣	fúchì	fūkhei
blind a.	瞎眼	syāyăn	haHtngáaHn (màaHnngáaHn)
blister n.	水泡	shwĕipàu	séuipaau (séuipōk)
blood n.			
-in the body	血	syĕ, sywè;	hyut;

-descent	血統	syĕttúng	hyuttúng
bloom v. i.	開花	kāihwā	hòifà
blossom v. i.	開花	kāihwā	hòifà
blot v. t.	塗抹	túmwŏ	tòuHmut
blow v. t.	吹	chwēi	chèui
blue a.	藍色	lánsè	lànHsìk
blunt a.			
-having a thick edge	鈍	dwùn;	deuHn;
-in manner	呆板	dāibăn;	ngòiHbáan;
-in speech	梗直	gĕngjf	gángjiHk
board n.			
-plank	板	băn;	báan;
-ministry	部	bù;	bouH;
-board of education	教育部	jyàuyùbù;	gaauyuHkbouH;
-board of foreign mission	西差會	syichāihwèi	sàichàniwúi
boast v. i.	誇口	kwākŏu;	kwàháu;
	自誇	dzkwā	jiHkwà
boat n.	船	chwán	syùHn
bobbin n.	線軸	syànjóu	sinjuHk
body n.			
physical	身體	shēntì;	sàntái;
-of flesh	肉體	ròutì	yuHktái
boil			
-v. t.	煮	jŭ;	jyú;
-n.	瘡	chwēng	chōng
bold a.	勇敢	yŭnggăn;	yúHnggám;
	大膽	dàdăn	daaiHdáam
bolt v. t.	閂	shwān	sàan
bomb			
-n.	炸彈	jàdàn;	jadáan;

-v. t.	轟炸	hūngjà	gwàngja
bondage n.	奴隸	núlì	nòuHdaiH
bonded p. a.	扣留	kòulyóu	kaulàuH
book n.	書	shū	syù
-book of filial piety	孝經	syàujìng	haaugìng
bookworm n.	書獃子	shūdāidz	syùngoiHji (syùchùHng)
border			
-n. frontier	邊界	byānjyè;	bìngaai;
-v. t. adjacent to	鄰接	línjyē	lèuHnjip
born v. t.	出生	chūshēng	chēutsàng (chēutsai)
-born again	重生	chúngshēng	chùHngsàng
borrow v. t.	借入	jyèrù	jeyaHp
bosom n.	懷	hwái;	wàaiH;
-bosom friend	知己	jrjǐ	jìgéi
boss n.	老板	lǎubǎn	lóuHbáan
botanical garden n.	植物園	jŕwùywán	jiHkmaHtyúm
both a.	二	èr;	yiH;
	兩	lyǎng	léuHng
bother v. t.			
-trouble	打擾	dǎrǎu;	dáyiuH (sòuyiuH);
-worry	煩惱	fánnǎu	fàaHnnóuH
bottle n.	瓶子	píngdz	pìHngji (jēun)
bottom n.	底	dǐ;	dái;
-bottomless pit	無底坑	wúdǐkēng	mòuHdáihàang
bow			
-v. t. bend head	低頭	dītóu;	dàitàuH;
-n. weapon	弓	gūng	gùng
bowl n.	碗	wǎn	wún
box n.			
-small	盒子	hédz;	haHpji (háp)
-large	箱子	syāngdz	sèungji (sēung)

boy n.

-child	男孩	nánhái;	nàaHmhòiH(nàaHmjái);
-waiter	茶房	cháfáng;	chàHfóng (siHjái);
-boy scouts n,	童子軍	túngdžjyūn;	tùHngjigwān;
-boyhood n.	兒童時代	értúng shídài	yìHtùHng sìHdoiH
bracelet n.	手鐲	shŏujwó	sáungáak
brain n.	腦	nău	nóuH
brake n.	閘	já	jaaHp
branch	樹枝	shùjī	syuHjì
brave a.	勇敢	yŭnggăn	yúHnggám
bread n.	麵包	myànbāu	miHnbāau
break v. t.	弄破	nùngpwò	luHngpo (jìngwaaiH)
-break a law	犯法	fànfă;	faaHnfaat;
-break off relations	斷絕關係	dwònjywégwōnsyì	tyúIInjyuIItgwàanhaiII
breast n.	胸	syūng	hùng
breath	呼吸	hūsyi	fūkēp
bribe u. t.	賄賂	hwèilù	fúilouH(béi hāakchín)
brick n.	磚	jwān	jyùn
bride n.	新婦	syïnfù;	sànfúH;
	新娘	syïnnyáng	sànnéung
bridegroom n.	新郎	syïnláng	sànlòHng
bridge n.	橋	chyáu	kìuH
brief a.	簡短	jyăndwăn	gáandyún
bright a.	光明	gwāngmíng;	gwòngmìHng;
-as textiles	鮮艷	syānyàn	sìnyiHm
brightness	光輝	gwānghwēi	gwòngfài
brimstone n.	硫磺	lyóuhwáng	làuHwòHng
bring	拿	ná;	nàH (nìng);

English	Chinese		
-rear	養	yăng	yéuHng
British a.	大不列顛	Dàbúlyèdyān	DaaiHbātliHtdīn
broad a.	寬	kwān;	fùn;
	闊	kwò;	fut;
	廣大	gwăngdà	gwóngdaaiH
broadcast v. t.	廣播	gwăngbwò	gwóngbo
brocade n.	織錦	jīrjǐn	jikgám
broker n.	經紀	jīngjì	gìnggéi
bronchitis n.	支氣管炎	jīrchìgwănyán	jiheigúnyìHm
bronze n.	青銅	chīngtúng;	chìngtùHng;
bronze age	銅器時代	túngchìshŕdài	tùHngheisìHdoiH
brooch n.	胸針	syūngjēn;	hùngjàm(sàmháujàm);
	別針	byéjēn	biHtjàm (kaujām)
brook n.	溪	syī	kài
broom n.	掃把	sàubă	soubá
brother n.	兄弟	syūngdì;	hìngdaiH;
-elder brother	哥哥	gēge;	gòHgo;
-younger brother	弟弟	dìdi	dàiHdái
brother-in-law n.			
-elder	姊夫	jyěfū;	jéfū;
-younger	妹夫	mèifū	muiHfū
brown a.	咖啡色	kāfēisè;	gafēsik;
	棕色	dzūngsè	jūngsik
bruise			
-v. i.	打傷	dăshāng;	dásèung;
-v. t.	碰青	pèngching	pungchèng
brush v./n.	刷	shwā;	chaat;
-Chinese brush	毛筆	máubǐ	mòuHbāt
budget n.	預算	yùswàn	yuHsyun

buffalo n.	水牛	shwĕiníu	séuingàuH
build v. t.	建造	jyàndzàu;	ginjouH;
	建築	jyànjù	ginjik
building n.	房屋	fángwū;	fòHngnguk;
	大樓	dàlóu	daaiHláu
bullet n.	子彈	dźdàn	jidáan
bundle n.	綑	kwŭn;	kwán;
	紮	jā	jaat
burden n.	重擔	jùngdàn	chúHngdaam
bureau n.	局	jyú;	guHk;
-bureau of public safety	公安局	gūngānjyú	gùngònguHk
burglar n.	夜盜	yèdàu	yeIIdouII
burial ceremony n.	葬禮	dzànglĭ	jongláiH
burn v. t.	燒	shāu;	sìu;
	燃燒	ránshāu	yìHusìu
bush n.	叢林	tsúnglín	chùHnglàHm
bushel n.	斗	dŏu	dáu
business n.			
-matter	事情	shìrching;	siHchìHng;
-trade	生意	shēngyì	sàangyi
busy a.	忙	máng	mòHng (m̀dākhàaHn)
but chnj.	但是	dànshr	daaHnsiH (daaHnhaiH)
butcher n.	屠夫	túfū	tòuHfù
butter n.	牛油	níuyóu	ngàuHyàuH
butterfly	蝴蝶	húdyé	wùHdip
button n.	扣	kòu	kau
buy v. t.	買	măi	máaiH
by prep.			
-near	近	jìn;	káIIn;
-past	經過	jīnggwò;	gìnggwo;
-with	用	yùng;	yuHng

-by and by	不久	bùjyǒu	bātgáu

C

cabbage n.	白菜	báitsài	baaHkchoi
cabin n.	房艙	fángtsāng	fòHngchōng
cabinet n.	櫃	gwèi	gwaiH
cablegram n.	海底電報	hǎidǐdyànbàu	hóidáidiHnbou
cafe n.	咖啡館	kāfēigwǎn	gafēgún (gafēsāt)
cage n.	鳥籠	nyǎulúng	níuHlùHng
cake n.	餅;	bǐng;	béng;
	糕	gāu	gōu
calamity n.	災難	dzāinàn	jòinaaHn
calcium n.	鈣	gài	koi
calculate v. t.	計算	jìswàn	gaisyun
calendar n.	日曆	rìlì	yaHtliHk
calf n.	小牛	syǎunyóu	sìungàuH (ngàuHjái)
calibre n.			
-of gun	口徑	kǒujìng	háuging
calico n.			
-plain white	白布;	bàibù;	baaHkbou;
-printed	花布	hwābù	fàbou
call v. t.			
-shout	叫;	jyàu;	giu;
-ask	請;	chǐng;	chíng (chéng);
-give a name to	稱呼	chēnghu	chìngfù
callous a.			
-hardened	變硬;	byànyìng	binngaaHn;
-hardened in mind	硬心腸;	yìngsyīncháng;	ngáaHnsàmchèuHng;
-unfeeling	無情	wúchíng	mòuHchìHng
calm a.			
-of the sea	平靜;	píngjìng;	pìHngjiHng;

-undisturbed	安ㄢ 靜ㄐㄧㄥ	ānjìng	ònjiHng
camel n.	駱ㄌㄨㄛ 駝ㄊㄨㄛ	lwòtwó	loktòH
camera n.	照ㄓㄠ 相ㄒㄧㄤ 機ㄐㄧ	jàusyàngjī	jiuséunggèi(yíngséunggēi)
camp n.	營ㄥ	yíng	yìHng
camphor n.	樟ㄓㄤ 腦ㄋㄠ	jānguŭlu	jĕunguóuH
campus n.	校ㄒㄧㄠ 園ㄩㄢ	syàuywán	haauHyùHn
can			
-v. t. able	能ㄋㄥ 夠ㄍㄡ	nénggou;	nàHnggau;
-n. metal	罐ㄍㄨㄢ	gwàn	gun
canal n.			
-drain	溝ㄍㄡ	gōu;	gàu;
-for navigation	運ㄩㄣ 河ㄏㄜ	yùnhé	waHnhòH
cancel v. t.			
-annul	取ㄑㄩ 消ㄒㄧㄠ	chyŭsyāu;	chéuisiu;
-obliterate	擦ㄘㄚ 掉ㄉㄧㄠ	tsāсhyàu	chaaidiuII (chaaijó)
cancer n.	癌ㄞ	yán	ngàaHm
candidate n.			
-for election	候ㄏㄡ 選ㄒㄩㄢ 人ㄖㄣ	hòusywănrén;	hauHsyúnyàHn;
-for position	申ㄕㄣ 請ㄑㄧㄥ 人ㄖㄣ	shēnchǐngrén	sànchíngyàHn
candle n.	蠟ㄌㄚ 燭ㄓㄨ	làjú	laaHpjūk
candlestick n	蠟ㄌㄚ 燭ㄓㄨ 台ㄊㄞ	làjútái	laaHpjūktòiH
candy n.	糖ㄊㄤ	táng;	tóng;
	糖ㄊㄤ 果ㄍㄨㄛ	tánggwŏ	tòHnggwó
cannon n.	大ㄉㄚ 礮ㄆㄠ	dàpàu	daaiHpaau
canteen n.			
-eating house	餐ㄘㄢ 室ㄕ	tsānshì;	chāansāt;
-flask for water	水ㄕㄨㄟ 壺ㄏㄨ	shwěihú	séuiwùH
canvas n.	帆ㄈㄢ 布ㄅㄨ	fānbù	fàaHnbou
canvass v. t.			
-for votes	徵ㄓㄥ 求ㄑㄧㄡ	jēngchyóu;	jìngkàuH;
-for goods	推ㄊㄨㄟ 銷ㄒㄧㄠ	twēisyāu;	tèuisiu;

-for funds	募捐	mùjywān	mouHgyùn
cap n.	帽子	màudz	mouHji(móu)
capable a.			
-able	能夠	nénggou;	nàHnggau;
-clever	本事	běnshr̀	búnsiH
capacity n.			
-ability	才能	tsáinéng;	chòiHnàHng;
-space	容量	rúnglyàng	yùHngleuHng
capital n.			
–city	首都	shǒudū;	sáudòu;
-money	資本	dz̄běn;	jibún;
-capitalism n.	資本主義	dz̄běnjǔyì;	jibúnjyúyiH;
-capitalist n.	資本家	dz̄běnjyā	jibúngā
capsize v. t.	翻	fān;	fàan;
-a boat	翻船	fānchwán	fàansyùHn
captain n			
-ship	船長	chwánjǎng;	syùHnjéung;
-team	隊長	dwèijǎng	deuiHjéung
captive n.	俘擄	fūlǔ	fùlóuH
capture			
-n.	戰利品	jànlìpǐn;	jinleiHbán;
-v. t.	俘擄	fūlǔ	fùlóuH
car n.	汽車	chìchē	heichè
carat n.			
-jewel	卡	kǎ;	kā;
-gold	開	kāi	hōi
caravan n.			
-of persons	隊商	dwèishāng;	deuiHsèung;
-wagon	篷馬車	péngmǎchē	pùHngmáHchè
carbon n.	炭	tàn	taan
-carbon dioxide	二氧化碳	èryǎnghwàtàn	yiHyéuHngfataan
card n.	卡片	kǎpyàn;	kātpín;

-visiting card	名片	míngpyàn;	mìHngpín;
invitation card	請帖	chǐngtyě	chéngtip
cardigan n.	短衣	dwǎnyī	dyúnyī (dyúnsāam)
care n.			
-heed	留心	lyóusyīn;	làuHsàm;
-care for one another	彼此相顧	bǐtsž syānggù	béichí sèunggu
career			
-n. occupation	職業	jíyè;	jìkyiHp;
-v. i. run rapidly	疾走	jídzǒu	jaHtjáu (jáudǔkfaai)
careful a.	小心	syǎusyīn	síusàm
cargo n.	貨物	hwòwù	fomaHt
carnal a.	屬血氣	shǔsyěchì;	suHkhyuthei;
-carnal desire	性慾	syìngyù	singyuHk
carpenter n.	木匠	mùjyàng	muHkjéung
carpet n.	地氈	dìtǎn	deiHjin
carriage n.	馬車	mǎchē	máHchè
carrot n.	紅蘿蔔	húnglwóbo	hùHnglòHbaaHk
carry v. t.			
-on one's back	背負	bēifù;	buifuH;
-in the hand	拿	ná;	nàH (nìk);
-on the shoulder	挑	tyāu	tìu (dàam)
cart n.	車	chē	chè
cartoon n.	卡通	kǎtūng;	kǎtūng,
	漫畫	mànhwà	maaHnwá
cartridge n.	子彈	dzždàn	jídáan
carve v. t.	彫刻	dyāukè	diuhāak
case v.			
-condition	情況	chíngkwàng;	chìHngfong;
-small box	盒	hé;	háp;

-event	事件	shìjyàn	siHgín
cash n.	現金	syànjīn;	yiHngàm;
	現款	syànkwǎn	yiHnfún
cast v. t.	丟	dyōu;	dìu;
-cast away	丟棄	dyōuchì	dìuhei
castle n.	堡壘	bǎulěi	bóuléuiH
casual a.			
-accidental	偶然	ǒurán;	ngáuHyìHn;
-irregular	臨時	línshí	làHmsìH
cat n.	貓	māu	māau
catalogue n.	目錄	mùlù	muHkluHk
catch v. t.			
-arrest	捉	jwō;	jūk;
-as a ball	接	jyē;	jip;
-as a contagious disease	傳染	chwánrán	chyùHnyíhm
category n.	類	lèi;	leuiH;
	種類	jǔnglèi	júngleuiH
cater v. i.	辦伙食	bànhwǒshí	baaHnfósiHk
caterpillar n.	毛蟲	máuchúng	mòuHchùHng
cathedral n.	禮拜堂	líbàitáng	láiHbaaitòHng
cause			
-n. reason	緣故	ywángù;	yùHngu;
-v. t. make	使	shǐ	sí (sáidou)
caution n.			
-care	留心	lyóusyīn;	làuHsàm;
-advice	忠告	jūnggàu	jùnggou
cave n.	洞	dùng	duHng
cease v. t.	停止	tíngjǐ	tiHngjí
-cease fire	停火	tínghwǒ	tiHngfó

ceiling n.	天花板	tyānhwābǎn	tīnfàbáan
celebrate v. t.	慶祝	chìngjù	hingjūk
cement n.	水泥	shwĕiní	séuinàiH
cemetery n.	公墓	gūngmù	gùngmouH
cent n.	分	fēn	fàn (sīn)
central a.	中間	jūngjyān	jūnggāan
-Central Bank	中央銀行	Jūngyāngyínháng	JùngyèungngàHnhòHng
centre n.			
-inside	中間	jūngjyān	jūnggāan;
-middle point	中心點	jūngsyīndyǎn	jùngsàmdím
century n.	世紀	shìjì	saigéi
ceremonial music n.	禮樂	lǐywè	láiHngoHk
reremony n.	典禮	dyǎnlǐ	dínláiH
-master of ceremonies	主禮人	jǔlirén	jyùláiHyàHn
certainty n.	確實性	chywèshfuyìng	koksaHtsing
certificate n.	證書	jèngshū;	jingsyù;
	執照	jŕjàu	jāpjiu
chaff n.	糠粃	kāngbǐ	hòngbéi
chain n.	鎖鍊	swǒlyàn	sólín
chair n.	椅子	yǐdz	yíji (yí)
chairman n.	主席	jǔsyí	jyújiHk
chalk n.	粉筆	fěnbǐ	fánbāt
challenge v. t.	挑戰	tyǎujàn	tiujin
chamber n.	寢室	chǐnshì	chàmsāt
champagne n.	香檳酒	syānbīnjyǒu	hēungbānjáu
chance n.	機會	jīhwèi	gèiwuiH
change v. t.			
-alter	改	gǎi;	gói;
-substitute	換	hwàn;	wuHn;

English	Chinese		
-transform	變化	byànhwà	binfa
channel n.	海峽	hǎisyá	hóihaaHp
chant v. t.	唱頌	chàngsùng	cheungjuHng
chapter n.	章	jāng	jèung
character n.			
-mental nature	品性	pǐnsyìng;	bánsing;
-Chinese word	字	dà;	jiH
-persons	人物	rénwù	yàHnmaHt
characteristic n.	特徵	tèjēng;	daHkjìng;
	特性	tèsyìng	daHksing
charcoal n.	木炭	mùtàn	muHktaan
charge v. t.	索價	swǒjyà	sokga (maaiHga)
-blame	責怪	dzégwài;	jaakgwaai;
-give orders	吩咐	fēnfù;	fànfu;
-entrust	交代	jyāudài;	gàaudoiH;
-free of charge	免費	myǎnfèi	míHnfai
charity n.	慈善	tszshàn	chìHsiHn
charming a.			
-giving pleasure	迷人	mírén;	màiHyàHn;
-delightful	可愛	kěài	hóoi
chart n.			
-tabular form	圖表	túbyǎu;	tòuHbíu;
-sea map	航海圖	hànghǎitú	hòHnghóitòuH
chase v. t.	追擊	jwēijí	jēuigìk
chaste a.	正經	jèngjing;	jinggìng;
	貞潔	jēnjyé	jìnggit
chat v. i.	閒談	syántán;	hàaHntàaHm(kìnggái)
	談話	tánhwà	tàaHmwaH
cheap a.	便宜	pyányì	biHnyìH (pèHng)

English	Chinese		
cheat			
-v. t.	欺騙	chīpyàn;	hèipin;
-n.	騙子	pyàndz	pinjí
cheek n.	嘴巴	dzwěibā	jéuibā (jéui)
cheer			
-n. mirth	愉快	yùkwài;	yuHfaai;
-v. t. gladden	歡樂	hwānlè;	túnloHk;
-v. t. applause	喝采	hètsǎi	hotchói
-cheer up!	抖起精神來	dǒuchǐjìngshénlái	dáuhéijìngsàHnlàiH
cheerful a.	愉快	yùkwài;	yuHfaai;
	高興	gāusyìng	gòuhing
chemist n.			
-skilled	化學家	hwàsywéjyā;	fahoHkgā;
-dispensing	藥劑師	yàujishr̄	yeuHkjāisi
chemistry n.	化學	hwàsywé	fahoHk
cheque n.	支票	jr̄pyàu	jīpiu
cherry n.	櫻桃	yingtáu	yìngtòuH
chess n.	棋	chí	kéi
-play chess	下棋	syàchí	haHkèiH (jūkkéi)
chest n.			
-breast	胸部	syūngbù;	hùngbouH;
-box	箱	syāng	sèung
chestnut n.	栗子	lìdz	leuHtjí (lùngléut)
chicken n.	雞	jī	gāi
chicken-pox n.	水豆	shwěidòu	séuidáu
chief a.			
-leader	首領	shǒulǐng;	sáulǐHng;
-first	第一	dìyi;	daiHyāt;
-main	主要	jǔyàu	jyúyiu

chiefly adv.

-above all 主要 jǔyàu; jyùyiu;

-mostly 大概 dàgài daaiHkói

chilblain n. 凍瘡 dùngchwāng dungchōng

child n. 孩子 háidz; hàaiHji;

小孩 syǎuhái siuhòiH (saimānjái)

children n.

-sons and
daughters 兒女 érnyǔ yìHnéuiH

children's Day 兒童節 értúngjyé yìHtùHngjit

chilly a. 寒冷 hánlěng hòHnláaHng

chimney n. 煙肉 yāntsung yìntūng

China n. 中國 Jūnggwó Jùnggwok

chinaware n. 瓷器 tszchì chìHhei

Chinese n. 中文 Jūngwén JùngmàHn

chisel

-v. t. 鑿 dzáu; joHk;

-n. 鑿子 dzáudz joHkji (jók)

chloroform n. 麻藥 máyàu màHyeuHk

choice n.

-choosing 選擇 sywǎndzé; syúnjaaHk;

-elite 精華 jìnghwá jìngwàH

choir n. 唱詩班 chàngshībān cheungsìbāan

choke v. t. 窒息 jìsyí jaHtsìk

choose v. t. 揀選 jyǎnsywǎn gáansyún

chord n.

-string 弦 sywán; yùHn;

-combination of
tones 和音 héyìn wòHyàm

chorus n. 副歌 fùgē fugō

Christmas n. 聖誕節 Shèngdànjyé Singdaanjit

church n. 教會 jyàuhwèi; gaauwúi;

禮拜堂 lǐbàitáng láiHbaaitòHng

-church building	教堂	jyàutáng	gaautòHng
cigar n.	雪茄煙	ɵywŏjyāyān	ɵyutgāyìn
cigarette n.	香煙	syāngyēn	hēungyìn
cinder			
n. ember	火屑	hwŏsyè;	fósit;
-v. t. burn	燒成灰	shāuchénghwēi	sìusìHngfùi
cinema n.			
-theatre	電影院	dyànyĭngywàn;	diHnyingyún;
-pictures	電影	dyànyĭng	diHnyíng
cinnamon n.			
-cassia	肉桂	róugwèi;	yuHkgwaı;
-cassia bark	桂皮	gwèipi	gwaipèiH
circle			
-n.	圈	chywān;	hyūn;
-n.	圓	ywán;	yùHn;
-v. i.	繞行	ràusyíng	yíuHhàHng
circulation n.			
-of the blood	循環	syúnhwán;	chèuHnwàaHn;
-of newspaper, etc.	銷路	syāulù	sìulouH
circumcision n.	割禮	gēlĭ	goｔláiII
circumstances n.			
-conditions	光景	gwāngjĭng;	gwòngging;
-surroundings	環境	hwánjìng	wàaHngíng
circus n.			
-company	馬戲團	măsyìtwán;	máIIheityùHn;
-show	馬戲	măsyì	máHhei
cistern n.			
-tank	水槽	shwĕitsáu;	séuichòuH;

English	Chinese		
-reservoir	水池	shwěichí	séuichìH
citizen n.	公民	gūngmín;	gùngmàHn;
	市民	shìmín	sìHmàHn
city n.	城市	chéngshì	sìHngsíH
-city wall	城牆	chéngchyáng	sìHngchèuHng
civil a.			
-pert. to citizen	公民	gūngmín;	gùngmàHn;
-polite	有禮	yǒulǐ;	yáuHláiH;
-civil law	民法	mínfǎ;	màHnfaat;
-civil war	內亂	nèilwàn	noiHlyuHn
civilization n.	文化	wénhwà;	màHnfa;
	文明	wénmíng	màHnmìHng
claim v. t.			
-maintain	主張	jǔjāng;	jyújèung;
-demand	要求	yāuchyóu	yìukàuH
clamour n.	亂嚷	lwànrǎng;	lyuHnyeuHng(lyuHngiu);
	吵鬧	chǎunàu	cháaunaauH
clap v. t.	拍	pāi	paak
clarity v. t.	澄清	chéngchīng	chìHngchìng
class n.			
-in school	年級	nyánjí;	nìHnkāp;
-caste	階級	jyējí;	gāaikāp;
-grade	等級	děngjí;	dángkāp;
-upper class	上流社會	shànglyóushèhwèi;	seuHnglàuHséhwúi;
-lower class	下層社會	syàtséngshèhwèi;	haHchàHngséHwúi;
-middle class	中產階級	chūngchǎnjyējí;	jùngcháangāaikāp;
-first class	第一等	dìyiděng;	daiHyātdáng;
-class leader	班長	bānjǎng	bāanjéung

classic a.

-in art   古典   gŭdyăn;   gúdín;

-of the first class   第一流   dìyilyóu   daiHyätlàuH

classicism n.   古典主義   gŭdyănjŭyì   gúdínjyúyiII

classification n.   分類   fēnlèi   fànleuiH

classmate n.   同學   túngsywé   tùHnghoHk

clause n.

-in gram.   子句   dz̄jyù;   jígeui;

-of treaty   條   tyáu   tiuH

claw n.   爪   jwă   jáau

clay n.   泥土   nítŭ   nàiHtóu

clean a.   乾淨   gānjìng   gònjeHng

cleanse v. t.   洗淨   syĭjing   sáijeHng

clear a.   清楚   chīngchu;   chìngchó;

-bright   亮   lyàng;   leuHng (gwòng);

-plain   明白   míngbai   mìHngbaaHk

cleave

-v. i. stick   黏貼   nyántyē;   nìHmtip;

-v. t. split   分裂   fēnlyè   fànliHt

clerk n.

-of a govt.   文員   wénywán;   màIInyùHn;

-of a hotel   管理員   gwănlĭywán;   gúnléiHyùHn;

-shop-assistant   店員   dyànywán   dimyùHn

clever a.

-in learning   聰明   tsūngmíng;   chùngmìHng;

-smart or quick   伶俐   línglì;   lìHngleiH;

-skilful   有本事   yŏubĕnshɩ̀   yáuHbúnsiH

client n.

-of a lawyer   當事人   dāngshɩ̀rén;   dòngsiHyàHn;

-of a shop	客人	kèrén	haakyàHn(yàHnhaak)
cliff n.	懸崖	sywányá;	yùHnngàaiH;
	山崖	shānyá	sàanngàaiH
climate n.	氣候	chìhòu;	heihauH;
	水土	shwěitǔ	séuitóu
climax n.			
-acme	頂點	dǐngdyǎn;	dǐngdím;
-in a play	高潮	gāucháu	gòuchìuH
climb v. t.	爬	pá	pàH
clinic n.	診所	jěngswǒ	chánsó
clock n.	鐘	jūng	jūng
close			
-v. t. as eyes	閉	bì;	bai (mèimàaiH);
-v. t. as door	關	gwān;	gwàan (sàan);
-a. near	接近	jyējìn	jipgaHn
cloth n.	布	bù	bou
clothe v. i.	穿	chwān	chyún (jeuk)
clothes n.	衣服	yìfu;	yìfuHk;
	衣裳	yìshang	yìsèuHng
cloud n.	雲	yún	wàHn
cloudy a.	陰天	yìntyān	yàmtìn
clove n.			
-cleft	裂隙	lyèsyì;	liHtgwìk;
-spice	丁香	dǐngsyāng	dìnghèung
clover n.	豐裕度日	fēngyùdùr	fùngyuHdouHyaHt
clown n.	小丑	syǎuchǒu	sìucháu
club n.	俱樂部	jyūlèbù	kèuiloHkbouH
clumsy a.			
-in manner	粗魯	tsūlǔ;	chòulóuH;
-not skiful	笨	bèn	baHn

clutch

-n. grasp	把握	báwò;	bángāak;
-v. t. disarrange	弄亂	nùnglwàn	luHnglyuHn (jìnglyuHn)

coach n.

-carriage	馬車	măchē;	máHchè;
-football, etc.	教練	jyàulyàn	gaauliHn

coal n. 煤 méi mùiH

coarse a.

-rough	粗	tsū;	chòu;
-rude	粗魯	tsūlŭ	chòulóuH

coast n.

	海岸	hăiàn;	hóingoHn;
	海邊	hăibyān	hóibin

coat n.

	外衣	wàiyī;	ngoiHyì;
	大衣	dàyī	daaiHyì (daaiHlāu)

cobweb n. 蜘蛛網 jrjūwăng jìjyùmóHng

cock n. 公雞 gūngjī gùnggài

-cock crow 雞叫 jījyàu gāigiu

cockroach n. 蟑螂 jānglàng jèunglòHng (gaHtját)

cocoanut n. 椰子 yédz yèHjí

cocoon n. 繭 jyăn gáan

code n. 法典 fădyăn faatdín

co-education n. 男女同校 nánnyŭtúngsyàu nàaHmnéuiHtùHng- haauH

co-existence n.

	並存	bìngtswún;	biHngchyùHn;
	共存	gùngtswún	guHngchyùHn

coffee n. 咖啡 kāfēi gafē

-coffee-house n. 咖啡店 kāfēidyàn gafēdim

coffin n. 棺材 gwēntsái gùnchòiH

cognate a.

-kindred by birth	同族	tùngdzú;	tùHngjuHk;
-allied	相聯	syānglyán	sèunglyùHn

co-herence n.

-connection 聯絡 lyánlwò; lyùHnlok;

-sticking together 黏合 nyánhé nìHmhaHp

coin n. 銅錢 túngchyán; tùHngchìHn;

硬幣 yìngbì ngaaHnbaiH

coincidence n. 碰巧 pèngchyǎu; punghǎau(yuHngāam);

巧合 chyǎuhé háauhaHp

cold a. 冷 lěng láaHng

co-living n. 共同生活 gùngtúngshēnghwó guHngtùHngsàngwuHt

collapse v. i.

-as a govt. 瓦解 wǎjyě; ngáHgáai;

-as a house 倒塌 dǎutà; dóutaap (lam)

-as plans 失敗 shībài sātbaaiH

collar n. 衣領 yilǐng yìléHng

colleague n. 同事 túngshr̀ tùHngsiH

collect v. t.

-as stamps 收集 shōují; sàujaaHp;

-receive 收 shōu sàu

collection n.

-gathering 集合 jíhé; jaaHphaHp;

college n. 學院 sywéywàn; hoHkyún;

大學 dàsywé daaiHhoHk

collision n.

-striking together 相撞 syēngjwàng; sèungjoHng;

-conflict 衝突 chūngtù chùngdaHt

colloquial a.

-not literary 土話 tǔhwà; tóuwá;

-informal 非正式 fēijèngshr̀ fèijingsìk

colonel n. 上校 shàngsyàu seuHnggaau

colony n.	殖民地	jímíndì	jiHkmàHndeiH
color n.	顏色	yánsè;	ngàaHnsìk;
-n. appearance	氣色	chìsè;	heisìk;
-v. t. put color on	上色	shàngsè	séuHngsìk
color blindness n.	色盲	sèmáng	sìkmàaHng
colt n.	駒	jyū;	kèui;
-v. t. befool	欺弄	chīnùng	hèiluHng
column n.			
-of characters	行	háng;	hòHng;
-newspaper	欄	lán;	làaHn;
-of soldiers	縱隊	dzùngdwèi	jùngdeuiH
comb			
-n.	梳子	shūdz;	sñjí (sñ);
-v. t.	梳	shū	sō
combine v. t.			
-join	聯合	lyánhé;	lyùIIuluaIIp,
-mix	攙	chāu;	chàm;
-of chemistry	化合	hwàhé	fahaHp
come v. i.	來	lái;	làiH;
	到	dàu	dou
-come again	再來	dzàilái	joilòiH (joilàiH)
comedy n.	喜劇	syǐjyù	héikeHk
comfort n./v. t.	安慰	ānwèi	ònwai
comfortable a.	舒服	shūfu;	syùtuHk;
	舒適	shūshì	syūsìk
comma n.	逗點	dòudyǎn;	dauHdím;
	一撇	yìpyě	yātpit
command v. t.			
-give orders	命令	mìnglìng;	miHngliHng;
-give instructions	吩咐	fēnfù	fànfu
commander-in-chief n.	總司令	dzǔngsžlìng;	júngsìliHng;
	元帥	ywánshwài	yùHnseui

commemoration n.	紀念	jìnyàn	geiniHm
-commemoration day	紀念日	jìnyànr̀	geiniHmyaHt
commence v. t.	開始	kāishǐ;	hòichí;
	起	chǐ	héi
commend v. t.			
-praise	稱讚	chēngdzàn;	chìngjaan;
-recommend	推薦	twēijyàn	tèuijin
commentary n.	評註	píngjù;	pìHngjyu;
	註解	jùjyě	jyugáai
commerce n.			
-between foreign countries	通商	tūngshāng	tùngsèung
commercial a.	商業	shāngyè	sèungyiHp
commission			
-n. duty	使命	shǐmìng;	simiHng;
-n. brokerage	佣金	yùngjìn;	yúnggēm;
-v. t. appoint	委任	wěirèn	wáiyaHm
commit v. t.			
-consign	交託	jyāutwō;	gàautok;
-perpetrate, as crime	犯法	fànfǎ;	faaHnfaat;
-commit sin	犯罪	fàndzwèi	faaHnjeuiH
committee n.			
-of a church	委辦會	wěibànhwèi;	wáiHbaaHnwúi;
-of a school	董事部	dǔngshɨbù	dúngsiHbouH
common a.			
-of things	普通	pǔtūng;	póutùng;
-usual	平常	píngcháng	pìHngsèuHng
-common people	平民	píngmín;	pìHngmàHn;
	老百姓	lǎubǎisyìng	lóuHbaaksing
-common saying	俗話	súhwà	juHkwá

-common sense	常識	chángshr̀	sèuHngsīk
commonwealth n.	共和政治	gùnghéjèngjr̀	guHngwòHjingjiH
commotion n.	騷動	sāudùng	sòuduHng
communicate v. t.			
-share in common	共享	gùngsyăng;	guHnghéung;
-convey	傳達	chwándá;	chyùHndaaHt;
-impart	分給	fēngěi;	fānkāp (fànbéi);
-be connected	相通	syāngtūng	sèungtùng
communism n	共產主義	gùngchănjŭyì	guHngcháanjyúyiH
communist party n.	共產黨	gùngchăndăng	guHngcháandóng
community n.			
-living together	共同生活	gùngtúngshēnghwó;	guHngtùHngsàngwuHt;
-common character	通性	tūngsyìng;	tùngsing;
-society	社會	shèhwèi	séHwúi
companion n.	同伴	túngbàn	tùHngbuHn
company n.			
-guest	賓客	bīnkè;	bànhaak;
-in business	公司	gūngsz̄;	gūngsi;
-group	隊	dwèi	deuiH
compare v. t.	比較	bĭjyău	béigaau
compass n.	指南針	jĭnánjēn;	jinàaHmjām;
	羅盤	lwópán	lòHpàHn
compassion n.			
-pity	憐憫	lyánmĭn;	lìHnmáHn;
-sympathy	同情心	túngchíngsyīn	tùHngchìHngsàm
compel v. t.	強逼	chyángbī;	kèuHngbīk;
	勉強	myănchyăng	míHnkéuHng

compensate

-v. i. make amend　　賠償　　péicháng;　　pùiHsèuHng;

-v. t. counter
　　　　balance　　相抵　　syāngdǐ　　sèungdái

compete v. i.

-try to get　　競爭　　jìngjēng;　　gingjàng;

-in a contest　　比賽　　bǐsài　　béichoi

competent a.

-adequate　　充分　　chūngfèn;　　chùngfaHn;

-fit　　適合　　shìhé;　　sìkhaHp;

-qualified　　合格　　hégé　　haHpgaak

competition n.　　競爭　　jìngjēng;　　gingjàng;

　　　　　　　　比賽　　bǐsài　　béichoi

complain v. t.

-murmur　　埋怨　　máiywàn;　　màaiHyun;

-censure　　指責　　jǐdzé　　jijaak

complement n.　　補語　　bǔyǔ;　　bóuyúH;

　　　　　　　　補充　　bǔchūng　　bóuchùng

complete

-v. t. finish　　完成　　wánchéng;　　yùHngsìHng;

-a. perfect　　完全　　wánchywán　　yùHnchyùHn

complex a.

-complicated　　複雜　　fùdzá;　　fūkjaaHp;

-composite　　混成　　hwǔnchéng　　waHnsìHng

complicate a.　　複雜　　fùdzá　　fūkjaaHp

compliment

-n. of admiration　　稱讚　　chēngdzàn;　　chìngjaan;

-n. greetings　　問候　　wènhòu;　　maHnhauH;

-v. t. congratulate　　恭喜　　gūngsyǐ　　gùnghèi

comply v. i.

-as a request　　答應　　dāyìng;　　daapying;

-as the rules　　服從　　fútsúng　　fuHkchùHng

component a

-composing　　組合　　dzǔhé;　　jóuhaHp;

-constituent	成分	chéngfèn	sìHngfaHn
compose v. t.			
-a song	作曲	dzwòchyǔ;	jokkūk;
-printing	排字	páidz̀;	pàaiHjiH;
-constitute	組織	dzǔjī	jóujik
composer n.	作曲家	dzwòchyǔjyā	jokkūkgā
composition n.	作文	dzwòwén;	jokmán;
	文章	wénjāng	màHnjèung
compound			
-n. composition	混合物	hwǔnhéwù;	waHnhaHpmaHt;
-v. t. a medicine	配藥	pèiyàu;	puiyeuHk;
-n. interest	複利	fùlì	fūkleiH
comprehend v. t.	瞭解	lyǎujyě;	líuHgáai;
	明白	míngbai	mìHngbaaHk
compress v. t.	壓	yā;	ngaat;
	壓搾	yājà	ngaatja
compulsory a.			
-compelled	強迫	chyángpwò;	kéuHngbāak (kéuHngbik),
-under obligation	義務	yìwù	yiHmouH
computer n.	電腦	dyànnǎu	diHnnóuH
concave a.	凹	wā	nāp
conceal v. t.			
-hide	隱藏	yǐntsáng;	yánchòHng;
-keep secret	隱瞞	yǐnmán	yánmùHn
conceit			
-n. of one's self	自誇	dz̀kwā;	jiHkwà;
-v. t. imagine	想像	syǎngsyàng	séungjeuHng
conceive v. t.			
-become pregnant	懷孕	hwáiyùn;	wàaiHyaHn;
-think of	想到	syǎngdàu	séungdou

concentrate v. t.

-to condense   集中   jíjūng;   jaaHpjùng;

-to give attention   專心   jwānsyīn   jyùnsàm

conception n.

-idea   概念   gàinyàn;   koiniHm;

-becoming pregnant   懷孕   hwáiyùn   wàaiHyaHn

concern

-n. interest in   關心   gwānsyīn;   gwàansàm;

-v. t. relate to   關涉   gwānshè   gwàansip

concerning prep.

-as regards   關於   gwānyú;   gwàanyù;

-relation to   有關   yǒugwān   yáuHgwàan

concert n.   音樂會   yīnywèhwèi   yàmngoHkwúi

concession n.

-yielding   讓步   ràngbù;   yeuHngbouH;

-grant   允許   yǔnsyǔ;   wàHnhéui;

-land   租界   dzūjyè   jòugaai

conciliate v. t. 調停   tyáutíng   tìuHtìHng

conclusion n.   結論   jyélwùn   gitleuHn

concordance n.

-index   索引   swǒyǐn;   sokyáHn;

-accordance   一致   yíjr   yātji

concrete

-a. not abstract   具體   jyùtǐ;   geuiHtái;

-n. beton   混凝土   hwǔnníngtǔ   waHnyìHngtóu (seHksì)

concubine n.   妾   chyè   chip (chipsiH)

concussion n.   震動   jèndùng   janduHng

condemn v. t.

-pronounce sentence 定罪   dìngdzwèi;   diHngjeuiH;

| -blame | 怪責 | gwàidzé | gwaaijaak |

condense v. t.

| -into fewer words | 縮短 | swōdwǎn; | sūkdyún; |
| -make denser | 凝結 | níngjyē | yìHnggit |

condition n.

| -state | 情形 | chíngsying; | chìHngyiHng; |
| -terms | 條件 | tyáujyàn | tìuHgín |

conduct

| -n. behaviour | 品性 | pǐnoyìng; | bànoing; |
| -v. t. direct | 指揮 | jǐrhwēi | jífài |

confederation n. | 聯邦 | lyánbāng | lyùHnbòng |

confer

| v. t. give | 給 | gěi; | kāp (béi), |
| v. i. consult with | 商量 | shānglyang | sèunglèuHng |

conference n. | 會議 | hwèiyì | wuiHyíH |

confess v. t. | 承認 | chéngrèn; | sìHngyiHng; |
| -a fault | 認錯 | rèntswò | yiHngcho |

confidence n.

| -faith | 信心 | syìnsyin; | seunsàm; |
| -trust | 信用 | syìngyùng | seunyuHng |

confidential a.

| -secret | 秘密 | mìmi; | beimaHt; |
| -written on envelope | 親展 | chinjǎn | chànjín |

confirm v. t.

-establish	證實	jèngshf;	jingsaHt;
-make certain	確定	chywèdìng;	kokdiHng;
-ratify	批准	pījwǔn	pàijéun

confiscate v. t. | 充公 | chūnggūng; | chùnggùng; |
| | 沒收 | mwòshōu | mutsàu |

conflict v. t.

-clash as opinions	衝突	chūngtù;	chùngdaHt;
-be different	矛盾	máudwùn	màauHtéuHn

Confucius n. 孔子 Kŭngdž Húngjí

confusion n.

-disorder	混亂	hwŭnlwàn;	waHnlyuHn;
-discomfiture	失意	shīyì	sātyi

congratulate z. t. 慶祝 chìngjù; hingjūk;

恭喜 gūngsyĭ gùnghéi

-congratulate on the New Year 拜年 bàinyán baainìHn

congratulations n. 祝詞 jùtsź jūkchìH

-congratulotions at Christmas 恭祝聖誕 gūngjù Shèngdàn gūngjūk Singdaan

congregate v. t. 會集 hwèijí; wuiHjaaHp;

聚會 jyùhwèi jeuiHwuiH

conjunction n. 連接詞 lyánjyētsź lìHnjipchìH

connect v. t.

-unite	連結	lyánjyē;	lìHngit;
-to link	串	chwàn	chyun

conquer v. t.

-gain dominion	征服	jēngfú;	jìngfuHk;
-overcome	克服	kèfú;	hāakfuHk;
-defeat	打敗	dăbài	dábaaiH

conscience n. 良心 lyángsyĭn lèuHngsàm

conscious a.

-of one's failing	自覺	dżjywé;	jiHgok;
-aware	覺悟	jywéwù	gokngH

consecutive a. 連續 lyánsyù lìHnjuHk

consent v. i.	同意	túngyì;	tùHngyi;
	贊成	dzànchéng	jaansìHng
consequence n.			
-result	結果	jyégwǒ;	gitgwó;
-effect	影響	yǐngsyǎng;	yìnghéung;
-relation	關係	gwānsyì	gwàanhaiH
conservatism n.	保守主義	bǎushǒujǔyì	bóusáujyúyiH
consider v. t.			
-think over	考慮	kǎulyù	háauleuiH;
-regard as	以為	yǐwéi	yíHwàiH
consist v. i.			
-composed	組成	dzǔchéng;	jóusìHng;
-comprised in	包含	bāuhán	bàauhàHm
consolation n.	安慰	ānwèi	ônwai
-consolation money	撫恤金	fǔsyùjīu	fúseutgām
consonant n.	輔音	fǔyīn;	fulIyāni;
	子音	dzǐyīn	jiyām
conspicuous a.			
-visible	可見	kějyàn;	hógin;
-prominent	顯著	syǎnjù	hínjyu
constantly adv.	時常	shícháng	sìHsèuHng (sìHsìH)
constitute v. t.			
-appoint	委任	wěirèn;	wáiyaHm;
-establish	設立	shèlì;	chitlaHp;
-form	組織	dzǔjī	jóujik
constitution n.			
-structure	構造	gòudzàu;	kaujouH;
-organic law	憲法	syànfǎ	hinfaat
construction n.			
-structure	結構	jyégòu;	gitkau
-of a sentence	句法	jyùfǎ	geuifaat
consul n.	領事	lǐngshì	líHngsɪ́

consulate n.	領事館	lǐngshìgwǎn	líHngsígún
consult v. t.			
-friend, etc.	商議	shāngyì;	sèungyíH;
-dictionary	查	chá	chàH
consume v. t.			
-destroy	消滅	syāumyè;	sìumiHt;
-waste	消耗	svāuhàu	sìuhou
contact v./n.	接觸	jyēchù	jipchūk
contagious a.	傳染	chwánrǎn	chyùHnyìHm
contain v. t.			
-comprise	包含	bāuhán;	bàauhàHm;
-include	在內	dzàinèi	joiHnoiH
contaminate v. t.	被污	bèiwū	beiHwù
contempt n.			
-despising	藐視	myǎushì;	mìuHsiH;
-shame	恥辱	chǐrù	chíyuHk
content			
-a. satisfied	滿足	mǎndzú;	múHnjūk;
-n. constituent	成分	chéngfèn;	sìHngfaHn;
-v. t. satisfy	使滿意	shǐmǎnyì	sìmúHnyìk(sáidou múHnyi)
contents n.			
-of a book, etc.	內容	nèirúng;	noiHyùHng;
-amount contained	容積	rúngji	yùHngjìk
contest v. t.			
-compete	比賽	bǐsài;	béichoi;
-dispute	爭論	jēnglwùn	jàngleuHn
continent n.	洲	jōu	jàu
continue v. t.			
-go on	繼續	jìsyù;	gaijuHk;
-extend	延長	yáncháng;	yìHnchèuHng;
-remain	仍舊	réngjyòu	yìHnggauH

contract

-n. agreement	契約	chìywē;	kaiyeuk;
-v. t. make contract	訂合同	dìnghétúng;	dinghaHptùHng;
-v. t. shorten	縮短	swōdwǎn	sūkdyún

contradict v. t.

-be contrary	矛盾	máudwùn;	màauHtéuHn;
-galusay	反駁	fǎnbwó	fóonbok

contrary a. 相反 syāngfǎn sèungfáan

contrast n.

	對照	dwèijàu;	deuijiu;
	對比	dwèibǐ	deuibéi

contribute v. t.

-money	捐助	jywānjù;	gyùnjoH;
-for newspaper	投稿	tóugǎu	tàuIIgóu

control v. t.

-hold in check	控制	kùngjǐ	hungjai;
-command	管轄	gwǎnsyá	gúnhaHt

convenient a.

	方便	fāngbyàn;	fòngbiHn
	利便	lìbyàn	leiHbiIIn

convention n.

-meeting	議會	yìhwèi;	yiIIwúi;
-agreement	條約	tyáuywē;	tiuHyeuk;
-custom	習慣	syígwàn	jaaHpgwaan

conversation n. 會話 hwèihwà wuiIIwá

convert v. t.

-as the heathen	回轉	hwéijwǎn;	wùiHjyún;
-form, state	改變	gǎibyàn;	góibin;
-use, purpose	改換	gǎihwàn	góiwuHn

convex lens n. 凸透鏡 tūtòujìng daHttaugeng

convince v. t.

  -persuade 說服 shwōfú; syutfuHk;

  -convict 証明有罪 jèngmíngyŏudzwèi jingmìHngyáuHjeuiH

conviction n.

  -of an offense 犯案 fànàn; faaHnon;

  -belief 信仰 syìnyăng seunyéuHng

  -conviction of sin 自覺有罪 dżjywéyŏudzwèi jiHgokyáuHjeuiH

convoy

  -v. t. accompany 護送 hùsùng; wuHsung;

  -n. protecting escort 護兵 hùbīng wuHbìng

convulsions n. 抽筋 chōujïn chàugàn

cook

  -n. person 厨子 chúdz; chyùHjí(fótáu);

  -v. t. food 煑飯 jŭfàn jyúfaaHn

cookie n. 餠 bĭng béng

cool a.

  -not hot 涼快 lyángkwài; lèuHngfaai(lèuHngsóng)

  -indifferent 冷淡 lĕngdàn láaHngdaaHm

coolie n. 苦力 kŭlì; fúliHk;

      工人 gūngrén gùngyàHn

co-operate v. i. 合作 hédzwò hahpjok

copper n.

  -metal 銅 túng; tùHng;

  -coin 銅錢 túngchyán tùHngchìHn

copy

  -v. t. imitate 學 sywé; hoHk;

  -v. t. transcribe 抄 chāu; chàau;

  -n. example 樣本 yàngbĕn yeuHngbún

copy book n. 習字本 syídżbĕn jaaHpjiHbún (jaaHpjiHbóu)

copyright n.	版權	bánchywán	báankyùHn
coral n.	珊瑚	shānhú	sàanwùH
cord			
-v. t.	綁	bǎng;	bóng;
-n.	繩子	shéngdz	sìHngji (sìng)
cork			
-v. t. stop up	塞住	sāijù;	sākjyuH;
-n. stopper	塞子	sāidz	sākjí (sāk)
cork-screw n.	酒鑽	jyǒudzwàn	jáujyun
corn n.			
-grain	五穀	wǔgǔ;	ńgHgūk;
-single grain	粒	lì;	nāp;
-on the foot	雞眼	jiyǎn	gāingáaHn
corner n.	角落	ivǎulwò	gokloHk (goklōktáu)
cornerstone n.	基石	jīshf	gèiseHk
cornet n.	喇叭	lābā	labā
corporal n.	班長	bānjǎng	bāanjéung
corporation n.	股份公司	gǔfèngūngsz	gúfaHngūngsi
corpse n.	屍首	shīshǒu;	sìsáu;
	屍體	shītǐ	sìtái
correct			
-v. t. make right	改正	gǎijèng;	góijeng;
-a. right	對	dwèi	deui (ngāam)
correlation n.	相關	syānggwān	sèunggwàan
correspond v. i.			
-agree	符合	fúhé;	fùHhaHp;
-by letters	通信	tūngsyìn	tùngseun
correspondence n.	通信	tūngsyìn	tùngseun
corridor n.	走廊	dzǒuláng	jáulòHuǵ
corrupt			
-a. morally bad	敗壞	bàihwài;	baaiHwaaiH;
-v. t. rotten	爛	làn	laaHn

corruptible a.	朽 壞	syŏuhwài;	náuwaaiH;
	腐 敗	fŭbài	fuHbaaiH
cost			
-v. t. worth	值 得	jŕde;	jiHkdāk;
-n. price	價 錢	jyàchyán	gachìHn
cosy a.	舒 服	shūfu	syùfuHk
cot n.	小 床	syăuchwáng	siuchòHng (chòHngjái)
cottage n.	茅 屋	máuwū	màauHngūk
cotton n.			
-raw	棉 化	myánhwā;	mìHnfà;
-cloth	棉 布	myánbù	mìHnbou
cough v. t.	咳 嗽	késòu	kātsou (kāt)
could p. p.	能 夠	nénggòu	nàHnggau
council n.	會 議	hwèiyì	wuiHyíH
councillor n.	議 員	yìywán	yíHyùHn
counsel n.			
-consultation	商 量	shānglyang;	sèunglèuHng;
-instruction	指 示	jĭshŕ	jísiH
counsellor n.			
-adviser	顧 問	gùwèn;	gumaHn;
-barrister	律 師	lyùshŕ	leuHtsi
count			
-v. t. reckon	計 算	jìswàn;	gaisyun;
-n. title	伯 爵	bwójywé	baakjeuk
countenance n.	容 貌	rúngmàu;	yùHngmaauH;
	相 貌	syàngmàu	seungmaauH
counter n.			
-of machine	計 算 機	jìswànji;	gaisyungèi;
-of shop	櫃 台	gwèitái	gwaiHtòiH
counterpart n.	副 本	fùbĕn	fubún

countess n.	女伯爵	nyŭbwójywó	néuiHbaakjeuk
country n.			
-nation	國家	gwójyā;	gwokgà;
-village	鄉村	syāngtswūn	hèungchyūn
-country-dance n.	土風舞	tŭfēngwŭ	tóufùngmóuH
-country-man	鄉下人	syāngsyàrén	hèungháyàHn
-country-side	野地	yĕdì	yélIdeiH
couple n.	夫婦	fūfù;	fùfúH;
-couple of days	兩天	lyăngtyān	léuHngtìn (lóuHngyaHt)
courage n.	勇氣	yŭngchì	yúHnghei
courageous a.	大膽	dàdăn;	daaiHdáam;
	勇敢	yŭnggăn	yúHnggám
course			
-instruction	課程	kòchéng;	fochlHng,
-road	路程	lùchéng;	louHchìHng;
-of course	當然	dāngrán	dòngyìIIn
court n.			
-tribunal	法庭	fātíng	faattìHng;
-yard	院子	ywàndz	yúnji (tìnjéng)
courteous a.	有禮貌	yŏulĭmàu;	yáuHláiHmaauII;
	客氣	kèchì	haakhei
courtyard n.	院子	ywàndz	yúnji (tìnjéng)
cousin n.			
-of father's	堂兄弟	tángsyūngdì;	tòHnghìngdaiH;
-of mother's	表兄弟	byăusyūngdì;	bíuhìngdaiH
covenant n.			
-agreement	契約	chìywē;	kaiyeuk;
-treaty	盟約	méngywē	màHngyeuk
cover			
-v. t. lay over	遮蓋	jēgài;	jèkoi (kám):
-v. t. as failing	遮掩	jēyăn;	jèyím;
-n. a lid	蓋子	gàidz;	goiji (goi)

-n. of book	封面	fēngmyàn	fùngmín
covet v. t.	貪戀	tānlyàn;	tàamlyún;
	貪心	tānsyīn	tàamsàm
cow n.	牛	nyóu;	ngàuH;
coward			
-a.	懦弱	nwòrwò;	noHyeuHk;
-n.	懦夫	nwòfū	noHfù
crab n.	蟹	syè;	háaiH;
	螃蟹	pángsyè	pòHnghháaiH
crack			
-v. i. break	破裂	pwòlyè;	poliHt;
-n. as in porcelain	裂紋	lyèwén	liHtmàHn
cracker n.			
-firework	炮仗	pàujàng;	paaujéung;
-biscuit	餅乾	bǐnggān	bénggōn
cradle n.	搖籃	yáulán	yìuHlàaHm
craft n.			
-guile	詭詐	gwěijà;	gwáija;
-skill	手藝	shǒuyì;	sáungaiH;
-crafty plans	奸謀	jyānmóu	gàanmàuH
cramp v. t.			
-affect with	抽筋	chōujīn;	chàugàn;
-prevent movement	擠滿	jǐmǎn	jàimúHn
crane n.			
-bird	鶴	háu;	hoHk (baaHk hók);
-machine	起重機	chǐjùngjī	héichúHnggèi
crash			
-v. ⁚. break	破碎	pwòswèi;	poseui;

-n. noise	砰聲	pēngshēng	pìngsèng
crate n.			
-basket	籃子	lándz;	làaHmjí (làaHm)
-wooden case	木箱	mùsyūng	muHksèung
crawl			
-v. i.	爬	pá;	pàH;
-n. swimming	自由式	dzyóushì	jiHyàuHsìk
crayon n.	顏色筆	yánsèbǐ,	ngàaIInsìkbāt,
	蠟筆	làbǐ	laaHpbāt
crazy a.	瘋狂	fēngkwáng	fùngkòHng
cream n.	奶油	nǎiyóu	náaIHyàuH
create v. t.	創造	chwàngdzàu;	chongjouH;
-cause	引起	yǐnchǐ	yáHnhéi
creature n.			
-living thing	生物	shēngwù;	sàngmaHt
-person	人	rén;	yàHn
-animal	動物	dùngwù	duHngmaHt
credit			
-n. confidence	信用	syìnyùng;	seunyuHng;
-v t. borrow	借貸	jyèdài	jetaai
creed n.	信條	syìntyáu	seuntìuH
creep			
-v. i- crawl	爬	pá;	pàH;
cremation n.	火葬	hwǒdzàng	fójong
crew			
-ship's	船員	chwánywán;	syùHnyùHn;
-aeroplane's	航空員	hángkūngywán	hòHnghùngyùHn
crime n.	罪	dzwèi	jouiH
criminal n.			
-case	刑事	syíngshì;	yìHngsiH;

-person	犯ㄈㄢ 人ㄖㄣ	fànrén	faaHnyàHn
criminology n.	犯ㄈㄢ 罪ㄗㄨㄟ 學ㄒㄩㄝ	fàndzwèisywé	faaHnjeuiHhoHk
crimson a.	朱ㄓㄨ 紅ㄏㄨㄥ;	jūhúng;	jyùhùHng;
	深ㄕㄣ 紅ㄏㄨㄥ	shēnhúng	sàmhùHng
crisis n.			
-in politics	危ㄨㄟ 機ㄐㄧ	wéijī;	ngàiHgèi;
-in illness	危ㄨㄟ 險ㄒㄧㄢ 期ㄑㄧ	wéisyănchí	ngàiHhímkèiH
crisp a.	脆ㄘㄨㄟ	tswèi	cheui
critical a.	危ㄨㄟ 急ㄐㄧ	wéijí	ngàiHgāp
criticize v. i.			
-judge	批ㄆㄧ 評ㄆㄧㄥ;	pīpíng;	pàipìHng;
-examine	監ㄐㄧㄢ 定ㄉㄧㄥ	jyàndìng	gaamdiHng
crocodile n.	鱷ㄜ 魚ㄩ	èyú	ngoHkyùH
crook			
-a. bent	彎ㄨㄢ 曲ㄑㄩ;	wānchyū;	wāankūk;
-n. swindler	騙ㄆㄧㄢ 子ㄗ	pyàndz	pinjí
crop			
-n. harvest	農ㄋㄨㄥ 作ㄗㄨㄛ 物ㄨ	núngdzwòwù	nùHngjokmaHt;
v. t. cut off	收ㄕㄡ 割ㄍㄜ	shōugē	sàugot
cross			
-n. gibbet	十ㄕ 字ㄗ 架ㄐㄧㄚ;	shŕdżjyà;	saHpjiHga;
-v. t. cancel	取ㄑㄩ 消ㄒㄧㄠ	chyŭsyāu;	chéuisìu;
-a. peevish	生ㄕㄥ 氣ㄑㄧ	shēngchì	sànghei (nàu)
cross-road n.	十ㄕ 字ㄗ 路ㄌㄨ	shŕdżlù	saHpjiHlouH
crow			
-n.	烏ㄨ 鴉ㄧㄚ;	wūyā;	wūngā;
-v. i.	叫ㄐㄧㄠ	jyàu	giu
crowd			
-n. of people	羣ㄑㄩㄣ 衆ㄓㄨㄥ;	chyúnjùng;	kwàHnjung
-v. t. press	擠ㄐㄧ	jĭ	jài (bĭk)

crown n.	冠 冕	gwānmyăn	gùnmíHn
crucial point n.	緊 急 關 頭	jǐnji gwāntóu	gángāp gwàantàuH
cruel a.	殘 酷	tsánkù;	chàaHnhouH;
	殘 忍	toánrĕn	chàaHnyán
cruise v. i.	巡 邏	syúnlwó	chèuHnlòH
crush v. t.			
-break	壓 碎	yāswèi;	ngaatseui;
-injure	壓 傷	yāshēng	ngaatsèung
crutch n.	拐 杖	gwăijàng	gwáaijéung
cry v. i.			
-weep	哭	kū;	hūk (haam);
-shout	叫	jyàu	giu
crystal			
-n. rock	水 晶	shwĕijǐng;	séuijìng;
-a. transparent	透 明	tòuming	taumìHng
cuff n.	袖 口	syōukŏu	jauHháu
cultivate v. t.			
-the mind	栽 培	dzāipéi;	jòipùiH;
-of fields	耕 種	gēngjùng	gàangjung
culture n.	文 化	wénhwà;	màHnfa;
	文 明	wénming	màHnmìHng
cunning a.	狡 猾	jyăuhwá	gáauwaaHt
cup n.	杯	bēi	būi
cupboard n.	碗 櫃	wăngwèi	wúngwaiH
curator n.	舘 長	gwănjăng	gúnjéung
cure v. t.			
-heal	治 療	jìlyáu;	jiHlìuH;
-preserve as meat	醃	yān	yìm
curfew n.	宵 禁	syāujìn	sìugam

curiosity n.

-desire to know 好奇心 hàuchísyïn; houkèiHsàm;

-curio 古董 gŭdŭng gúdúng

curl v./n. 鬈髮 jywănfă gyúnfaat

currency n.

-money 錢幣 chyánbì; chìHnbaiH;

-circulation 流通 lyóutūng làuHtùng

current a.

-common use 通用 tūngyùng; tùngyuHng;

-electric 電流 dyànlyóu; diHnlàuH;

-current account 活期存欵 hwóchìtswúnkwăn; wuHtkèiHchyùHnfún;

-current events 時事 shfshì; sìHsiH;

-current expenses 經費 jïngfèi; gìngfai;

-current thoughts 思潮 szcháu sìchìuH

curry n. 咖喱 kāli galēi

curriculum n. 課程 kèchéng fochìHng

curse

-v. t. scold 咒詛 jòudzŭ; jaujo;

-n. cause of misfortune 禍根 hwògēn woHgàn

curtain n.

-theatre 幕 mù; moHk;

-window 簾子 lyándz límji (lím)

curve

-v. t. bend 彎 wān; wāan;

-n. a line 曲線 chyūsyàn kūksin

cushion n. 椅墊 yǐdyàn yiHjin

custom n. 風俗 fēngsú fùngjuHk

customer n. 顧客 gùkè; guhaak;
　　　　　　 主顧 jŭgù jyúgu

custom-house n. 海關 hăigwān; hóigwāan;

	稅關	shwèigwān	seuigwāan

cut v. t.

-with knife	切	chyē;	chit;
-with scissors	剪	jyǎn;	jín;
-with axe	砍	kǎn	hám (pek)

cycle n.

-radio	週波	jōupwō,	jàubō,
-period of time	週期	jōuchī	jàukèiH

cyclone n.

	旋風	sywánfēng	syùHnfùng

cylinder n.

-pillar	圓柱	ywánjù;	yùHnchyúH;
-vessel	圓筒	ywántǔng	yùHntúng

cynical a.

-captious	吹毛求疵	chwēimáuchyóutsź;	chèuimòuHkàuHchī;
-sneering	兇暴	syūngbàu	hùngbouH

D

dad n.	爸爸	bàba	bàHbā
daily a.	每天	měityán	múiHtìn (múiHyaHt)
-daily interest	日利	ìlì	yaHtleiH
-daily life	日常生活	ìcháng shēnghwó	yaHtsèuHung sàngwuHt
-daily newspaper	日報	ìbàu	yaHtbou
dairy-man n.	送牛奶的	sùngnyóunǎide	sungngàuHnáaiHdik

damage v. t.

-harm	損害	swǔnhài;	syùnhoiH;
-injury	損傷	swǔnsháng	syúnsèung

damn

-v. i. condemn	定罪	dìngdzwèi;	diHngjeuiH;
-v. t. curse	罵	mà	maH (naauH)
damp a.	潮溼	cháushī	chìuHsāp

dance v. i.	跳舞	tyàuwǔ	tiumóuH
danger n.	危險	wéisyǎn	ngàiHhím
dare v. t.	敢	gǎn	gám
dark a.			
-without light	黑暗	hēiàn;	hāakngam;
-of the hair, skin, etc.,	黑	hēi;	hāak;
-dark ages	黑暗時代	hēiàn shídài;	hāakngam sìHdoiH;
-dark in mind	愚昧	yúmèi	yùHmuiH
darkness n.	黑暗	hēiàn	hāakngam
darling n.			
-person	愛人	àirén;	ngoiyàHn;
-child	寶寶	bǎubau	bóubóu
dash			
-v. t. strike	衝入	chūngrù;	chùngyaHp;
-n. mark in writing	畫	hwà	waaHk
date			
-n. appointed day	日期	rchí;	yaHtkèiH;
-n. engagement	約會	ywēhwèi	yeukwuiH;
-v. t. put a date on	寫日期	syěrchí	séyaHtkèiH
daughter n.	女兒	nyǔér	néuiHyìH
daughter-in-law n.	媳婦	syífù	sìkfúH (sànpóu)
dawn n.	天亮	tyānlyàng;	tìnleuHng (tìngwòng);
	黎明	límíng	làiHmìHng
day n.	天	tyān;	tìn;
	日子	rdz	yaHtjí
day-dream	白日夢	báirmèng	baaHkyaHtmuHng
daylight n.			
-sunlight	日光	rgwāng;	yaHtgwòng;
-dawn	天亮	tyānlyàng	tìnleuHng (tìngwòng)
daytime n.	白天	báityān	baaHktìn (yaHttáu)

	日間	ìjyān	yaHtgàan
deacon n.	執事	jíshr̀	jāpsiH
deaconess n.	女執事	nyŭjŕshr̀	néuiHjāpsiH
Jean a.	死	sž	sí (séi)
deaf a.	耳聾	ěrlúng	yíHlỳHng
deal v. i.	應付	yìngfù;	yingfuH;
-a good deal	許多	syŭdwo	hóuidò (hóudò)
dean n.	主任	jŭrèn	jyúyaHm
dear a.			
-beloved	親愛	chīnài;	chànngòi;
-costly	貴	gwèi	gwai
death n.	死	sž;	sí (séi)
	死亡	sžwáng	séimòHng
debate v./n.	辯論	byànlwùn	biHnleuHn
debt n.	債	jài	jaai
debtor n.	債戶	jàihù;	jaaiwuH;
	欠戶	chyànhù	himwuH
decade n.			
-of ten years	十年間	shínyánjyān;	saHpnìHngàan;
-of ten days	旬	syún	chèuHn
decadence n.			
-decay	衰頹	shwāitwéi;	sèuitèuiH;
-a falling away	凋零	dyāulíng	dìulìHng
decay			
-v. i. decline	衰敗	shwāibài;	sèuibaaiH;
-n. decomposition	腐爛	fŭlàn;	fuHlaaHn;
-v. t. impair	損傷	swŭnshāng	syúnsèung
decease			
-n. death	死亡	sžwáng;	séimòHng;
-v. i. depart from life	逝世	shr̀shr̀	saiHsai

deceit n.

  -fraud   欺ㄑ 騙ㄆㄧㄢ   chīpyàn;   hèipin;

  -trick   詭ㄍㄨㄟ 計ㄐㄧ   gwěijì   gwáigai

deceive v. t.

  -cheat   欺ㄑ 騙ㄆㄧㄢ   chīpyàn;   hèipin;

  -mislead   誤ㄨ 引ㄧㄣ   wùyǐn   ngHyáHn

December n.   十ㄕ 二ㄦ 月ㄩㄝ   Shfèrywé   SaHpyiHyuHt

decide v. i.

  -determine   決ㄐㄩㄝ 定ㄉㄧㄥ   jywédìng;   kyutdiHng;

  -settle   斷ㄉㄨㄢ 定ㄉㄧㄥ   dwàndìng   dyundiHng

decimal a./n.   十ㄕ 進ㄐㄧㄣ 數ㄨ   shfjìnshù   saHpjeunsou

decipher v. t.

  -explain   解ㄐㄧㄝ 釋ㄕ   jyěshì;   gáaisìk;

  -detect   探ㄊㄢ 明ㄇㄧㄥ   tànmíng;   taammìHng;

  -reveal   顯ㄒㄧㄢ 明ㄇㄧㄥ   syǎnmíng   hínmìHng

decision n.

  -judgment   斷ㄉㄨㄢ 定ㄉㄧㄥ   dwàndìng;   dyundiHng;

  -resoluteness   決ㄐㄩㄝ 定ㄉㄧㄥ   jywédìng   kyutdiHng

deck

  -n. of a ship   甲ㄐㄧㄚ 板ㄅㄢ   jyǎbǎn;   gaapbáan;

  -v. t. adorn   裝ㄓㄨㄤ 飾ㄕ   jwāngshì   jōngsìk

declaration n.

  -proclamation   宣ㄒㄩㄢ 告ㄍㄠ   sywāngàu;   syùngou;

  -notification   通ㄊㄨㄥ 告ㄍㄠ   tūnggàu   tùnggou

decline

  -v. i. refuse   推ㄊㄨㄟ 辭ㄘ   twēitsź;   tèuichìH;

  -v. i. sink   衰ㄕㄨㄞ 微ㄨㄟ   shwāiwéi;   sèuimèiH;

  -v. i. deviate   偏ㄆㄧㄢ 斜ㄒㄧㄝ   pyānsyé;   pìnchèH;

-v. t. turn aside	廢 止	fèijǐ	faiji
ecoration n.			
-decorating	裝 飾	jwāngshì;	jōngsìk;
-badge	動 章	syūnjāng	fànjèung
ecrease v. i.	減 少	jyǎnshǎu	gáamsiu
edicate v. t.	獻 給	syàngěi;	hinkāp (hinbéi);
	奉 獻	fèngsyàn	fuHnghihn
edication n.	奉 獻	fèngsyàn	fuHnghin
educt v. t.	減 除	jyǎnchú;	gáamchèuiH;
	扣 除	kòuchú	kauchèuiH
eed n.			
-act	作 為	dzwòwéi;	jokwàiH;
-agreement	契 據	chìjyù	kaigeui
eep a.	深	shēn	sàm
eer n.	鹿	lù	lúk
efeat			
-v. t. vanquish	打 敗	dǎbài;	dábaaiH;
-n. in battle	敗 仗	bàijàng	baaiHjeung
efend v. t.			
-guard	防 備	fánghèi;	fòHngbeiH;
-vindicate	辯 護	byànhù	biHnwuH
eficiency n.			
-lack	缺 乏	chywēfá;	kyutfaHt;
-defect	缺 點	chywēdyǎn	kyutdím
efinition n.	定 義	dìngyì	diIngyiH
eflation n.	通 貨 收 縮	tūnghwòshōuswō	tùngfosàusūk
efraud v. t.			
-cheat	欺 詐	chìjà	hèija;
-overreach	哄 騙	hǔngpyàn	huHngpin
efy v. t.			
-challenge	挑 戰	tyǎujàn;	tiujin;

-resist	抵抗	dǐkàng;	dáikong;
-disobey	不服從	bùfútsúng	bātfuHkchùHng
degeneration n.	退化	twèihwà	teuifa
degrade			
-v. i. degenerate	退化	twèihwà;	teuifa
-v. t. in rank	降級	jyàngjí;	gongkāp;
-v. t. of office	革職	géjŕ	gaakjik
degree n.			
-grade	等級	děngjí	dángkāp;
-extent	程度	chéngdù	chìHngdouH
delay			
-v. i. tarry	逗留	dòulyóu;	dauHlàuH;
-v. t. defer	遲延	chŕyán;	chìHyìHn;
-n. stop	停頓	tíngdwùn	tìHngdeuHn
delegation n.			
-appointment of	委派代表	wěipàidàibyǎu;	wáipaaidoiHbíu;
-body of	代表團	dàibyǎutwán	doiHbíutyùHn
deliberate			
-v. t. counsel	商議	shāngyì;	sèungyíH;
-v. t. consider	考慮	kǎulyù;	háauleuiH;
-a. on purpose	故意	gùyì	guyi
delicious a.	美味	měiwèi;	méiHmeiH;
	好吃	hǎuchŕ	hóuhek (hóusiHk)
delight v. i.	喜愛	syǐài;	héingoi;
	喜歡	syǐhwan	héifùn
delinquent n.	犯法	fànfǎ;	faaHnfaat;
-failing in duty	失職	shŕjŕ;	sātjik;
-neglect of duty	曠職	kwàngjŕ	kongjik
deliver v. t.			
-hand over	交付	jyāufù;	gàaufuH;
-rescue	拯救	jǎngjyòu	chínggau

delivery n.

| -parturition | 分娩 | fēnmyǎn; | fànmíHn; |
| -liberation | 釋放 | shìfàng | sìkfong |

delusion n.

| -deluding | 迷惑 | míhwò; | màiHwaaHk; |
| -misconception | 忘想 | wàngsyǎng | móHngséung |

demand

| -v. t. ask | 要求 | yāuchyóu; | yìukàuH; |
| -n. for goods | 需要 | syūyàu | sèuiyiu |

demobilize v. t. 解散軍隊 jyěsànjyūndwèi gáaisaangwàndéui

democracy n. 民主 mínjǔ màHnjyú

demolish v. t.

| -ruin | 毀壞 | hwěihwài; | wáiwaaiH; |
| -pull down | 拆毀 | chāihwěi | chàaiwái |

demon n.

| | 鬼 | gwěi; | gwái; |
| | 惡鬼 | ègwěi | ngokgwái |

demonology n. 鬼學 gwěisywé gwáihoHk

demonstrate v. t.

-show	指示	jǐshì;	jisiH;
-explain	說明	shwōmíng;	syutmìHng
-prove	証明	jèngmíng	jingmìHng

den n. 洞 dùng duHng

denomination n.

-religion	宗派	dzungpài;	jùngpaai;
-name	名稱	míngchēng;	mìHngchìng;
-kind	種類	jǔnglèi	júngleuiH

denote v. t.

| -indicate | 指明 | jǐmíng; | jimìIng; |
| -show | 表示 | byǎushì | bíusiH |

denounce v. t.

  -stigmatize 攻擊 gūngjí; gūnggǐk:

  -inform against 告發 gàufā; goufaat;

  -treaty 廢除 fèichú; faichèuiH

dense a.

  -crowded 稠密 chóumì; chàuHmaHt;

  -thick 濃厚 núnghòu nùHngháuH

dental

  -a. of the teeth 牙齒 yáchř; ngàHchǐ;

  -n. letter formed by 齒音 chǐyin chíyām

dentist n. 牙醫 yáyi ngàHyǐ

deny v. t.

  -say not true 否認 fǒurèn; fáuyiHng;

  -refuse 推辭 twēitsź teùichìH

depart v. i.

  -leave 離開 líkāi; lèiHhòi;

  -divide 分開 fēnkāi fànhòi

departure n.

  -start 出發 chūfā; chēutfaat;

  -going away 離開 líkái; lèiHhòi;

depend v. i. 倚靠 yǐkàu; yíHkaau;

   依賴 yilài yǐlaaiH

dependable a. 靠得住 kàudéjù; kaaudākjyuH;

   可靠 kěkàu hókaau

dependent n./a. 倚靠 yǐkàu yíHkaau

deport

  -v. t. exile 放逐 fàngjú; fongjuHk;

  -n. conduct 品行 pǐnsyìng bánhaHng

deposit v. t.

  -in bank 存欵 tswúnkwǎn; chyùHnfún;

  -bargain money 定錢 dìngchyán; deHngchìn;

  -as security 保証金 bǎujèngjǐn bóujinggàm

depot n.

  -storehouse 倉庫 tsāngkù; chòngfu;

-station	車站	chējàn	chèjaaHm
depression n.			
-financial	經濟不景氣	jīngji bùjǐngchì	gìngjai bātgìnghei
deprive v. t.			
-of rights	剝奪	bwódwó;	bokdyuHt;
-of office	革職	géjf	gaakjik
depth n.	深度	shēndù	sàmdouH
deputy n.	代表	dàibyǎu;	doiHbíu;
	委員	wěiywán	wáiyùHn
descend v. i.			
-come from above	降臨	jyànglín;	gonglàHm;
-move downward	降下	jyàngsyà	gonghaH
descendants n.	子孫	dɩ́swūn;	jísyùn;
	後裔	hòuyì	hauHyeuiH
describe v. t.			
-write	描寫	myáusyě;	mìuHsé;
-say	形容	syíngrúng	yìHngyùHng
desert			
-v. i. forsake	撇下	pyēsyà;	pithaH;
-n. barren tract	沙漠	shāmwò	sàmoHk
deserve v. t./v. i.			
-earn by service	應得	yìngdé;	yìngdāk;
-merit	當受	dāngshòu	dòngsauH
design			
-v. t.	設計	shèjì;	chitgai;
-n.	計劃	jìhwà	gaiwaaHk
desire			
-v. t. wish	指望	jɩ̌wàng;	jimoHng;
-n, longing	欲望	yùwàng;	yuHkmoHng;
-desire earnestly	切慕	chyèmù	chitmouH
desk n.	書桌	shūjwō	syùcheuk (syùtói)

desolate

-a. laid waste	荒涼	hwānglyáng.	fònglèuHng;
-v. t. ruin	毀滅	hwěimyè	wáimiHt

despair v. t.

	失望	shīwàng;	sātmoHng;
	絕望	jywéwàng	jyuHtmoHng

desperate a.

-little hope	絕望	jywéwàng;	jyuHtmoHng;
-irretrievable	不可救藥	bùkějyòuyàu	bāthógauyeuHk

despise v. t.

	輕看	chīngkàn;	hīnghon (táidài);
	看起不	kànbùchǐ	honkāthéi (táimhéi)

destination n.

-of place	目的地	mùdìdì;	muHkdìkdeiH;
-of purpose	宗旨	dzūngjǐ	jùngjí

destiny n.

-fate	命運	mìngyùn;	miHngwaHn;
-doom	定命	dìngmìng;	diHngmiHng;
-resistless power	天命	tyānmìng	tìnmiHng

destitute a.

-poor	貧窮	pínchyúng;	pàHnkùHng;
-not having	缺乏	chywēfá	kyutfaHt

destroy v. t.

-put an end	破壞	pwòhwài;	powaaiH;
-break	打壞	dǎhwài;	dáwaaiH.
-by fire	燒毀	shāuhwěi	sìuwái

destruction n.

-ruin	毀壞	hwěihwài;	wáiwaaiH;
-demolition	拆毀	chāihwěi	chàaiwái

detail n.

	詳細	syángsyì;	chèuHngsai;

	細ㄒ節ㄐㄧㄝ	syìjyé	saijit

detain v. t.

-hold back	留ㄌㄡ住ㄓㄨ	lyóujù;	làuHjyuH;
-seize	扣ㄎㄡ留ㄌㄧㄡ	kòulyóu	kaulàuH

detect v. t.

-find out	發ㄈㄚ現ㄒㄧㄢ	fāsyàn;	faatyiHn;
discover	發ㄈㄚ覺ㄐㄩㄝ	fājywé	faatgok

determination n.

-decision	決ㄐㄩㄝ定ㄉㄧㄥ	jywédìng;	kyutdiHng;
resolution	決ㄐㄩㄝ心ㄒㄧㄣ	jywésyin;	kyutsàm;
-of character	志ㄓ氣ㄑㄧ	jìchì	jihei

determine v. t.

-decide	決ㄐㄩㄝ定ㄉㄧㄥ	jywédìng;	kyutdiHng
-limit	限ㄒㄧㄢ定ㄉㄧㄥ	syàndìng	haaHndiHng

detest v. t.

-hate	恨ㄏㄣ	hèn;	haHn;
-abhor	討ㄊㄠ厭ㄧㄢ	tǎuyàn	tóuyim

detrimental a.

-harmful	損ㄙㄨㄣ害ㄏㄞ	swǔnhài;	syúnhoiH;
-mischievous	不ㄅㄨ幸ㄒㄧㄥ	búsyìng	bāthaHng

develop v. t.

-progress	發ㄈㄚ達ㄉㄚ	fādá;	faatdaaHt;
-body	發ㄈㄚ育ㄩ	fāyù;	faatyuHk;
-change into	變ㄅㄧㄢ成ㄔㄥ	byànchéng	binsìHng

development n.

	發ㄈㄚ展ㄓㄢ	fājǎn	faatjín

device n.

-stratagem	策ㄘㄜ略ㄌㄩㄝ	tsèlywè;	chaakleuk;
-means	方ㄈㄤ法ㄈㄚ	fāngfǎ;	fòngfaat;
-plan	計ㄐㄧ劃ㄏㄨㄚ	jìhwà	gaiwaaHk

devil n.

	魔ㄇㄛ鬼ㄍㄨㄟ	mwógwěi	mògwái

devise v. t.

-plan	籌算	chóuswàn;	chàuHsyun;
-invent	創作	chwàngdzwò	chongjok

devote v. t.

-pay attention	專心	jwānsyìn;	jyùnsàm;
-dedicate	獻身	syànshēn	hinsàn

devour v. t.

	吞	twūn	tàn

devout a.

-pious	虔誠	chyánchéng;	kìHnsìHng;
-earnest	懇切	kěnchyè	hánchit

dew n.

	露	lù;	louH;
	露水	lùshwěi	louHséui

diabetes n.

	糖尿病	tɛ́ngnyàubìng	tòHngniuHbeHng

diagnosis n.

	診斷	jěndwàn	chándyun

diagonal

-a.	非隣角	fɛilínjyǎu;	fèileuHnggok;
-n.	對角線	dwèijyǎnsyàn	deuigoksin

diagram n.

	圖表	túbyǎu	tòuHbíu

dial n.

-of sun	日規	ɽgwēi;	yaHtkwài;
-of watch	錶面	byǎumyàn;	bíumín;
-of clock	鐘面	jūngmyàn	jūngmín

dialect n.

	土話	tǔhwà;	tóuwá;
	方言	fāngyán	fòngyìHn

dialogue n.

	對話	dwèihwà	deuiwá

diameter n.

	直徑	jɽ́jìng	jiHkging

diamond n.

	鑽石	jwànshɽ́	jyunseHk

English	Chinese		
iarrhoea n.	瀉肚	syèdù	setóu (ngòtóu)
iary n.	日記	rìjì	yaHtgei
ice n.	骰子	shăidz	sìkjí (sìk)
ictation n.	默書	mwòshū	maaHksyù
ictionary n.	字典	dzdyăn	jiIIdǐn
ie v. i.	死	sž	séi
-about to die	臨終	lInjūng	làIIInjùng
-die together	同死	túngsž	tùHngséi
iesel express n.	柴油快車	cháiyóu kwàichē	chàaiHyàuHfaaichè
iet n.	節食	jyéshí	jitsiHk
iffer v. i.	不同	bùtúng	bāttùHng (m̀tùHng)
-differ in opinion	意見不同	yìyànbùtúng	yiginbāttùHng
ifference n.			
-unlike	不同	bùtúng;	bāttùHng (m̀tùHng)
-variation	各樣	gèyàng	gokyeuHng
differential a.	差別	chàbyé	chàbiHt
differentiate v. t.	分別	fεnbyé	fànbiHt
difficult a.			
-not easy	困難	kwùnán;	kwannàaHn;
-abstruse	深	shēn	sàm
difficulty n.			
-distress	難處	nέnchù;	nàaIInchyu;
-obstacle	妨礙	fέngài	fòHngngoiH
dig v. t.			
-down	挖	wā;	waak;
-deep	掘	jywέ	gwaHt
digest			
-v. t. as food	消化	syāuhwà;	sìufa;
-n. periodical abstract	文摘	wέnjāi	màHnjaaHk

dignity n.

 -nobleness　　　高《貴《　　　gīugwèi;　　　gòugwai;

 -worthiness　　　尊嚴　　　dzwūnyán　　　jyùnyìHm

dike n.　　　溝渠　　　gōuchyú　　　gàukèuiH (hàangkèuiH)

dilapidate v. t.　　　毀壞　　　hwěihwài　　　wáiwaaiH

dilemma n.　　　進退兩難　　　jìntwèiyǎngnán　　　jeunteuiléuHngnàaHn

diligence n.　　　殷勤　　　yīnchín;　　　yànkàHn;

　　　　　　勤勞　　　chínláu　　　kàHnlòuH

dilute v. t.　　　冲淡　　　chūngdàn　　　chùngtáaHm

dim a.

 -indistinct　　　朦朧　　　ménglúng;　　　mùHnglùHng;

 -dark　　　暗　　　àn　　　am

dime n.　　　一角　　　yìjyǎu　　　yātgok (yāthòuHjí)

diminish v. t.

 -lessen　　　減少　　　jyǎnshǎu;　　　gáamsiu;

 -make small　　　縮小　　　swōsyǎu　　　sūksiu;

dine v. i.　　　吃飯　　　chīfàn　　　hekfaaHn (siHkfaaHn)

dinner n.　　　正餐　　　jèngtsān;　　　jingchāan;

　　　　　　宴會　　　yànhwèi　　　yinwuiH

diocese n.　　　主教管轄區　　　jǔjyàugwǎnsyáchyū　　　jyúgaaugúnhaHtkèui

diploma n.　　　文憑　　　wénpíng　　　màHnpàHng

diplomatic a.

 -dexterous　　　機警　　　jïjǐng;　　　gèigíng;

 -artful　　　技巧　　　jìchyǎu　　　geiHháau

direct

 -a. not indirect　　　直接　　　jífjyē;　　　jiHkjip;

 -v. t. oversee　　　指揮　　　jǐhwēi;　　　jífài;

 -v. t. guide　　　指導　　　jǐdǎu　　　jídouH

direction n.	方向	fāngsyàng	fòngheung
director n.			
-one who directs	主管	jǔgwǎn;	jyúgún;
-manager	經理	jīnglǐ	gìngléiH;
-superintendent	監督	jyāndū	gāamdūk
dirty a.	汚穢	wūhwèi;	wùhwai (wùiòu)
	骯髒	āngdzāng	òngjòng (laaHttaat)
disable a.			
-cripple	殘廢	tsánfèi;	chàaHnfai;
-incapable	無用	wóyung	mòuHyuHng
disadvantage n.			
-unfavorable	不利	búlì;	bātleiH;
-damage	損害	sywǔnhài	syúnhoiH
disagree v. i.	不合	bùhó;	bāthaHp;
	不一致	bùyíjr̀	bātyātji
disagreeable a.	討厭	tǎuyàn	tóuyim
disappear v. i.	消失	syāushr̄;	sìusat;
	不見	bújyàn	bātgin (m̀gin)
disappoint v. t.			
-lose hope	失望	shr̄wàng;	sātmoHng;
-frustrate	妨礙	fángài	fòHngngoiH
disapprove v. t.			
-fail to approve	不贊成	búdzànchéng;	bātjaansìIng;
-dislike	嫌	syán;	yìHm;
-disallow	不准	bùjwǔn	bātjéun (m̀jéun)
disaster n.	災難	dzāinàn;	jòinaaIIn;
	災害	dzāihài	jòihoiH
disbelieve v. t.	不信	búsyìn	bātseun (m̀sèun)
discharge v. t.			
-of employment	免職	myǎnjŕ;	míHnjik;
-of army	退役	twèiyì;	teuiyiHk;

-of prisoner	釋放	shìfàng	sìkfong
disciple n.			
-apostle	門徒	méntú;	mùHntòuH;
-learner	門生	ménshēng	mùHnsàng
discipline			
-v. t. chastise	管教	gwǎnjyàu;	gúngaau;
-v. t. drill	操練	tsāulyàn;	chòuliHn;
-n. control	紀律	jìlyù	géileuHt
discontinue v. t.			
-stop	終止	jūngjǐ;	jùngjí;
-break off	斷絕	dwànjywé	tyúHnjyuHt
discount			
-n.	折扣	jékòu;	jitkau;
-v. t.	打折扣	dǎjékòu	dájitkau
discourage v. t.			
-dispirit	灰心	hwēisyin;	fùisàm;
-discountenance	挫折	tswòjé	chojit
discover v. t.			
-investigate	發覺	fājywé;	faatgok;
-find out	發現	fāsyàn;	faatyiHn;
-show	顯露	syǎnlù	hínlouH
discuss v. t.			
-talk	討論	tǎulwùn;	tóuleuHn;
-consider	商量	shānglyang	sèunglèuHng
disease n.	疾病	jibìng	jaHtbeHng
disgrace			
-v. t. shame	耻辱	chǐrù;	chíyuHk;
-n. loss of favor	失寵	shǐchǔng	sātchúng
disguise v. t.			
-by dress	假裝	jyǎjwāng;	gájòng;

-cloak	遮掩	jēyǎn	jèyím
disgust v. t.			
-distaste	討厭	tǎuyàn;	tóuyim;
-dislike	嫌	syán	yìHm
dish n.			
-plate	盤子	pándz;	pùHnjí (pùHn)
-saucer	碟子	dyédz	diHpjí (díp)
dishonest a.			
-insincere	不老實	bùlǎushf;	bātlóuHsaHt;
-fraudulent	狡猾	jyǎuhwá	gáauwaaHt
dishonor, dishonour			
-n. shame	羞辱	syōurù;	sàuyuHk;
-v. t. refuse to pay	拒付	jyùfù	kéuiīifuīī
disinfectant n.	消毒藥	syāudúyaǹ	siuduIIkyeuHk
dislike v. t.			
-hate	厭惡	yànwù;	yiṁwṳ;
-displease	不悅	búywè	bātyuHt (ṁhéifùn)
dismay v. t.			
-alarm	驚惶	jīnghwáng;	gìngwòHng;
-frighten	驚慌	jīnghwāng	gìngfòng
dismiss v. t.			
-from office, school	開除	kāichú;	hòichèuiH
-the class	下課	syàkè	haHfo (loHktòHng)
disobey v. t.	違背	wéibèi	wàiHbui;
	不服從	bùfútsúng	bātfuHkchùHng
disorder			
-n. irregularity	不規律	bùgwēilyù;	bātkwàileuHt;
-v. t. disturb	擾亂	rǎulwàn	yíuHlyuHn
dispatch			
-n. official	公文	gīngwén;	gùngmàHn;
-v. t. send off	送	sùng	sung

dispensary n.	藥房	yàufáng	yeuHkfòHng
disperse v. t.			
-scatter	散	sàn;	saan;
-break apart	解散	jyěsàn;	gáaisaan;
-disperse meeting	散會	sànhwèi	saanwúi
display v. t.			
-show	陳列	chénlyè;	chàHnliHtɨ
-expand	展開	jǎnkāi	jínhòi
disposal n.			
-arrangement	安排	ānpái;	ònpàaiH;
-set in order	整理	jěnglǐ;	jíngléiH;
-management	處理	chǔlǐ	chyúléiH
disposition n.			
-natural tendency	性情	syìngchíng;	singchìHng;
-temper	脾氣	píchì	pèiHhei
dispute v. t.			
-in argument	辯論	byànlwùn;	biHnleuHn;
-altercate	爭辯	jēngbyàn	jàngbiHn
disqualify v. t.			
-make unable	使不能	shǐbùnéng;	síbātnàHng(m̀hónàHng);
-for position	取消資格	chyǔsyāu dzge	chéuisiu jìgaak
disregard v. t.	不管	bùgwǎn;	bātgún;
	不理	bùlǐ;	bātléiH; (m̀léiH);
	不顧	búgù	bātgu
dissect v. t.			
-the body	解剖	jyěpōu;	gáaifáu;
-cut up	切開	chyēkāi	chithòi
dissipate			
-v. t. extravagance	浪費	làngfèi;	loHngfai;
-v. i. waste away	耗費	hàufèi	houfai
dissolve v. t.			
-liquefy	溶解	rúngjyě;	yùHnggáai;

-break up	解散	jyĕsàn	gáaisaan
distance n.			
-space	距離	jyùli;	ᴋéuiHlèiH;
-ramoteness	遠	ywăn	yúHn
distinction n.			
-difference	分別	fēnbyé;	fànbiHt;
-quality	特性	tòcyìng;	daHksing;
-eminence	優等	yōudĕng	yàudáng
distinguish v. t.	區別	chyūbyé;	kèuibiHt;
	辯別	byànbyé	biHnbiHt
distress n.			
-pain	痛苦	tùngkŭ;	tungfú;
-misery	苦難	kŭnàn;	fúnaaHn;
-sorrow	煩惱	fánnău	faaHnnóuII
distribute v. t.			
-arrange	分配	fēnpèi;	fànpui;
-give	分給	fēngĕi;	fànkăp (fànbéi);
-spread out	分佈	fēnbù	fànbou
district n.			
-of a city	區	chyū;	kèui;
-place	地方	dìfang	deiHfòng
disturb v. t.	攪擾	jyăurău;	gáauyíuH;
	打攪	dăjyău	dágáau
ditch n.	水溝	shĕigōu	séuigāu (hàangkèuiH)
dive v. i.			
-as submarine	潛水	chyénshwĕi	chìHmséui;
-search mentally into	研究	yánjyòu	yìHngau
divide v. i.	分開	fēnkāi	fànhòi
division n.			
-state of	區分	chyūfēn;	kèuifàn;
-segment	部分	bùfèn;	bouHfaHn;

Di

-Math.	除法	chúfǎ	chèuiHfaat
divorce v. i.	離婚	líhwūn	lèiHfàn
dizzy a.	頭暈	tóuyūn	tàuHwàHn
do v. t.			
-make	做	dzwò;	jouH;
-perform	辦	bàn	baaHn
dock n.	船塢	chwánwù	syùHnou
doctor n.			
-academic	博士	bwóshf;	boksiH;
-medical	醫生	yīshēng;	yīsāng;
-Doctor of Law	法學博士	fǎsywé bwóshf;	faathoHk boksiH;
-Doctor of Medicine	醫學博士	yīsywé bwóshḭ;	yìhoHk boksiH;
-Doctor of Philosophy	哲學博士	jésywé bwóshr̆;	jithoHk boksiH;
-Doctor of Theology	神學博士	shénsywé bwóshḭ	sàHnhoHk boksiH
doctrine n.			
-of church	道理	dàulǐ;	douHléiH;
-of politics	主義	jǔyì	jyúyiH
-doctrine of the mean (see Four Book)	中庸	jūngyūng	jùngyùHng
document n.	文件	wénjyàn;	màHngín;
	公文	gūngwén	gùngmàHn
doer n.	行爲者	syíngwéijĕ	hàHngwàiHjé
dog n.	狗	gǒu	gáu
dogmatic a.	武斷	wǔdwàn	móuHdyun
doll n.	娃娃	wáwá	wāwā (gūngjái)
dollar n.	一元	yìywán	yātyùHn (yātmēn)
domestic a.			
-pert. to house	家務	jyāwù;	gàmouH;
-intestine	國內	gwónèi	gwoknoiH

dominion n.

-sovereignty	統治權	tŭngjìchywán;	túngjiHkyùHn;
-land	領土	lĭngtŭ	lìHngtóu

donate v. t. 捐 jywān gyùn

donkey n. 驢子 lyúdz lòuHjí(lèuiH)

door n. 門 mén mùHn

doorkeeper n. 看門的 kānmónde hònmùHndik

dormitory n. 宿舍 sùshè sūkse

dose n. 劑 jì; jài;
服 fú fuhk

dot n. 點 dyăn dịm

double

-a. twofold	兩倍	lyăngbèi;	léuHngpúiH;
-v. t. increase	加倍	jyabèi	gàpúiH

doubt v. t.. 懷疑 hwáiyi; wàaiHyìH;
疑惑 yíhwò yìHwaaHk

dough n.

-moistened flour 生麵團 shēngmyàntwán; sàngmiHntyùHn;

-money 錢 chyán chín

dove n. 鴿子 gēdz gapjí (baaHkgáp)

dovetail n. 鳩尾 jyōuwĕi gàuméiH

down

-n. feathers 絨毛 rúngmáu; yùHngmòuH;

-adv. below 下 syà haH

-down town 進城 jìnchéng jeunsìHng (yaHpsèHng)

downcast a. 愁悶 chóumèn; sàuHmuHn;
煩悶 fánmèn fàaHnmuHn

downfall n.

-ruin 毀滅 hwĕimyè; wáimiHt;

-of rain	大雨	dàyǔ	daaiHyúH
downstairs adv.	樓下	lóusyà	làuHhaH
dowry n.	嫁妝	jyàjwāng	gajòng
dozen n.	一打	yídá	yātdā
draft			
-v. t. detach	調任	dyàurèn;	diuHyaHm;
-n. sketch	稿	gǎu	góu
-n. bill	滙票	hwèipyàu	wuiHpiu
drag v. t.	拉	lā;	làai;
	拖	twō	tō
dragon n.	龍	lúng	lùHng
drain			
-n. ditch	水溝	shwěigōu;	séuigāu;
-v. t. draw water off	排水	páishwěi	pàaiHséui
drama n.	戲劇	syìjyù	heikeHk
drape v. t.			
-fold	叠	dyé;	diHp (daaHp);
-hang	掛	gwà	gwa
draught n.			
-of air	通風	tūngfēng;	tùngfùng;
-of ship	吃水	chīshwěi;	hekséui (siHkséui);
-drinking	口	kǒu	háu (daaHm)
draw v. t.			
-attract	吸引	syyǐn;	kāpyáHn;
-as picture	畫畫	hwàhwà;	waaHkwá;
-retire	引退	yǐntwèi;	yáHnteui;
-draw near	親近	chīnjìn	chàngaHn
dread v. t.	懼怕	jyùpà;	geuiHpa;
	害怕	hàipà	hoiHpa

dream

-n.	夢ㄥˋ	mèng;	muHng;
-v. i.	做ㄗㄨㄛˋ夢ㄥˋ	dzwòmèng	jouHmuHng (faatmuHng)

dreg n.

-residue	渣ㄓㄚ滓ˇ	jādž;	jàjí;
-refuse.	廢ㄟˋ物ㄨˋ	fèiwù	faimaHt

dress

-n. clothes	衣ㄧ服ㄈㄨˊ	yīfu;	yìfuHk;
-v. t. wear	穿ㄔㄨㄢ	chwēn;	chyùn (jeuk);
-v. t. with medicine	敷ㄈㄨ藥ㄠˋ	fūyàu	fùyeuIIk

drill

-v. t. train	教ㄐㄠˋ練ㄌㄧㄢˋ	jyàulyàn;	gaauliHn;
-n. fabric	斜ㄒㄧㄝˊ紋ㄨㄣˊ布ㄅㄨˋ	syéwénbù	cheHmàHnbou

drink

-v. t.	喝ㄏㄜ	hē;	hot (yám);
-n. beverage	飲ㄧㄣˇ料ㄌㄧㄠˋ	yǐnlyàu;	yámliuH;
-n. liquor	酒ㄐㄧㄡˇ	jyǒu	jáu

drive v. t.

-vehicle	駕ㄐㄧㄚˋ駛ˇ	jyàshř;	gasái;
-expel	趕ㄍㄢˇ	gǎn	gón
driver n.	司ㄙ機ㄐㄧ	sžji	sìgèi

drop

-n. of fluids	滴ㄉㄧ	di;	diHk;
-v. t. in drops	滴ㄉㄧ下ㄒㄧㄚˋ	dīsyà;	diHkhnH (diHkloHk)
-v. t. by accident	跌ㄉㄧㄝˊ倒ㄉㄠˇ	dyédǎu;	ditdóu;
-v. t. omit	漏ㄌㄡˋ	lòu;	lauH;
-drops of blood	血ㄒㄧㄝˇ汗ㄏㄢˋ	syěhàn	hyuthoHn
drought n.	乾ㄍㄢ旱ㄏㄢˋ	gēnhàn	gònhóHn

drown v. t.

-in water	淹ㄧㄢ死ㄙˇ	yēnsž;	yìmséi (jaHmséi);
-in Hades	沉ㄔㄣˊ淪ㄌㄨㄣˊ	chénlwún	chàHmlèuHn

drug n.	中藥	jūngyàu;	jùngyeuHk;
	藥材	yàutsái	yeuHkchòiH
druggist n.	藥劑師	yàujishř	yeuHkjāisi
drum n.	鼓	gǔ	gú
drunkard n.	醉酒	dzwèijyǒu;	jeuijáu;
	酒徒	jyǒutú	jáutòuH (jáugwái)
dry a.			
-not wet	乾	gān;	gòn;
-of climate	乾燥	gāndzàu;	gònchou;
-thirsty	口渴	kǒukě;	háuhot (génghot);
-dry-clean	乾洗	gānsyǐ	gònsái
dubious a.			
-doubtful	懷疑	hwáiyí;	wàaiHyìH;
-unreliable	可疑	kěyí	hóyìH
duck n.	鴨	yā	ngáap
due			
-a. owing to	因為	yīnwei;	yànwaiH;
-a. payable	應付	yìngfù;	yìngfuH;
-abv. directly	向	syàng;	heung;
-due to	由於	yóuyú	yàuHyù
duet n.	二部合唱	èrbùhéchàng	yiHbouHhaHpcheung
duke n.	公爵	gūngjywé	gùngjeuk
dull a.			
-stupid	笨	bèn;	baHn;
-monotonous	無聊	wúlyáu;	mòuHliuH;
-not clear	模糊	mwóhú;	mòuHwùH;
-not active	死板	sžbǎn	séibáan
dumb a.	啞	yǎ	ngá
dungeon n.	地牢	dìláu	deiHlòuH
duplicate			
-a. twofold	兩倍	lyǎngbèi;	léuHngpúiH;
-n. document	副本	fùběn;	fubún;

-n. cheque	存根	tswúngēn	chyùHngàn
dust			
-n. of earth	塵	chén;	chàHn;
-n. ashes	灰	hwēi;	fùi;
-v. t. with cloth	抹	mwŏ	mut(maat)
duty n.			
-moral	責任	dzérèn;	jaakyaIIm;
-official	任務	rènwù;	yaHmmouH;
-tax	稅	shwèi	seui
dwell v. i.	住	iù;	jyuH;
	居住	jyūjù	gèuijyuH
-dwelling place	居所	jyūswŏ;	gèuisó;
	住處	jùchù	jyuHchyu
dye v. t.	染	răn	yíHm
dynamics n.	力學	lìsywé;	liHkhoHk;
	原動力	ywándùnglì	yùHnduHngliHk
dynamo n.	發電機	fādyànji	faatdiHngèi
dynasty n.	朝代	cháudài;	chìuHdoiH;
	朝	cháu	chìuH

E

each a.	各	gè;	gok;
	每	měi	múiH
eager a.			
-desirous	渴望	kĕwàng;	hotmoHng;
-ardent	熱心	rèsyin;	yiHtsàm;
-earnest	懇切	kĕnchyè	hánchit
eagle n.	鷹	yìng	yìng
ear n.	耳朵	ĕrdwo	yíHdéu (yiHjái)
earl n.	伯爵	bwójywé	baakjeuk
early a.	早	dzău	jóu
earn v. t.	賺錢	jwànchyán	jaaHnchìn

earnest a.

-eager	熱心	rèsyín;	yiHtsàm;
-serious	認眞	rènjēn;	yiHngjān;
-emphatic	懇切	kěnchyè	hánchit

earth n.

-Astron.	地球	dìchyóu;	deiHkàuH;
-world	世界	shìjyè;	saigaai
-ground	地	dì	deiH

earthen jars n.	石缸	shŕgēng	seHkgòng
earthenware n.	陶器	táuchì	tóuHhei
earthquake n.	地震	dìjèn	deiHjan

ease v. t.

-from labour	舒適	shūshŕ;	syūsìk;
-from care	安心	ānsyín;	ònsàm;
-loosen	放鬆	fàngsūng	fongsùng

east n.

	東	dūng;	dùng;
	東方	dūngfāng	dùngfòng

easy a.

-not difficult	容易	rúngyi;	yùHngyiH;
-at ease	舒服	shūfu	syùfuHk

eat v. t.	吃	chŕ;	hek (siHk);
-corrode	腐蝕	fŭshŕ	fuHsiHk

ebb v. i.

-as the tide	水退	shwĕitwèi;	séuiteui;
-to worse state	衰退	shwēitwèi	sèuiteui

ebony n.

	酸枝	swēnjŕ;	syùnjì;
	烏木	wūmù	wùmuHk

eccentric a.

-odd	古怪	gŭgwài;	gúgwaai;
-peculiar	特別	tèbyé	daHkbiHt

English	Chinese		
echo n.	應聲	yìngohong;	yíngseng;
	回聲	hwéishēng	wùiHsèng
eclipse n.	蝕	shf;	siHk;
-of the sun	日蝕	ìshf;	yaHtsiHk;
-of the moon	月蝕	ywèshf	yuHtsiHk
economic a.	經濟	jīngjì;	gìngjai;
-economic invasion	經濟侵畧	jīngji chīnlywè	gìngjai chàmleuk
economics n.	經濟學	jīngjìsywé	gìngjaihoHk
edge n.	邊	byēn;	bìn;
-of knife	刀口	dāukǒu;	dòuháu;
-of a lake	湖邊	húbyān	wùHbìn
editor n.			
-of newspaper	編輯	byānji;	pìnchэp;
-of book	編者	byēnjě	pìnjé
editor-in-chief	主筆	jǔbi	jyúbāt
eduction n.	教育	jyàuyù;	gaauyuHk;
-adult	成人教育	chéngɪénjyàuyù;	ɒiHngyòHngaauyuHk;
-elementary	小學教育	syǎusywéjyàuyù;	siuhoHkgaauyuHk;
-higher	高級教育	gāujìjyàuyù;	gōukāpgaauyuHk;
-moral	道德教育	dàudéjyàuyù;	douHdākgaauyuHk;
-physical	體育	tǐyù;	táiyuHk;
-primary	初級教育	chūjìjyàuyù;	chōkāpgaauyuHk;
-religious	宗教教育	dzūngjyàujyàuyù;	jùnggaaugaauyuHk;
-rural	鄉村教育	syāngtswūnjyàuyù;	hēungchyūngaauyuHk;
-vocational	職業教育	jíyèjyàuyù;	jìkyiHpgaauyuHk;
-education agency	教育機關	jyàuyùjìgwān;	gaauyuHkgèigwàan;
-education problem	教育問題	jyàuyùwèntí	gaauyuHkmaHntàiH

effect			
-n. efficiency	效ㄒㄧㄠˋ果ㄍㄨㄛˇ	syàugwǒ;	haauHgwó;
-v. t. bring to pass	實ㄕˊ現ㄒㄧㄢˋ	shŕsyàn;	saHtyiHn;
-v. t. accomplish	成ㄔㄥˊ就ㄐㄧㄡˋ	chéngjyòu	sìHngjauH
effective a.	有ㄧㄡˇ效ㄒㄧㄠˋ	yǒusyàu	yáuHhaauH
efficiency n.			
-Mech.	效ㄒㄧㄠˋ率ㄌㄩˋ	syàulyù;	haauHleuHt;
-competency	效ㄒㄧㄠˋ能ㄋㄥˊ	syàunéng	haauHnàHng
effort n.			
-of mind	努ㄋㄨˇ力ㄌㄧˋ	nǔlì;	nóuHliHk;
-of body	出ㄔㄨ力ㄌㄧˋ	chūlì	chēutliHk
egg n.	蛋ㄉㄢˋ	dàn;	dáan;
	鷄ㄐㄧ蛋ㄉㄢˋ	jīdàn	gàidáan
eggplant n.	茄ㄑㄧㄝˊ子ㄗ	chyédz	kéjí (ngáigwā)
eight a.	八ㄅㄚ	bā	baat
eighteen a.	十ㄕˊ八ㄅㄚ	shŕbā	saHpbaat
eighteenth a.	第ㄉㄧˋ十ㄕˊ八ㄅㄚ	dìshŕbā	daiHsaHpbaat
eightfold a.	八ㄅㄚ倍ㄅㄟˋ	bābèi	baatpúiH
eighth a.	第ㄉㄧˋ八ㄅㄚ	dìbā	daiHbaat
either..or..	不ㄅㄨˊ是ㄕˋ..就ㄐㄧㄡˋ是ㄕˋ..	búshr̀..jyòushr̀..	bātsiH..jauHsiH.. (m̀haiH..jauHhaiH..)
eject v. t.			
-drive out	趕ㄍㄢˇ出ㄔㄨ	gǎnchū;	gónchēut;
-evacuate	排ㄆㄞˊ出ㄔㄨ	páichū;	pàaiHchēut;
-of volcano	噴ㄆㄣ出ㄔㄨ	pēnchū	panchēut
elasticity n.	彈ㄊㄢˊ性ㄒㄧㄥˋ	tánsyìng;	daaHnsing;
	彈ㄊㄢˊ力ㄌㄧˋ	tánlì	daaHnliHk
elbow n.	肘ㄓㄡˇ	jǒu	jáu
elder a.	大ㄉㄚˋ	dà;	daaiH;
	長ㄓㄤˇ	jǎng;	jéung;
-elder brother	兄ㄒㄩㄥ	syūng;	hìng; (daaiHlóu);
	哥ㄍㄜ	gē;	gō (agō);

-elder of church	長老	jǎnglǎu	jéunglóuH
elect v. t.	選	sywǎn;	syún;
	選舉	sywǎnjyǔ	syúngéui
electricity n.	電	dyàn;	diHn;
-science	電器學	dyànchìsywé	diHnheihoHk
elegant a.			
-grace	優美	youmǔl;	yǎumélII,
-of persons	文雅	wényǎ;	màHnngáH;
-of things	精緻	jìngjr̀	jìngji
element n.			
-Chem.	元素	ywánsù;	yùHnsou;
-fig.	要素	yàusù	yiusou
elementary a.	初步	chūbù	chòbouH
elephant n.	象	syàng	jeuHng
elevator n.	昇降機	shēngjyàngjǐ;	sìnggonggèi;
	電梯	dyàntī	diHntài
eleven a.	十一	shŕyì	saHpyāt
eligible a.			
-suitable	適宜	shìyí;	sikyìH;
-desirable	合意	héyì	haHpyi
eliminate v. t.			
-take out	除去	chúchyù;	chèuiHheui
-discard	丟掉	dyōudyàu	dìudiuH (dámheui)
ellipse n.	橢圓	twǒywán	tóyùHn
eloquence n.	口才	kǒutsái	háuchòiII
else adv.			
-besides	另外	lìngwài;	liHngngoiH;
-otherwise	要不然	yàubùrán	yiubātyìHn (yeuIIkm̀haiII)
emancipation n.			
-release	解放	jyěfàng;	gáaifong;

-liberation	自主	dźjŭ	jiHjyú
embark v. t.			
-on ship	上船	shàngchwán;	séuHngsyùHn;
-engage	參加	tsānjyā;	chàamgà;
invest	投資	tóudž	tàuHjì
embarrass v. t.			
-in difficulty	爲難	wéinán;	wàiHnàaHn;
-abash	難爲情	nánwéichíng;	nàaHnwàiHchìHng;
-worry	煩惱	fánnău	fàaHnnóuH
embassy n.	大使舘	dàshřgwăn	daaiHsigún
emblem n.			
-device	徽章	hwēijāng;	fàijèung;
-symbol	標誌	byāujř	bìuji
embrace v. t.			
-in the arms	抱	bàu;	póuH;
-include	包括	bāukwò	bàaukwut
embroider v. t.	繡花	syòuhwē;	saufā;
	刺繡	tsżsyòu	chisau
emerge v. i.			
-appear	現出	syànchū;	yiHnchēut;
-from fluid	露出	lùchū	louHchēut
emergency n.			
-sudden necessity	緊急	jřnjí;	gángāp;
-occurrence	事變	shřbyàn	siHbin
emigrant n.	移民	yimín	yìHmàHn
eminent a.			
-distinguished	優秀	yōusyòu;	yàusau;
-prominent	傑出	jyéchū	giHtchēut

emotion n.

-agitation of mind	情緒	chíngsyù;	chìHngséuiH;
-deep feeling	感情	gănchíng	gámchìHng

emperor n. 皇帝 hwángdì wòHngdai

emphasize v. t.

-accentuate	加重語氣	jyājùng yŭchì;	gèchúHng yúHhei
-stress	強調	chyángdyàu;	kèuHngdiuH;
-into special prominence	注重	jùjùng	jyujuHng

empire n. 帝國 dìgwó daigwok

employ v. t.

-teacher	聘請	pìngchǐng,	pingchíng;
-servant	雇用	gùyùng;	guyuIng;
-use	用	yùng	yuHng

empty a.

-empty handed	空手	kūngshŏu;	hùngsáu;
-empty talk	虛談	syūtán;	hèuitàaHm;
-empty words	空話	kūnghwà	hùngwaH

enable v. t. 使能 shǐnéng sìnàHng (sáidou nàHnggau)

enchantment n. 妖術 法術 yāushù; fǎshù yìuseuHt; faatseuHt

encircle v. t.

-surround	圍繞	wéirău;	wàiHyíuH
-with arms	抱住	bàujù;	póuHjyuH;
-by enemy	包圍	bāuwéi	bàauwàiH

enclose v. t.

-by a fence	圍起	wéichǐ;	wàiHhéi;
-in a letter	附上	fùshàng	fuHséuHng

encourage v. t. 勉勵 鼓勵 myǎnlì; gŭlì mìHnlaiII, gúlaiH

encyclopedia n. 百科全書 băikēchywánshū baakfòchyùHnsyù

end

-n. of time	結局	jyéjú;	gitguHk;
-n. object in view	目的	mùdì;	muHkdik;
-v. t. cease	結束	jyéshù	gitchūk
-end of the world	世界末日	shìjyè mwòr	saigaai muHtyaHt

endeavour v. i.

-physical strength	盡力	jìnlì;	jeuHnliHk;
-intellectual power	努力	nǔlì;	nóuHliHk;
-attempt	試	shì	si

endorse v. t.　背書　bèishū　buisyù

endow v. t.

-as to an institution	捐助	jywānjù;	gyùnjoH;
-as a faculty	賦予	fùyǔ;	fuyùH;
-endowment fund	基金	jijīn	gèigàm

endure v. t.

	忍受	rěnshòu	yánsauH;
	忍耐	rěnnài	yánnoiH

enemy n.　仇敵　chóudí;　sàuHdiHk

-personel	仇人	chóurén;	sàuHyàHn;
-in war	敵人	dírén	diHkyàHn

energy n.

-spirit	精神	jīngshén;	jìngsàHn;
-strength	氣力	chìlì	heiliHk

enforce v. t.

-as laws	執行	jísyíng;	jāphàHng;
-compel	強逼	chyángbì	kéuHngbik

engage v. i.

-promise	約定	ywēdìng;	yeukdiHng;
-betroth	訂婚	dìnghwūn;	diHngfàn;
-undertake	擔任	dānrèn	dàamyaHm

engine n.

-machine	機器	jichí;	gèihei;

-motor	發動機	fādùngjī	faatduHnggèi
engineer n.	工程師	gūngchéngshr̄	gùngchìHngsi
English n.			
-language	英文	Yīngwén;	YìngmàHn;
-man	英國人	Yìnggwórén	YìnggwokyàHn
engrave v. t.			
-carve	彫刻	dyāukè;	dìuhāak;
-on memory	記住	jìjù	geijyuH
enjoy v. t.	享受	syǎngshou	héungsauH
enlarge v. t.			
-business	擴充	kwòchūng;	kongchùng;
-make larger	放大	fàngdà	fongdaaiH
enlist			
-v. i. oneself for military	當兵	dāngbīng;	dòngbìng;
-v. t. others for military	徵兵	jēngbīng	jìngbìng
enmity n.	敵意	díyì;	diHkyi;
	仇恨	chóuhèn	sàuHhaHn
enormous a.			
-size	巨大	jyùdà;	geuiHdaaiH;
-amount	很多	hěndwō	hándò (hóudò)
enough a.	足夠	dzúgòu	jūkgau
enquire v. i.			
-by search	打聽	dǎtīng;	dátìng;
-for information	查問	cháwèn	chàHmaHn
enroll v. t.			
-register	報名	bàumíng;	bouméng;
-record	登記	dēngjì	dànggei
entangle v. t.			
-as net	纏繞	chánrǎu;	chiHnyiuH;
-involve	連累	lyánlèi	lìHnleuiH

enter v. t.

  -go into · 進入 · jìnrù; · jeunyaHp;

  -join · 參加 · tsānjyā · chàamgà

enterprise n.

  -industrial · 企業 · chǐyè; · kéiHyiHp;

  -undertaking · 事業 · shìyè; · siHyiHp;

  -spirit of · 進取心 · jìnchyǔsyin · jeunchéuisàm

entertain v. t.

  -show hospitality · 招待 · jāudài; · jìudoiH;

  -give dinner-parties · 請客 · chǐngkè; · chénghaak;

  -amuse · 娛樂 · yúlè · yùHloHk

enthrone v. t. · 登記 · dēngjì · dànggei

enthusiasm n. · 熱心 · rèsyìn · yiHtsàm

entire a. · 完全 · wánchywán; · yùHnchyùHn;

  整個 · jěnggè · jìnggo

entrance n.

  -doorway · 入口 · rùkǒu; · yaHpháu;

  -door · 門 · mén; · mùHn;

  -passage · 路口 · lùkǒu · louHháu

entreat v. t. · 懇求 · kěnchyóu; · hánkàuH;

  請求 · chǐngchyóu · chǐngkàuH

entrust v. t.

  -commit · 託付 · twōfù; · tokfuH;

  -a duty, etc. · 委託 · wěitwō; · wáitok;

  -specified office · 委任 · wěirèn · wáiyaHm

entry n.

  -of a ship · 入港 · rùgǎng; · yaHpgóng;

  -in a register · 登記 · dēngjì; · dànggei;

  -on a form · 填寫 · tyánsě · tìHnsé

enumerate v. t.

  -count · 計算 · jìswàn; · gaisyun:

-relate	列舉	lyèjyŭ	liHtgéui
envelope n.	信封	syìnfēng	seunfūng
environment n.	環境	hwánjìng	wàaHngíng
envy v. t.	嫉妒 妒忌	jídù; dùjì	jaHtdouH; dougeiH
epidemic a.	流行病 傳染病	lyóusyìngbìng; chywánrănbìng	làuHàhHngbeHng; chyùHnyíHmbeHng
epilepsy n.	癲癇	dyānsyán	dìnhàaHn
equal a.			
-fair	公平	gūngpíng;	gùngpìHng;
-in position	相等	syāngdĕng;	sòungdáng;
-of a treaty	平等	píngdĕng	pìHngdáng
equality n.	平等	píngdèng	pìHngdáng
equilibrium n.	均衡 平衡	jyūnhéng; pínghéng	gwànhàHng; pìHnghàHng
era n.			
-chronological	紀元	jìywán;	géiyùHn;
-title of emperor's reign	年號	ngánhàu;	nìHnhouH;
-period	年代	nyándài	nìHndoiH
eraser n.	橡皮	syàngpí	jeuHngpèiH (gàauchaat)
erect			
-a. straight	直立	jŕlì;	jiHklaHp;
-v. t. establish to build	設立	shèlì	chitlaHp
err v. i.			
-go astray	失迷	shīmí;	satmàiH;
-make mistakes	做錯	dzwòtswò;	jouHcho;
-to sin	犯罪	fàndzwèi	faaHnjeuiH
errand n.	差使	chāishŕ	chàaisi

error n.

-fault	過失	gwòshī;	gwosāt;
-mistakes	錯誤	tswòwù	chongH

escalator v. t.　自動梯　dżdùngti̍　jiHduHngtài

escape v. i.

-free from	逃避	táubì;	tòuHbeiH;
-avoid	避免	bìmyǎn;	beiHmíHn;
-escape from calamity	避難	bìnàn	beiHnaaHn

escort

-v. t. go with	護送	hùsùng;	wuHsung;
-v. t. as prisoners	押送	yāsùng;	aatsung;
-n. guard	護衛	hùwèi	wuHwaiH

essay n.　論文　lwùnwén　leuHnmàHn

essence n.

-real substance	本質	běnjí;	búnjāt;
-distinctive character	要素	yàusù;	yiusou;
-scent	香味	syāngwèi	hèungmeiH

essential a.

-fundamental	根本	gēnběn;	gànbún;
-most important	主要	jǔyàu;	jyúyiu;
-required	必要	bìyàu	bìtyiu

establish v. t.

-as institution	設立	shèlì;	chitlaHp;
-a fact	確定	chywèdìng;	kokdiHng;
-establish a church	設立教會	shèlì jyàuhwèi	chitlaHp gaauwúi

estate n.　地產　dìchǎn　deiHcháan

-personal estate	動產	dùngchǎn;	duHngcháan;
-real estate	不動產	búdùngchǎn	bātduHngcháan

esteem v. t.

-appraise	估價	gūjyà;	gúga;

-to deem	以 為	yǐwéi;	yíHwàiH;
-prize	珍 貴	jēngwèi	jàngwai
esthetics n.	美 學	měisywé	méiHhoHk
estimate v. t.			
-appraise	評 價	píngjyà;	píHngga;
-judge	論 斷	lwùndwàn;	leuHndyun;
-price to be charged	預 算	yùswàn	yuHsyun
eternal a.	永 遠	yǔngywǎn	wiHngyúHn
ether n.	乙 太	yǐtài	yuttaai
ethics n.	倫 理 學	lwúnlǐsywé	leuHnleiHhoHk
etiquette n.	禮 節	lǐjyé	láiHjit
eugenics n.	優 生 學	yōushengsywé	yàusànghoHk
eunuch n.	太 監	tàijyàn	taaigaam
Eurasian n.	混 種 人	hwǔnjǔngrén	waHnjúngyàHn
European n.	歐 洲 人	Ōujōurén	AujàuyàHn
evacuate v. t.			
-troops	撤 退	chètwèi;	chitteui;
-civilians	疏 散	shūsàn	sòsaan
evaporate v. t.	蒸 發	jēngfā	jìngfaat
eve n.	前 夜	chyányè	chìHnyeH
-Christmas Eve	聖 誕 前 夕	Shèngdàn chyánsyi	Singdaan chiHnjiHk
-New-Year's Eve	新 年 前 夕	Syīnnyán chyánsyi	SànnìHn chìHnjiHk
even			
-a. level	平 坦	píngtǎn;	píHngtáan;
-a. equitable	公 平	gūngpíng;	gùngpíHng;
-adv. although	雖 然	swéirán	sèuiyìHn;
-even if	甚 至	shènjr̀	saHmji;

English	Chinese		
-even number	偶數	ǒushù	ngáuHsou
evening n.	黃昏;	hwánghwūn;	wòHngfàn;
	晚上	wǎnshàng	máaHnseuHng
event n.			
-thing that happened	事件	shɹ̀jyàn;	siHgín;
-in sports	項	syàng	hoHng
ever adv.	時常	shɹ́cháng	sìHsèuHng
-ever since	自從	dz̀tsúng;	jiHchùHng;
-for ever	永遠	yǔngywǎn	wíHngyúHn
evergreen			
-n.	冬青	dūngchǐng;	dùngchǐng;
-a.	常綠	chánglyù	sèuHngluHk
everlasting a.			
-endless	無窮;	wúchyúng;	mòuHkùHng;
-lasting forever	常存	chángtswún;	sèuHngchyùHn;
-everlasting life	永生;	yǔngshēng;	wíHngsàng;
-everlasting bitterness	永苦	yǔngkǔ	wíHngfú
every a.			
-each	各	gè;	gok;
-all	所有	swǒyǒu	sóyáuH
-everybody n.	每人;	měirén;	múiHyàHn;
	人人	rénrén;	yàHnyàHn;
-everyday n.	每日;	měir;	múiHyaHt;
	日常	ɹ̀cháng;	yaHtsèuHng
-everyone n.	各人	gèrén;	gokyàHn;
-everything n.	各事;	gèshɹ̀;	goksiH;
	萬事;	wànshɹ̀;	maaHnsiH
-every time	每次;	měits̀z;	múiHchi;
	每逢	měiféng;	múiHfùHng;
-everywhere adv.			
-in all places	各處;	gèchù;	gokchyu;

-thoroughly	全然	chywánrán	chyùHnyìHn
evidence n.			
-proof	証據	jèngjyù;	jinggeui;
-judicial	口供	kŏugūng	háugùng
evil a.			
-wicked	邪惡	syéè;	chèHngok;
-vicious	惡毒	èdú;	ngokduHk;
-evil desires	邪情	syéchíng;	chèHchìHng;
-evil doers	作惡的人	dzwòèderén;	jokngokdikyàIIn;
-evil heart	惡心	èsyin;	ngoksàm;
-evil nature	惡性	èsying;	ngoksing;
-evil person	惡人	èrén;	ngokyàHn;
-evil thoughts	惡念	èuyàn;	ngokniHm;
-evil words	壞話	hwàihwà	waaiHwá
evolution n.	進化	jìnhwà	jeunfa
exact a.			
-eaccurat	正確	jèngchywè;	jingkok;
-minute	精密	jingmì;	jingmaHt;
-of the time	準	jwŭn	jéun
exaggerate v. t.	誇張	kwājāng	kwàjèung
exalt v. t.			
-elevate	高舉	gāujyŭ;	gòugéui;
-praise	稱讚	chēngdzàn;	chìngjaan;
-exalt self	高擡自己	gāutái dzìjǐ	gòutòiH jiIIgéi
exalted p./a.	尊貴	dzwūngwèi;	jyùngwai;
	高尚	gāushàng	gòuseuHng
examination n.	考試	kăushì;	háausi;
	大考	dàkău	daaiHháau
-examination paper	試卷	shìjywàn	sigyún

examine v. t.

-test	考	kǎu;	háau;
-inspect	審查	shěnchá;	sámchàH;
-inquire	查問	cháwèn	chàHmaHn

example n.

-model	榜樣	bǎngyàng;	bóngyeuHng;
-pattern	樣子	yàngdz;	yeuHngji (yéung);
-precedent	實例	shílì	saHtlaiH

exceed v. t.

	過於	gwòyú;	gwoyù;
	超過	chāugwò	chìugwo

excellent a.

	佳美	jyāměi;	gàaiméiH;
	美好	měihǎu	méiHhóu

except prep.

	除非	chúfēi;	chèuiHfèi;
	除了以外	chúle...yǐwài	chèuiHlíuH...yíHngoiH (chèuiHjó...jì'ngoiH)

exception n.

	例外	lìwài	laiHngoiH

excessive a.

-in amount	過多	gwòdwō;	gwodò;
-in degree	過度	gwòdù;	gwodouH;
-too heavy	過重	gwòjùng;	gwochúHng;
-excessive luxury	過於奢侈	gwoyú shēchì	gwoyù chèchí

exchange v. t.

	交換	jyāuhwàn	gàauwuHn
-as money	換	hwàn;	wuHn;
-in place of	調換	dyàuhwàn	diuHwuHn

excite v. t.

-animate	興奮	syìngfèn;	hìngfáHn;
-stir	惹起	rěchì;	yéHhéi;
-stimulate	激勵	jilì	gìklaiH

exclaim v. t.

	喊	hǎn;	haam;
	叫	jyàu	giu

exclamatory a.

	感歎	gǎntàn	gámtaan

exclusion n.

-debarring	屏棄	píngchì;	pìHnghei;
-exclusion policy	排外政策	páiwài jèngtsè	pàaiHngoiH jingchaak
excommunicate v. t.	革除	géchú;	gaakchèuiH;
	開除	kāichú	hòichèuiH

excursion n.

-school children	遠足	ywăndzú;	yúHnjūk;
-recreation	旅行	lyűsyíng;	léuiHhàHng;
-pleasure	遊覽	yóulăn	yàuHláaHm

excuse

-v- t. exempt	原諒	ywánlyàng;	yùHnleuHng;
-n. apology offered	藉口	jyòkŏu	jiIIklău

execution n.

	執行	jŕsyíng;	jāphàHng;
	實行	shŕsyíng;	saHthàHng;
-execution ground	法塲	făchăng	faatchèuHng

executive a.

-of govt.	行政	syíngjèng;	hàHngjing;
-executive committee	執行委員會	jŕsyíngwĕiywánhwèi	jáphàHngwáiyùHnwúi

exempt a.

	免	myăn;	míHn;
-from army	免役	myănyì;	míHnyiHk;
-from taxes	免稅	myănshwèi	míHnseui

exercise

-v. t. use	運用	yùnyùng;	waIIuyuHug;
-v. t. practise	練習	lyànsyí;	liHnjaaHp;
-n. of body	運動	yùndùng;	waHnduHng;
-n. lesson	練習	lyànsyí	liHnjaaHp

exhausted p. a.

-tired out	疲乏	pífá;	pèiHfaIIt;

-spent	用盡	yùngjìn	yuHngjeuHn
exhibition n.			
-as goods	陳列	chénlyè;	chàHnliHt;
-as paintings	展覽	jănlăn;	jínláaHm;
-exposition	展覽會	jănlănhwèi	jínláaHmwúi
exhort v. t.			
-advise	勸告	chywàngàu;	hyungou;
-warn	警告	jînggàu;	gínggou;
-encourage	勉勵	myănlì	míHnlaiH
exhortation n.			
-advice	勸告	chywàngàu;	hyungou;
-admonition	勸誡	chywànjyè	hyungaai
exile			
-v. i. banish	放逐	fàngjú;	fongjuHk;
-n. person is sent away	流犯	lyóufàn	làuHfáan
exist v. i.			
-to be	存在	tswúndzài;	chyùHnjoiH;
-to have life	生存	shēngtswún	sàngchyùHn
existence n.	存在	tswúndzài;	chyùHnjoiH;
	存留	tswúnlyòu	chyùHnlàuH
exit n.	門口	mènkŏu;	mùHnháu;
	出口	chūkŏu	chēutháu
expand v. t.			
-develop	發展	fājăn;	faatjín;
-spread	張開	jāngkāi;	jèunghòi;
-swell	脹膨	péngjàng	pàHngjeung
expect v. t.			
-await	等待	děngdài;	dángdoiH;
-look for(mentally)	盼望	pànwàng;	paanmoHng;
-look forward to	希望	syīwàng	hèimoHng

expectation n.

-anticipation	預期	yùchī;	yuHkeiH;
-future	前途	chyántú	chìHntòuH

expedition n.

-scientific	探險	tànsyǎn;	taamhím;
-promptness	迅速	syùnsù;	seunchūk;
-troops	遠征	ywǎnjēng	yúHnjìng

expel v. t.

-exile	逐出	júchū;	juHkchēut;
-from school	開除	kāichú	hòichèuiH

expense n.

	費用	fèiyùng;	faiyuHng;
	經費	jīngfèi	gīngfai

expensive a.

	貴	gwèi	gwai

experience n.

	經驗	jīngyàn;	gìngyiHm;
	體驗	tǐyàn	táiyiHm

experiment n.

	試驗	shìyàn;	siyiHm;
	實驗	shfyàn	saHtyiHm

expert

-a. skilful	老練	lǎulyàn;	lóuHliHn;
-n. specialist	專家	jwānjyā;	jyūngā;
-n. in mining	技師	jìshī	geiHsi

explain v. t.

	解釋	jyěshì;	gáaisìk;
	說明	shwōmíng	syutmìHng

explanation n.

-description	說明	shwōmíng;	syutmìHng;
-meaning	意思	yìsz;	yisi;
-in excuse	聲明	shēngmíng	sìngmìHng

explode v. i.

-burst	爆炸	bàujà;	baauja;
-as a theory	推翻	twēifān	tèuifàan

export

-v. t.	出口	chūkǒu;	chēutháu;
-n.	出口貨	chūkǒuhwò	chēutháufo

exposition n.

-explain	釋義	shìyì;	sìkyiH;
-exposure	顯露	syǎnlù	hìnlouH

expound v. t.

-as a theory	發表	fābyǎu;	faatbíu;
-interpret	解釋	jyěshì	gáaisìk

express v. t.

-by words	表明	byǎumíng;	bíumìHng;
-opinion	表示	byǎushì;	bíusiH;
-express train	特別快車	tèbyé kwàichē	daHtbiHt faaichē

expression n.

-opinion	表示	byǎushì;	bíusiH;
-attitude	表情	byǎuchíng	bíuchìHng

extend v. t.

-as a principle	推廣	twēigwǎng;	tèuigwóng;
-prolong	延期	yánchì;	yìHnkèiH;
-enlarge	擴充	kwòchūng	kongchùng

extent n.

-compass	範圍	fànwéi;	faaHnwàiH;
-amout	總數	dzǔngshù;	júngsou;
-degree	程度	chéngdù	chìHngdouH

external a.

-outward	外表	wàibyǎu;	ngoiHbíu;
-from without	外來	wàilái;	ngoiHlòiH;
-external application	外用	wàiyùng;	ngoiHyuHng;
-external traffic	國外貿易	gwówài màuyì	gwokngoiH mauHyiHk

externalism n.	外界論	wàijyèlwùn	ngoiHgaaileuHn
extinguish v. t.			
-quench	熄滅	syímyè;	sikmilIt;
-nullify	取消	chyŭsyāu;	chéuisìu;
-obscure	蒙蔽	méngbì	mùIIngbai
extol v. t.			
-praise	稱頌	chēngsùng;	chìngjuHng;
-laud	讚美	dzànměi	jaanméiH
extort v. t.			
-exact	勒索	lèswŏ;	laHksok;
-wrest away	强奪	chyáugdwó	kèuIIngdyuHt
extra a.			
-additional	另外	lìngwàu;	liHngngoiH;
-pay	額外	éwài	ngaaHkngoiH
xtract			
-v. i. pull out	拔	bá;	baHt (màng);
-v. i. quote	選錄	swănlù;	syúnluHk;
-n. juice	汁	jī	jāp
xtraordinary a.			
-rare	稀有	syíyŏu;	hèiyáuH (síuyáuH);
-remarkable	非常	feicháng;	fèisèuHng;
-unusual	不平常	bùpíngcháng	bātpìlIngsèuHng
xtravagant a.	奢侈	shēchr;	chèchí;
	浪費	làngfèi	loHngfai
xtreme a.	極端	jidwān	giHkdyùn
xult v. i.			
-rejoice	高興	gūusyìng;	gòuhing;
-triumph	得勝	déshèng	dāksing
-ye n.	眼睛	yănjìng	ngáaHnjìng (ngáaHn)

eyeball n.	眼ㄢ 球ㄑ一ㄡ	yănchyóu;	ngáaHnkàuH;
	眼ㄢ 珠ㄓㄨ	yănjū	ngáaHnjyū
eyebrow n.	眼ㄢ 眉ㄟ	yănméi	ngáaHnmèiH
eye-glass n.	眼ㄢ 鏡ㄐ一ㄥ	yănjìng	ngáaHngéng
eyelash n.	睫ㄐ一ㄝ 毛ㄇㄠ	jyémáu	jitmòuH
eyelet n.	眼ㄢ 孔ㄎㄨㄥ	yănkŭng	ngáaHnhúng·
eyelid n.	眼ㄢ 皮ㄆ一	yănpí	ngáaHnpèiH
eyesight n.	眼ㄢ 光ㄍㄨㄤ	yăngwāng;	ngáaHngwōng;
	目ㄇㄨ 力ㄌ一	mùlì	muHkliHk

F

fable

-n. narration	寓ㄩ 言一ㄢ	yùyán;	yuHyìHn;
-v. i. talk idly	漫ㄇㄢ 談ㄊㄢ	màntán;	maaHntàaHm;
-v. t. invent	虛ㄒㄩ 造ㄗㄠ	syūdzàu	hèuijouH
fabric n.	布ㄅㄨ 疋ㄆ一	bùpĭ;	boupāt;
	織ㄓ 品ㄆ一ㄣ	jīpĭn	jikbán

fabricate v. t.

-devise falsely	偽ㄨㄟ 造ㄗㄠ	wĕidzàu;	ngaiHjouH;
-construct	構ㄍㄡ 造ㄗㄠ	gòudzàu	kaujouH
face n.	臉ㄌ一ㄢ	lyăn	líHm (miHn)
-lose face	丟ㄉ一ㄡ 臉ㄌ一ㄢ	dyōulyăn;	dìulíHm (sāt miHnjí);
-face to face	面ㄇ一ㄢ 對ㄉㄨㄟ 面ㄇ一ㄢ	myàndwèimyàn	miHndeuimiHn

facility n.

-ease	容ㄖㄨㄥ 易一	rúngyì;	yùHngyiH;
-expertness	熟ㄕㄨ 練ㄌ一ㄢ	shúlyàn;	suHkliHn;
-readiness	敏ㄇ一ㄣ 捷ㄐ一ㄝ	mĭnjyé;	máHnjit;
-facility of trade	旅ㄌㄩ 行ㄒ一ㄥ 便ㄅ一ㄢ 利ㄌ一	lyŭsyíngbyànlì	léuiHhàHngbiHnleiH
fact n.	事ㄕ 實ㄕ	shìshí	siHsaHt
-as a matter of fact	其ㄑ一 實ㄕ	chíshí	kèiHsaHt

factor n.

-reason	因素	yīnsù;	yànsou;
-constituent	成分	chéngfèn	sìHngfaHn

factory n.

	工廠	gūngchǎng;	gùngchóng;
	製造廠	jìdàuchǎng	jaijouHchóng

faculty n.

-ability	才能	tsáinéng;	chòiHnàHng;
-trade	行業	hángyè;	hòHngyiHp;
-professors	大專教授	dàjwānjyàushòu;	daaiHjyùngaausauH;
-dept. of university	科	kē;	fō;
-faculty meeting	教員會議	jyàuywán hwèiyì	gaauyùHn wuiHyiH

fade v. i.

-as colour	褪色	twèisè;	teuisìk;
-wither	凋殘	dyāutsán;	dìuchàaHn;
-as strength	衰老	shwāilǎu	sёuilóuI

fail v. i.

-not succeed	失敗	shībài;	sātbaaiH;
-in an exam.	不及格	bùjigé	bātkaHpgaak (mhaHpgaak)

failure n.

-want of success	失敗	shībài;	sātbaaiH;
-deficiency	缺點	chywēdyǎn	kyutdím

faint a.

-timorous	懦弱	nwòrwò;	noHyeuHk;
-swoon	頭暈	tóuyūn	tàuHwàHn

fair

-a. just	公平	gūngpíng;	gùngpìHng;
-a. moderate	中等	jūngděng;	jùngdáng;
-n. market	市場	shìchǎng	sìHchèuHng
fairy n.	神仙	shénsyān;	sàHnsìn;
	仙女	syānnyǔ	sìnnéui

fairyland n.	仙境	syānjìng	sìngíng
faith n.			
-trust	信心	syìnsyīn;	seunsàm;
-belief	信仰	syìnyǎng;	seunyéuHng;
-as religious belief	宗教信仰	dzūngjyàu syìn-yǎng	jùnggaauseunyéuHng
faithful a.			
-loyal	忠心	jūngsyīn;	jùngsàm;
-honest	誠實	chéngshr	sìHngsaHt
fake			
-a. false	假	jyǎ;	gá;
-a. pretended	假裝	jyǎjwāng;	gájòng;
-n. person	騙子	pyàndz	pìnji
fall			
-v. i. downward	落下	lwòsyà;	loHkhaH;
-v. i. lose dignity	墮落	dwòlwò;	doHloHk;
-v. i. spiritually	跌倒	dyédǎu;	ditdóu;
-n. autumn	秋季	chyōujì	chàugwai
false a.			
-not true	虛假	syūjyǎ;	hèuigá;
-dishonest	虛偽	syūwěi	hèuingaiH
fame n.			
-reputation	名譽	míngyù;	mìHngyuH;
-public report	公衆傳說	gūngjùngchwán-shwō	gùngjungchùHnsyut
familiar a.			
-acquainted	熟識	shúshr;	suHksìk;
-knowing about	精通	jīngtūng	jìngtùng
family n.			
-body of persons	家人	jyārén;	gàyàHn;

-household	家屬	jyāshǔ;	gàsuHk;
-happy family	幸福家庭	syìngfú jyātíng;	haHngfūk gàtìHng;
-tribe	族	dzú;	juHk;
-family tree	家譜	jyāpǔ	gàpóu
famine n.	饑荒	jīhwāng	gèifòng
famous a.	出名	chūmíng;	chēutméng;
	著名	jùmíng	jyumìHng
fan n.	扇子	shàndz	sinjí (sin)
fanaticism n.			
-excessive enthusiasm	狂熱	kwángrè;	kòHngyiHt;
-frenzy	狂亂	kwánglwàn	kòHnglyuHn
fancy v. i.			
-illusion	幻想	hwànsyǎng;	waaHnséung;
-not plain	華美	hwáměi	wàHméiH
far			
-a. not near	遠	ywǎn;	yúHn;
-adv. greatly	非常	fēicháng;	fèisèuHng;
-Far East	遠東	Ywǎndūng	YúHndūng
fare n.	費	fèi;	fai;
-by land	車費	chēfèi;	chèfai;
-by sea	船費	chwánfèi	syùHnfai
farewell interj.			
-see you again	再見	dzàijyàn;	joigìn,
-leave-taking	辭行	tszsyíng;	chìHhàHng;
-go well	一路平安	yílùpíngūn;	yātlouHpìHngòn;
-farewell party	歡送會	hwānsùnghwèi	fùnsungwúi
farm			
-n.	農塲	núngchǎng;	nùHngchèuHng;

-v. t.	耕種	gēngjùng	gàangjung
farmer n.	農夫	núngfū;	nùHngfù;
	農人	núngrén	nùHngyàHn
farther a.			
-distant	更遠	gèngywǎn;	gangyúHn;
-further	另外	lìngwài	liHngngoiH
Fascism n.	法西斯主義	Fǎsyis̀zjǔyi	FaatsàisìjyúyiH
fashion n.			
-style	時式	shfshr̀;	sìHsìk;
-shade	樣子	yàngdz	yeuHngjí (yéung)
fast			
-a. quick	快	kwài;	faai;
-a. tight	緊	jǐn;	gán;
-a. firm	耐久	nàijyǒu;	noiHgáu;
-v. i. not eat	禁食	jìnshf́	gamsiHk
fasten v. t.			
-fix firmly	結牢	jyéláu;	gitlòuH (dásaHt);
-cling	緊貼	jǐntyē;	gántip;
-tie	綁住	bǎngjù	bóngjyuH
fat a.			
-of meat	肥	féi;	fèiH;
-of person	胖	pàng	pun (fèiH)
fatal a.			
-mortal	致命	jr̀mìng;	jimiHng;
-fatal wound	致命傷	jr̀mìngshāng	jimiHngsèung
fatalism n.	定命論	dìngmìnglwùn	diHngmiHngleuHn
fate n.			
-destiny	命運	mìngyùn;	miHngwaHn;
-decree of Heaven	天數	tyānshù	tìnsou

ather n.	父	fù;	fuH;
	父親	fùchin;	fuHchàn;
-my father	家父	jyāfù;	gàfuII;
your father	令尊	lìngdzwūn:	liHngjyùn;
-Heavenly Father	天父	Tyānfù;	TìnfuH;
-deceased father	先父	syānfù	sìnfuH
atigue			
-n. weariness	疲勞	piláu;	pèiHlòuH;
-v. t. tire	困乏	kwùnfá	kwanfaHt
ault n.			
-wrong action	過失	gwòshŕ;	gwosāt;
-defect	缺點	chywĕdyàn;	kyutdìm;
-flaw	毛病	máubìng	mòuHbeHng
avor, favour n.			
-divine mercy	恩惠	ēnhwèi;	yànwaiH;
-partiality	情面	chìngmyàn;	chìHngmiHn;
-aid	幫忙	bāngmáng	bòngmòHng
favorite, favourite			
-n. partiality	寵愛	chŭngài;	chúngngoi;
-a. most liked	心愛	syīnài	sàmngoi
fear v. t.			
-alarm	恐懼	kŭngjyù;	húnggeuiH;
-fear God	敬畏神	jìngwèi Shén	gingwai SàHn
fearful a.			
-reverend	可畏	kĕwèi;	hówai;
-timid	膽怯	dănchyè	dáamhip
feast n.			
-banquet	宴會	yànhwèi;	yinwuiH;

-festival	節日	jyéŕ	jityaHt
feather n.	羽毛	yǔmàu	yúHmòuH
feature n.			
-appearance	面貌	myànmàu;	miHnmaauH;
-lineament	特色	tèsè	daHksik
federation n.			
-league	聯盟	lyánméng;	lyùHnmàHng;
-confederacy	聯邦	lyánbāng	lyùHnbòng
fee n.			
-charge	費	fèi;	fai;
feeble a.			
-weak	弱	rwò;	yeuHk;
-not intelligent	低能	dīnéng;	dàinàHng;
-weak in mind	意志薄弱	yìjìŕbwórwò	yijiboHkyeuHk
feed v. t.			
-give food	餵養	wèiyǎng;	waiyeuHng;
-nourish	飼養	szyǎng	jiHyéuHng
feel v. t.			
-touch	摸	mwō;	mó;
-affected	感覺	gǎnjywé;	gámgok;
-be concious	知道	jīdàu;	jìdou;
-be moved	感動	gǎndùng	gámduHng
feeling n.			
-sensations	知覺	jījywé;	jìgok;
-state of mind	心情	syīnching;	sàmchìHng;
-emotion	感情	gǎnching;	gámchìHng;
-kindness	人情	rénching	yàHnchìHng
fellowship			
-n. companionable-ness	友情	yǒuching;	yáuHchìHng;

-n. association	團體	twántǐ;	tyùHntái;
-v. t. in the church	交通	jyāutūng	gàautùng

female a.

-human	女	nyǔ;	néuiH;
-animal	雌	tž;	chì;
	母	mǔ	móuH

feminine gender n.

	陰性	yīnsyìng;	yàmsing;
	女性	nyǔsyìng	néuiHsing

fence n.

-hedge	籬笆	líhā;	lèiHbà;
-railing	欄杆	lángān	làaHngòn

ferry n.

-boat	渡船	dùchwán;	douHsyñHn;
-place	渡頭	dùtóu	douHtàuH

fertile a.

	肥沃	féiwò	fciHyūk

festival n.

	節期	jyéchi;	jitkèiH;
	節日	jyéṛ	jityaIIt

fetch v. t.

-bring	取	chyǔ	chéui (nìng, nǐk);
-sell for	賣	mài	maaiH

fetter

-n. for the feet	脚鐐	jyǎulyáu,	geuklíuH;
-v. t. restrain	約束	ywēshù	yeukchūk

fever

-v. t.	發燒	fāshāu;	faatsìu,
-n.	熱度	rèdù	yiHtdouH

sew a.

-small in number	少數	shǎushù;	siusou;
-several	幾個	jǐge;	géigo;
-quite a few	很多	hěndwō	hándò (hóudò)

fiancé n.	未婚夫	wèihwūnfū	meiHfànfù

fiancée n.   未婚妻   wèihwūnchī   meiHfànchài

fiber (fibre) n.

-plant   纖維   syānwéi;   chìmwàiH

-threadlike root   鬚根   syūgēn   sòugàn

fickle a.

-irresolute   反覆不定   fǎnfùbúdìng-   fáanfūkbātdiHng;

-not constant   輕浮   chīngfú;   hīngfàuH

-uncertain   靠不住   kàubújù   kaaubātjyuH(kaauǹjyuH

fiction n.

-novel   小說   syǎushwō;   sīusyut;

-story   故事   gùshr   gusiH

fidelity n.

faithfulness   忠實   jūngshŕ;   jùngsaHt;

-of wife   貞潔   jēngjyé   jīnggit

field n.

-arable   田地   tyándì;   tìHndeiH;

-athletic sports   運動塲   yùndùngchǎng   waHnduHngchèuHng

field-marshal n.   陸軍元帥   lùjyūnywánshwài;   luHkgwānyùHnseui;

   陸軍上將   lùjyūnshàngjyàng   luHkgwānseuHngjeung

fierce a.

-impetuous   狂暴   kwángbàu;   kòHngbouH;

-ferocious   兇狠   syūnghěn;   hùnghaHn;

-fierce anger   暴怒   bàunù   bouHnouH

fifteen a.   十五   shŕwǔ   saHpńgH

fifteenth a.   第十五   dìshŕwǔ   daiHsaHpńgH

fifth a.   第五   dìwǔ   daiHńgH

fiftieth a.   第五十   dìwǔshŕ   daiHńgHsaHp

fig n.

-fruit   無花果   wúhwāgwǒ;   mòuHfàgwó;

-tree	無ˣ 花ㄏㄚ 果ㄍㄨㄛ 樹ㄕㄨ	wúhwāgwǒshù	mòuHfàgwósyuH

fight

-v. t. with weapons	打ㄉㄚ 仗ㄓㄜ	dǎjàng;	dájeung;
-v. t. with hands	打ㄉㄚ 架ㄐㄧㄚ	dǎjyà;	dága (dágūau);
-n. battle	戰ㄓㄢ 爭ㄓㄜ	jànjēng	jinjàng

figure n.

-diagram	圖ㄊㄨ 形ㄒㄧㄥ	túsyíng;	tòuHyìHng;
-personage	姿ㄗ 態ㄊㄞ	dztài;	jìtaai;
-price	價ㄐㄧㄚ 錢ㄑㄧㄢ	jyàchyan;	gachìHn;
-digit	數ㄕㄨ 字ㄗ	shùdz;	soujiH;
-figure of speech	比ㄅㄧ 喻ㄩ	bǐyù;	béiyuH;
-figure out	計ㄐㄧ 算ㄙㄨㄢ	jìswàn	gaìsyun

file

-n. tool	銼ㄘㄨㄛ 刀ㄉㄠ	tswǒdāu;	chodōu;
-n. for letters	紙ㄓ 夾ㄐㄧㄚ	jǐjyá;	jigíp;
-n. row	行ㄏㄤ	háng;	hòHng;
-v. t. put on	存ㄘㄨㄣ 案ㄢ	tswúnàn	chyùHnon

filial a.

-dutiful	孝ㄒㄧㄠ 敬ㄐㄧㄥ	syàujìng;	haauging;
-piety	孝ㄒㄧㄠ 順ㄕㄨㄣ	syàushwùn;	haauseuHn;
-filial son	孝ㄒㄧㄠ 子ㄗ	syàudz	haauji

fill v. t.

-make full	充ㄔㄨㄥ 滿ㄇㄢ	chūngmǎn;	chùngmúHn;
-feed	餵ㄨㄟ 養ㄧㄤ	wèiyǎng;	waiyéuHng;
-as documents	填ㄊㄧㄢ 寫ㄒㄧㄝ	tyánsyě;	tìHnsé;
-as cups	倒ㄉㄠ	dàu	dóu

film n.

-photographic	膠ㄐㄧㄠ 捲ㄐㄩㄢ	jyāujywǎn;	gàaugyún (fēilám);
-on the eye	眼ㄧㄢ 膜ㄇㄛ	yǎnmwó	ngáaHnmók

filter

-n. for liquids	沙漏缸	shālòugāng;	sáláugōng;
-n. elec.	濾玻器	lyùbwōchì;	leuiHbōhei;
-n. photog.	濾光器	lyùgwāngchì;	leuiHgwōnghei;
-v. t. percolate	過濾	gwòlyù;	gwoleuiH;
-filter paper	濾紙	lyùjř	leuiHjí

filthy a.

-unclean	污穢	wūhwèi;	wùwai;
-dirty	骯髒	āngdzāng;	òngjòng (wùjôu);
-disgraceful	丟臉	dyōulyǎn	dìulím (sātmiHnjì)

fin n.

| | 魚鰭 | yúchí; | yúkèiH; |
| | 魚翅 | yúchr̀ | yùHchi |

final

-a. last	最後	dzwèihòu;	jeuihauH;
-a. ultimate	最終	dzwèijūng;	jeuijùng;
-n. of exams	大考	dàkǎu;	daaiHháau;
-n. game	決賽	jywésài	kyutchoi

finally adv.

-at the end	後來	hòulái;	hauHlòiH;
-ultimately	最後	dzwèihòu;	jeuihauH;
-lastly	末了	mwòlyǎu;	muHtlíuH;
-to sum up	總而言之	dzǔngéryánjř	júngyìHyìHnjì

finance

-n. of a state	財政	tsáijèng;	chòiHjing;
-n. money market	金融	jīnrúng;	gàmyùHng;
-v. t. conduct	管理財政	gwǎnlǐtsáijèng;	gúnléiHchòiHjing;
-v. t. provide	籌備資本	chóubèidzběn	chàuHbeiHjìbún

financial a.

| -financial independence | 經濟獨立 | jīngjìdúlì; | gìngjaiduHklaHp; |
| -financial support | 經濟援助 | jīngjìywánjù | gìngjaiwuHnjoH |

find v. t.

-look for	尋找	syúnjǎu;	chàHmjáau;
-discover	發現	fāsyàn	faatyiHn

fine

-a. minute	精細	jīngsyì;	jīngsai (yausai);
-a. refined	精製	jīngjt;	jìngjai;
-a. nice	好	hǎu;	hóu;
-n. mulct	罰金	fájin;	faHtgām;
-fine arts	美術	měishù;	méiHseuHt;
-fine scenery	美景	měijing	méiHging

finger n.

	手指	shǒujt;	sáují;
	指頭	jǐtou;	jitàuH;
-index finger	食指	shfjǐ;	siHkji;
-little finger	小指	syǎujǐ;	síuji;
-middle finger	中指	jūngjǐ;	jùngji;
-finger-print	指紋	jǐwén	jimàlIn

finish v. t.

-conclude	結束	jyéshù;	gitchūk;
-terminate	完	wán;	yùHn;
-complete	完成	wánchéng	yùHnsiHng

finite a.

-limited	有限	yǒusyàn;	yáuIIhaaHn;
-limit	限定	syàndìng	haaIIndiIIng

fir n.	樅樹	tsūngshù	chùHngsyuH

fire

-n.	火	hwǒ;	f6;
-v. t.	燃燒	ránshāu;	yìHnsìu;
-light a fire	點火	dyǎnhwǒ	dímf6
firebrigade n.	消防隊	syāufángdwèi	sìufòHngdéui

fireman n.	救火員	jyòuhwǒywán	gaufóyùHn
fireplace	壁爐	bìlú	bìklòuH
fire-proof a.	防火	fánghwǒ	fòHngfó
fires n.	火災	hwǒdzāi	fójòi
fire-set n.	火具	hwǒjyù	fógeuiH
firm			
-a. steady	堅定	jyāndìng;	gìndiHng;
-a. fixed	實	shf;	saHt;
-n. mercantile	商行	shāngháng	sèunghóng
first a.			
-in place	第一	dìyī;	daiHyāt;
-in time	先	syān;	sìn;
-first ancestor	始祖	shǐdzǔ;	chíjóu;
-first-born a.	初生	chūshēng;	chòsàang;
	頭生	tóushēng;	tàuHsàng;
-first cause	第一原因	dìyīwányīn;	daiHyātyùHnyàn;
-first class			
-of ticket	頭等	tóuděng;	tàuHdáng;
-quality	上等	shàngděng;	seuHngdáng;
-first & last	始終	shǐjūng	chíjùng
fish			
-n. animal	魚	yú;	yú;
-n. collectively	魚類	yúlèi;	yúleuiH;
-v. i. catch	打魚	dǎyú	dáyú (jūkyú)
fishbone n.	魚骨	yúgǔ	yùHgwāt
fisher-man n.	漁夫	yúfū	yùHfù
fishhook n.	魚鉤	yúgōu	yùHngàu
fishing n.	鉤魚	dyàuyú	diuyú
fist n.	拳頭	chywántóu	kyùHntàuH
fit			
-a. suitable	合適	héshì;	haHpsìk;
-n. convulsion	抽筋	chōujīn	chàugàn

Fitting

-n. on clothes	試ㄕ 樣ㄧ㍱	shìyàng;	siyéung;
-a. suitable	合ㄜ 適ㄕ	héshì	haHpsìk
five a.	五ㄨ	wǔ	ngH
fivefold a.	五ㄨ 倍ㄅ	wǔbèi;	ngHpúiH;
five grains	五ㄨ 穀ㄍㄨ	wǔgǔ;	ngHgūk;
five-year plan	五ㄨ 年ㄋㄧㄢ 計ㄐㄧ 劃ㄏㄨㄚ	wǔnyán jìhwà	ngHnìHn gaiwaaHk

fix v. t.

-determine	決ㄐㄩㄝ 定ㄉㄧㄥ	jywédìng;	kyutdiHng
-make firm	堅ㄐㄧㄢ 固ㄍㄨ	jyāngù;	gìngu;
-settle	安ㄢ 置ㄓ 妥ㄊㄨㄛ 當ㄉㄤ	ānjì twǒdàng	ònji tóHdong

fixed p. a.

-conventional	規ㄍㄨ 定ㄉㄧㄥ	gwēidìng;	kwàidiHng;
-fixed number	定ㄉㄧㄥ 額ㄜ	dìngé;	diHngngáak;
-fixed price	實ㄕ 價ㄐㄧㄚ	shíjyà	saHtga
flag n.	旗ㄑㄧ	chí	kèiH

flame

-n. burning gas	火ㄏㄨㄛ 焰ㄧㄢ	hwǒyán;	fóyìHm;
-v. t. inflame	燒ㄕㄠ	shāu	sìu
flannel n.	法ㄈㄚ 蘭ㄌㄢ 絨ㄖㄨㄥ	fǎlánrúng	faatlàaHnyúng

flap

n. pocket cover	袋ㄉㄞ 邊ㄅㄧㄢ	dàibyān;	doiHbìn;
-v. t. beat	拍ㄆㄞ	pāi	paak

flash v. i.

-of light	閃ㄕㄢ 光ㄍㄨㄤ	shǎngwāng;	sìmgwòng;
-as sword-blade	晃ㄏㄨㄤ	hwǎng	fòng
flash-light n.	電ㄉㄧㄢ 筒ㄊㄨㄥ	dyàntǔng	diHntúng

flat

-n. storey	一ㄧ 層ㄘㄥ 樓ㄌㄨ	yìtsénglóu;	yātchàHngláu;

-a. even	平	píng;	pìHng;
-a. uninteresting	平淡	píngdàn	pìHngdaaHm
flattery n.	諂媚	chǎnmèi;	chímméiH;
	奉承	fèngchéng	fuHngsìHng
flavor, flavour n.	滋味	dzwèi;	jìmeiH;
	香氣	syāngchì	hèunghei
flea n.	蝨	shī	sāt (sātná)
flee v. i.	逃避	táubì;	tòuHbeiH;
	逃走	táudzǒu	tòuHjáu
fleet			
-n. of warship	艦隊	jyàndwèi;	laaHmdéui;
-a. swift	快	kwài	faai
flesh n.			
-as opp. to spirit	肉體	ròutǐ;	yuHktái;
-bodily desires	情慾	chíngyù	chìHngyuHk
fleshly a.			
-lascivious	色慾	sèyù;	sikyuHk;
-worldly	世俗	shìsú;	saijuHk
-natural	屬乎血氣	shǔhū syěchì	suHkfùH hyuthei
flexible a.			
-soft	柔軟	róurwǎn;	yàuHyúHn;
-compliant	柔順	róushwùn;	yàuHseuHn;
-as language	伸縮	shēnswō	sānsūk
flight n.			
-flying	飛行	fēisyíng;	fèihàHng;
-running away	逃走	táudzǒu	tòuHjáu
fling v. t.			
-throw	扔	rēng;	yìng;
-toss	舉起	jyǔchǐ	géuihéi
flint n.	燧石	swèishf;	seuiHseHk;

		hwǒshŕ	fóseHk
float	火石		
-v. t.	浮	fú;	fàuH;
-n. life-buoy	浮水圈	fúhwěichywān,	fàuHséuihyūn;
-floating capital	流動資本	lyóudùng dzběn	làuHduHng jìbún
flock n.	群	chyún;	kwàHn;
-flock of sheep	羊群	yángchyún	yèuHngkwàHn
flood			
-n. water overflowing	洪水	húngshwěi,	hùHngséui;
-n. menstrual	血崩	syěběng;	hyutbàng;
-v. t. overflow	泛濫	fànlàn	faanlaaHm
floor n.			
-board	地板	dìběn;	deiHbáan;
-storey	層	tséng;	chàHng;
-the right to speak	發言權	fāyánchywán	faatyìHnkyùHn
florist n.	賣花人	màihwārén	maaiHfàyàHn
floss silk n.	絲棉	szmyán	sìmìHn
flour n.	麵粉	myànfěn	miHnfán
flourish v. i.			
-prosperous	昌盛	chāngshèng;	chèungsiHng;
-thrive	興旺	syingwàng	hìngwoHng
flow			
-v. i. as liquid	流動	lyóudùng;	làuHduHng;
-v. i. melt	熔化	rúnghwà;	yùHngfa;
-n. the tidal flood	潮漲	cháujàng	chìuHjeung
flower n.	花	hwā	fā
fluctuation n.	波動	bwōdùng;	bòduHng;
	搖動	yáudùng;	yìuHduHng;

	擺動	bǎidùng	báaiduHng
fluency n.	流利	lyóulì	làuHleiH
fluid a.	液體	yètǐ;	yiHktái;
	流質	lyóujǐ	làuHjāt
fluorescent light n.	日光燈	r̀gwāngdēng	yaHtgwōngdāng
flutter			
~v. i. flap wings	鼓翼	gǔyì;	gúyiHk;
~n. agitation	擾亂	rǎulwàn	yíuHlyuHn
fly			
~v. i. as birds	飛	fēi;	fèi;
~v. t. as kites	放	fàng;	fong;
~n. insect	蒼蠅	tsāngying;	chòngyiHng (wūyìng;)
-flying column	遊擊隊	yóujídwèi;	yàuHgikdéui;
-flying saucer	飛碟	fēidyé	fèidiHp
foam			
~n.	泡沫	pàumwò	paaumuHt;
~v. i.	起泡	chǐpàu	héipaau (héipōk)
focus n.	焦點	jyāudyǎn	jìudím
foe n.	仇敵	chóudí;	sàuHdiHk;
-personal	仇人	chóurén;	sàuHyàHn;
-in war	敵人	dírén;	diHkyàHn;
-hostile army	敵軍	díjyūn	diHkgwàn
fog n.	霧	wù	mouH
fold			
~v. t. over on itself	摺	jé;	jip;
~n. pen	欄	lán	làaHn
foliage n.	簇葉	tsùyè;	chūkyiHp;
	樹葉	shùyè	syuHyiHp
folk n.			
-people in general	民間	mínjyān;	màHngàan;
-one's family	家人	jyārén;	gàyàHn;

-folk dance	土 風 舞	tǔfēngwǔ	tóufùngmóuH
-folk-lore n.	民 傳	mínchwán	màHnchyùHn
-folk psychology n.	民 衆 心 理 學	mínjùng syīnlǐywé	màHnjung sàmléiHhoHk
-folk song n.	民 歌	míngē;	màHngō;
	民 謠	mínyáu	màHnyìuH
-follow v. t.			
-go after	跟 隨	gēnswéi;	gànchèuiH;
-go along	順 着	shwùnje;	seuHnjeuHk (seuHnjyuH);
-succeed	繼 續	jìsyù;	gaijuHk;
-obey	聽 話	tīnghwà;	tèngwaH;
-imitate	學	sywé	hoHk
-follower n.	信 徒	nyìntú;	seuntòuH;
	弟 子	dìdž	daiHjí
-following a.			
-succeeding	下 列	syàlyè;	haHliHt;
-next	第 二	dìer	daiHyiH
-folly n.			
-foolish act	愚 行	yúsyíng;	yùHhàHng;
-lewdness	淫 亂	yínlwàn	yàHmlyuHn
-fond a.			
-pleased	喜 歡	syǐhwan;	héifùn;
-tender	憐 愛	lyánài	lìHnoi
-font n.			
-batismal	聖 洗 缸	shèngsyǐgāng	singsáigōng;
-fountain	泉	chywán	chyùHn
-food n.			
-eatable	食 物	shŕwù;	siHkmaHt;
-provision	糧 食	lyángshŕ;	lèuHngsiHk;
-food &drink	飲 食	yǐnshŕ	yámsiHk

foodstuff n.	食料	shílyàu;	siHkliuH;
	食品	shípǐn	siHkbán
fool n.	愚人	yùrén;	yùHyàHn;
	傻子	shǎdz	sòHjí (sòHgwā)
foolish a.			
-without judgmdnt	糊塗	hútu;	wùHtòuH;
-silly	愚蠢	yúchwǔn	yùHchéun
foot n.			
-of the leg	脚	jyǎu;	geuk;
-of length	尺	chǐ;	chek;
-cubic foot	立方尺	lìfāngchǐ	laHpfōngchek
football n.	足球	dzúchyóu	jūkkàuH
foot-mark n.	脚印	jyǎuyìn	geukyan
foot-note n.	註解	jùjyě	jyugáai
footprint n.	脚印	jyǎuyìn;	geukyan;
	脚蹤	jyǎudzūng	geukjùng
footsteps n.	脚步	jyǎubù	geukbouH
footstool n.	脚凳	jyǎudèng	geukdang
for prep.			
-on behalf of	代替	dàitì;	doiHtai;
-for the sake of	因爲	yīnwei;	yànwaiH;
-for example	舉例	jyǔlì	géuilaiH
forbear v. t.			
-be patient	忍耐	rěnnài;	yánnoiH;
-not do	不要	búyàu	bātyiu (mhóu)
forbid v. t.	禁止	jìnjǐ;	gamji;
-forbidden book	禁書	jìnshū;	gamsyù;
-forbidden fruit	禁果	jìngwǒ	gamgwó
force			
~v. t. compel	強逼	chyángbī;	kéuHngbìk;

-n. strength for war	武 力	wŭlì;	móuHliHk;
-n. violence	暴 力	bàulì	bouHliHk
Fore a.			
-in time	前	chyán;	chìHn;
-in place	在 前	dzàichyán	joiHchìHn
Forearm n.	前 臂	chyánbì	chìHnbei
Forefathers n.	祖 先	dzŭsyān;	jóusin;
	列 祖	lyèdzŭ	liHtjóu
Forehead n.	前 額	chyáné	chìIInngaaHk
Foreign a.			
-alien	外 國	wàigwó;	ngoiHgwolıɟ
-western	西 洋	syiyáng	sàiyèuHng
Foreigner n.	外 國 人	wàigwórén	ngoiHgwokyàHn
Foreknowledge n.			
-previous knowledge	預 知	yùjī;	yuHjì;
-prescience	先 見	syānjyàn	singin
Foreman n.	工 頭	gūngtóu;	gùngtáu;
	監 工	jyāngūng	gaāmgūng
Forenoon n.	午 前	wŭchyán;	ńgHchìHn;
	上 午	shàngwŭ	seuHngńgH
Forest n.	森 林	sēnlín	sàmlàHm
Foreordination n.			
-predestination	預 定	yùdìng;	yuHdiHng;
-predetermination	預 決	yùjywé	yuHkyut
Forerunner n.	先 鋒	syānfēng;	sìnfùng;
	前 鋒	chyánfēng	chìHnfùng
Foresight n.			
-foreseeing	先 見	syānjyàn;	sìngin;

-provident care	遠ㄩㄢ 慮ㄌㄩ	ywǎnlyù	yúHnleuiH
foretell v. t.	預ㄩ 言ㄧㄢ;	yùyán;	yuHyìHn;
	預ㄩ 告ㄍㄠ	yùgàu	yuHgou
forever adv.			
-everlastingly	永ㄩㄥ 遠ㄩㄢ;	yǔngywǎn;	wíHngyúHn;
-always	常ㄔㄤ 常ㄔㄤ	chángcháng	sèuHngsèuHng (sìHsìH)
forfeit v. t.			
-rights	喪ㄙㄤ 失ㄕ;	sàngshī;	songsāt;
-property	沒ㄇㄛ 收ㄕㄡ	mwòshōu	mutsàu
forge			
—n. furnace	鍛ㄉㄨㄢ 冶ㄧㄝ 爐ㄌㄨ;	dwànyělú;	dyunyéHlòuH
—v. t. make falsely	僞ㄨㄟ 造ㄗㄠ;	wěidzàu;	ngaiHjouH;
—v. i. metals	鍛ㄉㄨㄢ 鍊ㄌㄧㄢ;	dwànlyàn	dyunliHn
forget v. t.	忘ㄨㄤ 記ㄐㄧ	wàngjì	mòHnggei (mgeidāk)
forgive v. t.			
-as a sin	赦ㄕㄜ 免ㄇㄧㄢ;	shèmyǎn;	semiHn;
-an inferior	饒ㄖㄠ 恕ㄕㄨ;	ráushù;	yìuHsyu;
-an equal	原ㄩㄢ 諒ㄌㄧㄤ	ywánlyàng	yùHnleuHng
-forgive sins	免ㄇㄧㄢ 罪ㄗㄨㄟ;	myǎndzwèi;	miHnjeuiH;
	赦ㄕㄜ 罪ㄗㄨㄟ;	shèdzwèi;	sejeuiH;
-forgive a debt	免ㄇㄧㄢ 債ㄓㄞ	myǎnjài	miHnjaai
forgivcness n.	赦ㄕㄜ 免ㄇㄧㄢ	shèmyǎn	semiHn
forgiving p. a.			
-disposed to forgive	寬ㄎㄨㄢ 容ㄖㄨㄥ;	kwānrúng;	fùnyùHng;
-merciful	仁ㄖㄣ 慈ㄘ	réntsź	yàHnchìH
form			
—n. figure	形ㄒㄧㄥ 狀ㄓㄨㄤ;	syíngjwàng;	yìHngjoHng;
—n. manner	形ㄒㄧㄥ 式ㄕ;	syíngshì;	yìHngsìk;
—n. formula	公ㄍㄨㄥ 式ㄕ;	gūngshì;	gūngsìk;
—n. class at school	年ㄋㄧㄢ 級ㄐㄧ;	nyánjí;	nìHnkāp;

-v. t. set up	設立	shèlì;	chitlaHp;
-v. t. organize	組織	dzŭjr;	jóujìk;
-v. t. combine	合	hé	haHp

Formal a.

-ceremonial	禮儀上	lĭyishàng;	láiHyìHseuHng;
-stiff	嚴格	yángé;	yìHmgaak;
-in due form	正式	jèngshr̀	jingsìk

Formalism n. 形式主義 syíngshr̀jŭyì yìHngsìkjyúyiH

Formality n.

-ceremony	儀式	yishr̀;	yìIIskì;
-customary	規矩	gwēijyu,	kwàigéui;
-procedure	手續	shŏusyù	sáujuHk

Former a.

	前者	chyánjĕ;	chìHnjó;
	以前	yĭchyán	yìIIchìHn
-former ages	前世紀	chyànshr̀jì;	chìHnsaigói;
-former occasion	前次	chyàntsz̀;	chìHnchi;
-former words	前言	chyànyán	chìHnyìHn

Formerly adv.

-times	從前	tsúngchyán;	chùHngchìHn;
-heretofore	一向	yìsyàng	yātheung

Formidable a.

-exciting fear	令人畏懼	lìngrénweijyù;	liHngyàHnwaigeuiH;
-frightful	驚恐	jìngkŭng	gìnghúng

Formula n.

-Math.	公式	gūngshr̀;	gūngsìk;
-set form	程式	chéngshr̀;	chìHngsìk;
-Med.	藥方	yàufāng;	yeuHkfōng;

Fornication n.

	淫行	yínsyíng;	yàIImhàHng;
	姦淫	jyānyín	gàanyàHm

Forsake v. t. 捨棄 shĕchì; séhei;

丢棄	dyōuchì;	diuhei;
抛棄	pāuchì	pàauhei
fort n. 炮臺	pàutái	paautòiH
forth adv. 向前	syàngchyán;	heungchìHn;
-and so forth 等等	děngděng;	dángdáng;
-back and forth 前後	chyánhòu;	chìHnhauH;
-burst forth (flower) 開放	kāifàng;	hòifong;
-stretch forth 伸長	shēncháng	sànchèuHng
fortify v. t.		
-strengthen 加力於	jyālìyú;	gàliHkyù;
-furnish power 施力	shīlì	sìliHk
fortnight n. 兩星期	lyǎngsyīngchì;	léuHngsìngkèiH;
十四日	shfszì	saHpseiyaHt
fortress n.		
-stronghold 要塞	yàusài;	yiuchoi;
-fortification 堡壘	bǎulěi	bóuléuiH
fortunate a.		
-lucky 幸運	syìngyùn;	haHngwaHn;
-auspicious 吉祥	jísyáng;	gātchèuHng;
-by good chance 僥倖	jyǎusyìng	hìuhaHng
fortune n.		
-fate 命運	mìngyùn;	miHngwaHn;
-luck 運氣	yùnchi;	waHnhei;
-wealth 財富	tsáifù;	chòiHfu;
-fortune teller 算命	swànmìng	syunmeHng (syunmeHnglóu)
forty a. 四十	szshf	seisaHp
forward		
-adv. onward 向前	syàngchyán;	heungchìHn;
-a. bold 大膽	dàdǎn;	daaiHdáam;
-v. t. send 送交	sùngjyāu	sunggàau

Foster v. t.

-rear	養	yăng;	yéuHng;
-encourage	獎勵	jyănglì	jéunglaiH

Found v. t.

-establish	創立	chwànglì;	chonglaHp;
-cast	鑄	jù	jyu

Foundation n.

-basis	基礎	jichŭ;	gèichó;
-principle	根本	gēnběn;	gànbún;
-endowment	基金	jijīn	gèigàm

Fountain n.

-spring	泉源	chywánywán;	chyùHnyùHn;
-reservoir	噴水池	pēnshwěichf	panséuichìH

Four a.	四	sż	sei
-Four Books	四書	sżshu	Seisyù
Fourfold a.	四倍	sżbèi	seipúiH
Fourscore a.	八十	bashf	baatsaHp
Foursquare a.	四方	sżfāng	seifòng
Fourteen a.	十四	shfsż	saHpsei
Fourteenth a.	第十四	dìshfsż	daiHsaHpsei
Fourth a.	第四	dìsż	daiHsei

Fowl n.

	家禽	jyāchín;	gàkàHm;
-chicken	鷄	jī	gāi

Fox n.	狐狸	húli	wùHléi

Fraction n.

-Arith.	分數	fēnshù;	faHnsou;
-part	部分	bùfen	bouHfaHn

Fracture n.	骨折	gŭjé	gwātjit

Fragile a.

easily broken	脆	tswèi;	cheui;
-weak	虛弱	syūrwò;	hèuiyeuHk;
-of one's will	薄弱	bwórwò	boHkyeuHk

fragment n.

-by cutting	片	pyàn;	pin;
-by breaking	碎片	swèipyàn	seuipín

fragrant a. 香 syāng; hèung;

-fragrant ointment 香膏 syānggāu hēunggōu

frail

-n. basket	蘆葦籃	lúwěilán;	lòuHwáiláam;
-a. fragile	脆	tswèi;	cheui;
-a. physically	虛弱	syūrwò;	hèuiyeuHk;
-a. mentally	懦弱	nwòrwò	noHyeuHk

frame

-n. of picture	架	jyà;	gá;
-n. bodily	骨骼	gǔgé;	gwātlok;
-v. t. compose	組織	dzǔjf;	jóujìk;
-v. t. fabricate	虛構	syūgòu	hèuikau

frantic a. 瘋狂 fēngkwáng; fùngkòHng;

發狂 fākwáng faatkòHng

fraternity n.

-brotherhood 兄弟關係 syūngdìgwānsyì; hìngdaiHgwàanhaiH

fraud n.

-deceit	欺騙	chīpyàn;	hèipin;
-trick	弊端	bìdwān	baiHdyùn

freak n.

-vagary 想入非非 syǎngrùfēifēi; séungyaHpfèiifèi;

-caprice 反覆無常 fǎnfùwúcháng fáanfūkmòuHsèuHng

free a.

-independent	自由	dzyóu;	jiHyàuH;
-gratis	免費	myǎnfèi;	míHnfai;

-untaxed	免稅	myǎnshwèi;	míHnseui;
-unrestrained	隨便	séuibyàn;	chèuiHbín;
-free man	自由人	dzyóurén;	jiHyàuHyàHn;
-free will	自由意志	dzyóu yìjr̀	jiHyàuH yiji
freedom n.	自由	dzyóu;	jiHyàuH;
-freedom of speech	發言自由	fāyán dzyóu;	faatyìHn jiHyàuH;
-freedom of religion	信仰自由	syìnyǎng dzyóu	seunyéuHng jiHyàuH
freeze v. i.			
-by cold	凍	dùng,	dung;
-into ice	結冰	jyébìng;	gitbìng;
-finance	凍結	dùngjyé;	dunggit;
-freeze to death	凍死	dùngsž	dungséi
freight n.			
-goods	貨	hwò;	fo;
-charge for transport	運費	yùnfèi	waHnfai
frequent			
-v. t. visit often	常去	chángchyù;	sèuHngheui;
-a. often	常常	chángcháng	sèuHngsèuHng (sìHsìH)
fresh			
-a. not stale	新鮮	syìnsyēn;	sànsìn;
-n. of water	淡水	dànshwěi;	táaHmséui;
-v. t. recruit	回復	hwéifù	wùiHfuHk
fret v. i.			
-worry	着急	jāuji;	jeuHkgāp;
-distress oneself	煩惱	fánnǎu	fàaHnnóuH
friction n.	摩擦	mwótsā	mòHchaat
Friday n.	禮拜五	Lǐbàiwǔ;	LáiHbaaingH;
	星期五	Syìngchīwǔ	SìngkèiHngH
friend n.	朋友	péngyou	pàHngyáuH
friendly			
-adv. amicably	和氣	héchì;	wòHhei;

-a. kind	仁慈	réntsź;	yàHnchìH;
a. favorable	有利	yǒulì	yáuHleiH

fright

-n. fear	恐怖	kǔngbù;	húngbou;
-v. t. affright	驚駭	jīnghài	gìnghoiH

frill n. 縐邊 jòubyān jaubìn

fringe n. 繸 swèi séui

frivolous a. 輕薄 chǐngbwó hìngboHk

frog n.

-land	青蛙	chǐngwā;	chìngwā;
-edible	田鷄	tyánjī	tìHngāi

from prep. 從 tsúng; chùHng;

由 yóu yàuH

-from antiquity 從古以來 tsúnggǔyǐlái chùHnggúyíHlòiH

front

-a.	前面	chyánmyàn;	chìHnmiHn(chìHnbiHn
-n. seat of war	戰區	jànchyū;	jinkèui;
-n. fighting line	戰線	jànsyàn;	jinsín;
-v. t. face toward	向	syàng	heung

frontier n. 邊界 byānjyè; bìngaai;

境界 jìngjyè gìnggaai

frost n. 霜 shwāng; sèung;

-frost bite 凍傷 dùngshāng dungsèung

froth

-n.	泡沫	pàumwò;	paaumút;
-v. i.	起泡	chǐpàu	héipaau (héipōk)
frown v. i.	縐眉頭	jòuméitóu;	jaumèiHtàuH;
	愁眉不展	chóuméibùjǎn	sàuHmèiHbātjǐn

frugal a.

-of persons	節省	jyéshěng;	jitsáang;
-of things	經濟	jǐngjì	gìngjai

fruit n.

	果子	gwŏdz;	gwójì;
	水果	shwěigwŏ	séuigwó (sàanggwó)

frustrate v t

-defeat	失敗	shībài;	sātbaaiH;
-baffle	作廢	dzwòfèi	jokfai

fry v. t.

-in deep oil	炸	já;	jaau;
-in a pan with fat	煎	jyān;	jìn;
-with gravy	炒	chǎu	cháau

fuel n.

-firewood	柴	chái;	chàaiH;
-any substance	燃料	ránlyàu	yìHnlíu

fugitive

-a. as from danger	逃難	táunàn;	tòuHnaaHn;
-n. refugee	難民	nànmín	naaHnmàHn

fulfil v. t.

-accomplish	成就	chéngjyòu;	sìHngjauH
-perform	履行	lyǚsyíng;	léiHhàHng;
-predictions	應驗	yìngyàn	yingyiHm

full a.

-filled up	充滿	chūngmǎn;	chùngmúHn;
-ample	充分	chūngfèn;	chùngfaHn;
-eaten enough	飽	bǎu	báau

fume n.

-smoke	煙	yān;	yìn;
-vapor	汽	chì;	hei;
-reek	蒸氣	jēngchì	jìnghei

fumigate v. t.

-smoke	燻煙	syūnyān;	fānyìn;
-perfume	燻香	syūnsyāng	fānhèung

fun n.

-sport	遊戲	yóusyì;	yàuHhei;
-merriment	歡樂	hwānlè;	fùnloHk;
-amusement	趣味	chyùwei	cheuimeiH

function n.

	功用	gūngyùng;	gùngyuHngj
-of an organ	機能	jīnéng;	gèinàHng;
-duty	職務	jífwù	jìkmouH

fundamental a.

-essential	主要	jǔyàu;	jyúyiu;
-basic	基本	jīběn;	gèibún;
-radical	根本	gēnběn;	gànbún;
-elementary	初步	chūbù	chòbouH

funeral n.

-affairs	喪事	sāngshì;	sòngsiH;
-burial	葬禮	dzànglǐ	jongláiH

fur n.

-hair	毛	máu;	mòuH;
-pelt	皮	pí	pèiH

furious a.

-full of fury	盛怒	shèngnù;	siHngnouH;
-frantic	狂暴	kwángbàu;	kòHngbouH;
-violent	激烈	jīlyè	gīkliHt

furnace n.

-kitchen	竈	dzàu;	jou;
-portable	爐	lú	lóu (fùnglóu)

furnish v. t.

-supply	供給	gūngjǐ;	gūngkāp;
-equip	設備	shèbèi	chitbeiH
furniture n.	傢具	jyājyù	gàgeuiH

furrow n.

-trench	溝《ㄡ	gōu;	kàu (hàangkèuiH);
-wrinkle	縐ㄓㄡ 紋ㄨㄣ	jòuwén	jaumàHn

further a.

-more distant	更《ㄥ 遠ㄩㄢ	gèngywǎn;	gangyúHn;
-additional	另ㄌㄧㄥ 外ㄨㄞ	lìngwài	liHngngoiH

fury n.

-rage	大ㄉㄚ 怒ㄋㄨ	dànù;	daaiHnouH;
-frenzy	發ㄈㄚ 狂ㄎㄨㄤ	fakwáng	faatkòHng

fuse

-v. t. melt	熔ㄖㄨㄥ	rúng;	yùHng;
-n. of a shell	藥ㄧㄠ 線ㄒㄧㄢ	yàusyàn;	yeuHksìn;
-n. fig.	導ㄉㄠ 火ㄏㄨㄛ 線ㄒㄧㄢ	dǎuhwǒsyàn;	douHfósìn;
-n. Elec.	保ㄅㄠ 險ㄒㄧㄢ 絲ㄙ	bǎusyǎnsž	bóuhimsi

fuss v. i.

-overbusy about trifles	小ㄒㄧㄠ 題ㄊㄧ 大ㄉㄚ 做ㄗㄨㄛ	syǎutídàdzwò;	siutàiHdaaiHjouH;
-unduly anxious about trifles	大ㄉㄚ 驚ㄐㄧㄥ 小ㄒㄧㄠ 怪ㄍㄨㄞ	dàjingsyǎugwài	daaiHgìngsiugwaai

future

-a. not past or present	將ㄐㄧㄤ 來ㄌㄞ	jyānglái;	jèunglòiH;
-n. prospects	前ㄑㄧㄢ 途ㄊㄨ	chyántú	chìHntòuH

G

gabble v. i.

-talk idly	閒ㄒㄧㄢ 談ㄊㄢ	syántán;	hàaHntàaHm;
-prate	空ㄎㄨㄥ 談ㄊㄢ	kūngtán	hùngtàaHm

gaiety n.

-cheerfulness	快ㄎㄨㄞ 活ㄏㄨㄛ	kwàihwo;	faaiwuHt;
-amusement	歡ㄏㄨㄢ 樂ㄌㄜ	hwānlè;	fùnloHk

gain

-v. t. get	得ㄉㄜ 到ㄉㄠ	dèdàu;	dākdóu;

-v. t. earn	賺	jwàn;	jaaHn;
-n. benefit	利益	lìyì	leiHyìk
gale n.	大風	dàfēng;	daaiHfùng;
	狂風	kwángfēng	kòHngfùng
gallant a.			
-brave	勇敢	yŭnggăn;	yúHnggám;
-chivalrous	豪爽	háushwăng;	hòuHsóng;
-gay in dress	華美	hwáměi;	wàHméiH;
-courtly	慇懃	yīnchín	yànkàHn
gallop v. t.	跑	pău	páau (jáu)
gallows n.	絞架	jyăujyà;	gáaugá;
	絞臺	jyăutái	gáautòiH
gamble v. t.	賭錢	dŭchyán;	dóuchín;
	賭博	dŭbwó	dóubok
game n.			
-play	遊戲	yóusyì;	yàuHhei;
-sports	運動	yùndùng;	waHnduHng;
-contest	比賽	bĭsài	béichoi
gang n	黨	dăng;	dóng;
-robbers	匪徒	fěitú;	féitòuH;
-ruffians	歹徒	dăitú	cháutòuH
gangrene n.	腐爛	fŭlàn;	fuHlaaHn;
gangway n.	跳板	tyàubăn	tiubáan
gaol n.	監獄	jyēnyù;	gēamyuHk;
	監牢	jyēnláu	gēamlòuH
gap n.	洞	dùng;	duHng;
	裂縫	lyèfèng	liHtfùHng
garage n.			
-shed	車房	chēfáng;	chèfòHng;

-repairing	汽車行	chìchēháng	heichèhóng
garbage n.	垃圾	lèsè	laaHpsaap
garden n.	花園	hwāywán	fàyún
gargle			
-v. i.	漱口	shùkŏu;	souháu (lóngháu);
-n. liquid	漱口水	shùkŏushwĕi	souháuséui (lóngháuséui)
garlic n.	蒜	swàn	syun
garrison			
-v. t. supply	駐防	jùfáng;	jyufòHng;
-troops	駐軍	jùjyūn	jyugwàn
gas n			
-Chem.	氣	chì;	hei;
-coal	煤氣	méichì;	mùiHhei;
-poison	毒氣	dúchì	duHkhei
gasoline n.	汽油	chìyóu	heiyàuH
gasp v. i.	喘	chwăn;	chyún;
	喘氣	chwănchì	chyúnhei
gastric ulcer n.	胃潰瘍	wèikwèiyáng	waiHkwáiyèuHng
gate n.	大門	dàmén	daaiHmùHn
gather v. t.			
-meet	聚集	jyùjí;	jeuiHjaaHp;
-flowers	摘	jāi;	jaaHk;
-harvest	收成	shōuchéng;	sàusìHng;
-gather up	拾起	shíchì	saHphéi (jɐphéi)
gaze v. i.	注視	jùshì	jyusiH
gay a.			
-merry	快樂	kwàilè;	faailoHk;
-cheerful	高興	gāusyìng;	gòuhing;
-showy	華美	hwáměi	wàHméiH
gear n.	齒輪	chǐlwún	chílèuHn
gem n.	寶石	băushí	bóuseHk

gender n.	性	syìng	sing
genealogy n.	家譜	jyāpŭ;	gàpóu;
	族譜	dzúpŭ	juHkpóu
general			
-n. of army	大將軍	dàjyāngjyūn;	daaiHjèunggwàn;
-a. common	一般	yìbān	yātbùn
-general good	公益	gūngyì	gūngyìk
generally adv.			
-usually	平常	píngcháng;	pìHngsèuHng;
-commonly	普通	pŭtūng;	póutùng;
-not detail	大概	dàgài	daaiHkói
generation n.			
-in genealogy	世代	shìdài;	saidoiH;
-period of age	時代	shŕdài	sìHdoiH
generous a.			
-not mean	慷慨	kăngkài;	hóngkoi;
-noble	大量	dàlyàng	daaiHleuHng
genius n.	天才	tyāntsái	tìnchòiH
gentile n.	外邦人	wàibāngrén	ngoiHbòngyàHn
gentle a.			
-mild	溫柔	wēnróu;	wànyàuH;
-not rough	文雅	wényă;	màHnngáH;
-tame	馴良	syúnlyáng	sèuHnlèuHng
gentleman n.	君子	jyūndž	gwànjí;
	紳士	shēnshŕ	sànsiH
genuine a.			
-real	眞	jēn;	jàn;
-sincere	眞誠	jēnchéng;	jànsìHng;
-frank	正直	jèngjŕ	jingjiHk
geography n.	地理	dìlĭ	deiHléiH
geometry n.	幾何	jǐhé	géihòH

germ n.

-microbe	微生物	wéishēngwù;	mèiHsàngmaHt;
-bacillus	細菌	syìjyùn;	saikwán;
-of disease	病菌	bìngjyùn	beHngkwán

gesture n.

| with the body | 姿勢 | dźshì; | jìsai; |
| -with the hand | 手勢 | shŏushì | sáusai |

get v. t.

-obtain	得	dé;	dāk;
-fetch	拿	ná;	nàH (nìng);
-purchase	買	mǎi;	máaiH;
-have	有	yŏu;	yáuH;
-win	贏	yíng;	yèHng;
-beget	生	shēng;	sàang;
-learn	學	sywé;	hoHk;
-arrive	到	dàu	dou

giant n.

| | 巨人 | jyùrén; | geuiHyàHn; |
| | 偉人 | wěirén | wáiHyàHn |

gift n.

-present	禮物	lǐwù;	láiHmaHt;
-talent	恩賜	ēntsż	yànchi
-gift of healing	醫病的恩賜	yìbìngdeēntsż	yìbeHngdìkyànchi

| **giggle v. i.** | 嘻嘻笑 | syìsyìsyàu | hèihèisiu |

| **gild v. t.** | 鍍金 | dùjìn | douHgàm |

| **ginger n.** | 薑 | jyāng | gèung |

| **girl n.** | 女子 | nyŭdz; | néuiHjí (néuijái) |
| -girl guide | 女童子軍 | nyŭtúngdzjyūn | néuiHtùHngjígwān |

give v. t.

-generally	給	gěi;	kāp (béi):
-as present	送	sùng;	sung;
-give away	讓步	ràngbù;	yeuHngbouH;

-give heed	留心	liusyīn	làuHsàm
glad a.			
-pleased	喜歡	syǐhwan;	héifùn;
-happy	快樂	kwàile	faailoHk
glance v. t.	轉眼	jwǎnyǎn	jyúnngáaHn
gland n.	腺	syàn	sin
glare v. i.			
-shine	閃光	shǎngwāng;	sǐmgwòng;
-stare angrily	怒視	nùshr̀	nouHsiH
glass n.			
-substance	玻璃	bwōli;	bōlēi;
-for drinking	玻璃杯	bwōlibēi;	bōlēibūi;
-mirror	鏡子	jìngdz;	gengji (geng);
-as spectacles	眼鏡	yǎnjìng	ngáaHngéng
glimpse n.			
-flash	閃	shǎn;	sǐm;
-trace	痕跡	hénjì;	hàHnjik;
-a short view	瞥見	pyějyàn	pitgin
glitter v. i.	發光	fāgwāng;	faatgwòng;
	閃耀	shǎnyàu	sǐmyiuH
globe n.	地球	dìchyóu	deiHkàuH
gloomy a.			
-of a house	暗	àn;	ngam;
-of a person	憂鬱	yōuyù	yāuwāt
glory n.	榮耀	rùngyàu	wìHngyiuH
glove n.	手套	shǒutàu	sáutou
glow			
-v. i. burn	燒	shāu;	sìu;
-n. earnestness	熱誠	rèchéng	yiHtsìHng
glucose n.	葡萄糖	pútáutáng	pòuHtòuHtòHng

glue

-n.	膠水	jyāushwěi;	gàauséui;
-v. t.	黏	nyán	nìHm
glutton n.	貪食	tānshŕ;	tàamsiHk;
	貪吃	tānchī	tàamhek
gnash the teeth	切齒	chyěchŕ	chitchí
go v. i.			
-generally	去	chyù;	heui;
-walk away	走	dsŏuȷ	jáu (hàaHng);
-be off	走開	dzŏukāi	jáuhòi (hàaHnghòi)
goal n.			
-purpose	目的	mùdiȷ	muHkdik;
-of a race	終點	jūngdyǎn,	jùngdímȷ
-football	球門	chyóumén	kàuHmùHn
godliness n.	敬虔	jìngchyán	gingkìHn
gold n.	金	jīn;	gàm;
	黃金	hwángjīn	wòHnggàm
golden a.	金	jīn	gàm
-golden age	黃金時代	hwángjīnshŕdài	wòHnggàmsìHdoiH
gong n.	鑼	lwó;	lòH;
	銅鑼	tùnglwó	tùHnglòH
good a.	好	hǎu;	hóu;
-of a child	乖	gwāi;	gwàai;
-kind	仁慈	réntsź;	yàHnchìH;
-good seed	好種	hǎujǔng;	hóujúng;
-good deeds	善行	shànsyíng;	siHnhàHng;
-good and evil	善惡	shànè;	siHnngok;
Good Friday	受難節	Shòunànjyé	SauHnaaHnjit

goodness n.

-of conduct	良善	lyángshàn;	lèuHngsiHn;
-excellence	優點	yōudyǎn	yàudím

goose n.   鵝   é   ngòH

gorge

-v. t. feed greedily	貪食	tānshí;	tàamsiHk;
-n. pass	山峽	shānsyá	sàanhaaHp

gorgeous a.

-showy	華麗	hwálì;	wàHlaiH;
-magnificent	堂皇	tánghwáng	tòHngwòHng

gossip

-n. idle talk	閒話	syánhwà;	hàaHnwá;
-v. i. tattle	搬弄是非	bānnùngshìfēi	bùnnuHngsiHfèi

govern v. t.

-with authority	治理	jìlǐ;	jiHléiH;
-as one's temper	控制	kùngjì	hungjai

governor n.

-of province	省長	shěngjǎng;	sáangjéung;
-of colony	總督	dzǔngdū	júngdūk

grace n.

-of God	恩典	ēndyǎn;	yàndín;
-beauty	美麗	měilì;	méiHlaiH;
-refinement	文雅	wényǎ	màHnngáH

grade

-n. of school	年級	nyánjí;	nìHnkāp;
-n. degree	等	děng;	dáng;
-v. t. arrange in classes	分級	fēnji	fānkāp (fānbāan)

gradual a.   漸漸   jyànjyàn;   jiHmjím;

         逐漸   jú
jyàn   juHkjím

graduate

-n. from school	畢業生	bìyèshēng;	bātyiHpsāng;
-v. i. academical	畢業	bìyè	bātyiHp

grain

-n. cereals	五穀	wŭgŭ;	ngHgŭk;
-n. classifier	粒	lì	nāp

grammar n. 文法 wénfă màlInfaat

gramophone n. 留聲機 lyóushēngjī làuHsìnggèi

granary n. 穀倉 gŭtsāng; gūkchōng;
農倉 núngtsāng nùHngchōng

grand a.

-great	偉大	wĕidà;	wáiHdaaiH;
-exalted	高	gāu;	gòu;
-splendid	講究	jyăngjyòu	gónggau

granite n. 青石 chīngshí; chèngseHk;
花崗石 hwāgāngshí fàgòngseHk

grant v. t.

-give	賜給	tsàgĕi,	chìtāpi
-of a petition	批准	pījwŭn	pàijéun

grape n. 葡萄 pútáu pòuHtòuH (pòuHtàiHji)

grasp v. t.

-with the hand	抓	jwā;	jáau (jà);
-with the mind	明白	míngbai	mìHngbaaHk
grasp power	掌權	jăngchywán	jéungkyùHn

grass n. 草 tsău chóu

grateful a. 感謝 gănsyè; gámjeH;
感激 gănjí gámgìk

grave

-n. tomb	墳墓	fénmù;	fàHnmouH;
-a. severe	嚴肅	yánsù	yìHmsūk

gravy n. 肉汁 ròujī yuHkjāp

graze

-v. i. feed	吃草	chītsǎu;	hekchóu;(siHkchóu);
-v. t. tend sheep	放羊	fàngyáng	fongyèuHng(hònyèuHng

grease

-v. t.	上油	shàngyóu;	séuHngyàuH;
-n.	油	yóu	yàuH

great a.

-of personality	偉大	wěidà;	wáiHdaaiH;
-big	大	dà;	daaiH;
-Great wall	長城	Chángchéng	ChèuHngsìHng

greedy a.

-of food	貪吃	tānchī;	tàamhek (waiHsiHk);
-covetous	貪心	tānsyīn;	tàamsàm;
-of gain	貪錢	tānchyán	tàamchín

green a.

-dark	綠	lyù;	luHk;
-plant like	青	chīng;	chèng;
-inexperienced	沒有經驗	méiyǒujīngyàn;	muHtyáuHgìngyiHm;
-raw	生	shēng;	sàang;
-unripe	不熟	bǔshú	bātsuHk (msuHk)

greet v. t.

-to a superior	問安	wènān;	maHnòn;
-when meeting	問候	wènhòu	maHnhauH

grenade n.

	手留彈	shǒulyóudàn	sáulàuHdáan

grief n.

	憂愁	yōuchóu;	yàusàuH;
	煩惱	fánnǎu	fàaHnnóuH

grieve v. i.

	悲哀	bēiāi;	bèingòi;
	悲傷	bēishāng	bèisèung

grill v. t.

	燒	shāu;	sìu;
	烤	kǎu	hāau (hong)

grin

-v. i. show the teeth	露齒	lùchǐ;	louHchí;
-n. snare	網羅	wǎnglwó	móHnglòH

| grind v. t. | 磨 | mwó | mòH |
| grip v. t. | 抓 | jwā | jáau (jāpjyuH) |

grit

-n. sand	沙	shā;	sà;
-v. t. grate	磨擦	mwótsā	mòHchaat
groan v. i.	呻吟	shēnyín	sànyàHm
groom n.	新郎	syinláng	sànlòHng

groove n.

| -channel | 溝 | gōu; | gàu; |
| -furrow | 槽 | tsáu | chòuH |

ground

-n. earth	土地	tŭdì;	tóudeiH;
-n. reason	原因	ywányīn;	yùHnyàn;
-n. foundation	基礎	jichŭ;	gèichó;
-v. i. of ship	擱淺	gēchyǎn	gokchín

group n.

	團	twán;	tyùHn;
	組	dzŭ;	jóu;
	群	chyún	kwàHn

grow

-v. i. increase in size	生長	shēngjǎng;	sàngjéung;
-v. i. advance	發達	fādá;	faatdaaHt;
-v. i. become	養成	yǎngchéng;	yéuHngsìHng;
-v. t. of plants	種	jùng;	jung;
-v. t. of beard	留	lyóu	làuH
-grow up	長大	jǎngdà	jéungdaaiH

grub

| -v. i. dig | 掘 | jywé; | gwaHt; |
| -n. larva | 幼蟲 | yòuchúng | yauchùHng |

grumble v. i.

| -murmur | 怨恨 | ywànhèn; | yunhaHn; |
| -at fate | 怨命 | ywànmìng | yunmeHng |

guarantee

-v. t. warrant	擔保	dānbǎu;	dàambóu;
-n. cash	保證金	bǎujèngjīn;	bóujinggām;
-n. person	保證人	bǎujèngrén	bóujingyàHn

guard

-v. t. watch	看守	kānshǒu;	hònsáu;
-v. t. protect	保護	bǎuhù;	bóuwuH;
-v. t. preserve	護庇	hùbì;	wuHbei;
-n. of person	衞兵	wèibīng;	waiHbìng;
-n. basket ball	後衞	hòuwèi	hauHwaiH

guardian n.

-watchman	守衞	shǒuwèi;	sáuwaiH;
-protector	監護人	jyānhùrén	gàamwuHyàHn

guess v. t. 猜   tsāi   chàai (gú)

guest n.

	客人	kèrén;	haakyàHn;
	來賓	láibīn	lòiHbàn

guide

-v. t. instruct	引導	yǐndǎu;	yáHndouH;
-v. t. show the way	帶路	dàilù;	daailouH;
-n. for tourist	嚮導	syǎngdǎu	héungdouH

guile n.

-subtlety	詭詐	gwěijà;	gwáija;
-treachery	奸謀	jyānmóu	gàanmàuH

guilt n.

	罪	dzwèi;	jeuiH;
	罪債	dzwèijài	jeuiHjaai

gum n.

-of tree	樹膠	shùjyāu;	syuHgàau;
-of mouth	牙牀	yàchwáng	ngàHchòHng

gun n.

-rifle	鎗	chyāng;	chēung;

-fowl ng	獵鎗	lyèchyāng	liHpcheung
gunboat n.	炮艦	pàujyàn	paaulaaHm
gymnasium n.			
-hall	體育舘	tǐyùgwǎn;	táiyuHkgún;
-room	健身房	jyànshēnfáng	giHnsànfóng

H

ha	哈	hā	hā
habit n.			
-personal	習慣	syígwàn;	jaaHpgwaan;
-custom	風俗	fēngsú	fùngjuHk
habitual a.			
-customary	慣於	gwànyú;	gwaanyù;
-usual	習常	syícháng	jaaIIpsèuHng
Hades n,	陰間	Yǐnjyān;	Yàngàan;
	陰府	Yǐnfǔ	Yàmfú
haemorrhage n.	出血	chūsyě	chēuthyut
hail n.	雹	báu	boHk
hair n.			
-in general	毛	máu;	mòuH;
-of the head	頭髮	tóufa	tàuHfaat
hall n.	廳	tǐng;	tēng;
	堂	táng	tòIIng
hallo int.	喂	wèi!	wai!
hallow v. t.			
-make holy	成聖	chéngshèng;	sìHngsing;
-set apart for holy	分別爲聖	fēnbyéwéishèng	fànbiHtwàiHsing
halt v. i.			
-stop	停	tíng;	tìHng;
-cease marching	止步	jǐbù	jíbouH

halter n.

-n. death by hanging 　吊死　　　　dyàusž;　　　diuséi;

-v. t. hang 　吊　　　　　　dyàu　　　　　diu

hammer

-n. 　鎚子　　　　　chwéidz;　　　chèuiHjí (chéui);

-v. t. 　鎚　　　　　chwéi　　　　　chèuiH

hand n.

-of body 　手　　　　　shǒu;　　　　sáu;

-of a clock 　針　　　　　jēn;　　　　　jàm;

-hand down 　留傳　　　　líuchwán　　　làuHchyùHn

handicap v. t. 妨礙　　　　　fángài;　　　fòHngngoiH;

障礙　　　　　jàngài　　　　jeungngoiH

handiwork n. 手工　　　　　shǒugūng　　　sáugùng

handkerchief n. 手帕　　　　　shǒupà　　　　sáupaak (sáugēnjái)

handle

-n. shaft 　柄　　　　　bǐng;　　　　beng;

-n. of teapot, cup 　耳　　　　　ěr;　　　　　yǐH;

-v. t. manage 　處理　　　　chǔlǐ;　　　chyúHléiH;

-v. t. deal with 　應付　　　yìngfù　　　yingfuH

handsome a. 英俊　　　　yǐngjyùn　　　yìngjeun

hang v. t.

-suspend 　掛　　　　　gwà;　　　　gwa;

　　　　吊　　　　　dyàu;　　　　diu;

-kill by 　吊死　　　　dyàusž　　　diuséi

hangar n.

-shed for aeroplane 飛機庫　　　fēijīkù　　　fèigèifu

happen v. i.

-meet 　遇見　　　　yùjyàn;　　　yuHgin;

-chance 　碰巧　　　pèngchyǎu;　　punghǎau (yuHngāam);

-take place 　發生　　　fāshēng　　　faatsàng

happiness n.	幸福	syìngfú;	haHngfúk;
	福分	fúfèn	fūkfaHn
harbour			
-n. port	港口	gǎngkǒu;	gónghàu;
-v. t. conceal	隱藏	yǐntsáng	yáuchòIIng
hard a.			
-solid	剛硬	gūngyìng;	gòngngaaHng;
-difficult	難	nán;	nàaHn;
-distressing	困難	kwùnnán	kwannàaHn
hardly adv.			
-scarcely	僅有	jǐnyǒu;	gányáuH;
-with difficulty	困難	kwùnnán;	kwannàaHn;
-not probably	恐不	kǔngbù	húngbāt (hùngpam̀wúiH)
hardship n.	艱難	jyānnán;	gàannàaHn;
	辛苦	syinkǔ	sànfú
harlot n.	娼	chāng;	chēung;
	妓	jì	geiH
harm			
-v. t. bodily	傷	shāng;	sèung;
-v. t. morally	害	hài;	hoiH;
-n. injury	損害	swǔnhài;	syúnhoiH;
-n. misfortune	不幸	búsyìng	bāthaHng
harmonize			
-v. i. music or color	調和	tyáuhé;	tiuHwòH;
-v. i. agree	相合	syānghé;	sèunghaHp;
-v. t. of persons	調停	tyáutíng	tiuHtìHng
harmony n.			
-musical	和諧	hésyé;	wòHhàaiH;
-agreement	一致	yíjì;	yātji;
-between persons	和睦	hémù	wòHmuHk

harness

-n. armor	盔甲	kwēijyǎ;	kwàigaap;
-v. t. arm	武裝	wǔjwāng	móuHjōng

harp n.

-lute	琴	chín;	kàHm;
	豎琴	shùchín	syuHkàHm

harrow n.

-rake	耙子	pádz	pàHji (pàH)

harsh a.

-rough	粗	tsū;	chòu;
-of taste	苦	kǔ;	fú;
-stern	嚴厲	yánlì;	yìHmlaiH;
-cruel	刻薄	kèbwó;	hāakboHk;
-stiff	强硬	chyángyìng	kèuHngngaaHn

harvest

-n.	收成	shōuchéng;	sàusìHng;
-n.	莊稼	jwāngjyà;	jòngga;
-v. i.	收割	shōugē	sàugot

haste n.

-swiftness	快捷	kwàijyé;	faaijit;
-hurry	急速	jísù	gāpchūk

hat n.	帽子	màudz	mouHji (móu)
hatch v. t.	孵蛋	fūdàn	fùdáan

hate v. t.

-detest	厭惡	yànwù;	yimwu;
-abbor	憎恨	dzēnghèn	jànghaHn

haul

-v. t. pull	拉	lā;	làai
-v. t. drag	拖	twō;	tò;
-v. i. shift	轉移	jwǎnyí	jyúnyìH

haunted a.	有鬼	yǒugwěi;	yáuHgwái;

	鬧鬼	nàugwěi	naauHgwái
ave v. t.	有	yǒu	yáuH
avoc n.			
-destruction	破壞	pwòhwài;	powaaiH;
-waste	荒廢	hwāngfèi;	fòngfai;
-damage	損害	syǔnhài	syúnhoiH
awk n.	鷹	yǐng;	yìng;
	老鷹	lǎuyǐng	lóuHyǐng
awker n.			
-pedlar	小販	syǎufàn	síufaan
ay n.			
-dried grass	乾草	gāntsǎu;	gònchóu;
-fodder	草料	tsǎulyàu	chóuliulI
azard n.			
-risk	冒險	màusyǎn;	mouHhím;
-peril	危難	wēinán	ngàiHnàaHn
aze n.	霧	wù	mouH
e pron.	他	tā;	tà (kéuiH);
-he-goat	公羊	gūngyáng	gùngyèuHng
ead n.			
-of body	頭	tóu;	tàuH;
-chief	首領	shǒulǐng;	sáulíHng;
-of ship	船頭	chwántóu	syùHntàuH
eadquarters n.			
-of political party	總部	dzǔngbù;	júngbouH;
-of military	司令部	sīlìngbù	sìliHngbouH
eal v. t.	醫治	yìjì	yìjiH
ealth n.	健康	jyànkāng;	giHnhòng;
	健全	jyànchywán	giHnchyùHn

hear v. t.	聽	tǐng;	tèng;
	聽見	tǐngjyàn	tènggin
hearsay n.			
-report	報告	bàugàu;	bougou;
-rumor	傳說	chwánshwō;	chyùHnsyut;
-common talk	常談	chángtán	sèuHngtàaHm
hearse n.	柩車	jyòuchē;	gauHchè;
	棺材車	gwēntsáichē	gùnchòiHchè
heart n.	心	syǐn;	sàm;
-spirit	心靈	syǐnlíng;	sàmlìHng;
-love	愛心	àisyǐn;	oisàm;
-centre	中心	jūngsyǐn	jùngsàm
heat n.			
-hotness	熱	rè;	yiHt;
-degree of	熱度	rèdù	yiHtdouH
heathen n.	異教人	yìjyàurén;	yiHgaauyàHn;
	外邦人	wàibāngrén	ngoiHbòngyàHn
heaven n.			
-sky	天	tyēn;	tìn;
-of Buddhists	西天	syityēn;	sàitìn;
-Christian	天堂	tyēntáng	tìntòHng
heavy a.	重	jùng;	chúHng;
-of rain	大	dà;	daaiH;
-heavy burden	重担	jùngdàn	chúHngdaam
hedge n.	籬笆	líbā	lèiHbā
heedful a.	愼重	shènjùng;	saHnjuHng;
	小心	syǎusyǐn	síusàm
heel n.	脚跟	jyǎugēn	geukgàn(geukjàang)

height n.	高	gāu;	gòu;
-altitude	高度	gāudù	gòudouH
heir n.	後嗣	hàusz̀;	hauHjiH;
	承繼人	chéngjìrén	sìHnggaiyàHn
helicopter n.	直昇機	jíshēngjī	jiHksìnggèi
hell n.	地獄	dìyù	deiHyuHk
helmet n.	頭盔	tóukwēi	tàuHkwài
help v. t.	幫助	bāngjù;	bòngjoH;
	幫忙	bāngmáng	bòngmòHng
hem			
-n. doubled-back	緄邊	gwŭnbyēn;	gwánbin;
-n. edge	邊緣	byānywán;	binyùHn;
-v. t. surround	包圍	bāuwéi	bàauwàiH
hemp n.	麻	má;	màH;
	大麻	dàmá	daaiHmàH
hen n.			
-of fowl	母鷄	mŭjī;	móuHgāi;
-of other birds	母	mŭ	móuH
henceforth adv.	從今以後	tsúngjìnyĭhòu	chùHnggàmyíHhauH
herb n.	草	tsăuu	chóu
herd n.	羣	chyún;	kwàHn;
-v. t. unite as beasts	成羣	chéngchyún;	sìHngkwàHn;
-v. t. look after	看	kān	hòn
here adv.			
-this place	這裏	jèlĭ;	jéHléuiH (nìsyu)
-hither	至此	jìtsz̆;	jichí;
-now	現今	syànjìn	yiHngām
hereditary a.			
-of business	祖傳	dzŭchwán;	jóuchyùHn;
-of rank	世襲	shz̀syí;	saijaaHp;
-of disease	遺傳	yíchwán	wàiHchyùHn

heresy n.	異端	yìdwān	yiHdyùn
heretofore adv.			
-hitherto	從來	tsúnglái;	chùHnglòiH;
-in time past	從前	tsúngchyán	chùHngchìHn
heritage n.	遺產	yíchǎn	wàiHcháan
hermit n.	隱士	yǐnshṛ	yánsiH
hero n.	英雄	yīngsyúng	yìnghùHng
hesitate v. s.	猶豫	yóuyù;	yàuHyùH;
	躊躇	chóuchú	chàuHchyúH
hiccup v. i.	打嗝	dǎgé;	dágaak;
	打噎	dǎyē	dáyìt (dásìyik)
hide v. t.	隱藏	yíntsáng;	yánchòHng;
-oneself	躲	dwǒ;	dó (nèimàaiH);
-a thing	藏	tsáng	chòHng
high a.	高	gāu;	gòu;
-of price	貴	gwèi	gwai
hill n.	山	shān	sàan
hinder v. t.	阻止	dzǔjṛ;	jójí;
	防礙	fángài	fòHngngoiH
hinge n.	鉸鏈	jyǎulyàn	gáaulín
hint v. t.	暗示	ànshṛ	ngamsiH
hip n.	大腿	dàtwěi	daaiHtéui
hire v. t.			
-as men	請	chǐng;	chéng;
-of things	租	dzū	jòu
his pron.	他的	tāde	tādìk (kéuiHge)
history n.	歷史	lìshṛ;	liHksí;
-personal experiences	經歷	jīnglì;	gìngliHk;
-record attached to a curio	來歷	láilì	lòiHliHk
hit v. t.			
-with a blow	打	dǎ;	dá;

-as a mark	打ㄉㄚ 中ㄓㄨㄥ	dǎjùng;	dájung;
-guess right	猜ㄘㄞ 中ㄓㄨㄥ	tsāijùng	chāaijung
ive n.	蜂ㄈㄥ 巢ㄔㄠ	fēngcháu	fūngchàauH

oard

-n. treasure	財ㄘㄞ 物ㄨ	tsáiwù;	chòiHmaHt;
-v. t. hide	藏ㄘㄤ	tsáng;	chòHng;
-v. t. as money	積ㄐㄧ	jī;	jīk (chóuH);
-v. t. as goods	囤ㄊㄨㄣ 積ㄐㄧ	twúnjī	deuHnjīk

oarse a.

-raucous	啞ㄧㄚ 聲ㄕㄥ	yǎshēng;	ngáoòng;
-harsh	粗ㄘㄨ 厲ㄌㄧ	tsūlì	chòulaiH (chòulóuH)
obby n.	嗜ㄕ 好ㄏㄠ	shìhàu	sihou

oe

| -n. | 鋤ㄔㄨ 頭ㄊㄡ | chútóu; | chòHtàuH; |
| -v. t. | 鋤ㄔㄨ | chú | chòII |

old v. t.

-grasp	拿ㄋㄚ	ná;	nàH (nīk);
-as a ceremony	舉ㄐㄩ 行ㄒㄧㄥ	jyǔsyíng;	géuihàHng;
-contain	裝ㄓㄨㄤ	jwāng;	jòng;
-restrain	約ㄩㄝ 束ㄕㄨ	ywēshù;	yeukchūk;
-support	支ㄓ 持ㄔ	jrchf;	jichìlI;
-hold fast	守ㄕㄨ 住ㄓㄨ	shǒujù	sáujyuH

ole n.

| -aperture | 洞ㄉㄨㄥ | dùng; | duHng; |
| -in the ground | 坑ㄎㄥ | kēng | hàang |

oliday n.

| -ordinary | 假ㄐㄧㄚ 日ㄖ | jyàr; | gayaHt; |
| -festival | 節ㄐㄧㄝ 日ㄖ | jyér | jityaHt |

oliness n.

| | 聖ㄕㄥ 潔ㄐㄧㄝ | shèngjyé; | sìnggit; |
| | 神ㄕㄣ 聖ㄕㄥ | shénshèng | sàHnsing |

ollow

| -a. empty | 空ㄎㄨㄥ | kūng; | hùng; |

-a. sunken	凹	wā;	nāp;
-n. cavity	洞	dùng	duHng(lūng)
home n.	家	jyā;	gà;
-house	房子	fángdz;	fòHngjí (ngūk);
-residence	住家	jùjyā;	jyuHgà;
-native place	家鄉	jyāsyāng	gàhèung
homogeneous a.	同種	túngjǔng;	tùHngjúng;
	同類	túnglèi	tùHngleuiH
homosexuality n.	同性戀愛	túngsyìnglyànài	tùHngsinglyúnngoi
honest a.	老實	lǎushf;	lóuHsaHt;
	誠實	chéngshf	sìHngsaHt
honey n.	蜜	mì;	maHt;
	蜂蜜	fēngmì	fūngmaHt (maHttòHn
Hong Kong n.	香港	Syānggǎng	Hèunggóng
honor, honour			
-v. t. respect	尊重	dzwūnjùng;	jyùnjuHng;
-n. fame	名譽	míngyù;	mìHngyuH;
-n. glory	光榮	gwāngrúng	gwòngwìHng
honorable a.	尊貴	dzwūngwèi	jyùngwai
honorary a.	名譽	míngyù	mìHngyuH
hook n.	鈎	gōu	ngāu
hoop n.	鐵環	tyěhwán	titwàaHn (tithyūn)
hop v. i.	獨脚跳	dújyǎutyàu	duHkgeuktiu
hope v. t.	希望;	syìwàng;	hèimoHng;
	盼望	pànwàng	paanmoHng
horizon n.	水平線;	shwěipíngsyàn;	séuipìHngsin;
	地平線	dìpíngsyàn	deiHpìHngsin
horoscope n.	八字	bādż;	baatjiH;

生辰八字 shēngchénbādz sàangsàHnbaatjiH

orrible a.			
-shocking	可怕	kěpà;	hópa;
-unpleasing	討厭	tǎuyàn	tóuyim
orse n.	馬	mǎ	máH
ose n.			
-tube	水管	shwǎigwǎn;	séuigún;
-stockings	長襪	chángwà	chèuHngmaHt
ospitable a.			
-fond of receiving guests	好客	hàukè;	houhaak,
-good service	招待周到	jāudàijōudàu	jiudoiHjàudou
ospital n.	醫院	yìwàn	yìyún
ospitality n.	招待	jāudài;	jiudoiH;
	欵待	kwǎndài	fúndoiH
ost n.	主人	jǔrén	jyúyán
ostage n.	人質	rénjí	yàHnjat
ostel n.			
-for students	宿舍	sùshè;	sūkse;
-hostelry	客寓	kèyù	haakyuH
ostile			
-a. unfriendly	惡意	èyì;	ngokyi;
-n. enemy	仇敵	chóudí	sàuHdiHk
ot a.			
-of temperature	熱	rè;	yiHt;
-feverish	燒	shāu;	sìu;
-pungent	辣	là;	laaHt;
-as argument	激烈	jīlyè	gikliHt
otel n.	旅舘	lyǔgwǎn;	léuiHgún;
	飯店	fàndyàn	faaIndim
our n.	小時	syǎushf;	síusìH;
	鐘頭	jūngtóu	jùngtàuH
ouse n.	房屋	fángwū;	fòHngngūk;

English	Chinese		
-family	家	jyā	gà
household n.	家族	jyādzú;	gàjuHk;
-family	一家人	yìjyārén	yātgàyàHn
housekeeper n.	看家	kānjyā;	hòngà (hōnngūk);
	女管家	nyǔgwǎnjyā	néuiHgúngà
housewife n.	主婦	jǔfù	jyúfúH
how adv.			
-in what way	怎樣	dzěmyàng;	jámyeuHng (dímyéung)
-by what means	怎麼	dzěmma;	jámmō (dím);
-to what extent	多麼	dwóme;	dōmō (géigam);
-how great	何等大	héděng dà;	hòHdáng daaiH;
-how much more	何況	hékwàng	hòHfong
however			
-adv. in whatever manner	任何情形	rènhéchíngsying;	yaHmhòHchìHngyìHn;
-adv. although	然而	ránér;	yìHnyìH;
-adv. to whatever extent	無論如何	wúlwùnrúhé;	mòuHleuHnyùHhòH;
-conj. nevertheless	雖然	swéirán	sèuiyìHn
howl v. i.			
-as animals	叫	jyàu;	giu;
-of the wind	怒號	nùhǎu;	nouHhouH;
-of men	喊叫	hǎnjyàu	haamgiu (giu)
hub n.			
-nave	輪轂	lwúngǔ;	lèuHngūk;
-centre	中心	jūngsyīn	jùngsàm
hug v. t.			
-put arms round	攬	lǎn;	láam;
-embrace closely	擁抱	yǔngbàu	yúngpóuH (póuH)
huge a.	大	dà	daaiH
hulk n.			
-heavy clumsy ship	笨重之船	bènjùngjīchwán;	baHnjuHngjìsyùHn;

-body of ship	船身	chwánshēn	syùHnsàn
ull			
-n. husk	壳	ké;	hok;
	皮	pí;	pèiH;
-v. t. take peas, etc.	剝壳	bāuké;	mōkhok;
	剝皮	bāupí	mōkpèiH
m v. i.	哼	hēng	hàng
man a.	人	rén;	yàHn;
-human life	人類生活	rénlèi shēnghwó;	yàHnleuiH sàngwuHt;
-human personality	人格	réngé;	yàHngaak;
-human race	人種	rénjŭng	yàHnjúng
human rights	人類公權	rénlèigūngchywán,	yàHnleuiHgùngkyùHn;
-human society	人類社會	rénlèiohòhwòi	yàHnleuiHsóHwfii
manism n.	人道主義	réndàujŭyì	yàHndouHjyúyiH
mane a.	好心	hăusyīn;	hóusàm;
	仁慈	réntsź	yàHnchìH
mble a.			
-not proud	謙卑	chyānbēi;	hìmbèi;
-modest	謙虚	chyānsyu	hìmhèui
mid a.	濕	shī;	sāp;
	潮濕	cháushī	chiuHsāp
miliate v. t.	丟臉	dyōulyăn;	dìulím;
	侮辱	wŭrù	móuHyuHk
mility n.			
-act of submission	服從	fútsúng;	fuHkchùHng;
-humbleness	謙遜	chyānsyùn	hìmseun
mour n.			
-moisture	濕氣	shīchì;	sāphei;
-disposition	性情	syìngchíng;	singchìHng;
-mood	心情	syinchíng	sàmchìHng

humorous a.	幽默	yōumè;	yàumaaHk;
	滑稽	hwáji	waaHtkài
hundred a.	百	bǎi	baak
hunger n.	饑餓	jīè	gèingoH
hunt			
~v. i. follow game	打獵	dǎlyè;	dáliHp;
~v. t. search for	尋找	syúnjǎu	chàHmjáau (wán)
hurricane n.	暴風	bàufēng;	bouHfùng;
	颶風	jyùfēng	geuiHfùng
hurry v. t.	催	tswēi;	chèui;
	趕快	gǎnkwài	gónfaai
hurt v. t.			
-mental	傷害	shānghài;	sèunghoiH;
-bodily	傷	shāng	sèung
husband n.	丈夫	jàngfu	jeuHngfù
husbandman n.	農夫	núngfū	nùHngfù
husl. int.	別出聲	byéchūshēng;	biHtchēutsèng (m̀hóu chēutsèng);
	別響	byésyǎng	biHthéung (m̀hóuchò
husk n.			
-as of rice	糠	kāng;	hòng;
-of beans, etc.	壳	ké	hok
husky voice n.	沙聲	shāshēng	sàsèng (dauHsàhàuH
hut n.			
-thatched	茅屋	máuwū;	màauHngūk;
-hovel	棚	péng	pàaHng
hydrant n.	消防水栓	syāufángshwān-	sìufòHngséuisàan
hydralic engineering	水利工程	shwěiligūngchéng	séuileiHgùngchìHng
hydrogen n.	氫	chīng;	hìng;
	氫氣	chīngchì	hìnghei
hygiene n.	衛生	wèishēng	waiHsāng

ymn n.	聖詩	shèngshī:	singsi;
	讚美詩	dzànměishī	jaanméiHsi
ymnal n.	聖詩集	shèngshījí	singsijaaHp
ymnology n.	聖詩學	shèngshīsywé	singsihoHk
yphen n.	連號	lyánhàu	liHnhouH
ypnotism n.	催眠術	tswēimyánshù	chèuimiHnseuHt
ypocrite n.	假冒為善	jyǎmàuwéishàn;	gámouHwàiHsiHn;
	偽君子	wèijyūndž	ngaiHgwànji
ypodermic injection n.	皮下注射	písyàjùshè	pèiHhaHjyuseh
ypothesis n.	假設	jyǎshè;	gáchit;
	假定	jyǎdìng	gádiHng
yssop n.	牛膝草	nyóusyitsǎu	ngàuIɪsātchóu
ysteria n.	精神失常	jìngshénshrcháng;	jìngsàHnsātsèuHng;
	歇斯特里症	syěsztèlǐjèng	hitsidaHkléiHjing
pron.	我	wǒ;	ngóH;
-polite term	鄙人	bǐrèn	péiyàHn
e n.	冰	bīng	bīng
ilng n.	糖衣	tángyǐ	tòHngyì
on n.	神像	shénsyàng	sàHnjeuHng
onoclast n.	毀壞偶像	hwěihwàiðusyàng	wáiwaaiHngáuHjeuHng
ea n.			
-opinion	意思	yìsz;	yisi;
-imagination	想像	syǎngsyàng	séungjeuHng
eal a.			
-fit for a model	理想	lǐsyǎng;	léiHséung;
-aim	目的	múdi	muHkdik

identical a.	相同	syāngtúng;	sèungtùHng;
	同樣	túngyàng	tùHngyéung
identity n.			
-oneness	同一	túngyi;	tùHngyāt;
-resemblance	相似	syāngsz̀	sèungchíH
ideology n.			
-science of ideas	觀念學	gwān nyànsywé;	gùnniHmhoHk;
-idle theorizing	空論	kūnglwùn	hùngleuHn
idiom n.	成語	chéngyŭ	siHngyúH
idiot n.	白癡	báichī	baaHkchì
idle			
-a. doing no work	空閒	kŭngsyán;	hùnghàaHn;
-a. lazy	懶惰	lăndwò;	láaHndoH;
-v. i. saunter idly	閒蕩	syándàng	hàaHndoHng
idol n.	偶像	ŏusyàng	ngáuHjeuHng
if conj.	如果	rúgwŏ;	yùHgwó;
	假如	jyărú	gáyùH
ignorance n.	愚昧	yúmèi;	yùHmuiH;
	無知	wújī	mòuHjì
ignore v. t.	不理	bùlĭ;	bātléiH (m̀léiH);
	不顧	búgù	bātgu
ill			
-a. sick	病	bìng;	beHng;
-a. unconfortable	不舒服	bùshùfu;	bātsyùfuHk(m̀syùfuHk
-adv. badly	不好	bùhău	bāthóu (m̀hóu)
illegal a.	犯法	fànfă;	faaHnfaat;
	非法	fēifă	fèifaat
illegidle a.			
-difficult to read	難讀	nándú;	nàaHnduHk;
-not legible	不明白	bùmíngbai	bātmìHngbaaHk (m̀mìHngbaaHk)

illegitimate child n.   私ㄙ生ㄥ子ㄦ   sīshēngdž   sìsàngji

illiterate a.

   -ignorant of letters   文ㄨㄣ盲ㄇㄤ   wénmáng;   màHnmàaHng;

   -unlearned   失ㄕ學ㄒㄩㄝ   shīsywé   sāthoHk

illness n.

   -disease   病ㄅㄧㄥ   bìng;   beiIng;

   -wickedness   惡ㄜ意ㄧ   èyì   ngokyi

illumine v. t.   光ㄍㄨㄤ照ㄓㄠ   gwēngjàu;   gwòngjiu;

     照ㄓㄠ亮ㄌㄧㄤ   jàulyàng   jiuleuHng

illusion n.

   -delusion   妄ㄨㄤ想ㄒㄧㄤ   wàngoyàng;   móHngséung;

   -psychol.   錯ㄘㄨㄛ覺ㄐㄩㄝ   tswòjywé   chogok

illustrate v. i.

   -make clear   說ㄕㄨㄛ明ㄇㄧㄥ   shwōmíng;   syutmìHng;

   -provide wit pictures   圖ㄊㄨ解ㄐㄧㄝ   tújyě   tòuHgáai

image n.

   -effigy   形ㄒㄧㄥ像ㄒㄧㄤ   syíngsyàng;   yìHngjeuHng;

   -mental   想ㄒㄧㄤ像ㄒㄧㄤ   syǎngsyàng;   séungjeuHng;

   -reflection   影ㄧㄥ子ㄦ   yǐngdz   yíngjí (yíng)

imagination n.   幻ㄏㄨㄢ想ㄒㄧㄤ   hwànsyǎng   waaHnséung

imitate v. t.

   -as a model   效ㄒㄧㄠ法ㄈㄚ   syàufǎ;   haauHfaat;

   -counterfeit   假ㄐㄧㄚ冒ㄇㄠ   jyǎmàu   gámouH

immanence n.

   -indwelling   內ㄋㄟ在ㄗㄞ   nèidzài;   noiHjoiH;

   -inherence   固ㄍㄨ有ㄧㄡ   gùyǒu   guyáuH

immediate a.

   -instant   立ㄌㄧ刻ㄎㄜ   lìkè;   laHphāak (jikhāak);

   -direct   直ㄓ接ㄐㄧㄝ   jŕjyē   jiHkjip

immersion n.	浸禮	jìnlǐ;	jamláiH;
	水禮	shwěilǐ	séuiláiH
immigrant n.	移民	yímín	yìHmàHn
immoral a.			
-morally wrong	不道德	búdàudé;	bātdouHdāk;
-dissolute	淫蕩	yíndàng	yàHmdoHng
immovable a.			
-fixed	堅定不移	jyāndìngbùyí;	gìndiHngbātyìH;
-of intention	決定	jywédìng	kyutdiHng
immutability n.	不變性	búbyànsyìng	bàtbinsing
impair v. t.			
-damage	損壞	swǔnhwài;	syúnwaaiH;
-make worse	弄壞	nùnghwài	luHngwaaiH(jíngwaaiH
impart v. t.			
-make known	通知	tūngjī;	tùngjì;
-communicate	傳達	chwándá	chyùHndaaHt
impatient a.			
-lacking forbearance	性急	syìngjí;	singgāp;
-uneasy	着急	jāují	jeuHkgāp
imperative mood n.	命令法	mìnglìngfǎ	miHngliHngfaat
impersonal a.	無人格	wúréngé;	mòuHyàHngaak;
	非人	fēirén	fèiyàHn
impersonate v. t.	化裝	hwàjwāng;	fajōng;
	扮演	bànyǎn	baaHnyín
impertinent a.			
-not pertinent	不適當	búshìdàng;	bātsìkdong(m̀sikdong)
-not to the point	不及	bùjí;	bātkaHp;
-irrelevant	不適用	búshìyùng	bātsìkyuHng (m̀sikyuHng

impetuous a.

-rushing with violence	猛 撞	měngjwàng;	máaHngjoHng;
-furious	忿 激	fènjī;	fáHngĭk;

implicate v. t. 連 累　lyánlèi　lìHnleuiH

imply v. t.

hint	暗 示	ànshì;	ngamsiH;
-mean	含 意	hányì	hàHmyi

import v. t.

	進 口	jìnkǒu;	jeunháu(yaHpháu);
	輸 入	shùrù	syùyaHp

important a.

	要 緊	yàujĭn;	yiugán;
	重 要	jùngyàu	juHngyiu

impose v. t.

-place	放	fàng;	fong;
-of fine	罰 錢	fáchyán	faHtchín

impossible a.

	不 可 能	bùkěnéng;	bàthónàHng;
	做 不 到	dzwòbúdàu	jouHbātdou(jouHm̀dou)

impostor n. 欺 詐 者　chìjàjě　hèijajé

impotent a.

-weak	無 力	wúlì;	mòuHliHk;
-feeble	虛 弱	syùrwò	hèuiyeuHk

impress v. t.

-print	印	yìn;	yan;
-as a seal	蓋 印	gàiyìn;	goiyan (kāpyan);
-the feelings of	感 動	gǎndùng	gámduHng

impression n. 印 象　yìnsyàng　yanjeuHng

imprison v. t.

	被 囚	bèichyóu;	beiHchàuH;
	坐 監	dzwòjyān	chóHgūam

improbable a.

-not probable	未 必	wèibì;	meiHbit;
-not to be expected	不 期 望	bùchīwàng	bātkèiHmoHng (m̀hèimoHng)

improve v. t.

-make better   改良   gǎiliáng;   góilèuHng;

-progress   進步   jìnbù;   jeunbouH;

-by revision   改正   gǎijèng   góijing

improvise v. t.   臨時作成   línshŕdzwòchéng   làHmsìHjoksìHng

impudent a.

-showing no respect   大膽   dàdǎn;   daaiHdáam;

-in a shameless way   臉皮厚   lyǎnpíhòu;   líHmpèiHháuH (miHnpèiHháuH)

-rash   魯莽   lǔmǎng   lóuHmóHng

impulse n.   衝動   chūngdùng;   chùngduHng;

   激動   jídùng   gìkduHng

in prep.   裏面   lǐmyàn;   léuiHmiHn;

-not out   在家   dzàijyā   joiHgà (háikéi)

inaugurate v. t.

-into office   就職   jyòujŕ;   jauHjĭk;

-as an undertaking   創辦   chwàngbàn;   chongbaaHn;

-as a movement   提倡   tíchàng;   tàiHchèung;

-as a new era   開始   kāishř;   hòichí;

-as a building   落成   lwòchéng;   loHksìHng;

-as a society   開幕   kāimù   hòimoHk

Incarnation n.   道成肉身   dàuchéngròushēn   douHsìHngyuHksàn

incense n.   香   syāng   hèung

incentive

-a. inciting   激發   jífā;   gìkfaat;

-a. kindling   着火   jáuhwǒ;   jeuHkfó;

-n. motive   動機   dùngjĭ   duHnggèi

inch n.   英寸   yingtswùn   yìngchyun

include v. t.   包括   bāukwǒ;   bàaukwut;

	包含	bāuhán	bàauhàHm
inclusive a.			
comprising	包括	bāukwò;	bàaukwut;
surrounding	包圍	bāuwéi	bàauwàiH
incognito a.	匿名	nìmíng;	nìkmìHng;
	隱名	yǐnmíng	yánmìHng
income n.	收入	shōurù;	sàuyaHp;
-tax	所得稅	swǒdéshwèi	sódākseui
incommunicative a.			
-silent	緘默	jyǎnmwò;	gáammaaHk;
-reserved	保留	bǎulyóu	bóulàuH
incomparable a.			
-beyond comparable	無此	wúbǐ;	móuHbéi;
-matchless	無敵	wúdí	móuHdiHk
incompetent a.			
-incapable	無能	wúnéng;	móuHnàHng;
-disqualified	不合格	bùhégé	bāthaHpgaak
incomplete a.			
-not complete	不完全	bùwánchywán;	bātyùHnchyùHn;
-not finished	未完	wèiwán;	meiHyùHn;
-defective	有缺點	yǒuchywēdyǎn	yáuHkyutdím
incomprehensible a.	不能了解	bùnénglyǎujyě	bātnàHnglíuHgáai
inconceivable a.			
-not conceivable	不可思議	bùkěszyì;	bāthósìyìH;
-unimaginable	不可想像	bùkěsyǎngsyàng;	bāthóséungjeuHng;
-unbelievable	不可信	bùkěsyìn	bāthóseun
inconsiderable a.			
-trivial	不足取	bùdzúchyǔ;	bātjūkchéui;
-not considerable	不考慮	bùkǎulyù	bātháauleuiH
inconvenient a.	不便	búbyàn;	bātbiHn;

不方便	bùfāngbyàn	bātfòngbiHn(m̀fòngbiHn

incorporate v. t.

| -unite | 聯合 | lyánhé; | lyùHnhaHp; |
| -form | 組合 | dzǔhé | jóuhaHp |

incorrect a.

-faulty	錯誤	tswòwù;	chongH;
-inaccurate	不正確	bùjèngchywè;	bātjingkok;
-untrue	不眞	bùjēn	bātjān(m̀ngāam)

incorruptible a.

| -of material things | 不能朽壞 | bùnéngsyǒuhwài; | bātnàHngnáuwaaiH; |
| -as an officer | 清廉 | chǐnglyán | chìnglìHm |

increase v. t.

-add	增加	dzēngjyā;	jànggà;
-in size	加大	jyādà;	gàdaaiH;
-in price	起價	chǐjyà	héiga

incredible a.

| -unbelievable | 難信 | nánsyìn; | nàaHnseun; |
| -exaggerated | 荒唐 | hwāngtáng | fòngtòHng |

incriminate v. t.

| -in ordinary parlance | 歸罪於 | gwēidzwèiyú; | gwàijeuiHyù; |
| -accuse | 控告 | kùnggàu | hunggou |

incurable a.

| -disease | 不治 | búj̀ì; | bātjiH; |
| -habit, evils | 不可救藥 | bùkějyòuyàu | bāthógauyeuHk |

indeed adv.

| | 果然 | gwǒrán; | gwóyìHn; |
| | 實在 | shŕdzài | saHtjoiH |

indefinite a.

| -uncertain | 不確定 | búchywèdìng; | bātkokdiHng; |

-not fixed	不固定	búgùdìng;	bātgudiHng;
-vague	含糊	hànhu	hàHmwùH

ndependent a.

-autonomous	獨立	dúlì;	duHklaHp;
-not supported by others	自立	dzìlì;	jiHlaHp

ndex n.

	索引	swǒyin;	sokyáHn;
	目錄	mùlù	muHkluHk

ndicate v. t.

-show	指示	jřshì;	jísıH;
-point out	指出	jřchū	jichēut

ndifferent a.

-inenthusiasm	冷淡	lěngdàn;	láaHngdaaHm;
-unconcerned	不關心	bùgwānoyin;	hātgwàansàm;
-not caring for	不理	bùlǐ	hātléiH (m̀léiH)

ndigenous a.

	土生的	tǔshēngde;	tóusàngdìk;
-people	土人	tǔrén	tóuyàHn

ndigested a.

-undigested	不消化	bùsyāuhwà;	bātsıufa (m̀sıufa);
-confused	雜亂	dzálwàn	jaaHplyuHn

ndignant a.

	動怒	dùngnù;	duHngnouH;
	怒……	fènnù	fáHnnouH

ndirect a.

	間接	jyànjyē	gaanjip

ndispensable a.

-not dispensable	不可避免	bùkěbìmyǎn;	bāthóbeiHmíHn;
-absolutely necessary	必須	bìsyū;	bitsèui;
-essential	必要	bìyàu	bityiu

ndividual a.

	個別	gèbyé;	gobiHt;
	個人	gèrén	goyàHn

ndulge

-v. t. as a child	縱容	dzùngrúng;	jungyùHng;

-v. i. oneself	放縱	fàngdzùng	fongjung
industrious a.			
-assiduous	勤勉	chínmyǎn;	kàHnmíHn;
-skilful	熟練	shúlyàn	suHkliHn
industry n.	工業	gūngyè	gùngyiHp
ineffective a.	無效	wúsyàu	mòuHhaauH
inevitable a.	不可避免	bùkěbìmyǎn;	bāthóbeiHmíHn;
	不能避免	bùnéngbìmyǎn	bātnàHngbeiHmíHn
inexhaustible a.	無窮	wúchyúng;	mòuHkùHng;
	用不完	yùngbùwán	yuHngbātyùHn (yuHngmìyùHn)
infallible a.			
-unerring	無誤	wúwù;	mòuHngHȩ
-indubitable	無疑	wúyí	mòuHyìH
infant n.	嬰孩	yīnghái	yìnghòiH
infantry n.	步兵	bùbīng	bouHbìng
infatuate v. t.			
-affect with folly	迷惑	míhwò;	màiHwaaHk;
-foolish love	迷戀	mílyàn	màiHlyún
infection n.	傳染	chwánrǎn	chyùHnyíHm
infer v. t.	推論	twēilwùn;	tèuileuHn;
	推測	twēitsè	tèuichāak
inferior a.			
-of poor quality	卑劣	bēilywè;	bèilyut;
-in rank	下級	syàjí	haHkāp
infest v. t.	擾亂	rǎulwàn;	yíulyuHn;
	騷擾	sāurǎu	sòuyíuH
infinite a.	無限	wúsyàn;	mòuHhaaHn;

	無窮	wúchyúng	mòuHkùHng

infinitive a.

| -undefined | 不定 | búdìng | bātdiHng; |
| -unlimited | 無限 | wúsyàn; | mòuHhaaHn |

inflate

| -v. t. distend | 伸長 | shēncháng; | sànchèuHng; |
| -v. i. puff up | 意氣揚揚 | yìchìyángyáng | yiheiyèuHngyèuHng |

inflict v. t.

| -strike | 打 | dǎ; | dá; |
| -punish | 罰 | fá | faHt |

infliction n.

| | 苦痛 | kǔtùng | fútung |

influence

| -v. t. affect | 影響 | yǐngsyǎng; | yínghé·ung; |
| -n. power | 勢力 | shìlì | sailiHk |

influenza n.

| | 流行性感冒 | liúsyíngsyìng gǎnmàu | làuHhàHngsinggámmouH |

inform

| -v. t. notify | 通知 | tūngjr̄; | tùngjì; |
| -v. t. inspire | 激勵 | jīlì; | gīklaiH; |

information n.

| -notification | 通知 | tūngjr̄; | tùngjì; |
| -instruction | 教誨 | jyàuhwěi | gaaufui |

informal a.

| -not usual form | 非正式 | feijèngshr̀; | fèijingsik; |
| -without ceremony | 不拘禮 | bùjyúlǐ | bātkèuiláiII |

infuse v. t.

| -pour in | 冲 | chūng; | chùng; |
| -steep in | 泡 | pàu | pᴀau |

ingenious a.

| -skilful | 技巧 | jìchyǎu; | geiHháau; |
| -clever | 聰明 | tsūngmíng; | chùngmìHng; |

-inventive	有天才	yǒutyāntsái	yáuHtìnchòiH
inglorious a.			
-shameful	可恥	kěchǐ;	hóchí;
-humble	卑微	bēiwèi	bèimèiH
ingratitude n.	忘恩負義	wàngēnfùyì	mòHngyànfuHyiH
ingredient n.			
-component	成分	chéngfèn;	sìHngfaHn;
-constituent	要素	yàusù	yiusou
inhabit v. t.	居住	jyūjù	gèuijyuH
inhale v. t.	吸	syī;	kāp;
-and exhale	呼吸	hūsyi	fūkāp
inherit v. t.			
-as an heir	繼承	jìchéng;	gaisìHng;
-by birth	遺傳	yíchwán;	wàiHchyùHn;
-a profession	承受	chéngshòu	sìHngsauH
inheritance n.	產業	chǎnyè;	cháanyiHp;
	遺產	yíchǎn	wàiHcháan
inhuman a.			
-unfeeling	無情	wúchíng;	mòuHchìHng;
-brutal	無人道	wúréndàu;	mòuHyàHndouH
-cruel	殘忍	tsánrěn	chàaHnyán
iniquity n.			
-unjust	不正	bújèng;	bātjing;
-sin	罪惡	dzwèiè	jeuiHngok
initial			
-a. commencing	初辦	chūbàn;	chòbaaHn;
-n. lst letter of a word	第一字母	dìyidzmǔ	daiHyātjiHm6uH
initiate v. t.			
-begin	發起	fāchǐ;	faathéi;
-originate	起始	chǐshǐ	héichí
initiation n.	入會式	rùhwèishr̀	yaHpwúisǐk
injection n.	注射	jùshè	jyuseH(dájām)

injure v. t.

-damage	損害	swǔnhài;	syúnhoiH;
-harm	害	hài;	hoiH;
-hurt	傷	shāng	sèung

injustice n.

-unfairness	不公平	hùgūngpíng;	būtgùngpìHng;
-unrighteousness	不義	búyì	bātyiH

ink n.

	墨水	mèshwěi	maHkséui

inland a.

	內地	nèidì;	noiHdeiH;
	國內	gwónèi	gwoknoiH

inn n.

	客店	kèdyàn;	haakdim;
	旅舘	lyǔgwǎn	léuiHgún

inner a.

	內在	nèidzài;	noiHjoiH;
	裏面	lǐmyàn;	léuiHmiHn (léuiHbiHn);
-inner life	內心生活	nèisyìnshēnghwó	noiHsàmsàngwuHt

innkeeper n.

	店主	dyànjǔ	dimjyú

innocent a.

-guiltless	無罪	wúdzwèi;	mòuHjeuiH;
-as a child	天眞	tyānjēn	tìnjàn

innumerable a.

	無數	wúshù;	mòuHsou;
	數不清	shǔbùchǐng	sóubātchìng (sóumching)

innutritious a.

	營養不良	yíngyǎngbùlyáng	yìHngyéuHngbātlèuHng

inoffensive a.

-harmless	無害	wúhài;	mòuHhoiH
-giving no offense	不觸犯	búchùfàn	bātchūkfaaHn

inordinate a.

-excessive	過度	gwòdù;	gwodouH;
-intemperate	不節制	bùjyéjìr	bātjitjai

inorganic a.

	無機	wújī	mòuHgèi

inquest n.

-offocial inquiry	審問	shěnwèn;	sámmaHn;
-by coroner	驗屍	yánshī	yiHmsì

inquire

-v. t. ask about	訪問	fǎngwèn;	fóngmaHn;
-v. t. question	質問	jǐfwèn;	jātmaHn;
-v. i. examine	考問	kǎuwèn;	háaumaHn;
-v. i. investigate	查問	cháwèn	chàHmaHn

inquiry n.

	詢問	syúnwèn;	sèunmaHn;
-inquiry office	問詢處	wènsyúnchù	maHnsèunchyu

insane a.

	瘋狂	fēngkwáng;	fùngkòHng;
-insane asplum	精神病院	jingshénbìngywàn	jìngsàHnbeHngyún

insanitary a.

-not sanitary	不衞生	búwèishēng;	bātwaiHsāng;
-unhealthy	不健康	bújyànkāng	bātgiHnhòng

inscribe v. t.

-engrave	彫刻	dyāukè;	tiuhāak;
-write	書寫	shūsyě	syùsé (sé)

insect n.

	昆蟲	kwūnchúng	kwànchùHng

insecure a.

-unsafe	不安全	bùǎnchywán	bātònchyùHn;
-not secure	不安穩	bùānwěn	bātònwán

insert v. t.

	挿入	chārù	chaapyaHp

inside a.

	裏面	lǐmyàn;	léuiHmiHn(léuiHbiHn)
	裏頭	lǐtou	léuiHtàuH

insist v. i.

-persist	堅持	jyānchí;	gìnchìH;
-make firm demand	偏要	pyānyàu	pìnyiu

insolent a.

	無禮	wúlǐ;	mòuHláiH;
-haughty	傲慢	àumàn;	ngouHmaaHn;

-overbearing	驕橫	jyāuhèng	gìuwàaHng
inspect v. t.			
-as goods	檢查	jyǎnchá;	gímchàH;
-as by customs	查驗	cháyàn;	chàHyiHm;
-school, factory	視查	shìchá;	siHchàH;
-troops	檢閲	jyǎnywè	kímyuHt
inspiration n.	靈感	línggǎn	lìHnggám
inspire v. t.			
-affect	感化	gǎnhwà;	gámfa;
-inhale	吸入	syìrù	kāpyaHp
install v. t.			
-in an office	就職	jyòujf;	jauHjìk;
-as light, etc.	裝	jwāng	jòug
instalment n.	分期付欵	fēnchifùkwǎn	fànkèiHfuHfún
instance			
-n. example	實例	shflì;	saHtlaiH;
-n. request	要求	yāuchyóu;	yìukàuH;
-v. t. cite	引證	yǐnjèng	yáHnjing
instant			
-a. immediate	立刻	lìkè;	laHphāak;
-n. the present month	本月	běnywè;	búnyuHt;
-a. urgent	緊急	jǐnjí	gángāp
instead adv.			
-in the place	代替	dàitì;	doiHtai;
-in lieu	更代	gēngdài	gàngdoiH
instigate v. t.			
-urge forward	唆使	swōshř;	sòsí (tìubuHt);
-foment	煽動	shāndùng	sinduHng
instinct n.	本能	běnnéng;	búnnàHng;
	天性	tyānsyìng	tìnsing

institute

-n. college　　學院　　sywéywàn;　　hoHkyún;

-v. t. establish　　設立　　shèlì;　　chitlaHp;

-v. t. originate　　創辦　　chwàngbàn　　chongbaaHn

instruct v. t.

-direct　　指導　　jǐdǎu;　　jídouH;

-teach　　教授　　jyàushòu;　　gaausauH;

-inform　　通知　　tūngjr̄;　　tùngjì;

-admonish　　教訓　　jyàusyùn　　gaaufan

instruction n.

-teaching　　教訓　　jyàusyùn;　　gaaufan;

-precept　　教條　　jyàutyáu　　gaautìuH

instrument n.

-tool　　器具　　chìjyù;　　heigeuiH;

-scientific　　儀器　　yíchì;　　yìHhei;

-of labourers　　工具　　gūngjyù　　gùnggeuiH

insubordinate a.

-not subordinate　　不服從　　bùfútsúng;　　bātfuHkchùHng;

-disobedient　　不順從　　búshwùntsúng;　　bātseuHnchùHng;

-mutinous　　叛亂　　pànlwàn　　punlyuHn

insufficient a.　　不足　　bùdzú;　　bātjūk;

　　　　不夠　　búgòu　　bātgau(m̀gau)

insult v. t.

-with contempt　　侮辱　　wǔrù;　　móuHyuHk;

-with irreverence　　褻瀆　　syèdú　　sitduHk

insurance n.　　保險　　bǎusyǎn　　bóuhím

insure v. t.

-make sure　　確實　　chywèshf;　　koksaHt;

-guarantee　　擔保　　dānbǎu　　dàambóu

intact a.

-uninjured　　　　　未損傷　　　　　wèiswǔnshāng;　　　meiHsyúnsèung;

-left entire　　　　依然完全　　　　yiránwánchywán　　　yìyìIInyùHnchyùHn

integrity n.

-honesty　　　　　誠實　　　　　　chéngshf;　　　　　sìHngsaHt;

-moral soundness　品行端正　　　　pìnsyíngdwānjèng　hánhaHngdyùnjing

intellectual a.

-the intellect　　　智力　　　　　　jrlì;　　　　　　　jiliHk;

-understanding　　理解力　　　　　lìjyelì　　　　　　léiHgáalliHk

intelligence n.

-mental acuteness　聰明　　　　　　tsūngmíng;　　　　chùngmìHng;

-intellect　　　　智力　　　　　　jrlì;　　　　　　　jiliHk;

-sagacity　　　　伶俐　　　　　　língli;　　　　　　lìHngleiH;

-news　　　　　新聞　　　　　　syinwón;　　　　　sànmàHn;

-information　　　情報　　　　　　chíngbàu　　　　　chìHngbou

intend v. t.

-plan　　　　　　打算　　　　　　dáswàn;　　　　　dásyun;

-purpose　　　　企圖　　　　　　chìtú;　　　　　　kéiHtòuH;

-stretch　　　　　仲展　　　　　　shēnjǎn　　　　　sànjín

intensity n.

-quality of being
　intense　　　　　烈性　　　　　　lyèsyìng;　　　　　liHtsing;

-strength　　　　強力　　　　　　chyánglì　　　　　kèuHngliHk

intension n.

-intensity　　　　強度　　　　　　chyángdù;　　　　kèuHngdouH;

-strain　　　　　緊張　　　　　　jǐnjāng;　　　　　gánjèung;

-determination　　決心　　　　　　jywésyin　　　　　kyutsàm

intention n.

-meaning　　　　意思　　　　　　yìsz;　　　　　　yisi;

-purpose　　　　目的　　　　　　mùdi;　　　　　　muHkdik;

-design	主意	jŭyì	jyúyi
interaction n.	互相作用	hùsyāngdzwòyùng	wuHsèungjokyuHng
intercept v. t.			
-interrupt communication	攔住	lánjù;	làaHnjyuH;
-seize by the way	截住	jyéjù;	jiHtjyuH;
-hinder	阻止	dzŭjĭr	jójí
intercession n.	代求	dàichyóu;	doiHkàuH;
	調停	tyáutíng	tiuHtìHng
interchange			
-v. t. exchange	交換	jyāuhwàn;	gàauwuHn;
-v. i. alternate	輪流	lwúnlyóu	lèuHnlàuH
intercourse n.			
-sexual connection	性交	syìngjyāu;	singgàau;
-communication	交通	jyāutūng;	gàautùng;
-commerce	通商	tūngshāng	tùngsèung
interesting a.			
-spicy	興趣	syìngchyu;	hingcheui;
-to listen to	好聽	hăutíng	hóutèng
interfere v. i.	干涉	gānshè	gònsip
interior a.			
-inner	內在	nèidzài;	noiHjoiH;
-inland	內地	nèidì	noiHdeiH
intermarriage n.	通婚	tūnghwūn	tùngfàn
intermediate a.	中間	jūngjyēn	jūnggāan
internal a.			
-inward	內中	nèijūng;	noiHjùng;
-interior	內部	nèibù;	noiHbouH;
-as country	國內	gwónèi	gwoknoiH

international a.	國際	gwójì	gwokjai
interpolation n.	插入句	chārùjyù	chaapyaHpgeui
interpret v. t.			
-translate	傳譯	chwányì;	chyùHnyiHk;
-explain	解釋	jyěshr̀	gáaisìk
interpreter n.	翻譯員	fānyìywán	fàanyiHkyùHn
interrogate v. t.	問	wèn	maHn
interrogative a.	疑問	yíwèn;	yìHmaHn;
	發問	fāwèn	faatmaHn
interrupt v. t.			
-the continuity of	中斷	jūngdwàn;	jùngtyúHn;
-hinder	妨害	fánghài;	fòHnghoiH;
-stop	暫停	jàntíng	jaaHmtìHng
intersection n.	交切點	jyāuchyēdyǎn;	gàauchitdím;
	橫切	héngchyē	wàaHngchit
interval n.			
-space of time	間隔	jyāngé;	gaangaak;
-music	音程	yinchéng	yàmchìHng
interview v. t.			
-see	會見	hwèijyàn;	wuiHgin;
-with dignitary	謁見	yèjyàn;	yitgin;
-of dignitary	接見	jyējyàn;	jipgin;
-of pressmen	訪問	fǎngwèn	fóngmaHn
intestine n.	腸	cháng;	chèuHng;
-large	大腸	dàcháng	daaiHchèuHng
intimate a.			
-of friendship	親密	chīnmì;	chànmaHt;
-of acquaintance	熟	shóu, shú;	suHk;
-intimate friend	知己	jr̄jǐ	jìgéi

intimidate v. t.

-make fearful 畏縮 wèiswō; waisūk;

-overawe 威壓 wēiyā; wàingaat;

-cow 威嚇 wēihè wàihaak

into prep. 進入 jìnrù; jeunyaHp(yaHpheui);

進去 jìnchyu jeunheui(yaHpheui)

intolerable a. 不堪 bùkān; bāthàm;

不能忍受 bùnéngrěnshòu bātnàHngyánsauH

intolerant a.

-not enduring 不能忍耐 bùnéngrěnnài; bātnàHngyánnoiH;

-bigotted 執迷 jímí jāpmàiH

intonation n. 語調 yǔdyàu yúHdiuH

intoxicate v. t. 醉 dzwèi jeui

intransitive a.

-not passing over 不及物 bùjíwù; bātkaHpmaHt;

-not transitive 不移行 bùyísyíng bātyìHhàHng

intrigue n.

-plot 陰謀 yìnmóu; yàmmàuH;

-amour 風流艶事 fēnglyóuyànshì fùnglàuHyiHmsiH

introduce v. t. 介紹 jyèshàu; gaaisiuH;

-one who introduces 介紹人 jyèshàurén gaaisiuHyàHn

introduction n.

-of a book 緒言 syùyán; séuiHyìHn;

-treatise 初步 chūbù; chòbouH;

-letter of introduction 介紹信 jyèshàusyìn gaaisiuHseun

introvert v. t.

-turn the mind 省心 shěngsyìn; sìngsàm;

-turn inward 內轉 nèijwǎn noiHjyún

intrude v. i.

-in a conversation 插嘴 chādzwěi; chaapjéui;

-of a mob	闖進	chwǎngjìn;	chòngjeun;
-disturb	打擾	dǎrǎu;	dáyíuH;
-encroach	侵略	chǐnlywè	chàmleuk
intrust v. t.	委託	wěitwō	wáitok
intuition n.			
-cognition	直覺	jŕjywé;	jiHkgok;
-insight	洞察	dùngchá	duHngchaat
inunction n.	敷油	fūyóu	fùyàuH
inundate v. t.	淹	yūn	yìm
invade v. t.			
-with armed forces	侵略	chǐnlywè;	chàmleuk;
-infringe	侵犯	chǐnfàn	chàmfaaI ìn
invalid			
-a. weak	虛弱	syūrwò;	hèuiyeuHk;
-a. sickly	有病	yǒubìng;	yáuHbeHng;
-a. null	作廢	dzwòfèi;	jokfai;
-n. sick person	病人	bìngrén;	beIIngyàIIn;
-invalided soldiers	傷兵	shāngbìng	sèungbìng
invaluable a.	無價之寶	wújyàjŕbǎu	mòuHgajibóu
invasion n.	侵略	chǐnlywè;	chàmleuk;
	征伐	jēngfá	jìngfaHt
invent v. t.			
-originate	發明	fāmíng;	faatmìHng;
-fabricate	捏造	nyèdzàu	niHpjouH
inventory n.	清單	chǐngdēn;	chingdāan;
-inventory of presents	禮單	lǐdān	láiIIdūan

inverse

-a.   相⊥反ㄈㄢ   syāngfǎn;   sèungfáan;

-n.   反ㄈㄢ面ㄇㄧㄢ   fǎnmyàn;   fáanmiHn;

-inverse proportion   反ㄈㄢ比ㄅㄧ   fǎnbǐ   fáanbéi

invest v. t.

-lay out   投ㄊㄡ資ㄗ   tóudz̄;   tàuHjì;

-clothe   穿ㄔㄨㄢ   chwān;   chyùn;

-besiege   圍ㄨㄟ困ㄎㄨㄣ   wéikwùn   wàiHkwan

investigate v. t.

-study   研ㄧㄢ究ㄐㄧㄡ   yánjyòu;   yìHngau;

-a matter   調ㄉㄧㄠ查ㄔㄚ   dyàuchá;   diuHchàH;

-legal cases   審ㄕㄣ查ㄔㄚ   shěnchá   sámchàH

invincible a.   無ㄨ敵ㄉㄧ   wúdí   mòuHdiHk

invisible a.

-not visible   看ㄎㄢ不ㄅㄨ見ㄐㄧㄢ   kànbújyàn;   honbātgin (táimgin)

-without form   無ㄨ形ㄒㄧㄥ   wúsyíng;   mòuHyìHng;

-invisible church   無ㄨ形ㄒㄧㄥ教ㄐㄧㄠ會ㄏㄨㄟ   wúsyíngjyàuhwèi   mòuHyìHnggaauwúi

invitation n.

-inviting   邀ㄧㄠ請ㄑㄧㄥ   yāuchǐng;   yìuchíng;

-solicitation   請ㄑㄧㄥ求ㄑㄧㄡ   chǐngchyóu;   chíngkàuH;

-invitation card   請ㄑㄧㄥ帖ㄊㄧㄝ   chǐngtyē   chéngtip

invite v. t.   邀ㄧㄠ請ㄑㄧㄥ   yāuchǐng   yìuchíng

invocation n.

-magical formula   昭ㄓㄠ示ㄕ   jāushr̀;   jiusiH;

-prayer   禱ㄉㄠ告ㄍㄠ   dǎugàu   tóugou

invoice n.   發ㄈㄚ票ㄆㄧㄠ   fāpyàu;   faatpiu;

-invoice of account   清ㄑㄧㄥ單ㄉㄢ   chǐngdān   chǐngdāan

invoke v. t.   祈ㄑㄧ求ㄑㄧㄡ   chíchyóu;   kèiHkàuH;

	懇求	kěnchyóu	hánkàuH
involve v. t.			
-contain	包含	bāuhán;	bànuhàHm;
-implicate	連累	lyánlèi;	lìHnleuiH;
-wind	纏繞	chánrǎu;	chìHnyíuH;
-engage thoroughly	專心	jwānsyin	jyùnsàm
inward a.			
-thoughts	內心	nèisyin;	noiHsàm;
-interior	內部	nèihù;	noiHhouH;
-inland	內地	nèidì	noiHdeiH
iodine n.	碘酒	dyǎnjyǒu	dínjáu
iron			
-n. metal	鐵	tyě;	tit;
-n. flat	熨斗	tòngdǒu;	tongdáu;
-v. t. clothing	熨	tàng;	tong;
-Iron Age	鐵器時代	tyěchìshfdài	titheisìHdoiH
irregular a.			
-to rules	不規則	bùgwēidzé;	bātkwaijak;
-to natural laws	亂	lwàn;	lyuHn;
-uneven	不整齊	bùjěngchí	bātjíngchàiH(m̀chàiHjíng)
irreverent a.			
-blasphemous	褻漫	syèmàn;	sitmaaHn;
-not reverent	不敬	bújìng	bātging
irrigate v. t.	灌溉	gwàngài	gunkoi
irritable a.	易怒	yìnù	yiHnouH
is v. i.	是	shì;	siH (haiH);
-is it or is it not	是否	shìfǒu	siHfáu
island n.	島	dǎu;	dóu;
-in the sea	海島	hǎidǎu;	hóidóu;
-in the river	洲	jōu	jàu

islet n.	小島	syăudău	síudóu
isolate v. t.			
-infected persons	隔離	gélí;	gaaklèiH;
-place apart	隔開	gékāi	gaakhòi
issue			
–v. t. of books, etc.	發行	fāháng;	faathòHng;
–v. t. make public	發表	fābyău;	faatbíu;
–v. t. discharge	流出	lyóuchū	làuHchēut;
–n. final result	結果	jyégwŏ	gitgwó
it pro.			
-inanimate	它	twō;	tà;
-lower animal	牠	tā	tà (kéuiH)
italics n.	斜體字	syétĭdż	chetáijiH
itch n.	癢	yăng	yéuHng (hàHn)
item n.	項	syàng;	hòHng;
	條	tyáu	tìuH
itinerary n.	遊程	yóuchéng	yàuHchìHng
itself pro.	他自已	tā dżjĭ	tà jiHgéi(kéuiH jiHgé
ivory n.	象牙	syàngyá	jeuHngngàH
J			
jacket n.	短外衣	dwănwàiyĭ;	dyúnngoiHyĭ (dyúnngoiHtou);
	夾克	jyákè	gaaphāak(jēkkeHk)
jade n.	玉	yù	yuHk
jail n.	監牢	jyēnláu;	gàamlòuH;
	監獄	jyēnyù	gàamyuHk
jailer n.	禁卒	jìndzú;	gamjēut;
	獄吏	yùlì	yuHkleiH
January n.	正月	Jēngywè;	JìngyuHt;
	一月	Yĭywè	YātyuHt

jar n.

-bottle	瓶	píng;	píHng (jēun);
-of large dimensions	缸	gēng;	gòng;
-deep vessel	罐	gwàn	gun、

jaundice n. 黃膽病 hwángdǎnbìng wòHngdáambeHng

jaw n. 牙床 yáchwáng ngàHchòHng

jealous a. 嫉妒 jídù; jaHtdou;
妒忌 dùji dougeiH

jealousy n. 妒忌心 dùjìsyīn dougeiHsàm

jeep n. 吉普車 jipǔchē gātpóuchè

jelly n. 果醬 gwǒjyàng; gwójeuHng;
-made from agar-agar 涼粉 lyángfěn lèuHngfán

jet v. i. 噴射 pēnshè panseH

jewel n.

-precious stone	寶石	bǎushí;	bóuseHk;
-gem	寶玉	bǎuyù;	bóuyúk;
-collectively	珠寶	jūbǎu	jyùbóu

jingle n. 叮噹聲 dīngdāngshēng dīngdōngsèng

job n.

-employment	職業	jíyè;	jikyiHp;
-piece of work	工作	gūngdzwò	gùngjok

join v. t.

-club, etc.	加入	jyōrù;	gàyaHp;
-unite	聯合	lyánhé;	lyùHnhaHp;
-as bones	接	jyē;	jip;
-join together	聯合	lyánhé	lyùHnhaHp

joint n.

-of bones	關節	gwēnjyé;	gwàanjit;
-Mech.	接合	jyēhé	jiphaHp

joke

-n.   笑話   syàuhwà;   siuwá;

-v. i.   開玩笑   kāiwánsyàu   hòiwuHnsiu (gónsíu)

jolly a.

-joy   快樂   kwàile;   faailoHk;

-delightful   高興   gāusying   gòuhing

journal n.

-daily register   日誌   ɽjɽ;   yaHtji;

-daily newspaper   日報   ɽbàu;   yaHtbou;

-of a legislative body   議事錄   yìshɽlù   yíHsiHluHk

journalist n.   新聞記者   syīnwénjìjě   sànmàHngeijé

journey n.

-distance travelled   路程   lùchéng;   louHchìHng;

-trip   旅行   lyǔsyíng   léuiHhàHng

joy n.

-delight   喜樂   syǐlè;   héiloHk;

-gladness   愉快   yùkwài   yùHfaai

joyful a.   快樂   kwàile;   faailoHk;

-joyful news   喜信   syǐsyìn   héiseun

jubilee n.   五十週年紀念   wǔshɽjōunyánjìnyàn;   ńgHsaHpjàunìHngéiniHm;

-jubilee meeting   紀念會   jìnyànhwèi;   geiniHmwúi;

-Jubilee Year   禧年   syǐnyán   héiniHn

judge

-v. t. in a court   審判   shěnpàn;   sámpun;

-v. t. estimate   估價   gūjyà;   gúga;

-v. t. as work of art   鑑定   jyàndìng;   gaamdiHng;

-n. judicial officer   審判官   shěnpàngwān;   sámpungùn;

-n. magistrate   推事   twēishɽ;   tèuisí;

-n. umpire   裁判員   tsáipànywán   chòiHpunyùHn

judgement n.

-act of judging	審判	shěnpàn;	sámpun;
-faculty	判斷力	pàndwànlì	pundyunliHk

juice n. 汁 — jī — jāp

July n. 七月 — chīywè — chātyuHt

jump v. i. 跳 — tyàu — tiu

jumper n. 長衫 — chángdzáu — chèuHngjoHk

June n. 六月 — lyòuywè — luHkyuHt

jungle n. 叢林 — tsúnglín — chùHnglàHm

junior

-a. younger	年幼	nyányòu;	nìHnyau;
-n. by generation	後輩	hòubèi	hauHbui
-junior middle school	初中	chūjūng	chòjùng

junk n.

-Chinese	帆船	fānchwán;	fàaIIusyùHn;
-2nd hand article	舊貨	jyòuhwò;	gauHfo;
-waste paper	廢紙	fèijř	faijí

jurisdiction n.

-upon a case	裁判權	tsáipànchywán;	chòiHpunkyùHn;
-judical function	司法權	sžfáchywán	sífaatkyùHn

jury n. 陪審員 — péishěnywán — pùiHsámyùHn

just

-a. impartial	公平	gūngpíng;	gùngpìHng;
-a. upright	正直	jèngjŕ;	jingjiHk;
-adv. exactly	剛才	gāngtsái;	gòngchòiH;
-just come	剛來	gānglái	gònglòiH (ngāamngāamlàiH)

justice n.

-rectitude	正義	jèngyì;	jingyiH;
-fairness	公道	gūngdàu;	gùngdouH;
-impatiality	公平	gūngpíng	gùngpìHng

justification n.	稱義	chēngyì	chìngyiH
justify v. t.			
-vindicate	證明	jèngmíng;	jingmìHng;
-warrant	保證	báujèng	bóujing

K

kaleidoscope n.	萬花筒	wànhwātŭng	maaHnfàtùHng
kapok n.	木棉	mùmyán	muHkmìHn
keel n.	龍骨	lúnggŭ	lùHnggwāt
keep v. t.			
-observe	遵守	dzwūnshŏu;	jèunsáu;
-maintain	維持	wéichŕ;	wàiHchìH;
-watch	看守	kānshŏu;	hònsáu;
-keep morning watch	守晨更	shŏuchénggēng;	sáusàHngàng;
-keep in order	保持整齊	băuchŕ jĕngchŕ;	bóuchìH jĭngchàiH;
-keep quiet	安靜	ānjìng	ònjiHng
keeper n.	看門的	kānménke	hònmHndĭk
kennel n.	狗房	gŏufáng;	gáufòHng(gáungūk);
	狗窩	gŏuwō	gáuwō
kerosene n.	煤油	méiyŏu	mùiHyàuH
kettle n.	水壺	shwĕihú	séuiwú
key			
-n. of a lock	鑰匙	yàushr;	yeuHksìH(sósìH);
-n. to a problem	解答	jyĕdá;	gáaidaap;
-a. chief	主要	jŭyàu;	jyúyiu;
-a. fundamental	基本	jībĕn	gèibún
key-note n.	基音	jīyīn	gèiyàm
khaki n.	黃斜布	hwángsyébù	wòHngchébou
kick v. t.	踢	tī;	tek;
-kick ball	踢球	tīchyóu	tekkàuH(tekbō)
kidnap v. t.			
-seize for ransom	綁票	băngpyàu;	bóngpiu;

English	Chinese		
-decoy away	拐帶	gwǎidài	gwáaidaai
kidney n.	腎	shèn;	saHn;
	腎臟	shèndzàng	saHnjoHng
kill v. t.			
-slay	殺	shā;	saat;
-by a blow	打死	dǎsž;	dáséi;
-by a fall	跌死	dyésž;	ditséi;
-by collision	撞死	jwàngsž	joHngséi
kilogram (2,2046pds.) n.	仟克	chyēnkè	chìnhāak
kilometer (3,280.8ft.) n.	仟米	chyānmǐ	chìnmáiH
kind			
-a. gracious	仁慈	réntsź;	yàHnchìH;
-n. sort	種類	jǔnglèi;	júngleuiH;
-a. friendly	和氣	héchì;	wòHhei;
-kind intention	美意	měiyì	méiHyi
kindergarten n.	幼稚園	yòujìrywán	yaujiHyún
kindle v. t.			
-as firecrackers	點	dyǎn;	dím;
-as passions	發火	fāhwǒ	faatfó
kindness n.			
-beneficence	善行	shànsyíng;	siIInhàIIng;
-good will	仁愛	rénài	yàHnngoi
kindred n.			
-relationship	親族	chìndzú;	chànjuHk;
-by blood	內親	nèichìn;	noiHchàn;
-by marriage	外戚	wàichì	ngoiHchìk
king n.	國王	gwówáng;	gwokwòHng;
-king's palace	王宮	wánggūng	wòHnggùng

kinsfolk n.

  -relative   親戚   chǐnchi;   chānchìk;

  -kindred   親族   chǐndzú   chànjuHk

kiss

  -v. t.   接吻   jyēwěn;   jipmáHn;

          親嘴   chǐndzwěi;   chànjéui;

  -n.   吻   wěn   máHn

kitchen n.   廚房   chúfáng   chèuiHfóng

kite n.   風箏   fēngjēng   fùngjàng(jíyíu)

kitten n.   小貓   syǎumāu   síumāau(māaujái)

knee n.   膝   syǐ   sāt(sāttàuHgō)

kneel v. i.   跪   gwèi;   gwaiH;

          屈膝   chyūsyǐ(lit.)   wātsāt(lit.)

knife n.   刀   dāu   dōu

knight n.

  -ranking   爵士   jywéshr̀;   jeuksiH;

  -rider   騎士   chíshr̀   kèHsiH

knit v. t.   織   jr̄   jik

knock v. t.   打   dǎ;   dá;

  -knock the door   叩門   kòumén;   kaumùHn (paakmùH

          打門   dǎmén   dámùHn (paakmùHn

knot n.   結   jyé   git(lit)

know v. t.

  -as a fact   知道   jr̄dau;   jìdou;

  -understand   明白   míngbai;   mìHngbaaHk;

  -acquainted with   相識   syāngshr̀;   sèungsìk;

  -recognise   認得   rènde   yiHngdāk

knowledge n.

  -learning   知識   jr̄shr;   jìsìk;

  -experience   學識   sywéshr̀;   hoHksìk;

-understanding	認識	rènshr	yiHngsik
know-nothing adv.	一無所知	yìwúswǒjr̄	yātmòuHsójì
knuckle n.	指節	jr̄jyé	jíjit

L

ladel

-n. slip	標籤	byāuchyān;	bìuchìm;
-v. t. tag	貼紙	tyējr̄	tipjí
labor, labour n.			
-fatigue	勞力	láulì;	lòuHliHk;
-hard work	苦工	kǔgūng;	fúgūng;
-parturition	分娩	fēnmyǎn;	fànmiHn;
toiloome	勞苦	láukǔ	lòuHfú
laboratory n.	實驗室	shŕfyànshr̀	saHtyìHmsàt
lace n.	花邊	hwābyān	fābìn
lack			
-v. t. want	缺少	chywēshǎu;	kyutsíu;
-v. i. be short	短少	dwǎnshǎu;	dyúnsíu;
-n. deficiency	不足	bùdzú	bātjūk (m̀gau)
lacquer			
-n.	油漆	yóuchì;	yàuHchāt;
-v. t.	上漆	shàngchì	sóuHngchāt
ladder n.	梯	tī	tài
ladle n.	長柄勺	chángbìngsháu	chèuHngbengcheuk
lady n.	女郎	nyǔláng;	néuiHlòHng;
	少女	shàunyǔ	siunéuiH
laity n.	平信徒	píngsyìntú	pìHngseuntòuH
lake n.	湖	hú	wùH
lamb n.	羔羊	gāuyáng;	gòuyèuHng;
	小羊	syǎuyang	siuyèuIIng (yèuHngjái)

lame a.	瘸腿	chywétwěi	kèHtéui (bàigeuk)
lamp n.	燈	dēng;	dāng;
-light a lamp	點燈	dyàndēng	dímdāng

land

-n. as dist. from sea	陸地	lùdì;	luHkdeiH;
-n. ground	土地	tǔdì;	tóudeiH;
-v. t. from boat	上岸	shàngàn;	séuHngngoHn;
-v. t. from plane	降落	jyànglwò;	gongloHk;
-by land	由陸路	yóu lùlù	yàuH luHklouH
landing n.	登陸	dēnglù;	dàngluHk;
	上岸	shàngàn	séuHngngoHn

landlord n.

-of land	地主	dìjǔ;	deiHjyú;
-of field	田主	tyánjǔ;	tìHnjyú;
-of house	房東	fángdūng;	fòHngdūng;
-of property	業主	yèjǔ	yiHpjyú
landmark n.	界石	jyèshŕ	gaaiseHk

landscape n.

-picture	山水	shānshwěi;	sàanséui;
-scenery	風景	fēngjǐng	fùnggíng
lane n.	小巷	syàusyàng	siuhoHng
language n.	語言	yǔyán	yúHyìHn
-literary language	文言	wényán;	màHnyìHn;
-colloquial language	白話	báihwà;	baaHkwá;
-spoken language	口語	kǒuyǔ	háuyúH

lantern n.

-paper	燈籠	dēnglúng;	dānglùHng;
-portable	手燈	shǒudēng;	sáudāng;
-street light	街燈	jyēdēng;	gāaidāng;
-lantern feast	元宵節	ywánsyāujyé	yùHnsiujit

ap n.	膝部	syìbù	sātbouH
ap-dog n.	膝狗	syìgǒu	sātgáu
arceny n.	偷竊	tōuchyè	tàusit
ard n.	猪油	jūyóu	jyùyàuH
arge n.	大	dà	daaiII
ark n.	百靈鳥	bǎilíngnyǎu	baaklìHngnìuH
ash v. t.			
-beat	打	dǎ;	dá;
-flog	鞭打	byāndǎ	bìndá
ast a.			
-final	最後	dzwèihòu;	jeuihauH;
-most recent	最近	dzwèijìn;	jeuigaIIn;
-last month	上個月	shànggcywè;	seuHnggoyuHt;
-last week	上個禮拜	shànggelǐbài;	seuHnggolǎiHbaaïŋ
-last day	末日	mwòɩ;	muHtyaHt;
-lasting forever	永遠長存	yǔngywǎncháng-tswún	wíHngyúHnchèuHng-chyùHn
latch n.	插梢	chāshāu	chaapsìu
late a.	遲	chf;	chìH;
-recent	最近	dzwèijìn;	jeuigaHn;
-of an office	前任	chyánrèn	chìHnyaHm
lately adv.	近來	jìnlái;	gaHnlòiH;
	最近	dzwèijìn	jeuigaHn
latent a.			
-hidden	隱藏	yìntsáng;	yánchòHng;
-latent power	潛勢力	`chyánshìlì;	chìHmsailiHk;
-latent period	潛伏期	chyánfúchì	chìHmfuHkkèiH
later adv.	較晚	jyàuwǎn;	gaaumáaHn (gaauchìH);
-sooner or later	早晚	dzǎuwǎn	jóumáaHn(chìHjóu)
latitude n.	緯度	wěidù	wáiHdouH

latter a.

  -last 最後 dzwèihòu; jeuihauH;

  -opp. to former 後者 hòujě hauHjé

laugh

  –v. i. smile 笑 syàu; siu;

  –v. t. ridicule 嘲笑 cháusyàu jāausiu(gèisiu)

laughable a. 可笑 kěsyàu hósiu

launch

  –n. 汽艇 chìtǐng; heitéHng;

  –v. t. 下水 syàshwěi haHséui(loHkséui)

laundry n. 洗衣房 syǐyìfáng; sáiyìfòHng;

           洗衣店 syǐyìdyàn sáiyìdim

lavatory n.

  -for washing hands 盥洗室 gwànsyǐshr̀; gunsáisāt;

  -w. c. 厠所 tsèswǒ chisó

lavish v. t. 浪費 làngfèi loHngfai

law n. 法律 fǎlyù; faatleuHt;

           律法 lyùfǎ; leuHtfaat;

  -science 定律 dìnglyù; dihngleuHt;

  -governmental law 政府法律 jèngfǔ fǎlyù; jingfú faatleuHt;

  -canon law 宗教法 dzūngjyàufǎ; jùnggaaufaat;

  -moral law 道德律 dàudélyù douHdākleuHt

lawful a. 合法 héfǎ haHpfaat

lawless a. 無法 wúfǎ; mòuHfaat;

           非法 fēifǎ; fèifaat;

           違法 wéifǎ wàiHfaat

lawlessness n. 不法 bùfǎ bātfaat

lawsuit n. 訟事 sùngshr̀; juHngsiH;

           案件 ànjyàn ongiHn

lawyer n. 律師 lyùshī leuHtsī

lay v. t.

-set down	放	fàng;	fong;
-spread	舖	pū;	pòu;
-as bricks	砌	chì	chai;
-lay hown	放下	fàngsyà;	fonghaH(fongdài);
-lay hold of	拿住	nájù;	nàHjyuH(jūkjyuH);
-lay hands on	按手	ànshǒu	onsáu
-do violence	動手	dùngshǒu	duHngsáu(yūksáu)

layman n.

-laity	平信徒	píngsyìntú;	pìHngseuntòuII;
-non-expert	外行	wàiháng;	ngoiHhòHng;
-Budd.	居士	jyūshì	gèuisiH

lazy a.

-disliking exertion	懶惰	lǎndwò;	láaHndoH;
-loafing	遊手好閒	yóushǒuhàusyán	yàuIIsáuhouhàaIIn

lead

-v. t. instruct	引導	yǐndǎu;	yáHndouH;
-v. t. direct	指揮	jǐhwēi;	jífài;
-n. mineral	鉛	chyān	yùHn

leader n.

-chief	領袖	lǐngsyòu;	líHngjauH;
commanding officer	隊長	dwèijǎng;	deuiIIjéung;
-leader of meeting	主席	jǔsyí	jyńjiHk

leaf n.

-of a book	頁	yè;	yiHp;
-of tree	樹葉	shùyè;	syuHyiHp;
-of a door	扇	shàn	sin

league n.

-association	聯盟	lyánméng;	lyùHnmàHng;
-party	黨	dǎng;	dóng;

La

-league of nations	國際聯盟會	gwójìlyánménghwèi	gwokjailyùHnmàHngwú
leak			
-n. a crack	漏洞	lòudùng;	lauHduHng;
-v. i. of electricity	漏電	lòudyàn	lauHdiHn
lean			
-v. i. incline	靠	kàu;	kaau;
-a. thin	瘦	shòu;	sau;
-lean meat	瘦肉	shòuròu;	sauyuHk;
-lean against	靠住	kàujù	kaaujyuH
leap v. i.	跳	tyàu	tiu
learn v. t.	學習	sywésyí	hoHkjaaHp
learned a.			
-having knowledge	有學問	yǒusywéwèn;	yáuHhoHkmaHn;
-clever	聰明	tsūngming	chùngmìHng
learning n.	學問	sywéwèn;	hoHkmaHn;
	學識	sywéshr̀;	hoHksìk;
	才學	tsáisywé	chòiHhoHk
lease v. t.			
-land, building	租	dzū;	jòu;
-territory	租借	dzūjyè	jòuje
least a.			
-in quantity	最少	dzwèishǎu;	jeuisíu;
-in size	最小	dzwèisyǎu;	jeuisíu;(jeuisai);
-at least	至少	jr̀shǎu	jisíu
leather n.	皮革	pígé;	pèiHgaak;
	皮	pí	pèiH
leave			
-v. t. quit	退	twèi;	teui;
-v. t. desert	拋棄	pàuchì;	pàauhei;

-v. t. of a ship, train	開ㄎㄞ	kāi;	hòi;
-n. holiday	放ㄈㄤ 假ㄐㄚ	fàngjyà;	fongga;
-leave behind	留ㄌㄡ 下ㄒㄚ	lyóusyà	làuHhaH(làuHdài)
leaves n.	樹ㄕㄨ 葉ㄧㄝ	shùyè	syuHyiHp
leaven			
-n.	酵ㄒㄠ	syàu;	hàau;
-v. t.	發ㄈㄚ 酵ㄒㄠ	fāsyàu	faathàau
lecture n.	演ㄧㄢ 講ㄐㄤ	yǎnjyǎng	yíngóng
ledge n.			
-raised edge	高ㄍㄠ 邊ㄅㄢ	gāubyēn;	gōubin;
-shelf	架ㄐㄚ	jyà	gá
ledger n.	總ㄗㄨㄥ 賬ㄓㄤ	dzǔngjàng;	júngjeung;
	分ㄈㄣ 類ㄌㄟ 賬ㄓㄤ	fēnlèijàng	fànleuiHjeung
leek n.	韭ㄐㄧㄡ 菜ㄘㄞ	jyǒutsài	gáuchoi
left a.	左ㄗㄨㄛ	dzwǒ	jó
leg n.			
-as of pork	腿ㄊㄨㄟ	twěi;	téui;
-whole leg	腳ㄐㄧㄠ	jyǎu;	geuk;
-knee to ankle	小ㄒㄧㄠ 腿ㄊㄨㄟ	syǎutwǒi;	siutéui:
-thigh	大ㄉㄚ 腿ㄊㄨㄟ	dàtwěi	daaiHtéui
legacy n.	遺ㄧ 贈ㄗㄥ	yídzèng	wàiHjaHng
legal a.			
-lawful	合ㄏㄜ 法ㄈㄚ	héfǎ;	haHpfaat;
-based on law	律ㄌㄩ 法ㄈㄚ 上ㄕㄤ	lyùfǎshàng;	leuHtfaatseuHng;
-fixed by law	法ㄈㄚ 定ㄉㄧㄥ	fǎdìng	faatdiHng
legalism n.	律ㄌㄩ 法ㄈㄚ 主ㄓㄨ 義ㄧ	lyùfǎjǔyì	leuHtfaatjyúyiH
legend n.	傳ㄔㄨㄢ 奇ㄑㄧ	chwánchí;	chyùHnkèiH;
	古ㄍㄨ 談ㄊㄢ	gǔtán	gútàaHm
legislative a.	立ㄌㄧ 法ㄈㄚ	lìfǎ;	laIIpfaat;

-Legislative Assembly	立法院	Lìfǎywàn	LaHpfaatyún;
-legislative body	立法部	lìfábù	laHpfaatbouH
legitimate a.			
-lawfully begotton	嫡出	díchū;	diHkchēut;
-real	眞實	jēnshf;	jànsaHt;
-lawful	合法	héfǎ	haHpfaat
leisure n.	閒暇	syánsyá;	hàaHnhaH (dākhàaHn)
	空閒	kūngsyán	hùnghàaHn
lemon n.	檸檬	nìngméng	nìHngmūng
lend v. t.	借出	jyèchū;	jechēut;
-lend a hand	幫忙	bāngmáng	bòngmòHng
length n.			
-opp. to breadth	長度	chángdù;	chèuHngdouH;
-of timd	長久	chángjyǒu	chèuHnggáu
lengthen v. t.			
-by adding	加長	jyācháng;	gàchèuHng;
-by pulling	拉長	lācháng;	làaichèuHng;
-as time	延長	yáncháng	yìHnchèuHng
lenient a.			
-generous	寬容	kwānrúng;	fùnyùHng;
-mild	溫和	wēnhé;	wànwòH;
-tolerant	大量	dàlyàng	daaiHleuHng
Leninism n.	列寧主義-	Lyèníngjǔyì	LiHtnìHngjyúyìH
lens n.			
-camera	透鏡	tòujìng;	taugeng;
-Anat.	水晶體	shwěijingtǐ	séuijingtái
leopard n.	豹	bàu	paau
leper n.	大痲瘋	dàmáfēng	daaiHmàHfūng
leprosy n.	痲瘋病	máfēngbìng	màHfūngbeHng

less

-a. in quantity	較ㄐㄠ 少ㄕㄠ	jyàushǎu;	gaausíu;
-a. in size	較ㄐㄠ 小ㄒㄠ	jyàusyǎu;	gaausíu (gaausai);
-prep. minus	減ㄐㄢ	jyǎn;	gáam;
-far less	遠ㄩㄢ 不ㄅㄨ 及ㄐ	ywǎnbùji;	yúHnbātkaHp;
-less & less	越ㄩㄝ 來ㄌㄞ 越ㄩㄝ 少ㄕㄠ	ywèláiywèshǎu	yuHtlàiHyuHtsíu

lesson n.

-reading	功ㄍㄨㄥ 課ㄎㄜ	gūngkè;	gùngfo;
-teaching	教ㄐㄠ 訓ㄒㄩㄣ	jyàuoyùn	gaaufan

lest conj. 免ㄇㄧㄢ 得ㄉㄜ — myǎnde — míHndāk

let v. t.

-allow	准ㄓㄨㄣ	jwǔn;	jéun;
-for hire	出ㄔㄨ 租ㄗㄨ	chūdzū	chēutjòu

letter n. 信ㄒㄧㄣ — syìn; — seun;

-a letter	一ㄧ 封ㄈㄥ 信ㄒㄧㄣ	yīfēngsyìn;	yātfùngseun;
-send a letter	寄ㄐ 信ㄒㄧㄣ	jìsyìn;	geiseun;
-ordinary letter	平ㄆㄧㄥ 信ㄒㄧㄣ	píngsyìn;	pìHngseun;
-registered letter	掛ㄍㄨㄚ 號ㄏㄠ 信ㄒㄧㄣ	gwàhàusyìn;	gwahouHseun;
-letter of alphabet	字ㄗ 母ㄇㄨ	dzìmǔ;	jiHmóuH;
-letter of introduction	介ㄐㄧㄝ 紹ㄕㄠ 信ㄒㄧㄣ	jyèshàusyìn	gaaisiuIIseun

lettuce n. 生ㄕㄥ 菜ㄘㄞ — shēngtsài — sāangchoi

level n.

-horizontal	水ㄕㄨㄟ 平ㄆㄧㄥ	shwěipíng;	séuipìHng;
-rank	程ㄔㄥ 度ㄉㄨ	chéngdù;	chìHngdouH;
-standard	水ㄕㄨㄟ 準ㄓㄨㄣ	shwěijwǔn	séuijéun

lever n. 槓ㄍㄤ 桿ㄍㄢ — gànggǎn — gonggòn

liability n. 責ㄗㄜ 任ㄖㄣ — dzérèn; — jaakyaHm;

義ㄧ 務ㄨ — yìwù — yiHmouH

liar n. 說ㄕㄨㄛ 謊ㄏㄨㄤ 的ㄉㄜ — shwōhwǎngde — syutfōngdik (góngdaaiHwaHge)

libel n.	破壞名譽	pwòhwàimíngyù	powaaiHmìHngyuH

liberal a.

-generous	慷慨	kǎngkài;	hóngkoi;
-from narrow ideas	大量	dàlyàng	daaiHleuHng;
-liberal arts	文藝	wényì;	màHnngaiH;
-liberal party	自由黨	dzyóudǎng;	jiHyàuHdóng;
-liberal translation	意譯	yìyì	yiyiHk

liberty n.

-freedom	自由	dzyóu;	jiHyàuH;
-liberty bond	獎券	jyǎngjywàn;	jéunggyun;
-liberty & quality	自由平等	dzyóu píngděng;	jiHyàuH pìHngdáng;
-liberty, Statue of	自由神	dzyóushén	jiHyàuHsàHn

library n.

-public	圖書館	túshūgwǎn;	tòuHsyùgún;
-reading room	書房	shūfáng;	syùfóng;
-series of books	文庫	wénkù	màHnfu

licence n.

| -document | 執照 | jŕjàu; | jāpjiu; |
| -permission | 許可證 | syúkějèng | héuihójing |

| lick v. t. | 舐 | ιyǎn | tíHm |

| lid n. | 蓋 | gài | goi |

lie

| -v. i. | 說謊 | shwōhwǎng; | syutfòng (góngdaaiHwaH); |
| -n. | 謊話 | hwǎnghwà | fòngwaH(daaiHwaH) |

life n.

-of animate existence	命	mìng;	meHng;
	生命	shēngmìng;	sàngmiHng;
	性命	syìngmìng;	singmiHng;
-manner of living	生活	shēnghwó;	sàngwuHt;
-biography	生平	shēngpíng	sàngpìHng

lifeblood n.	心 血	syīnsywě;	sàmhyut;
	精 力	jīnglì	jīngliHk
lifeboat n.	救 生 船	jyòushēngchwán	gausàngsyùHn
lifeless a.			
-spiritless	無 生 氣	wúshēngchì;	mòuHsànghei (móuHmāthéisik)
-dead	死 的	szde	séidik (séige)
lifetime n.	一 生	yìshēng;	yātsàng;
	終 身	jūngshēn	jūngsàn
lift			
-v. t. anything heavy	舉	jyǔ;	géui;
-v. t. with both hands	擡	tái;	tòiH;
-v. t. as a lid	打 開	dǎkāi;	dáhòi;
-n. elevator	電 梯	dyànti;	diHntài;
-lift up the head	擡 頭	táitóu;	tòiHtàuH (dàamgòugotàuII);
-lift up the eyes	舉 目	jyǔmù	géuimuHk
light			
-n. opp. of darkness	光	gwāng;	gwòng;
-a. bright	光 亮	gwānglyàng;	gwòngleuHng;
-a. not heavy	輕	chīng;	hèng;
-a. in colour	淺	chyǎn;	chín;
-v. t. illuminate	照	jàu;	jiu;
-v. t. as a lamp	點	dyǎn;	dím;
-light a lamp	點 燈	dyǎndēng	dímdēng
lighthouse n.	燈 塔	dēngtǎ	dāngtaap
lightning n.	閃 電	shǎndyàn	símdiHn
like			
-v. t. please	喜 歡	syǐhwan;	héifùn (jùngyi)
-a. alike	像	syàng;	jeuHng (chíH);

-just like	好像	hăusyàng;	hóujeuHng (hóuchíH);
-like manner, in	照樣	jàuyàng;	jiuyéung;
-like-minded	同心同意	túngsyĭntúngyì	tùHngsàmtùHngyi

likeness n.

-shape	形狀	syíngjwàng;	yìHngjoHng;
-copy	樣式	yàngsh̀;	yeuHngsĭk;
-photo	相片	syàngpyăn;	seungpin;

llly n. 百合花 băihéhwā baakhaHpfā

limb n. 手足 shŏudzú; sáujūk;

-Prot. 肢體 jr̄tĭ jìtái

lime n.

-from rock	石灰	shŕhwēi;	seHkfùi;
-fruit	萊姆	láimŭ	lòiHmóuH

limit

-n. boundary	界限	jyèsyàn;	gaaihaaHn;
-v. t. restrict	限制	syànjr̀;	haaHnjai;
-within the limit of	範圍內	fànwéinèi;	faaHnwàiHnoiH;
-without limit	無限	wúsyàn;	mòuHhaaHn;
-limited period	期限	chĭsyàn	kèiHhaaHn

limitless a.

-having no limits	無限	wúsyàn;	mòuHhaaHn;
-boundless	無邊	wúbyān	mòuHbĭn

limp v. i. 瘸着走 chywéjedzŏu kèHjeuHkjáu
(bàiháHhàaHng)

line n.

-thread	線	syàn;	sin;
-stroke	畫	hwà;	waaHk;
-row	行	háng;	hòHng;
-line, straight	直線	jŕsyàn;	jiHksìn;

-line of vision	視線	shìsyàn	siHsin
linen n.	麻布	mábù	màHbou
linger v. i.			
-delay	躭擱	dānge;	dàamgok;
-loiter	遲延	chfyán;	chìHyìHn;
-saunter	漫步	mànbù;	maaHnbouH;
-a lingering illness	纏綿的疾病	chánmyándejíbìng	chìHnmìHndikjaHtbeHng
linguist n.	語言學家	yǔyánsywéjyā	yúHyìHnhoHkgā
link			
-n. of a chain	環	hwán;	wàaHn;
-v. t. join	連	lyán	lìHn
lining n.	襯裏	chànlǐ	chanléiH
-every cloud has a silver lining	禍中必有福	hwò-jūng-bì-yǒu-fú	woII-jùng-bìt-yáuH-fūk
lion n.	獅子	shīdz,	sijí,
-a den of lions	獅子洞	shīdzdùng	sìjíduHng
lioness n.	母獅	mǔshī	móuHsi
lip n.	嘴唇	dzwěichwín	jéuiseuIIn
liquid n.	液體	yìtǐ or yètǐ	yiHktái
liquor n.	酒	jyǒu	jáu
list n.			
-roll	表	byǎu;	bíu:
-catalogue	目錄	mùlù;	muHkluHk;
-list, make a	列單	lyèdān	liHtdāan
listen v. i.	聽	tìng	tèng
listener n.	聽衆	tìngjùng	tèngjung
litany n.	應答祈禱	yìngdá chídǎu	yingdaap kèiHtóu
literacy n.	文字教育	wéndzìjyàuyù	màHnjiHgaauyuHk
literal a.	照字面	jàudzìmyàn;	jiujiHmín;
-literal translation	直譯	jfyì;	jiHkyiHk;

-literal sense	字面的意義	dzmyànde yìyi	jiHmíndikyiyiH
literary a.	文學	wénsywé;	màHnhoHk;
-literary essays	文章	wénjēng;	màHnjèung;
-literary man	文人	wénrén;	màHnyàHn;
-literary talents	文學天才	wénsywé tyāntsái	màHnhoHk tìnchòiH
literature n.	文學	wénsywé	màHnhoHk
litter n.			
-rubbish	垃圾	lèsè;	laaHpsaap;
-of pigs	一窩	yìwō;	yātwò;
-stretcher	擔架	dānjyà	dàamga
little a.			
-few	少	shău;	síu;
-small	小	syău;	síu (sai);
-not much	沒有多少	méiyou dwōshău	muHtyáuH dòsíu (móuHgéidò)
live v. i.			
-alive	活的	hwóde;	wuHtdik;
-exist	生存	shēngtswún;	sàngchyùHn;
-dwell	住	jù;	jyuH;
-live in peace and prosperity	安居樂業	ēn-jyū-lè-yè;	òn-gèui-loHk-yiHp
-live peacefully	安居	ānjyū	òngèui
livelihood n.	生計	shēngjì;	sànggai;
	生活	shēnghwó	sàngwuHt
lively a.			
-active	活潑	hwópwo;	wuHtput;
-full of life & spirit	精神飽滿	jīngshénbăumăn;	jìngsàHnbáaumúHn;
-lively hope	活潑的盼望	hwópwode pànwàng	wuHtputdik paanmoH
liver n.	肝	gān;	gòn;
	肝臟	gāndzàng	gònjoHng

living a.

-alive	活的	hwóde;	wuHtdìk;
-livelihood	生活	shēnghwó;	sàngwuHt;
living stones	活石	hwóshf;	wuHtseHk;
-living way	活路	hwólù	wuHtlouH(sàanglouH)

load n.

-coolie's	擔	dàn;	daam;
-vehicle's	車	chē;	chè;
-ship's	載	dzài;	joi;
-heavy load	重擔	jùngdàn	chúHngdaam

loan

-v. t. lend	借出	jyèchū;	jechēut;
-n. money	借款	jyékwǎn;	jefún;
-n. raised by a state	公債	gūngjài	gùngjaai

lobster n.   龍蝦   lúngsyā   lùHnghā

local a.

-of a particular place	本地	běndì;	búndeiH;
-confined to a part	局部	jyúbù;	guHkbouH;
-local church	地方教會	dìfāng jyàuhwèi;	deiHfòng gaauwúi;
-local government	地方自治	dìfāng dz̀j̀	deiHfòng jiHjiH

location n.

-site	地點	dìdyǎn;	deiHdím;
-place	地方	dìfang;	deiHfòng;
-position	位置	wèijr	waiHji

lock n.   鎖   swǒ;   só;

-lock the door	鎖門	swǒmén;	sómùHn;
-a lock	一把鎖	yìbǎ swǒ	yātbá só

locomotive n.   火車頭   hwǒchētóu   fóchètàuH

locus n.

-Plane Geom.	軌跡	gwěiji;	gwáijìk;

-a place	地	dì;	deiH;
-locality	場 所	chǎngswǒ	chèuHngsó
locust n.	蝗 蟲	hwángchúng	wòHngchùHng
lodge			
-v. t. for keeping	寄 存	jìtswún;	geichyùHn;
-n. hut	茅 屋	máuwū;	màauHngūk;
-v. i. dwell temporarily	暫 住	jànjù	jaaHmjyuH
log			
-n. timber	大 木	dàmù;	daaiHmuHk (muHkchaam);
-v. t. to fell	伐 木	fámù	faHtmuHk
logic n.	論 理 學	lwùnlǐsywé;	leuHnléiHhoHk;
	邏 輯	lwójì	lòHchāp
loiter v. i.			
-linger	逗 留	dòulyóu;	dauHlàuH;
-dawdle	偷 懶	tōulǎn	tàuláaHn
lonely a.			
-without companions	寂 寞	jímwò;	jiHkmoHk;
-alone	單 獨	dāndú;	dàanduHk;
-feeling sad	淒 涼	chīlyáng	chàilèuHng
long			
-a. not short	長	cháng;	chèuHng;
-a. of distance	遠	ywǎn;	yúHn;
-a. of time	久	jyǒu;	gáu (noiH);
-v. i. wish	希 望	syīwàng;	hèimoHng;
-long ago	從 前	tsúngchyán;	chùHngchìHn;
-long face	憂 悶	yōumèn;	yàumuHn;
-long for	渴 慕	kěmù;	hotmouH;
-long live China	中 國 萬 歲	Jūnggwó wànswèi	Jùnggwok maaHnseui
longevity n.	長 壽	chángshòu;	chèuHngsauH;
	長 命	chángmìng	chèuHngmeHng

longing n.	切望	chyèwàng;	chìtmoHng;
-longing eyes	望穿秋水	wàngchwānchyōu shwěi	moHngchyùnchàuséui
longitude n.	經線	jìngsyàn	gìngsin
longsighted a.	遠視	vwǎnshì	yúHnsiH
long-suffering a.	堅忍	jyānrěn	gìnyáHn

look v. i.

-see	看	kàn;	hon (tái);
-pay attention	注意	jùyi;	jyuyi;
-look for	尋找	syúnjǎu;	chàHnjáau;
-look up to	仰望	yǎngwàng	yéuHngmoHng

lookout n.

-take care	注意	jùyi;	jyuyi;
-the place	瞭望臺	lyáuwàngtái	lìuHmoHngtòlH

loose

-a. not tight	鬆	sūng;	sùng;
-v. t. make loose	放鬆	fàngsūng;	fongsùng;
-v. t. unbind	打開	dǎkāi;	dáhòi;
-v. t. untie	解開	jyěkāi	gáaihòi

loot

-v. t. plunder	搶刼	chyǎngjyé;	chéunggip;
-v. t. by corruption	舞弊	wǔbì;	móuHbaiH;
-n. taken in war	戰利品	jànlìpǐn	jìnleiHbán

lose v. t.

-not to win	輸	shū;	syù;
-die	喪失	sàngshī;	songsāt;
-by mislaying	遺失	yíshr;	wàiHsāt;
-lose life	喪命	sàngmìng;	songmiHng;
-lose courage	喪膽	sàngdǎn;	songdáam;
-lose oneself	迷路	mílù	màiHlouH

loss n.

-by dropping	遺失	yíshr;	wàiHsāt;
-pecuniary. etc.	損失	swǔnshr;	syúnsāt;
-of a right. etc.	喪失	sàngshr;	songsāt;
-casualties	死傷	szshāng	séisèung

lot n.

-fate	命運	mìngyun;	miHngwaHn;
-lottery	籤	chyān;	chìm;
-a lot of	許多	syǔdwō;	héuidò (hóudò);
-cast lots	抽籤	chōuchyān	chàuchìm

lottery n.

	獎券	jyǎngjywàn;	jéunggyun;
	彩票	tsǎipyàu	chóipiu(máHbiu)

lotus n.

	蓮	lyán;	lìHn;
	荷	hé	hòH

loud a.

	大聲	dàshēng	daaiHsèng

louse n.

	蝨子	shrdz	sātjí (sātná)

lovable a.

	可愛	kěài	hóngoi

love v. t.

	愛	ài;	ngoi;
-love in compassion	愛惜	àisyí;	ngoisik;
-love & cherish	親愛	chīnài	chànngoi
-pitying love	憐愛	lyánài;	lìHnngoi;
-love one another	彼此相愛	bǐtszsyāngài	béichísèungngoi

lover n.

-one in love	愛人	àirén;	ngoiyàHn;
-paramour	情人	chíngrén	chìHngyàHn

low a.

-not high	低	dī;	dài;
-base	卑賤	bēijyàn;	bèijiHn;
-not tall	矮	ǎi;	ngái;

-not deep 淺 chyǎn chín

ower

-v. t. as things suspended 放低 fàngdi; fongdài;

-v. t. as price of goods 減 jyǎn; gáam;

-v. i. fall to a lower stage 跌 dyé; dit;

-lower classes 下流社會 syàlyóushèhwèi haHlàuHséHwúi

owly a.

-humble 卑微 bēiwéi; bèimèiH;

-modest 溫和 wēnhé; wànwòH;

-inferior 下等 syàděng haHdáng

oyal a. 忠心 jūngsyin jùngsàm

uck n. 運氣 yùnchì; waHnheı;

-bad(or ill)luck 不幸 búsyìng; bāthaHng;

-by(good)luck 幸運 syìngyùn haHngwaHn

uggage n. 行李 syínglǐ hàHngléiH

ukewarm a.

-tepid 不冷不熱 bùlěngbúrè; bātláaHngbātyiHt;

-moderately warm 溫和 wēnhé; wànwòH;

-slightly warm 半冷半熱 bànlěngbànrè bunláaHngbunyiHt

umber n. 木料 mùlyàu muHkliuH

uminous a.

-brilliant 發光 fāgwāng; faatgwòng;

-shining 照耀 jàuyàu jiuyiuH

ump

-n. mass 團 twán; tyùHn;

-v. t. unite 集合 jíhé; jaaHphaHp;

-v. i. force 勉強 myǎnchyǎng míHnkéuHng

funar calendar n. 農曆 núnglì; nùHngliHk;

	陰曆	yīnlì	yàmliHk
lunatic n.	精神病人	jīngshénbìngrén	jìngsàHnbeHngyàHn
lunch n.	午餐	wŭchān	ńgHchāan (ngaanjau)
lung n.	肺	fèi	fai
lust n.			
-desire	私慾	sźyù	sìyuHk
luxury n.	奢侈	shēchr	chèchí

M

ma	媽	mā	mā (màHmā)
macaroni n.	通心粉	tūngsyīnfĕn	tùngsàmfán
machine n.	機器	jīchì	gèihei
mad a.			
-insane	癲狂	dyānkwáng;	dìnkòHng;
-frenzied	狂妄	kwángwàng	kòHngmóHng
madam n.	婦人	fùren	fúHyàHn
madhouse n.	瘋人院	fūngrénywàn	fùngyàHnyún
magazine n.	雜誌	dzájr̀	jaaHpji
magic n.			
-charm	魔力	mwólì	móliHk;
-evil	法術	fàshù	faatseuHt;
-enchantment	魔術	mwóshù	mòseuHt
magistrate n.	法官	fàgwān	faatgùn
Magna Carta n.	大憲法	dàsyànfă	daaiHhínfaat
magnet n.			
-natural	磁石	tsźshf̀;	chìHseHk;
-steel bar	吸鐵	syītyĕ	kāptit
magneto n.	磁電	tsźdyàn	chìHdiHn
magnificent a.			
-great	偉大	wĕidà;	wáiHdaaiH;
-grand	堂皇	tánghwáng;	tòHngwòHng;

-splendid	華麗	hwálì;	wàHlaiH;
-pompous	豪華	háuhwá	hòuHwàH

magnify v. t.

-ampligy	擴充	kwòchīng;	kongchùng;
-as by a microscope	放大	fàngdà	fongdaaiH

mahogany n. 紅木 húngmù hùHngmuHk

maid n.

-female servant	女僕	nyŭpú;	néuiHbuHk;
young girl	少女	shàunyŭ;	siunéuiH;
-maiden	女童	nyŭtúng	néuiHtùHng

maiden n.

-maid	女童	nyŭtúng;	néuiHtùHng;
-virgin	處女	chùnyŭ;	chyunéuiH;
-maiden name	本性	bĕnsyìng	búnsing

mail

-v. t.	郵寄	yóujì	yàuHgei;
-n.	郵件	yóujyàn	yàuHgiHn

main a.

-chief	主要	jŭyàu;	jyúyiu;
-important	重要	jùngyàu;	juHngyiu;
-powerful	有勢	yŏushì	yáuHsṇi

mainland n. 大陸 dàlù daaiHluHk

maintain v. t.

-support	支持	jīchf;	jìchìH;
-keep up	維持	wéichf;	wàiHchìHi;
-continue	繼續	jìsyù;	gaijuIIk;
-assert	主張	jŭjāng	jyújèung

maize n. 玉蜀黍 yùshŭshŭ yuHksuHksyú

majestic a.

-dignified	威嚴	wēiyán;	wàiyìHm;
-noble	高貴	gāugwèi	gòugwai

majesty n.

-exalted dignity   尊嚴   dzwūnyàn;   jyùnyìHm;

-grandeur & dignity   威嚴   wēiyán;   wàiyìHm;

-Her Majesty   皇后陛下   hwánghòubìsyà   wòHnghauHbaiHhaH

major n.

-Mil.   少校   shàusyàu;   siugaau;

-chief   主要   jǔyaù;   jyúyiu;

-major general   少將   shàujyàng;   siujeung:

-major scale   長音階   chángyīnjyē   chèuHngyàmgàai

majority n.

-more than half   過半數   gwòbànshù;   gwobunsou;

-of age   成年   chéngnyán;   sìHngnìHn;

-the greater number   多數   dwōshù   dòsou

make v. t.

-construct   做   dzwò;   jouH;

-manufacture   製造   jr̀dzàu;   jaijouH;

-cause   使   shř   sái (sáidou)

malaria n.   瘧疾   mywèjí   yeuHkjaHt

male a.

-of men   男性   nánsyìng;   nàaHmsing;

-of beasts   公   gūng   gùng

malice n.

-malevolence   惡意   èyì;   ngokyi;

-evil heart   毒心   dúsyìn   duHksàm

malnutrition n.   營養不良   yíngyǎngbùlyáng   yìHngyéuHngbātlèuH

mam(m)a n.   媽媽   māma   màHmā

mammal n.   哺乳動物   púrǔdùngwù   bouHyúHduHngmaH

mammy   媽媽   māma   màHmā

man   男人   nánrén   nàaHmyán

anage v. t.

-administer	辦理	bànlǐ;	baaHnléiH;
-govern	處理	chǔlǐ;	chyúléiH;
-handle	料理	lyàulǐ	liuHléiH

anager n.

-of shop, bank	經理	jīnglǐ;	gìngléiH;
-of property	管理人	gwǎnlǐrén	gúnléiHyàHn

andarin language n. 國語   gwóyǔ   gwokyúH

andate n. 訓令   syùnlìng   fanliHng

ange n. 疥瘡   jyèchwāng   gaaichōng

anger n. 馬槽   mǎtsáu   máHchòuH

ango n. 芒果   mánggwǒ   mònggwǒ

anhood n.

-being man	爲人	wéirén;	wàiHyàHn;
-manly quality	男子氣概	nándzchìgài	nàaHmjíheikoi

ania n.

-derangement of mind	神志錯亂	shénjìtswòlwàn;	sàHnjicholyuHn;
-furore	狂熱	kwángrè	kòHngyiHt

anicure n. 修指甲   syōujǐjya   sàujigaap

anifest

-a. obvious	明瞭	mínglyǎu;	mìHngliuH;
-v. t. appear	顯現	syǎnsyàn;	hínyiHn;
-v. t. display	顯示	syǎnshì;	hínsiH;
-v. t. prove	證明	jèngmíng	jingmìHng

anifold a.

-multifarious	各種	gèjǔng;	gokjúng;
-various	各式	gèshì	goksik

anipulate v. t. 弄   nùng   luHng

mankind n.

-human race 人類 rénlèi yàHnleuiH

manner n.

-fashion 樣子 yàngdz; yeuHngji (yéung);

-method 方法 fāngfǎ; fòngfaat;

-conduct 行爲 syíngwéi; hàHngwàiH;

-style, of a painter 筆法 bǐfǎ bātfaat

manners n.

-customs 風俗 fēngsú; fùngjuHk;

mansion n.

大厦 dàsyà; daaiHhaHj

大樓 dàlóu daaiHláu

manual n.

-handbook 手册 shǒutsè; sáuchaak;

-text book 教科書 jyàukēshū gaaufōsyÙ

manufacture v. t. 製造 jǐdzàu jaijouH

manure

-n. dung 糞 fèn; fan;

-n. artificial 肥料 féilyàu; fèiHlíu;

-v. t. apply to 施肥 shiféi sìfèiH

manuscript n. 稿本 gǎuběn; góubún;

原稿 ywángǎu yùHngóu

many a. 多 dwō dò

-great many 許多 syǔdwō héuidò (hóudò)

-many thanks 多謝 dwōsyè dòjeH

map n. 地圖 dǐtú deiHtòuH

Marathon race 馬拉松賽跑 Mǎlāsūngsàipǎu MáHláaisūngchoipáau

marble n. 大理石 dàlǐshf; daaiHléiHseHk;

雲石 yúnshf; wàHnseHk;

-play thing 彈珠 dànjū daaHnjyū (bōjí)

march

-v. i. as soldiers do 行軍 syíngjyūn; hàHnggwàn;

-v. i. proceed	進行	jìnsyíng;	jeunhàHng;
-n. frontier	邊境	byānjìng	binging
March n.	三月	Sānywè	SàamyuHt
margin n.			
-a border	邊	byān;	bin;
-difference	差額	chàè	chàngáak
-margin of the page	頁邊	yèbyān	yiHpbin
marine a.			
-naval	海軍	hǎijyūn;	hóigwān;
-maritime	海上	hǎishàng	hóiseuHng
marionette n.	傀儡	kwéiléi	faailéuiH
mark n.			
-trace left	痕跡	hénjī;	hàHnjīk;
-dot	點	dyǎn;	dím;
-sign	記號	jìhàu;	geihouH;
-in an exam.	分數	fēnshù;	fēnsou;
-seal impressed	印	yìn	yan
market n.			
-place	市場	shìchǎng;	síHchèuHng;
-demand for goods	銷路	syāulù	siulouH
marriage n.	結婚	jyéhwūn;	gitfàn;
	婚姻	hwūnyin	fànyàn
-marriage ceremony	婚禮	hwūnlǐ;	fànláiH;
-marriage witnesses	證婚人	jènghwūnrén	jingfànyàHn
marrow n.	骨髓	gúswéi	gwātséuiH
marry v.			
-general term	結婚	jyéhwūn;	gitfàn;
-have a husband	嫁	jyà;	ga;

-have a wife	娶	chyǔ	chéui
marshal n.			
-military commander	陸軍司令	lùjyūnsžlìng;	luHkgwànsìliHng;
-field marshal	陸軍元帥	lùjyūnywánshwài	luHkgwànyùHnseui
martial a.	軍隊的	jyūndwèide;	gwàndéuidìk;
	武的	wǔde	móuHdìk
-martial law	軍法	jyūnfǎ	gwànfaat
martyr n.			
-of a religion	殉道	syùndàu;	sèundouH;
-of a country	烈士	lyèshì	liHtsiH
marvellous a.			
-wonderful	奇怪	chígwài;	kèiHgwaai;
-incredible	難信	nánsyìn	nàaHnseun
Marxism n.	馬克斯主義	Mǎkèsžjǔyı	MáHhāaksìjyúyiH
masculine	男性	nánsyìng	nàaHmsìng
mask n.	面具	myànjyù;	miHngeuiH;
-against poison gas	防毒面具	fángdúmyànjyù	fòHngduHkmiHngeuiH
-fig.	假面具	jyǎmyànjyù	gámiHngeuiH
mass n.			
-lump	團	twán;	tyùHn;
-bulk	大量	dàlyàng;	daaiHleuHng;
-crowd of people	羣衆	chyúnjùng	kwàHnjung
massacre n.	屠殺	túshā	tòuHsaat
mast n.	桅杆	wéigān	wàiHgòn
master			
-n. employer	老板	lǎubǎn;	lóuHbáan;
-n. owner	主人	jǔrén;	jyúyán;
-v. t. become adept in	精通	jīngtūng;	jìngtùng;

-master of the family	家ㄐㄚ主ㄓㄨ	jyājŭ;	gàjyú;
-Master of Arts	文ㄨㄣ學ㄒㄩㄝ碩ㄕㄛ士ㄕ	wénsywéshwòshr̀;	màHnhoHkseHksiH;
-master of ceremonies	主ㄓㄨ禮ㄌㄧ人ㄖㄣ	jŭlĭrén	jyúláiHyàHn
mat n.			
-for lying	蓆ㄒㄧ子ㄌ	syídz;	jeHkjí (jeHk);
-door	門ㄇㄣ墊ㄌㄧㄢ	méndyàn	mùHndìn
match			
-n. antagonist	對ㄉㄨㄟ手ㄕㄡ	dwèishŏu;	deuisáu;
-n. marriage	婚ㄏㄨㄣ姻ㄧㄣ	hwūnyin;	fànyàn;
-n. lucifer	火ㄏㄨㄛ柴ㄔㄞ	hwŏchái;	fócháai;
-v. t. mate	配ㄆㄟ合ㄏㄜ	pèihé;	puihaHp;
-v. t. contest	比ㄅㄧ賽ㄙㄞ	bĭsài	béichoi
material n.			
-substance	材ㄘㄞ料ㄌㄧㄠ	tsáilyàu;	chòiHlíu;
-books	教ㄐㄧㄠ材ㄘㄞ	jyàutsái;	gaauchòiH;
-fabric	料ㄌㄧㄠ子ㄌ	lyàudz	liuHjí (líu)
Materialism n.	唯ㄨㄟ物ㄨ論ㄌㄨㄣ	wéiwùlwùn	wàiHmaHtleuHn
mathematics n.	數ㄕㄨ學ㄒㄩㄝ	shùsywé	souhoHk
matriculate			
-v. t. enroll	報ㄅㄠ名ㄇㄧㄥ	bàuméng;	bouméng;
-v. i. to a university	考ㄎㄠ入ㄖㄨ學ㄒㄩㄝ試ㄕ	kăudàsywéshr̀	háaudaaiHhoHksi
matrimony n.	婚ㄨㄣ姻ㄧㄣ	hwūnyin;	fànyàn;
	結ㄐㄧㄝ婚ㄏㄨㄣ	jyéhwūn	gitfàn
matron n.			
-of hospital	護ㄏㄨ士ㄕ長ㄓㄤ	hùshr̀jăng	wuHsiHjéung
-of dormitory	舍ㄕㄜ監ㄐㄧㄢ	shèjyān	segāam

matter n.

-substance	物質	wùjf;	maHtjāt;
-affair	事情	shìchíng;	siHchìHng;
-subject	問題	wèntí;	maHntàiH;
-as a matter of fact	事實上	shìshfshàng;	siHsaHtseuHng;
-in the matter of	關於	gwānyú;	gwàanyù;
-no matter who	不論何人	búlwùnhérén	bātleuHnhòHyàHn

mattress n. 褥子 rùdz yuHkjí (jinyúk)

mature a.

-ripen	熟	shóu;	suHk;
-of person	成人	chéngrén	siHngyàHn

maxim n.

	格言	géyán;	gaakyìHn;
	座右銘	dzwòyòumíng	joHyauHmíHng

maximum n.

-in quantity	最多	dzwèidwō;	jeuidò;
-in degree	最高	dzwèigāu	jeuigōu

may v. i.

-can	可以	kěyǐ;	hóyíH;
-as a wish	願	ywàn;	yuHn;
-to be allowed	或者	hwòjě	waaHkjé

May n. 五月 wǔywè NgHyuHt

mayor n. 市長 shìjǎng siHjéung

me pron. 我 wǒ ngóH

meadow n.

	草地	tsǎudì;	chóudeiH;
	牧場	mùchǎng	muHkchèuHng

meal n.

-repast	餐	tsēn;	chàan;
-food	飯	fàn	faaHn
-take a meal	吃一頓飯	chīyídwùnfàn	hekyātdeuHnfaaHn (siHk yātchàanfaaHn)
-to serve a meal	開飯	kāifàn	hòifaaHn
-a foreign meal	西餐	syìtsēn	sàichāan

ean

-a. ordinary	平常	píngcháhg;	pìHngsèuHng;
-a. base	下賤	syàjyàn;	haHjiHn;
-a. ignoble	卑鄙	beibì;	bèipéι;
-a. stingy	小氣	syăuchì;	síuhei;
-v. t. intend	想	syăng;	séung;
-v. t. signify	意思	yìsz	yisi
eaning n.	意思	yìsz	yisi
eans n.			
-wealth	財產	tsáichăn;	chòiHcháan;
-capital	資本	dzbĕn;	jìbún;
-method	方法	fāngfă	fòngfaat
eantime adv.	同時	túngshŕ;	tùHngsiH;
	當時	dāngshŕ	dòngsìH
easles n.	麻疹	májĕn	máHchán
easure			
-v. t. take dimensions	量	lyáng;	lèuHng;
-n. length	尺寸	chŕtswùn;	chekchyun;
-n. degree	程度	chéngdù	chìHngdouH
-beyond	非常	fēicháng	fèisèuIIng
eat n.	肉	ròu	yuHk
echanic n.	機工	jīgūng	gèigùng
echanics n.	機器	jĭchì	gèihei
edal n.			
-as a reward	獎章	jyăngjăng;	jéungjēung;
-memento	紀念章	jìnyànjăng	geiniHmjēung
eddle v. i.	干涉	gānshè	gònsip
edical a.	醫藥	yìyàu	yìyeuHk
-medical corps.	軍醫部	jyūnyìbù	gwànyìbouH
-medical treatment	醫療	yìlyáu	yìliuH

medicine n.

-drug	藥	yàu;	yeuHk;
-fluid	藥水	yàushwěi;	yeuHkséui;
-ointment	藥膏	yàugāu;	yeuHkgōu;
-pill	藥丸	yàuwán;	yeuHkyún;
-plaster	膏藥	gāuyàu;	gòuyeuHk;
-powder	藥粉	yàufěn	yeuHkfán

medieval history n.   中古史   jūnggǔshř   jùnggúsí

medium

-n. agency	媒介	méijyè;	mùiHgaai;
-n. means	方法	fāngfǎ;	fòngfaat;
-a. moderate	中等	jūngděng;	jùngdáng;
-a. average	普通	pǔtūng	póutùng

meek a.

-mild	溫和	wēnhé;	wànwòH;
-gentle	斯文	szwén;	sìmàHn;
-humble	謙卑	chyānbēi	hìmbèi

meet v. t.

-encounter	遇見	yùjyàn;	yuHgin;
-assemble	聚集	jyùjí;	jeuiHjaaHp
-by appointment	見面	jyànmyàn;	ginmiHn;
-as difficulties	遭遇	dzāuyù	jòuyuH

meeting n.   會   hwèi   wúi

-meeting adjourned	散會	sànhwèi	saanwúi
-meeting of welcome	歡迎會	hw ānyínghwèi	fùnyiHngwúi

melancholic a.

	憂鬱	yōuyù;	yàuwāt;
	愁悶	chóumèn	sàuHmuHn

melody n.

-tunefulness	佳調	jyādyàu;	gàaidiuH;

-sweet music	好音樂	hǎuyìnywè;	hóuyàmngoHk;
-rhythmical	旋律	sywánlyù;	syùHnleuHt;
-song	曲	chyǔ;	kūk;
-tune	調	dyàu	diuH
melon n.	瓜	gwā;	gwā;
-water melon	西瓜	syìgwā	sāigwā
melt v. t.			
-liquid	溶解	rúngjyě;	yùHnggáai;
-metal	熔化	rúnghwà	yùHngfa
member n.			
-limb	肢體	jītǐ	jìtái
-member of committee	委員	wěiywán	wáivùHn
-member of meeting	會員	hwèiywán	wáiyùHn
-member of an organization	董事	dǔngshr̀	dúngsiH
memorandum n.			
-a note	備忘錄	bèiwànglù;	beiHmòHnglúk;
-informal letter	便箋	byànjyān;	biHnjìn;
-record	記錄	jìlù	geiluHk
memorial			
-a. commemorative	紀念	jìnyàn;	geiniHm;
-n. petition	請願書	chǐngywànshū;	chingyuHnsyù;
-n. memento	紀念品	jìnyànpǐn;	geiniHmbán;
-n. monument	紀念碑	jìnyànbēi;	geiniHmbèi
-memorial service	追悼會	jwēidàuhwèi	jèuidouHwái
memory n.			
-power of	記性	jìsyìng;	geising;
-remembrance	記憶	jìyì	geiyìk

menace

-v. t. threaten	威赫	wēihè;	wàihaak;
-n. danger	危險	wéisyǎn;	ngàiHhím;
-n. evil	禍害	hwòhài	woHhoiH

mend v. t.

-repair	補	bǔ;	bóu;
-put right	改好	gǎihǎu;	góihóu;
-mend nets	補網	bǔwǎng	bóumóHng

meningitis n. 腦膜炎 ǹǎumwóyán nóuHmókyìHm̀

menses n. 月經 ywèjīng yuHtgìng

mental a.

-of the mind	心理上	syînlǐshàng;	sàmléiHseuHng;
-spiritual	精神上	jīngshénshàng;	jìngsàHnseuHng;
-mental arithmetic	心算	syînswàn;	sàmsyun;
-mental disorder	精神錯亂	jìngshéntswòlwàn;	jìngsàHncholyuHn;
-mental energy	智能	jìnéng	jinàHng

mention v. t.

-raise a point	提出	tíchū;	tàiHchēut;
-in speech	說到	shwōdàu;	syutdou (góngdou);
-writing	寫到	syědàu	sédou

menu n. 荣單 tsàidān choidāan

merchandise n. 貨 hwò; fo;

	貨物	hwòwù;	fomaHt;
	商品	shāngpǐn;	sèungbán;

merchant n. 商人 shāngrén sèungyàHn

mercy n. 慈悲 tsźbēi; chìHbèi;

	仁慈	réntsź;	yàHnchìH;
-show mercy	開恩	kāiēn	hòiyàn

mere a.

-simple	單一	dānyǐ;	dāanyāt;

-nothing else	僅ㄐㄧ有ㄧㄡ	jǐnyǒu;	gányáuII;
-no more	不ㄅㄨ過ㄍㄨㄛ	búgwò	bātgwo
-rge v. t.	合ㄏㄜ併ㄅㄧㄥ	hébìng	haHpbing
-rit n.			
-efficacy	功ㄍㄨㄥ勞ㄌㄠ	gūngláu;	gùnglòuH;
-deserve	應ㄧㄥ得ㄉㄜ	yìngdé	yìngdāk
-rry a.	快ㄎㄨㄞ樂ㄌㄜ	kwàilè;	faailoHk;
-Merry Christmas	聖ㄕㄥ誕ㄉㄢ快ㄎㄨㄞ樂ㄌㄜ	Shèngdànkwàilè	SingdaanfaailoHk
-ssage n.	消ㄒㄧㄠ息ㄒㄧ	syāusyí	siusìk
-ssenger n.			
-bears a message	送ㄙㄨㄥ信ㄒㄧㄣ	sùngsyìn;	sungseun;
-dispatch bearer	使ㄕ者ㄓㄜ	shǐjě;	sijé;
-office servant	聽ㄊㄧㄥ差ㄔㄞ	tìngchāi	tìngchàai
-tal n.	五ㄨ金ㄐㄧㄣ	wǔjīn;	ńgHgàm;
	金ㄐㄧㄣ屬ㄕㄨ	jīnshǔ	gàmsuHk
-taphor n.	比ㄅㄧ喻ㄩ	bǐyù;	béiyuH;
	隱ㄧㄣ喻ㄩ	yǐnyù	yányuH
-ter n.	計ㄐㄧ量ㄌㄧㄤ器ㄑㄧ	jìlyángchì;	gailèuHnghei
-gas meter	瓦ㄨㄚ斯ㄙ計ㄐㄧ量ㄌㄧㄤ器ㄑㄧ	wǎsżjìlyángchì	ngáHsigailèuHnghei
-thod n.	法ㄈㄚ子ㄗ	fádz;	faatjí;
	方ㄈㄤ法ㄈㄚ	fāngfǎ	fòngfaat
-crobe n.	微ㄨㄟ生ㄕㄥ蟲ㄔㄨㄥ	wéishēngchúng	mèiHsàngchùHng
-crophone n.	播ㄅㄛ音ㄧㄣ機ㄐㄧ	bwòyinjī;	boyāmgèi;
	擴ㄎㄨㄛ音ㄧㄣ器ㄑㄧ	kwòyinchì	kongyāmhei
-croscope n.	顯ㄒㄧㄢ微ㄨㄟ鏡ㄐㄧㄥ	syǎnwéijìng	hinmèiHgeng
-dday n.	中ㄓㄨㄥ午ㄨ	jūngwǔ;	jùngńgH;
	正ㄓㄥ午ㄨ	jèngwǔ	jingńgH
-ddle a.	中ㄓㄨㄥ間ㄐㄧㄢ	jūngjyān;	jūnggāan;

-Middle Ages	中世紀	jūngshŕjì;	jùngsaigéi;
-middle school	中學	jūngsywé	jùnghoHk
midnight n.	半夜	bànyè	bunyé
midway a.	半路	bànlù;	bunlóu;
	中途	jūngtú	jùngtòuH
midwife n.	接生	jyēshēng;	jipsāng;
	助產士	jùchǎnshŕ	joHcháansiH
might n.			
-power	權力	chywánlì;	kyùHnliHk;
-strength	力量	lìlyàng;	liHkleuHng;
-might as well	可能	kěnéng	hónàHng
mighty a.			
-powerful	有勢力	yǒushŕlì;	yáuHsailiHk;
-great	偉大	wěidà	wáiHdaaiH
mild a.			
-of behaviour	斯文	sžwén;	sìmàHn;
-of disposition	溫柔	wēnróu;	wànyàuH;
-of weather	溫和	wēnhé	wànwòH
mildew			
-n.	霉	méi;	mùiH;
-v. i.	發霉	fāméi	faatmùiH (faatmòu)
mile n.	英里	yīnglǐ;	yīngléiH;
	哩	lǐ	léiH
militarism n.	武功主義	wǔlìjǔyì	móuHliHkjyúyiH
military n.	軍事	jyūnshŕ;	gwànsiH;
	陸軍	lùjyūn;	luHkgwàn;
-military academy	陸軍士校	lùjyūnshŕsyàu;	luHkgwànsiHhaauH
-military age	徵兵年齡	jēngbīngnyánlíng;	jìngbìngnìHnliHng;
-military band	陸軍軍樂隊	lùjyūnjyūnywèdwèi;	luHkgwàngwànngoǵdeuiH
-military discipline	軍紀	jyūnjì;	gwàngéi;

-military law	軍法	jyūnfǎ;	gwànfaat;
-military officer	陸軍將校	lùjyūnjyàngsyàu;	luHkgwānjeunggaau;
-military police	憲兵	syànbìng;	hìnbìng;
-military review	閱兵	ywèbìng;	yuHtbìng;
-military service	兵役	bìngyì;	bìngyiHk;
-military weapons	兵器	bìngchì	bìnghei
ilk n.	奶	nǎi	náaiH
ilky Way n.	銀河	Yínhé	NgàHnhòH
ill n.			
-for grinding	磨	mwó;	mòH;
-workshop	工廠	gūngchǎng;	gùngchóng;
-manufactory	製造廠	jìdzàuchǎng	jaijouHchóng
illennium n.	千禧年	Chyānsyīnyán	chìnhēiniHn
illion n.	百萬	bǎiwàn	baakmaaHn
illionaire n.	百萬富翁	bǎiwànfùwūng	baakmaaHnfuyūng
illstone n.	磨力石	mwódàushf	mòHdōuseHk
imic v. t.	模仿	mwófǎng;	mòuHfóng;
	學樣	sywéyàng	hoHkyéung
ind			
-v. t. look after	照顧	jàugù;	jiugu;
-v. t. heed	注意	jùyì;	jyuyi;
-v. t. feel concern	担心	dānsyīn;	dàamsàm;
-n. opinion	意見	yìjyàn;	yigìn;
-never mind	不要緊	búyàujǐn	bātyiugán (ṁyiugán)
indful a.			
-bearing in mind	記住	jìjù;	geijyuH;
-regardful	留心	lyóusyīn;	làuHsàm;
-attentive	注意	jùyì	jyuyi
ine			
-pron.	我的	wǒde;	ngóHdìk (ngóHge)

-n. place	礦	kwàng;	kong;
-n. a rich source	富源	fùywán;	fuyùHn;
-coal mine	煤礦	méikwàng	mùiHkong

mineral

-a. organic	無機	wúji;	mòuHgèi;
-n. chemical element	礦物	kwàngwù	kongmaHt
minimum a.	最少	dzwèishǎu;	jeuisíu;
	最低	dzwèidi	jeuidài

minister n.

-pastor	牧師	mùshī;	muHksǐ;
-of a democratic state	部長	bùjǎng;	bouHjéung;
-of an empire	大臣	dàchén;	daaiHsàHn;
-diplomatic	公使	gūngshǐ	gùngsi

ministry n.

-board	部	bù;	bouH;
-the cabinet	內閣	nèigé;	noiHgok;
-of foreign affairs	外交部	wàijyāubù	ngoiHgàaubouH
mink n.	水獺毛皮	shwěilàimáupí	séuilaaimòuHpèiH

minor a.

-small	小	syǎu;	síu;
-music	短	dwǎn;	dyǔn;
-minor scale	短音階	dwǎnyīnjyē	dyúnyāmgāai

mint

-n. a coin	錢幣	chyánbì;	chìHnbaiH;
-v. t. fabricate money	鑄幣	jùbì	jyubaiH

minus a.

-less	減	jyǎn;	gáam;
-elec.	陰	yīn	yàm

-a. very small	微⟨⟩小⟨⟩	wéisyǎu;	mèiHsíu;
-a. detailed	詳⟨⟩細⟨⟩	syángsyì;	chèulIngsai;
-a. accurate	精⟨⟩密⟨⟩	jìngmì;	jìngmaHt;
-n. part of an hour	分⟨⟩	fēn;	fàn;
-in a minute	一會兒⟨⟩	yìhwěr	yātwuiHyìH (yātjalInggɑ̄m)
minutely adv.	精⟨⟩細⟨⟩	jìngsyì	jìngsai
minutes n.	議⟨⟩事⟨⟩錄⟨⟩	yìshìlù;	yíHsiHluHk;
	記⟨⟩錄⟨⟩	jìlù	gcilulIk
miracle n.	奇⟨⟩蹟⟨⟩	chíjì;	kèiHjìk;
	神⟨⟩蹟⟨⟩	shénjì	sàHnjik
miraculous a.	不⟨⟩可⟨⟩思⟨⟩議⟨⟩	bùkěszyì;	bāthósìyiH;
	神⟨⟩奇⟨⟩莫⟨⟩測⟨⟩	shénchímwòtzè	sàHnkèiHmoHkchāak
mire n.	濕⟨⟩地⟨⟩	shīdì;	sāpdeiII,
	泥⟨⟩坑⟨⟩	nìkōng	nàlHhaang
mirror n.	鏡⟨⟩子⟨⟩	jìngdz	gengjí (geng)
misapply v. t.	用⟨⟩錯⟨⟩	yǔngtswò	yuHngcho
misapprehend v. t.	誤⟨⟩會⟨⟩	wùhwèi	ngHwuiH
misbehave v. t./v. i.	行⟨⟩爲⟨⟩不⟨⟩正⟨⟩	syíngwéibújèng	hàHngwàiHbātjing
miscarriage n.			
-mismanagement	處⟨⟩置⟨⟩不⟨⟩善⟨⟩	chǔjìrbúshàn;	chyújibātsiHn;
-abortion	流⟨⟩產⟨⟩	lyóuchǎn	làuHcháan
mischief n.			
-harm	傷⟨⟩害⟨⟩	shānghài;	sèunghoiH;
-foolish behaviour	胡⟨⟩鬧⟨⟩	húnàu	wùHnaauH(dóulyuHn`
misconduct n.	違⟨⟩法⟨⟩行⟨⟩爲⟨⟩	wéifǎsyíngwéi	wàiHfaathàHngwàiH
miser n.	守⟨⟩財⟨⟩奴⟨⟩	shǒutsáinú;	sáuchòiHnòuH;
	小⟨⟩氣⟨⟩鬼⟨⟩	syǎuchìgwěi	síuheigwái
miserable a.			
-wretched	悲⟨⟩慘⟨⟩	bēitsǎn;	bèicháam;

-pitiable	可憐	kĕlyán	hóliHn
misery n.			
-distress	困苦	kwùnkŭ;	kwanfú;
-wretchedness	不幸	búsyìng	bāthaHng
misfortune n.			
-bad luck	不幸	búsyìng;	bāthaHng
-mischance	災禍	dzāihwò	jòiwoH
misprint n.	印錯	yìntswò	yancho
miss			
-n. title	小姐	syăujyĕ;	síujé;
-n. loss	損失	swŭnshī;	syúnsāt;
-v. t. omit	遺漏	yílòu;	wàiHlauH;
-v. i. fail	失敗	shībài	sātbaaiH
missing p. a.			
-absent	不在	búdzài;	bātjoiH(m̀háisyu);
-wanting	缺乏	chywēfá	kyutfaHt
mission n.			
-errand	使命	shĭmìng;	simiHng;
-society	差會	chāihwèi;	chàaiwúi;
-duty	任務	rènwù;	yaHmmouH;
-persons sent	特派員	tèpàiywán;	daHkpaaiyùHn;
-mission policy	宣教策略	sywānjyàutsèlywè	syùngaauchaakleuk
missionary n.			
-male	宣教師	sywānjyàushī;	syùngaausī;
-female	傳教士	chwánjyàushī̀	chyùHngaausiH
misspell v. t.	拼錯	pìntswò	pìngcho (chyuncho)
mist n.	霧	wù	mouH
mistake			
-v. t. misunderstand	誤會	wùhwèi;	ngHwuiH;

-v. i. err in recognising	認与 錯ち	rèntswò;	yiHngcho;
-n. error	錯ち	tswò	cho
mister(abbr. Mr.) n.	先T 生ア	syānsheng	sìnsàang

mistress(abbr, Mrs.)n.

-wife	太ち 太ち	tàitai;	taaitáai;
-of family	主业 婦口	jŭfù;	jyúfúH;
-of shopkeeper	老ㄌ 板ㄅ 娘ㄋ	lăubănnyáng	lóuHbáannèuHng

misunderstand v. t.

-mishear	聽ㄊ 錯ち	tīngtswò;	tèngcho;
-take in wrong sense	誤ㄨ 會ㄏ	wùhwèi	ngHwuiH

misuse v. t.

-use wrongly	用ㄩ 錯ち	yùngtswò;	yuHngcho;
-of official authority	濫ㄌ 用ㄩ	lànyùng	láaHmyuHng

mix v. t.

-by stirring	攪ㄐ	jyău;	gáau;
-become blended	攙ㄔ	chān;	chàm;
-associate with	來ㄌ 往ㄨ	láiwăng;	lòHngwóHng;
-confuse	混ㄏ 亂ㄌ	hwŭnlwàn	waHnlyuHn

mixture n.

-medley	雜ㄗ 色ㄙ	dzásè;	jaaHpsìk;
-medicine	藥ㄧ 水ㄕ	yàushwĕi;	yeuHkséui;
-a compound	組ㄗ 合ㄏ 物ㄨ	dzŭhéwù	jóuhaHpmaHt
moan v. i.	哼ㄏ	hēng;	hàng;
	吟ㄧ 呻ㄕ	shēnyín	sànyàHm

mob

-n. rabble	暴ㄅ 民ㄇ	bàumín;	bouHmàHn;
-v. t. attack	暴ㄅ 動ㄉ	bàudùng	bouHduHng
mobile a.	可ㄎ 動ㄉ	kĕdùng	hóduHng
mobilization n.	動ㄉ 員ㄩ	dùngywán	duHngyùHn

mock v. t.

-ridicule	譏笑	jīsyàu;	gèisiu;
-despise	輕視	chĭngshr̀	hìngsiH

modal a. 外形 wàisyíng; ngoiHyìHng;

-modal auxillaries 法助動詞 fǎjùdùngtsź faatjoHduHngchìH

mode n.

-style	樣子	yàngdz;	yeuHngjí (yéung);
-way	方法	fōngfǎ;	fòngfaat;
-mood	語氣	yŭchì	yúHhei

model n.

-example	榜樣	bǎngyàng;	bóngyeuHng;
-as of a ship	模型	mwósyíng;	mòuHyìHng;
-imitated	模範	mwófàn;	mòuHfaaHn;
-person for artists	模特兒	mwótèér	mòuHdaHkyìH

moderate a.

-not excessive	不過分	búgwòfèn;	bātgwofaHn (m̀gwofaH
-of action	溫和	wēnhé;	wànwòH;
-mediocre	普通	pŭtūng;	póutùng;
-moderate prices	低廉價格	dīlyánjyàgé;	dàilìHmgagaak;
-moderate terms	適度條件	shr̀dùtyáujyàn	sìkdouHtìuHgfn

modern a.

	現代	syàndài;	yiHndoiH;
	時髦	shŕmáu;	sìHmòuH;
	摩登	mwódēng	mōdāng

modernism n. 現代主義 syàndàijŭyì yiHndoiHjyúyiH

modernist n. 現代派 syàndàipài yiHndoiHpaai

modest a.

-shy	怕羞	pàsyōu;	pasàu (pacháu);
-humble	謙虛	chyānsyū;	hìmhèui;
-of actions	客氣	kèchì;	haakhei;

-of dress	樸素	púsù	poksou
modifier n.			
-one who modifies	修改者	syōugǎijě;	sàugóijé;
-Gram.	修飾語	syōushìyǔ	sāusìkyúH
modify v. t.			
-qualify	形容	syíngrúng;	yìHngyùHng;
-alter	更改	gēnggǎi;	gànggói;
-change	改變	gǎibyàn	góibin
moist a.	濕	shr̄;	sāp;
	潮濕	cháushr̄	chìuHsāp
moisture n.			
-wetness	濕氣	shr̄chì;	sāphei;
-water vapour	水分	shwěifèn	sóuifaHn
mold, mould			
-n. soil	泥土	nítǔ;	nàiHtóu;
-n. mildew	霉	méi,	mùiH (mòu);
-v. t. cover with	發霉	fāméi;	faatmùiH (faatmòu);
-v. t. to cast	鑄	jù	jyu
molest v. t.			
-trouble	煩擾	fánrǎu;	fàaHnyíuH;
-annoy	煩腦	fánnǎu;	fàaHnnóuH;
-interfere	干涉	gānshè	gònsip
moment n.			
-an instant	一會兒	yìhwěr;	yātwuiHyìH (yātjaHn-gāan);
-a period	時候	shíhou	sìHhauH
momentary a.			
-only a moment	片時	pyànshf;	pinsìH;
-transitory	暫時	jànshf	jaaImsìII
monarch n.			
-king	王	wáng;	wòHng;
-emperor	皇帝	hwángdì	wòHngdai

monastery n.

-of medieval Europe	修道院	syōudàuywàn;	sàudouHyún;
-Buddhist	佛寺	fwósz̀;	faHtjí;
-Taoist	道觀	dàugwān	douHgùn
Monday n.	禮拜一	lǐbàiyī;	láiHbaaiyāt;
	星期一	syīngchíyi	sìngkèiHyāt
money n.	錢	chyán	chín
-money bag	錢袋	chyándài	chìHndói
-make money	賺錢	jwànchyán	jaaHnchín

money-order n.

-as issued	滙票	hwèipyàu;	wuiHpiu;
-postal	郵滙	yóuhwèi;	yàuHwuiH;
-telegraphic	電滙	dyànhwèi	diHnwuiH
monitor n.	班長	bēnjǎng	bāanjéung
monk n.	修士	syōushr̀;	sàusiH;
-Buddhist	和尚	héshàng	wòHséung
monkey n.	猴子	hóudz	hàuHjí (máHlāu)
monogamy n.	一夫一妻	yìfūyìchī	yātfùyātchài
monogram n.	徽	hwāi	fài

monopoly n.

-the right	專利權	jwēnlìchywán;	jyùnleiHkyùHn;
-commodity	專賣品	jwēnmàipǐn	jyùnmaaiHbán
monosyllable n.	單音字	dānyìndz̀	dāanyāmjiH
monotone n.	單調	dāndyàu	dàandiuH
monster n.	妖怪	yāugwài;	yiugwaai;
	怪物	gwàiwù	gwaaimaHt
month n.	月	ywè	yuHt
-last month	上月	shàngywè	seuHngyuHt

-next month	下月	syàywè	haHyuHt
-current month	本月	běnywè	búnyuHt
-first of the month	月初	ywèchū	yuHtchō
-end of the month	月底	ywèdǐ	yuHtdái

monthly a.

-magazine	月刊	ywèkān;	yuHthón;
-salary	月薪	ywèsyïn	yuHtsàn

monument n.

-arch	牌坊	páifāng;	pàaiHfōng;
-bronze statue	銅像	tîngsyàng;	tùHngjeuHng;
-tombstone	石碑	shfbēi	seHkbēi

mood n.

Gram.	語氣	yŭchì;	yúHhei;
-temper	脾氣	píchì;	pèiHhei;
-state of mind	心情	syinchíng;	sāmchìHng;
-emotion	情緒	chíngsyù	chìHngséui;
-change one's mood	轉換心情	jwǎnhwànsyinchíng	jyúnwuHnsāmchìIIng

moon n.	月亮	ywèlyàng	yuHtleuHng
moonlight n.	月光	ywègwāng	yuHtgwōng

mop

-n. an implement	地拖	dìtwō;	deiHtō;
-v. t. wipe with	拖地	twōdì	tòdeiH

moral

-n. lesson	教訓	jyàusyùn;	gaaufan;
-a. virtue	道德	dàudé;	douHdāk;
-moral law	道德律	dàudélyù;	douHdākleuHt;
-moral liberty	道德自由	dàudédzỳóu;	douHdakjiHyàuHf;
-moral sense	是非之心	shffēijīsyin	siHfēijisām

moralist n.	道德家	dàudéjyā;	douHdakgā;

	德青家	déyùjyā	dākyuHkgā
morality n.	道德	dàudé;	douHdāk;
	道義	dàuyì	douHyiH
more a.	更	gèng;	gang;
	越	ywè	yuHt
-all the more	更加	gèngjyā	ganggà
-more & more	越發	ywèfā	yuHtfaat
-more or less	多少	dwōshǎu	dòsíu
-how much more	何況	hékwàng	hòHfong
moreover adv.	而且	érchyě;	yìHché;
	況且	kwàngchyě;	fongché;
	並且	bìngchyě	biHngché
morning n.	早晨	dzǎuchén;	jóusàHn;
-morning prayers	早禱	dzǎudǎu;	jóutóu;
-good morning	早安	dzǎuān;	jóungōn;(jóusàHn);
-morning star	晨星	chénsyǐng	sàHnsing
morphia n.	嗎啡	māfēi	māfē
morse n.	電碼	dyànmǎ	diHnmáH
mortal a.			
-subject to death	致死	jìrsž;	jiséi;
-fatal	致命	jìrmìng;	jimiHng;
-man is mortal	人必有死	rénbìyǒusž;	yàHnbìtyáuHséi;
-mortal wound	致命傷	jìrmìngshāng	jimiHngsèung
mortar n.			
-cement	水泥	shwěiní;	séuinàiH;
-for pounding	臼子	jyòudz	kaují
mortgage v. t.	押	yā;	ngaat;
	抵押	dǐyā	dáingaat
mortification n.	克己	kèjǐ;	hāakgéi;

	制 慾	jìyù	jaiyuHk

mortuary n.

-burial place	葬 地	dzàngdì;	jongdeiH;
-morgue	檢 屍 場	jyǎnshīchǎng	kímsìchèuHng

mosaic n.	剪 嵌 細 工	jyǎnchyánsyìgūng;	jínkìHmsaigūng

mosquito n.	蚊 子	wéndz	mānji (mān)

moss n.	青 苔	chīngtāi	chìngtòiH

most a.

-superlative sign	最	dəwèi;	jeui;
-nearly all	大 概	dàgài	daaiHkói;
-most. at the	至 多	jìdwō	jidò

mostly adv.

-usually	大 概	dàgài;	daaiHkói;
-almost all	多 半	dwōbàn	dòbun (daaiHbun)

moth .n	蛾 子	édz	ngòHji (ngòH)

mother n.	母 親	mǔchin	móuHchàn

-Mother's Day	母 親 節	mǔchinjyé;	móuHchànjit;
-mother-in-law	岳 母	ywèmǔ	ngoHkmóuH

motion n.

-movement	動 作	dùngdzwò;	duHngjok;
-proposal	提 議	tíyì;	tàiHyíH;
-application	申 請	shēnchǐng;	sànchíng;
-of the bowels	大 便	dàbyàn;	daaiHbiHu;
-accelerated motion	加 速 運 動	jyāsùyìndùng	gāchūkwaHnduHng
-curvilinear motion	曲 線 運 動	chyūsyànyùndùng	kūksinwaHnduHng

motive n.

-object	動 機	dùngjì;	duHnggèi;
-reason	理 由	lǐyóu	léiHyàuH

motor

-n. Elec.	發動機	fādùngjī;	faatduHnggèi;
-v. i. travel	坐汽車	dzwòchìchē	chóHheichē
motorboat n.	汽船	chìchwán	heisyùHn
motorcar n.	汽車	chìchē	heichē
motorcycle n.	機器脚踏車	jīchìjyǎutàchē	gèiheigeukdaaHpchē (diHndāanchē)
motto n.	格言	géyán;	gaakyìHn;
	座右銘	dzwòyòumíng	joHyauHmíHng

mould—see mold

mount

-v. t. on a horse	騎馬	chímǎ;	kèHmáH;
-v. t. ascend	上	shàng;	séuHng;
-v. t. as jewels	鑲	syāng;	sèung;
-n. mountain	山	shān	sàan
mountain n.	山	shān	sàan
-ascend a mountain	上山	shàngshān	séuHngsàan
-descend a mountain	下山	syàshān	haHsàan (loHksàan)
-mountain stream	山溪	shānsyī	sàankài

mourn v. i.

-cry	哭	kū;	hūk (haam);
-feel grief	悲傷	bēishāng;	bèisèung;
-lament	哀悼	āidàu	ngòidouH

mourning n.

-lamentation	悲痛	bēitùng;	bèitung;
-clothing	喪服	sāngfú	sòngfuHk
mouse n.	老鼠	lǎushǔ	lóuHsyú
moustache n.	鬚子	húdz	wùHjí (wùHsòu)
mouth n.	口	kǒu;	háu;
	嘴	dzwěi	jéui
mouthful n.	一口	yìkǒu	yātháu
movable a.	活動	hwódùng	wuHtduHng

English	Chinese		Romanization	
-movable property	動ㄉㄨㄥˋ	產ㄔㄢˇ	dùngchǎn	duHngcháan
move v. t.				
-set in motion	動ㄉㄨㄥˋ		dùng;	duHng;
-push with the hand	推ㄊㄨㄟ		twūi;	tèui;
-remove as goods	搬ㄅㄢ		bān;	bùn;
-as troops	調ㄉㄧㄠˋ	動ㄉㄨㄥˋ	dyàudìng;	diuHduHng;
-propose	提ㄊㄧˊ	議ㄧ	tíyì;	tàiHyìH;
-as feelings	感ㄍㄢˇ	動ㄉㄨㄥˋ	gǎndùng	gámduHng
movement n.				
-behavior	行ㄒㄧㄥˊ	動ㄉㄨㄥˋ	syíngdùng;	hàHngduHng;
-for special purpose	運ㄩㄣˋ	動ㄉㄨㄥˋ	yùndùng	waHnduHng
movie n.	電ㄉㄧㄢˋ	影ㄧㄥˇ	dyànyǐng	diHnyíng
mow v. t.				
-cut down	割ㄍㄜ	下ㄒㄧㄚˋ	gēsyà;	gothaH;
-cut grass	鏟ㄔㄢˇ	草ㄘㄠˇ	chǎntsǎu	cháanchóu
much adv.	多ㄉㄨㄛ		dwō	dò
-as much as possible	盡ㄐㄧㄣˋ	量ㄌㄧㄤˋ	jìnlyàng	jeuHnleuHng
mud n.	泥ㄋㄧˊ		ní;	nàiH;
-soft	爛ㄌㄢˋ	泥ㄋㄧˊ	lànní;	laaHnnàiH;
-sticky	泥ㄋㄧˊ	巴ㄅㄚ	níbā	nàiHbā (nàiHbaaHn)
muddle				
-v. t. cloud	蒙ㄇㄥˊ	蔽ㄅㄧ	méngbì;	mùHngbai;
-n. mess	雜ㄗㄚˊ	亂ㄌㄨㄢˋ	dzálwàn	jaaHplyuHn
mulberry n.				
-tree	桑ㄙㄤ	樹ㄕㄨˋ	sāngshù;	sōngsyuH;
-fruit	桑ㄙㄤ	葚ㄕㄣˋ	sāngshèn	sōngsaHm
mule n.	騾ㄌㄨㄛˊ	子ㄗ	lwódz	lòHjí
multiple				
-a. manifold	多ㄉㄨㄛ	種ㄓㄨㄥˇ	dwōjǔng;	dòjúng;

-n. Math.	倍數	bèishù;	púiHsou;
-common multiple	公倍數	gūngbèishù	gùngpúiHsou

multiply

-v. t. increase	加多	jyādwō;	gàdò;
-v. i. Math.	乘	chéng;	sìHng;
-v. t. by generation	繁殖	fánjŕ	fàaHnjiHk

multitude n.

-crowd	羣集	chyúnjí;	kwàHnjaaHp;
-a great number	許多	syŭdwō	héuidò

mum

-a. silent	靜	jìng;	jiHng;
-a. not speaking	不說話	bùshwōhwà;	bātsyutwaH(ìnchēutsèng
-int. be silent	蕭靜	sùjìng	sūkjiHng

mummy n.

-embalmed body	木乃伊	mùnăiyĭ	muHknáaiHyì
mumps n.	痄腮	jàsāi;	jasòi;
	腮腺炎	sāisyànyán	sòisinyìHm
municipal a.	自治上	dzjŕshàng;	jiHjiHseuHng;
	內政上	nèijèngshàng	noiHjingseuHng

munition n.

-fortification	礮臺	pàutái;	paautòiH;
-stronghold	要塞	yàusài;	yiuchoi;
-ammunition	軍用品	jyūnyùngpĭn	gwànyuHngbán
murder v. t.	殺人	shārén;	saatyàHn;
-premeditated	謀殺	móushā;	màuHsaat;
-unpremeditated	誤殺	wùshā	ngHsaat
murderer n.	兇手	syūngshŏu	hùngsáu

murmur v. i.

-complain	發牢騷	fāláusāu;	faatlòuHsòu;
-grumble	埋怨	máiywàn	màaiHyun

English	Chinese		
muscle n.	肌 肉	jīròu	gèiyuHk
museum n.	博 物 館	bwówùgwăn;	bokmaHtgún;
	博 物 院	bwówìywàn	bokmaHtyún
mushroom n.	多 菇	dūnggū	dūnggū
music n.	音 樂	yīnywè;	yàmngoIIk;
-notes	樂 譜	ywèpŭ	ngoHkpóu
musical a.	音 樂 上	yīnywèshàng;	yàmngoHkseuHng;
-musical instruments	樂 器	ywèchì	ngoHkhei
musician n.			
-professional	樂 師	ywèshī;	ngoHksì;
-skilled	音 樂 家	yīnywèjyā;	yàmngoHkgā;
-composer	作 曲 家	dəwòchyŭjyā	jokkūkgᾱ
must v. i.	必 須	bìsyū;	bìtsèui;
	要	yàu	yiu
mustard n.	芥 辣	jyèlà	gaaılaaHt
mute			
-a. speechless	無 語	wúyŭ;	mòuHyúH;
-n. one who is silent	不 發 言 者	bùfāyánjě	bātfaatyìHnjé (m̀góngsyutwaH)
mutilate v. t.			
-maim	殘 毀	tsánhwĕi;	chàaHnwái;
-hack	砍 斷	kăndwàn	hámtyúHn
mutiny			
-n. tumult	騷 亂	sāulwàn;	sòulyuHn;
-n. strife	爭 鬥	jēngdòu;	jàngdau;
-v. i. rebel	反 叛	fănpàn	fáanpun
utter			
-v. i. growl	咆 哮	pàusyāu;	pàauHhàau;
-v. t. murmur	含 糊 而 言	hánhúéryán	hàHmwùHyìHyìHn
mutton n.	羊 肉	yángròu	yèuHngyuHk
mutual a.	相	syāng;	sèung;

	互相	hùsyāng	wuHsèung

muzzle n.

| -of a quadruped | 口 | kǒu; | háu; |
| -fastening for the mouth | 口罩 | kǒujàu | háujaau (háulāp) |

my prep. | 我的 | wǒde | ngóHdĭk (ngóHge) |

myself pro. | 我自己 | wǒdzìjǐ | ngóHjiHgéi |

mysterious a. | 神秘 | shénmì | sàHnbei |

mystery n. | 奧秘 | àumì; | oubei; |

mystic

| -a. | 神秘 | shénmì; | sàHnbei; |
| -n. | 通神家 | tūngshénjyā | tùngsàHngā |

myth n. | 神話 | shénhwà | sàHnwá |

mythology n.

| -myth | 神話 | shénhwà; | sàHnwá; |
| -the science | 神話學 | shénhwàsywé | sàHnwáhoHk |

N

nag

| -v. t. by faultfinding | 吹毛求疵 | chwēimáuchyóutsz̄; | chèuimòuHkàuHchì; |
| -n. pony | 駒 | jyū | kèui |

nail

-n. of metal	釘	dǐng;	dǐng;
-n. of fingers	指甲	j̆ĭjyǎ;	jígaap;
-n. claw	爪	jwǎ;	jáau;
-v. t.	釘	dìng	dèng

naked a.

| -of body | 裸體 | lwótǐ; | lótái (mōkchìng;) |
| -naked truth | 明白眞理 | míngbáijēnlǐ | mìHngbaaHkjànléiH |

name n.

| -of a person | 名字 | míngdz̀; | mìHngjiH; |

-of a thing	名稱	míngchēng;	mìHngchìng;
-designation	名目	míngmù	mìHngmuHk
-baby name	乳名	rŭmíng	yúHmɛ́ng
-family name	姓	ʂyìng	sìng
namely adv.			
-to wit	就是	jyòushř;	jauHsiH (jauHhaiH);
-that is to say	換句話說	hwànjyùhwàshwō	wuHngeuiwaHsyut
nap			
-v. I.	微睡	wéishwèi;	mèiHseuiH;
-n.	午睡	wŭshwèi	ńgHseuiH (fanngaangaau)
napkin n.	餐巾	tsānjin	chāangān
narcotic n.	麻醉劑	mádzwèiji	màHjeuijāi
narration n.			
-recital	誦讀	ʂùngdú;	juHngduHk;
-story	故事	gùshř	gusiH
narrative n.			
-recital	傳記	jwànjì;	jyuHngei;
-account	講述	jyăngshù	góngseuHt
narrow a.	窄	jăi	jaak
nasty a.			
-unpleasant	討厭	tăuyàn;	tóuyim;
-indecent	下流	syàlyóu	haHlàuH
nation n.			
-country	國家	gwójyā;	gwokgà;
-people	民族	míndzú	màHnjuHk
national a.	屬國家	shŭgwójyā;	suHkgwokgà;
- atio al la guage	國語	gwóyŭ	gwokyúH

-national flag	國旗	gwóhchí	gwokkèiH
-national goods	國貨	gwóhwò	gwokfo
-national anthem	國歌	gwógē	gwokgō
-national religion	國教	gwójyàu	gwokgaau
nationality n.			
-member of a nation	國籍	gwójí;	gwokjiHk;
-one's birthplace	籍貫	jígwàn	jiHkgun
native a.			
-as indigenous	本國	běngwó	búngwok
-as of a country	本地人	běndìrén	búndeiHyàHn
-inborn	天賦	tyānfù	tìnfu
-inherent	固有	gùyǒu	guyáuH
natural a.			
-conferred by birth	生成	shēngchéng;	sàangsìHng;
-not made by men	天然	tyānrán;	tìnyìHn;
-natural features	地勢	dìshì	deiHsai
-natural history	博物學	bwówùsywé	bokmaHthoHk
nature n.			
-character	天性	tyānsyìng;	tìnsing;
-universe	自然界	dzìránjyè;	jiHyìHngaai;
-qualities	性質	syìngjí	singjāt
-human nature	人性	rénsyìng	yàHnsing
naughty a.			
-bad	壞	hwài;	waaiH;
-mischievous	頑皮	wánpí	wàaHnpèiH (baakyim
naval a.	海軍的	hǎijyūnde	hóigwāndìk
navel n.	肚臍	dùchí	tóuHchìH
navigate v. t.	航海	hánghǎi	hòHngháoi

navy n. 　海軍   hǎijyūn   hóigwān

  -navy blue 　深藍   shēnlán   sàmlàaHm

nay adv. 　不   bù;   bāt (m̀);

  　不然   bùráu   batyìHn

near a./adv.

  -not far off 　近   jìn;   gaHn;

  -in proximity 　附近   fùjìn;   fuHgaHn;

  -Near East 　近東   Jìndūng   GaHndùng

nearly adv. 　差不多   chàhùdwō;   chābūtdōɪ;

  　大約   dàywē;   daaiHyeuk;

  　將近   jyāngjìn   jèunggaHn

nearsighted a. 　近視   jìnshɨ   gaHnsiH

neat a.

  -clean 　乾淨   gānjìng;   gòngjeHng;

  -in good order 　整齊   jěngchí   jíngchàiH

necessary a.

  -indispensable 　必須   bìsyū;   bìtsèui;

  -unavoidable 　難免   nánmyǎn   nàaHnmíHn

  -not necessary 　不必   búbì   bātbit

necessity n.

  -inevitableness 　不免   bùmyǎn;   bātmíHn;

  -campulsion 　強廹   chyángpwò   kèuHngbāak(kéuIIngbìk)

neck n. 　頸   jǐng   góng

necktie n. 　領帶   lǐngdài   léHngdáai (léHngtāai)

need v. t.

  -require 　要   yàu;   yiu;

  -must 　必須   bìsyū;   bìtsèui;

  -in want of 　需要   syūyàu   sèuiyiu

needle n. 　針   jēn   jàm

needless a.

  -not needed   不需要   bùsyūyàu;   bātsèuiyiu;

  -unnecessary   非必要   fēibìyàu   fèibìtyiu

needle-work n.   針線   jēnsyàn;   jàmsin;

                 女紅   nyǔgūng   néuiHhùHng

negative

  -a. refusing assent   否認   fǒurèn;   fáuyiHng;

  -a. opp. to positive   消極   syāují;   sìugiHk;

  -a. Math.   負   fù;   fuH;

  -a. Chem.   陰   yin;   yàm;

  -n. Photog.   底片   dǐpyàn   dáipin

neglect v. t.

  -pay no attention   不理   bùlǐ;   bātléiH (m̀léiH);

  -give not enough care   忽略   hūlywè;   fātleuk;

  -by carelessness   大意   dàyì   daaiHyi

negro n.   黑人   hēirén   hāakyàHn

neighbour n.   鄰居   línjyū;   lèuHngèui;

                 街坊   jyēfāng   gāaifōng

neighbourhood n.

  -neighbourliness   友好   yǒuhǎu;   yáuHhóu;

  -vicinity   鄰近   línjìn;   lèuHngaHn;

  -neighbour   鄰居   línjyū   lèuHngèui

neither a./conj.

  -not either   都不   dōubù;   dōubāt;

  -followed by nor   不... 也不...   bù...yěbù...   bāt...yáHbāt...

nephew n.

  -brother's son   姪兒   jíér;   jaHtyìH(jaHt);

  -sister's son   外甥   wàishēng   ngoiHsàng

nerve n.

  -nerve centre   神經中樞   shénjingjūngshū   sàHngìngjùngsyù

-nerve strain	神經過勞	shénjinggwòláu	sàHnginggwolòuH
nervous a.			
-nbout	不放心	búfàngsyìn;	bātfongsàm (m̀fongsàm);
-timid	膽小	dǎnsyǎu;	dáamsíu;
-over-excitable	神經過敏	shénjinggwòmǐn	sàHnginggwomáHn
nervous system	神經系	shénjingsyì	sàHnginghaiLL
est n.	窩	wō	wō (chàauH)
et n.	網	wǎng	móHng
-fishing net	魚網	yúwǎng	yùHmóHng
-mosquito net	蚊帳	wénjàng	mānjeung
eurotic a.	神經質	shénjingjf	sàHngìngjāt
euter a.			
-gender	中性	jūngsying	jùngsìng
eutrality n.	中立	jūnglì	jùnglaHp
eutralize v. t.			
-Chem.	中和	jūnghé;	jùngwòH;
-counteract	抵消	dǐsyāu	dáisìu
ever adv.			
-in regard to the past	從不	tsúngbù;	chùHngbāt;
-in regard to the future	永不	yǔngbù;	wíHngbāt;
-certainly not	不會	búhwèi;	bātwuiH (m̀wúi);
-never mind	不要緊	búyàujǐn	bātyiugán (m̀yiugán)
evertheless adv.			
-however	雖然	swéirán;	sèuiyìHn;
-still	還是	háishr̀	wàaHnsiH (juHnghaiLL)
ew a.	新	syìn	sàn
-new civilization	新文化	syìnwénhwà	sànmàHnfa
-new life movement	新生活運動	Syìnshēnghwó-yùndùng	SànsàngwuHtwaHn-duHng

-New Year's congratulation	恭賀新年	gūnghèsyìnnyán	gùnghoHsànnìHn
news n.			
-newspaper	新聞	syìnwén;	sànmàHn;
-correspondent	通訊	tūngsyùn	tùngséun
newsagency n.	通訊社	tūngsyùnshè	tūngseunséH
newspaper n.	報紙	bàujǐ	boují
next			
-a. following	第二	dìèr;	daiHyiH;
-a. after that	然後	ránhòu;	yìHnhauH;
-prep. nearest to	隔壁	gébì	gaaklik (gaaklèiH)
-next time	下次	syàtsz̀	haHchi
-next month	下月	syàywè	haHyuHt
-the week after next	下下一個星期	syàsyàyígesyìngchi	haHhaHyātgosìngkèiH
nib n.	筆尖	bǐjyēn	bātjìm
nice a.			
-good	好	hǎu;	hóu;
-of taste	味道好	wèidàuhǎu;	meiHdouHhóu;
-pleasing	和氣	héchì;	wòHhei;
-fine	精巧	jīngchyǎu	jìngháau
-nicelooking	好看	hǎukàn	hóuhon (hóutái)
nickname n.	綽號	chwòhàu;	cheukhouH;
	花名	hwāmíng	fàméng
nicotine u.	尼古丁	nígǔdǐng;	nèiHgúdǐng;
	煙草精	yāntsǎujīng	yìnchóujìng
niece n.			
-brother's daughter	姪女	jínyǔ;	jaHtnéui;
-sister's daughter	外甥女	wàishēngnyǔ	ngoiHsàngnéui
nigh a.	近	jìn	gaHn (káHn)

ight n.	晚上	wǎnshàng	máaHnseuHng
-night & day	晝夜	jòuyè	jauyeH
-night school	夜校	yèsyàu	yeHhaauH
ihilism n.	虛無論	Syūwúlwùn	HèuimòuHleuHn
ll n.	零	líng;	lìHng;
	無	wú	mòuII
ine a.	九	jyǒu	gáu
ineteen a.	十九	shfjyǒu	saHpgáu
ineteenth a.	第十九	dìshfjyǒu	dàiHsaHpgáu
inetieth a.	第九十	dìjyǒushí	daiHgáusaHp
inety a,	九十	jyǒushf	ghusaHp
inth a.	第九	dìjyǒu	daiIIgáu
ip v. t.			
-pinch	捏	nyē;	nip;
-as a crab does	鉗	chyán;	kiHm;
-as a dog does	咬	yǒu;	ngáauH;
-with an instrument	鉗	chyán	kiHm
ipple n.	奶頭	nǎitóu	náaiHtàuH
itrate n.	硝酸鹽	syāusywānyán	siusyùnyìHm
-nitrate of silver	硝酸銀	syāusywānyín	siusyùnngàHn
itrogen n.	氮	dàn;	daaHm;
	淡氣	dànchì	daaIImhei
-nitrogen dioxide	二氧化氮	èryǎnghwàdàn	yiHyéuHngfadaaHm
no			
-a. not any	沒有	méiyou;	muHtyáuH (móuH);
-adv. not	不	bù	bāt (m̀)
oble a.			
-aristocratic	貴族	gwèidzú;	gwaijuHk;

English	Chinese		
-magnanimous	高尚	gāushàng	gòuseuHng
nobody n.			
-no person	無人	wúrén;	mòuHyàHn (móuHyàHn);
-of no importance	無名小卒	wúmíngsyǎudzú	mòuHmìHngsíujeut
nod v. i.	點頭	dyǎntóu	dímtàuH
noise n.			
-sound	聲音	shēngyin	sìngyàm
noisy a.	吵鬧	chǎunàu;	cháaunaauH;
-bustling	熱鬧	rènau	yiHtnaauH
nomad			
-n.	遊牧民族	yóumùmíndzú;	yàuHmuHkmàHnjuHk
-a.	遊牧	yóumù	yàuHmuHk
nominal a.	名義上	míngyìshang;	mìHngyiHseuHng;
	掛名	gwàmíng	gwamìHng
nor.e a.	沒有	méiyou;	muHtyáuH (móuH);
	都沒	dōuméi	dōumuHt (dōumóuH)
nonsense n.	胡說	húshwō	wùHsyut (lyúngóng)
noodles n.	麵	myàn	miHn
noon n.	中午	jūngwǔ	jùngnǵH
-forenoon	上午	shàngwǔ	seuHngnǵH
-afternoon	下午	syàwǔ	haHńgH
normal a.			
-natural	正常	jèngcháng;	jingsèuHng;
-usual	平常	píngcháng	pìHngsèuHng
-normal temperature	標準溫度	byāujwǔnwēndù	bìujéunwāndouH
north n.	北	běi;	bāk;
	北方	běifāng	bākfòng
-north latitude	北緯	běiwěi	bākwáiH
-north pole	北極	běijí	bākgiHk

northeast n.	東北	dūngběi	dūngbāk
northern a.	北方的	běifāngde	bākfòngdìk
-northern lights	北極光	běijígwāng	hākgiHkgwòng
northwest n.	西北	syībēi	sàibāk
nose n.	鼻子	bídz	beiHji (beiHgō)
nostril n.	鼻孔	bíkŭng	beiHhúng (beiHgōlūng)
not adv.	不	bùi	bàt (m),
-not included	不在內	búdzàinèi	bātjoiHnoiH
notable a.			
-remarkable	值得注意	jídejùyi;	jiHkdākjyuyi;
-distinguished	有名	yǒumíng	yáuHméng
note n.			
-mark	記號	jìhàu;	geihouH;
-short record	筆記	bǐjì;	bātgei;
-annotation	註解	jùjyě;	jyugáai;
-short letter	條子	tyáudz;	tìuHji;
-paper money	鈔票	chāupyàu;	chàaupiu;
-tone	音調	yīndyàu,	yāmdìuH;
-musical	音符	yinfú;	yàmfùH;
-v. t. heed	注意	jùyì	jyuyi
nothing n.	無事	wúshr̀	mòuHsiH (móuHsiH)
notice			
-v. t. heed	注意	jùyì;	jyuyi;
-v. t. notify	通知	tūngjī;	tùngji;
-n. posted up	佈告	bùgàu	bougou
notify v. t.			
-inform generally	通知	tūngjī	tùngji
notorious a.	有名	yǒumíng,	yáuHméng;
	著名	jùmíng	jyumìHng (chēutméng)
notwithstanding prep.	雖然	swéirán	sèuiyìHn

noun n.	名詞	míngtsź	mìHngchìH
nourish v. t.			
-furnish nutriment	滋養	dz̄yăng;	jìyéuHng;
-feed well	補養	bŭyăng	bóuyéuHng
novel n.	小說	syăushwō	síusyut
November n.	十一月	shŕyiywè	saHpyātyuHt
novice n.			
-beginner	初學	chūsywé;	chòhoHk;
-tyro	生手	shēngshŏu	sàangsáu
now adv.	現在	·syàndzài;	yiHnjoiH (yìHgā);
	目前	mùchyán;	muHkchìHn;
-now & then	時時	shŕshŕ	sìHsìH
nowadays adv.			
-at the present time	目前	mùchyán;	muHkchìHn;
-now	現今	syànjīn;	yiHngām;
-recently	近來	jìnlái	gaHnlòiH
nowhere adv.	無處	wúchù	mòuHchyu (móuHdeiHfòng)
nucleus n.	核	hé or hŕ	waHt
nude a.	裸體	lwótĭ	lótái
nuisance n.			
-action	麻煩	máfàn;	màHfàaHn;
·thing or person	討厭	tăuyàn	tóuyim
nullify v. t.			
-make invalid	作廢	dzwòfèi;	jokfai;
-cancel	取消	chyŭsyāu	chéuisìu
numb			
-v. t.	麻痺	mábì;	màHbei;
-a. benumbed	麻痺	mábì;	màHbei;
-a. insensible	麻木	mámù	màHmuHk

umber n.

-sum	數目	shùmu;	soumuHk;
-symbol	數字	shùdz;	soujiH;
-for telephone	號	hàu;	houH;
-even number	雙數	shwāngshù	sèungsou
-odd number	單數	dānshù	dāansou
-total number	總數	dzǔngshù	júngsou
umerous a.	很多	hěndwō;	hándò (hóudò);
	許多	syǔdwō	héuidò (hóudò)

urse

-n. for the sick	看護	kānhù;	hònwuH;
	護士	hùshr;	wuHsiH;
-n. of children	保姆	bǎumǔ;	bóumóuH;
-v. t. feed	餧奶	wèinǎi	waináaiH
-dry nurse	保姆	bǎumǔ	bóumóuH
-wet nurse	奶媽	nǎimā	náaiHmā
ursery n.	育嬰室	yùyingshr;	yuHkyìngsāt;
	托兒所	twōérswǒ	tokyìHsó
ut n.	胡桃	hútáu;	wùHtòuH (haHptòuH);
	栗子	lìdz	leuIItjí (fùngléut)
utritious a.	有營養	yǒuyíngyǎng	yáuHyìHngyéuHng
ylon n.	尼龍	nílúng	nèiHlùHng

)

ak n.	橡樹	syàngshù	jeuIIngsyuII
ar n.	槳	jyǎng;	jéung;
	櫓	lǔ	lóuH
ath n.	誓	shr	saiH
atmeal n.	麥片	màipyàn	maaHkpin
bedience n.	順從	shwùntsúng;	seuHnchùHng;
	服從	fútsúng	fuHkchùHng

English	Chinese	
-obedience to master	服從主人	fútsúngjŭrén	fuHkchùHngjyúyàHn
-obedience to parents	孝順父母	syàushwùnfùmŭ	haauseuHnfuHmóuH
obeisance n.			
-low bow	鞠躬	jyúgūng;	gūkgùng;
-with hands in front	作揖	dzwòyĭ;	jokyāp;
-kneeling	跪	gwèi	gwaiH
obey v. t.			
-give ear to	聽話	tīnghwà;	tèngwaH;
-submit to	服從	fútsúng;	fuHkchùHng;
-a law	遵守	dzwūnshŏu	jèunsáu
-obey the laws	守法	shŏufă	sáufaat
obituary notice n.	訃聞	fùwén	fuHmàHn
object			
-n. aim	目的	mùdi;	muHkdik;
-n. of a scheme	宗旨	dzūngjĭ;	jùngjí;
-n. article	物質	wùjf;	maHtjāt;
-n. motive	目標	mùbyāu;	muHkbīu;
-v. i. oppose	反對	făndwèi	fáandeui
objection n.	反對	făndwèi	fáandeui
objective a.			
-final aim	後果	hòugwo;	hauHgwó;
-opp. to subjective	客觀	kègwān	haakgùn
-objective case	受格	shòugé	sauHgaak
obligation n.	本分	bĕnfèn;	búnfaHn;
	義務	yìwù	yiHmouH
oblige v. t.			
-compel	強迫	chyángpwò;	kèuHngbāak;
-do a favour	幫忙	bāngmáng	bòngmòHng(kéuHng

oblong n.	長方形	chángfāngsyíng	chèuHngfōngyìHng
obscene a.	猥褻	wěisyè;	waisit;
-obscene books	淫書	yínshū;	yàHmsyù;
-obscene language	粗話	tsūhwà	chòuwá
obscure a.			
-dark	暗	àn;	ngam;
-indistinct	模糊	mwóhú;	mòuHwùH;
-not easily under-stand	含糊	hánhú	hàHmwùH
observation n.			
-notice	觀察	gwānchá;	gùnchaat;
-watching	監視	jyānshr̀	gàamsiH
observe v. t.			
-see	看	kàn;	hon (tái);
-notice	注意	jùyi;	jyuyi;
-inspect	觀察	gwānchá;	gùnchaat;
-obey	遵守	dzwūnshǒu;	jèunsáu;
-observe the rules	守規矩	shǒugwēijyu	sáukwàigéui
obsolete a.			
-disused	不用	búyùng;	bātyuHng (m̀hyuHng);
-out of date	過時	gwòshŕ	gwosìH
obstacle n.	障礙	jàngài;	jeungngoiH;
	妨害	fánghài	fòHnghoiH
obstinate a.	頑固	wángù;	wàaHngu;
	固執	gùjr̀	gujēp
obstruct v. t.			
-hinder	妨礙	fángài;	fòHngngoiH;
-as a passage	塞住	sāijù;	sākjyuH;
-interrupt	阻止	dzǔjŕ	jójí
obtain v. t.			
-gain	得到	dédàu;	dākdou;
-attain	達到	dádàu;	daaHtdou;

-arrive at	到	dàu	dou
obvious a.	明白	míngbai;	mìHngbaaHk;
	明顯	míngsyǎn	mìHnghín
occasion n.			
-opportunity	機會	jīhwèi;	gèiwuiH;
-time	次	tsż;	chi;
-reason	理由	lǐyóu;	léiHyàuH;
-need	必要	bìyàu	bìtyiu
occasionally adv.	偶然	ǒurán;	ngáuHyìHn;
-sometimes	有時	yǒushí	yáuHsìH
occidental a.	西方	syīfāng;	sàifòng;
	西洋	syīyáng	sàiyèuHng
occupy			
~v. t. take possession of	佔領	jànlǐng;	jimlíHng;
~v. t. possess	佔有	jànyǒu;	jimyáuH;
~v. t. engage the service	從事	tsúngshì;	chùHngsiH;
~v. i. reside	居住	jyūjù;	gèuijyuH;
-occupied territory	淪陷區	lwúnsyànchyū	lèuHnhaaHmkèui
occupant n.			
-of a honse	房客	fángkè;	fòHnghaak;
-possessor	所有人	swǒyǒurén	sóyáuHyàHn
occupation n.			
-calling	職業	jíyè;	jíkyiHp;
-employment	工作	gūngdzwò;	gùngjok;
-business	事情	shìching	siHchìHng
occur v. i.			
-happen	發生	fāshēng;	faatsàng;
-meet with	碰着	pèngje;	pungjeuHk (pungdóu)
-come to one's mind	想起	syǎngchǐ	séunghéi
ocean n.	海洋	hǎiyáng	hóiyèuHng

-Atlantic Ocean	大西洋	Dàsyiyáng	DaaiHsàiyèuHng
-Pacific Ocean	太平洋	Tàipíngyáng	TaaipìHngyeuHng
o'clock n.	… 點鐘	...dyǎnjūng	...dímjūng
octave n.			
-Music	第八音	dìbāyin	daiHbaatyām
October n.	十月	shíywè	saHpyuHt
octopus n.	章魚;	jāngyú;	jèungyùH
	八爪魚	bājwǎyú	baatjáauyùH
oculist n.	眼科醫生	yǎnkēyishēng	ngáaHnfōyisāng
odd a.			
-strange	奇怪	chígwài;	kèiHgwaai;
-eccentric	占怪	gǔgwài	gúgwaai
-odd number	單戠	dānshù	daansou
-odds & ends	零碎	língswèi	lìHngseui
odour n.	味	wèi	meiH
of prep.	… 的	...de	...dīk (ge)
-of course	當然	dāngrán	dòngyìHn
off a./adv.			
-far off	遠	ywǎn;	yúHn;
-away from	離開	líkāi	lèiHhòi
offend v. t.			
-somebody	得罪	dédzwèi;	dākjeuiH;
-make angry	發怒	fānù;	faatnouH;
-transgress	犯法	fànfǎ	faaHnfaat
offer v. t.			
-as a present	送	sùng;	sung;
-as a price	出	chū;	chēut;
-as an idea	貢獻	gùngsyàn;	gunghin;
-propose	提出	tíchū	tàiHchēut
-offer gifts	獻禮物	syànlǐwù	hinláiHmaHt

office n.

-in general	辦公室	bàngūngshr̀;	baaHngūngsāt;
-of the govt.	政府機關	jèngfǔjigwān;	jingfúgèigwàan;
-shop	店	dyàn;	dim;
-firm	行	háng;	hóng;
-branch office	支店	jr̄dyàn;	jìdim;
	分行	fēnháng;	fànhóng;
	分局	fēnjyú	fàngúk
-head(or main)office	總店	dzǔngdyàn;	júngdim;
	總行	dzǔngháng;	júnghóng;
	總局	dzǔngjyú	júnggúk

officer n.

-govt.	公務員	gūngwùywán;	gùngmouHyùHn;
-of a company	職員	jŕywán;	jikyùHn;
-mil. & nav.	軍官	jyūngwān	gwāngūn

official a.

-formal	正式	jèngshr̀;	jingsik;
-authoritative	官方	gwānfāng;	gùnfòng;
-public	公	gūng;	gùng;
-official letter	公文	gūngwén	gùngmàHn
-official residence	官邸	gwāndǐ	gùndái

offspring n.

-descendants	後裔	hòuyì;	hauHyeuiH;
-produce	出產	chūchǎn;	chēutcháan;
-issue	結果	jyégwǒ	gitgwó

often adv.

	常常	chángcháng	sèuHngsèuHng (sìHsìH

ogre n.

-a monster	食人鬼	shŕréngwěi;	siHkyàHngwái;
-cruel man	惡徒	ètú	ngoktòuH

Oh int.

-denoting sorrow	哎呀	āiyà;	àiyà;
-denoting surprise	哦	ế	ốH

oil n. 油 yóu yàuH

| -machine oil | 機油 | jīyóu | gèiyàuH |
| -mineral oil | 鑛油 | kwàngyóu | kongyàuH |

ointment n. 藥膏 yàugāu yeuHkgōu

| -apply an ointment | 敷藥膏 | fūyàugāu | fùyeuHkgōu |

old a.

-of persons	老	lǎu;	lóuH;
-of things	舊	jyòu;	gauH;
-ancient	古	gǔ	gú
-old-fashioned	舊式	jyòushì;	gauHsìk;
	古老	gǔlǎu	gúlóuH

olive n. 橄欖 gǎnlǎn; gáamláaHm;
青果 chìnggwǒ chìnggwó

| -olive oil | 橄欖油 | gǎnlǎnyóu | gáamláaHmyàuH |

Olympic Games 世運 shìyùn saiwaHn

omelette n. 炒蛋 chǎudàn; cháaudáan;
煎蛋捲 jyāndànjywǎn jìndaaHngyún

omen n. 預兆 yùjàu; yuHjiuH;
兆頭 jàutóu jiuHtàuH

ominous a.

| -foreshadowing evil | 預兆 | yùjàu; | yuHjiuH; |

omit v. t.

| -unintentionally | 漏 | lòu; | lauH; |
| -intentionally | 省 | shěng | sáang |

omnibus n. 公共汽車 gūnggùngchìchē gùngguHngheichè

omnipotent a. 全能 chywánnéng; chyùHnnàHng;
無所不能 wúswǒbùnéng mòuHsóbātnàHng

omnipresent a. 無所不在 wúswǒbúdzài mòuHsóbātjoilI

omniscient a.   無ⅹ 所ㄥㄛ 不ㄅㄨ 知ㄓ   wúswŏbùjī   mòuHsóbātjì

on prep.

-indicating position or time   在ㄗㄞ   dzài;   joiH (hái);

-the upper part   在ㄗㄞ 上ㄕㄤ 面ㄇㄧㄢ   dzàishàngmyàn   joiHseuHngmiHn (háiseuHngbiHn)

-on & on   不ㄅㄨ 停ㄊㄧㄥ   bùtíng   bāttìHng (m̀tìHng)

-on behalf of   代ㄉㄞ 替ㄊㄧ   dàitì   doiHtai

-on no account   千ㄑㄧㄢ 萬ㄨㄢ 不ㄅㄨ   chyānwànbù   chīnmaaHnbāt

once adv.

-one time   一 次ㄘ   yítsż;   yātchi;

-formerly   從ㄘㄨㄥ 前ㄑㄧㄢ   tsúngchyán;   chùHngchìHn;

-before   以 前ㄑㄧㄢ   yĭchyán   yíHchìHn

-once upon a time   從ㄘㄨㄥ 前ㄑㄧㄢ   tsúngchyán   chùHngchìHn

one a.   一   yĭ   yāt

-one another   彼ㄅㄧ 此ㄘ   bĭtsż;   béichí;

   互ㄨ 相ㄒㄧㄤ   hùsyāng   wuHsèung

-one & the same   全ㄑㄩㄢ 然ㄖㄢ 相ㄒㄧㄤ 同ㄊㄨㄥ   chywánránsyāngtúng   chyùHnyìHnsèungtùHn

-one day   有ㄧㄡ 一 天ㄊㄧㄢ   yŏuyìtyān   yáuHyāttìn (yáuHyātyaHt)

-one family   一 家ㄐㄧㄚ 人ㄖㄣ   yìjyārén   yātgàyàHn

-One Way Street   單ㄉㄢ 行ㄒㄧㄥ 路ㄌㄨ   dānsyínglù   dāanhàaHnglouH

onion n.

-spring onions   蔥ㄘㄨㄥ   tsūng;   chūng;

-the bulb   蔥ㄘㄨㄥ 頭ㄊㄡ   tsūngtóu   chūngtàuH

only a.

-one alone   只ㄓ 有ㄧㄡ 一   jĭyŏuyĭ;   jiyáuHyāt;

-merely   只ㄓ 是ㄕ   jĭshż;   jísiH;

-but   但ㄉㄢ 是ㄕ   dànshż   daaHnsiH (daaHnhaiH

onus n.

-burden   負ㄈㄨ 擔ㄉㄢ   fùdān;   fuHdàam;

-obligation	義務	yìwù;	yiHmouH;
-charge	責任	dzérèn	jaakyaHm
onward a./adv.			
-moving forward	前進	chyánjìn;	chìHnjeun;
-forward	向前	syàngchyán	heungchìHn
opaque a.	不透明	bútòumíng	bāttaumìHng (m̀tau-mìHng)
open v. t.			
-as a door	開	kāi;	hòi;
-as a book	掀開	syānkāi;	kínhòi;
-as a letter	拆開	chāikāi;	chaakhòi;
-undo	解開	jyěkāi	gáaihòi
opening n.			
-a breach	裂口	lyèkǒu;	liItháu;
-commencement	開始	kǎishǐ;	hòichí;
-of exhibition	開幕	kāimù;	hòimoHk;
-of a railway	通車	tūngchē	tùngchè
-opening day	開幕日	kāimùr	hòimoHkyaHt
opera n.	歌劇	gējyù	gōkeHk
-comic opera	喜劇	syǐjyù	héikeHk
-tragic opera	悲劇	bēijyù	bèikeHk
operation n.			
-process	手續	shǒusyù;	sáujuHk;
-surgery	手術	shǒushù;	sáuseuHt;
-Math.	演算	yǎnswàn	yínsyun
operator n.	電話生;	dyànhwàshēng;	diHnwaHsāng;
	接線生	jyēsyànshēng	jipsinsāng
opinion n.	意見	yìjyàn;	yigin;
-different opinions	見解不同	jyànjyěbùtúng	gingáaibattùHng
opium n.	鴉片	yāpyàn;	ngàpin;

	鴉片烟	yāpyànyān	ngàpinyin
opponent n.			
-antagonist	敵手	díshǒu;	diHksáu;
	對手	dwèishǒu	deuisáu
opportunity n.	機會	jīhwèi	gèiwuiH
oppose v. t.	反對	fǎndwèi;	fáandeui;
-resist	反抗	fǎnkàng;	fáankong;
-by physical force	抵抗	dǐkàng;	dáikong;
-in argument	抗議	kàngyì;	kongyíH
-obstruct	阻擋	dzǔdǎng	jódóng
opposite a.			
-contrary	相反	syāngfǎn;	sèungfáan;
-facing	對面	dwèimyàn	deuimiHn
oppress v. t.			
-tyrannically	壓制	yājì;	ngaakjai;
-severely	虐待	nywèdài	yeuHkdoiH
optic ne ve n.	視神經	shìshénjīng	siHsàHngìng
optics n.	光學	gwāngsywé	gwònghoHk
optimism n.	樂觀	lègwān;	loHkgùn;
	樂觀主義	lēgwānjǔyì	loHkgùnjyúyiH
optimistic a.	樂觀	lègwàn	loHkgùn
option n.	買賣權	mǎimaìchywán	máaiHmaaiHkyùHn
or conj.	或者	hwòjě;	waaHkjé;
-alternatively	還是	háishì;	wàaHnsiH(juHnghaiH)
-else	不然	bùrán	bātyìHn
oral a.	口說	kǒushwō;	háusyut;
	口述	kǒushù	háuseuHt
-oral method	口授法	kǒushòufǎ	háusauHfaat

orange n.	橙子	chéngdz	cháangjí (cháang)
orator n.	演說家	yǎnshwōjyā	yínsyutgā
orbit n.			
-Anat.	眼眶	yǎnkwàng;	ngáaHnkwōng;
-Astron.	軌道	gwěidàu	gwáidouH
orchard n.	果園	gwǒywán	gwóyùHn
orchestra n.	樂隊	ywèdwèi	ngoHkdeuiH
orchid n.	蘭花	lánhwā	làaHnfā
ordain v. t.	按牧	ànmù;	onmuHk;
	授聖職	shòushèngjf	sauHsingjik
order			
-n. command	命令	mìnglìng;	miHngliHng;
-n. injunction	禁令	jìnlìng;	gamliHng;
-n. for money	滙票	hwèipyàu;	wuiHpiu;
-n. discipline	紀律	jìlyù;	géileuHt;
-n. arrangement	次序	tsżsyù;	chijeuiH;
-v. t. for goods	定貨	dìnghwò;	diHngfo;
-v. t. bid	吩咐	fēnfù	fànfu
-in order to	爲 … 起見	wèi...chǐjyàn	waiH...héigin
ordinance n.	法令	fǎlìng	faatliHng
ordinary a.			
-usual	平常	píngcháng;	piHngsèuHng;
-commonplace	普通	pǔtūng	póutùng
ore n.	礦物	kwàngwù;	kongmaHt;
	礦石	kwàngshf	kongseHk
organ n.			
-musical instrument	風琴	fēngchín	fùngkàHm

-Biol.	器官	chìgwān	heigùn
-organization	機關	jīgwān	gèigwàan
-sexual organs	生殖器官	shēngjŕchìgwān	sàngjiHkheigùn
organic a.	有機	yǒujī	yáuHgèi
-organic chemistry	有機化學	yǒujīhwàsywé	yáuHgèifahoHk
organize v. t.	組織	dzǔjŕ	jóujĭk
orgies n.	歡宴	hwànyàn;	fùnyin;
	狂飲	kwángyǐn	kòHngyám
Orient n.	東方	dūngfāng	dùngfòng
origin n.			
-beginning	起源	chǐywán;	héiyùHn;
-as of a custom	原本	ywánběn;	yùHnbún;
-cause	原因	ywányin;	yùHnyàn;
-source	根本	gēnběn	gànbún
original a.	原來	ywánlái;	yùHnlòiH;
	本來	běnlái;	búnlòiH;
	最初	dzwèichū	jeuichò
originally adv.	原來	ywánlái;	yùHnlòiH;
	本來	běnlái	búnlòiH
ornament			
-n. decoration	裝飾	jwāngshŕ;	jōngsĭk;
-v. t. decorate	裝飾	jwāngshŕ	jōngsĭk
orphan n.	孤兒	gūér	gùyìH
orphanage n.	孤兒院	gūérywàn	gùyìHyún
Orthodoxy n.	正教	jèngjyàu	jinggaau
ostentation n.			
-show	外觀	wàigwān;	ngoiHgùn;
-display	誇耀	kwāyàu	kwàyiuH
ostracize v. t.	放逐	fàngjú	fongjuHk

other a.	別的	byéde;	biHtdik (daiHyiHdĭ);
	第二	dìer	daiHyiH
-other business	其他的事	chítàdeshr̀	kèiHtàdiksiH (kèiHtàgesiH)
-every other day	隔日	gér̀	gaakyaHt
otherwise adv.	要不然	yàubùrán;	yiubātyìHn (yeuHkm̀haiH);
	否則	fŏudzé	fáujāk
ought v.	應該	yìnggāi;	yìnggòi;
	應當	yìngdāng	yìngdòng
ounce n.	安士	ànshr̀	ònsí
our pro.	我們的	wŏmende	ngóIImùHndik (ngóHdeiHge)
ourselves pro.	我們自己	wŏmon dàjĭ	ngóIImùIIu jiIIgéi (ngóHdeiH jiHgéi)
out adv.	外	wài;	ngoiH;
-outside	外面	wàimyàn;	ngoiHmiHn (ngoiIIbiIIu)
-not at home	不在家	búdzàijya	bātjoiHgà (r̀hháikéi)
outdoor a.	戶外	hùwài;	wuHngoiH;
	屋外	wūwài	ngūkngoiH
outer a.	外	wài;	ngoiH;
	外面	wàimyàn	ngoiHmiHn (ngoiHbiHn)
-outer garment	外衣	wàiyi	ngoiHyì (ngoiHtou)
outlet n.			
-exit	出路	chūlù;	chèutlouH;
-vent	出口	chūkŏu;	chèutháu;
a letting out	放出	fàngchu	tongchēut
outline n.			
-contour	輪廓	lwúnkwò;	lèuHngok;
-essential points	大綱	dàgēng	daaiHgòng
outrage v. t.	強姦	chyángjyān	kèuHnggàan
outside adv./prep./a.	外面	wàimyàn;	ngoiHmiHn (ngoiHbiHn);
	在外	dzàiwài	joiHngoiH (háingoiHbiHn)

outwardly adv.

-outward	向外	syàngwài;	heungngoiH;
-of appearance	外表	wàibyǎu;	ngoiHbíu;
-apparently	顯然	syǎnrán	hínyìHn

oval a. 蛋形 — dànsyíng — dáanyìHng

ovary n. 卵巢 — lwǎncháu — léunchàauH

ovation n. 喝采 — hētsǎi; — hotchói;

-an easy victory	小凱旋	syǎukǎisywán;	síuóisyùHn;
-popular reception	民衆歡迎	mínjùnghwēnyíng	màHnjungfùnyìHng

oven n. 爐 — lú; — lòuH;

火爐 — hwǒlú; — fólòuH

over prep.

-across	過	gwò;	gwo;
-on the opposite side	對面	dwèimyàn;	deuimiHn;
-above	上面	shàngmyàn;	seuHngmiHn (seuHngbiHn);
-more than	多過	dwōgwo	dògwo

overcoat n. 大衣 — dàyi — daaiHyi (daaiHlāu)

overcome v. t.

-as difficulties	克服	kéfú;	hāakfuHk;
-as enemies	打敗	dǎbài	dábaaiH

overflow

-v. i. as with water	水滿	shwěimǎu;	séuimúHn;
-v. i. flood	泛濫	fànlàn;	faanlaaHm;
-v. i. superabound	過多	gwòdwō;	gwodò;
-n. a flood	大水	dàshwěi	daaiHséui

over-look v. t.

-from above	往下看	wàngsyàkàn;	wóHnghaHhon (táihaHbiHn);
-omit to see	漏看	lòukàn;	lauHhon (lauHjótái);

-fail to notice	沒注意	méijùyì;	muHtjyuyi (móuHjyuyi);
-neglect	忽略	hūlywè;	fātleuk;
-excuse	原諒	ywánlyàng	yùHnleuHng
over-population n.	人口過多	rénkŏugwòdwō	yàHnháugwodò
over-production n.	生產過剩	shēngchǎngwòshèng;	sàngcháangwosiHng;
	供過於求	gunggwóyúchyóu	gùnggwoyùkàuH
over-sea			
-a. beyond the sea	海外	hǎiwài;	hóingoiH
over-see v. t.			
-look over	視察	shìchá;	siHchaat;
-superintend	監督	jyāndū	gāamdūk
owe v. t.	欠	chyàn	him
owing to	因爲	yīnwei	yànwaiH
owl n.	貓頭鷹	māutóuyìng	māautàuHyìng
own			
-a. one's	自己的	dźjǐde;	jiHgéidìk (jiHgéige);
-v. t. possess	有	yǒu	yáuH
-my own	我自己的	wǒdżjǐde	ngóHjiHgéidìk (ngóHjiHgéige)
owner n.	主人	jŭrén;	jyúyán;
	物主	wùjŭ	maHtjyú
ownership n.	所有權	swǒyǒuchywán	sóyáuHkyùHn
ox n.	公牛	gūngnyóu	gùngngàuH
oxygen n.	氧;	yǎng;	yéuHng;
	氧氣	yǎngchì	yéuIInghei
oyster n.	蠔	háu;	hòuH;
	牡蠣	mŭlì	máauHlaiH
p			
pace n.	步	bù	bouH
pacify v. t.			
-soothe	安慰	ànwèi	ònwai

package n.	包裹	bāugwǒ;	bàaugwó;
	包件	bāujyàn	bàaugiHn
pact n.	合約	héywē	haHpyeuk
pad n.			
-cushion	墊子	dyàndz;	dinjí (dín);
-of blotting paper	吸墨紙	syīmèjř	kāpmaaHkjí
padlock n.	掛鎖	gwàswǒ	gwasó
pagan n.	異教徒	yìjyàutú	yiHgaautòuH
page n.	頁	yè;	yiHp;
	面	myàn	miHn
pagoda n.	塔	tǎ	taap
pail n.	桶	tǔng	túng
pain n.			
-bodily	痛	tùng;	tung;
-mental	痛苦	tùngkǔ;	tungfú;
-labour	勞苦	láukǔ	lòuHfú
paint			
-n. pigment in cake form	顏料	yánlyàu;	ngàaHnlíu;
-n. house-painter's	油漆	yóuchǐ;	yàuHchāt;
-v. t. as house	油漆	yóuchǐ;	yàuHchāt;
-v. t. picture	畫	hwà	waaHk
painter n.			
-artist	畫家	hwàjyā;	wágā;
-artisan	油漆匠	yóuchǐjyàng	yàuHchātjéung
painting n.	畫	hwà	wá
pair n.			
-of chopsticks	對	dwèi;	deui;
-of spectacles	副	fù;	fu;

-of trousers	條	tyáu;	tìuH;
-of scissors	把	bá	bá
palace n.	宮殿	gūngdyàn;	gùngdiHn;
	王宮	wánggūng	wòHnggùng
pale a.	青	chīng;	chèng;
	青白	chīngbái	chìngbaaHk
palm n.	棕樹	dzūngshù	jùngsyuH
palpitate v. i.	心跳	syīntyàu	sàmtiu
palsy n.			
-paralysis	癱瘓	tānhwàn;	tāanwuHn (táan);
of one side	半身不遂	bànshēnbùswéi	bunsànhātseuiH
pamphlet n.	小冊	syăutsè	síuchaak
pan n.	鍋	gwō	woHk
pane n.	窗格	chwānggé	chēunggaak
pangolin n.	穿山甲	chwāngshānjyă	chyùnsàangaap
panic n.	恐怖;	kŭngbù;	húngbou;
	恐慌	kŭnghwāng	húngfòng
pantomime n.	啞劇	yăjyù	ngákeHk
pants n.	短褲	dwănkù	dyúnfu
papa n.	爸爸	bàba	bàHbā
papacy n.	教皇制	jyàuhwángjr̀	gaauwòHngjai
papaya n.	木瓜	mùgwā	muHkgwā
paper n.	紙	jr̆	jí
-sensitized paper	感光紙;	găngwōngjr̆;	gámgwōngjí;
-test paper	試驗紙	shr̀yànjr̆	siyiHmjí
parable n.			
-allegory	比喻;	br̆yù;	béiyuH;

-fable	寓言	yùyán	yuHyìHn
parachute n.	降落傘	jyànglwòsǎn	gongloHksaan
parade n.	閱兵	ywèbìng	yuHtbìng
paradise n.			
-Christian	樂園	lèywán;	loHkyùHn;
-Budd.	極樂世界	jílèshìjyè	giHkloHksaigaai
paraffin	石蠟	shílà	seHklaaHp
paragraph n.	段	dwàn;	dyuHn;
	節	jyé	jit
parallel a.	平行	píngsyíng	pìHnghàHng
paralysis a.	瘋癱	fēngtān;	fùngtáan;
	痲痺	mábì	màHbei
parcel n.	包	bāu;	bàau;
	包裹	bāugwǒ	bàaugwó
parchment n.	羊皮紙	yángpíjǐ	yèuHngpèiHjí
pardon v. t.			
-forgive	饒恕	ráushù;	yiùHsyu;
-excuse	原諒	ywánlwàng;	yùHnleuHng;
-overlook	寬恕	kwānshù	fùnsyu
-pardon me	對不起	dwèibùchǐ	deuibāthéi (deuim̀jyuH
parenthesis n.	括弧	kwòhú	kwutwùH
parents n.	父母	fùmǔ;	fuHmóuH;
	雙親	shwāngchīn	sèungchàn
parish n.	教區	jyàuchyū;	gaaukèui;
	牧師區	mùshīchyū	muHksìkèui
-parish clerk	教區助理	jyàuchyūjùlǐ	gaaukèuijoHléiH
-parish register	教友名冊	jyàuyǒumíngtsè	gaauyɛ́uHmìHngchaak
park n.	公園	gūngywán	gùngyùHn

-park a car	停車	tíngchē	tìHngchè
parliament n.	國會	gwóhwèi	gwokwúi
parlour n.	客廳	kèting	haaktēng
parrot n.	鸚鵡	yīngwǔ	yìngmóuII
part			
-v. t. divide	分開	fēnkāi,	fànhòl;
-n. portion	部分	bùfèn	bouHfaHn
take v. i.			
-take part	參加	tоànjyā;	chàamgà;
-have a share	有分	yǒufèn	yáuHfán
artial v. i.			
-not entire	一部分	yíbùfèn;	yātbouHfaHn;
-biased	偏心	pyānsyīn	pìnsàm
artiality n.	偏心	pyānsyīn;	pìnsàm;
	偏見	pyānjyàn	pìngin
articipate v. i.	參加	tsānjyā	chàamgà
articiple n.	分詞	féntsź	fànchìH
article n.			
-least amount	少量	shǎulyàng;	síuleuHng;
-Meth.	分子	fèndž	faHnjí
articular a.			
-individual	個人	gèrén;	goyàHn;
-special	特別	tèhyé;	daHkbiHt;
-in detail	詳細	syángsyì;	chèuHngsai;
-precise	講究	jyǎngjyòu	gónggau
artition n.	隔開	ᴋékāi	gaakhòi
artly adv.	部分	bùfèn	bouIIfaHn
artner n.			
-companion	伴侶	bànlyǔ;	buIInléuiIT;

-in business	股東	gǔdūng;	gúdūng;
-in games	對手	dwèishǒu	deuisáu
partnership n.			
-association	聯合	lyánhé;	lyùHnhaHp;
-participation	協同	syétúng;	hiHptùHng;
-joint possession	共有	gùngyǒu	guHngyáuH
party n.			
-organization	黨派	dǎngpài;	dóngpaai;
-dinner	宴會	yànhwèi	yinwuiH
pass			
–v. i. go forward	走	dzǒu;	jáu (haàHng);
–v. i. in an exam.	及格	jígé;	kaHpgaak;
–v. i. release, a custom house	放行	fàngsyíng;	fonghàHng;
–n. passage	通路	tūnglù;	tùnglouH;
–n. licence to	通行證	tūngsyíngjèng;	tùnghàHngjing;
–n. ticket of admission	入塲劵	rùchǎngjywàn	yaHpcheùHnggyun
-pass a motion	通過	tūnggwò	tùnggwo
-pass the night	過夜	gwòyè	gwoyeH
-pass through	經過	jīnggwò	gìnggwo
pass book n.	存摺	tswúnjé	chyùHnjip
passage n.			
-act of passing	通行	tūngsyíng;	tùnghàHng;
-passing to & fro	來往	láiwǎng;	lòiHwóHng;
-in a house	走廊	dzǒuláng;	jáulòHng;
-fare	路費	lùfèi;	louHfai;
-paragraph	段	dwàn	dyuHn
passenger n.	搭客	bākè;	daaphaak;

	乘客	chèngkè	sìHnghaak

passion n.

-anger	怒氣	nùchì;	nouHhei;
-sexual	情慾	chíngyù;	chìHngyuHk;
-emotion	情感	chínggǎn;	chìHnggám;
-inordinate desire	熱情	rèchíng	yiHtchìHng

passionate a.

-irascible	易怒	yìnù;	yiHnouH;
-ardent	奮激	fènjí;	fáHngik;
-enthusiastic	狂熱	kwángrè	kòHngyiHt

passive a.

-inactive	被動	bèidùng	beiHduHng
-passive resistance	消極抵抗	syāujídìkàng	sìugiHkdáikong
-passive voice	被動式	bèidùngshì	beiHduHngsik

passport n.

	護照	hùjàu;	wuHjiu;
	通行證	tūngsyíngjèng	tùnghàHngjing

password n.

	暗號	ànhàu;	ngamhouH;
	口號	kǒuhàu	háuhouH

past

-a. gone by	已往	yǐwǎng;	yíHwóHng;
-n. former facts	往事	wǎngshì;	wóHngsiH;
-adv. by	經過	jìnggwò;	gìnggwo;
-prep. beyond	超過	chāugwò	chìugwo
-past tense	過去式	gwòchyùshì	gwoheuisik

paste

-n.	漿糊	jyànghu;	jèungwùH;
-v. t.	黏	nyán;	nìHm;
-v. t.	貼	tyē	tip

pastel n.

| | 粉筆 | fěnbì | fánbāt |

pastime n.

-amusement	娛樂	yúlè;	yùHloHk;
-hobby	消遣	syāuchyǎn;	siuhín;
-game	遊戲	yúusyì	yàuHhei

pastor n. 牧師　mùshī　muHksī

pastry n. 點心　dyǎnsyin　dímsām

pasture

-n. grazing land	草地	tsǎudì;	chóudeiH;
	牧場	mùchǎng;	muHkchèuHng;
-v. i. eat the grass	吃草	chītsǎu	hekchóu (siHkchóu)

pat

-v. t./v. i. tap	輕拍	chīngpāi;	hìngpaak;
-n. sound of tap	拍聲	pāishēng	paaksèng

patch

-v. t. mend	補	bǔ;	bóu;
-n. cloth to repair	補布	bǔbù;	bóubou;
-n. a scrap	碎布	swèibù	seuibou

patent a. 專賣　jwānmài　jyùnmaaiH

-patented article	專賣品	jwānmàipǐn	jyùnmaaiHbán
-patent medicine	專賣藥	jwānmàiyàu	jyùnmaaiHyeuHk
-patent office	專賣局	jwānmàijyú	jyùnmaaiHgúk

paternity n. 爲父者　wéifùjě　wàiHfuHjé

path n. 路　lù　louH

pathologist n. 病理學家　bìnglǐsywéjyā　beHngléiHhoHkgā

pathology n. 病理　bìnglǐ;　beHngléiH;

病理學　bìnglǐsywé　beHngléiHhoHk

patience n. 忍耐　rěnnài;　yánnoiH;

忍心　rěnsyin　yánsàm

patient

-a.	忍耐	rěnnài;	yánnoiH;

-n.	病人	bìngren	beHngyàHn
-patient disposition	耐性	nàisyìng	noiHsing
patriot n.	愛國者	àigwójě	ngoigwokjé
patriotism n.	愛國心	àigwósyìn	ngoigwoksàm
patrol v. t.	巡邏	syúnlwó	chèuHnlòH
patron n.			
-of a society	贊助人	dzànjùrén;	jaanjoHyàHn;
-promoter	發起人	fáchǐrén;	faathóiyàHn;
-customer	顧客	gùkè	guhaak
pattern n.			
-model	樣子	yàngdz;	yeuHngjí (yéung);
-sample	樣本	yàngběn;	yeuHngbún;
figure	模樣	mwóyàng;	mòuHyeuHng;
-good example	模範	mwófàn	mòuIIfaaIIn
pauper n.	乞丐	chǐgài	hātkoi (hātyì)
pause v. i.			
-stop	停止	tíngjǐ;	tìHngjí;
-hesitate	猶豫不決	yóuyúbùjywé	yàuHyuHbātkyut
pave v. t.			
-as with stone	舖	pū;	pòu;
-prepare	安排	ānpái	ònpàniH
pavement n.	人行道	rénsyíngdàu	yàHnhàaHngdouH
paw n.	爪	jwǎ,	jáau;
	掌	jǎng	jéung
pawn v. t.	當	dàng	dong
pawnshop n.	當舖	dàngpù	dongpou
pay			
-v. t. as a debt	還	hwán;	wàaHn;
-v. t. as wages	發	fā;	faat;
-v. t. indemnify	賠償	péicháng;	pùiHsèuIIng;

-n. of clerks, etc.	薪水	syìnshwěi;	sànséui;
-n. of servants, etc.	工錢	gūngchyán	gùngchìHn
-pay respects to	拜望	bàiwàng	baaimoHng
-pay taxes	納稅	nàshwèi	naaHpseui
payee n.	收欵人	shōukwǎnrén	sàufúnyàHn
payer n.	付欵人	fùkwǎnrén	fuHfúnyàHn
pea n.	豌豆	wāndòu;	wāandáu;
	青豆	chìngdòu	chèngdáu
peace n.	平安	píngān;	pìHngòn;
	太平	tàipíng;	taaipìHng;
	和平	hépíng	wòHpìHng
-universal peace	天下太平	tyānsyàtàipíng	tìnhaHtaaipìHng
peacemaker n.	調停者	tyáutíngjě;	tìuHtìHngjé;
	和事老	héshìlǎu	wòHsiHló̀uH
peach n.	桃	táu	tóu
peacock n.	孔雀	kǔngchywè	húngjeuk
peak n.	山頂	shāndǐng;	sàandéng;
	山峰	shānfēng	sàanfùng
peanut n.	花生	hwāshēng;	fàsàng;
-peanut butter	花生醬	hwāshēngjyàng;	fàsàngjeung;
-peanut oil	花生油	hwāshēngyóu	fàsàngyàuH
peapod n.	豆莢	dòujyá	dauHhaap
pear n.	梨	lí	léi
pearl n.			
-genuine	珠珍	jēnjū;	jānjyū;
-beads	珠子	jūdz	jyūjí (jyū)
peasant n.	農民	núngmín	nùHngmàHn
pebble n.	石子	shŕdz	seHkjí (seHkjái)

-n. a measure	斗𠇍	dǒu;	dáu;
-v. i. of birds	啄𡆦	jwó	deuk

peculiar a.

-characteristic	特殊	tèshū;	daHksyùH;
-special	特別	tèbyé;	daHkbiHt;
-strange, odd	古怪	gūgwài	gúgwaai
pedagogy n.	教授法	jyàushòufǎ	gaausauHfaat
pedal n.	踏板	tàbǎn	taapbáan
-pedal surface	垂足面	chwéidzúmyàn	sèuiHjūkmiHn
pedant n.	腐儒	fǔrú;	fuHyùH;
	學究	sywéjyōu	hoHkgau
peddler n.	小販	syǎufàn	síufáan
pedestrian n.	行人	syíngrén	hàHngyàHn
pediatrician n.	兒科醫生	érkēyìshēng	yìHfōyìsāng
pedicab n.	三輪車	sānlwúnchē	sàanlèuHnchè
pedlar n.	小販	syǎufàn	síufáan

peel

-n. skin, etc.	皮	pí;	pèiH;
-v. t. to skin	剝皮	bāupí;	mōkpèiH;
-v. t. with a knife	削皮	syāupí	seukpèiH
peep v. i.	偷看	tōukàn	tàuhon (tàutái)
peer n.	貴族	gwèidzú	gwaijuHk
Pekingman n.	北京人	Běijìngrén	BākgìngyàHn
pelvis n.	骨盤	gǔpán	gwātpùHn
pen n.	筆	bǐ	bāt

penalty n.

-punishment	刑罰	syíngfá;	yìHngfaHt;
-fine	罰欵	fákwǎn;	faHtfún;

-retribution	報應	bàuyìng	bouying
pence n.	辨士	byànshr̀	biHnsiH
pencil n.	鉛筆	chyānbǐ	yùHnbāt
pendant n.	垂飾	chwéishr̀	sèuiHsìk
pendulum n.	擺	bǎi	báai
penetrate v. t.			
-enter into	進入	jìnrù;	jeunyaHp;
-of a liquid	滲入	shènrù;	samyaHp;
-understand	了解	lyǎujyě;	líugáai;
-see through	看穿	kànchwān	honchyùn (táichyùn)
penguin n.	企鵝	chǐé	kéiHngòH
penicillin n.	盤尼西林	pánnísyilín	pùHnnèiHsàilàHm
peninsula n.	半島	bàndǎu	bundóu
penknife n.	小刀	syǎudāu	síudōu (dōujái)
penmanship n.	習字	syídz̀;	jaaHpjiH;
	書法	shūfǎ	syùfaat
pennant n.	三角旗	sānjyǎuchí	sàamgokkèiH
penniless a.	一文不名	yìwénbùmíng	yātmàHnbātmìHng
penny n.	辨士	byànshr̀	biHnsiH
pension n.	退休金	twèisyōujǐn	teuiyàugām
pentagon n.	五邊形	wǔbyānsyíng	ńgHbìnyìHng
peon n.	聽差	tīngchāi;	tīngchàai;
	雜役	dzáyì	jaaHpyiHk (jaaHpchàai)
peony n.	牡丹花	mǔdānhwā;	máauHdāanfā;
	富貴花	fùgwèihwà	fugwaifā
people n.			
-in general	人	rén;	yàHn;

-the nation	國民	gwómín;	gwokmàHn;
-citizen	百姓	bǎisyìng;	baaksing;
-race	民族	míndzú;	màHnjuHk;
-people's commune	人民公社	rénmíngūngshè	yàHnmàHngùngséH
epper n.	胡椒	hújyāu	wùHjiu
er prep.			
-through	由	yóu;	yàuH;
-for each	每	měi	múiH
erceive v. t.			
-generally	發覺	fajywé;	faatgok,
-see	看見	kànjyàn;	hongin (táidóu)
-feel	覺得	jywéde	gokdāk
ercentage n.			
-Math.	百分法	bǎifēnfǎ;	baakfaHufaat;
-proportion	比率	bǐlyù;	béileuHt;
-as in examination	分數	fēnshù	fansou
erception n.			
-cognition	識別力	shíbyéli;	sikbiHtliHk;
-apprehension	理解力	lǐjyěli	léiHgáailiHk
erch			
-v. i. as a bird	歇	syē;	hit (yāusìk);
-n. fish	鱸魚	lúyú	lòuHyùH
erfect			
-a. complete	完全	wánchywán;	yùHnchyùHn;
-a. not defective	無缺	wúchywē;	mòuHkyut;
-a. flawless	完美	wánměi;	yùHnméiH;
-v. t. complete	完成	wánchéng	yùHnsìHng
erform v. t.			
-do	做	dzwò;	jouH;

-an obligation	履行	lyŭsyíng;	léuiHhàHng;
-a ceremony	舉行	jyŭsyíng;	géuihàHng;
-duty of office	執行	jŕsyíng;	jāphàHng;
-perform ceremony	行禮	syínglĭ	hàHngláiH

performance n.

-execution	執行	jŕsyíng;	jāphàHng;
-of a contract	履行	lyŭsyíng;	léuiHhàHng;
-theatrical	戲	syì;	hei;
-musical	演奏	yăndzòu	yínjau

perfume n.

| -smell | 香味 | syāngwèi; | hèungmeiH; |
| -liquid | 香水 | syāngshwĕi | hèungséui |

perhaps adv.

	或者	hwòjĕ;	waaHkjé;
	也許	yĕsyŭ;	yáHhéuï;
	可能	kĕnéng	hónàHng

peril n.

| -danger | 危險 | wéisyăn; | ngàiHhím; |
| -injury | 損害 | swŭnhài | syúnhoiH |

period n.

-epoch	時代	shŕdài;	sìHdoiH;
-a set time	時期	shŕchì;	sìHkèiH;
-end of time	期限	chìsyàn;	kèiHhaaHn;
-term of years	年限	nyánsyàn	nìHnhaaHn

periodical n. | 定期刊物 | dìngchikānwù | diHngkèiHhónmaHt |

perish v. i.

-be destroyed	毀滅	hwĕimyè;	wáimiHt;
-be ruined	滅亡	myèwáng;	miHtmòHng;
-die	死	sž	séi

erjury n.	偽ㄨㄟˊ 誓ㄕˋ	wèishr̀	ngaiHsaiH
ermanent a.			
-opp. to temporary	永ㄩㄥˇ 久ㄐㄧㄡˇ	yǔngjyǒu;	wíHnggáu;
-fixed	固ㄍㄨˋ 定ㄉㄧㄥˋ	gùdìng;	gudìHng;
-wave	電ㄉㄧㄢˋ 髮ㄈㄚˇ	dyànfǎ	diHnfaat
ermission n.	許ㄒㄩˇ 可ㄎㄜˇ	syǔkě;	héuihó;
	准ㄓㄨㄣˇ 許ㄒㄩˇ	jwǔnsyǔ	jéunhéui
ermit			
~v. t. consent	准ㄓㄨㄣˇ 許ㄒㄩˇ	jwǔnsyǔ	jéunhéui;
~v. t. tolerate	寬ㄎㄨㄢ 容ㄖㄨㄥˊ	kwānrúng;	fùnyùHng;
~v. i. allow	允ㄩㄣˇ 准ㄓㄨㄣˇ	yǔnjwǔn	wáHnjéun
erpendicular a.	垂ㄔㄨㄟˊ 直ㄓ	chwéijf̄	sèuiHjiHk
erpetrate v. t.	犯ㄈㄢˋ	fàn	faaHn
erpetual a.	永ㄩㄥˇ 久ㄐㄧㄡˇ	yǔngjyǒu	wíHnggáu
-perpetual calendar	萬ㄨㄢˋ 年ㄋㄧㄢˊ 日ㄖˋ 曆ㄌㄧˋ	wànnyánr̀lì	maaHnnìHnyaHtliHk
erplex v. t.			
-puzzle	弄ㄋㄨㄥˋ 不ㄅㄨˋ 清ㄑㄧㄥ	nùngbùchīng;	luHngbātchīng (gáaum̀chìngchó);
-embarrass	爲ㄨㄟˊ 難ㄋㄢˊ	wéinán	wàiHnàaHn
ersecute v. t.	逼ㄅㄧ 迫ㄆㄛˋ	bīpwò;	bikbāak;
	迫ㄆㄛˋ 害ㄏㄞˋ	pwòhài	bāakhoiH
ersecution n.	迫ㄆㄛˋ 害ㄏㄞˋ	pwòhái;	bāakhoiH;
	虐ㄋㄩㄝˋ 待ㄉㄞˋ	nywèdài	yeuHkdoiH
erseverance n.	耐ㄋㄞˋ 性ㄒㄧㄥˋ	nàisyìng;	noiHsing;
	毅ㄧˋ 力ㄌㄧˋ	yìlì	ngaiHliHk
ersevere v. i.	忍ㄖㄣˇ 耐ㄋㄞˋ	rěnnài;	yánnoiH;
	堅ㄐㄧㄢ 持ㄔˊ	jyānchf̄	gìnchìH
ersimmon n.	柿ㄕˋ 子ㄗ	shr̀dz	chíjí (chí)
ersist v. i.	堅ㄐㄧㄢ 持ㄔˊ	jyānchf̄	gìnchìH

person n.	人ㄖㄣ	rén	yàHn
personal a.			
-individual	個ㄍㄜ 人ㄖㄣ	gèrén;	goyàHn;
-done by	親ㄑㄧㄣ 身ㄕㄣ	chīnshēn;	chànsàn;
-private	私ㄙ 人ㄖㄣ	sīrén	sìyàHn
-personal freedom	個ㄍㄜ 人ㄖㄣ 自ㄗ 由ㄧㄡ	gèréndzyóu	goyàHnjiHyàuH
-personal interview	面ㄇㄧㄢ 洽ㄑㄧㄚ	myànchyà	miHnhāp
perspiration n.			
-sweat	汗ㄏㄢ	hàn;	hoHn;
-perspiring	出ㄔㄨ 汗ㄏㄢ	chūhàn	chēuthoHn
perspire v. i.	出ㄔㄨ 汗ㄏㄢ	chūhàn;	chēuthoHn;
	流ㄌㄧㄡ 汗ㄏㄢ	lyóuhàn	làuHhoHn
persuade v. t.	勸ㄑㄩㄢ	chywàn	hyun
pertaining to	屬ㄕㄨ 於ㄩ	shǔyú	suHkyù
pervade v. t.	佈ㄅㄨ 滿ㄇㄢ	bùmǎn	boumúHn
perverse a.	變ㄅㄧㄢ 態ㄊㄞ	byàntài	bintaai
pessimism n.	悲ㄅㄟ 觀ㄍㄨㄢ	bēigwān	bèigùn
pessimistic a.	悲ㄅㄟ 觀ㄍㄨㄢ	bēigwān;	bèigùn;
	消ㄒㄧㄠ 極ㄐㄧ	syāují	sìugiHk
pest n.			
-plague	黑ㄏㄟ 死ㄙ 病ㄅㄧㄥ	hēisžbìng;	hāaksíbeHng;
-insect	害ㄏㄞ 蟲ㄔㄨㄥ	hàichúng	hoiHchùHng
pestilence n.	瘟ㄨㄣ 疫ㄧ	wēnyì	wànyiHk
pet n.	寶ㄅㄠ 貝ㄅㄟ	bǎubèi;	bóubui;
	心ㄒㄧㄣ 愛ㄞ 動ㄉㄨㄥ 物ㄨ	syīnàidùngwù	sàmoiduHngmaHt
petal n.	花ㄏㄨㄚ 瓣ㄅㄢ	hwābàn	fàfaan
petition n.			
-request	請ㄑㄧㄥ 求ㄑㄧㄡ	chǐngchyóu;	chíngkàuH;
-parl., etc.	請ㄑㄧㄥ 願ㄩㄢ 書ㄕㄨ	chǐngywànshū	chíngyuHnsyù

petrify v. t.	硬化	yìnghwà	ngaaHngfa
petrol n.	汽油	chìyóu	heiyàuH
petty a.			
-small	小	syǎu;	síu (sai);
-trifling	瑣碎	swǒswèi	sóseui
pharmacist n.	藥劑師	yàujìshī	yeuHkjūisi
pharmacy n.			
-dispensary	藥房	yàufáng	yeuHkfòHng
phase n.			
-aspect	方面	fāngmyàn;	fòngmiHn;
-stage	時期	shíchí	siHkèiH
phenomenon n.	現象	syànsyàng	yiHnjeuHng
philanthropy n.			
-love of mankind	博愛	bwóài;	bokoi;
-benevolence	慈善	tsźshàn	chìHsiHn
philosopher n.	哲學家	jésywéjyā	jithoHkgā
philosophy n.	哲學	jésywé	jithoHk
phoenix n.	鳳凰	fènghwáng	fuHngwòHng
phonetic a.	注音	jùyīn;	jyuyām;
-alphabet	注音字母	jùyīndzìmǔ;	jyuāmjiHmóuH;
-symbols	注音符號	jùyīnfúhàu	jyuyāmfùHhouH
phonetics n.	語音學	yǔyīnsywé	yúHyāmhoHk
phonograph n.	留聲機	lyóushēngjī	làuHsìnggèi (cheunggèi)
photograph			
-n.	照片	jàupyàn;	jiupín;
-v. t.	照相	jàusyàng	jiuséung (yíngséung)
photographer n.	攝影師	shèyǐngshī	sipyíngsi
phrase n.	短句	dwǎnjyù	dyúngeui
phthisis n.	肺病	fèibìng;	faibeHng;

	肺勞	fèiláu	failòuH
physical a.			
-material	物質	wùjf;	maHtjāt;
-bodily	身體	shēntǐ	sàntái
-physical constitution	體格	tǐgé	táigaak
-physical examination	體格檢查	tǐgéjyǎnchá	táigaakgímchàH
-physical exercise	體操	tǐtsāu	táichòu
-physical science	自然科學	dżránkēsywé	jiHyìHnfòhoHk
-physical strength	體力	tǐlì	táiliHk
-physical world	自然界	dżránjyè	jiHyìHngaai
physician n.	醫生	yishēng	yisāng
-as opp. to surgeon	內科醫生	nèikēyisnēng	noiHfōyisāng
physicist n.	物理學家	wùlìsywéjyā	maHtléiHhoHkgā
physics n.	物理學	wùlìsywé	maHtléiHhoHk
physiognomy n.	相術	syàngshù;	seungseuHt;
	相法	syàngfǎ	seungfaat
physiology n.	生理學	shēnglìsywé	sàngléiHhoHk
physique n.	體格	tǐgé	táigaak
pianist n.	鋼琴師	gāngchínshr	gongkàHmsì
piano n.	鋼琴	gāngchín	gongkàHm
pick v. t.			
-choose	選	sywǎn;	syún (gáan);
-as fruit, flower	摘	jāi;	jaaHk;
-collect here & there	拾	shf;	saHp (jāp);
-as one's teeth	剔	ti	tik
pickles n.	醃菜	yāntsái	yìmchoi (hàaHmchoi)
picnic n.	旅行	lyǔsyíng;	léuiHhàHng;
	野餐	yětsān	yéHchāan
pictograph n.	象形文字	syàngsyíngwéndż	jeuHngyìHngmàHnjiH
picture n.	畫	hwà;	wá;

i	圖畫	túhwà	tòuHwá
icul n.	擔	dàn	daam
ie n.			
-pastry	饅頭	mántou,	maaHntàuH;
-meat	肉糕	ròugāu;	yuHkgou;
-fruit	果糕	gwŏgāu	gwógōu
iece n,			
-a piece of cloth (a classifier)	一塊布	yíkwàibù	yātfaaibou
ier n.	碼頭	mătóu	máHtàuH
ierce v. t.			
-of pointed instruments	刺	tsż;	chi;
-bore through	穿進	chwānjìn	chyùnjeun (jeukyaHp)
iety n.			
-towards God	虔誠	chyánchéng;	kìHnsìHng;
-towards parents	孝順	syàushwùn	haauseuHn
ig n.	豬	jū	jyū
igeon n.	鴿子	gēdz	gapjí (yúHgap)
igment n.	顏料	yánlyàu	ngàaHnlíu
ile			
-n. post	椿子	jwāngdz;	jòngjí (jōng);
-n. heap	堆	dwēi;	dèui;
-v. t. drive	打椿	dăjwāng	dájōng
iles n.	痔瘡	jìchwāng	jiHchōng
ilferer n.	小偷	syăutōu	síutāu (pàHsáu)
iling n.	打椿	dăjwāng	dájōng
ill n.	藥丸	yàuwán;	yeuHkyún;
	藥片	yàupyàn	yeuHkpìn
illage v. t.	打刼	dăjyé;	dágip;

	搶扱揤	chyǎngjyé	chéunggip
pillar n.	柱	jù;	chyúH;
	柱子	jùdz	chyúHjí (chyúH)
pillow n.	枕頭	jěntóu	jámtàuH
pillowcase n.	枕頭套	jěntóutàu	jámtàuHtou (jámtàuHdói)
pilot n.			
-port	領港人	lǐnggǎngrén;	líHnggóngyàHn;
-of aeroplane	飛機師	fēijishr̄	fēigēisī
pimple n.	小膿泡	syǎunúngpàu	síunùHngpaau (pōkjái)
pin n.			
-ordinary	大頭針	dàtóujēn;	daaiHtàujām;
-safety	扣針	kòujēn;	kaujām;
-hair	夾子	jyādz;	gáapjí (dénggáap);
-drawing	圖釘	túdǐng	tòuHdēng
pincers n.			
-forceps	鑷子	nyèdz;	nípjí (níp);
-pliers	鉗子	chyándz	kímjí (kím)
pinch v. t.			
-fingers	捏	nyē;	nip;
-finger-nails	掐	chyā;	hap;
-pincers	夾	jyā	gaaHp
pine n.	松樹	sūngshù	sùngsyuH
pineapple n.	菠蘿	bwōlwó;	bòlòH;
	鳳梨	fènglí	fuHnglèiH
ping-pong n.	乒乓球	bīngbāngchyóu	bingbōngkàuH (bingbōngbō)
pink a.	粉紅色	fěnhúngsè;	fánhùHngsìk;
	淡紅色	dànhúngsè	táaHmhùHngsìk

innacle n.	小尖塔	syăujyāntă	síujimtaap
int n.	品脫	pĭntwō	bántyut
loneer n.			
-Mil.	工兵	gūngbĭng;	gùngbĭng;
-fig.	開路先鋒	kāilùsyānfēng	hòilouHsinfùng
ious a.	虔敬	chyánjĭng	kìHnging
ip n.	小種子	syăujŭngdz	síujúngjí (júngjái)
ipe n.			
-tube	管	gwăn;	gún;
-flute	笛子	dídz;	deHkjí (dék);
-smoking	煙斗	yāndŏu	yĭndáu
-pipe organ	風琴	fēngchín	fùngkàHm
irate n.	海盜	hăidàu	hóidouH
istol n.	手鎗	shŏuchyāng	sáuchēung
it n.			
-of a mine	坑	kēng;	hàang;
-trap	陷阱	syànjĭng;	haHmjiHng;
-of the stomach	心窩	syĭnwō	sāmwō
itch			
-v. t. throw	扔	rēng;	yìng (dám);
-v. t. arrange	排	pái;	pàaiH;
-n. music	音調	yĭndyàu	yāmdıuH
itcher n.	水壺	shwĕihú	séuiwùH
tiable a.			
-rousing pity	可憐	kĕlyán;	hólìHn;
-of occurrences	悽慘	chĭtsăn	chàicháam
ittance n.	賙濟物	jōujìwù	jàujaimaHt
ty v. t.	可憐	kĕlyán	hólìHn

-what a pity	可惜	kěsyi	hósik
place			
-n. space	地方	dìfang;	deiHfòng;
-n. rank	身份	shēnfèn;	sànfán;
-v. t. put	放	fàng	fong
placenta n.	胎衣	tāiyī	tòiyì
placid a.			
-quiet	安靜	ānjìng;	ònjiHng;
-gentle	溫柔	wēnróu	wànyàuH
plague n.	瘟疫	wēnyì	wànyiHk
plain			
-a. evident	明白	míngbai;	mìHngbaaHk;
-a. simple	簡單	jyǎndān;	gáandàan;
-a. straight forward	老實	lǎushf;	lóuHsaHt;
-n. level ground	平地	píngdì;	pìHngdeiH;
-n. moor	平原	píngywán	pìHngyùHn
plait n.	辮子	byàndz	bìnjí (bìnjái)
plan			
-v. t. design	設計	shèjì;	chitgai;
-v. t. intend	打算	dǎswàn;	dásyun;
-n. scheme	計劃	jìhwà;	gaiwaaHk;
-n. project	設計	shèjì;	chitgai;
-n. plane figure	平面圖	píngmyàntú	pìHngmiHntòuH
plane			
-a. level	平	píng;	pìHng;
-n. Geom.	平面	píngmyàn;	pìHngmiHn;
-n. aeroplane	飛機	fēiji	fèigèi
planet n.	行星	syíngsyíng	hàHngsing
plank n.	木板	mùbǎn	muHkbáan

ant

-n. tree	樹	shù;	syuH;
-n. opp. to animal	植 物	jíwù;	jiHkmaHt;
-v. t. put in the ground	種	jùng	jung

aster n.

-for walls	灰	hwēi;	fùi;
-Med.	膏 藥	gāuyàu	gòuyeuHk
astic n.	塑 膠	sùjyāu	sokgàau
ate n.	淺 碟	chyǎndyé;	chíndiHp;
-n. sheet of metal	板	bǎn;	báan;
-n. photo	底 片	dǐpyàn;	dáipin;
-v. t.	鍍	dù	douH
ateau n.	高 原	gāuywàn	gòuyùHn
atform n.	臺	tái;	tòiH,
-railway	月 臺	ywètái;	yuHttòiH;
-for lecturing	講 臺	jyǎngtái;	góngtòiH;
-on a roof	露 臺	lùtái;	louHtòiH;
-theatrical	戲 臺	syìtái	heitòiH
atinum n.	白 金	báijīn;	baaHkgām
	鉑	bwó	baaHk

ay

-v. t. as a game	玩	wán;	wáan;
-n. dramatic composition	演 戲	yǎnsyì	yínhei (jouHhei)
-play cards	打 牌	dǎpái	dápáai
-play an instrument	彈 琴	tánchín	tàaHnkàHm
ayground n.	操 場	tsāuchǎng	chòuchèuHng

— n.

-excuse	口 實	kǒushí;	háusaIIt;
-defendant's answer	答 辯	dábyàn	daapbiHn

plead v. i.

-beg earnestly	懇求	kěnchyóu;	hánkàuH;
-árgue	辯論	~~byànlwùn;~~	biHnleuHn;
-in one's defence	辯護	byànhù	biHnwuH

pleasant a.

-pleasing	可愛	kěài;	hóoi;
-agreeable	和藹可親	héǎikěchīn;	wòHóihóchàn;
-cheerful	高興	gàusyìng	gòuhing

please v. t.

-request	請	chǐng;	chéng;
-give pleasure	使人歡喜	shǐrénhwānsyǐ;	síyàHnfùnhéi;
-be willing	喜歡	syǐhwan	héifùn

pleasure n.	快樂	kwàile	faailoHk
pleat n.	摺	jé	jip
plebiscite n.	議決權	yìjywéchywán	yíHkyutkyùHn

pledge

-v. t. pawn	抵押	dǐyā;	dáiaat;
-n. thing pawned	抵押品	dǐyāpǐn;	dáiaatbán;
-n. security	保証	bǎujèng	bóujing
plenipotentiary n.	全權大使	chywánchywán-dàshǐ	chyùHnkyùHndaaiHs

plenty

-n.	豐富	fēngfù;	fùngfu;
-adv.	充分	chūngfèn	chùngfaHn

pleurisy n.	肋膜炎	lèmwóyán	laHkmókyìHm
pliable a.	柔軟	róurwǎn	yàuHyúHn
pliers n.	鉗子	chyándz	kìHmjí (kìHm)
plight n.	情境	chíngjìng	chìHnggíng

plot

~v. t. plan	企圖	chìtú;	kéiHtòuH;
~v. t. against a ruler	謀反	móufǎn;	màuHfáan;
~n. conspiracy	陰謀	yìnmóu	yàmmàuH
plough n.	犁	lí	làiH
pluck v. t.			
-pull off	拔	bá;	baIIt;
-flowers	摘	jāi	jaaHk
plug			
~n. electric	插頭	chātóu;	chaaptàuH (chaapsōu);
~v. t. stop	塞住	sāijù	oākjyuII
plum n.	李	lǐ	léi
plumber n.	鉛管匠	chyāngwǎnjyàng	yùHngúnjeuHng
plumb line	錘線	chwéisyàn	sèuiHsin
plume n.	毛	máu;	mòuII;
	羽毛	yǔmáu	yúHmòuH
plunder v. t.	搶劫	chyǎngjyé;	chéunggip;
	打劫	dǎjyé	dágip
plunge v. t.	跳	tyàu	tiu
plural number	多數	dwōshù	dòsou
plus a.	加	jyā	gà
plywood n.	膠合板	jyāuhébǎn	gàauhaHpháan
pneumatic a.	空氣的	kūngchìde	hùnghcidìk
pneumonia n.	肺炎	fèiyán	faiyiIIm
poach v. t.			
-an egg	煮	jǔ;	jyú;
-to trespass	偷捕	tōubǔ	tàubouH
pocket n.	袋	dài	dói
pocketbook n.	筆記簿	bǐjìbù;	bātgeibóu;
	袖珍本	syòujēnběn	jauHjānbún
pocketknife n.	小刀	syǎudāu	síudōu (dōujái)

pockmark n.	麻子	mádz	màHjí (dauHpèiH)
pod n.	豆莢	dòujyá	dauHhaap
poem n.	詩	shr̄	sí
poet n.	詩人	shr̄rén	síyàHn
poetry n.	詩	shr̄	sí
point			
-n. dot	點	dyǎn;	dím;
-n. purpose	目的	mùdi;	muHkdìk;
-v. t. direct	指	jǐ	jí
poise n.	秤坨	chèngtwó	chingtòH
poison			
-n.	毒	dú;	duHk;
-v. t.	下毒藥	syàdúyàu	haHduHkyeuHk (loHkduHkyeuHk)
poisonous snake	毒蛇	dúshé	duHksèH
poke v. t.	戳	chwō	cheuk (dūk)
poker n.	撲克	pūkè	pokhāak (pūkká)
polar a.	極	jí;	giHk;
-polar bear	白熊	báisyúng;	baaHkhùHng;
-polar star	北極星	běijísyïng	bākgiHksïng
pole			
-n. for flying a flag	旗杆	chígān;	kèiHgòn;
-v. t. push along	撐	chēng	chàang
police n.	警察	jǐngchá	gíngchaat
-military police	憲兵	syànbïng	hinbïng
-police station	警察局	jǐngchájyú	gingchaatgúk
policy n.	政策	jèngtsè	jingchaak
polish v. t.	擦	tsā	chaat
polite a.	有禮貌	yǒulǐmàu;	yáuHláiHmaauH;
	斯文	sz̄wén	sìmàHn
political a.	政治上	jèngjřshàng	jingjiHseuHng

politican n.

-good sense	政治家	jèngjɨjyā;	jingjiHgā;
-bad sense	政客	jèngkò	jinghaak
politics n.	政治學	jèngjɪsywé	jɪngjiHhoHk
poll n.	選舉	sywǎnjyǔ;	syúngéui;
	投票	tóupyàu	tàuHpiu
pollute v. t.	汚辱	wūrù	wùyuHk
polo n.	馬球	mǎchyóu	máHkàuII
polygamy n.	一夫多妻	yìfūdwōchī	yātfùdòchài
polytechnic n.	工藝學院	gūngyìsywéywàn	gùngngaiHhoHkyún
pomegranate n.	石榴	shílyóu	seHkláu
pomade n.	髮油	fǎyóu	laatyàuII
pomelo n.	柚子	yòudz	yáují (lūkyáu)
pomp n.	壯觀	jwànggwān;	jonggùn;
	盛列	shènglyè	siHngliHt
pompous a.	繁華	fánhwá	fàaHnwàH
pond n.	池	chɨ;	chìH;
	塘	táng	tòHng
ponder v. i.			
-think over	考慮	kǎulyù;	háauleuiH;
-think of the past	回憶	hwéiyì	wùiHyik
pongee n.	府綢	fǔchóu	fúcháu
pony n.	小馬	syǎumǎ	síumáH (máHjái)
pool n.	池	chɨ	chìH
poor a.			
-poverty	貧窮	pínchyúng;	pàHnkùHng;
-in quality	粗	tsū;	chòu;
-pity	可憐	kělyán;	hólìHn;

-unskilled	生手	shēngshǒu	sàangsáu
pop corn n.	熱爆玉蜀黍	rèbàuyùshúshǔ	yiHtbaauyuHksuHksyú (baausūkmáiH)
popeyed a.	突眼	tūyǎn	daHtngáaHn
poplar n.	白楊	báiyáng	baaHkyèuHng
poplin n.	毛葛	máugé	mòuHgok
poppy n.	罌栗	yīngsù	yīngsūk
popular a.			
-fashionable	流行	lyóusyíng;	làuHhàHng;
-not abstruse	通俗	tūngsú	tùngjuHk
popularize v. t.	通俗化	tūngsúhwà	tùngjuHkfa
population n.	人口	rénkǒu	yàHnháu
porcelain n.	瓷器	tszchì	chìHhei
porch n.	門廊	ménláng	mùHnlòHng
porcupine n.	豪豬	háujū	hòuHjyū
pore n.	毛孔	máukǔng	mòuHhúng
pork n.	猪肉	jūròu	jyūyuHk
porous a.	多孔	dwōkǔng	dòhúng (dòlūng)
porridge n.	粥	jōu	jūk
port n.			
-harbour	港口	gǎngkǒu;	góngháu;
-town	商埠	shāngfù	sèungfauH
-closed port	河港	hégǎng	hòHgóng
-free port	自由港	dzyóugǎng	jiHyàuHgóng
-naval port	軍港	jyūngǎng	gwàngóng
-open port	通商港	tūngshānggǎng	tùngsèunggóng
-port office	港務局	gǎngwùjyú	góngmouHgúk
portable a.	手提	shǒutí	sáutàiH
portage n.	搬運	bānyùn;	bùnwaHn;
	運費	yùnfèi	waHnfai
porter n.			
-luggage-carrier	挑夫	tyāufū;	tǐufù (gūlēi);

-door-keeper	守門	shǒumén	sáumùHn (hòngāng)
portfolio n.	公事包	gūngshìbāu	gùngsiHbāau
portion n.			
-part	部分	bùfèn;	bouHfaHn;
-share	份	fèn	faHn
portmanteau n.	皮箱	písyāng	pèiHsēung
portrait n.	肖像	syàusyàng;	chiujeuHng;
	畫像	hwàsyàng	wájeuHng
portray v. t.	扮演	bànyǎn	baaHnyín
pose n.			
gesture	姿勢	dzshì;	jìsai;
-attitude	態度	tàidù	taaidouH
position n.			
-place	位置	wòijì	waiIIji;
-rank	地位	dìwèi	deiHwaiH
positive a.			
-opp. to negative	積極	jíjí;	jikgiHk;
-absolute	絕對	jywédwèi;	jyuHtdeui;
-positive electricity	陽電	yángdyàn	yèuHngdiHn
-positive pole	陽極	yángjí	yèuHnggiIIk
possess v. t.	有	yǒu	yáuH
possession n.	財產	tsáichǎn;	chòiHcháan;
	所有	swǒyǒu	sóyáuH
possibility n.	可能性	kěnéngyìng	hónàHngsing
possible a.	可能	kěnéng;	hónàIIng;
	可為	kěwéi	hówàiH
possibly adv.	或者	hwòjě;	waaHkjé;
	也許	yěsyǔ	yáHhéui
post n.			
-box	郵筒	yóutǔng;	yàuHtúng;
-office	郵政局	yóujèngjyú	yàuHjinggúk

-post-cord	明信片	míngsyìnpyàn	mìHngseunpín
-postman	郵差	yóuchāi	yàuHchàai
postage n.	郵費	yóufèi	yàuHfai
poster n.	招貼	jāutyē	jìutip (gàaijìu)
posterity n.	子孫	dž̌swūn	jísyūn
posthumous a.	死後的	sž̌hòude	séihauHdĭk
postpone v. t.	延期;	yánchí;	yìHnkèiH;
	展期	jǎnchí	jínkèiH
postscript n.			
-to a letter	再者	dzàijě;	joijé;
-to a book	附錄	·fùlù	fuHluHk
posture n.			
-gesture	姿勢;	dž̌shì;	jìsai;
-attitude	態度	tàidù	taaidouH
pot n.			
-for beverage	壺	hú;	wùH;
-for flowers	瓶	píng;	pìHng;
-jar	罐	gwàn	gun
potato n.	馬鈴薯	mǎlíngshǔ	máHlìHngsyú (syùHjái)
potent a.	有勢	yǒushì;	yáuHsai;
	有能	yǒunéng	yáuHnàHng
potential n.	可能性	kěnéngsyìng	hónàHngsing
-potential difference	電位差	dyànwèichā	diHnwaiHchà
-potential mood	可能法	kěnéngfǎ	hónàHngfaat
potter n.	陶匠	táujyàng	tòuHjeuHng
pottery n.	陶器	táuchì	tòuHhei
pouch n.	袋	dài	doiH
poultice n.	膏藥	gāuyàu	gòuyeuHk
poultry n.	家禽	jyāchín	gàkàHm
pound n.	英鎊	yìngbàng	yìngbóng

pour v. t.

-heavily	倒	dàu;	dóu;
-gently	斟	jēn	jàm
poverty n.	貧窮	pínchyúng	pàIInkùHng
powder n.	粉	fĕn	fán

power n.

-ability	能力	nénglì;	nàHngliHk;
-authority	權柄	chywánbìng	kyùHnbing
influence	勢力	shìlì	sailiHk
powerful a.	有勢	yŏuchì	yáuIIsaI
practical a.	實際	shíjì;	saHtjai;
	實用	shíyùng	saHtyuHng
practise v. t.	練習	lyànǥyí	liHnjaaIIµ

praise v. t.

-a person	稱讚	chēngdzàn;	chìngjaan;
God	讚美	dzànmëi	jaanmëiH
pram n.	搖籃車	yáulánchē	yìuHlàaHmchē
prawn n.	蝦	syā	hā

pray v. i.

-beg	求	chyóu;	kàuH;
-to God	祈禱	chídău	kèiHtóu
-pray with hope	祈望	chíwàng	kèiHmoHng
prayer n.	祈禱	chídău;	kèiHtóu;
	禱告	dăugàu	tóugou
preach v. t.	傳道人	chwándàu;	chyùIIndouII,
	講道	jyǎngdàu	góngdouH
preacher n.	傳道人	chwándàurén	chyùHndouHyàHn
preannounce v. t.	預告	yùgàu	yuHgou
prearrange v. t.	預定	yùdìng	yuHdiHng
precaution n.	預防	yùfáng	yuHfòHng

precede v. t.

-in front	在前	dzàichyán;	joiHchìHn;

-in rank	職位高	jíwèigāu	jikwaiHgòu
precedent n.	例子	lìdz;	laiHjí
	先例	syānlì	sìnlaiH
precept n.	律例	lyùlì	leuHtlaiH
precious a.	寶貴	bǎugwèi;	bóugwai;
	貴重	gwèijùng	gwaijuHng
-precious stone	寶石	bǎushŕ	bóuseHk
precipice n.	懸崖	sywányái	yùHnngàaiH
precipitous a.	險峻	syǎnjyùn	hímjeun
precis n.	大意	dàyì;	daaiHyi;
	摘要	jāiyàu	jaaHkyiu
precise a.			
-exact	確實	chywèshŕ;	koksaHt;
-accurate	正確	jèngchywè;	jingkok;
-detailed	詳細	syángsyì	chèuHngsai
precocious a.	早熟	dzǎushú	jóusuHk
predecessor n.	前人	chyánrén;	chìHnyàHn;
-in office	前任	chyánrèn	chìHnyaHm
predetermine v. t.	預定	yùdǐng	yuHdiHng
predicament n.	逆境	nìjìng	yiHkgíng
predicate n.	述語	shùyǔ	seuHtyúH
predict v. t.	預言	yùyán;	yuHyìHn;
	預告	yùgàu	yuHgou
predominant a.	優勢	yōushŕ	yàusai
pre-eminent a.	優秀	yōusyòu;	yàusau;
	卓越	jwóywè;	cheukyuHt;
	出衆	chūjùng;	chēutjung;
	超群	chāuchyún	chìukwàHn

preface n.	序	syù;	jeuiH;
	序文	syùwén	jeuiHmàHn
prefer v. t.	寧願	nìngywàn;	nìHngyún;
	情願	chíngywàn	chìHngyún
preferential right	優先權	yōusyānchywán	yàusìnkyùHn;
prefix n.	接頭詞	jyētóutsź	jiptàuHchìH
pregnant a.	懷孕	hwáiyùn;	wàaiHyaHn;
-pregnant woman	孕婦	yùnfù;	yaHnfúII;
prehistoric a.	史前	shíchyán	sìchìHn
prejudice n.			
-bias	偏見	pyānjyàn;	pìngin;
-in favour	偏心	pyānsyìn	pìnsàm
preliminary a.	初步	chūbù	chòbouH
prelude n.	前奏曲	chyándzòuchyŭ	chìHnjaukūk
premature a.	早熟	dzăushú	jóusuHk
premier n.	首相	shŏusyàng	sáuseung
premiere n.			
-1st performance	首次公演	shŏutsżgūngyăn	sáuchigùngyín
premise n.	前提	chyántí	chìHntàiH
premium n.	保險費	băusyănfèi	bóuhímfai
prepaid a.	預付	yùfù;	yuHfuH;
	先付	syānfù	sìnfuH
preoccupied a.			
-engrossed	專心	jwānsyìn;	jyùnsàm;
-absorbed	專注	jwānjù;	jyùnjyu;
-lost in thought	凝思	yísż	yìHngsì
preparation n.	預備	yùbèi;	yuHbeiH;
	準備	jwŭnbèi	jéunbeiH

preparatory class 預ㄩ 科ㄎㄜ 班ㄅㄢ　　yùkēbān;　　yuHfōbāan;

先ㄒㄧㄢ 修ㄒㄧㄡ 班ㄅㄢ　　syānsyōubān　　sinsāubāan

prepare v. t.

  -get ready 預ㄩ 備ㄅㄟ　　yùbèi　　yuHbeiH;

  -as in cooking 煮ㄓㄨ　　jǔ　　jyú

prepay v. t. 先ㄒㄧㄢ 付ㄈㄨ　　syānfù;　　sinfuH;

預ㄩ 付ㄈㄨ　　yùfù　　yuHfuH

preposition n. 前ㄑㄧㄢ 置ㄓ 詞ㄘ　　chyánjìrtsź　　chìHnjichìH

presage n. 預ㄩ 兆ㄓㄠ　　yùjàu　　yuHjiuH

prescribe v. t.

  -by law 規ㄍㄨㄟ 定ㄉㄧㄥ　　gwēidìng;　　kwàidiHng;

  -medical 開ㄎㄞ 藥ㄧㄠ 方ㄈㄤ　　kāiyàufāng　　hòiyeuHkfōng

prescription n. 藥ㄧㄠ 方ㄈㄤ　　yàufāng　　yeuHkfōng

presence n.

  -being present 出ㄔㄨ 席ㄒㄧ　　chūsyí;　　chēutjiHk;

  -as a witness 在ㄗㄞ 場ㄔㄤ　　dzàichǎng　　joiHcheùHng

present

  -a. in place 在ㄗㄞ 塲ㄔㄤ　　dzàichǎng;　　joiHchèuHng;

  -a. of time 目ㄇㄨ 前ㄑㄧㄢ　　mùchyán;　　muHkchìHn;

  -v. t. hand in 交ㄐㄧㄠ 給ㄍㄟ　　jyāugěi;　　gāaukāp (gàaubéi);

  -v. t. introduce 介ㄐㄧㄝ 紹ㄕㄠ　　jyèshàu;　　gaaisiuH;

  -n. a gift 禮ㄌㄧ 物ㄨ　　lǐwù　　láiHmaHt

presentation n. 贈ㄗㄥ 送ㄙㄨㄥ　　dzéngsùng　　jaHngsung

preserve

  -v. t. keep safe 保ㄅㄠ 存ㄘㄨㄣ　　bǎutswún;　　bóuchyùHn;

  -n. in sugar 蜜ㄇㄧ 餞ㄐㄧㄢ　　mìjyàn　　maHtjin

preside v. i.

  -act as chairman 做ㄗㄨㄛ 主ㄓㄨ 席ㄒㄧ　　dzwòjǔsyí;　　jouHjyújHk;

主ㄓㄨ 持ㄔ　　jǔchŕ　　jyúchìH

president n.

-of republic	總統	dzŭngtŭng;	júngtúng;
-at a meeting	主席	jŭoyí;	jyújiHk;
of a bank	行長	hángjăng;	hòHngjéung;
-of a company	董事長	dŭngshìjăng;	dúngsiHjéung;
-of a society	會長	hwèijăng;	wuiHjéung;
-of a university	大學校長	dàsywésyáujăng	daaiHhoHkhaauHjéung

press

-v. t. downwards	壓	yā;	ngaat;
-v. t. together	夾	jyá;	gaaHp;
-v. t. as by crowd	逼	bī;	bīk;
-v. t. force	強逼	chyángbī;	kéuHngbīk;
-n. printing house	印刷場	yìnshwāchăng;	yauchaatchóng;
-n. newspaper	報紙	bàujŕ	bouji
pressure n.	壓力	yālì	ngaatliHk
prestige n.	名譽	míngyù;	mìHngyuH;
	名望	míngwàng	mìHngmoHng

presume v. i.

-take for granted	假定	jyădìng;	gádiHng;
-suppose	想	syăng	sóung
presumption n.	假定	jyădìng	gádiILng
pretend v. t.	假裝	jyăjwāng	gájòng
pretext n.	藉口	jyèkŏu	jiHkháu
pretty a.	美麗	mĕilì;	méiHlaiH;
	漂亮	pyàulyang	piuleuHng (leng)

prevail v. i.

-gain victory	得勝	déshèng;	dāksing;
-have effect	有效	yŏusyàu;	yáuHhaauH;

English	Chinese		
-prevail for nothing	徒勞無益	túláuwúyì	tòuHlòuHmòuHyìk
prevalent a.	流行	lyóusyíng	làuHhàHng
prevent v. t.			
-hinder	阻止	dzǔjř;	jójǐ;
-keep from happening	預防	yùfáng	yuHfòHng
previous a.	先	syān;	sìn;
	前	chyán	chìHn
pre-war a.	戰前	jànchyán	jinchìHn
prey n.			
-victim	犧牲品	syīshēngpǐn;	hèisàngbán;
-booty	戰利品	jànlìpǐn	jinleiHbán
price n.	價錢	jyàchyán;	gachìHn;
	價格	jyàgé	gagaak
prick			
-v. t. pierce	刺	tsż;	chi;
-n. thorn	刺	tsż	chi
pride n.			
-haughtiness	驕傲	jyāuàu;	gìungouH;
-arrogance	傲慢	àumàn	ngouHmaaHn
primary a.	第一	dìyī;	daiHyāt;
	最初	dzwèichū	jeuichò
primitive man	原始人	ywánshǐrén	yùHnchíyàHn
prince n.	太子	tàidz	taaijí
princess n.	公主	gūngjǔ	gùngjyú
principal a.			
-most important	主要	jǔyàu	jyúyiu
-principal clause	主句	jǔjyù	jyúgeui
-principal tone	主音	jǔyīn	jyúyām
-principal of school	校長	syàujǎng	haauHjéung

rinciple n.

-as of navigation	原理	ywánlǐ;	yùHnléiH;
-doctrine	主義	jǔyì	jyúyiH

rint v.t. 印 yìn; yan;

-printed matter 印刷品 yìnshwəpǐn yanchaatbán

rior a. 先 syān; sìn;

前 chyán chìHn

rise v. t. 撬 chyàu hiu (giuH)

rism n. 三稜鏡 sōnlíngjìng oàamlìIIuggeng

rison n. 監牢 jyānláu; gàamlòuH;

監獄 jyānyù gaamyuHk

risoner n. 犯人 fànrén; faaIIuyàHn;

囚犯 chyóufàn chàuHfáan

rivate a.

-belong to oneself	私人	sīrén;	sìyàHn;
-as a school	私立	sīlì	sìlaHp

rivation n.

-a depriving 剝奪 bwódwó; mōkdyuHt;

-destitution 貧乏 pínfá pàHnfaHt

rivilege n. 權利 chywánlì kyùHnleiH

Privy Council n. 樞密院 Shūmìywàn SyūmaHtyún

rivy seal n. 玉璽 yùsyǐ yuIIksái;

御璽 yùsyǐ yuHeói

rize n.

-monetary 獎金 jyǎngjīn; jéunggām;

-non-monetary 獎品 jyǎngpǐn jéungbán

ro & con 贊成與反對 dzànchéng yǔ jaansìHng yúH fáandeui
fǎndwèi

robably adv. 大概 dàgài; daaiHkói;

或者 hwòjě; waaHkjé;

	也 許	yĕsyŭ	yáHhéui
probation n.	試 用	shìyùng;	siyuHng;
	見 習	jyànsyí	ginjaaHp
probe v. t.	調 查	dyàuchá	diuHchàH
problem n.	問 題	wèntí	maHntàiH
procedure n.	手 續	shŏusyù;	sáujuHk;
	程 序	chéngsyù	chìHngjeuiH
proceed v. i.			
-go on	繼 續	jìsyù;	gaijuHk;
-take measures	進 行	jìnsyíng	jeunhàHng
proceeds n.	收 入	shōurù;	sàuyaHp;
-net proceeds	淨 益	jìngyì	jiHngyìk
process n.			
-method	方 法	fāngfă;	fòngfaat;
-of manufacture	製 法	jìfă	jaifaat
procession n.	遊 行	yóusyíng	yàuHhàHng
proclaim v. t.	宣 佈	sywānbù;	syùnbou;
	宣 稱	sywānchēng	syùnchìng
proclamation n.	告 示	gàushr̀;	gousiH;
	佈 告	bùgàu;	bougou;
	宣 言	sywānyán	syùnyìHn
procrastinate v.i./v.t.	遲 延	chŕyán	chìHyìHn
procurator n.	檢 察 官	jyănchágwān	gímchaatgùn
procure v. t.	取 得	chyúdé	chéuidāk (lódóu)
prodigal a.	浪 費	làngfèi;	loHngfai;
	奢 華	shēhwá	chèwàH
-prodigal son	浪 子	làngdž	loHngjí
prodigy n.	神 童	shéntúng	sàHntùHng
produce v. t.			
-bring about	發 生	fāshēng;	faatsàng;

Pr

-manufacture	出產	chūchǎn	chēujcháan
producer n.	生產者	shēngchǎnjě	sàngcháanjó
production n.			
-of crops	出產	chūchǎn;	chēutcháan;
-of goods	製造	jìdzàu;	jaijouH;
-of art	作品	dzwòpǐn	jokbán
profane v. t.	褻瀆	syèdú	sitduHk
profess v. t.	認	rèn;	yiHng;
	承認	chéngrèn	sìHngyiHng
profession n.	職業	jíyè	jikyiHp
professional a.			
-opposed to amateur	職業	jíyè;	jikyiHp;
specialize	專門	jwānmén	jyùnmùHn
professor n.	教授	jyàushòu	gaausauH
proficient			
-a.	精通	jīngtūng;	jìngtùng;
-n.	專家	jwānjyā	jyùngà
profile n.	半面	bànmyàn	bunmiHn
profit n.			
-benefit	利益	lìyì;	leiHyìk;
-good points	好處	hǎuchù	hóuchyu
profligate			
-a.	放蕩	fàngdàng;	fongdoHng;
-n.	浪子	làngdž	loHngjí
pro forma invoice	估價單	gūjyàdān	gúgadāan
profound a.	深	shēn	sàm
profuse a.	浪費	làngfèi;	loHngfai;
	奢侈	shechř	chèchí
program(me) n.			
-plan	計劃	jìhwà;	gaiwaaHk;
-theatrical	節目	jyémù	jitmuHk

progress v. i.	進步	jìnbù	jeunbouH
progressive form	進行式	jìnsyíngshŕ	jeunhàHngsìk
prohibit v. t.	禁止	jìnjǐ	gamjí
prohibition n.	禁止	jìnjǐ;	gamjí;
	禁令	jínlìng	gamliHng
project n.	計劃	jìhwà;	gaiwaaHk;
	設計	shèjì	chitgai
projector n.	放映機	fàngyǐngjī	fóngyínggèi
prolapse v. i./n.	脫落	twōlwò	tyutloHk (tyutlāt)
prolapsus n.	脫肛	twōgāng	tyutgòng
prolific a.	有生產力	yǒushēngchǎnlì	yáuHsàngcháanliHk
prologue n.			
-of a book	序	syù;	jeuiH;
-of a play	開場白	kāichǎngbái	hòichèuHngbaaHk
prolong v. t.	延長	yáncháng	yìHnchèuHng
promenade n.	行人道	syíngréndàu	hàHngyàHndouH
prominent a.			
-projecting	突出	tūchū;	daHtchēut;
-distinguished	傑出	jyéchū	giHtchēut
promise			
-v. t.	答應	dāyìng;	daapying;
-n.	應許	yìngsyǔ;	yìnghéui;
-break a promise	失信	shīsyìn;	sātseun;
-keep a promise	守約	shǒuywē;	sáuyeuk;
-make a promise	約定	ywēdìng	yeukdiHng
promising a.	有希望	yǒusyīwàng;	yáuHhèimoHng;
	有前途	yǒuchyántú	yáuHchìHntoùH
promissory note	欠單	chyàndàn;	himdāan;
	期票	chīpyàu	kèiHpiu

romote v. t.

-in rank	升級	shēngjí;	sìngkāp;
-interests, etc.	增進	dzēngjìn;	jàngjeun;
-as arts, ect.	提倡	tíchàng	tàiHchèung
romotion examination	升級考試	shēngjíkăushŕ	sìngkāpháausi

rompt a.

-quick	快	kwài	faai;
-without delay	立刻	lìkè	laHphàak
rompter n.	提示者	tíshŕjě	tàiHsiHjé
ronoun n.	代名詞	dàimíngtsź	doiHmìHngchìH
ronounce v. i.	宣佈	sywānbù;	syùnbou;
	發表	fābyău	faatbíu
ronounciation n.	發音	fāyin	faatyām

roof n.

-evidence	証據	jèngjyù;	jinggeui;
-documentary	字據	dżjyù;	jiHgeui;
-for correction	稿	gău	góu
ropaganda n.	宣傳	sywānchwán	syùnchyùHn

ropagate v. t.

-animals	繁殖	fánjŕ;	fàaHnjiHk;
-opinions	傳達	chwándá	chyùHndaaHt
ropel v. t.	推進	twēijìn	tèuijeun
ropeller n.	螺旋漿	lwósywánjyăng	lòHsyùHnjéung

roper a.

-correct	正確	jèngchywè;	jingkok;
-suitable	適當	shŕdàng	sìkdong

roperty n.

-things owned	財產	tsáichăn;	chòiHcháan;
-estate	產業	chănyè	cháanyiHp
rophecy n.	預言	yùyán	yuHyìHn

| prophesy v. i. | 預言 | yùyán | yuHyìHn |
| propitious a. | 吉利 | jíli | gàtleiH |

proportion n.

| -ratio | 比例 | bǐlì; | béilaiH; |
| -symmetry | 相稱 | syāngchèng | sèungching |

proposal n.

-suggestion	建議	jyànyì;	ginyíH;
-motion	提案	tíàn;	tàiHon;
-of marriage	求婚	chyóuhwūn	kàuHfàn

propose v. t.

-suggest	提議	tíyì;	tàiHyíH;
-intend	想	syǎng;	séung;
-offer marriage to	求婚	chyóuhwūn	kàuHfàn

proprietor n.

-owner	主人	jǔrén;	jyúyàHn;
-of house	屋主	wūjǔ;	ngūkjyú;
-of land	地主	dìjǔ;	deiHjyú;
-of shop	店主	dyànjǔ	dimjyú
propriety n.	禮	lǐ;	láiH;
	禮節	lǐjyé	láiHjit
pro rata	照分	jàufēn	jiufàn
prose n.	散文	sǎnwén	sáanmàHn

prosecute v. t.

| -a scheme | 實行 | shfsyíng; | saHthàHng; |
| -sue | 控告 | kùnggàu | hunggou |

prospect n.

-view	景色	jǐngsè;	gíngsík;
-hope	希望	syīwàng;	hèimoHng;
-of a trade, etc.	前途	chyántú	chìHntòuH
prosper v. i.	興旺	syīngwàng;	hìngwoHng;

	發達	fādá	faatdaaHt
rosperity n.			
-success	成功	chénggūng;	siHnggùng;
-good fortune	幸運	ąyìngyùn;	haIIngwaIIu,
-wealth	富貴	fùgwèi;	fugwai;
-flourishing condition	興旺	syìngwàng	hìngwoHng
rosperous a.	興旺	syìngwàng;	hìngwoHng;
	發達	fādá	faatdaaHt
rostate gland	攝護腺	shèhùsyàn	sipwuHsin
rostitute n.	妓女	jìnyŭ	geiHnéuiH
rostrate v. t.	俯伏	fŭfú	fúfnHk
rotect v. t.			
-keep safe	保護	bāuhù;	bóuwuH;
-guard	防衞	fángwèi;	fòHngwaiII;
-of the gods	保佑	băuyòu	bóuyauH
rotein n.	蛋白質	dànbáijí	dáanbaaHkjāt
rotest v. i./v. t.	主張	jŭjāng;	jyújèung;
	抗言	kàngyán	kongyìHn
rotocol n.	草約	tsăuywē	chóuyeuk
roton n.	質子	jídz	jātjí
rototype n.	模範	mwófàn;	mòuHfaaHn;
	標準	byānjwŭn	biujéun
rotrude v. t./v. i.	伸出	shēnchū;	sànchēut;
	突出	tūchū	daHtchēut
roud a.	驕傲	jyāuàu	gìungouH
rove v. t.	証明	jèngmíng	jingmìHng
roven a.	應驗	yìngyàn	yingyiHm
roverb n.	俗語	súyŭ;	juHkyúH;
	成語	chéngyŭ	sìHngyúH
rovide v. t.			
-prepare	預備	yùbèi;	yuHbeiH;

-supply	供給	gūngjǐ	gūngkāp
provided conj.	倘若	tǎngrwò;	tóngyeuHk;
	假如	jyǎrú	gáyùH
province n.	省	shěng	sáang
provincial a.	省的	shěngde;	sáangdǐk;
-school	省立學校	shěnglìsywésyàu	sáanglaHphoHkhaauH
provision n.	糧食	lyángshf;	lèuHngsiHk;
	食品	shfpǐn	siHkbán
provisional a.	臨時	línshf	làHmsìH
provoke v. t.	觸怒	chùnù;	chūknouH;
	挑撥	tyǎubwó	tìubuHt
prow n.	船頭	chwántóu	syùHntàuH
prowess n.			
-bravery	勇敢	yǔnggǎn;	yúHnggám;
-martial	功勞	gūngláu	gùnglòuH
prowl v. i./v. t.	密查	mìchá	maHtchàH
proximity n.	最近	dzwèijìn;	jeuigaHn;
	貼近	tyējìn	tipgaHn
proxy n.	代理人	dàilǐrén	doiHléiHyàHn
prudence n.			
-caution	謹慎	jǐnshèn;	gánsaHn;
-forethought	遠慮	ywǎnlyù	yúHnleuiH
prudent a.	小心	syǎusyin	síusàm
prune			
-v. t. cut	修剪	syōujyǎn;	sàujín;
-n. plum	梅乾	méigān	mùiHgòn
pry v. i.			
-inquisitively	打聽	dǎting;	dáting;

-prize	攟	chyàu	giuH
seudonym n.	筆名	bǐmíng	bātméng
shaw int.	呸	pèi	pèi
ychiatrist n.	精神病學家	jīngshénbìng sywéjyā	jīngsàHnhoHng hoHkgā
ychologist n.	心理學家	syinlǐsywéjyū	sàmléiHhoHkgà
ychology n.	心理學	syinlǐsywé	sàmléiHhoHk
omaine n.	屍毒	shīdú	sìduHk
uberty n.	春情期	chwūnchíngchī	chèunchìHngkàiH
blic a.	公共	gūnggùng;	gùngguHng;
-public welfare	公益	gūngyì	gūngyìk
blication n.	刊物	kānwù;	hónmaHt;
	讀物	dúwù	duHkmaHt
blish v. t.	出版	chūbǎn;	chēutbáan;
	發行	fāháng	faathòHng
dding n.	布丁	bùdǐng	boudīng
ff n.	吹	chwēi;	chèui;
	噴	pèn	pan
ll v. t.			
-draw	拉	lā;	làai;
-draw out	拔	bá	baHt
lley n.	滑車	hwáchē;	waaHtchè;
	滑輪	hwálwún	waaHtléun
lmonary a.	肺的	fèide	faidīk
lp n.			
-of fruit	果肉	gwǒròu;	gwóyuHk;
-to make paper	紙漿	jǐjyāng	jíjēung
lpit n.	講壇	jyǎngtán	góngtàaHn
lsate v. i.	跳	tyàu	tiu

pulse n.	脈	mài	maaHk
pump n.	喞筒	jitŭng	jìktúng
pumpkin n.	南瓜	nángwā	nàaHmgwā
punch n.	拳擊	chywánji	kyùHngìk
punctual a.	準時;	jwŭnshí;	jéunsìH;
	按時	ànshí	onsìH
punctuation n.	標點 .	byāudyăn	bīudím
puncture			
-n.	刺孔	tsżkŭng;	chihúng;
-v. t.	刺	tsż	chi
punish v. t.	罰;	fá;	faHt;
	處罰	chŭfá	chyúfaHt
punishment n.	刑罰	syíngfá	yìHngfaHt
pupil n.			
-student	學生;	sywésheng;	hoHksāang;
-of eye	瞳孔	túngkŭng	tùHnghúng
puppet n.	傀儡	kwéilĕi	faailéuiH
puppy n.	小狗	syăugŏu	síugáu (gáujái)
purchase v. t.	買	măi	máaiH
pure a.	純潔	chwúnjyé	sèuHngit
purge v. t.	洗刷	syĭshwā	sáichaat
purify v. t.	潔淨	jyéjìng	gitjiHng
purple a.	紫色	dźsè	jísìk
purpose n.			
-objective	目的;	mùdi;	muHkdìk;
-intention	主意	jŭyì	jyúyi
purse n.	錢包	chyánbāu	chìHnbāau
purser n.	船務長	chwánwùjăng	syùHnmouHjéung

ursue v. t.	追	jwēi	jèui
us n.	膿	núng	nùHng
ush v. t.	推	twēi;	tèui;
-in a crowd	擠	jǐ	jài (bǐk)
ut v. t.	放	fàng	fong
-put into practice	實行	shísyíng	saHthàHng
utrefy v. i./v. t.	腐敗	fǔbài	fuHbaaiH
utty n.	油灰	yóuhwēi	yàuHfùi
uzzle			
-n. test thinking	謎	mí;	màiH;
-n. problem	難題	nántí;	nàaHntàiH;
-v. t. perplex	迷惑	míhwò	màiHwaaHk
ajamas n.	睡衣	shwèiyi	seuiHyi
lon n.	標柱	byūujù	bìuchyúH
ramid n.	金字塔	jǐndztǎ	gāmjiHtaap
thon n.	蟒蛇	mǎngshé	móHngsèH

ack n.	鴨叫聲	yājyàushēng;	ngaapgiusèng;
-in medicine	庸醫	yūngyi	yùHngyi
adrangle n.	四角形	sżjyǎusyíng;	seigokyìHug;
	四邊形	sżbyānsyíng	seibìnyìHng
adruped n.	四足獸	sżdzúshòu	seijūksau
aint a.			
-peculiar	古怪	gǔgwài;	gúgwaai;
-strange	奇怪	chígwài	kèiHgwaai
ake v. i.			
-shake	震動	jèndùng;	janduHng;

-tremble	發抖	fàdǒu	faatdáu
qualification n.	資格	dzge	jìgaak
qualify a.	合格	hégé	haHpgaak
quality n.			
-grade	等	dǎng;	dáng;
-essential nature	品質	pǐnjŕ;	bánjāt;
-desirable traits	好處	hǎuchù	hóuchyu
quandary n.	困惑	kwùnhwò	kwanwaaHk
quantity n.	數量	shùlyàng;	souleuHng;
	分量	fènlyàng	faHnleuHng
quarantine n.	檢疫所	jyǎnyìswǒ	kímyiHksó
quarrel v. i.	吵架	chǎujyà	cháauga (chòuHgāau)
quart n.	夸爾	kwāěr	kwàyíH
quarter n.			
-¼	四分之一	sżfènjŕyi;	seifaHnjiyāt;
-15 min.	一刻	yíkè;	yāthāak (yātgogwāt);
-district	區	chyū	kèui
quartet(te) n.	四重唱	sżchúngchàng	seichùHngcheung
quarto n.	四開	sżkāi	seihòi
quartz n.	石英	shŕfyìng;	seHkyìng;
	水晶	shwěijìng	séuijìng
quay n.	碼頭	mǎtóu	máHtàuH
queen n.			
-wife of king	皇后	hwánghòu;	wòHnghauH;
-reigning	女王	nyǔwáng	néuihwòHng
queer a.	奇怪	chígwài	kèiHgwaai
quench v. t.	熄滅	syímyè;	sìkmiHt;
-a light	熄燈	syídēng	sìkdāng
question			
-n. problem	問題	wèntí;	maHntàiH;

-v. t. inquire about	問ㄨㄣ	wèn	maHn
questionnaire n.	詢ㄒㄩㄣ 問ㄨㄣ 事ㄕ 項ㄒㄧ�★	syúnwènshìsyàng	sèunmaHnsiHhoHng
queue n.	辮ㄅㄧㄢ 子口	byàndz	bìnjí (bìnjái)
quick a.	快ㄎㄨㄞ	kwài	faai
quiet a.			
-soundless	安ㄢ 靜ㄐㄧㄥ	ānjìng;	ònjiHng;
-calm	平ㄆㄧㄥ 靜ㄐㄧㄥ	píngjìng;	pìHngjiHng;
-disposition	溫ㄨㄣ 和ㄏㄜ	wēnhé;	wānwòH;
-place	清ㄑㄧㄥ 靜ㄐㄧㄥ	chīngjìng	chìngjiHng
quietly adv.	靜ㄐㄧㄥ 靜ㄐㄧㄥ 地ㄉㄜ	jìngjìngde	jiHngjìngdéi
quilt n.			
-bed-cover	被ㄅㄟ 單ㄉㄢ	bèidāu,	péiHdāan;
-cotton	棉ㄇㄧㄢ 被ㄅㄟ	myánbèi	mìHnpéiH
quinine n.	奎ㄎㄨㄟ 寧ㄋㄧㄥ	kwéiníng	kwàiniHng
quintet(te) n.	五ㄨ 重ㄔㄨㄥ 唱ㄔㄤ	wǔchúngchàng	ńgHchùHngcheung
quire n.	刀ㄉㄠ	dāu;	dòu;
-one quire of paper	一 刀ㄉㄠ 紙ㄓ	yìdāujǐ	yātdòují
quit v. t.			
-stop	停ㄊㄧㄥ 止ㄓ	tíngjǐ;	tìHngjí;
-leave	離ㄌㄧ 開ㄎㄞ	líkāi	lèiHhòi
quite adv.	很ㄏㄣ	hěn;	hán (géi);
	相ㄒㄧㄤ 常ㄔㄤ	syāngdāng	sèungdòng
quiz			
-n. burlesque	笑ㄒㄧㄠ 話ㄏㄨㄚ	syàuhwà;	siuwá;
-v. t. test	測ㄘㄜ 驗ㄧㄢ	tsèyàn	chāakyiHm
quorum n.	法ㄈㄚ 定ㄉㄧㄥ 人ㄖㄣ 數ㄕㄨ	fǎdìngrénshù	faatdiHngyàHnsou
quota	份ㄈㄣ 額ㄜ	fēné;	faHnngáak;
	比ㄅㄧ 額ㄜ	bǐé	béingáak
quotation n.	引ㄧㄣ 言ㄧㄢ	yǐnyán;	yáHnyìHn;

	引證	yǐnjèng	yáHnjing
quote v. t.	引用	yǐngyùng	yáHnyuHng

R

rabbit n.	兔子	tùdz	toují (toujái)
rabble n.	烏合之衆	wūhéjrjùng	wùhaHpjìjung
rabies n.	狂犬病	kwángchywǎnbìng	kòHnghyúnbeHng
race n.			
-of men	種族	jǒngdzú;	júngjuHk;
-run a race	賽跑	sàipǎu	choipáau
rack n.	架	jyà	ga
radar n.	雷達	léidá	lèuiHdaaHt
radiant a.			
-shining	發光	fāgwāng;	faatgwòng;
-bright	光明	gwāngmíng	gwòngmìHng
radiate v. t./v. i.			
-as heat	放射	fàngshè;	fōngseH;
-Mech.	輻射	fúshè	fūkseH
radiator n.	輻射體	fúshètǐ	fūkseHtái
radical			
-a. fundamental	基本	jiběn;	gèibún;
-n. Chinese character	部首	dúshǒu	boųHsáu
radio n.	收音機	shōuyinjǐ;	sàuyàmgèi;
	無線電	wúsyàndyàn	mòuHsindihn
radium n.	鐳	léi	lèuiH
radius n.			
-Geom.	半徑	bànjǐng;	bunging;
-Anat.	橈骨	nǎugǔ	nàauHgwāt
raffle			
-n.	彩票	tsǎipyàu;	chóipiu;

-v. t.	搖彩	yáutsăi	yıuHchói
aft n.	木排	mùpái	muHkpàaiH
ag n.	破布;	pwòbù;	pobou;
	爛布	lànbù	laaHnbou
age			
-n. anger	忿怒;	fènnù;	fáHnnouH;
-v. i. get angry	發怒	fānù	faatnouII
aid			
-n. of troops	突擊;	tūjí;	daHtgĭk;
-v. t. of police	搜查	sōuchá	sáuchàH
ake			
-n.	耙子;	pádz;	pàHjí (pá);
-v. t.	耙	pá	pàH
ailroad n.	鐵路	tyĕlù	titlouH
ailway n.	鐵路	tyĕlù	titlouH
-railway station	火車站	hwŏchējàn	fóchèjaaHm
ally n.	民衆大會	mínjungdàhwèi	màHnjungdaaiHwuiH
aiment n.	衣服	yīfu	yìfuHk
ain			
-n.	雨	yŭ;	yúH;
-v. i.	下雨	syàyŭ	haHyúH (loHkyúH)
ainbow n.	天虹	tyānhúng	tìnhùHng
aincoat n.	雨衣	yŭyī	yúHyī
aise v. t.			
make higher	高升;	gāushōng;	gòusìng;
-lift	舉	jyŭ;	géui;
-as cattle	養	yăng	yéuHng
amble v. i.	散步	sànbù	saanbouH
amp n.	斜道	syédàu	chèHdouH
anch n.	畜牧場	syùmùchăng	chŭkmuHkchèuHng

random n.

-at random	隨便	swéibyàn	chèuiHbín

rank n.

| -class | 階級 | jyēji; | gāaikāp; |
| -position | 地位 | dìwei | deiHwaiH |

ransack v. t. 搜刼 sōujyé sáugip

ransom

-n.	贖金	shújĭn;	suHkgām;
-v. t.	贖回	shúhwéi	suHkwùiH (suHkfàan)
-ransom price	贖價	shújyà	suHkga

rape v. t. 強姦 chyángjyān kèuHnggàan

rapid a. 快 kwài faai

rare a.

| -seldom | 稀有 | syiyŏu; | hèiyáuH (síuyáuH); |
| -wonderful | 希奇 | syichí | hèikèiH |

rascal n. 流氓 lyóumáng làuHmàHn

rash n.

| -eruption of the skin | 疹子 | jĕndz; | chánjí (chán); |
| -reckless | 粗心 | tsūsyin | chòusàm |

rat n. 老鼠 lăushŭ lóuHsú

rate n.

-proportion	比率	bĭlyù;	béileuHt;
-degree	程度	chéngdù;	chìHngdouH;
-of exchange	行情	hángchíng;	hòHngchìHng;
-at any rate	無論如何	wúlwùnrúhé	mòuHleuHnyùHhòH

rather adv. 寧可 níngkě; nìHnghó;
不如 bùrú bātyùH

ratify v. t.

| -confirm | 承認 | chéngrèn; | sìHngyiHng; |

English	Chinese		
-sanction	批准	pījwǔn	pàijéun
atio n.	比	bǐ;	béi;
	比例	bǐlì;	béilaiH;
	比率	bǐlyù	béileuHt
ation n./v. t.	配給	pèiji	puikāp
ational a.			
-reasonable	講理	jyǎnglǐ	gònglèiH
ationalization n.	合理化	hélǐhwà	haHpléiHfa
attan n.	籐	téng	tàHng
attle n.			
-n. body rattle	撥浪鼓	bwōlànggǔ;	buHtloHnggú;
-v. t. shake	搖	yáu	yìuH
avage v. t/v. i.			
-plunder	搶刼	chyǎngjyé	chéunggip
ave v. I.	怒號	nùháu	nouHhouH
aw a.	生	shēng;	sàang;
-raw fish	生魚	shēngyú	sàangyú
ay n.			
-of light	光線	gwāngsyàn	gwòngsin
ayon n.	人造絲	réndzàusz̄	yàHnjouHsì
azor n.	剃刀	tìdāu	taidòu
each v. t.	到	dàu;	dou;
-reach out	伸	shēn	sàn
eact v. i.	反應	fǎnyìng	fáanyìng
eactionary n.	反動份了	fǎndùngfèndz	fáandulIngfalIuji
ead v. t.			
-aloud	讀	dú;	duHk;
-silently	看	kàn;	hon (tái);
-read in unison	同聲讀	túngshēngdú	tùHngsìngduHk
eadily adv.			
-immediately	立刻	lìkè;	laHphāak;

-willingly	願意	ywànyì	yuHyi
ready a.	預備好	yùbèihǎu	yuHbeiHhóu
readymade a.	現成	syànchéng	yiHnsìHng
real a.			
-actual	實在	shŕdzài;	saHtjoiH;
-genuine	眞	jēn	jàn
reality n.			
-being real	眞實	jēnshŕ;	jànsaHt;
-facts	事實	shŕshŕ	siHsaHt
-reality of facts	實際	shŕjì	saHtjai
realization n.	實行	shŕsyíng;	saHthàHng;
	實現	shŕsyàn	saHtyiHn
realize v. t.			
-effectuate	實行	shŕsyíng;	saHthàHng;
-come to understand	覺悟	jywéwù	gokngH
really adv.	眞的	jēnde;	jāndìk (jànge);
	實在	shŕdzài	saHtjoiH
ream n.	令	líng	lǐng
reap v. t.			
-harvest	收割	shōugē;	sàugot;
-gather	收成	shōuchéng	sàusìHng
rear			
-n. back part	後面	hòumyàn;	hauHmiHn (hauHbiHn)
-v. t. breed	撫養	fǔyǎng	fúyéuHng
reason n.			
-ground	理由	lǐyóu;	léiHyàuH;
-cause	原因	ywányin	yùHnyàn
reasonable a.			
-proper	合理	hélǐ;	haHpléiH;
-of price	公道	gūngdàu	gùngdouH

easoning n.	推 論	twēilwùn;	tèuileuHn;
	理 論	lĭlwùn	léiHleuHn
ebate n.			
-deduction	扣	kòu;	kau;
	打 折 扣	dăjékòu	dájitkau
ebel			
-v. i.	反 叛	fǎnpàn;	fáanpun;
-n.	叛 徒	pàntú	puntòuH
-rebel troops	叛 軍	pànjyūn	pungwan
ebellion n.	謀 反	móufǎn;	màuHfáan;
	判 逆	pànnì	punyiHk
ebellious a.	判 逆 的	pànnìde	punyiHkdik (fáanpunge)
buke v. t.	罵	mà;	mauH (muuuH);
	責 備	dzébèi	jaakbeiH
ecall v. t.			
-call back	叫 回	jyàuhwéi;	giuwùiH (giufàan);
-cancel	取 消	chyŭsyāu;	chéuisiu;
-recall to mind	回 憶	hwéiyì	wùiHyìk
eceipt n.	收 條	shōutyáu;	sàutiuH;
	收 據	shōujyù	sàugeui
-receipt	存 根	tswúngēn	chyùHngàn
eceive v. t.			
-a guest	接 客	jyēkè;	jiphaak;
-a letter	收 信	shōusyìn;	sàuseun;
-a prize	領 獎	lĭngjyǎng;	líHngjéung
-a pupil	收 學 生	shōusywéshēng	sàuhoHksāang
ecently adv.	近 來	jìnlái	gaHnlòiH
eception n.			
-welcome	歡 迎 會	hwānyínghwèi;	fùnyìHngwúi;

-tea party	茶會	cháhwèi;	chàHwúi;
-parents of school	懇親會	kěnchìnhwèi	hánchànwúi
recess n.	休息	syōusyi	yāusik
recipe n.			
-prescription	處方	chùfāng;	chyufōng;
-for preparing dish	食譜	shífpǔ	siHkpóu
recital n.	背誦	bèisùng;	buijuHng;
-solo	獨唱	dúchàng;	duHkcheung;
-of piano	獨奏	dúdzòu	duHkjau
recite v. t.	背誦	béisùng	buijuHng
reckless a.	粗心	tsūsyin;	chòusàm;
	不小心	bùsyǎusyin	bātsiusàm (m̀siusàm)
reckon v. t.	數	shǔ;	sóu;
	計算	jìswàn	gaisyun
reclaim v. t.			
-demand the return of	收回	shōuhwéi	sàuwùiH;
-land	開荒	kāihwāng	hòifòng
recline v. i.			
-lean	靠	kàu;	kaau;
-lie down	躺	tǎng;	tóng (fāndài)
recognize v. t.			
-identify	認	rèn;	yiHng;
-admit	承認	chéngrèn	sìHngyiHng
recollect v. t.	記	jì	gei
recommend v. t.	介紹	jyèshàu;	gaaisiuH;
	推薦	twēijyàn	tèuijin
recompense v. t.			
-for service	報酬	bàuchóu;	bouchàuH;
-for loss	賠償	péicháng;	pùiHsèuHng;
-for good	報答	bàudá;	boudaap;

English	Chinese		
-for evil	報應	bàuyìng	bouying
econcile v. t.			
-back to harmony	和好	héhǎu;	wòHhóu;
-agree	和解	héjyě	wòHgáai
econciliation n.	和睦	hémù	wòHmuHk
econstruct v. t.	整頓	jěngdwùn;	jìngdeuHn;
	重建	chúngjyàn	chùHnggin
ecord			
–v. t. notedown	記	jì;	gei;
–v. t. of a document	登記	dēngjì;	dànggei;
–n. of gramophone	唱片	chàngpyàn;	cheungpín;
–n. personal career	履歷	lyǔlì;	léuiHliHk;
–n. historical	記載	jìdzài;	geijoi;
–n. sporting	紀錄	jìlù	geiluHk
ecover v. t.			
-return to normal condition	恢復	hwēifù;	fùifuHk;
-from sickness	復原	fùywán	fuHkyùHn
recruit n.	新兵	syīnbīng	sànbìng
ectangular a.	長方形的	chángfāngsyíngde	cheùHngfòngyìHngdìk
ectify v. t.			
-to put right	改正	gǎijèng	góijeng
recuperate v. t./v. i.	復原	fùywán	fuHkyùHn
recurrent a.	循環	syúnhwán	chèuHnwàaHn
-recurrent fever	回歸熱	hwéigwēirè	wùiHgwàiyiHt
red a.	紅色	húngsè	hùHngsìk
redeem v. t.	贖	shú;	suHk;
	贖回	shúhwéi;	suHkwùiH (suHkfàan);
	救贖	jyòushú	gausuHk
redouble v. t./v. i.	倍加	bèijyā	púiHgà

redtape n.	官樣文章	gwēnyàngwénjāng	gùnyeuHngmàHnjèung
reduce v. t.			
-Chem.	還原	hwánywán;	wàaHnyùHn;
-lower	減低	jyǎndǐ	gáamdài
reduced prices	廉價	lyánjyà	lìHmga
reduction n.			
-in size	減少	jyǎnshǎu;	gáamsíu;
-of penalty	減輕	jyǎnchīng	gáamhèng
redundant a.	多餘	dwōyú;	dòyùH;
	滿溢	mǎnyì	múHnyaHt
reed n.	水草	shwěitsǎu;	séuichóu;
	蘆草	lútsǎu	lòuHchóu
reel n.	線軸	syànjóu	sinjuHk
refer v. t.			
-give in charge	委託	wěitwō;	wáitok;
-to books	參考	tsānkǎu	chàamháau
referee n.	裁判員	tsáipànywán;	chòiHpunyùHn;
	評判員	píngpànywán	pìHngpunyùHn
reference n.			
-book of reference	參考書	tsānkǎushū	chàamháausyù
-in reference to	關於	gwānyú	gwàanyù
refine v. t.	提煉	tílyàn;	tàiHliHn;
-refine gold	煉金	lyànjīn	liHngām
refined a.	文雅	wényǎ;	màHnngáH;
	斯文	sžwén	sìmàHn
reflect v. t./v. i.			
-mentally	回想	hwéisyǎng;	wùiHséung;
-reflect light	反光	fǎngwāng	fáangwòng

reform v. t.

-morals	改《ㄞ 過ㄍㄛ	găigwò;	góigwo;
-manners	矯ㄐㄠ 正ㄓㄥ	jyŭujèng;	kíujing,
-a profligate	感《ㄞ 化ㄏㄨㄚ	gănhwà;	gámfa;
-a process	改《ㄞ 良ㄌㄧㄤ	găilyáng;	góilèuHng;
-politics	改《ㄞ 革《ㄜ	găigé	góigaak
reformation n.	改《ㄞ 革《ㄜ	găigé;	góigaak;
	改《ㄞ 善ㄕㄢ	găishàn	góisiHn
reformatory n.	感《ㄞ 化ㄏㄨㄚ 院ㄩㄢ	gănhwàywàn	gámfayún
refrain v. t./v. i.	禁ㄐㄧㄣ 戒ㄐㄧㄝ	jìnjyè;	gamgaai;
	制ㄓ 止ㄓ	jrjř	jaijí
refresh v. t./v. i.	休ㄒㄧㄡ 養ㄧㄤ	syōuyăng	yàuyéuHng
refreshment n.	點ㄉㄧㄢ 心ㄒㄧㄣ	dyănsyín;	dímsām;
	茶ㄔㄚ 點ㄉㄧㄢ	chádyăn	chàHdím
refrigerator n.	冰ㄅㄧㄥ 箱ㄒㄧㄤ	bĭngsyāng	bingsēung (syutgwaiH)

refuge n.

-protection	保ㄅㄠ 護ㄏㄨ	băuhù;	bóuwuH;
-place of	避ㄅㄧ 難ㄋㄢ 所ㄙㄨㄛ	bìnànswŏ	beiHnaaHnsó
refugee n.	難ㄋㄢ 民ㄇㄧㄣ	nànmín	naaHnmàHn
refund v. t.	退ㄊㄨㄟ 還ㄏㄨㄢ	twèihwán	teniwàaHn

refuse

-v. t. decline	推ㄊㄨㄟ 辭ㄘ	twēitsź;	tèuichìH;
-v. t. reject	拒ㄐㄩ 絕ㄐㄩㄝ	jyùjywé;	kéuijyuHt;
-n.	垃ㄌㄚ 圾ㄙㄜ	lèsè	laaHpsaap

regain v. t.

-concrete things	收ㄕㄡ 回ㄏㄨㄟ	shōuhwéi;	sàuwùiH;
-things abstract	恢ㄏㄨㄟ 復ㄈㄨ	hwēifù;	fùifuHk;

-get back	得回	déhwéi	dākwùiH (dākfàan)

regard v. t.

-look upon	看	kàn;	hon (tái);
-pay attention to	注意-	jùyi;	jyuyi;
-consider	以爲	yǐwéi	yíHwàiH

regardless a.

| | 不顧 | búgù; | bātgu (m̀léiH); |
| | 不管 | bùgwǎn | bātgún |

regenerate v. t.

| -reform oneself | 改過自新 | gǎigwòdz̀syìn; | góigwojiHsàn; |
| -reborn | 再生 | dzàishēng | joisàng (fàansàang) |

region n.

| -district | 地方 | dìfang; | deiHfòng; |
| -sphere | 範圍 | fànwei | faaHnwàiH |

register v. t.

-at a school	註册	jùtsè;	jyuchaak;
-at a hotel	登記	dēngjì-	dànggei;
-at a hospital	掛號	gwàhàu;	gwahouH;
-a letter	掛號	gwàhàu	gwahouH

registrar n.

| | 註册主任 | jùtsèjǔrèn; | jyuchaakjyúyaHm̀; |
| | 總務主任 | dzǔngwùjǔrèn | júngmouHjyúyaHm |

registry n.

| | 註册局 | jùtsèjyú | jyuchaakgúk |

regret v. t.

| -repent of | 後悔 | hòuhwěi; | hauHfui; |
| -sorry for | 抱歉 | bàuchyàn | póuhip |

regular a.

| -usual | 照常 | jàucháng; | jiusèuHng; |
| -orderly | 有秩序 | yǒujr̀syu | yáuHdiHtjeuiH |

regulation n.

| -rule | 章程 | jāngchéng; | jèungchìHng; |
| -order or law | 法令 | fǎlìng | faatliHng |

rehearsal n.	排演	páiyǎn;	pàaiHyín;
	預習	yùsyí	yuHjaaHp
reign vi i.	統治	tǔngjì	túngjiH
reimburse v. t.	償還	chánghwán;	sèuHngwàaHn;
	付還	fùhwán	fuHwàaHn
ein n.			
-of horse	韁繩	jyāngshéng	gèungsìHng
einforce v. t.	援兵	ywánbìng	wuHnbìng
einstate v. t.	復職	fùjf	fuHkjìk
eject v. t.			
-a proposal	拒絕	jyùjywé;	kéuiHjyuHt;
-goods, etc.	退回	twèihwéi;	teuiwùiH;
-a petition	駁回	bwóhwéi	bokwùiH (bokfàan)
ejoice v. i.	歡喜	hwānsyǐ;	fùnhéi;
	高興	gāusyìng	gòuhìng
elapse v. i.			
-of sickness	再發	dzàifā	joifaat
elate v. i.	講	jyǎng	góng
elating to	關於	gwānyú	gwàanyù
elation n.	關係	gwānsy	gwàanhaiH
elationship n.	關係	gwānsyì,	gwàanhaiH;
	親屬關係	chīnshǔgwānsyì	chànsuHkgwàanhaiH
elative n.	親戚	chīnchi	chānchìk
elax v. t.			
-slacken	放鬆	fangsūng;	fongsùng;
-from work	休息	syōusyi	yāusìk
elaxation n.	鬆弛	sūngchì;	sùngchìH;

| | 舒ㄕㄨ 暢ㄔㄤ | shūchàng | syùcheung |

release v. t.

| -set free | 釋ㄕ 放ㄈㄤ | shìfàng; | sìkfong; |
| -let go | 放ㄈㄤ 行ㄒㄧㄥ | fàngsyíng | fonghàHng |

relent v. i. 發ㄈㄚ 慈ㄘ 悲ㄅㄟ   fātszbēi   faatchìHbèi

relief n.

-of mind	放ㄈㄤ 心ㄒㄧㄣ	fàngsyin;	fongsàm;
-help	幫ㄅㄤ 助ㄓㄨ	bāngjù;	bòngjoH;
-of besieged places	援ㄩㄢ 助ㄓㄨ	ywánjù;	wùHnjoH;
-goods or money	救ㄐㄧㄡ 濟ㄐㄧ	jyòujì	gaujai

religion n. 宗ㄗㄨㄥ 教ㄐㄧㄠ   dzūngjyàu   jùnggaau

religious a. 宗ㄗㄨㄥ 教ㄐㄧㄠ 上ㄕㄤ   dzūngjyàushang   jùnggaauseuHng

| -religious education | 宗ㄗㄨㄥ 教ㄐㄧㄠ 教ㄐㄧㄠ 育ㄩ | dzūngjyàujyàuyù | jùnggaaugaauyuHk |
| -religious liberty | 宗ㄗㄨㄥ 教ㄐㄧㄠ 自ㄗ 由ㄧㄡ | dzūngjyàudzyóu | jùnggaaujiHyàuH |

relinquish v. t.

| -to give up | 放ㄈㄤ 棄ㄑㄧ | fàngchì | fonghei |

reluctant a.

| -unwilling | 捨ㄕㄜ 不ㄅㄨ 得ㄉㄜ | shěbùdé; | sébātdāk (m̀sédāk): |
| -disinclined | 勉ㄇㄧㄢ 強ㄑㄧㄤ | myǎnchyǎng | míHnkéuHng |

rely v. i.

| -lean on | 靠ㄎㄠ | kàu; | kaau; |
| -put faith in | 信ㄒㄧㄣ 任ㄖㄣ | syìnrèn | seunyaHm |

remain v. i.

| -stay | 住ㄓㄨ | jù; | jyuH; |
| -after subtraction | 剩ㄕㄥ | shèng | jiHng |

remainder a. 剩ㄕㄥ 下ㄒㄧㄚ 的ㄉㄜ   shèngsyàde   jiHnghaHdǐk (jiHngfàange)

remand v. t. 退ㄊㄨㄟ 回ㄏㄨㄟ   twèihwéi   teuiwùiH

remark v. t.

| -observe | 看ㄎㄢ | kàn; | hon (tái); |
| -notice | 注ㄓㄨ 意 | jùyi; | jyuyì; |

-say	說話	shwōhwà	syutwaH (góngsyutwaH)
remarkable a.	非常	fēicháng	fèisèuHng
remedy n.			
-means	辦法	bànfǎ;	baaHnfaat;
-redress	補救	bǔjyòu;	bóugau;
-cure	醫治	yījɨ	yìjiH
remember v. t.	記得	jìde	geidak
remind v. t.			
-put in mind	想起	syǎngchɨ;	séunghéi;
-cause to remember	提醒	tísyǐng	tàiHsíng
remission n.			
-pardon	赦免	shèmyǎn;	semíHn;
-of a tax	免	myǎn	míHn
remnant n.			
-residue	剩餘	shèngyú;	siHngyùH;
-fragment	零碎	língswei;	lìHngseui;
-of cloth	碎布	swèibù	seuibou
remorse n.	後悔	hòuhwěi;	hauHfui;
	悔恨	hwěihèn	fuihaHn
remove			
-v. t. to another place	搬	bān;	bɨn;
-v. t. take away	拿去	náchyu;	nàHheui (nìkheui);
-v. i. change house	搬家	bānjyā	bùngà (būnngūk)
renaissance n.			
-ref. to Asia	新思潮	syīnszcháu;	sànsìchiuH;
-ref. to Europe	文藝復興	wényìfùsyíng	màHnngaiHfuHkhìng
renew v. t.			
-revive	復新	fùsyǐn;	fuHksàn;

-as a license	換ㄏㄨㄢˋ	hwàn	wuHn
renounce v. t.			
-surrender	棄ㄑㄧˋ 權ㄑㄩㄢˊ	chìchywán	heikyùHn
renovate v. t.			
-make new again	裝ㄓㄨㄤ 修ㄒㄧㄡ	jwāngsyōu	jòngsàu
rent			
-a torn	破ㄆㄛˋ 爛ㄌㄢˋ	pwòlàn;	polaaHn;
-n. hole	裂ㄌㄧㄝˋ 縫ㄈㄥˊ	lyèfèng;	liHtfùHng;
-v. t. hire	租ㄗㄨ	dzū	jòu
repair v. t.			
-of buildings, etc.	修ㄒㄧㄡ 理ㄌㄧˇ	syǒulǐ;	sàuléiH;
-as a puncture	補ㄅㄨˇ	bǔ	bóu
repay v. t.			
-money	還ㄏㄨㄢˊ	hwán;	wàaHn;
-requite	報ㄅㄠˋ 答ㄉㄚˊ	bàudá;	boudaap;
-indemnify	賠ㄆㄟˊ 償ㄔㄤˊ	péicháng;	pùiHsèuHng;
-repay debt	還ㄏㄨㄢˊ 債ㄓㄞ	hwánjài	wàaHnjaai
repeat v. t.			
-do again	再ㄗㄞˋ 做ㄗㄨㄛˋ	dzàidzwò;	joijouH;
-say over again	再ㄗㄞˋ 說ㄕㄨㄛ	dzàishwō	joisyut (joigóng)
repeatedly adv.	再ㄗㄞˋ 三ㄙㄢ	dzàisān;	joisàam;
	屢ㄌㄩˇ 次ㄘˋ	lyǔtsż	léuiHchi;
repent v. i.	悔ㄏㄨㄟˇ 改ㄍㄞˇ	hwěigǎi;	fuigói;
	悔ㄏㄨㄟˇ 過ㄍㄨㄛˋ	hwěigwò	fuigwo
repentance n.	悔ㄏㄨㄟˇ 罪ㄗㄨㄟˋ	hwěidzwèi;	fuijeuiH;
	悔ㄏㄨㄟˇ 過ㄍㄨㄛˋ	hwěigwò	fuigwo
repetition n.	重ㄔㄨㄥˊ 復ㄈㄨˋ	chúngfù	chùHngfūk

replace v. t.

-in the former place 放 回   fànghwéi;   fongwùiH (fóngfàan);

-supplant 代 替   dàitì   doiHtai

reply v. i.

-verbal 回 答   hwéidá;   wùiHdaap;

-written 回 信   hwéisyìn;   wùiHseun;

-as to a toast 答 辭   dátsź   daapchìH

report v. t./n. 報 告   bàugàu;   bougou;

-n. rumour 謠 言   yáuyán;   yìuIIyìIIn;

-n. to a superior 呈 報   chéngbàu   chìHngbou

reporter n. 記 者   jìjě   geijé

represent v. t.

-persons 代 表   dàibyǎu;   doiHbíu;

-act for another 代 理   dàilǐ;   douHléiH;

-stand for 代 替   dàitì   doiHtai

reprieve

-v. t. 暫 緩 執 行   jànhwǎnjfsyíng;   jaaHnwuHnjāphàHng;

-n. 緩 行   hwǎnsyíng   wuHnhàHng

reprimand v. t. 罵   mà;   maH (naauH);

責 備   dzébèi   jaakbeiH

reprisal n. 報 復   bàufù   boufuHk

reproach v. t. 罵   mà;   maH (naauH);

責 備   dzébèi   jaakbeiH

republic n. 共 和 國   gùnghégwó   guHngwòIIgwok

-Republic of China 中 華 民 國   Jūnghwámíngwó   JùngwàHmàHngwok

repulsive a. 擊 退 的   jítwèide   gikteuidìk

reputation n. 名 譽   míngyù   mìHngyuII

request v. t.

-formally apply for 請 求   chǐngchyóu;   chíngkàuH;

-the opinions of	徵求	jēngchyóu;	jìngkàuH;
-peremptorily	要求	yāuchyóu	yìukàuH
require v. t.	要	yàu;	yiu;
	需要	syūyàu	sèuiyiu
rescue v. t.	救	jyòu;	gau;
-from poverty	救濟	jyòujì	gaujai
research v. t.	研究	yánjyòu	yìHngau
-research student	研究生	yánjyòushēng	yìHngausāng
-research worker	考據者	kǎujyùjě	háaugeuijé
resemblance n.	像	syàng	jeuHng
resemble v. t.	類似	lèisز	leuiHchíH
resent v. t.	憤怒	fènnù;	fáHnnouH;
	怨恨	ywànhèn	yunhaHn
reserve v. t.			
-put by	留	lyóu;	làuH;
-book	定	dìng	deHng
reserved p. a.	預定	yùdìng;	yuHdiHng;
	保留	bǎulyóu	bóulàuH
reservoir n.	水庫	shwěikù;	séuifu;
	水池	shwěichî	séuichìH
residence n.	住宅	jùjái	jyuHjaaHk
residential area	住宅區	jùjáichyū	jyuHjaaHkkèui
resign v. i.			
-from office	辭職	tsزjî;	chìHjik;
-from school	退學	twèisywé	teuihoHk
resigned p. a.	告退	gàutwèi;	gouteui;
	放棄	fàngchì	fonghei
resist v. t.			
-attack disease	抵抗	dǐkàng	dáikong

| esistance n. | 反抗 | fánkàng; | fáankong; |
| | 抵抗力 | dǐkànglì | dáikongliHk |

esolution n.

-firmness	堅決	jyānjywé;	gìnkyut;
-purpose formed	決心	jywésyìn;	kyutsàm;
-adopted by a meeting	議決	yìjywé	yíHkyut

esolve v. t.

-a problem	解決	jyějywé;	gáaikyut;
-decide	決定	jywédìng;	kyutdiIIug;
-by vote	表決	byǎujywé	bíukyut

esort n.

| summer resort | 避暑地 | bìshǔdì | beiHsyúdeiH |

esources n.

| -of a country | 資源 | džywán; | jìyùHn; |
| -pecuniary means | 財力 | tsáilì | chòiHliHk |

espect v. t.

| -as persons | 尊敬 | dzwūnjìng; | jyùnging; |
| -as another's rights | 尊重 | dzwūnjùng | jyùnjuHng |

| espectable a. | 可敬的 | kějìngde | hógingdìk (hogingge) |

espond v. i.

-answer	回答	hwéidá;	wùiHdaap;
-to treatment	反應	fǎnyìng;	fáanying;
-act in response	響應	syǎngyìng	héungying

esponse n.	答辭	dátsź	daapchìH
responsibility n.	責任	dzérèn	jaakyaHm
-bear responsibility	負責	fùdzé	fuHjaak

est

| -v. i. repose | 休息 | syōusyi; | yāusìk; |
| -n. remainder | 其他 | chítā | kèiHtà |

restitution n.

-repayment	賠償	péicháng;	pùiHsèuHng;
-reparation	恢復	hwēifù	fùifuHk

restless a.

-unable to rest	睡不着	shwèibùjáu;	seuiHbātjeuHk (fanm̀jeuHk);
-never stopping	不停	bùtíng	bāttìHng (m̀tìHng)

restore v. t.

-give back	拿回	náhwéi;	nàHwùiH (nikfàan);
-repair	修理	syōulǐ;	sàuléiH;
-town	光復	gwāngfù	gwòngfuHk

restrain v. t.

-restrict	限制	syànjì;	haaHnjai;
-control	約束	ywēshù	yeukchūk

result n.

-consequence	結果	jyégwǒ;	gitgwó;
-of an experiment	成績	chéngji	sìHngjik

resume v. t.

-go on with	繼續	jìsyu	gaijuHk

resurrection n.

	復活	fùhwó	fuHkwuHt

retail v. t.

	零賣	língmài;	lìHngmaaiH;
	零售	língshòu	lìHngsauH

retire v. i.

-withdraw	退	twèi;	teui;
-from service	退休	twèisyōu	teuiyàu

retirement n.

	退職	twèijf	teuijik

retreat v. i.

	退	twèi;	teui;
-summer retreat	避暑地	bìshǔdì	beiHsyúdeiH

retribution n.

-divine justice	報應	bàuyìng;	bouying;
-recompense	賞罰	shǎngfá	séungfaHt

retrospect n. 回想 hwéisyǎng wùiHséung

return v. i.

-come back	回來	hwéilái;	wùiHlòiH (fàanlàiII)
-go back	回去	hwéichyù;	wùiHheui (fàanheui);
-give back	還	hwán	wàaHn

reveal v. t.

-let out, as a secret	洩漏	syèlòu;	sitlauH;
-of a deity	啓示	chìshr̀;	káisiH,
-uncover	顯明	syǎnming	hínmìHng

revelation n. 默示 mèshr̀; maaHksiH;
啓示 chìshr̀ káisiH

revenge v. t. 報仇 bàuchóu bouchàuH

revenue n. 收入 shōurù sàuyaHp

reverence n. 尊敬 dzwūnjìng; jyùnging;
敬重 jingjùng gingjuHng

reverend

-a. respectful 可敬 kějing hóging

reverent a. 恭敬 gūngjìng gùngging

reverse v. t.

-face in opp. direction	反轉	fǎnjwǎn;	fáanjyun;
-contrary	相反	syāngfǎn	sèungfáan

review v. t.

a lesson	溫習	wēnsyí;	wànjaaHp;
-troops	檢閱	jyǎnywè	kímyuHt

revile v. t.

-rail at 罵 mà maH (naauH)

revise v. t.

-manuscript	校訂	jyàuding;	gaauding;
-proofs	校對	jyàudwèi	gaaudeui

revive v. i./v. t.

-bring back to consciousness	甦醒	sūsyǐng	sòusíng

revival n.

	復興	fùsyíng	fuHkhìng

revolt v. i.

-rebel	叛變	pànbyàn;	punbin;
-riot	暴動	bàudùng	bouHduHng

revolution n.

-Astron., rotation	自轉	dzìjwǎn;	jiHjyún;
-political	革命	gémìng;	gaakmiHng;
-of machine	旋轉	sywánjwǎn	syùHnjyún

revolve v. i.

-rotate	轉	jwǎn;	jyun;
-round a circle	旋轉	sywánjwǎn	syùHnjyún

revolver n.

	手鎗	shǒuchyāng;	sáuchēung;
-pistol	左輪	dzwǒlwún	jóléun

reward

-v. t. as a merit	獎賞	jyǎngshǎng;	jéungséung;
-v. t. recompense	酬謝	chóusyè;	chàuHjeH;
-n.	報仇	bàuchóu	bouchàuH

rhetoric n.	修辭	syōutsź	sàuchìH
rheumatic n.	風濕	fēngshī	fūngsāp
rhinoceros n.	犀牛	syǐnyóu	sàingàuH

rhyme

-n.	韻	yùn;	wáHn;

-v. i.	押韻	yāyún	aatwáHn
rhythm n.	旋律	sywánlyù;	syùHnleuHt;
	節奏	jyɛ́dzòu	jitjau
rib n.			
-Anat.	肋骨	lègŭ;	laHkgwāt;
-cookery	排骨	páigŭ	pàaiHgwāt
ribbon n.			
-of silk	絲帶	sēdài,	sìdáai;
-of satin	緞帶	dwàndài	dyuHndáai
rice n.			
-growing	稻	dàu;	douH;
-paddy	穀	gŭ;	gūk;
-hulled	米	mĭ;	máiH;
-boiled	飯	fàn	faaHn
rich a.	有錢	yŏuchyán;	yáuHchín;
	富有	fùyŏu	fuyáuH
riches n.			
-treasures	錢財	chyántsái	chìHnchòiH
rickets n.	傴僂病	yŭlóubíng	yúHláubeHng (tòHbui)
ricksha n.	人力車	rénlìchē	yàHnliHkchè (chèjái)
rid v. t.			
-get rid of	除去	chúchyù	chèuiHheui
riddle n.	謎	mí;	màiH;
	謎語	míyŭ	màiHyúH
ride v. i.			
-as a horse	騎	chí;	kèII;
-in a car	坐	dzwò	chóH
ridicule v. t.	嘲笑	cháusyàu;	chìuHsiu (gèisiu);
	戲弄	syìnùng	heiluHng
rifle n.	步鎗	bùchyāng;	bouHchēung;

	來福鎗	láifúchyāng	lòiHfūkchēung

right

-a. not mistaken	對	dwèi;	deui (ngāam);
-a. not left	右	yòu;	yauH;
-a. proper	正當	jèngdàng;	jingdong;
-n. be entitled	權利	chywánlì	kyùHnleiH

rigid a.

| -stiff | 硬 | yìng; | ngaaHng; |
| -strict | 嚴格 | yángé | yìHmgaak |

rigorous a.

-stern	嚴格	yángé;	yìHmgaak;
-harsh	嚴厲	yánlì;	yìHmlaiH;
-minutely accurate	精密	jīngmì	jīngmaHt

rim n.

| | 邊 | byān | bīn |

ring

-n. a circle	圈	chywān;	hyūn;
-n. worn on a finger	戒指	jyèjr;	gaaijí;
-v. i. as bells	響	syǎng	héung

riot v. i.	暴動	bàudùng	bouHduHng
rioter n.	暴徒	bàutú	bouHtòuH
ripe a.	熟	shú;	suHk;
	成熟	chéngshú	sìHngsuHk

ripple

| -n. | 波紋 | bwōwén; | bòmàHn; |
| -v. i. | 起波紋 | chǐbwōwén | héibòmàHn |

rise v. i.

-stand up	站起來	jànchǐlái;	jaaHmhéilòiH (kéiHhéisàn);
-of the sun	日出	rchū;	yaHtchēut;
-of prices	漲價	jǎngjyà;	jeungga (héiga)
-ascend	上升	shàngshēng	seuHngsìng

risk n.	危險	wéisyăn	ngàiHhím
-run a risk	冒險	màusyăn	mouHhím
rite n.	禮;	lĭ;	láiH;
	儀式	yíshr̀	yiHsìk
rival n.			
-competitor	對手;	dwèishŏu;	deuisáu
	敵手	díshŏu	diHksáu
river n.	河;	hé;	hòH;
	江	jyūng	gòng
rivet n	鉚釘	máuding	máauHdeng
road n.	路	lù	louH
roar n.			
-of lion	咆哮;	páusyàu;	pàauHhàau;
-of sea	嘯聲	syàusheng	siusìng
roast v. t.	烤	kău	hāau (hong)
rob v. t.	搶;	chyăng;	chóung;
	搶劫	chyăngjyé	chéunggip
robe n.	袍	páu	pòuH
robber n.	賊;	dzéi;	chaaHk
	強盜	chyángdàu	kèuHngdouII
robust a.	強壯	chyángjwàng	kèuHngjong
rock			
-n.	石頭;	shŕtou;	seHktáuH;
-v. i.	搖	yáu	yìuH
rocket n.	火箭	hwŏjyàn	fójin
rod n.	棍杖;	gwùn (or) jàng;	gwan (or) jeuHng;
-fishing	魚竿	yúgān	yùHgòn
role n.	角色	jyănsè	goksìk

roll

–v. t. as a ball	滾	gwǔn;	gwán (lūk);
–v. t. rock	搖	yáu;	yìuH;
–n. attendance	點名	dyǎnmíng	dímméng
romance n.	浪漫	làngmàn	loHngmaaHn
romantic a.	浪漫	làngmàn	loHngmaaHn
roof n.	屋頂	wūdǐng	ngūkdéng
room n.	房	fáng;	fóng;
	房間	fángjyān	fòHnggàan

root

–n.	根	gēn;	gàn;
–v. t.	除根	chúgēn	chèuiHgàn
rope n.	繩子	shéngdz	sìHngjí (síng)

rose

–n. flower	玫瑰花	méigwàihwā;	mùiHgwaifā;
–a. pink	粉紅	fěnhúng	fánhùHng
rot v. i.	爛	làn	laaHn
rota n.	名册	míngtsè	mìHngchaak
rotary a.	轉	jwǎn;	jyun;
	旋轉	sywánjwǎn	syùHnjyún

rotten a.

-decayed	腐爛	fǔlàn;	fuHlaaHn;
-by damp	霉爛	méilàn	mùiHlaaHn

rough a.

-of surface	粗	tsū;	chòu;
-rude	粗魯	tsūlǔ;	chòulóuH;
-of the sea	風浪大	fēnglàngdà	fùngloHngdaaiH
round a.	圓	ywán	yùHn

rouse v. t.

-as anger	惹氣	rěchí;	yéHhei (gǐkhei);

-waken	叫醒	jyàusyǐng	giusćng
route n.	路	lù	louH
routine n.	慣例	gwànlì;	gwaanlaiH
	例行公事	lìsyínggūngshf	laiHhàHnggùngsiH
row n.	行	háng;	hòHng;
	排	pái	pàaiH
-row a boat	搖船	yáuchwán	yìuHsyùHn
royal a.	王的	wángde	wòHngdǐk
			(suIIkyù wòHngge)
rub v. t.			
-between two hands	搓	tswō;	chò;
-out, off	擦	tsā;	chaat
-on	搽塗	chá (or) tú	chàH (or) tòuH
rubber n			
-caoutchouc	樹膠	shùjyāu;	syuHgàau;
-eraser	橡皮	syàngpi	jeuIIngpèiḤ
rubbish n.			
-refuse	垃圾	lèsè;	laaHpsaap;
-things of no value	廢物	fèiwù	faimaHt
ruby n.	紅寶石	húngbǎushf	hùHngbóuseHk
rude a.	粗魯	tsūlǔ;	chòulóuH;
	魯莽	lǔmǎng	lóuHmóHng
rudiment n.			
-of learning	初步	chūbù;	chòbouH;
-the 1st principles	原理	ywánlǐ	yùHnléiH
rug n.	地毯	dìtǎn	deiHjin
rugged a.			
-not smooth	粗	tsū;	chòu;
-uneven	不平	bùpíng	bātpìIIng (m̀pìIIng)
ruin			
-v. t. destroy	毀壞	hwěihwài;	wáiwaaiH;

-n. decayed	毀滅	hwĕimyè	wáimiHt
rule			
-n. regulation	規則	gwèidzé;	kwàijāk;
-v. t. a country	統治	tŭngj ̀	túngjiH
ruler n.			
-sovereign	元首	ywánshŏu;	yùHnsáu;
-for ruling lines	尺	chĭ	chek
rumor (our) n.	謠言	yáuyán	yìuHyìHn
run v. i.			
-of men	跑	pău;	páau;
-of machinery	走	dzŏu	jáu (hàaHng)
runway n.	跑道	păudàu	páudouH
rupture			
-v. t. of peace	破裂	pwòlyè;	poliHt;
-v. t. burst	爆	bàu;	baau;
-n. hernia	小腸氣	syăuchángchì	síuchèuHnghei
rural a.	鄉村的	syāngtswūnde	hēungchyūndìk
rush v. i.			
-in	闖	chwăng;	chóng (joHng);
-out	衝	chūng	chùng;
rusty a.	生銹	shēngsyòu	sàangsau
rut n.	車印	chēyìn	chèyan
rye n.	小麥	syăumài	síumaaHk

S

sabotage n.	損壞	swŭnhwài;	syúnwaaiH;
-of employer's property	破壞行動	pwòhwàisyíngdùng;	powaaiHhàHngduHng
-refusal to work	怠工	dàigūng	tóiHgùng
sack n.	袋	dài;	doiH;

		Mandarin	Cantonese
	包	bāu	bàau
ackcloth n.	麻布	mábù	màHbou
acred a.	聖	shèng	sing
acrifice v. t.	犧牲	syishēng	hèisàng
ad a.	憂愁;	yōuchóu;	yàusàuH;
	煩悶	fánmèn	fàaHnmuHn
addle n.	馬鞍	mǎān	màHōn
dism n.	虐待狂	nywèdàikwáng	neuHkdoiHkòHng
fe			
-a. free from danger	安全	ānchywán;	ònchyùHn;
-a. reliable	穩當;	wěndàng;	wándong;
-n. for money	保險箱	bǎusyǎnsyāng	bóuhìmsēung (gaapmaaHn)
g v. i.	傾斜	chīngsyé	kìngchèH
ge n.			
-herb	鼠尾草	shūwěitsǎu;	syúméiHchóu,
-wise person	聖人	shèngrén	singyàHn
il			
-n.	帆	fān;	fàaHn;
-v. i.	開船	kāichwán	hòisyùHn
ilor n.	水手	shwěishǒu	séuísáu
ke n.	米酒	mǐjyǒu	máiHjáu
lad n.	生菜	shēngtsài	sāangchoi
lary n.	薪水	syīnshwěi	sànséui
le n.			
-of goods for money	賣	mài;	maaiH;
-at low prices	大減價	dàjyǎnjyà	daaiHgáamga
liva n.	口水	kǒushwěi	háuséui
lmon n.	薩門魚	sàményú	saatmùHnyùH
lt n.	鹽	yán	yìHm
lty a.	鹹	syán	hàaHm

salute v. t.

-greet	行禮	syínglǐ;	hàaHngláiH;
-bow	鞠躬	jyúgūng	gūkgùng

salvage

-n.	救護	jyàuhù;	gauwuH;
-v. t.	搶救	chyǎngjyòu	chéunggau

same a.

	一樣	yíyàng;	yātyeuHng;
	同樣	túngyàng	tùHngyéung

sample n.

	樣本	yàngběn;	yeuHngbún;
	樣品	yàngpǐn	yeuHngbán

sanatorium n.

-hospital	療養院	yáuyǎngywàn;	lìuHyéuHngyún;
-health resort	療養地	yáuyǎngdì	lìuHyéuHngdeiH

sanctify v. t. 成聖 chéngshèng sìHngsing

sanction n./v. t.

-approval	批准	pǐjwǔn;	pàijéun;
-penalty	制裁	r̀tsái	jaichòiH

sand n. 沙 shā sà

sandal n. 涼鞋 lyángsyé lèuHnghàaiH

sandwich n. 三文治 sānwénjr̀ sàammàHnjiH

sane a. 穩健 wěnjyàn wéngiHn

sanitation n. 衛生設備 wèishēngshèbèi waiHsàngchitbeiH

sanity n. 神清氣爽 shénchǐngchì shwǎng sàHnchìngheisóng

Santa Claus n. 聖誕老人 Shèngdànlǎurén SingdaanlóuHyàHn

sap n. 汁 jr̄ jāp

sapphire n. 藍寶石 lǎnbǎushŕ làaHmbóuseHk

sarcastic a.

	譏笑	jīsyàu;	gèisiu;
	諷刺	fèngtsż	fungchi

sardine n. 沙丁魚 shàdǐngyú sādǐngyú

satchel n.	書包	shūbāu	syùbàau
satellite n.	衞星	wèisyìng;	waiHsìng;
-man-made	人造衞星	réndzàuwèisyìng	yàHnjouHwaiHsing
satisfactory a.			
-giving satisfaction	滿意	mǎnyì;	múHnyiʮ
-sufficient	滿足	mǎndzú	múHnjūk
satisfy v. t.			
-make content	滿足	mǎndzú;	múHnjūk;
-satiate	吃飽	chřbǎu	hekbáau (siHkbáau)
saturate v. t.	浸濕	jìnshř;	jamsāp;
-Chem.	飽和	bǎuhé	báauwòH
Saturday n.	禮拜六	lǐbàilyòu;	láiHbaailuHk;
	星期六	syìngchǐlyòu	sìngkèiHluHk
sauce n.	醬油	jyàngyóu	jeungyàuH (siHyàuH)
saucer n.	碟	dyé	diHp
sausage n.	臘腸	làcháng;	laaHpchéung;
	香腸	syāngcháng	hèungchéung
savage			
-a. ferocious	野蠻	yěmán;	yéHmàaHn;
-a. cruel	殘忍	toánrěn;	cháaHnyán;
-n. uncivilised person	野人	yěrén	yéHyàHn
save v. t.			
-economize	省	shěng;	sáang (hàan);
-rescue	救	jyòu	gau
savoury			
-a.	美味	měiwèi;	méiHmeiH;
-n.	香物	syūngwù	hèungmaHt
saw			
-v. t.	鋸	jyù;	geu;
-n.	鋸子	jyùdz	geuijí (geui)

say v. t.	說	shwō;	syut;
	講	jyǎng	góng
scaffold n.	架子	jyàdz	gají (gá)
scald v. t.			
-burn with hot liquid	燙	tàng;	tong (luHk);
-rinse with boiling water	冲	chūng	chùng
scalp n.	頭頂	tóudǐng;	tàuHdéng;
	頭皮	tóupí	tàuHpèiH
scale n.			
-of a fish	魚鱗	yúlín;	yùHlèuHn;
-standard	準音	byāujwǔn;	bǐujéun;
-music	音階	yǐnjyē	yàmgàai
scandal n.	醜事	chǒushr̀;	cháusiH;
-wicked talk	是非	shr̀fēi	siHfèi
scar n.			
-scab	疤	bā;	bà;
-mark	痕	hén	hàHn
scarce a.			
-contrary of plentiful	少	shǎu;	síu;
-rare	希罕	syīhǎn	hèhón
scare v. t.	嚇	syà	haak
scarf n.	圍巾	wéijǐn	wàiHgān
scarlet a.	大紅	dàhúng;	daaiHhùHng;
	深紅	shēnhúng;	sàmhùHng;
-scarlet fever	猩紅熱	syīnghúngr̀	sìnghùHngyiHt
scatter v. t.	散開	sànkāi;	saanhòi;
	分散	fēnsàn	fànsaan
scavenger n.	清道夫	chīngdàufū	chìngdouHfù
scanery n.	風景	fēngjǐng;	fùnggíng;

-on a stage	佈景	bùjǐng	bougíng
cent n.	香味	jyāngwèi	hèungmeiH
cheme v. t.	計劃	jìhwà	gaiwaaHk
cholar n.			
-student	學生	sywésheng;	hoHksāang;
-learned man	學者	sywéjě	hoHkjé
cholarship n.			
-as learning	學識	sywéshr;	hoHksik;
-as support	獎學金	jyǎngsywéjin	jéunghoHkgām
chool n.	學校	sywésyàu	hoHkhaauII
-middle school	中學	jūngsywé	jùnghoIIk
-primary school	小學	syǎusywé	síuhoHk
-school term	學期	sywéchí	hoHkkèiH
chooling n.	學費	sywéfèi	hoHkfai
cience n.	科學	kēsywé	fòhoHk
cientist n.	科學家	kēsywéjyā	fòhoHkgā
cissors n.	剪子	jyǎndz	jínjí (gaaujín)
cold v. t.	罵	mà	maH (naauII)
cope n.			
-sphere	範圍	fànwéi	faaHnwàiH;
-opportunity	機會	jīhwèi	gèiwuiH
corch v. t.	燒焦	shāujyāu	sìujìu (sìunùng)
core			
-v. i. mark points	記分	jìfēn;	geifān;
-n. 20	二十	èrshf;	yiHsaHp;
-n. mark	分數	fēnshù	fànsou
corn v. t.	藐視	myǎushì	míuHsiH

scotch v. t./v. i.	燒焦	shāujyāu	sìujìu (sìunùng)
scoundrel n.	惡棍	ègwùn;	ngokgwan;
	無賴	wúlài	mòuHláai
scout n.	童軍	túngjyūn	tùHnggwàn
scowl			
-n.	怒容	nùrúng;	nouHyùHng;
-v. i.	不悅	búywè	bātyuHt
scrap n.	零碎	língswèi	lìHngseui
scrape v. t.	削	syāu;	seuk;
	刮	gwā	gwaat
scratch v. t.			
-an itching place	抓	jwā;	jáau (jūk);
-scrape	刮	gwā	gwaat
scream			
-v. i.	喊叫	hǎnjyàu;	haamgiu;
-n.	尖叫聲	yānjyàushēng	jìmgiusèng
screen n.			
-standing	屏風	píngfēng;	pìHngfùng;
-hanging	簾	lyán;	lím;
-of a cinema	銀幕	yínmù	ngàHnmoHk
screw			
-n. spike	螺絲刀	lwósždāu;	lòHsìdōu (lòHsìpài);
-v. t. twist	擰	nǐng	niHng
scribble v. t.	草寫	tsǎusyě	chóusé
scribe n.			
-clerk	文書	wénshū;	màHnsyù;
-Bible	文士	wénshŕ	màHnsiH

cript n.	書 寫 體	shūsyětǐ	syùsétái
cripture n.	聖 經	Shèngjīng	Singgìng
croll n.	卷	jywàn	gyún
crub v. t.	擦	tsā	chaat
cruples n.	顧 慮	gùlyù;	guleuiH;
	自 責	dz̀dzé	jiHjaaḳ
crutinize v. t.	查	chá;	chàH;
	檢 查	yǎnchá	gímchàH
culpture v. t.	雕 刻	dyāukè	dìuhāak
cythe n.	鐮 刀	yándāu	lìHmdōu
ea n.	海	hǎi	hói
eal			
-n.	印	yìn;	yan;
-v. t.	蓋 印	gàiyìn	koiyan (kāptòuHjēung)
-seal a door	封 門	fēngmén	fùngmùHn
eam			
-n.	縫	féng	fùHng;
-v. t.	縫 上	féngshàng	fùHngséuHng (lyùHnmàaiH)
eaman n.			
-sailor	水 手	shwěishǒu;	séuisáu;
-worker on the ship	船 員	chwánywán	syùHnyùHn
eaport n.	海 港	hǎigǎng	hóigóng
earch v. i.	找	jǎu;	jáau (wán);
	找 尋	syúnjǎu	chàHmjáau
eashore n.	海 岸	hiàn	hóingoHn
easick a.	暈 船	yūnchwán	wàHnsyùHn
eason			
n.	季	jì;	gwai;
-v. t. render palatable	調 味	tyáuwèi	tìuHmeiH

seasoning n.	調味品	tyáuwèipǐn	tìuHmeiHbán
seat n.			
-pew	座位	dzwòwèi;	joHwaiH;
-chair	椅子	yǐdz	yíji (yí)
seaweed n.	海草	hǎitsǎu;	hóichóu;
-edible	海帶	hǎidài	hóidaai
second			
-n. in number	第二	dìèr;	daiHyiH;
-n. of time	秒	myǎu;	míuH;
-v. t. agree	贊成	dzànchéng	jaansìHng
secret a.	秘密	mìmì	beimaHt
secretary n.	書記	shūjì;	syùgei;
	秘書	mìshū	beisyù
section n.			
-part	部分	bùfèn;	bouHfaHn;
-of a dept.	部	bù;	bouH;
-of a road	段	dwàn	dyuHn;
-paragraph	段	dwàn	dyuHn
security n.			
-safety	安全	ānchywán;	ònchyùHn;
-bill	保證金	bǎujèngjīn	bóujinggām
sediment n.	渣子	jādz	jàji (jà)
seduce v. t.			
-for bad purpose	引誘	yǐnyòu;	yáHnyáuH;
-for women	勾引	gōuyǐn	ngàuyáHn
see v. t.			
-look at	看	kàn;	hon (tái);
-understand	明白	míngbai	mìHngbaaHk
-interview	見	jyàn;	gin;
-visit	看	kàn	hon (taam)

eed n.

-of a plant	種子	jŭngdz;	júngjí;
-of fruit	核	hú	waHt

seek v. t. 尋找 syúnjău; chàHmjáau;

-seek for aid 求助 chyóujù kàuHjoH

seem v. t. 好像 hăusyàng hóujeuHng (hóuchiH)

egment n.

-piece broken off	斷片	dwànpyàn;	dyuHnpin;
-part	部分	bùfen	bòuHfaHn

segregate v. t. 分離 fēnlí fànlèiH

seize v. t. 抓住 jwājù; jáaujyuH;

-seize for ransom 綁票 băngpyàu bóngpiu

eldom adv. 很少 hěnshău; hánsíu (hóusíu);

少有 shăuyŏu síuyáuH

elect v. t. 挑選 tyāusywăn tìusyún;

選擇 sywăndzé syúnjaaHk

elf n. 自己 dżjĭ; jiHgéi;

自身 dżshēn jiHsàn

-self-confidence 自信心 dżsyìnsyin jiHseunsàm

elf-control n. 自制 dżjì; jiHjai;

克己 kèjĭ hāakgéi

elf-deceit a. 自欺 dżchi jiHhèi

elf-evident a. 自然明白 dżránmíngbai jiHyìHnmìHngbaaHk

elf-governing a. 自治的 dżjìrde jiHjiHdĭk

elf-important a. 自大 dżdà; jiHdaaiH;

自尊 dżdzwūn jiHjyùn

elfish a. 自私 dżsż jiHsì

ell v. t. 賣 mài maaiH

emester n. 學期 sywéchi hoHkkèiH

emicolon n. 分號 fēnhàu; fànhouH;

	半支點	bànjřdyăn	bunjìdím
seminary n.	神學院	shénsywéywàn	sàHnhoHkyún
send v. t.			
-a. present	送	sùng;	sung;
-a. person	派	pài;	paai;
-a. letter	寄	jì	gei
senior			
-a. in office	高級	gāují;	gōukăp;
-n. in age	長輩	jăngbèi	jéungbui
seniority n.	資歷	dẓlì;	jìliHk;
-seniority in age	長輩	jăngbèi	jéungbui
sensation n.			
-feeling	感覺	gănjywé;	gámgok;
-emotion	感動	găndùng	gámduHng
sense n.			
-perception	知覺	jřjywé;	jìgok;
-feeling	感覺	gănjywé;	gámgòk;
-significance	意義	yìyi;	yiyiH;
-five senses	五官	wŭgwān	ńgHgùn
sensible a.			
-aware	知道	jřdàu;	jìdou;
-possessing sense	有理性	yŏulìsyìng	yáuHléiHsìng
sensitive a.	神經過敏	shénjīnggwòmĭn	sàHngìnggwomáHn
sensual a.	肉感	ròugăn;	yuHkgám;
	淫蕩	yíndàng	yàHmdoHng
sentence			
-v. t. judge	判決	pànjywé;	punkyut;
-n. Gram.	句子	jyùdz	geuijí (geui)

entiment n.

-feelings	感情	gănchíng;	gámchìHng;
-emotion	情緒	chíngsyù	chìHngséuiH

entry n. 哨兵 shàubing saaubing

eparate v. t.

-keep apart	分開	fēnkāi;	fànhòi;
-of persons	離開	líkāi;	lèiHhòi;
-as by partition	隔開	gékāi;	gaakhòi;
-differentiate	分別	fēnbyé	fànbiHt

eptember n. 九月 Jyŏuywè GáuyuHt

epulchre n. 墳墓 fénmù fàHnmouH

equel n.

-what follows after 繼起 jìchĭ gaihéi

equence n.

-succession	相連	syānglyán	sèunglìHn
-in regular sequence	順次	shwùntsż	seuHnchi

erial a. 連續 lyánsyù lìHnjuHk

eries n.

-succession	連續	lyánsyù;	lìHnjuHk;
-of books	叢書	tsúngshū	chùHngsyù

erious a.

-important	重要	jùngyàu;	juHngyiu;
-solemn	嚴肅	yánsù;	yìHmɛūk;
-of a situation	嚴重	yánjùng;	yìImjuHng;
-of an illness	嚴重	yánjùng;	yìHmjuHng

erpent n. 蛇 shó sèH

erum n. 血清 sywěching hyutchíng

ervant n.

	用人	yùngrén;	yuHngyàHn (gùngyàHn);
	僕人	púrén	buHkyàHn

serve v. t.

-wait upon	服侍	fúshr̀;	fuHksiH;
-work for	服務	fúwù;	fuHkmouH;
-as guests	招待	jāudài	jiudòiH

service n.

-servant status	服侍	fúshr̀;	fuHksiH;
-worship	做禮拜	dzwòlǐbài;	jouHláiHbaai:
-assistance rendered	服務	fúwù	fuHkmouH

session n.

-meeting	會議	hwèiyì;	wuiHyíH;
-class period	上課時間	shàngkèshŕjyān	séuHngfosìHgaan

set

–v. t. place	放	fàng;	fong;
–v. t. fix	定	dìng;	diHng;
–v. t. as jewels	鑲	syāng;	sèung;
–n. of books	套	tàu;	tou;
–n. of china	副	fù	fu

set square n.	三角板	sānjyǎubǎn	sàamgokbáan
settee n.	長靠椅	chángkàuyǐ	chèuHngkaauyí

settle v. t.

-decide	決定	jywédìng	kyutdiHng;
-adjust an affair	解決	jyějywé	gáaikyut

settlement n.

-of questions	解決	jyějywé;	gáaikyut;
-colony	殖民地	jŕmíndì	jiHkmàHndeiH

seven a.	七	chī	chāt
seventh a.	第七	dìchī	daiHchāt
seventy a.	七十	chīshŕ	chātsaHp

sever v. t.

-cut off	分開	fēnkāi;	fànhòi;

-friendship	斷絕	dwànjywé	tyúHnjyuHt
several a.	幾	jǐ	géi
severe a.			
strict	嚴格	yángé;	yìIImgaak,
-stern	莊嚴	jwāngyán;	jòngyiHm;
-not light	重	jùng;	chúHng;
-not lenient	嚴厲	yánlì	yiIImlaiII
sew v. t.	縫	féng	fùHng(lyùHn)
sewage n.	溝內污物	gōunèiwūwù	gàunoiHwùmaHt
sewer n.	暗溝	àngōu	ngamgàu
sex n.	性	syìng	sing;
	性別	syìngbyé	singbiHt
sexual desire	性慾	syìngyù;	singyuHk;
shabby a.	破爛	pwòlàn;	polaaHn;
-as clothes	襤褸	lánlyǔ	làaHmlóuiH
shade n.			
-shadow	影子	yǐngdz;	yíngjí (yíng);
-depth of colour	色度	sèdù	sikdouH
shadow n.	影子	yǐngdz	yíngjí (yíng)
shake v. t.			
-move	搖	yáu;	yìuH;
-tremble	發抖	fādǒu;	faatdáu;
-of the earth	震動	jèndùng	janduHng
shall v. aux.			
-future tense	將要	jyāngyàu;	jèungyiu;
-must	必須	bìsyū	bìtsèui
shallow a.	淺	chyǎn	chín
sham a.			
-not real	假	jyǎ;	gá;
-pretend to be	假裝	jyǎjwāng	gájòng

shame n.

-disgrace	羞恥	syōuchǐ;	sàuchí;
-humiliation	貶降	byǎnjyàng	bíngong
shameful a.	丟臉	dyōulyǎn	dìulíHm (móuHmín)
shameless a.	無恥	wúchǐ	mòuHchí
shampoo v. t.	洗頭	syǐtóu	sáitàuH
shape n.	樣子	yàngdz	yeuHngjí (yéung);
	形狀	syíngjwàng	yìHngjoHng

share

-n. portion	分	fèn;	faHn;
-n. in firm	股份	gǔfèn;	gúfaHn;
-v. t. partake	參加	tsānjyā;	chàamgà;
-v. t. use together	公用	gūngyùng	gùngyuHng
shark n.	鯊魚	shāyú	sàyú
sharp a.	尖	jyān;	jìm;
-not blunt	利	lì	leiH

shave v. t.

-with a razor	剃	tì;	tai;
-with a plane	刨	páu	pàauH
she pro.	她	tā	tà (kéuiH)
shear v. t.	剪	jyǎn;	jín;
-shear sheep	剪羊毛	jyǎnyángmáu	jínyèuHngmòuH

shed n.

-for storing things	棚	péng;	pàaHng;
-workshop	工塲	gūngchǎng	gùngchèuHng
-shed blood	流血	lyóusyě	làuHhyut
-shed tears	流淚	lyóulèi	làuHleuiH
sheep n.	羊	yáng;	yèuHng;
	綿羊	myányáng	mìHnyèuHng

sheepfold n.	羊圈	yángjywan	yèuHnggyun
sheet n.			
-for a bed	牀單	chwángdān;	chòHngdāan;
-piece	片	pyàn;	pin;
-of paper	張	jāng	jèung
shelf n.	書架	shūjyà	syùgá
shell n.			
-zool. etc.	殼	ké;	hok;
-projectile	砲彈	pàudàn	paudáan
shelter			
-v. t. screen	遮	jē;	jè;
-v. t. protect	保護	bǎuhù;	bóuwuH;
-v. i. take shelter	躲避	dwǒbì	dóbeiH
shepherd			
-n.	牧人	mùrén;	muHkyàHn;
-v. t.	牧羊	mùyáng	muHkyèuHng
shield n.	盾牌	dwùnpái	téuHnpàaiH
shift			
-v. t. move	移	yí;	yìH;
-v. t. change	換	hwàn;	wuHn;
-n. daily working period	輪班	lwúnbān	lèuHnbāan
shilling n.	先令	syānlìng	sinlíng
shin n.	脛骨	jìnggǔ	ginggwāt
shine v. i.	照	jàu;	jiu;
	發光	fāgwāng	faatgwòng
ship			
-n.	船	chwán;	syùHn;
-v. t.	運	yùn	waHn

shirk v. t.

  -lazy 偷懶 tōulǎn; tàuláaHn;

  -as danger 躲避 dwǒbì; dóbeiH;

  -as difficulties 避免 bìmyǎn; beiHmíHn;

  -as responsibilities 推辭 twēitsź tèuichìH

shirt n. 襯衫 chènshān chansāam

shiver v. i. 發抖 fādǒu faatdáu

shock v. t. 震動 jèndùng janduHng

shoe n. 鞋 syé hàaiH

shoot v. t.

  -as an arrow 射箭 shèjyàn; seHjin;

  -as a gun 開鎗 kāichyāng hōichēung

shop n. 店 dyàn; dim;

  鋪子 pùdz poují (poutáu)

shopkeeper n. 店主 dyànjǔ; dimjyú;

  老板 lǎubǎn lóuHbáan

shore n. 岸 àn; ngoHn;

  海岸 hǎiàn hóingoHn

short a.

  -in length 短 dwǎn; dyún;

  -in time 短 dwǎn; dyún;

  -in height 矮 ǎi ngái

shortcoming n. 缺點 chywēdyǎn; kyutdím;

  短處 dwǎnchù dyúnchyu

shortsighted a. 近視 jìnshr̀; gaHnsiH;

  近視眼 jìnshìyǎn gaHnsiHngáaHn

shot n. 子彈 dźdàn; jídáan;

  -crack shot 鎗手 chyāngshǒu chēungsáu

should v. aux.

  -ought to   應該   yìnggāi;   yìnggòi;

  -must   必須   bìsyū   bitsèui

shoulder n.   肩膀   jyāngbǎng   gyùnbóng (boktàuH)

shout

  -v. i. speak loudly   大聲叫   dàshēngjyàu;   daaiHsènggiu;

  -n. for joy   歡呼   hwānhū   fùnfù

shovel n.   鏟子   chǎndz   cháanjí (cháan)

  -shovel up   鏟   chǎn   cháan

show

  -v. t. allow to be seen   給 … 看   gěi...kàn;   kāp...hon (béi...tái)

  -v. t. prove   証明   jèngmíng;   jingmìHng;

  -v. t. point out   指出   jřchū;   jíchēut;

  -n. an exhibition   展覽會   jǎnlǎnhwèi   jínláaīīmwúi

shower n.   陣雨   jènyǔ   jaHnyúH

shred v. t.   切片   chyēpyàn;   chitpin

   切細   chyēsyì   chitsai (chityau)

shrewd a.

  -sharp-witted   敏捷   mǐnjyé;   máHnjit;

  -sagacious   精明   jīngmíng   jingmìHng

shriek

  -v. i.   尖叫   jīyānjyàu;   jīmgiu;

  -n.   吱吱聲   jřjřshēng   jìjìsèng

shrimp n.   蝦   syā   hā

shrink v. i.

  -contract   收縮   shōuswō;   sāusūk;

  -in size   縮小   swōsyǎu   sūksiu

shroff n.   收銀人   shōuyínrén   sàungányàHn

shrub n.

  -small tree 小樹 syăushù; síusyuH (syuHjái);

  -bush 灌木 gwànmù gunmuHk

shudder v. i. 震顫 jènchàn; janjin;

        發抖 fādŏu faatdáu

shuffle v. t. 洗牌 syĭpái sáipáai

shut v. t.

  -as a door, window 關 gwān; gwàan (sàan);

  -as books 合 hé; haHp;

  -as eyes 閉 bì; bai (mèi);

  -as ears 掩 yăn yím (kám)

shutter n.

  -venetian blind 百葉窗 băiyèchwān; baakyiHpchēung;

  -Photog. 開關 kāigwān hòigwàan

shuttle n. 梭 swō sò

shy a.

  -bashful 怕羞 pàsyōu; pacháu;

  -timid 膽小 dănsyāu dáamsíu

sick a. 病 bìng; beHng;

        有病 yŏubìng yáuHbeHng

side

  -n. border 邊 byān; bin (biHn);

  -v. i. take one's part 袒護 tănhù táanwuH

sidewalk, sideway n. 行人道 syíngréndàu; hàaHngyàHndouH;

  -adv. 側面 tsèmyàn; jākmiHn;

        橫斜 héngsyé wàaHnchèH

siege v. t. 包圍 bāuwéi; bàauwàiH;

        圍攻 wéigūng wàiHgùng

sieve

-n.	篩子	shāidz;	sàijí (sài);
-v. t.	篩	shāi	sài

sigh v. i. | 嘆氣 | tànchì | taanhei

sight n.

-power of seeing	眼力	yǎnlì;	ngáaHnliHk;
-view	風景	fēngjǐng	fùnggíng

sign

-n. visible mark	記號	jìhàu;	geihouH;
-n. indication	表示	byǎushì;	bíusiH;
-v. t. one's name	簽名	chyānmíng	chìmméng

signal

-n. serves to start action	信號	syìnhàu;	seunhouII,
-n. with flags	旗號	chíhàu;	kèiHhouH;
-v. i. with the hand	做手勢	dzwòshǒushì	jouHsáusai

signature n.

	簽名	chyānmíng;	chìmméng;
	簽字	chyāndz̀	chìmjí

signboard n. | 招牌 | jāupái | jìupàaiH

significant a.

-important	重要	jùngyàu;	juHngyiu;
-having a meaning	有意義	yǒuyìyi	yáuHyiyiH

sigify v. t.

-make known	通知	tūngjr̄;	tùngjì;
-express	表示	byǎushì;	bíusiH;
-show by sign	指	jř	jí

silence n.

-absence of sound	無聲	wúshēng;	mòuHsìng (móuHsèng);
-absence of speech	靜默	jìngmè	jiHngmaaHk

silk n.

-material	絲	sz̄;	sì;

English	Chinese		
-fabric	綢	chóu;	cháu;
-thin glazed	絹	jywàn	gyun
silly a.	傻	shǎ;	sòH
	愚 蠢	yúchwǔn	yùHchéun
silver n.	銀	yín	ngàHn
silversmith n.	銀 匠	yínjyàng	ngàHnjeuHng
silverware n.	銀 器	yínchì	ngàHnhei
similar a.	相 似	syāngsz̀;	sèungchíH;
	類 似	lèisz̀	leuiHchíH
simmer v. i./v. t.	慢 慢 煮 開	mànmànjǔkāi	ɯáaHnmáanjyúhòi (maaHnmáanjyúgwán
simple a.			
-not complicated	簡 單	jyǎndān;	gáandàan;
-easy	容 易	rúngyì;	yùHngyiH;
-not luxurious	樸 素	pǔsù;	poksou;
-weak in intellect	老 實	lǎushŕ	lóuHsaHt
simplify v. t.	簡 化	yǎnhwà	gáanfa
simply adv.	不 過	búgwò;	bātgwo;
	無 非	wúfēi	mòuHfèi
-simply because	只 因 爲	jřyïnwei	jíyànwaiH
simultaneous a.	同 時	túngshŕ	tùHngsìH
sin n.	罪	dzwèi;	jeuiH;
	罪 惡	dzwèiè	jeuiHngok
since conj.	旣 然	jìrán;	geiyìHn;
	… 以 來	…yïlái;	…yíHlòiH;
	自 從 …	dz̀tsúng…	jiHchùHng…
sincere a.	忠 誠	jūngchéng;	jùngsìHng;
	誠 懇	chéngkěn	sìHnghán
sinful a.	有 罪	yǒudzwèi	yáuHjeuiH
sing v. t.	唱	chàng;	cheung;

	唱歌	chànggē	cheunggō

single a.

-only one	單獨	dāndú;	dàanduHk;
-not double	單	dān;	dàan;
-alone	獨白	dúdź	duHkjıH

singular a.

	單	dān;	dàan;
-singular number	單數	dūnshù	dāansou

sinister a.

-evil omen	凶兆	syūngjàu;	hùngjiuH;
-malignant	不吉的	bùjíde	bātgātdǐk

sink

-v. i.	沉	chén;	chàHm;
-n.	磁盆	tszpén	chìHpùHn

sinking n.

sink down	沉下	chénsyà;	chàHmhaH;
-weak	衰弱	shwāirwò	oùuiycuHk

sinless a.

	無罪	wúdzwèi;	mòuHjeuiH;
	無辜	wúgū	mòuHgù

sinner n.

	罪人	dzwèirén	jeuiHyàHn

sip v. t.

-taste	嚐	cháng,	sèuHng;
-of liquid	啜	chwò	jyut

siphon

-n.	虹吸管	húngsyǐgwǎn;	hùHngkāpgún;
-v. t.	虹吸	húngsyǐ	hùHngkāp

sir n.

-in addressing	先生	syānsheng;	sìnsàang;
-knight's title	爵士	jywéshì	jeuksiH

sister n.

-elder	姊姊	jyějye	jeHjē;

-younger	妹ʅ 妹ʅ	mèimei;	mùiHmúi;
-convent	修ᐪ 女ʮ	syōunyŭ	sàunéui
sit v. t.	坐ᵖˣᵋ	dzwò	ҫhóH
site	地ㄉ˙ 點ㄉ˙	dìdyăn	deiHdím
situation n.			
-locality	地ㄉ 點ㄉ˙	dìdyăn;	deiHdím;
-position	地ㄉ 位ˣ	dìwei;	deiHwaiH;
-condition	情˙ 形ㄒ˙	chíngsying;	chìHngyìHng;
-circumstance	境ㄐ˙ 遇ㄩ	jìngyù	gìngyuH
six a.	六ㄌˣ	lyòu	luHk
sixteen a.	十ㄕ 六ㄌˣ	shflyòu	saHpluHk
sixteenth a.	第ㄉ 十ㄕ 六ㄌˣ	dìshflyòu	daiHsaHpluHk
sixty a.	六ㄌˣ 十ㄕ	lyòushf	luHksaHp
size n.			
-bigness	大ㄉˊ 小ㄒ˙	dàsyău;	daaiHsíu;
-of a piece of land	面ㄇˋ 積ㄐ˙	myànji;	miHnjìk;
-of shirts, shoes. etc.	號ㄏˋ	hàu	houH
skate			
-v. i.	溜ㄌˣ 冰ㄅ˙	lyōubǐng;	làuhbǐng;
-n.	溜ㄌˣ 冰ㄅ˙ 鞋ㄒ˙	lyōubǐngsyé	làuHbǐnghàaiH
skeleton n.			
-human	骨ㄍˣ 骼ㄍˋ	gŭgé;	gwātlok;
-of an animal	骨ㄍˣ	gŭ;	gwāt;
-outline	輪ㄌˣ 廓ㄎˣ	lwúnkwò	lèuHngok
sketch n.			
-quick drawing	素ㄙˋ 描ㄇ˙	sùmyáu;	soumìuH;
-rough drawing	畫ㄏˋ 稿ㄍˋ	hwàgău;	wágóu

-dramatic	短劇	dwǎnjyù	dyúnkeHk
skewer n.	捲線針	jywǎnsyànjēn	gyúnsinjām
skid			
-n.	止動器	jǐdùngchì	jíduHnghei;
-v. i.	制住	jìjù	jaijyuH
skiful a.			
-experienced	熟練	shúlyàn;	suHkliHn;
-well-versed	精巧	jīngchyǎu	jīngháau
skill n.	技術	jìshù;	geiHseuHt;
	技能	jìnéng	geiHnàHng
skin n.	皮	pí;	pèiH;
	皮膚	pífu	pèiHfù
skirt n.	裙子	chyúndz	kwàHnjí (kwàHn)
skull n.	頭蓋骨	tóugàigǔ	tàuHkoigwāt
sky n.	天	tyān	tìn
slam v. t.	摔門	shwāimén	sēutmùHn (dengmùHn)
slander v. t.	毀謗	hwěibàng	wáipong
slang n.	俚語;	lǐyǔ;	lèiHyúH;
	俗語	súyǔ	juHkyúH
slap v. t.	打	dǎ	dá
slate n.	石板	shífbǎn	seHkbáan
slaughter v. t.			
-kill	殺	shā	saat;
-massacre	屠殺	túshā	tòuHsaat
slave n.	奴隸;	núlì;	nòuHdaiH;
	奴僕	núpú	nòuHbuHk
slavery n.	奴役;	núyì;	nòuHyiHk;
	苦役	kǔyì	fúyiHk
slay v. t.	殺死;	shāsž;	saatséi;
	打死	dǎsž	dáséi
sleep v. i.	睡	shwèi;	seuiH (fan);

	睡覺	shwèijyàu	seuiHgaau (fangaau)
sleeve n.	袖子	syòudz	jauHjí (jauH)

slender a.

-not stout	柔軟	róurwǎn;	yàuHyúHn;
-lean & small	瘦小	shòusyǎu	sausíu

slice

-n. thin, flat piece	片	pyàn;	pin;
-n. large, thick piece	塊	kwài;	faai;
-v. t. cut into pieces	切片	chyēpyàn	chitpin

slide

-n. inclined plane	滑板	hwábǎn;	waaHtbáan;
-n. of magic lantern	幻燈片	hwàndēngpyàn;	waaHndāngpin;
-n. of a microscope	玻璃片	bwōlípyàn;	bōlēipin;
-v. i. slip	滑	hwá	waaHt

slight a.

-not serious	小	syǎu;	síu;
-small in quantity	少	shǎu;	síu;
-light	輕	chǐng;	hèng;
-not deep	淺	chyǎn	chín

slim a.

-of figure	苗條	myáutyau	míuHtíuH

slip v. i.

-of the foot	滑	hwá;	waaHt;
-error	錯	tswò	cho
slipper n.	拖鞋	twōsyé	tōháai

slit

-v. t. cut	割	gē;	got;
-n. narrow opening	縫	féng	fùHng (lyùHn)

slogan n.

-battle cry	口號	kǒuhàu;	háuhouH;
-printed sheet	標語	byāuyū	bìuyúH

slope n. 斜坡 — syépwō — chèHbò

slot n. 放錢口 — fàngchyánkǒu — fongchínháu

-of letter box	信筒口	syìntǔngkǒu	seuntúngháu

slothful a. 懶惰 — lǎndwò — láaHndoH

slouch

v. i. droop	垂下	chwéisyà;	sèuiHhaH (sèuiHdài);
v. t. stand badly	蹣跚	mánshān	mùHnsàan

slow a. 慢 — màn — maaHn

slug n.

	鼻涕蟲	bítichúng	beiHtaichùHng
	蝸牛	wōnyóu	wòngàuH

slum n. 貧民區 — pínmínchyū — pàHnmàHnkèui

slumber v. i. 睡覺 — shwèijyàu — seuiHgaau (fangaau)

slump n.

-in prices	暴跌	bàudyé;	bouHdit;
-in businesss prosperity	不景氣	bùjǐngchì	bātgínghei

sly a. 狡猾 — jyǎuhwá — gáauwaaHt

smack v. t.

-of the lips	咂嘴	dzādzwěi;	jàpjéui;
-slap	打	dǎ	dá

small a.

-in size	小	syǎu;	síu (sai),
in quantity	少	shǎu	síu

smallest a. 最小 — dzwèisyǎu — jeuisíu (jeuisai)

smallpox n.	天花	tyānhwā	tìnfà
smart a.			
-intelligent	聰明	tsūngmíng;	chùngmìHng;
-shrewd	伶俐	línglì	lìHngleiH
smell			
n. odour	氣味	chìwèi;	heimeiH;
-n. unpleasant	臭味	chòuwèi;	chaumeiH;
-v. t. perceive	聞	wén	màHn
smile			
-v. i.	笑	syàu;	siu;
-n.	微笑	wéisyàu	mèiHsiu
smoke			
-n.	煙	yān;	yin;
-v. i.	吸煙	syīyān	kāpyin (siHkyin)
smooth a.			
-level	平	píng	pìHng;
-polished	光滑	gwānghwá;	gwòngwaaHt;
-as matters	順利	shwùnlì	seuHnleiH
smother v. i.	悶死	mènsž	muHnséi
smoulder v. i./v. t.	冒煙	màuyān	mouHyìn
smudge			
-n.	熏火	syūnhwǒ	fànfó;
-v. i.	熏煙	syūnyān	fànyìn
smuggle v. t.	走私	dzǒusž	jáusì
snack n.	點心	dyǎnsyīn	dímsām
snag n.			
-unexpected obstacle	枝節	jīrjyé	jìjit
snake n.	蛇	shé	sèH

snap v. t.

-as wood, string	斷ㄉㄨㄢˋ	dwàn;	tyúHn;
-with teeth	咬ㄧㄠˇ	yău	ngáauH

snare n.

-net	網ㄨㄤˇ	wăng;	móHng;
-trap	陷ㄒㄧㄢˋ阱ㄐㄧㄥˇ	syànjĭng	haaHmjiHng

snarl v. i.

-baring the teeth	齜ㄗ牙ㄧㄚˊ	dẓyá;	jìngàH;
-growl	嗥ㄏㄠˊ叫ㄐㄧㄠˋ	háujyàu	hòuIIgiu

snatch v. t.

-seize	搶ㄑㄧㄤˇ	chyăng;	chéung;
-grab	抓ㄓㄨㄚ	jwā	jáau (jūkjyuH)

sneak v. i. 溜ㄌㄧㄡ走ㄗㄡˇ   lyōudẕŏu   làuHjáu

sneer

-n.	冷ㄌㄥˇ言ㄧㄢˊ冷ㄌㄥˇ語ㄩˇ	lěngyánlěngyŭ;	láaHngyìHnláaHngyúH;
-v. i.	冷ㄌㄥˇ笑ㄒㄧㄠˋ	lěngsyàu	láaHngsiu

sneeze v. i. 打ㄉㄚˇ嚏ㄊㄧˋ噴ㄆㄣ   dătipen   dátaipan (dáhātchì)

sniff v. i.

-take in air	吸ㄒㄧ	syĭ;	kāp;
-take a smell	聞ㄨㄣˊ	wén	màHn

snip v. t. 剪ㄐㄧㄢˇ   jyăn   jín

snob n. 假ㄐㄧㄚˇ紳ㄕㄣ士ㄕˋ   jyăshenshɨ   gásànsiH

snore v. i. 發ㄈㄚ鼾ㄏㄢ聲ㄕㄥ   fāhānshēng   faathòHnsèng (beiHhòHn)

snow

-n.	雪ㄒㄩㄝˇ	sywě;	syut;
-v. i.	下ㄒㄧㄚˋ雪ㄒㄩㄝˇ	syàsywě	haHsyut (loHksyut)

snub v. t. 叱ㄔˋ責ㄗㄜˊ   chɨdzé   chîkjaak

so adv.

in that degree	那ㄋㄚˋ麼ㄇㄛ	nàme;	náHmō (gámyóung);

in this degree	這麼	jème;	jéHmō (gámyéung);
-therefore	因此	yìntsž	yànchí
-so and so	某某	mŏumŏu	máuHmáuH
soak v. t.	浸	jìn	jam
soap n.	肥皂	féidzàu	fèiHjouH (fàangáan)
sob v. i.	啜泣	chwòchì	jyutyāp
sober a.	清醒	chǐngsyǐng	chǐngsíng
social a.			
-pert. to society	社會上	shèhwèishàng;	séHwúiseuHng;
-pert. to relationship	交際上	jyàujìshàng	gàaujaiseuHng
-social ethics	社會倫理	shèhwèilwúnlǐ	séHwúilèuHnléiH
-social reform	社會改良	shèhwèigǎilyáng	séHwúigóilèuHng
-social service	社會服務	shèhwèifúwù	séHwúifuHkmouH
socialism n.	社會主義	shèhwèijǔyì	séHwúijyúyiH
society n.	社會	shèhwèi	séHwúi
sociology n.	社會學	shèhwèisywé	séHwúihoHḳ
sock n.	短襪	dwǎnwà	dyúnmaHt
soda n.	蘇打	sūdá	sōudá
-bicarbonate	碳酸鈉	tànswānnà	taansyūnnaaHp
sofa n.	沙發	shāfā	sàfaat (sōfáyí)
soft a.			
-not hard	軟	rwǎn;	yúHn;
-as voice	溫柔	wēnróu;	wànyàuH;
-mild	溫和	wēnhé	wànwòH
soil			
-n. earth	土地	tǔdì;	tóudeiH;
-v. t. make dirty	弄髒	nùngdzāng	luHngjòng (jíngwùjòu
solar calendar n.	陽曆	yánglì	yèuHngliHk

solder			
-n.	銲藥	hànyàu;	hoHnyeuHk;
-v. t.	銲接	hànjyē	hoHnjip
soldier n.	兵	bǐng	bìng
sole			
-a. one and only	單獨	dándú,	dàanduHk;
-n. of foot	脚板	jyǎubǎn;	geukbáan;
-n. of shoe	鞋底	syédǐ	hàaiHdái
solemn a.	嚴肅	yánsù;	yìHmsūk;
	莊嚴	jwāngyán	jòngyìHm
solicit v. t.	懇求	kěnchyóu	hánkàuH
solicitor n.	律師	lyùshř	leuHtsī
solid a.			
-compact	結實	jyēshf;	gitsaHt;
-opp. of liquid	固體	gùtǐ	gutái
solitary a.			
-alone	寂寞	jímwò;	jiHkmoHk;
-of places	偏僻	pyānpì	pìnpik
soluble a.			
-in a fluid	溶解	rúngjyě;	yùHnggáai;
-as a problem	解決	jyějywé	gáaikyut
solution n.			
-of problem	解決	jyějywé;	gáaikyut;
-liquid	溶液	rúngyè;	yùHngyiHk;
-Math.	解答	jyědá	gáaidaap
solve v. t.			
-settle	解決	jyějywé;	gáaikyut;
-explain	解釋	jyěshř	gáaisik

some a.

-of numbers	幾	jǐ;	géi;
-of quantities	一些	yìsyē;	yātsè (yātdǐ);
-not all	有的	yǒude	yáuHdǐk (yáuHdǐ)
somebody n.	有人	yǒurén	yáuHyàHn
somehow adv.	想法	syǎngfǎ;	séungfaat;
	總要	dzǔngyàu	júngyiu

something

-n. not named	有些東西	yǒusēdūngsyi;	yáuHsèdūngsāi (yáuHdiyéH);
-n. a matter	有事	yǒushì;	yáuHsiH;
-adv. about	大約	dàywē;	daaiHyeuk
sometimes adv.	有時	yǒushí	yáuHsìH
somewhat adv.	稍微	shāuwéi;	sáaumèiH;
	有點	yǒudyǎn	yáuHdím (yáuHdǐ)
somewhere adv.	某處	mǒuchù	máuHsyu
son n.	兒子	érdz	yìHjí
song n.	歌	gē;	gō;
	曲	chyǔ	kūk

soon adv.

-early	早	dzǎu;	jóu;
-in a short time	不久	bùjyǒu	bātgáu (móuHnoiH)
-as soon as	一俟	yísż	yātjiH
soot n.	煤煙	méiyān	mùiHyìn
soothe v. t.	安慰	ànwèi	ònwai
soothsayer n.	預言者;	yùyánjě;	yuHyìHnjé;
	卜者	bǔjě	būkjé

soprano n.

-of women	女高音	nyǔgāuyìn;	néuiHgòuyàm;
-of boys	男高音	nángāuyìn	nàaHmgòuyàm
socrery n.	法術	fǎshù	faatseuHt
sordid a.	不潔	bùjyé;	bātgit (mgònjeHng);

	污ㄨ穢ㄏㄨㄟ	wūhwèi	wùwai (wùjòu)

ore

| -a. painful | 痛ㄊㄨㄥ | tìng; | tung; |
| -n. ulcer | 瘡ㄔㄨㄤ | chwāng | chōng |

orrow n.

-grief	憂ㄧㄡ 愁ㄔㄡ	yōuchóu;	yàusàuH;
-sadness	愁ㄔㄡ 悶ㄇㄣ	chóumèn;	sàuHmuHn;
-cause of grief	心ㄒㄧㄣ 事ㄕ	syīnshì	sàmsiH

orry a.

-feeling regret	難ㄋㄢ 過ㄍㄨㄛ	nángwò;	nàaIIngwo;
-distressed in mind	心ㄒㄧㄣ 煩ㄈㄢ	syīnfán;	sāmfàaHn;
-I am sorry (for a fault)	對ㄉㄨㄟ 不ㄅㄨ 起ㄑㄧ	dwòibùchǐ	dcuibāthói (dcuimjyuII)

ort

-v. t. select	揀ㄐㄧㄢ	jyǎn;	gáan;
-v. t. classify	分ㄈㄣ 類ㄌㄟ	fēnlèi;	fànleuiH;
-n. species	種ㄓㄨㄥ 類ㄌㄟ	jǔnglèi	júngleuiH

S. O. S.

| | 求ㄑㄧㄡ 救ㄐㄧㄡ 信ㄒㄧㄣ 號ㄏㄠ | chyóujyòusyìnhàu | kàuHgauseunhouH |

Soul n.

| | 靈ㄌㄧㄥ 魂ㄏㄨㄣ | línghwún | lìHngwàHn |

Sound

-n. noise	聲ㄕㄥ 音ㄧㄣ	shēngyin;	sìngyàm;
-a. healthy	健ㄐㄧㄢ 全ㄑㄩㄢ	jyànchywán;	giHnchyùHn;
-v. i. seem	好ㄏㄠ 像ㄒㄧㄤ	hǎusyàng	hóujeuHng

soup n.

| | 湯ㄊㄤ | tāng | tòng |

sour a.

| | 酸ㄙㄨㄢ | swān | syùn |

source n.

-origin	來ㄌㄞ 源ㄩㄢ	láiywán;	lòiHyùHn;
-fountain	源ㄩㄢ 頭ㄊㄡ	ywántóu	yùHntàuH
-of news	方ㄈㄤ 面ㄇㄧㄢ	fāngmyàn	fòngmiHn

south n.	南	nán;	nàaHm
	南方	nánfāng	nàaHmfòng
southeast n.	東南	dūngnán	dùngnàaHm
southwest n.	西南	syinán	sàinàaHm
souvenir n.	紀念品	jìnyànpǐn	geiniHmbán
sovereign n.			
-supreme ruler	元首	ywánshǒu;	yùHnsáu;
-king	國王	gwówáng;	gwokwòHng;
-emperor	皇帝	hwángdì	wòHngdai
sow			
-n. f. pig	母豬	mǔjū;	móuHjyū;
-v. t. seed	撒種	sǎjǔng	saatjúng
space n.			
-as opposed to time	空間	kūngjyān;	hùnggàan;
-room	空地	kūngdì;	hùngdeiH;
-area	地方	dìfang	deiHfòng
spade			
-n.	鏟子	chǎndz;	cháanjí (cháan);
-v. t.	鏟	chǎn	cháan
span			
-n. of the hand	一拃	yìjǎ;	yētjaH;
-v. t. bridge	跨過	kwàgwò	kwàgwo
spanner n.			
-wrench	搬子	bāndz	bùnjí (kím)
spare			
-a. superfluous	多餘	dwōyú;	dòyùH;
-a. extra	另外	lìngwài;	liHngnoiH;
-v. t. give to others	給	gěi	kāp (béi)
spark n.	火花	hwǒhwā;	fófā;

| | | hwǒsyìng | fósìng |

sparkle v. i.

-as champagne	起泡	chǐpàu;	hóipōk;
-emit sparks	發火星	fahwǒsyìng;	taattósing;
-shine	發光	fāgwāng;	faatgwòng;
-as stars	閃爍	shǎnshwò	sìmlik
sparrow n.	麻雀	máchywè	màHjénk
spasm n.	抽筋	chōujìn;	chàugàn,
	痙攣	jìnglywán	ginglyùHn
speak v. i.	說	shwō;	syut;
	講	jyǒng	góng
speaker n.	講者	jyǎngjě;	góngjé;
	發言人	fāyánrén	faatyìHnyàHn
-loud speaker	擴音器	kwòyinchì	kongyāmhei
spear n.	鎗	chyūng	chēung
special a.	特別	tèbyé;	daIIkbiHt;
	特殊	tèshū	daHksyùH
specialist n.	專家	jwānjyā	jyūngā
specially adv.	特意	tèyì	daHkyi (jyūndāng)
species n.	種類	jǔnglèi	júngleuiH
specific a.	特殊	tèshū;	daIIksyùII,
-specific gravity	比重	bǐjùng;	béichúIIng;
-specific heat	比熱	bǐrè;	beiyiHt;
-specific medicine	特效藥	tèsyànyàu	daHkhaauHyeuHk

specification n.

| -explanation | 說明 | shwōmíng; | syutmìHng; |
| -designation | 指定 | jǐdìng | jidiHng |

specimen n.

-sample	樣本	yàngběn;	yeuHngbún;
-model	標本	byāuběn	bĭubún

spectacles n. 眼鏡   yǎnjìng   ngáaHngéng

speculate v. i.

-commerce	投機	tóujī;	tàuHgèi;
-theorise	推測	twēitsè	tèuichāak

speech n.

-language	話	hwà;	wá;
-address	演說	yǎnshwō	yínsyut

speechless a.

-not speaking	不說話	bùshwōhwà;	bātsyutwaH (m̀góngwá)
-dumb	啞吧	yǎbā	ngábā (ngá)
speed n.	速度	sùdù;	chūkdouH;
	快慢	kwàimàn	faaimaaHn

spell

-v. t.	拚音	pīnyīn;	pīngyām;
-n. charm	符咒	fújòu	fùHjau
spelling n.	拚法	pīnfǎ	pīngfaat

spend v. t.

-consume	用	yùng;	yuHng;
-pass, as time	過	gwò	gwo

sphere n.

-globe	地球	dìchyóu;	deiHkàuH;
-scope	範圍	fánwéi	faaHnwàiH
spice n.	香料	syānglyàu	hèunglíu
spider n.	蜘蛛	jīrjū	jìjyū
spike n.	道釘	dàudǐng	douHdēng

pill

-v. t. let liquid out	流	lyóu;	làuH;
-n. for lighting	紙 媒	jǐméi	jímùiH

pin v. t.

-as thread	紡	fǎng;	fóng;
-of silk worms	吐 絲	tùsź	tousì

pinach n. 菠 菜 bwōtsái bòchoi

pinal column n. 脊 柱 jǐjù jekchyúH

pine n. 脊 骨 jǐgǔ jekgwāt

pinster n.

-unmarried	未 婚 女 子	wèihwūnnyǔdž;	meiHfànnéuiHjí;
-virgin	處 女	chùnyǔ	chyunéuiH

piral a. 螺 旋 lwósywán lòHsyùHn

pire n. 尖 塔 jyāntǎ jìmtaap

piril n.

-ghost	鬼 怪	gwěigwài;	gwáigwaai;
-as opp. to flesh	精 神	jīngshén	jìngsàHn

pit

-n. saliva	口 水	kǒushwěi;	háuséui;
-v. i. expectorate	吐 痰	tùtán	toutàaHm

pite n. 怨 恨 ywànhèn yunhaHn

-in spite of	不 管	bùgwǎn	bātgún

lash v. t. 濺 jyàn jin (jìt)

lendid a.

-fine	好	hǎu;	hóu;
-glorious	光 榮	gwāngrúng;	gwòngwìHng;
-showy	華 麗	hwálì	wàHlaiH

lendour n. 光 榮 gwàngrúng; gwòngwìHng;

	榮 華	rúnghwá	wìHngwàH

splice v. t.	絞接	jyǎujyē	gáaujip;
	結繩	jyēshéng	gitsíng
splint n.	夾板	jyábǎn	gaapbáan
splinter n.			
-of wood	刺	tsż;	chi;
-of shell	彈片	dànpyàn	daaHnpin
split v. t.			
-rend	裂開	lyèkāi;	liHthòi;
-cleave	劈	pi;	pek;
-as a party	分裂	fēnlyè	fànliHt
spoil			
⁓v. t. damage	弄壞	nùnghwài;	luHngwaaiH;
⁓v. t. as a child	縱壞	dzùnghwài;	jungwaaiH
⁓v. i. as food	變壞	byànhwài;	binwaaiH;
⁓n. booty	戰利品	jànlìpǐn	jinleiHbán
spoke n.			
-of wheel	輪輻	lwúnfú;	lèuHnfūk;
-of ladder	梯級	tíjí;	tāikāp;
-spoken language	白話	báihwà	baaHkwá
sponge n.	海綿	hǎimyán	hóimìHn
sponsor n.	擔保人	dānbǎurén;	dàambóuyàHn;
	保證人	bǎujèngrén	bóujingyàHn
spontaneous a.			
-without motive	自然	dżrán;	jiHyìHn;
-plants	天生	tyānshēng	tìnsàang
spool n.	捲	jywǎn	gyún
spoon n.	匙子	chʹdz;	chìHjí (chìHgāng);
	調羹	tyáugēng	tiuHgāng

sport n.

-frolic	遊戲	yóusyì;	yàuHhei;
-game	運動	yùndùng	waHnduHng

sportsman n.　運動家　yùndùngjyā　waHnduHnggā

spot n.

-speck	點	dyǎn;	dím;
-on character	污點	wūdyǎn;	wùdím;
-region	地方	dìfang	deiHfòng

spout

-v. t. in a jet	噴	pēn;	pan;
-n. of a gutter pipe	水管	shwěigwǎn	séuigún

spram v. i.　扭　nyǒu;　náu;

扭傷　nyǒushāng　náusèung

spray v. t.　噴　pēn　pan

spread v. I.

-as a carpet	鋪	pū;	pòu;
=smear	搽	chá;	chàH;
-as news	傳	chwán;	chyùHn;
-as a disease	傳染	chwánrǎn	chyùHnyíHm

spring n.

-season	春季	chwūnjì;	chèungwai;
-as of chair, bed	彈簧	tánhwáng;	daaHnwòHng (daaHn-gung);
-of clocks	發條	fātyáu;	faattíu;
-of water	泉水	chywánshwěi;	chyùHnséui;
-v. i. jump	跳	tyàu	tiu

sprinkle v. t.

-fluid	灑	sǎ;	sá;
-powder	撒	sǎ	saat

sprout

-n.	芽	yá;	ngàH;
-v. i.	發芽	fāyá	faatngàH

spy

-n. one sent to watch	偵探	jēngtàn;	jìngtaam;
-n. of a belligerent	間諜	jyāndyé;	gaandiHp;
-v. i.	偵探	jēngtàn	jìngtaam

squalid a.	不潔	bùjyé;	bātgit (m̀gònjeHng);
	污穢	wūhwèi	wùwai (wùjòu)
squander v. t./v. i.	浪費	làngfèi	loHngfai
square a.	四方	sżfāng;	seifōng;
-instrument	曲尺	chyūchǐ;	kūkchek;
-in a city	廣場	gwǎngchǎng	gwóngchèuHng

squash v. t.

-crush	壓壞	yāhwài;	ngaatwaaiH;
-into a pulp	壓爛	yālàn	ngaatlaaHn

squatter n.	違法居住著	wéifǎjyūjùjě	wàiHfaatgèuijyuHjé

squeak v. i./n.

-as a mouse	吱吱叫	jijìjyàu	jijigiu

squeal v. i./n.

-as a child	尖叫	jyānjyàu	jìmgiu

squeeze v. t.

-embrace	抱	bàu;	póuH;
-wring	絞擰扭	jyǎn,nǐng,nyǒu	gáau,níng,náu
-extort	勒索	lèswǒ	laHksok

squib n.	爆仗	pàujàng;	paaujéung;
	小花爆	syǎuhwāpàu	síufāpaau
squirm v. t./v. i.	蜿蜒	wǎnyán	yúnyìHn
squirt v. t./v. i.	噴出	pēnchū	panchēut
stab v. t.	刺	tsż	chi

tability n.	穩固	wěngù;	wángu;
	穩定	wěndìng	wándiHng
table			
-a. established	穩定	wěndìng;	wándiHng;
-n. building for horses	馬房	mǎfáng	máHfòHng
tadium n.	運動場	yùndùngchǎng	waHnduHngchèuHng
taff n.			
-used to walk with	拐杖	gwǎijàng;	gwáaijeuIIng;
-of an office	職員	jfywán	jìkyùHu
tage n.			
-elevated platform	臺	ţái;	tòiH;
-for theatricals	戲臺	syìtái;	heitòiH;
-oratorium	講臺	jyàngtái	góugtòiII
tagger v. i.	瞞跚	mánshān;	mùIInsàan;
	搖擺	yáubǎi	yìuHbáai
tagnate v. i.	停滯	tíngjì	tìHngjaiH
tain			
-v. t. soil	弄髒	núngdzāng;	luHngjòng (jìngwùjòu);
-v. t. dye	染	rǎn;	yíHm;
-n. dirty mark	髒	dzāng	jòng (wùjòu)
tair n.	級	jí	kāp
tale a.	不新鮮	bùsyìnsyān	bātsànsìn (m̀sànsìn)
tall n.			
-for selling things	攤	tān;	tāan;
-stable	馬房	mǎfáng;	máHfòHng;
-in theatre	特別位	tèbyéwèi	daHkbiHtwái
tamina n.	精力	jīnglì	jìngliHk
tammer v. i.	口吃	kǒují	háunāk (nākngá)
tamp			
-n. a chop	印章	yìnjāng;	yanjēung;

-n. of letters	郵票	yóupyàu;	yàuHpiu;
-v. i. tread	踹	tsǎi	cháai

stand

-v. t. on feet	站	jàn;	jaaHm;
-v. t. endure	忍	rěn;	yán;
-n. put things on	架	jyà	ga

standard n.

-model	標準	byāujwǔn;	biujéun;
-stage	程度	chéngdù	chìHngdouH
standpoint n.	立場	lìchǎng;	laHpchèuHng;
	論點	lwùndyǎn	leuHndím

staple a.	主要	jǔyàu;	jyúyiu;
-staple diet	主食	jǔshf;	jyúsiHk;
-staple commodity	主要商品	jǔyàushāngpǐn;	jyúyiusèungbán;
-staple fibre	人造棉	réndzàumyán	yàHnjouHmìHn

star n.	星	syīng	sìng

starch

-n. food	澱粉	dyànfěn;	diHnfán;
-n. solution	漿粉	jyāngfěn;	jèungfán;
-v. t.	漿	jyāng	jèung
stare v. i.	注視	jùshr̀;	jyusiH;
	凝視	níngshr̀	yìHngsiH (moHngsaHt,

start v. t.

-begin	開始	kāishř;	hòichí;
-on a journey	出發	chūfā;	chēutfaat
-starting po!nt	起點	chǐdyǎn;	héidím;

startle v. t.

-surprise	驚奇	jīngchí;	gìngkèiH;

-frighten	懼怕	jyùpà;	geuiHpa;
-astonish	吃驚	chrījing	hekgìng (gìngfòng)
starve v. t.	餓	è	ngoH
state			
-n. country	州	jōu;	jàu;
-n. condition	情形	chíngsying;	chìHngyìHng;
-v. t. in speech	說	shwō	syut (góng)
statement n.			
-verbal	說	shwō;	syut (góng);
-written	字	dzè;	jiH;
-before a court	口供	kǒugūng	háugùng
statesman n.	政治家	jèngjìjyū	jingjiHgā
station			
-n. as of a bus	站	jàn;	jaaHm;
-n. social position	身份	shēnfèn;	sànfán;
-v. t. as troops	駐	jù	jyu
stationary n.	文具	wénjyù	màHngeuiH
statistics n.			
-shown by numbers	統計	tǔngjì;	túnggai;
-the science	統計學	túngjìsywé	túnggaihoHk
statue n.			
-bronze	銅像	túngoyàng;	tùHngjouHng;
-stone	石像	shísyàng	seHkjeuHng
status n.	身份	shēnfèn;	sànfán;
	地位	dìwei	deiHwaiH
statute n	身材	shēntsái	sànchòiH
stay v. i.	住	jù;	jyuH;
-stay overnight	過夜	gwòyè	gwoyeH
steadfast a.	穩定	wěndìng;	wándiHng;

	堅定	jyāndǐng	gìndiHng
steady a.	穩安	wéntwó;	wántóH;
	堅固	jyāngù	gìngu

steak n.

| -beaf steak | 牛排 | nyóupái | ngàuHpáai (ngàuHpá) |

| **steal v. t.** | 偷 | tōu | tàu |

steam

-n. vapour	汽	chì;	hei;
-v. t. in double boiler	蒸	jēng;	jìng;
	燉	dwùn	daHn

| **steamboat n.** | 汽艇 | chìtǐng | heitéHng |

| **steel n.** | 鋼 | gāng | gòng |

steep

| -a. slope | 懸崖 | sywányái; | yùHnngàaiH; |
| -v. t. soak in liquid | 浸漬 | jìnjì | jamjìk |

| **steeple n.** | 禮拜堂尖塔 | lǐbàitángjyāntǎ | láiHbaaitòHngjìmtaap |

| **steer v. t.** | 駕駛 | jyàshǐ | gasái |

| **stem n.** | 樹幹 | shùgàn; | syuHgon; |
| | 樹莖 | shùjìng | syuHging |

stencil

-v. t.	油印	yóuyìn;	yàuHyan;
-n. plate	印花板	yìnhwābǎn;	yanfábáan;
-n. paper	蠟紙	làjǐ	laaHpjí

| **stenograph n.** | 速記員 | sùjìywán | chūkgeiyùHn |

step

-v. i. walk	走	dzǒu;	jáu (hàaHng);
-n. a apace	步	bù;	bouH;
-n. of rank	級	jí;	kāp;
-n. of a staircase	級	jí	kāp

stepmother n.	繼母	jìmŭ	gaimóuH
sterile a.			
-unfruitful	瘦瘠	shòují	saujek
sterilize v. t.			
-of female beings	不受孕	búshòuyùn;	bātsauHyaIIn;
-Bacteriology	殺菌	shājyùn	saatkwán
tern			
-a. severe	嚴厲	yánlì;	yiHmlaiH;
-a. strict	嚴格	yángé;	yìHmgaak;
-n. of a ship	船尾	chwánwěi	syùHnméiH
tew v. t.			
-in an open pot	燉	dwùn;	daHn;
-in a closed pot	燜	mēn	mān
teward n.	管家	gwǎnıyā;	gùngā;
	招待員	jāudàiywán	jiudoiHyùHn
tick			
-n.	杖	jàng;	jeuHng;
-v. i. adhere	貼	tyē;	tip;
-v. i. as to an opinion	堅持	jyānchí	ginchìH
ticky a.	黏	nyán	nìHm
iff a.			
-as collar	硬	yìng;	ngaaHn;
-difficult	難	nán	nàaHn
ifle v. t.	窒息	jísyí;	jaHtsìk;
	悶死	mènsž	muHnséi
igma n.			
-branded mark	烙印	làuyìn;	lokyan;
-Biblical	印記	yìnjì	yangei
ill			
-adv. yet	還	hái;	wàaHn (juHng);

English	Chinese		
-adv. even	甚至	shènjr̀;	saHmji;
-a. quiet	靜	jìng	jiHng
stimulate v. t.			
-encourage	鼓勵	gǔlì;	gúlaiH;
-Physiology	刺激	tsz̀ji;	chigik;
-excite	興奮	syìngfèn	hìngfáHn
sting			
-n.	針刺	jēn, tsz̀;	jām, chi;
-v. t. as a bee	螫	jē;	chik (gāk);
-v. t. as a mosquito	叮	dìng;	dèng;
-v. t. as a nettle	刺	tsz̀	chi
stink			
-v. i.	臭	chòu;	chau;
-n.	臭味	chòuwèi	chaumeiH
stipulate v. t.	約定	ywēdìng;	yeukdiHng;
	訂約	dìngywē	dingyeuk
stir v. t.			
-mix	攙	chān;	chàm;
-with a spoon	攪	jyǎu	gáau
stock			
-n. of goods	存貨	tswúnhwò;	chyùHnfo;
-n. shares	股份	gǔfèn;	gúfaHn;
-v. t. store	存	tswún;	chyùHn;
-live-stock	家畜	jyāchū	gāchūk
stomach n.	胃	wèi;	waiH
-belly	肚子	dùdz	tóuHjí (tóuH)
stone n.	石	shŕ;	seHk;
	石頭	shŕtou	seHktàuH
-Stone Age	石器時代	shŕchìshŕdài	seHkheisìHdoiH
stool n.	凳子	dèngdz	dangjí (dang)

toop v. i.

-the body	彎ㄨㄢ 腰ㄧㄠ	wānyāu;	wāanyìu;
-the head	點ㄉㄧㄢ 頭ㄊㄡ	dyǎntóu	dímtàuH

top v. t.

	停ㄊㄧㄥ	tíng;	tìHng;
	停ㄊㄧㄥ 止ㄓ	tíngjǐ	tìHngjí

tore

-n. shop	鋪ㄆㄨ 子ㄗ	pùdz;	poují (poutáu);
-v. t. save	儲ㄔㄨ 蓄ㄒㄩ	chǔsyù	chyúHchūk
torehouse n.	倉ㄘㄤ 庫ㄎㄨ	tsāngkù	chōngfu
storey n.	層ㄘㄥ	tséng	chàIIng
torm n.	暴ㄅㄠ 風ㄈㄥ	bàufēng;	bouHfùng;
	風ㄈㄥ 雨ㄩ	fēngyǔ	fùngyúH
tory n.	故ㄍㄨ 事ㄕ	gùshr	gusìH

tout a.

-fat	胖ㄆㄤ	pàng;	pun (fèiH);
-robust	強ㄑㄧㄤ 壯ㄓㄨㄤ	chyángjwàng	kèuHngjong
stove n.	爐ㄌㄨ	lú;	lòuH;
	火ㄏㄨㄛ 爐ㄌㄨ	hwǒlú	fólòuH

straight a.

-as a line	直ㄓ	jf;	jiHk;
-upright	正ㄓㄥ 直ㄓ	jèngjf	jingjiHk

straightforward a.

-honest	正ㄓㄥ 直ㄓ	jèngjf;	jingjiHk;
-frank	直ㄓ 爽ㄕㄨㄤ	jfshwǎng	jiHksóng

strain

-v. t. nervous	緊ㄐㄧㄣ 張ㄓㄤ	jǐnjāng;	gánjèung;
-n. extreme vigour	過ㄍㄨㄛ 勞ㄌㄠ	gwòláu	gwolòuH

strange a.

-rare	少ㄕㄠ 見ㄐㄧㄢ	shǎujyàn;	síugin;
-unusual	奇ㄑㄧ 怪ㄍㄨㄞ	chígwài	kèiHgwaai

stranger n.	生人 陌生人	shēngrén; mèshēngrén	sàangyàHn; maaHksàangyàHn (sàangbóuyàHn)
strangle v. t.			
-with hand	勒死	lēsž;	laHkséi;
-with a noose	絞死	jyǎusž	gáauséi
strap n.	皮帶	pídài;	pèiHdáai;
-of a bus	吊帶	dyàudài	diudáai
strategy n.	戰略	jànlywè	jinleuk
straw n.			
-of grain	稻草	dàutsǎu;	douHchóu;
-for beverages	水草	shwěitsǎu	séuichóu
stray v. i.			
-lose one's way	迷路	mílù;	màiHlouH;
-do wrong	墮落	dwòlwò	doHloHk
streak n.	紋	wén	màHn
stream n.	溪	syï	kài
street n.	街	jyē	gāai
strength n.			
-bodily	力	lì;	liHk;
-power	力量	lìlyang	liHkleuHng
strenuous a.			
-energetic	熱心	rèsyïn;	yiHtsàm;
-putting force	努力	nǔlì	nóuHliHk
stretch c. t.			
-the limbs	伸	shēn;	sàn;
-as leather gloves	拉長	lācháng	làaichèuHng
stretcher n.	擔架	dānjyà	dàamga
strict a.			
-severe	嚴格	yángé;	yìHmgaak;

-exact	精確	jīngchywè	jīngkok
-strictly prohibited	嚴禁	yánjìn	yìHmgam

stride

-v. i.	大步走	dàbùdzŏu;	daaiHbouHjáu (daaiHbouHhàaHng);
-n.	大步	dàbù	daaiHbouH

strike v. t.

-beat	打	dă;	dá;
-as labourers	罷工	bàgūng;	baHgùng;
-as students	罷課	bàkè	baHfo

string n.

-rope	繩子	shéngdz;	sìHngjí (síng);
-musical	絃	syán;	yùHn;
-string of pearls	一串珍珠	yìchwànjēnjū	yātchyunjēnjyū

strip

-n. as of cloth	條	tyáu;	tìuH;
-v. t. undress	脫	twō	tyut

stripe n.

-streak	條紋	tyáuwén;	tìuHmàHn;
-line	條	tyáu	tìuH

strive v. i.

-try hard	努力	nŭlì	nóuHliHk

stroke

-n. blow	一拳	yìchywán;	yātkyùHn;
-n. of the pen	畫	hwà;	waaHk;
-v. t.	撫摸	fŭmwó	fúmó

strong a.

-physically	強壯	chyángjwàng;	kèuHngjong;
-solid	結實	jyēshŕ;	gitsaHt;

St

-of policy	強ㄑㄧㄤˊ 硬ㄧㄥˋ	chyángyìng	kèuHngngaaHng

structure n.

-a bldg.	建ㄐㄧㄢˋ 築ㄓㄨˊ 物ㄨˋ	jyànjùwù;	ginjūkmaHt;
-construction	構ㄍㄡˋ 造ㄗㄠˋ	gòudzàu;	kaujouH;
-arrangement	結ㄐㄧㄝˊ 構ㄍㄡˋ	jyēgòu	gitkau

struggle v. i.

-against difficulties	奮ㄈㄣˋ 鬥ㄉㄡˋ	fèndòu;	fáHndau;
-for existence	掙ㄓㄥ 扎ㄓㄚˊ	jēngjá;	jàngjaat;
-contend with	競ㄐㄧㄥˋ 爭ㄓㄥ	jìngjēng	gingjàng
stubborn a.	頑ㄨㄢˊ 固ㄍㄨˋ	wángù;	wàaHngu;
	固ㄍㄨˋ 執ㄓˊ	gùjŕ	gujāp

stud n.

-large headed nail	包ㄅㄠ 釘ㄉㄧㄥ	bāudĭng;	bàaudèng;
-press stud	揿ㄑㄧㄣˋ 扣ㄎㄡˋ	chìnkòu;	gaHmkau (bāknáu);
-as horse breeding	養ㄧㄤˇ 馬ㄇㄚˇ 場ㄔㄤˇ	yăngmăchăng	yéuHngmáHchèuHng
student n.	學ㄒㄩㄝˊ 生ㄕㄥ	sywésheng	hoHksāang

studio n.

-of an artist	畫ㄏㄨㄚˋ 室ㄕˋ	hwàshř;	wásāt;
-of a photographer	照ㄓㄠˋ 相ㄒㄧㄤˋ 館ㄍㄨㄢˇ	jàusyànggwăn;	jiuséunggún;
-of a film company	製ㄓˋ 片ㄆㄧㄢˋ 廠ㄔㄤˇ	jìpyànchăng	jaipinchóng
studious a.	勤ㄑㄧㄣˊ 學ㄒㄩㄝˊ	chìnsywé;	kàHnhoHk (kàHnliH
	用ㄩㄥˋ 功ㄍㄨㄥ	yùnggūng	yuHnggùng

study

-v. t. in school	讀ㄉㄨˊ 書ㄕ	dúshū;	duHksyù;
-v. t. learn	學ㄒㄩㄝˊ 習ㄒㄧˊ	sywésyí;	hoHkjaaHp;
-n. room	書ㄕ 房ㄈㄤˊ	shūfáng	syùfóng
-study abroad	留ㄌㄧㄡˊ 學ㄒㄩㄝˊ	lyóusywé	làuHhoHk

stuff

-n. material	材料	tsáilyàu;	chòiHlíu;
-v. t. to fill cushion	塞	sāi	sāk

stuffy a.

	悶熱	mènrè;	muHnyiHt;
-atmosphere	氣不流通	chìbùlyóutūng	heibātlàuHtùng

stumble v. i.

	摔倒	shwāidǎu;	sēutdóu (ditdóu);
	絆倒	bàndǎu	buHndóu

stump n.

-of a tree	樹椿子	shùjwangdz	syùHjòngjí (syuIItàuII)

stun v. t.

-knock senseless	氣絕	chìjywé	heijyuHt

stunt n.

-trick	把戲	bǎsyì;	báhei;
-feat	技藝	jìyì	gciHngaiH

stupendous a.

-amazing	驚人	jīngrén;	gìngyàHn;
-by size or degree	巨大	jyùdà	geuiHdaaiH

stupid a.

	愚蠢	yúchwǔn;	yùHchéun;
	糊塗	hútu	wùHtòuH

stupor n.

	昏迷	hwūnmí;	fànmàiH;
-dazed state	人事不省	rénshìbùsyǐng	yàHnsiHbātsíng

sturdy a.

	強壯	chyángjwàng	kèuHngjong

stutter v. t.

	口吃	kǒují	háunāk (nākngá)

style n.

-manner of doing	態度	tàidu;	taaidouH;
-fashion	樣子	yàngdz;	yeuHngjí (yéung);
-of penmanship	筆法	bǐfǎ	bātfaat

stylish a.

-fashionable	時式	shíshr̀;	sìHsìk;

-modish	時髦	shŕmáu;	sìHmòuH;
-smart	漂亮	pyàulyang	piuleuHng

subdue v. t.

-as an enemy	打敗	dăbài;	dábaaiH;
-as passion	壓制	yājŕ	ngaatjai

subject

-v. t. subdue	服從	fútsúng;	fuHkchùHng;
-n. of study	科目	kēmù;	fōmuHk;
-n. Gram.	主詞	jŭtsź;	jyúchìH;
-n. person	一人	yìrén;	yātyàHn;
-n. theme	題目	tìmù	tàiHmuHk

sublime a.

-high quality	高尚	gāushàng;	gòuseuHng;
-great	宏壯	húngjwàng	hùHngjong

submarine n.   潛水艇   chyánshwĕitĭng   chìHmséuitéHng

submerge v. t.

-put under liquid	浸	jìn;	jam;
-sink from sight	沉	chén	chàHm

submit v. i.

-yield	服從	fútsúng;	fuHkchùHng;
-surrender	投降	tóusyáng;	tàuHhòHng;
-acquiesce	遷就	chyānjyòu	chìnjauH

subordinate a.

-of another person	手下	shŏusyà;	sáuhaH;
-under a certain command	部下	bùsya	bouHhaH

subpoena

-n. writ	傳票	chwánpyàu;	chyùHnpiu;
-v. t. to appear at court	傳	chwán	chyùHn

subscribe v. i.

-contribute	捐	jywān;	gyùn;
-for newspaper	訂	dìng;	deHng;
-sign	簽名	chyānmíng	chìmméng
subsequent a.	後來的	hòuláide;	hauHlòiHdìk;
	接着的	jyējede	jipjeuHkdìk

subside v. i.

sink	沈澱	chéndyàn;	chàHmdiHn;
quiet	平靜	píngjìng	pìHngjiHng

subsidiary a.

-supplementary	補助	bǔjù	bóujoH
subsidize v. t.	津貼	jīntyē	jèuntip

subsist v. i.

-exist	存在	tswúndzài;	chyùHnjoiH;
-pass days	度日	dùr	douHyaHt
substance n.	物質	wùjf	maHtjāt

substantial a.

-a large amount	大量	dàlyàng;	daaiHleuHng;
-commercially sound	有信用	yǒusyìnyùng	yáuHseunyuHng

substantiate v. t.

-prove the truth	證實	jèngshf	jingsaHt
substitute v. t.	代替	dàiti;	doiHtai;
-man	代理人	dàilǐrén;	doiHléiHyàHn;
-article	代用品	dàiyùngpǐn	doiHyuIIngbán

subtle a.

-cunning	狡猾	jyǎuhwá;	gáauwaaHt;
-crafty	陰險	yīnsyǎn	yàmhím

subtract v. t.

  -deduct   扣   kòu;   kau;

  -Arith.   減   jyǎn   gáam

suburb n.   郊外   jyāuwài   gàaungoiH;

               近郊   jìnjyāu   gaHngàau

subvention n.   補助金   bǔjùjīn;   bóujoHgām;

               援助   ywánjù   wuHnjoH

subway n.   隧道   swèidàu   seuiHdouH

succeed v. i.

  -continue   繼續   jìsyu;   gaijuHk;

  -inherit   承繼   chéngjì;   sìHnggai;

  -accomplish   成功   chénggūng   sìHnggùng

successful a.   成功   chénggūng   sìHnggùng

successor n.   繼承人   jìchéngrén   gaisìHngyàHn

such a.

  -like this   這樣   jèyàng;   jéHyeuHng (gámyéung

  -of this sort   這種   jèjǔng   jéHjúng (nìtìng)

  -such and such   某某   mǒumǒu   máuHmáuH

suck v. t.

  -with the mouth   咂   dzá;   jaap;

  -by suction   吸   syī   kāp

suction n.

  -a pump   吸   syī   kāp

suds n.   肥皂水   féidzàushwěi   fèiHjouHséui (gáansé

suddenly adv.   忽然   hūrán;   fātyìHn;

               突然   túrán   daHtyìHn

sue v. t.

  -prosecute   控告   kùnggàu;   hunggou;

  -beg   求   chyóu   kàuH

suffer v. t.

-pain	忍痛	rěntùng;	yántung;
-hardship	受苦	shòukǔ;	sauHfú;
-loss	受損失	shòuswǔnshř	sauHsyúnsāt

sufficient a.

	足夠	dzúgòu;	jūkgau;
	充分	chūngfèn	chùngfaHn

suffix n.

	字尾	dżwěi;	jiHméiH;
-Gram.	接尾詞	jyēwěitsź	jipméiHchìH

suffocate v. t.

-by stopping respiration	悶死	mènsž;	muHnséi (guHkséi);
-by smoke	燻死	syūnsž;	fànséi;
-by water	淹死	yānnǎ	yìmséi

sugar n.

	糖	táng	tòHng

suggest v. t.

-theory or plan	提出	tíchū	tàiHchēut

suggestion n.

	提議	tíyì;	tàiHyíH;
	建議	jyànyì	ginyíII

suicide n.

	自殺	dżshā	jiHsaat

suit

-n. of clothing	套	tàu;	tou;
-n. blouse	襯衫	chènshān;	chansāam;
-v. i. be fitted to	適合	shřhé	sìkhaIIp

suitable a.

-agreeable	適合	shřhé;	sìkhaHp
-appropriate	相當	syāngdāng	sèungdòng

suite n.

-of furniture	一套家具	yítàujyājyù	yattougàgeuiII

suitor n.

-in marriage	求婚者	chyóuhwūnjě	kàuHfànjé

sulk v. i.	不高興	bùgāusyìng	bātgòuhing (m̀fùnhéi)
sullen a.	憂悶	yōumèn;	yàumuHn;
	愁眉不展	chóuméibùjǎn	sàuHmèiHbātjín
sulphur n.	硫黃	lyóuhwáng	làuHwòHng
sultry a.	悶熱	mènrè	muHnyiHt (guHkyiHt)
sum			
-n. amount	數目	shùmu;	soumuHk;
-v. t. add	加	jyā	gà
summary n.	大綱	dàgāng;	daaiHgòng;
	概要	gàiyàu	koiyiu
summer n.	夏天	syàtyān;	haHtìn;
	夏季	syàjì	haHgwai
-summer vacation	暑假	shǔjyà	syúga
summit n.	頂	dǐng	déng
summon v. t.			
-call	叫	jyàu;	giu;
-of law	傳	chwán	chyùHn
summons n.	傳票	chwánpyàu	chyùHnpiu
sun n.	太陽	tàiyang;	taaiyèuHug;
	日	r̀	yaHt (yaHttáu)
sunbeam n.	日光	r̀gwāng	yaHtgwōng
sunburn n.	日晒	r̀shài	yaHtsaai
Sunday n.	禮拜日	lǐbàir̀;	léiHbaaiyaHt;
	星期日	syìngchìr̀	sìngkèiHyaHt
sundry a.	各種	gèjǔng;	gokjúng;
	繁雜	fándzá	fàaHnjaaHp
sunlight n.	日光	r̀gwāng;	yaHtgwōng;
	陽光	yánggwāng	yèuHnggwōng

sunrise n.	日ᴰ 出ᵍ	r̀chū	yaHtchēut
sunset n.	日ᴰ 落ᵍ	r̀lwò	yaHtloHk
sunshine n.	日ᴰ 光ᴷ	r̀gwāng;	yaHtgwōng;
	陽ᵞ 光ᴷ	yánggwāng	yèuHnggwōng

superb a.

-best	最ᵍ 好ᴴ	dzwèihǎu;	jeuihóu;
-magnificent	壯ᵍ 麗ᴸ	jwànglì	jonglaiII
superintendent n.	監ᴶ 督ᴰ	jyōndū	gāamdūk

superior

-a. in excellence	上ˢ 等ᵀ	shàngděng;	seuHngdáng;
-a. aesthetically	優ᵞ 秀ˢ	yōusyòu;	yàusau;
n. in rank	上ˢ 級ᴶ	shàngjí	seuHngkāp
supernatural a.	超ᶜ 自ᴶ 然ᴺ	chāudzìráu;	chìujiHyìHn;
	不ᴮ 可ᴷ 思ˢ 議ᵞ	bùkěszyì	bathósìyíH
superstitious a.	迷ᴹ 信ˢ	mísyìn	màiHseun
supper n.	晚ᵂ 飯ᶠ	wǒnfàn;	máaHnfaaHn;
	晚ᵂ 餐ᶜ	wǎntsān	máaHnchāan
supple a.	柔ᴿ 軟ᴿ	róurwǎn;	yàuHyúHn;
	柔ᴿ 順ˢ	róushwùn	yàuHseuHn

supplement

-n. to a book	附ᶠ 錄ᴸ	fùlù;	fuHluHk;
-n. to a magazine	附ᶠ 刊ᴷ	fùkān;	fuIIhón;
-v. t.	補ᴮ 充ᶜ	bǔchūng	bóuchùng
supply v. t.	供ᴷ 給ᴶ	gūngjí;	gūngkāp;
	供ᴷ 應ᵞ	gūngyìng	gùngying

support v. t.

| -maintain | 支ᴶ 持ᶜ | jr̄chf; | jìchìH; |
| -second | 贊ᴶ 成ᶜ | dzànchéng; | jaamsìHng; |

-keep from falling	托住	twōjù;	tokjyuH
-pay for keep	養	yǎng	yéuHng

suppose v. t.

-think	以爲	yǐwéi;	yíHwàiH;
-if	假如	jyǎrú	gáyùH

supposition n. 假定　jyǎdìng;　gádiHng

suppress v.t.

-subdue	壓制	yājǐ;	ngaatjai;
-rebellion	鎮壓	jènyā;	janngaat;
-forbid	禁止	jìnjǐ	gamji

supreme a.	最高	dzwèigāu;	jeuigòu;
	至上	jìshàng	jiseuHng
surcharge n.	過載	gwòdzài;	gwojoi;
	加重	jyājùng	gàchúHng
sure a.	一定	yídìng;	yātdiHng;
	確實	chywèshf	koksaHt
surf n.	浪花	lànghwā	loHngfā
surface n.	面	myàn;	miHn (mín);
	表面	byǎumyàn	bǐumiHn
surgeon n.	外科醫生	wàikēyishēng;	ngoiHfōyisāng;
-Mil. and Nav.	軍醫	jyūnyǐ	gwànyǐ
surgery n.	外科	wàikē;	ngoiHfō;
-operating room	手術室	shǒushùshî;	sáuseuHtsàt;
-consulting room	診症室	jěnjèngshî	chánjingsāt

surmise v. t.

-make a guess	推測	twēitsè	tèuichāak
surname n.	姓	syìng	sing

surpass v. t.

-excel	勝過	shènggwo;	singgwo;
-exceed	超過	chāugwo	chiugwo
surplus a.	多餘	dwoyú;	dòyùH;
	過剩	gwòshèng	gwosiHng

surprise v. t.

-astonish	驚奇	jīngchí;	gìngkèiH;
-strike with wonder	驚訝	jīngyà	gìngnga

surrender v. i.

-to the enemy	投降	tóusyáng;	tòuHhòHng;
-hand over	交出	jyāuchu	gàaucheut
surround v. t.	圍住	wéijù;	wàiHjyuH;
	包圍	bauwéi	bàauwàiH

survey v. t.

-of land	測量	tsèlyáng;	chāaklèuHng;
-scan	檢查	jyǎnchá	kímchàH
survive v. i.	生存	shēngtswún;	sàngchyùHn;
	未死	wèisž	meiHséi

susceptible a.

-sensitive	敏感	mǐngǎn;	máHngám;
-impressionable	易感	yìgǎn	yiHgám

suspect v. t.

-doubt	懷疑	hwáiyí;	wàaiHyìH;
-imagine to be guilty	嫌疑	syányí	hìHmyìH

suspense n.

-anxiety	掛念	gwànyàn;	gwaniHm;

-as of judgment	懸案	sywánàn	yùHnon
suspicion n-	懷疑	hwáiyi;	wàaiHyìH;
	疑心	yìsyin	yìHsàm
sustain v. t.			
-a loss, etc.	受	shòu;	sauH;
-bear	忍受	rěnshòu;	yánsauH;
-support	支持	jrchf	jìchìH
swagger v. i.	傲慢	àumàn;	ngouHmaaHn;
	誇張	kwājāng	kwàjèung
swallow			
-n. zool	燕子	yàndz;	yinjì;
-v. t.	吞	twūn	tàn
swamp n.	濕地	shīdì;	sāpdeiH;
	沼澤	jàudzé	jiujaaHk
swanky a.	出風頭	chūfēngtóu;	chēutfùngtàuH;
	擺架子	bǎijyàdz	báaigaji
swarm n.			
-of bees	羣	chyún;	kwàHn;
-of things	堆	dwēi	dèui
swat n.	蒼蠅	tsāngying	chòngyìHng
sway v. i.			
-lean unsteadily	搖擺	yáubǎi;	yìuHbáai;
-have influence over	揮舞	hwēiwǔ	fàimóuH
swear v. i.	發誓	fāshr̀;	faatsaiH;
	誓願	shr̀ywàn	saiHyuHn
sweat			
-n.	汗	hàn;	hoHn;
-v. i.	出汗	chūhàn	chēuthoHn
sweep v. t.	掃	sǎu	sou

sweet

-a. of taste	甜	tyán;	tìHm;
-a. of sound	好 聽	hăutīng,	hóutèng;
-a. lovable	可 愛	kĕài;	hóoi;
-n. candy	糖	táng	tòHng
swell v. i.	腫	jŭng	júng

swerve v. i.

-change direction	轉 向	jwănsyàng	jyúnheung
swift a./adv.	快	kwài	faai
swim v. i.	游 泳	yóuyŭng	yàuIIwiHng (yàuHséui)
swine n.	豬	jū	jyū

swing

-n. apparatus	鞦 韆	chyōuchyān,	chàuchìn;
-v. i. in a swing	打 鞦 韆	dăchyōuchyān;	dáchàuchìn;
-v. i. as a pendulum	搖 擺	yáubăi	yíuHbáai
switch n.	開 關	kāigwān	hòigwàan
swivel n.	旋 環	sywánhwán	syùHnwàaHn

swoop v. t.

-as bird of prey	突 然 下 攫	tùránsyàjywé	daHtyìHnhaHfok
sword n.	劍	jyàn	gim
syllable n.	音 節	yinjyé	yāmjit
syllabus n.	課 程	kèchéng	fochìHng
symbol n.	記 號	jìhàu;	geihouH;
	符 號	fúhàu;	fùHhouH;
	象 徵	syàngjēng	jeuIIngjìng
sympathy n.	同 情	túngchíng;	tùHngchìHng;
	同 情 心	túngchíngsyìn	tùHngchìHngsàm

symphony n.	交響樂	jyāusyǎngywè	gàauhéungngoHk
symptom n.	症狀	jèngjwàng	jingjoHng
syndicate			
-n. company	企業公司	chìyègūngsz̄;	kéiHyiHpgūngsi;
~v. t. combine	聯合	łyánhé	lyùHnhaHp
synonym n.	同義字	túngyìdz̀	tùHngyiHjiH
syntax n.	造句法	dzàujyùfǎ	jouHgeuifaat
syphilis n.	梅毒	méidú	mùiHduHk
syringe n.	藥針;	yàujēn;	yeuHkjām;
	注射器	jùshèchì	jyuseHhei
syrup n.	糖水	tángshwěi	tòHngséui
system n.			
-administrative	制度	jr̀dù;	jaidouH;
-organization	組織	dzǔjf;	jóujìk;
-orderly sequence	秩序	jr̀syù;	diHtjeuiH;
Biol.	系統	syìtǔng	haiHtúng

T

tab n.	懸垂片	sywánchwéipyàn	yùHnsèuiHpin
table n.			
-furniture	桌子	jwōdz;	jeukjí (tói);
-list	表	byǎu	bíu
tableau n.	活人畫	hwórénhwà	wuHtyàHnwá
table d'hote n.	客飯;	kèfàn;	haakfaaHn;
	和菜	hétsài	wòHchoi
tablespoon n.	茶匙;	cháchf;	chàHchìH (chàHgāng)
	湯匙	tāngchf	tòngchìH (tōnggāng)
tablet n.	藥片	yàupyàn	yeuHkpin
tabulate v. t.	製成表	jr̀chéngbyǎu;	jaisìHngbíu;

列表		lyèbyău	liHtbíu
tacit a.			
-implied	默契	mèchì;	maaIIkkai;
-understood but not stated	沉默	chénmè	chàHmmaaHk
tack n.			
-flat-headed nail	圖釘	túdīng;	tòuHdēng;
-long stitches	針路	jēnlù	jāmlouH
tackle n.			
-for sailing	船具	chwánjyù;	syùHngeuiH;
-for fishing	漁具	yújyù	yùHgeuiH
tact n.	機警	jijǐng;	gèigíng;
-mus. beat	拍子	paidz	paakjí
tactics n.			
-Mil. and Nav.	戰術	jànshù;	jinoouHt;
-fig.	手段	shǒudwàn	sáudyuHn
tadpole n.	蝌蚪	kēdǒu	fòdáu
tail n.	尾	wěi	méiH
tailor n.	裁縫	tsáiféng	chòiHfúng
take v. t.			
-generally	拿	ná;	nàH (nìng);
-as medicine	吃	chī;	hek (siHk);
-take care of	照顧	jàugù;	jiugu;
-take charge of	擔任	danren	dàamyaIIm
talcum powder n.	爽身粉	shwǎngshēnfēn	sóngsànfán
tale n.	故事	gùshř	gusiH
talent n.	天才	tyāntsái;	tìnchòiH;
	才幹	tsáigàn	chòiHgon
talk v. i.			
-speak	說話	shwōhwà	syutwaH (góngsyutwaH);

-chat	談話	tánhwà	tàaHmwá
tall a.	高	gāu	gòu
tally			
-n. piece of notched wood	符木	fúmù;	fùHmuHk;
-n. account or score	計算	jìswàn;	gaisyun;
-v. t. to check list against goods	算賬	swànjàng	syunjeung
tame			
-a.	馴良	syúnlyáng;	sèuHnlèuHng;
-v. t.	養馴	yǎngsyún	yéuHngsèuHn
tamper v. i.			
-interfere	干涉	gānshè;	gònsip;
-use bribery	賄賂	hwèilù	kwúilouH
tan			
-a. yellowish brown	棕色	dzūngsè;	jūngsìk;
-v. t. to sun-burn	曬黑	shàihēi	saaihāak
tangerine n.	橘子	jyúdz	gwātji (gam)
tangible a.	確實	chywèshf;	koksaHt;
-Law	有形的	yǒusyíngde	yáuHyìHngdik
tangle v. t.			
-involve	連累	lyánlèi;	lìHnleuiH;
-entangle	纒住	chánjù	chìHnjyuH
tank n.			
-reservoir	水池	shwěichf;	séuichìH;
-Mil.	坦克車	tǎnkèchē	táanhāakchē
tantrum n.	發怒	fānù;	faatnouH;
	發脾氣	fāpichì	faatpèiHhei
tap			
-n. of a water pipe	水龍頭	shwěilúngtóu;	séuilùHngtàuH;

-v. t. rap	拍	pāi	paak
tape n.	帶子	dàidz;	daaiji (dáai);
-magnetic	錄音帶	lùyindài	luHkyāmdáai
tapestry n.	掛錦	gwàjǐn	gwagám
tar n.	柏油	bwóyóu	buuHkyáu
target n.			
-archery	靶子	bǎdz;	báji (bá);
-thing aimed at	目標	mùbyāu	muHkbìu
tariff n.			
-tax	稅	shwèi;	seui;
-list of charges	收費表	shōufèibyǎu	sàufaibíu;
-price list	價目表	jyàmùbyǎu	gamuHkbíu
tarnish v. t.	失光澤	shīgwāngdzé	sātgwōngjaaHk
tarpaulin n.	油布	yóubù;	yàuHbou;
	漆布	chíbù	chātbou
tart n.	果漿包子	gwǒjyāngbāudz	gwójeungbāaují (gwójeungbāau)
taste			
-n. flavour	味道	wèidàu;	meiHdouH;
-n. for art	嗜好	shìhàu;	sihou;
-v. t. by eating	嚐	cháng	sèuHng (si)
tasteful a.	美味	méiwèi	méiHmeiH
tasteless a.	無味	wúwèi	mòuHmeiH
taunt v. t.	侮辱	wǔrù	móuHyuHk
taut a.	緊張	jǐujāng	gánjèung
tawdry a.	俗氣	súchì	juHkhei (juHk)
tax			
-n. duty	稅	shwèi;	seui;
-v. t. exacting taxes	抽稅	chōushwèi	chàuseui
taxi n.	出租汽車	chūdzūchìchē	chēutjòuheichè(dīksí)

tea n.	茶		chá	chàH
-tea party	茶 會		cháhwèi	chàHwúi
teach v. t.	教		jyāu	gaau
teacher n.	先生		syāngsheng;	sìnsàang;
	老師		lǎushr̄;	lóuHsī;
	教員		jyàuywán;	gaauyùHn;
	教師		jyàushr̄	gaausī
teacup n.	茶杯		chàbēi	chàHbùi
teak n.	麻栗樹		málishù	màHleuHtsyuH
team n.	隊		dwèi	deuiH
tear				
-n. of the eye	眼淚		yǎnlèi;	ngáaHnleuiH
-v. t. as clothes	撕破		szpwò;	sìpo(sìlaaHn);
-shed tears	流淚		lyóulèi	làuHleuiH
tease v. t.	開玩笑		kāiwánsyàu;	hòiwuHnsiu;
	戲弄		syìnùng	heiluHng
teaspoon n.	茶匙		cháchŕ	chàHchìH (chàHgāng)
technical a.				
-specialize	專門		jwānmén;	jyùnmùHn;
-skilful	技術		jìshù;	geiHseuHt;
-technical school	工業學校		gūngyèsywésyàu	gùngyiHphoHkhaauH
-technical skill	專門技術		jwānménjìshù	jyùnmùHngeiHseuHt
-technical term	術語		shùyǔ	seuHtyúH
technique n.	技術		jìshù;	geiHseuHt;
	技巧		jìchyǎu	geiHháau
tedious a.				
-dull	沉悶		chénmèn;	chàHmmuHn;
-wearisome	煩悶		fánmèn	fàaHnmuHn

teens n.	十ᵖ 多ㄨㄛ 歲ㄥㄨㄟ	shŕdwōswèi	saHpdòseui (saHpgéiseui)
telegram n.	電ㄉㄧㄢ 報ㄅㄠ	dyànbàu	diHnbou

telegraph

-n. apparatus	電ㄉㄧㄢ 報ㄅㄠ 機ㄐㄧ	dyànbàuJi;	diIubougèi,
-n. telegram	電ㄉㄧㄢ 報ㄅㄠ	dyànbàu;	diInbou;
-v. t.	打ㄉㄚ 電ㄉㄧㄢ 報ㄅㄠ	dădyànbàu	dádiHnbou
telepathy n.	千ㄑㄧㄢ 里ㄌㄧ 眼ㄧㄢ	chyānlĭyăn	chìnléiHngáaHn

telephone

-n.	電ㄉㄧㄢ 話ㄏㄨㄚ	dyànhwà;	diHnwá;
-v. t.	打ㄉㄚ 電ㄉㄧㄢ 話ㄏㄨㄚ	dădyànhwà	dádiIInwá
telescope n.	望ㄨㄤ 遠ㄩㄢ 鏡ㄐㄧㄥ	wàngywănjìng	moHngyúHngeng
television n.	電ㄉㄧㄢ 視ㄕ	dyànshŕ	diHnsiH

tell v. t.

-utter	告ㄍㄠ 訴ㄙㄨ	gàusu;	gousou;
-order	叫ㄐㄧㄠ	jyàu;	giu;
-distinguish	分ㄈㄣ 別ㄅㄧㄝ	fēnbyé	fànbiIIt
temper n.	脾ㄆㄧ 氣ㄑㄧ	píchi	pèiHhei

temperament n.

| -character | 性ㄒㄧㄥ 質ㄓ | syìngjr; | singjāt; |
| -adjustment | 調ㄊㄧㄠ 節ㄐㄧㄝ | tyáujyé | tìuHjit |

temperance n.

-moderation	節ㄐㄧㄝ 制ㄓ	jyéjŕ;	jitjai;
-control	自ㄗ 制ㄓ	dżjŕ	jiHjai
temperate a.	節ㄐㄧㄝ 制ㄓ	jyéjŕ;	jitjai;
	溫ㄨㄣ 和ㄏㄜ	wēnhé	wànwòH

temperature n.

| -of weather | 氣ㄑㄧ 溫ㄨㄣ | chìwēn; | heiwān; |

-of body	熱度	rèdù	yiɪttdouH
temple n.			
-for worship	廟	myàu;	míu;
-of the head	太陽穴	tàiyángsywè	taaiyèuHngyuHt
temporary a.			
-transient	暫時	jànshŕ;	jaaHmsìH;
-provisional	臨時	línshŕ	làHmsìH
tempt v. t.	引誘	yǐnyòu;	yáHnyáuH;
	誘惑	yòuhwò	yáuHwaaHk
temptation n.	試探	shɪ̀tàn	sitaam
ten a.	十	shŕ	saHp
tenant n.			
-of a house	租戶	dzūhù	jòuwuH;
-of a farm	佃戶	dyànhù;	diHnwuH;
-of ground	租地人	dzūdìrén	jòudeiHyàHn
ténd			
-v. t. watch over	看管	kāngwǎn;	hòngún (hònjyuH);
-v. i. be directed	向	syàng	heung
tender			
-n. offer in writing	提供	tígūng;	tàiHgùng;
-a. of meat-not tough	嫩	nwùn;	nyuHn;
-a. tender hearted	仁慈	réntsź	yàHnchìH
tennis n.	網球	wǎngchyóu	móHngkàuH
tense			
-a. of strained news	緊張	jǐnjāng;	gánjèung;
-a. tense the muscles	拉緊	lājǐn;	làaigán;
-n. gramm. time form of verb	時態	shŕtài	sìHtaai

:ension n.

-strain	緊張	jǐnjāng	gánjèung
tent n.	帳棚	jàngpéng;	jeungpàHng
	帳篷	jàngpéng	jeungpùHng

tentative a.

-experimental	試驗	shìyàn;	siyiIIm;
-trial offer	假定	jyǎdìng	gádiHng
enth a.	第十	dìshf	daiHsaHp
:epid a.	微溫	wéiwen;	mèiHwàn;
	暖的	nwǎnde	nyúIІadìk (nyúHnnyúndéi)

erm n.

-name	名詞	míngtsź;	mìHngchìH;
-time	期間	chíjyān;	kèiHgàan;
-semester	學期	sywéchi;	huHkkèiH;
-condition	條件	tyáujyàn	tiuHgín
erminal n.	終點	jūngdyǎn;	jùngdím;
	終端	jūngdwān	jùngdyùn

erminate v. t.

-end	完	wán;	yùHn;
-conclude	結束	jyéshù;	gitchūk;
-cease	停止	tíngjǐ;	tìHngjí;
-a contract	解除	jyěchú	gáaichèuiH
ermite n.	白蟻	báiyǐ	baaHkngáiH
errace n.	陽臺	yángtái	yèuHngtòiH (kèHláu)

errible a.

-awful	可怕	kěpà;	hópa;
-severe	厲害	lìhai;	leiHhoiH;
-tremendous	很大	hěndà	hándaaiH (hóudaaiH)

terrific a.

-terrible	可怕	kĕpà;	hópa;
-very great	很大	hĕndà;	hándaaiH (hóudaaiH)
-excessive	非常	fēicháng	fèisèuHng

terrify v. t.

	驚嚇	jīnghè;	gìnghaak;
	威脅	wēisyé	wàihip

territory n.

-land	土地	tŭdì;	tóudeiH;
-region	地方	dìfang;	deiHfòng;
-of a state	領土	lĭngtŭ	líHngtóu

terror n.

	恐佈	kŭngbŭ	húngbou

terrorist n.

	暴徒	bàutú	bouHtòuH

test

-v. t. try	試	shì;	si;
-v. t. examine	試驗	shìyàn;	siyiHm;
-n. trial	試驗	shìyàn;	siyiHm;
-n. quiz	測驗	tsèyàn	chāakyiHm

testament n.

	遺囑	yíjŭ;	wàiHjūk;
	遺言	yíyán	wàiHyìHn

testify v. t.

-bear witness	作證	dzwòjèng;	jokjing;
-certify	證明	jèngmíng	jingmìHng

testimonial n.

-of character	證明書	jèngmíngshū;	jingmìHngsyù;
-presentation	獎狀	jyăngjwàng	jéungjoHng

testimony n.

-as evidence	證據	jèngjyù;	jinggeui;
-in court of law	口供	kŏugūng	háugùng

tether

-n. rope or halter	繩	shéng;	síng;

-v. t. tie animal	綁住	bǎngjù	bóngjyuH
ext n.			
-original	原文	ywánwén;	yùHnmàHn;
-topic	題目	tímù	tàiHmuHk
extbook n.	課本	kèběn;	fobún;
	教科書	jyàukēshū	gaaufōsyù
exture n.			
-structure of material	質	jí	jàt (jàtdéi)
han conj.	比	bǐ;	béi;
	比較	bǐjyǎu	héigaau
hank v. t.	多謝	dwōsyè;	dòjeH;
	感謝	gǎnsyè;	gámjeH;
	謝謝	syèsye	jeHjeH
hat pro.	那	nà;	náH (gó);
	那個	nàge	náHgo (gógo)
he (def. article)		Is usually untranslated in Chinese.	
heatre n.			
-plays, operas	戲院	syìywàn;	heiyún;
-motion pictures	電影院	dyànyǐngywàn	diHnyíngyún
theft n.			
-stealing	偷竊	tōuchyè;	tàusit;
-larceny	偷竊罪	tōuchyèdzwèi	tàusitjeuiH
their pro.	他們的	tāmende	tàmùHndìk
them pro.	他們	tāmen	tàmùHn (kéuiHdeiH)
theme n.			
-subject	題目	tímù;	tàiHmuHk;
-essay	論文	lwùnwén	leuHnmàHn
themselves pro.	他們自己	tāmen dzìjǐ	tàmùHn jiHgéi (kéuiHdeiHjiHgéi)
then adv.			
-at that time	當時	dāngshí;	dòngsìH;

-afterwards	後來	hòulái;	hauHlòiH;
-in that case	那麼	nàme;	náHmō (gámyéung);
-consequently	就	jyòu	jauH
thence adv.	從那裏	tsúngnàli;	chùHngnáHléuiH (háigósyu);
	因此	yìntsž	yànchí
theory n.	理論	lǐlwùn;	léiHleuHn;
	學理	sywéli	hoHkléiH
there			
-adv. in that place	在那裏	dzàinàli;	joiHnáHléuiH (háigósy
-int.	那！	nà!	nàH!
-see that!	你瞧！	nǐchyáu!	néiHchìuH (néiHtáihá!
therefore adv.	所以	swǒyǐ;	sóyíH;
	因此	yìntsž	yànchí
thermometer n.	溫度計	wēndùjì;	wàndouHgai;
	寒暑表	hánshǔbyǎu	hòHnsyúbíu
thermos flask n.	熱水瓶	rèshwěipíng;	yiHtséuipìHng;
	暖水壺	nwǎnshwěihú	nyúHnséuiwú
they pro.	他們	tāmen	tàmùHn (kéuiHdeiH)
thick a.			
-not thin	厚	hòu;	háuH;
-of liquids	濃	núng;	nùHng;
-dense	密	mì;	maHt;
-of mist	大	dà;	daaiH;
-of hair	多	dwō	dò
thief n.	賊	dzéi	chaaHk
thigh n.	大腿	dàtwěi	daaiHtéui
thimble n.	頂針	dǐngjēn	déngjēm
thin a.			
-not thick	薄	bwó;	boHk;

-not dense	稀	syï;	hèi;
-lean	瘦	shòu	sau
thing n.			
-abstract	事	shї;	siH;
-concrete	物	wù	maHt
think v. t.	想	syǎng	séung
third a.	第三	dìsān	daiHsàam
thirst n.	口渴	kǒukě;	háuhot (génghot);
-thirst after	渴望	kěwàng	hotmoHng
thirsty a.	渴	kě;	hot;
	口渴	kǒukě	háuhot (génghot)
thirteen a.	十三	shísān	saHpsàam
thirteenth a.	第十三	dìshísān	daiHsaHpsàam
thirtieth a.	第三十	dìsānshí	daiHsàamsaHp
thirty a.	三十	sānshí	sàamsaHp
this a.	這	jè;	jéII (nĭ),
	這個	jège	jéHgo (nigo)
thorn n.	刺	tsž;	chi;
	荆棘	jīngjí	gïnggïk
thoroughly adv.	徹底	chèdĭ;	chitdái;
	充分	chūngfèn	chùngfaHn
those a.	那些	nàsyē	náHsè (gódi)
though adv.	雖然	swéirán	sèuiyìHn
thought n.			
-thinking	思想	sžsyǎng;	sìséung,
-idea	意思	yìsz;	yisi;
-reflection	想像	syǎngsyàng	séungjeuHng
thoughtless a.	不加思考	bùjyāszkǎu	bātgàsìháau
thousand a.	千	chyān	chìn
-ten thousand	一萬	yíwàn	yātmaaHn
thrash v. t.	打穀	dǎgŭ	dágŭk

thread

-n.	線	syàn;	sin;
-v. i.	穿	chwān	chyùn
threat n.	恐嚇	kŭnghè;	húnghaak;
	威脅	wēisyé	wàihip
threaten v. t.	威脅	wēisyé;	wàihip;
	恐嚇	kŭnghè	húnghaak
three a.	三	sān	sàam
threefold a.	三倍	sānbèi	sàampúiH
thresh v. t.			
-beat out corn	打麥	dămài	dámaaHk
threshold n.	門檻	ménkăn	mùHnkáaHm
thrice adv.			
-three times	三次	sāntsż;	sàamchi;
-threefold	三倍	sānbèi	sàampúiH
thrifty a.	節省	jyéshěng	jitsáang
thrive v. i.	興旺	syìngwàng;	hìngwoHng;
-of plants	茂盛	màushèng	mauHsiHng
throat n.	喉嚨	hóulung	hàuHlùHng
throb v. i.	跳動	tyàudùng	tiuduHng
thrombosis n.	血液凝結	syéyènìngjyé	hyutyiHkyìHnggit
throne n.	王位	wángwèi;	wòHngwaiH;
	寶座	băudzwò	bóujoH
throng v. i.	擁擠	yūngjǐ;	yúngjài (jàiyúng);
	擠滿	jǐmăn	jàimúHn
throttle			
-v. t. to strangle	勒斃	lēbì;	laHkbaiH (laHkséi);
-n.	咽喉	yānhóu	yìnhàuH

through prep.

-one end to the other	通過	tūnggwò;	tùnggwo;
-by means of	由	yóu	yàuH

throw v. t.

-cast	扔	rēng	yìng;
-fling	丟	dyōu	dìu (dám)
-throw away	丟掉	dyōudyàu	dìudiuH (dámjóheui)

thrust v. t.

-push	推	twēi;	tèui;
-pierce	刺	tsż	chi

thud n. 硼聲 péngshēng pèHngsèng

thumb n. 拇指 mǔjř móuHjí

thunder

-n.	雷	léi;	lèuiH
-v. i.	打雷	dǎléi	dáléuiH

Thursday n. 禮拜四 lǐbàisż; láiHbaaisei;

星期四 syīngchīsż sìngkèiHsei

thus adv. 這樣 jèyàng; jéHyeuHng (gámyéung);

這麼 jème; jéHmō (gám)

thwart v. t. 挫折 tswòjé chojit

thyme n. 百里香 bǎilǐsyāng baakléiHhēung

tick n.

-v. t. sound of watch	滴答聲	dīdāshēng	dīkdaatsèng;
-n. small mark	小記號	syǎujìhàu	sìugeihouH

ticket n. 票 pyàu piu

tickle v. t. 膈肢 gójr gaakjì (jit)

tide n. 潮水 cháushwěi chìuHséui

tidings n. 消息 syāusyi siusìk

tidy a. 整齊 jěngchí jìngchàiH

tie

-v. t. fasten 綁 băng; bóng;

-v. t. a knot 打結 dăjyé; dágit;

-n. necktie 領帶 lĭngdài léHngdáai (léHngtāai)

tiger n. 老虎 lăuhŭ lóuHfú

tight a.

-not loose 緊 jĭn; gán;

-not leaking 密 mì maHt

tile n.

-for roof 瓦 wă; ngáH;

-for floor 磚 jwān jyùn

till

-prep. 等到 dĕngdàu; dángdou;

-v. t. of land 耕 gēng gàang

tilt v. i.

-incline 斜 syé; che;

-tjp 歪 wāi mé

timber n. 木料 mùlyàu muHkliuH

time n. 時間 shŕjyān; sìHgaan;

-number, as repetitions 次 tsż chi

timetable n. 時間表 shŕjyānbyău sìHgaanbíu

timid a.

-easily frightened 膽小 dănsyău dáamsíu;

-shy 怕羞 pàsyōu pasàu (pacháu)

tin n.

-metal 錫 syī; sek;

-can 罐 gwàn gun

tinkle n. 叮噹聲 dĭngdāngshēng dingdongsèng

tint n.	顏色	yánsè;	ngàaHnsik;
	彩色	tsăisè	chóisik
tiny a.	很小	hěnsyău	hánsíu (hóusíu)
tip n.			
-end	頭	tóu;	tàuH;
-sharp point	尖	jyān;	jìm;
-gratuity	小費	syăufèi	síufai
tiptoe n.	腳尖	jyăujyān	geukjìm
tire v. i.	疲乏	pífá;	pèiHfaHt;
	疲倦	píjywàn	pèiHgyuHn
tiresome a.			
-tedious	厭倦	yànjywàn;	yimgyuHn;
annoying	討厭	tăuyàn	tónyim
tissue n.	織物	jřwù;	jíkmaHt;
-Biol.	組織	dzŭjr	jóujik
title n.			
-name	名	míng;	méng;
-topic	標題	byāutí	bìutàiH
to prep.			
-towards	向	syàng;	heuug;
-motion towards	到	dàu	dou
-to and fro	來來去去	láiláichyùchyù	lòiHlòiHheuiheui
toad n.	蛤蟆	háma	gapmàH (hàmòuH)
toast v. t.			
-by heating	烤	kău;	hàau (hong;)
-drink to the health of	乾杯	gānbēi	gònbùi;
-n. the speech	祝詞	jùtsź	jūkchìH
tobacco n.	煙草	yāntsău	yìnchóu
today n.	今天	jĭntyan;	gāmtĭn;

	今ㄐㄣ 日ㄖ	jinr	gàmyaHt
toddle v. i.	蹣ㄇㄢ 跚ㄕㄢ 行ㄒㄥ 走ㄗㄡ	mǎnshānsyíngdzǒu	múHnsàanhàHngjáu
toe n.			
-of the foot	脚ㄐㄠ 趾ㄓ	jyǎujř;	geukjí;
-of a shoe	鞋ㄒㄧㄝ 尖ㄐㄢ	syéjyān	hàaiHjim
toenail n.	脚ㄐㄠ 趾ㄓ 甲ㄐㄚ	jyǎujřjyǎ	geukjígaap
together adv.	一ㄧ 同ㄊㄨㄥ	yìtúng;	yāttùHng;
	一ㄧ 齊ㄑㄧ	yìchí	yātchàiH
toil			
-v. i. labor	勞ㄌㄠ 碌ㄌㄨ	láulù	lòuHlūk;
-n. hardship	勞ㄌㄠ 苦ㄎㄨ	láukǔ;	lòuHfú
toilet n.			
-dressing	服ㄈㄨ 裝ㄓㄨㄤ	fújwāng;	fuHkjōng;
-bathroom	浴ㄩ 室ㄕ	yùshr;	yuHksāt;
-make up	化ㄏㄨㄚ 裝ㄓㄨㄤ	hwàjwāng;	fajòng;
-W. C.	厠ㄘ 所ㄙㄨㄛ	tsèswǒ	chisó
token n.			
-symbol	記ㄐ 號ㄏㄠ	jìhàu;	geihouH;
-souvenir	紀ㄐ 念ㄋㄢ 品ㄆㄣ	jìnyànpǐn	geiniHmbán
tolerate v. t.			
-endure	忍ㄖㄣ 耐ㄋㄞ	rěnnài;	yánnoiH;
-permit	允ㄩㄣ 許ㄒㄩ	yǔnsyǔ	wáHnhéui
toll n.	鐘ㄓㄨㄥ 聲ㄕㄥ	jūngshēng	jūngsìng
tomato n.	番ㄈㄢ 茄ㄑㄧㄝ	fānchyé	fàanké
tomb n.	墓ㄇㄨ	mù;	mouH;
	墳ㄈㄣ 墓ㄇㄨ	fénmù	fàHnmouH
tombstone n.	墓ㄇㄨ 碑ㄅㄟ	mùbēi	mouHbèi
tomorrow n./adv.	明ㄇㄥ 天ㄊㄧㄢ	míngtyan,	mìHngtìn;

	明日	míngr̂	mìHngyaHt(tìngyaHt)
on n.	噸	dwūn	dēun
one n.			
-sound	聲音	shēngyin;	sìngyàm;
-modulation of sound	音調	yìndyàu;	yàmdiuH;
tenor, as of remarks	口氣	kŬuchî	hǎuhei
ongue n.	舌頭	shétou;	siHttàuH (leiH);
-language	話	hwà;	waII;
-dialect	方言	fāngyán	fòngyìHu
onic			
-a. giving vigour	滋補	dz̄bŭ	jìbóu;
-n. Med.	補藥	hйyàu	bóuyeuHk
onight n./adv.	今晚	jǐnwăn	gàmmáaHn
oo adv.			
-more than	太	tài;	taai;
-like wise	也	yě	yáH
tool n.	工具	gūngjyù	gùnggeuiH;
tooth n.	牙	yá;	ngàH;
	牙齒	yáchř	ngàHchí
toothache n.	牙痛	yátùng	ngàHtung
toothbrush n.	牙刷	yáshwā	ngàHcháat
toothpick n.	牙簽	yáchyān	ngàHchìm
top n.			
-summit	頂	dǐng;	déng;
-surface	上面	shàngmyan;	seuHngmiHn (seuIIngbiHn);
-toy	陀螺	twólwó	tòHlòH
topic n.	題目	tímù;	tàiHmuHk;
	標題	byūutí	bĭutàiH

torch n.	火把	hwŏbǎ;	fóbá;
	火炬	hwŏjyù	fógeuiH
torment v. t.			
-torture	拷問	kǎuwèn;	háaumaHn;
-afflict	折磨	jémwó	jitmòH
tornado n.	旋風	sywánfēng	syùHnfùng
torpid a.	麻痺	mábì	màHbei
torrent n.	急流	jílyóu	gāplàuH
tortoise n.	龜	gwēi	gwài
torture			
-v. t. bodily	毒打	dúdǎ;	duHkdá;
-v. t. ill-treat	虐待	nywèdài;	yeuHkdoiH;
-n. punishment	刑罰	syíngfá	yìHngfaHt
toss v. t.	扔	rēng	yìng
total a.	總共	dzŭnggùng;	júngguHng
	共計	gùngjì	guHnggai
totalizator n.	計算器	jìsywànchì	gaisyunhei
totter v. i.	蹣跚	mánshān;	múHnsàan;
	搖動	yáudùng	yìuHduHng
touch v. t.			
-feel with the hand	摸	mwō;	mó;
-affect the feelings	感動	gǎndùng;	gámduHng;
-touch stone	試金石	shìjīnshí	sigāmseHk
touching a.	動情	dùngchíng;	duHngchìHng;
	感動	gǎndùng	gámduHng
tough a.			
-stiff	硬	yìng;	ngaaHn;

-vigorous	強壯	chyángjwàng;	kèuHngjong;
-stubborn	固執	gùjr	gujáp
tour v. i.	遊歷	yóulì;	yàuHliHk;
	觀光	gwāngwāng	gùngwòng
tourist n.	遊客	yóukè	yàuHhaak
tout v. t.			
-pester customers	招生意	jāushēngyì	jiusàangyi;
-for votes	拉票	lāpyàu	làaipiu
tow v. t.			
-pull	拉	lā;	làai;
-drag	拖	twō	tō
towards prep.			
-in the direction of	向	syàng;	heung;
-speaking of time	到	dàu	dou
towel n.			
-face	面巾	myànjin;	miHngān;
-bathing	毛巾	máujin	mòuHgān
tower n.	塔	tă	taap
town n.	鎭	jèn;	jan;
	市鎭	ohrjèn	oíjan
toy n.	玩具	wánjyù	wuHngeuiH
trace n.			
-footprint	脚印	jyăuyìn;	geukyan;
-mark	痕跡	hénjì;	hàHnjìk;
-trail	蹤跡	dzūngjì	jūngjìk
-v. t. follow the course of	追究	jwēijyòu	jèuigau
track n.			
-railway	軌道	gwĕidàu;	gwáidouH;

-series of marks	痕跡	hénjì	hàHnjik
tractor n.	拖拉機	twōlāji	tōlàaigèi
trade			
~n. commerce	貿易	màuyì;	mauHyiHk;
~v. i. buy and sell	做生意	dzwòshēngyì	jouHsàangyi
tradition n.	傳統	chwántŭng	chyùHntúng
traffic			
~v. i. buy and sell	做生意	dzwòshēngyì;	jouHsàangyi;
~n. communication	交通	jyāutūng;	gàautùng;
~n. vehicles	車	chē	chè
tragedy n.			
-of drama	悲劇	bēijyù;	bèikeHk;
-tragic events	慘事	tsánshr̀	cháamsiH
tragic a.	悲慘	bēitsăn;	bèicháam;
	不幸	búsyìng	bāthaHng
trail n.	足跡	dzújì;	jūkjìk;
-trailer	預告片	yùgàupyàn	yuHgoupín
train			
~n. of railway	火車	hwŏchē;	fóchè;
~v. t. by practice	訓練	syùnlyàn	fanliHn
training n.	訓練	syùnlyàn;	fanliHn;
-training class	訓練班	syùnlyànbān	fanliHnbāan
traitor n.	賣國賊	màigwódzéi	maaiHgwokchaaHk
tram n.	電車	dyànchē	diHnchè
tramp			
~v. i. walk heavily	踐踏	jyàntà;	chíndaaHp;
~n. vagrant	流氓	lyóumáng	làuHmàHn

trample v. t.

-tread on heavily	踐踏	jyàntà;	chindaaHp;
-injure by treading	踹壞	tɐǎihwài	chàaiwaaiH

tranquil a.

-peaceful	平靜	píngjìng;	pìHngjiHng;
-free from care	安心	ānsyìn	ònsàm
transact v. t.	辦	hàn;	baaHn;
	辦理	bànlǐ	baaHnléiH
transcribe v. t.	抄寫	chāusyě;	chàausé;
	謄寫	téngsyě	tàHngsé

transfer v. t.

-as things	搬	bān;	bùn;
-as persons	調	dyàu;	diuΔ,
-hand over	交	jyāu	gàau

transform v. t.

-the shape	變形	byànsyíng;	binyìHng;
-the nature	改變	gǎibyàn	góibin

transit

-v. t. being conveyed	過境	gwòjìng;	gwoging;
-n. conveyance	運輸	yùnshū;	waHnsyù;
-transit visa	過境簽證	gwòjìngchyāujèng	gwogingchìmjing
translate v. t.	繙譯	fānyì	fàanyiHk
translator n.	繙譯	fānyì;	fàanyiHk;
	譯者	yìjě	yiHkjé
transliterate v. t.	譯音	yìyìn	yiHkyām
transparent a.	透明	tòumíng	taumìHng
transport v. t.	運	yùn;	waHn;
	運輸	yùnshū	waHnsyù

trap

-n. pitfall	陷阱	syànjǐng;	haHmjiHng;
-v. t. catch	捉	jwō;	jūk;
-v. t. ensnare	陷害	syànhài	haHmhoiH
trash n.	廢物	fèiwù;	faimaHt;
	垃圾	lèsè	laaHpsaap
travel v. i.	旅行	lyǔsyíng	léuiHhàHng
-travel by land	陸路	lùlù	luHklouH
-travel by water	水路	shwěilù	séuilouH
traveller n.	旅客	lyǔkè	léuiHhaak
-travelling expenses	旅費	lyǔfèi	léuiHfai
trawl v. t.	拖網	twōwǎng	tòmóHng
tray n.	盤	pán	pùHn
treacherous a.			
-disloyal	奸詐	jyānjà;	gàanja;
-deceiving	欺騙	chīpyàn;	hèipin;
-false	虛偽	syūwěi	hèuingaiH
tread v. t.	踐踏	jyàntà	chíndaaHp
treason n.	謀反	móufǎn;	màuHfáan;
	判逆	pànnì	punyiHk
treasure n.			
-collectively	財寶	tsáibǎu;	chòiHbóu;
-valuable thing	寶物	bǎuwù	bóumaHt
treasurer n.	會計	kwàijì;	wuiHgai;
	財政	tsáijèng;	chòiHjing;
	出納	chūnà	chēutnaaHp
treasury n.	寶庫	bǎukù;	bóufu;
-of a country	國庫	gwókù;	gwokfu;
-stone-house	倉庫	tsāngkù	chōngfu

treat v. t.

-act towards	待	dài;	doiH;
-deal with	對待	dwèidài;	deuidoiH;
-consider as	當做	dàngdzwò	dongjouH

treatment n.

-of a problem	處理	chǔlǐ;	chyúIIléiH;
-medical	治療	jìlyáu	jiHlìuH

treaty n.	條約	tyáuywē	tiuHyeuk
tree n.	樹	shù	syuH
-tree branch	樹枝	shùjī	syuHjì
-tree root	樹根	shùgēn	syuHgàn
-tree leaves	樹葉	shùyè	syuHyiHp
tremble v. i.	發抖	fādǒu	faatdáu

tremendous a.

-extraordinary	非常	fēicháng;	fòisèuHng;
-enormous	很大	hěndà	hándaaiH (hóudaaiH)

trend

-v. i. in a particular direction	傾向	chingsyàng;	kìngheung;
-tendency	趨勢	chyūshì;	chèuisai;
-movement	潮流	cháulyóu	chìuHlàuH

trespass v. i.

-enter unlawfully	侵入	chinrù;	chàmyaHp;
-commit an offence	犯罪	fàndzwèi	faaHnjeuiH
trestle n.	架橋	jyàchyáu	gakìuH

trial n.

-exam. by test	試煉	shìlyàn;	siliHn;
-inquiry into a case	審判	shěnpàn	sámpun
triangle n.	三角	sānjyǎu;	sàamgok;
	三角形	sānjyǎusyíng	sàamgokyìHng

tribe n.

-race	民族	míndzú;	màHnjuHk;
-of a family	支派	jīpài	jipaai
tribulation n.	苦難	kǔnàn	fúnaaHn
tribunal n.	法庭	fǎtíng	faattìHng
tribute n.	貢獻	gùngsyàn;	gunghin;
	貢物	gùngwù	gungmaHt

trick n.

-n. mischief	詭計	gwěijì;	gwáigai;
-n. artifice	手段	shǒudwàn;	sáudyuHn;
-v. t. cheat	欺騙	chīpyàn	hèipin

trikle

-v. i.	滴下	dīsyà;	diHkhaH;
-n.	滴	dī	diHk

trifle n.

	小事	syǎushr̀;	síusiH;
	瑣事	swǒshr̀	sósiH
trigger n.	引發機	yǐnfājī	yáHnfaatgèi
trim v. t.	剪	jyǎn	jín
trimming n.	裝飾	jwāngshr̀	jōngsik

trip n.

-as to the seaside	旅行	lyǔsyíng;	léuiHhàHng;
-organized by students	遠足	ywǎndzú	yúHnjūk
triple a.	三倍	sānbèi	sàampúiH
triplicate n.	三份	sānfèn	sàamfaHn
triumph v. i.	得勝	déshèng	dāksing
triumphant a.	得勝;	déshèng;	dāksing;
	誇勝	kwāshèng	kwàsing
trivial a.	平凡;	píngfán;	pìHngfàaHn;

	通俗	tūngsú	tùngjuHk
troop n.	軍隊	jyūndwèi	gwàndéui
tropics n.	熱帶	rèdài	yiHtdaai
trouble			
-v. t. disturb	打攪	dǎjyǎu;	dágáau;
-v. t. cause inconvenience	麻煩	máfán;	màHfàaHn;
-n. disturbance	擾亂	rǎulwàn;	yíuHlyuHn;
-n. distress	煩惱	fánnǎu	fàaHnnóuH
trousers n.	褲子	kùdz	fuji (fu)
truant v. i.	逃學	táusywé	tòuHhoHk
truck n.	貨車;	hwòchē;	fochè;
	卡車	kǎchē	kāchè
true a.			
-not false	眞	jēn;	jàn;
-true facts	眞相	jēnsyàng	jànseung
trumpet n.	喇叭	lǎbā	labā
truncheon n.	警棍	jǐnggwùn	gínggwan
trunk n.	樹身;	shùshēn;	syuHsàn;
-telephone call	長途電話	chángtúdyànhwà	chèuHngtòuHdiHnwá
trust v. t.			
-believe	相信	syāngsyìn;	sèungseun;
-have confidence in	信任	syìnrèn	seunyaHm
trustee n.	受託人	shòutwōrén	sauHtokyàHn
trustworthy a.	可靠;	kěkàu;	hókaau;
	靠得住	kàudejù	kaaudākjyuH
truth n.			
-that which is true	眞實	jēnshí;	jànsaHt;
-accomplished fact	事實	shìshr;	siHsrHt;
-as in the Bible	眞理	jēnlǐ	jànléiìI

try v. t.			
-as a method	試	shr̀	si;
-as an accused	審	shěn	sám
-try a case	審案	shěnàn	sámngon
tug v. t.	拖	twō;	tò;
-n. boat to tow vessels	拖船	twōchwán	tòsyùHn
tuition n.			
-fee	學費	sywéfèi;	hoHkfai;
-instruction	教授	jyàushòu	gaausauH
tulip n.	鬱金香	yùjinsyāng	wātgāmhēung
tumble v. i.	跌倒	dyédǎu	ditdóu
tumour n.	瘤	lyóu	láu
tumult n.	吵鬧	chǎunàu;	cháaunaauH;
	騷動	sāudùng	sòuduHng
tune n.	音	yīn;	yām;
	調	dyàu	diuH
tunnel n.			
-underground	隧道	swèidàu;	seuiHdouH;
-through mountain	山洞	shāndùng	sàanduHng
turkey n.	火雞	hwǒjī	fógāi
turn v. t.			
-revolve	轉	jwǎn;	jyún;
-of milk, etc.	變	byàn;	bin;
-as a key	開	kāi	hòi
turnip n.	蘿蔔	lwóbwo	lòHbaaHk
turpentine n.	松節油	sūngjyéyóu	chùHngjityàuH
turtle n.	鼈	byē;	bit;

	龜	gwēi	gwāi
tutor n.	家教	jyājyàu	gàgaau
tweezers n.	鑷子	nyèdz	nipjí (níp)
twelfth a.	第十二	dìshfèr	daiHsaHpyiH
twelve a.	十二	shfèr	saHpyiH
twenty a.	二十	èrshf	yiHsaHp
twice adv.			
-2 times	兩次	lyǎngtsż;	léuHngchi;
-doubly	兩倍	lyǎngbèi	léuHngpúiH
twig n.	小枝	syǎujr̄	síujī
twilight n.	曙光	shǔgwāng	syùHgwòng
twins n.	雙胞胎	shwāngbāutāi;	sèungbàautöi;
	雙生	shwāngshēng	sèungsàng (mājái)
twist v. t.			
-contort	扭	nyǒu;	náu;
-distort	弄歪	nùngwāi	luHngmé (jíngmé)
two a.			
-in counting	二	èr;	yiH;
-as things	兩	lyǎng	léuHng
two-edged a.	兩刃	lyǎngrèn	léuHngyaHu
twofold a.	兩倍	lyǎngbèi	léuIngpúiH
type			
-n. model	樣	yàng;	yéung;
-v. i.	打字	dǎdż	dájiH
typewriter n.	打字機	dǎdżjī	dájiHgēi
typhoon n.	颱風	táifēng	tòiHfùng
typical a.	典型	dyǎnsyíng	dínyìHng
typify v. t.	代表	dàibyǎu;	doiHbíu;

	預表	yùbyǎu	yuHbíu
typist n.	打字員	dǎdżywán	dájiHyùHn
tyranny n.	虐政	nywèjèng	yeuHkjing
tyrant n.	暴君	bàujyūn	bouHgwàn

U

udder n.

  -of cow   乳房   rǔfáng   yúHfòHng

ugly a.

  -to sight   醜   chǒu;   cháu;

  -unpleasant   不好   bùhǎu   bāthóu (m̀hóu)

ulcer n.   潰瘍   kwèiyáng   kúiyèuHng

ulterior a.

  -of motives   秘密   mìmi;   beimaHt;

  -situated beyond   在彼方   dzàibǐfān   joiHbéifòng (háigóbiHn)

ultimate a.

  -final   最後   dzwèihòu   jeuihauH

ultimatum n.

  -cannot be rejected   最後通牒   dzwèihòutūngdyé   jeuihauHtùngdiHp

umbrella n.   傘   sǎn   saan (jē)

umpire n.

  -sports   裁判員   tsáipànywán   chòiHpunyùHn

unable a.

  -physically   不能   bùnéng;   bātnàHng (m̀nàHnggau);

  -skilled   不會   búhwèi   bātwúiH (m̀wúiH)

unaccomplished a.   未完成   wèiwánchéng   meiHyùHnsìHng

unaccustomed a.   不慣   búgwàn   bātgwaan (m̀gwaan)

nacquainted a.	不認得	bùrènde	bātyiHngdāk (m̀yiHngdāk)
nafraid a.	不怕	búpà;	bātpa (m̀pa);
	無懼	wújyù	mòuHgeuiH
nanimous a.	意見一致	yìjyànyíjı̀	yiginyātji
nashamed a.	不以爲耻	bùyĭwéichı̆	bātyíHwàiHchí
navoidable a.	難免	nánmyǎn;	nàaHnmíHn;
	不得已	bùdéyĭ	bātdākyíH
naware a.	不知不覺	bùjı̆rbùjywé;	bātjı̀bātgok;
	意外	yı̀wàı	yi'ngoiII
nbelief n.	不信	búsyìn;	bātseun (m̀seun);
	疑惑	yíhwò	yìHwaaHk
nceasing a.	不停	bùtíng	bāttìHng (m̀tìHng)
ncertain a.			
-not certain	含糊	hánhú;	hàHmwùH;
-indefinite	不一定	bùyídìng;	bātyātdiIIng (m̀yātdiHng);
-doubtful	有疑問	yǒuyíwèn	yáuHyìHmaHn
ncivilized a.	未開化	wèikāihwà;	meiHhòifa;
	野蠻	yěmán	yéHmàaHn
ncle n.			
-father's elder brother	伯父	bwófù;	baakfuH;
-father's younger brother	叔父	shúfù;	sūkfuH;
-mother's brother	舅父	jyòufù	káuHfú
nclean a.	不乾淨	bùgānjìng	bātgònjeHng (m̀gònjeHng)
ncommon a.	不平常	bùpíngcháng;	bātpìHngsèuHng (m̀pìHngsèuHng);
	罕有	hǎnyǒu	hónyáuH (síuyáuH)
ncouth a.			
-uncultured	荒僻	hwāngpì;	fōngpìk;
-uncivlized conduct	粗笨	tsūbèn	chòubaHn

under prep.

-below	在⋯下面	dzài...syàmyan;	joiH...haHmiHn (hái...haHbiHn);
-less than	以下	yǐsyà	yíHhaH
underclothing n.	內衣	nèiyī;	noiHyī (dáisāam);
	襯衣	chènyī	chanyī (chansāam)
undercurrent n.	潛流	chyánlyóu	chímlàuH
underfoot			
-a.	被踐踏	bèijyàntà;	beiHchíndaaHp;
-adv.	脚下	jyǎusvà	geukhaH
undergo v. t.			
-experience	受	shòu;	sauH;
-pass through	經過	jìnggwò	gìnggwo
underground a.	地下	dìsya	deiHhá
underhand adv.			
-clandestinely	秘密地	mìmìde;	beimaHtdeiH;
-not openly	暗中	ànjūng	ngamjūng
underline n.	字下線	dzsyàsyàn	jiHhaHsin
undermine v. t.			
-wear away base	下掘	syàjywé	haHgwaHt
underneath adv.	在⋯下面	dzài...syàmyàn	joiH...haHmiHn (hái...haHbiHn)
undershirt n.	汗衫	hànshān	hoHnsāam (sinsāam)
understand v. t.	明白	míngbai;	mìHngbaaHk;
	領會	lǐnghwèi	líHngwuiH
understanding n.	了解	lyǎujyě;	líuHgáai;
	理解力	lǐjyělì	léiHgáailiHk
understatement n.			
-inadequate	減輕口氣	jyǎnchìngkǒuchì	gáamhèngháuhei

undertake v. t.	擔任	dānrèn	dàamyaHm
undertaker n.			
-conduct funerals	殯儀-館	bìnyígwǎn	banyìHgún
uneasy a.			
-uncomfortable	不舒服	bùshūfu;	bātsyùfuHk (m̀syùfuHk);
-anxious	擔心	dānsyīn	dàamsàm
unending a.			
infinite	無窮	wúchyúng;	mòuHkùHng;
	無盡	wújìn	mòuHjeuHn
unequal a.			
-not fair	不平等	bùpíngděng;	bātpìHngdáng (m̀pìHngdáng);
-not uniform	不一律	bùyílyù;	bātyātleuHt (m̀yātleuIlt),
-not the same	不同	bùtúng	bāttùHng (mtùHng)
unexpected a.	想不到	syǎngbúdàu;	séungbātdou (séungm̀dou);
	意外	yìwài	yi'ngoiH
unfair a.	不公平	bùgūngpíng	bātgùngpìHng (m̀gúngpìHng)
unfaithful a.	不忠	bùjūng	bātjúng (m̀jùngsàm)
unfamiliar a.	不熟悉	bùshóusyi	bātsuHksìk (m̀suHk)
unfit a.	不適合	búshìhhó	bātsìkhaHp (m̀haHpsìk)
unfold v. t.			
-as newspaper	打開	dǎkāi;	dáhòi;
-as buds	開	kāi	hòi
unfortunate a.	不幸	búsyìng	bāthaHng
ungrateful a.	忘恩負義	wàngēnfùyì	mòHngyànfuHyiH
unhappy a.			
-not happy	不快樂	bukwàile;	bātfaailoHk (m̀faailoHk);
-not glad	不高興	bùgāusying	bātgòuhing (m̀gòuhing);
-sad	煩悶	fánmèn;	fàaHnmuHn;

-not fortunate	不ㄅㄨ幸ㄒㄥ	búsyìng	bàthaHng
unhealthy a.			
-of persons	不ㄅㄨ健ㄐㄢ康ㄎㄤ	bújyànkāng;	bātgiHnhòng (m̀giHnhòng);
-unsound	不ㄅㄨ健ㄐㄢ全ㄑㄢ	bújyànchywán	bātgiHnchyùHn (m̀giHnchyùHn)
uniform			
-n. of school, etc.	制ㄓ服ㄈㄨ	jìfu;	jaifuHk;
-a. same	一律ㄌㄩ	yílyù	yātleuHt
unify v. t.	統ㄊㄨㄥ一	tǔngyì	túngyāt
unimaginable a.	不ㄅㄨ能ㄋㄥ想ㄒㄤ像ㄒㄤ	bùnéngsyǎngsyàng	bātnàHngséungjeuHng
unimportant a.	不ㄅㄨ重ㄓㄨㄥ要ㄧㄠ	bújùngyàu	bātjuHngyiu (m̀gányiu)
union n.			
-combination	聯ㄌㄢ合ㄏㄜ	lyánhé;	lyùHnhaHp;
-league	聯ㄌㄢ盟ㄇㄥ	lyánméng;	lyùHnmàHng;
-amalgamation of countries	聯ㄌㄢ邦ㄅㄤ	lyánbāng	lyùHnbòng
unique a.	無ㄨ比ㄅ	wúbǐ;	mòuHbéi;
	無ㄨ雙ㄕㄨㄤ	wúshwāng	mòuHsèung
unit n.			
-std. quantity	單ㄉㄢ位ㄨ	dānwèi;	dàanwái;
-a group of soldiers	部ㄅㄨ隊ㄉㄨ	bùdwèi	bouHdeuiH
unite v. t.			
-join together	合ㄏㄜ併ㄅㄥ	hébìng;	haHpbing;
-combine	聯ㄌㄢ合ㄏㄜ	lyánhé;	lyùHnhaHp;
-link together	連ㄌㄢ結ㄐㄝ	lyánjyé;	lìHngit;
-for common action	團ㄊㄨㄢ結ㄐㄝ	twánjyé	tyùHngit
unity n.			
-concord	一致ㄓ	yíjr̀;	yātji;
-identity	同ㄊㄨㄥ樣ㄧㄤ	túngyàng;	tùHngyéung;

-centralisation	統一	tǔngyï	túngyāt
universal a.			
-affecting all	普遍	pǔpyàn;	póupin;
-general	普通	pǔtūng	póutùng
universe n.	宇宙	yǔjòu;	yúHjauH;
	天地	tyāndì	tìndeiH
university n.	大學	dàsywó	daaiHhoHk
unjust a.	不公平	bùgūngpíng	hātgùngpìHng (m̀gùngpìHng)
unkempt a.			
-dishevelled	蓬亂	pénglwàn	pùHnglyuIIn
unkind a.	無情	wúchíng;	mòuHchìHng;
	殘忍	tsánrěu	chàaHnyán
unknown a.	不知道	bùjīdau;	bātjìdou (m̀jìdou)
-unknown nationality	不明國籍	bùmínggwójí	batmìHnggwokjiHk
unlawful a.	不法	bùfǎ;	bātfaat
-unlawful act	不法行爲	bùfǎsyíngwéi	bātfaathàHngwàiH
unless conj.	除非	chúfēi	chèuiHfèi
unlike a.	不像	búsyàng	bātjeuHng (m̀chíH)
unlimited a.	無限	wúsyàn;	mòuHhaaHn;
	不受限制	búshòusyànjï	bātsauHhaaHnjai
unload v. t.			
-take the load from	起貨	chǐhwò;	hóifo;
-discharge of a load	卸貨	syèhwò	sefo
unlock v. t.	開鎖	kāiswǒ	hòisó
unlucky a.	不幸	búsyìng;	bāthaHng;
	不吉利	bùjílì	hātgātleiH (m̀laiHsiH)

unmarried a.	未ㄟ 婚ㄣ	wèihwūn;	meiHfàn;
	單ㄢ 身ㄣ	dānshēn	dàansàn (duHksàn)
unnecessary a.	不ㄨ 需ㄩ 要ㄠ	bùsyūyàu	bātsèuiyiu (m̀sèuiyiu)
unquestionable a.	不ㄨ 成ㄥ 問ㄣ 題ㄧ	bùchéngwèntí	bātsìHngmaHntàiH
unravel v. t.	解ㄝ 糾ㄡ 紛ㄣ	jyějyōufēn	gáaidáufàn
unreasonable a.	不ㄨ 合ㄜ 理ㄌ	bùhélǐ	bāthaHpléiH
unreliable a.	靠ㄠ 不ㄨ 住ㄨ	kàubújù	kaaubātjyuH (kaaum̀jyuH)
unroll v. t.	展ㄢ 開ㄞ	jǎnkāi	jínhòi
unsafe a.	不ㄨ 安ㄢ 全ㄩ	bùānchywán	bātònchyùHn (m̀ònchyùHn)
unseasonable a.	不ㄨ 合ㄜ 時ㄭ	bùhéshŕ	bāthaHpsìH(m̀haHpsìH)
unseen a.	未ㄟ 見ㄢ	wèijyàn	meiHgin
untable a.			
-of persons	反ㄢ 覆ㄨ 無ㄨ 常ㄤ	fǎnfùwúcháng;	fáanfūkmòuHsèuHng;
-of human affairs	千ㄧ 變ㄢ 萬ㄢ 化ㄚ	chyānbyànwànhwà;	chìnbinmaaHnfa;
-of things	不ㄨ 安ㄢ 定ㄥ	bùāndìng	bātòndiHng (m̀òndiHng)
unspeakable a.	難ㄢ 以ㄧ 形ㄥ 容ㄥ	nányǐsyíngrúng;	nàaHnyíHyìHngyùHng
	說ㄛ 不ㄨ 盡ㄣ	shwōbújìn	syutbātjeuHn (góngm̀jeuHn)
unsteady a.	不ㄨ 安ㄢ 定ㄥ	bùāndìng;	bātòndiHng (m̀ondiHn
	不ㄨ 穩ㄨ 固ㄨ	bùwěngù	bātwángu (m̀wánjaHn)
untie v. t.	解ㄝ 開ㄞ	jyěkāi	gáaihòi
until prep.	等ㄥ 到ㄠ	děngdàu	dángdou
unto prep.	至ㄓ	jr̀;	ji;
	到ㄠ	dàu	dou
untrue a.			
-false	假ㄚ	jyǎ;	gá;
-incorrect	不ㄨ 對ㄨ	búdwèi;	bātdeui (m̀ngāam);
-unfaithful	不ㄨ 忠ㄨ 實ㄭ	bùjūngshŕ	bātjùngsaHt (m̀jùngsa
unusual a.			
-uncommon	不ㄨ 普ㄨ 通ㄊ	bùpǔtūng;	bātpóutùng (m̀póutùn

-unfamiliar	不尋常	bùsyúncháng;	bātchàHmsèuHng (m̀piHngsèuHng)
-strange	奇怪	chígwài;	kèiHgwaai;
-exceptional	例外	lìwài;	laiHngoiH
-remarkable	非常	fēicháng	fèisèuHhg

unwieldy a.

-clumsy	笨重	bènjùng;	baHnjuIIng;
-awkward	不便利	búhyànlì;	bātbiHnleiH;
-difficult to use	難用	nánvùng	nàaHnyuHng

unworthy a.

	不值得	bùjŕde;	bātjiHkdāk (m̀jiHkdāk);
-not fit	不配	búpèi	bātpui (m̀pui)

unyielding a.

	不服從	bùfútsúng;	bātfuHkchùHng (m̀fuIIkchùHng)
	不屈服	bùchyūfú	bātwātfuHk (m̀wātfuHk)

up adv.

	在上面	dzàishàngmyàu	joiIIseuIIngmiHn (háiseuHngbiHn);
-up and down	上下	shàngsyà	seuHnghaH

uphill adv.

	上斜	shàngsyé;	séuHngche;
	上山	shàngshān	séuHngsàan

uphold v. t.

-hold up	擡高	táigāu;	tòiHgòu;
-give moral 'support	支持	jīchf	jìchìH

upholster v. t.

-furniture	置備	jìbèi;	jibeiH;
-rooms	佈置	bùjr	bouji

upmost a.

	最高	dzwèigāu	jeuigòu

upon prep.

	在 … 上	dzài...shàng;	joiH...seuHng;
-upon my word	我敢發誓	wŏgănfāshŕ	ngóHgámfaatsaiH

upper a.

-in place	上頭	shàngtou;	seuHngtàuH (seuHngbiHn)
-in rank	上級	shàngjí	seuHngkāp

uppermost a.

	最上	dzwèishàng;	jeuiseuHng;

	最高	dzwèigāu	jeuigòu

upright a.
| -in conduct | 正直 | jèngjí; | jingjiHk; |
| -vertical | 直 | jí | jiHk |

uproar n.
| | 騷動 | sāudùng; | sòuduHng; |
| | 吵鬧 | chăunàu | cháaunaauH |

upset v. t.
-as by bad news	煩腦	fánnău;	fàaHnnóuH;
-overthrow	推翻	twēifān;	tèuifàan;
-as another's plan	破壞	pwòhwài	powaaiH

upside down a.
| -reverse | 顛倒 | dyāndău; | dìndóu; |
| -topsy turvy | 亂七八糟 | lwànchíbādzāu | lyuHnchātbaatjòu |

upstart n.
| | 暴發戶 | bàufāhù | bouHfaatwuH |

upstairs adv.
| | 樓上 | lóushàng | làuHseuHng |

upwards adv.
| | 向上 | syàngshàng; | heungseuHng; |
| | 以上 | yìshàng | yíHseuHng |

uranium n.
| | 鈾 | yóu | yàuH |

urban a.
| -of town or city dweller | 城市 | chéngshì | sìHngsíH; |
| | 市區 | shìchyū | síHkèui |

urchin n.
| | 頑童 | wántúng | wàaHntùHng |

urge v. t.
| | 催促 | tswēitsù; | chēuichūk; |
| | 催逼 | tswēibì | chēuibīk |

urgent a.
-immediate	緊急	jĭnjí;	gángāp;
-important	緊要	jĭnyàu;	gányiu;
-urgent need	急用	jíyùng	gāpyuHng

urine n.	小便	syǎubyàn;	sìubiHn
	尿	nyàu	niuH
urn n.	甕	wùng;	ung;
-to store human ashes	屍灰甕	shīhwēiwùng	sìfùiung
urologist n.	泌尿科醫生	mìnyàukēyishēng	beiniuHfōyìsāng
usage n.			
-use	用法	yùngfǎ;	yuIngfaat;
-custom	風俗	fēngsú	fùngjuHk
use			
-n.	用	yùng;	yuHng;
-n.	用處	yùngchu;	yuHngchyu;
-v. t.	用	yùng	yuHng
useful a.	有用	yǒuyùng	yáuHyuHng
usher			
-n.	招待員	jāudàiywán;	jìudoiHyùHn;
-v. t.	招待	jāudài	jìudoiH
usual a.	平常	píngcháng;	pìHngsèuHng;
-common	普通	pǔtūng	póutùng
usurp v. t./v. i.	篡奪	tswàndwó;	saandyuHt;
	侵佔	chīnjàn	chàmjim
utensil n.	器皿	chìmǐng;	heimíIHng;
-kitchen	廚房用具	chúfángyùngjyù	chyùHfòHng yuIHnggeuiH
utilitarianism n.	功利主義	gūnglìjǔyì	gùngleiHjyúyiH
utilize v. t.	利用	lìyùng	leiIyuHng
utmost a.			
-greatest	最	dzwèi;	jeui;
-most possible	最多	dzwèidwō	jeuidò

utter

| -v. t. express in words | 說 | shwō; | syut (góng); |
| -a. total | 完全 | wánchywán | yùHnchyùHn |

uttermost

| -a. | 至極 | j̀rjí; | jigiHk; |
| -n. | 到極點 | dàujídyǎn | dougiHkdím |

| **uvula n.** | 小舌 | syǎushé | síusiHt |

V

vacancy n.

-unoccupied place	空位	kūngwèi;	hùngwái;
-of an official post	空缺	kūngchywē	hùngkyut
vacant a.	空	kūng	hùng
vacation n.	假期	jyàchí	gakèiH
vaccinate v. t.	種痘	jùngdòu	jungdáu
vacuum n.	眞空	jēnkūng;	jànhùng;
-vacuum cleaner	吸塵機	syíchénjī;	kāpchàHngèi;
-vacuum tube	眞空管	jēnkūnggwǎn	jànhùnggún

vagabond n.

-wanderer	流浪者	lyóulàngjě;	làuHloHngjé;
-rascal	流氓	lyóumáng	làuHmàHn
vague a.	模糊	mwóhu;	mòuHwùH;
	含糊	hánhu	hàHmwùH

vain a.

-empty	空虛	kūngsyū;	hùnghèui;
-conceited	自高	dz̀gāu;	jiHgòu;
-useless	無用	wúyùng	mòuHyuHng (móuHyuHng)

valence n.	原ㄩㄢˊ 子ㄗ˙ 價ㄐㄧㄚˋ	ywándzjyà	yùHnjíga
valid a.			
-ratified	有ㄧㄡˇ 效ㄒㄧㄠˋ	yŏusyàu;	yáuHhaauH;
-confirmed	正ㄓㄥˋ 確ㄑㄩㄝˋ	jèngchywè	jingkok
valley n.	山ㄕㄢ 谷ㄍㄨˇ	shāngǔ	sāangūk
valuable a.			
-precious	寶ㄅㄠˇ 貴ㄍㄨㄟˋ	băugwèi;	bóugwai;
-costly	貴ㄍㄨㄟˋ 重ㄓㄨㄥˋ	gwèijùng	gwaijuIIng
value			
-n. price	價ㄐㄧㄚˋ	jyà;	ga;
-n. worth	價ㄐㄧㄚˋ 值ㄓ	jyàjí,	gujiHk;
-v. t. fix the price	估ㄍㄨ 價ㄐㄧㄚˋ	gūjyà	gúga
valve n.			
-Elec.	眞ㄓㄣ 空ㄎㄨㄥ 管ㄍㄨㄢˇ	jēnkūnggwăn;	jànhùnggún;
-Anat.	瓣ㄅㄢˋ	bàn	faan
van n.	有ㄧㄡˇ 蓋ㄍㄞˋ 貨ㄏㄨㄛˋ 車ㄔㄜ	yŏugàihwòchē	yáuHgoifochè
vandalism n.	暴ㄅㄠˋ 行ㄒㄧㄥˊ	bàusyíng	bouHhàHng
vanilla n.	香ㄒㄧㄤ 蘭ㄌㄢˊ	syānglán	hèunglàaHn
vanish v. i.			
-disappear	消ㄒㄧㄠ 失ㄕ	syāushr̄;	sìusāt;
-as smoke	消ㄒㄧㄠ 散ㄙㄢˋ	syāusàn;	sìusaan;
-pass out of existence	消ㄒㄧㄠ 滅ㄇㄧㄝˋ	syāumyè	sìumiHt
vanity n.			
-vainglory	虛ㄒㄩ 榮ㄖㄨㄥˊ	syūrúng;	hèuiwìHng;
-conceit	自ㄗˋ 負ㄈㄨˋ	dz̀fù;	jiHfuH;
-unrealness	空ㄎㄨㄥ 虛ㄒㄩ	kūngsyū	hùnghèui

vapor, vapour n.

-rising from water	汽	chì;	hei;
-fog	霧	wù;	mouH;
-Phys.	氣體	chìtǐ	heitái

varicose a. 靜脈擴張 jìngmàikwòjāng jiHngmaHkkongjèung

variety n. 各式各樣 gèshìgèyàng goksìkgokyeuHng

various a.

	各種	gèjǔng;	gokjúng;
	各樣	gèyàng;	gokyeuHng;
	各色	gèsè	goksìk

varnish

-n.	漆	chì;	chāt;
-v. t.	油漆	yóuchì	yàuHchāt

vary v. t.

-alter	換	hwàn;	wuHn;
-Biol.	變	byàn;	bin;
-differ	不同	bùtúng	bāttùHng (m̀tùHng)

vase n. 花瓶 hwāpíng fàpìHng (fājēun)

vaseline n. 凡士林 fánshìlín fàaHnsiHlàHm

vast a. 大 dà daaiH

vat n. 大桶 dàtǔng daaiHtúng

veal n. 乳牛肉 rǔnyóuròu yúHngàuHyuHk

veer v. t./v. i. 轉方向 jwǎnfāngsyàng jyunfòngheung

vegetable n.

	菜	tsài	choi;
	蔬菜	shūtsài	sòchoi

vegetation n. 植物 jŕwù jiHkmaHt

vehicle n. 車 chē chè

veil n.

-curtain	幕	mù;	moHk;
-for the face	面紗	myànshā	miHnsà

vein n.

-as opp. to artery	靜脈	jìngmài;	jiHngmaaHk;
-blood vessel	血管	syĕgwăn	hyutgún

velocity n. 速度 sùdù chūkdouH

velvet n. 天鵝絨 tyānérúng tìnngòHyúng

veneer v. t.

-cover with this cooting of wood	包板	bāubăn;	bàaubáan;
-polish of manner	可敬	kĕjìng	hóging

venerate v. t. 尊敬 dzwūnjìng; jyùnging;

敬重 jìngjùng gingjuHng

vengeance n. 報復 bàufù; houfuHk;

報仇 bàuchóu bousàuH

venom n. 毒物 dúwù; duHkmaHt;

-liquid 毒液 dúyè duHkyiHk

vent n. 孔 kŭng; húng (lūng);

-opening 出口 chūkŏu chēutháu

ventilate v. t. 通風 tūngfēng tùngfùng

venture v. i.

-risk	冒險	màusyăn;	mouHhím;
-dare	敢	găn	gám

Venus n. 金星 jīnsyīng gàmsìng

verandah n. 走廊 dzŏuláng jáulòIIng

verb n. 動詞 dùngtsź duHngchìH

verbatim adv.

-word for word 逐字地 júdżde juHkjiHdeiH

verdict n. 判決 pànjywé punkyut

verdigris n. 銅綠 túnglyù tùHngluHk

verge n.

-extreme edge 邊緣 byānyán; bìnyùHn;

-borderline	邊界	byānjyè	bīngaai
verify v. t.			
-confirm	證實	jèngshf;	jingsaHt;
-fulfil	應驗	yìngyàn	yingyiHm
vermin n.			
-insects	害蟲	hàichúng;	hoiHchùHng;
-parasites	寄生蟲	jìshēngchúng	geisàngchùHng
vernacular n.	方言	fāngyán	fòngyìHn
versatile a.	多才多藝	dwōtsáidwōyì	dòchòiHdòngaiH
verse n.			
-as opp. to prose	詩	shī;	sī;
-Pros.	句	jyù;	geui;
-Bib.	節	jyé	jit
version n.	譯文	yìwén	yiHkmàHn
vertebrate n.	脊椎動物	jíjwēidùngwù	jekjēuiduHngmaHt
vertical a.	直立	jílì;	jiHklaHp;
	垂直	chwéijf	sèuiHjiHk
vertigo n.			
-dizziness	暈	yūn	wàHn
very adv.	很	hěn;	hán (hóu);
	十分	shrfēn	saHpfàn
vessel n.			
-utensil	器皿	chìmǐng;	heimíHng;
-receptacle	容器	rúngchì;	yùHnghei;
-ship	船	chwán	syùHn
vest n.			
-undershirt	汗衫	hànshān;	hoHnsāam (sinsāam);
-for women	襯衣	chènyī	chanyī (chansāam)
vet n.	獸醫	shòuyī	sauyī
veteran n.	宿戰士	sùjànshr	sūkjinsiH

-ex-serviceman	退伍軍人	twèiwǔjyūnrén	teuíngHgwànyàHn
eto n.	否決權	fǒujywéchywán	fáukyutkyùHn
ex v. t.			
-annoy	煩惱	fánnǎu;	fàaHnnóuH;
-irritate	惹人生氣	rérénshēngchì	yéHyàHnsàanghei (gìknāu)
iaduct n.	天橋	tyānchyáu	tìnkìuH
ibrate v. i.	震動	jèndùng;	janduHng;
	顫動	chàndùng	jinduIng
ice n.			
-deputy	副	fù;	fu;
-evil conduct	惡行	èsyíng;	ngokhàHng;
-tool	老虎鉗	láuhǔchyán	lóuHfúkìIm
iceroy n.	總督	dzǔngdū	júngdūk
ice versa adv.	到轉	dàujwǎn	doujyun
icinity n.	附近	fùjìn;	fuHgaHn;
	鄰近	línjìn	lèuHngaHn
icious a.			
-depraved	邪惡	syéè;	chèHngok;
-malignant	惡毒	èdú;	ngokduHk;
-wicked	壞	hwài	waaiH
ctim n.			
-to a deity	犧牲	syīshēng;	hèisàng;
-of a disaster	遭難者	dzāunnànjě	jòunaaHnjé
ictimize v. t.	犧牲	syīshēng	hèisàng
ictory n.	勝利	shènglì;	singleiH;
	戰勝	jànshèng	jinsing
ie v. i.	競爭	jìngjēng,	gingjàng;

	競賽	jìngsài	gingchoi
view			
~v. t. see	看	kàn;	hon (tái);
~v. t. survey	觀察	gwānchá;	gùnchaat;
~n. opinion	意見	yìjyàn;	yigin;
~n. sight	風景	fēngjǐng	fùnggíng
vigour n.			
-mental	精神	jīngshén;	jìngsàHn;
-physical	精力	jīnglì;	jìngliHk;
-energy	氣力	chìlì	heiliHk
vile a.			
-depraved	邪惡	syéè;	chèHngok;
-mean	下賤	syàjyàn	haHjiHn
village n.	鄉村	syāngtswūn;	hēungchyūn;
	鄉下	syāngsyà	hèunghá
villain n.	惡漢	èhàn;	ngokhon;
	流氓	lyóumáng	làuHmàHn
vindicate v. t.	辯護	byànhù;	biHnwuH;
	辯明	byànmíng	biHnmìHng
vindictive a.	報復心	bàufùsyīn;	boufuHksàm;
	仇念	chóunyàn	sàuHniHm
vine n.	葡萄樹	pútáushù	pòuHtòuHsyuH
vinegar n.	醋	tsù	chou
vineyard n.	葡萄園	pútáuywán	pòuHtòuHyùHn
violent a.			
-cruel	強暴	chyángbàu;	kèuHngbouH;
-forcible	猛烈	měnglyè;	máangliHt;

| -of language | 激烈 | iĭlyè | gĭkliHt |

iolet n.

| plant | 紫羅蘭 | džlwólán; | jilòHlàaHn; |
| -colour | 青蓮色 | chinglyánsè | chĭngliHnsĭk |

iolin n.

| | 小提琴 | syäutíchín | síutàiHkàHm |

iper n.

| | 毒蛇 | dúshé; | duHksèH; |
| | 蝮蛇 | fùshé | fūksèH |

irgin n.

| | 處女 | chŭnyŭ; | chyunéuiH; |
| | 童女 | túngnyŭ | tùHngnéuiH |

irile a.

| | 男性 | nánsyìng | nàaIImsing |

irtue n.

| -goodness | 美德 | mĕidé; | mÉiHdāk; |
| -clastity | 貞潔 | jēngjyé | jìnggit |

irtuous a.

| -good | 善良 | shànlyáng; | siHnlèuHng; |
| -chaste | 貞潔 | jēngjyé | jìnggit |

irus n.

| -of disease | 病毒 | bìngdú; | beHngduHk; |
| -for inoculation | 痘苗 | dòumyáu | dauHmìuH |

isa n.

| | 簽證 | chyānjèng | chìmjing |

is-a-vis n.

| | 相向 | syàngsyàng | sèungheung |

iscose n.

| | 黏合劑 | nyánhéjì | niHmhaHpjāi |

isible a.

| | 能見 | néngjyàn; | nàHnggin (táidóu); |
| | 顯著 | syănjù | hínjyu |

ision n.

| -visual power | 眼力 | yănlì; | ngáaHnliHk; |
| -imagination | 幻想 | hwànsyäng; | waaHnséung; |

-prophetic sight	異像	yìsyàng	yiHjeuHng
visit v. t.			
-superiors	拜訪	bàifǎng;	baaifóng;
-of sightseeing	觀光	gwāngwāng;	gùngwòng;
-inspect	參觀	tsāngwān;	chàamgùn;
-delegation	訪問	fǎngwèn	fóngmaHn
visitation n.	訪問	fǎngwèn	fóngmaHn
vital a.			
-of life	有生命	yǒushēngmìng;	yáuHsàngmiHng;
-fatal	致命	jìmìng	jimiHng
-vital force	活力	hwólì	wuHtliHk
vitamin n.	維他命	wéitāmìng	wàiHtàmiHng
vitriol n.	硫酸	lyóuswān	làuHsyùn
vivacious a.	活潑	hwópwo;	wuHtput;
	有生氣	yǒushēngchì	yáuHsàanghei
vivid a.			
-lively	活潑	hwópwo;	wuHtput;
-animated	生動	shēngdùng;	sàangduHng;
-of colours	顯明	syǎnmíng;	hínmìHng;
-of light	光亮	gwānglyàng	gwòngleuHng
vivisection n.	活體解剖	hwótǐjyěpōu	wuHttáigáaifáu
vocabulary n.	字彙	dzìhwèi;	jiHwuiH;
	語彙	yǔhwèi	yúHwuiH
vocal a.	有聲	yǒushēng;	yáuHsìng;
-vocal cord	聲帶	shēngdài	sìngdáai
vocation n.	職業	jŕyè	jīkyiHp
vogue n.	流行	lyóusyíng;	làuHhàHng;

	時與	shísyǐng	sìHhìng
voice n.	聲	shēng;	sēng;
	聲音	shēngyin	sìngyàm
void a.			
-empty	空	kūng;	hùng;
-null	無效	wúsyàu	móuIIhaauH (móuHhaauH)
volcans n.	火山	hwǒshān	fósàan
volt n.	伏特	fútè	fuHkdaHk;
-voltage	電壓單位	dyànyādānwèi	diHnngaatdāanwái
voluble a.			
-fluent	流暢	lyóuchàng;	làuHcheung
-talking a lot	善辯	shànbyàn	siHnbiHn
volume n.			
-of a solid body	體積	tǐjī;	táijīk;
-of a gas	容積	rúngjī;	yùHngjīk;
-of a book	卷	jywàn	gyún
voluntarily adv.	自願	dzywàn;	jiHyuHn;
	任意	rènyì;	yaHmyi;
	自動	dzdùng	jiHduHng
volunteer n.	志願者	jrywànjě;	jiyuIIujé,
-Mil.	義勇軍	yìyǔngjyūn	yiHyúnggwān
voluptuous a.	好色	hàuoè;	housìk;
	肉慾	ròuyù	yuHkyuHk;
vomit v.t.	嘔	ǒu;	ngáu;
	吐	tù	tou
voracious a.	貪食	tānshf	tàamsiHk
vote n.			
-in regard to election	選舉	sywǎnjyǔ;	syúngéui;
-in regard to passing resolution	表決	byǎujywé;	bíukyut;

-ticket used in voting	選票	sywănpyàu	syúnpiu
vouch v.t.			
-confirm	保證	băujèng	bóujing;
-uphold	斷定	dwàndìng	dyundiHng
voucher n.	收據	shōujyù	sàugeui
vow			
-n. an oath	誓	shr̀;	saiH;
-v.t. make an oath	發誓	fāshr̀;	faatsaiH;
-fulfil a vow	還願	hwánywàn	wàaHnyuHn
vowel n.	母音	mŭyin	móuHyām
voyage			
-v.i. travel by sea	航行	hángsyíng;	hóHnghàHng;
-n. journey by sea	水路	shwĕilù	séuilouH
vulgar a.			
-low	下流	syàlyóu;	haHlàuH;
-base	下賤	syàjyàn;	haHjiHn;
unrefined	粗魯	tsūlŭ;	chòulóuH;
-common	通俗	tūngsú	tùngjuHk
vulnerable a.	可損害	kĕswŭnhài	hósyúnhoiH
vulture n.	兀鷹	wùying	ngaHtyìng

W

wad n.	襯墊	chèndyàn	chandin
wadding n.	塡物	tyánwù;	tìHnmaHt;
	木棉	mùmyán	muHkmìHn
waddle v.i.	蹣跚而行	mănshānérsyíng;	múHnsàanyìHhàHng;
	搖擺而行	yáubăiérsyíng	yìuHbáaiyìHhàHng
wade v.i.	涉水	shèshwĕi	sipséui

afer n.	薄 煎 餅	bwójyānbíng	boHkjìnbéng
ag v.t.	搖	yáu	yìuH
ages n.	工 錢	gūngchyán;	gùngchìHn;
	工 資	gūngdz̄	gùngjì
aggon n.	貨 車	hwòchē	fochè
aif n.	流 浪 兒 童	lyóulàngértúng	làuHloHngyìHtùHng
ail v.i.	哭	kū	hūk (haam)
aist n.	腰	yāu;	yìu;
	腰 部	yāubù	yìuhouH
ait v.i.	等	děng;	dáng;
	等 候	děnghòu	dánghauH
aiter n.	侍 者	shìjě;	sìHjé (sìHjái);
	茶 房	cháfáng	chàHfóng (bōi)
aive v.t.	放 棄	fàngchì;	fonghei;
	棄 權	chìchywán	heikyùHn
wake v.t.	醒	syǐng	séng
alk v.i.	走	dzǒu;	jáu (hàaHng);
	走 路	dzǒulù	jáulouH(hàaHnglouH)
vall n.	牆	chyáng	chèuHng
vallet n.	皮 夾	píjyá;	pèiIgáap;
	錢 袋	chyándài	chìHndói (ngàHnbāau)
valnut n.	胡 桃	hútáu	wùHtòuH (haHptòuH)
wander v.i.	流 浪	lyóulàng	làuHloHng (pìulàuIî)
wane v.i.			
-decrease	減 少	jyǎnshǎu;	gáamsíu;
-decline	衰 落	shwāilwò	sèuiloHk
want v.t.			
-desire	要	yàu;	yiu;
-need	需 要	syūyàu;	sèuiyiu;
-lack	缺 少	chywēshǎu	kyutsíu

wanton a.	淫⁻ᵥ 蕩ᵈₐᵧ	yíndàng	yàHmdoHng
war			
-n.	戰ᵗʰ 爭ᵗʰ	jànjēng;	jinjàng;
-v.t.	打ᵈᵧ 仗ᵗʰ	dǎjàng	dájeung
-declare war	宣ᵀᵁ 戰ᵗʰ	sywānjàn	syùnjin
warden n.	監ⁱⁱ 護ʰ 員ᵘ	jyānhùywán	gàamwuHyùHn
warder n.	看ᵏ 守ˢ	kānshǒu	hònsáu
wardrobe n.	衣⁻ 櫥ᵍ;	yìchú;	yìchyùH;
	衣⁻ 櫃ᵍ	yìgwèi	yìgwaiH
wares n.	貨ʰ 品ᵖ	hwòpǐn	fobán
warm a.	暖ⁿ;	nwǎn;	nyúHn;
	溫ˣ 暖ⁿ	wēnnwǎn	wànnyúHn
warn v.t.	警ʲ 告ᵍ	jǐnggàu	gínggou
warning u.	警ʲ 告ᵍ;	jǐnggàu;	gínggou;
	警ʲ 戒ʲ	jǐngjyè	gínggaai
warp v.t./v.i.	彎ˣ 曲ᵏ	wānchyū	wāankūk
warrant n.			
-for arrest	拘ʲ 票ᵖ;	jyūpyàu;	kèuipiu;
-to attend	傳ᵍ 票ᵖ	chwánpyàu	chyùHnpiu
warrior n.	戰ᵗʰ 士ˢ	jànshì	jinsiH
warship n.	戰ᵗʰ 艦ⁱ	jànjyàn	jinlaaHm
wart n.	贅ᵗʰ 瘤ᵈ	jwèilyóu	jeuiláu
wash v.t.	洗ᵀ	syǐ	sái
washer n.	洗ᵀ 淨ʲ 器ᵍ	syǐjingchì	sáijiHnghei
wasp n.	黃ʰ 蜂ᵍ	hwángfēng	wòHngfūng
waste			
-v.t. squander	浪ᵈ 費ᵍ;	làngfèi;	loHngfai
-v.t. consume	消ᵀ 耗ʰ;	syāuhàu;	sìuhou;

-a. desolate	荒廢	hwāngfèi	fòngfai
watch			
-n. timepiece	手錶	shǒubyǎu;	sáubiu,
-n. of the night	更	gēng;	gung,
-v.t. tend	看守	kānshǒu	hònsáu
watchful a.	留心	lyóusyìn;	làuHsàm;
	謹慎	jǐnshèn	gánsaHn
water			
-n.	水	shwěi;	séui;
-v.t.	洒水	sǎshwěi	sáséui
-water jar	水缸	shwěigāng	séuigōng
waterfall n.	瀑布	pùbù	boHkbou
waterpower n.	水力	shwǐilì	séuiliHk
waterproof a.	防水	fángshwěi	tòHngséui
watt n.	瓦特	wǎtè	ngáHdaHk
wave			
-v.t. sway	搖	yáu;	yìuH;
-v.t. brandish	舞	wǔ;	móuII;
-n. of the sea	浪	làng	loHng
wax n.	蠟	là	laaHp
way n.			
-road	路	lù;	louH;
-method	方法	fāngfǎ;	fòngfaat
-manner	樣子	yàngdz	yeuHngjí(yéung)
wayward a.	任性	rènsyìng;	yaHmsing;
-capricious	反覆無常	fǎnfùwúchàng	fáanfūkmòuHsèuHng
we pron.	我們	wǒmen	ngóHmùlIn(ngóHdeiII)
weak a.			
-feeble	軟弱	rwǎnrwò;	yúHnyeuHk;

-debilitated	衰弱	shwāirwò;	sèuiyeuHk;
-fig.	懦弱	nwòrwò	noHyeuHk
weakness n.	懦弱	nwòrwò;	noHyeuHk;
-lacking	缺點	chywēdyǎn;	kyutdím;
-weak points	弱點	rwòdyǎn;	yeuHkdím;
-defect	短處	dwǎnchù	dyúnchyu
wealth n.	錢財	chyántsái	chìHnchòiH
wean v.t.	斷奶	dwànnǎi	tyúHnnáaiH
weapon n.	武器	wǔchǐ;	móuHhei;
	軍械	jyūnsyè	gwànhaaiH

wear v.t.

-clothes, socks, etc.	穿	chwān;	chyùn (jeuk);
-hat, spectacles,etc.	戴	dài	daai

weary a.

-tired	疲倦	píjywàn;	pèiHgyuHn;
-of something	討厭	tǎuyàn	tóuyim
weather n.	天氣	tyānchì	tìnhei

weave v.t.

-cloth	織	jī;	jīk;
-baskets	編	byān	bìn
weaver n.	織工	jīgūng	jikgūng
web n.	織物	jīwù;	jìkmaHt;
-of spider	蜘蛛網	jījūwǎng	jìjyūmóHng
webbing n.	蹼	pú	buHk
wedding n.	婚禮	hwūnlǐ	fànláiH

wedge

-n.	楔子	syèdz;	sitjí (sit);

-v.t.	楔ㄒㄧㄝ	syè	sit
Wednesday n.	禮ㄌㄧ拜ㄅㄞ三ㄙㄢ	líbàisān;	láiHbaaisàam;
	星ㄒㄧㄥ期ㄑㄧ三ㄙㄢ	syìngchisān	sìngkèiHsàam
weed			
-n.	野ㄧㄝ草ㄘㄠ	yětsău;	yáHchóu;
-v.t.	除ㄔㄨ草ㄘㄠ	chútsău	chèuiHchóu
week n.	禮ㄌㄧ拜ㄅㄞ	líbài;	láiHbaai;
	星ㄒㄧㄥ期ㄑㄧ	syìngchi	sìngkèiH
-in compounds	週ㄓㄡ	jōu;	jàu;
-week end	週ㄓㄡ末ㄇㄛ	jōumwò	jàumuIIt
weekday n.	週ㄓㄡ日ㄖ	jōuṛ	jàuyaHt
weekly			
-a./adv.	每ㄇㄟ週ㄓㄡ一一次ㄘ	měijōuyítsż,	múiIIjàuyātchi;
-n.	週ㄓㄡ刊ㄎㄢ	jōukān	jàuhón
weep			
-v.i. cry	哭ㄎㄨ	kū,	hūk (haam);
-v.t. shed, as tears	流ㄌㄧㄡ淚ㄌㄟ	lyóulèi	làuHleuiH (làuHngáaHnséui)
weft n.	緯ㄨㄟ	wěi	wáiII
weigh v.t.	稱ㄔㄥ	chèng	ching
weight n.			
-degree of heaviness	重ㄓㄨㄥ量ㄌㄧㄤ	jùnglyàng;	chúHngleuHng;
-metal piece	法ㄈㄚ碼ㄇㄚ	fămă;	faatmáH;
-of a balance	稱ㄔㄥ坨ㄊㄨㄛ	chèngtwó	chingtòH
weir n.	堰ㄧㄢ	yàn	yim
welcome v.t.	歡ㄏㄨㄢ迎ㄧㄥ	hwānyíng	fùnyìHng
weld v.t./v.i.	鍛ㄉㄨㄢ接ㄐㄧㄝ	dwànjyē	dyunjip
welfare n.	福ㄈㄨ利ㄌㄧ	fúlì;	fūkleiH;
	幸ㄒㄧㄥ福ㄈㄨ	syìngfú	haHngfūk
well			
-n.	井ㄐㄧㄥ	jĭng;	jéng;

We

-a. in health	好ㄏㄠ	hǎu	hóu
west n.	西ㄒㄧ	syī;	sài;
	西ㄒㄧ 方ㄈㄤ	syīfāng	sàifòng
wet a.	濕ㄕ	shī;	sāp;
	潮ㄔㄠ 濕ㄕ	cháushī	chìuHsāp
-wet nurse	奶ㄋㄞ 媽ㄇㄚ	nǎimā	náaiHmā
wharf n.	頭ㄊㄡ 碼ㄇㄚ	mǎtou	máHtàuH
what a.			
-interrog.	甚ㄕㄣ 麼ㄇㄛ	shénme;	saHmmō (mātyéH);
-that or those which	所ㄙㄨㄛ	swǒ	só
whatever pro.	無ㄨ 論ㄌㄨㄣ	wúlwùn;	mòuHleuHn;
	無ㄨ 論ㄌㄨㄣ 如ㄖㄨ 何ㄏㄜ	wúlwùnrúhé	mòuHleuHnyùHhòH
wheat n.	麥ㄇㄞ 子ㄗ	màidz;	maHkjí;
	小ㄒㄧㄠ 麥ㄇㄞ	syǎumài	síumaHk
wheel n.	輪ㄌㄨㄣ 子ㄗ	lwúndz;	lèuHnjí (léun);
-of a cart	車ㄔㄜ 輪ㄌㄨㄣ	chēlwún;	chèléun;
-of a ship	舵ㄉㄨㄛ 輪ㄌㄨㄣ	dwòlwún;	tòHlèuHn;
-spinning wheel	紡ㄈㄤ 車ㄔㄜ	fǎngchē	fóngchè
when adv.			
-interrog;	何ㄏㄜ 時ㄕ	héshf;	hòHsìH;
-at the moment that	當ㄉㄤ 時ㄕ	dāngshf;	dòngsìH;
-during the time that	那ㄋㄚ 時ㄕ	nàshf	náHsìH (gójaHnsí)
whenever adv.	無ㄨ 論ㄌㄨㄣ 何ㄏㄜ 時ㄕ	wúlwùnhéshf;	mòuHleuHnhòHsìH;
	隨ㄙㄨㄟ 時ㄕ	swéishf	chèuiHsìH
where adv.			
-at what place	何ㄏㄜ 處ㄔㄨ	héchù;	hòHchyu;
-at the place in which	… 的ㄉㄜ 地ㄉㄧ 方ㄈㄤ	…dedìfang	…dikdeiHfòng (gedeiHfòng)
whether conj.	或ㄏㄨㄛ 是ㄕ	hwòshf;	waaHksiH(yeuHkhaiH)
	要ㄧㄠ 是ㄕ	yàushf	yiusiH(yeuHkhaiH)
which pro.	那ㄋㄚ 個ㄍㄜ	nǎge;	náHgo (bīngo);

那_ㄋ一^一個_ㄜ　　　　　　nǎyíge　　　　náHyātgo (bǐnyātgo)

while

-n. time	時ㄕ 候ㄏ	shíhou;	oiHhauH;
-conj. during the time that	在ㄗㄞ … 的ㄜ 時ㄕ 候ㄏ	dzài...deshíhou	joiH...dǐksìIhauH (hái...gesìHhauH

him n.

-fancy	高ㄍㄠ 興ㄒㄥ	gāusyìng;	gòuhing;
-thought	意ㄧ 思ㄙ	yìsz	yisi
vhlmper n./v. i.	啜ㄔㄨㄛ 泣ㄑㄧ	chwōchì;	jyntyāp;
	嗚ㄨ 咽ㄧㄢ	wūyān	wūyìn
vhine v. i./v. t.	哀ㄞ 聲ㄕㄥ	āishēng	ngòisèng

whip

-v. t. strike	打ㄉㄚ	dǎ;	dá;
-n. plaited cord	鞭ㄅㄧㄢ 子ㄗ	hyāndz	bìnjí (bìn)
whirl v. i.	旋ㄒㄩㄢ 轉ㄓㄨㄢ	sywánjwǎn	syùHnjyún
whisk n.	掃ㄙㄠ 帚ㄓㄡ	sàujou;	soujáau (soubá);
-v. t. sweep	掃ㄙㄠ	sǎu;	sou;
-v. t. beat	打ㄉㄚ	dǎ	dá
whiskers n.	鬍ㄏㄨ 子ㄗ	húdz	wùHjí (wùHsòu)
whisper n./v. t./v. i.	耳ㄦ 語ㄩ	ěryǔ;	yíHyúH;
	私ㄙ 語ㄩ	szyǔ;	sìyúH

whistle

-n. instrument	口ㄎㄡ 哨ㄕㄠ	kǒushàu;	háusaau;
-v. i. with the lips	吹ㄔㄨㄟ 口ㄎㄡ 哨ㄕㄠ	chwēikǒushàu	chèuiháusaau
white a.	白ㄅㄞ	bái	baaHk
-white race	白ㄅㄞ 種ㄓㄨㄥ 人ㄖㄣ	báijǔngrén	baaHkjúngyàHn

who pro.

-interrog.	誰ㄕㄟ	shéi;	sèuiH (bǐngo);
-the relative	那ㄋㄚ 個ㄍㄜ 人ㄖㄣ	nàgerén;	náHgoyàHn (gógoyàHn);
-Who's who	現ㄒㄧㄢ 代ㄉㄞ 名ㄇㄧㄥ 人ㄖㄣ 錄ㄌㄨ	syàndàimíngrénlù	yiHndoiIImìIIng-yàHnluHk

whole a.

-all	所有	swŏyŏu;	sóyáuH
-entire	整個	jĕngge	jínggo
wholesale n.	批發	pīfā	pàifaat

wholesome a.

-good	有益	yŏuyì;	yáuHyìk;
-moral health	合衛生	héwèishēng	haHpwaiHsāng
wholeheartedly adv.	專心	jwānsyin;	jyūnsàm;
	奮力	fènlì	fáHnliHk

whom pro.

-interrog.	誰	shéi;	sèuiH (bingo);
-relative	那個	nàge	náHgo (gógo)
whose pro.	誰的	shéide	sèuiHdìk (bingoge)

why adv.

-interrog.	爲什麼	wèishénme;	waiHsaHmmō;
-the reason for which	···的原因	...deywányin	...dìkyùHnyàn (...geyùHnyàn)

wick n.

-of lamp	燈心	dēngsyin;	dàngsàm;
-of candle	蠟燭心	làjúsyin	laaHpjūksàm

wicked a.

-evil	邪惡	syéè;	chèHngok;
-spiteful	惡毒	èdù	ngokduHk

wide a.

-as breadth	寬	kwān;	fùn (fut);
-as clothes	肥大	féidà	fèiHdaaiH
widow n.	寡婦	gwăfù	gwáfúH
widower n.	鰥夫	gwānfū	gwāanfù
width n.	寬	kwān;	fùn (fut);

	闊ㄎㄨㄛ	kwò	fut
wife n.	妻ㄑㄧ子ㄗ	chǐdz;	chàijí;
	太ㄊㄞ太ㄊㄞ	tàitai	taaitáai
wig n.	假ㄐㄧㄚ髮ㄈㄚ	jyǎfǎ	gáfaat
wild a.			
-of animals	野ㄧㄝ	yě	yéH;
-of plants	野ㄧㄝ生ㄕㄥ	yěshēng;	yéHsàang;
-licentious	荒ㄏㄨㄤ唐ㄊㄤ	hwāngtáng	fòngtòHng
wilderness n.	曠ㄎㄨㄤ野ㄧㄝ	kwàngyě;	kòngyéH;
	荒ㄏㄨㄤ野ㄧㄝ	hwāngyě	fòngyéH
wilful a.	故ㄍㄨ意ㄧ	gùyì	gnyi;
-self-will	任ㄖㄣ性ㄒㄧㄥ	rènsyìng;	yaHmsing;
-headstrong	頑ㄨㄢ強ㄑㄧㄤ	wánchyáng;	wàaImkèuHng;
-obstinate	頑ㄨㄢ固ㄍㄨ	wángù	wàaHngu
will			
-v. i. of the future	要ㄧㄠ	yàu;	yiu;
-v. i. wish	要ㄧㄠ	yàu;	yiu;
-n. deliberate intention	主ㄓㄨ意ㄧ	júyi·	jyúyi;
-n. testament	遺ㄧ囑ㄓㄨ	yíjǔ;	wàiHjūk;
-n. of God	旨ㄓ意ㄧ	jǐ˙	jíyi
willing a.	肯ㄎㄣ	kᴜ,	háng;
	願ㄩㄢ意ㄧ	ywànyi	yuHnyi
willow n.	柳ㄌㄧㄡ	lyǒu;	lánH;
	楊ㄧㄤ柳ㄌㄧㄡ	yánglyǒu	yèuHngláuH
wilt v. t./v. i.			
-wither as plant	枯ㄎㄨ萎ㄨㄟ	kūwěi;	fùwái;
	凋ㄉㄧㄠ謝ㄒㄧㄝ	dyāusyè	diujeH
win v. i.			
-as money	贏ㄧㄥ	yíng;	yèHng;

-as a battle	打勝仗	dăshèngjàng	dásingjeung
wince v. i.			
-with pain	避縮	bìswō	beiHsūk
wind			
-n. air in motion	風	fēng;	fùng;
-v. t. as thread on a spool	捲	jywǎn;	gyún;
-v. t. twist	扭	nyǒu;	náu;
-wind a clock	開鐘	kāijūng;	hōijūng;
-wind a watch	上錶鏈	shàngbyǎulyàn	séuHngbiulín
-wind intrument	管樂器	gwǎnywèchì	gúnngoHhei
winding a.	彎曲	wānchyū	wāankūk
window n.	窗	chwāng	chēung
windy a.	有風	yǒufēng;	yáuHfùng;
	多風	dwōfēng	dòfùng
wine n.			
-of grain	酒	jyǒu;	jáu;
-of grape	葡萄酒	pútáujyǒu	pòuHtòuHjáu
wing n.			
-of aerial flight	翅膀	chìbǎng	chibóng;
-of aeroplane	翼	yì	yiHk;
-Arch.	廂房	syāngfáng	sēungfóng
wink v. i.	眨眼	jáyǎn	jáamngáaHn
winnow v. t.	簸	bwǒ;	bo;
	篩	shāi	sài
winter n.	冬天	dūngtyan;	dūngtǐn;
	冬季	dūngjì	dùnggwai
wipe v. t.	擦	tsā;	chaat;

	抹ᄆ	mwǒ	mut (maat)
wire n.	電ᄃ 線ᅵ	dyànsyàn;	diHnsin;
-n. telegraphic	電ᄃ 報ᄎ	dyànbàu;	diHnbou;
-v. i. send message	打ᄃ 電ᄃ 報ᄎ	dǎdyànbàu;	dádiHnbou
wireless n.	無ᄉ 線ᅵ 電ᄃ 報ᄎ	wúsyàndyànbàu	mòuHsindiHnbou
wisdom n.	智ᄌ 慧ᄒ	jìhwèi	jiwai
wise a.	聰ᄎ 明ᄆ	tsūngming	chùngmìHng
wish v. t.			
-want	要ᅵ	yàu;	yiu;
-hope	希ᅵ 望ᄇ	syīwàng	hèimoHng
wistful a.	想ᅵ 望ᄇ	syǎngwàng;	séungmoHng;
meditate	默ᄆ 想ᅵ	mèsyǎng	maIIkséung
wit n.			
-intelligence	智ᄌ 慧ᄒ	jìhwèi;	jiwai;
-quickness of mind	機ᄀ 警ᄀ	jījǐng	gèigìng
witch n.	女ᄂ 巫ᄇ	nyǔwū;	néuiHmòuH;
	巫ᄇ 婆ᄇ	wūpwó	mòuHpòH
witchcraft n.	邪ᄉ 術ᄉ	syéshù	chèHseuHt
with prep.			
-in company of	同ᄐ	túng;	tùHng;
-by means of	用ᄋ	yùng	yuHng;
withdraw v. t.			
-take back	收ᄉ 回ᄒ	shōuhwéi;	sàuwùiH;
-as a motion	收ᄉ 回ᄒ	shōuhwéi;	sàuwùiH;
-as the troops	退ᄐ	twèi	teui
wither v. i.			
-of plants	枯ᄏ	kū;	fù;

-of flowers	謝	syè	ŝeH

without prep.

-outside	在外	dzàiwài;	joiHngoiH (hái-ngoiHbiHn)
-not having	沒有	méiyou	muHtyáuH (móuH)

withstand v. t./v. i.

-oppose	反對	făndwèi;	fáandeui;
-be patient	忍耐	rěnnài	yánnoiH

witness

-n. person	證人	jèngrén;	jingyàHn;
-v. i. prove	證明	jèngmíng	jingmìHng

wizard n.

-magician	術士	shùshг̀	seuHtsiH
wizened a.	枯萎	kūwěi	fùwái

woe n.

-calamity	災禍	dzāihwò	jòiwoH
wolf n.	狼	láng	lòHng
woman n.	女人	nyǔrén;	néuiHyán;
	婦女	fùnyǔ	fúHnéuiH

womb n.

-uterus	子宮	džgūng	jígūng

wonder

-n. strange event	奇事	chíshг̀;	kèiHsiH;
-n. miracle	奇蹟	chíji;	kèiHjìk;
-v. t. uncertain	不知	bùjг̄	bātjì (m̀jì)

wonderful a.

-marvellous	奇怪	chígwài;	kèiHgwaai;
-excellent	好極	hăují	hóugiHk

wood n.

-timber	木料	mùlyàu;	muHkliuH;

-forest	樹林	shùlín	syuHlàHm
wool n.			
-of sheep	羊毛	yángmáu	yèuHngmòuII
word n.			
-spoken	話	hwà;	waH;
-written	字	dż	jiII
work n./v. i.	工作	gūngdzwò	gùngjok
workman n.	工人	gūngrén	gùngyàHn
workshop n.	工場	gūngchǎng	gùngchèuHng
world n.			
-the earth	世界	shrjyè;	saigaai,
-society	社會	shèhwèi;	séHwúi;
-Budd.	紅塵	húngchén	hùIIngchàHn
worldly a.	屬世	shŭshŕ;	suHksai;
	世俗	shŕsú	saijuHk
worm n.	蟲	chúng	chùHng
worry v. i.	煩惱	fánnǎu;	fàaHnnóuH;
	擔心	dānsyīn	dàamsàm
worse a.	更壞	gènghwài	gangwaaiH
worship v. t.	拜	bài;	baai;
-adore	崇拜	chúngbài	sùIIngbaai
worth a.	值得	jŕde	jiIIkdāk
worthy a.	有價值	yŏujyàjr;	yáuHgajiHk;
	值得	jŕde	jiHkdāk
would v. aux.	想要	syǎngyàu	séungyiu
wound			
-n.	傷	shāng	sèung;

-v. t.	受傷	shòushāng	sauHsèung
wrangle v. i.	吵架	chǎujyà;	cháauga (chòuHgāau);
	爭論	jēnglwùn	jàngleuHn
wrap v. t.	包	bāu	bàau
wrath n.	震怒	jènnù;	jannouH;
	憤怒	fènnù	fáHnnouH
wreath n.	花圈	hwāchywān	fāhyūn
wreck n.			
-broken ship	破船	pwòchwán;	posyùHn
-as a plan	破壞	pwòhwài	powaaiH
wrench v. t.	扭轉	nyǒujwǎn	náujyún
wrestle v. i.	搏鬥	bwódòu;	bokdau;
	蟀絞	shwāijyāu	seutgāau (ditdóu)
wretched a.	可憐	kělyán;	hólìHn;
	悽慘	chìtsǎn	chàicháam
wriggle v. t.	扭	nyǒu	náu
wring v. t.	絞	jyǎu;	gáau;
	扭	nyǒu	náu
wrinkle n.	縐紋	jòuwén;	jaumàHn;
-v. t.	縐	jòu	jau
wrist n.	手腕	shǒuwàn	sáuwún
writ n.	票	pyàu	piu
write v. t.	寫	syě	sé
writer n.	作者	dzwòjě;	jokjé;
	作家	dzwòjyā	jokgā
writhe v. i.	扭曲	nyǒuchyū;	náukūk
writing n.	書寫	shūsyě;	syùsé;

	筆跡	bǐjì	bātjik

wrong

-a. not right	錯	tswò;	cho,
-v. t. judge unfairly	冤枉	ywanwang	yùnwóng
wry a.	歪曲	wāichyū	wāaikūk

X

X-ray

-n.	愛克斯光	àikèszgwāng;	oihāaksigwōng;
-v. t.	照愛克斯光	jàuàikèszgwāng	jiuoihāaksigwōng

Y

yacht n.

-racing	快艇	kwàitǐng;	faaitéHng;
-pleasure	遊艇	yóutǐng;	yàuHtéHng
yale lock n.	彈簧鎖	tánhwángswǒ	daaHnwòHngsó (daaHngūngsó)
yap v. i.	小狗叫	syǎugǒujyàu	síugáugiu (gáujáigiu)

yard n.

-unit of measure	碼	mǎ;	máH;
-enclosed ground	院子	ywàndz;	yúnjí (yún);
-yard stick	碼尺	mǎchǐ	máHchek
yarn n.	線	syàn;	sin;
	紗	shā	sà
yawn v. i.	打哈欠	dǎhāchyàn	dáhāhim (dáhaamlouH)
year n.	年	nyán;	nìHn;
-of man's age	歲	swèi	seui
-last year	去年	chyùnyán	heuinìHn (gauHnín)

-new year	新年	syīnnyán	sànnìHn
yearbook n.	年鑑	nyánjyàn	nìHngaam
yearly adv.	每年	měinyán;	múiHnìHn
	年年	nyánnyán	nìHnnìHn
yeast n.			
-Chem.	酵母	syàumǔ;	haaumóuH
-ferment	酒母	jyǒumǔ;	jáumóuH
yell v. i.			
-cry out	叫	jyàu;	giu;
-shout	大聲喊	dàshēnghǎn	daaiHsènghaam
yellow a.	黃	hwáng;	wòHng;
	黃色	hwángsè	wòHngsìk
yelp v. i.	汪汪叫	wāngwāngjyàu	wòngwònggiu
yes adv.			
-contrasted with no	是	shì;	siH (haiH);
-expressing agreement	好	hǎu	hóu
yesterday n.	昨天	dzwótyan;	joHktìn (kàHmyaHt)
	昨日	dzwóï	joHkyaHt
yet adv.			
-still	還	hái;	wàaHn;
-nevertheless	但是	dànshì	daaHnsiH (daaHnhaiH
yield			
-v. i. surrender	屈服	chyūfú;	wātfuHk;
-v. t. produce	生	shēng	sàang
yoke n.	軛	è	ngāak
yolk n.	蛋黃	dànhwáng	daaHnwóng
yonder adv.	那邊	nàbyān	náHbìn (góbiHn)

you pro.			
-sing.	你	nǐ;	néiH;
-plur.	你們	nǐmen	néiHmùHn (néiHdeiH)
young a.			
-of men	年輕	nyánchīng;	nìHnhèng;
-of animals	小	syǎu	síu (sai)
-young people	青年人	chīngnyánrén	chīngnìHnyàHn
youngster n.			
-youth	少年	shàunyán;	siunìHn;
-child	小孩子	syǎuhàidz	síuhàaiHjí (saimānjái)
your pro.			
-sing.	你的	nǐde;	néiHdīk (néiHge);
-plur.	你們的	nǐménde	néiHmùHndīk (néiHdeiHge)
yours=**your**			
yourself pro.	你自己	nǐdžjǐ	néiHjiHgéi
youth n.			
-period	少年時代	shàunyánshŕdài;	siunìHnsìHdoiH;
-young person	少年人	shàunyánrén	siunìHnyàHn

Z

zeal n.	熱心	rèsyīn;	yiHtsàm;
	熱誠	rèchéng	yiHtsìHng
zealous a.	熱心的	rèsyīnde	yiHtsāmdīk (yiHtsàmge)
zero n.			
-Arith.	零	líng;	lìHng;
-of thermometer	零度	língdù	lìHngdouH
zebra n.	斑馬	bānmǎ;	bàanmáH;

-zebra line	斑馬線	bānmǎsyàn	bàanmáHsin
zig-zag a.	曲折	chyūjé	kūkjit
zinc n.	鋅	syìn	sàn
zipper n.	拉鍊	lālyàn	làailín
zodiac n.	黃道帶	hwángdàudài	wòHngdouHdaai
zone n.			
-belt, area	地帶	dìdài;	deiHdaai;
-in compounds	帶	dài	daai
zoo n.	動物園	dùngwùywán	duHngmaHtyún
zoology n.	動物學	dùngwùsywé	duHngmaHthoHk

APPENDIX OF RELIGIOUS TERMS

A

Aaron n.	亞倫	Yǎlwún	AlèuHn
abbot n.	修道院長	syōudàuyùnjǎng	sàudouHyúnjéung
Abel n.	亞伯	Yǎbwó	Abaak
abhor v. t.	怒恨	nùhèn	nóuHhaHn
abomination n.	憎惡	dzēngwù	jàngwu
Abraham n.	亞伯拉罕	Yǎbwólāhǎn	Abaaklàaihón
Absalom n.	押沙龍	Yāshālúng	AatsàlùHng
absolution n.	赦罪	shèdzwèi	sejeuiH
abstinence n.	齋戒	jāijyè	jàaigaai
abyss n.			
-hell	陰間	yīnjyōn	yàmgàan
-bottomless gulf	深淵	shēnywān	sàmyùn
acclamation n.	歡呼文	hwōnhūwén	fùnfùmàHn
accurse v. t.	咒詛	jòudzǔ	jaujo
acolyte n.	輔祭	fǔjì	fuHjai
actualism n.	現實論	syànshílwùn	yiHnsaHtleuHn
Adam n.	亞當	Yǎdāng	Adòng
advent n.	降臨節	jyànglínjyó	gonglàHmjit
Advocate			
-n.Comforter	保惠師	Bǎuhwèishī;	BáuwaiHsī;
-v. t. defend	辯護	byànhù	biHnwuH
aestheticism n.	唯美主義	wéimǎijǔyì	wàiHmóiHjyúyiH
agnosticism n.	不可知論	bùkějīlwùn	bāthójìleuHn
agony n.	傷痛	shāngtùng	sèungtung
Allah n.	阿拉	Alā	Alāai

All Saints'Day n.	諸聖日	Jūshèngr̀	JyùsingyaHt
All Souls'Day	追思日	Jwēiszr̀	JèuisìyaHt
almighty a.	全能	chywánnéng;	chyùHnnàHng
	無所不能	wúswǒbùnéng	mǒuHsóbātnàHng
alms n.	賙濟	jōujì;	jàujai;
	施捨	shīshě	sìsé
Alpha n.	阿拉法	Alāfā	Alàaifaat
altar n.	祭壇	jìtán;	jaitàaHn;
-book	禮儀書	lǐyíshū;	láiHyìHsyū;
-bread	祭餅	jìbǐng;	jaibéng;
-cards	禮文表	lǐwénbyǎu;	láiHmàHnbíu;
-cover	聖桌布	shèngjwōbù	singjeukbou(singtóibou)
amen int.	阿們	àmen	amùHn
ambo n.	讀經台	dújìngtái	duHkgìngtói
Ambrose, St. n.	聖安波羅修	Shèngānbwōlwó-syōu	SingònbòlòHsàu
Anabaptists n.	重洗派	Chúngsyǐpài	ChùHngsáipaai
anchorite n.	隱士	yǐnshr̀	yánsiH
Andrew n.	安得烈	Āndélyè	NgōndākliHt
angel n.			
-Prot.	天使	tyānshǐ;	tìnsi;
-R. Cath.	天神	tyānshén	tìnsàHn
angelology n.	天使論	tyānshǐlwùn	tìnsileuHn
Anglican Church n.	聖公會	Shènggūnghwèi	Singgùngwúi
Anointed One n.	受膏者	Shòugāujě	SauHgòujé
anomaly n.	反常	fāncháng	fáansèuHng
anti-Christ n.	敵基督者	díJīdūjě	diHkGēidūkjé
Antioch	安提阿	Āntíà	Ngòntàiha
antiphon n.	對應唱和	dwèiyìngchànghé	deuiyingcheungwòH

apocrypha n.	次經	tsżjïng;	chigìng;
	旁經	pángjïng	pòHnggìng
apostasy n.	背教	bèijyàu	buigaau
apostle n.	使徒	shītú	sitòuH
Apostle's Creed n.	使徒信經	shītú syìnjïng	sitòuH seunging
apostolic age n.	使徒時代	shītú shīdài	sitòuH sìHdoiH
Arabia n.	亞拉伯	Yălābwó	Alāaibaak
Aramaic n.	亞蘭文	Yălánwén	AlàaHnmàHn
archaeology n.	考古學	kăugŭsywé	háaugúhoHk
archangel n.	天使長	tyānshījăng	tìnsijéung
archbishop n.	大主教	dàjŭjyàu	daaiHjyúgaau
archdeacon n.	會吏總	hwèilìdzŭng	wuiHletHjúng
ark of the Covenant n.	約櫃	ywēgwăi	yeukgwaiH
articles of faith n.	信條	syìntyáu	seuntìuH
ascension n.	升天	shēngtyān	sìngtìn
Ash Wednesday n.	蒙灰日	ménghwēir	mùHngfùiyaHt
assemblies of God	神召會	Shénjàuhwèi	SàHnjiuHwúi
Assumption, Feast of the	聖母升天節	Shèngmŭshēng- tyānjyé	SingmóuHsìngtìnjit
atonement n.	贖罪	shúdzwèi	suHkjeuiH
Augustine n.	奧古斯丁	Aùgŭszdïng	Ougúsidìng
Authorised Version	欽定譯本	Chīndìngyìbĕn	YàmdiIIngyiIIkbún
auto-suggestion n.	自己提示	dżjītíshì	jiHgéitàiHsiH
Ave Maria n.	聖母頌	Shèngmŭsùng	SingmóuHjuHng

B

Baal n.	巴力	Bālì	BàliHk
babe n.	嬰孩	yïnghái	yìnghòiH
Babel n.	巴別	Bābyé	BàbiHt

Babylon n.	巴比倫	Bābǐlwún	BàbéilèuHn
backslider n.	退後信徒	twèihòu syìntú	teuihauH seuntòuH
banns n.	結婚預告	jyēhwūnyùgàu	gitfànyuHgou
baptismal a.			
-candidate	預備受洗者	yùbèishòusyǐjě	yuHbeiHsauHsáijé
-certificate	洗禮証	syǐlǐjèng	sáiláiHjing
-name	受洗名	shòusyǐmíng	sauHsáiméng
Baptist Church n.	浸信會	Jìnsyìnhwèi	Jamseunwúi
Barabbas n.	巴拉巴	Bālābā	Bālāaibā
beatitudes n.	八福	bāfú	baatfūk
behold v. t.	看哪	kàn na	hon a
believers n.	信徒	syìntú	seuntòuH
belonging n.	相屬性	syāngshǔsyìng	sèungsuHksing
belong to the Lord	屬主	shǔ Jyǔ	suHk Jyú
beloved Son n.	愛子	àidž	ngoijí
benediction n.	祝福	jùfú	jūkfūk
benevolence n.	仁愛	ránài	yàHnoi
bereaved p. a.	遺族	yídzú	wàiHjuHk
bereavement n.	喪失	sàngshř	songsāt
Bethany n.	伯大尼	Bwódàní	BaakdaaiHnèiH
Bethlehem n.	伯利恒	Bwólìhéng	BaakleiHhàHng
betrothal n.	訂婚禮	dìnghwūnlǐ	diHngfànláiH
Bible n.	聖經	Shèngjǐng	Singgìng
-Bible characters n.	聖經人物	Shèngjǐngrénwù	SinggìngyàHnmaHt
-Bible class	查經班	chájǐngbān	chàHgìngbàan
bill of divorce	休書	syōushū	yàusyù
Billy Graham n.	葛培理	Gěpéilǐ	GotpùiHléiH
birth control n.	節育	jyéyù	jityuHk

birthright n.	長子的名分	jăngdždemíngfèn	jáungjidìkmìHngfaHn
black magic n.	黑法術	hēifăshù	hāakfaatseuHt
blessed p. a.	蒙福	méngfú	mùHngfūk
Book of Common Prayer n.	公禱書	gūngdăushū	gùngtóusyù
Book of Life n.	生命册	Shēngmìngtsè	SàngmiHngchaak
Book of Odes n.	詩經	Shrjìng	Sìgìng
Brahmanism n.	婆羅門教	Pwólwóménjyàu	PòHlòHmùHngaan
break bread	擘餅	bwōbǐng	maakbéng
breviary n.	日課經	rkèjìng	yaHtfogìng
Buddha n.	佛	Fwó	FaHt
Buddhism n.	佛教	Fwójyàu	FaHtgaau
burning bush	火燒荆棘	hwŏshāujìngjí	fósługìnggǐk
burnt offering	燔祭	fánji	fàaHnjai

C

Caesar n.	該撒	Gāisā	Gòısaat
Cain n.	該隱	Gāiyǐn	GòiyáHn
call of God	蒙召	méngjàu	mùHngjiuH
calling (vocation)	神召	shénjàu;	sàHnjiuII;
	呼召	hūjàu	fùjiuH
Calvin n.	加爾文	Jyāěrwén	GàyíHmàHn
Calvinism n.	加爾文主義	Jyāěrwénjŭyì	GàyíHmàHnjyúyiII
camp meeting	露天聚會	lùtyānjyùhwèi	louHtìnjeuiHwuiH
Cana n.	迦拿	Jyāná	GànàH
Canaan n.	迦南	Jyānán	GànàaHm
Capernaum n.	迦百農	Jyābăinúng	GàbaaknùHng
canon n.	法典	fădyăn;	faatdǐn;
-in liturgy	祝聖文	jùshèngwén;	jūksingmàHn;
-law	教規	jyàugwēi;	gaaukwài;

-office	法政會長	fǎjènghwèijǎng	faatjingwuiHjéung
canticle n.	頌	sùng	juHng
cardinal n.	紅衣主教	húngyijūjyàu	hùHngyìjyúgaau
-principles	基本原則	jìběnywándzé	gèibúnyùHnjāk
Carmel, Mount	迦密山	Jyāmìshān	GàmaHtsàan
carol n.	樂歌	lègē	loHkgō
cassock n.	禮袍	lǐpáu	láiHpòuH
cast out devils	趕鬼	gǎngwěi	góngwái
catacombs n.	墓窟	mùkū	mouHfāt (mouHduHng)
catechism n.	要理問答	yàulǐwèndá	yiuléiHmaHndaap
cathedral n.	座堂	dzwòtáng	joHtòHng
catholic n.			
-universal	大公教會	dàgūngjyàuhwèi	daaiHgùnggaauwúi
-Roman Catholic	天主教	Tyānjǔjyàu	Tìnjyúgaau
celibacy n.	獨身制	dúshēnjǐ	duHksànjai
centurian	百夫長	bǎifūjǎng	baakfùjéung
ceremonies, assistant in	輔禮人	fǔlǐrén	fúHláiHyàHn
ceremony of dedication	告成之禮	gàuchéngjǐlǐ	gousìHngjìláiH
chalice n.	聖餐杯	shèngtsānbēi	singchāanbūi
chancel n.	聖所	shèngswǒ	singsó
chaos n.	混沌	hwùndwùn	waHndeuHn
chapel n.	小禮拜堂	syǎulǐbàitáng	síuláiHbaaitòHng
chaplain n.	特務牧師	tèwùmùshī	daHkmouHmuHksī
-in the army	軍中牧師	jyūnjūngmùshī	gwànjùngmuHksī
chasten v. t.	懲戒	chěngjyè;	chìHnggaai;
	懲罰	chěngfá	chìHngfaHt
chastity n.	貞潔	jēngjyé	jìnggit
cherish v. t.			
-nurture	撫育	fǔyù;	fúyuHk;

-take care of	照顧	jàugù	jiugu
Cherubim	噎略咱	Jilùbwó	GèilouHbaak
chief pastor	牧長	mùjăng	muHkjéung
chief priests	祭司長	jìsžjăng	jaisìjéung
chosen people	選民	sywănmín	syúnmàHn
chosen vessel	蒙選的器皿	múngsywănde chìming	mùHngsyúndikheimiHng
Christ n.	基督	Jĭdū	Gēidūk
-agony of	基督傷痛	Jidūshāngtùng	Gēidūksèungtung
-coming again of	基督再來	Jidūdzàilái	GēidūkjoilóıH
-example of	基督的榜樣	Jidūdebăngyàng	GēidūkdikbóngyeuHng
-geneology of	基督家譜	Jĭdūjyāpŭ	Gēidūkgàpóu
-the Lordship of	基督為首	Jidūwéishŏu	GēidūkwàiHsáu
christian n.	基督徒	jidūtú	gēidūktòuH
-call	蒙召	méngjàu	mùIIngjiuH
-education	基督教教育	Jĭdūjyàujyàuyù	GēidūkgaaugaauyuHk
-soldier	基督精兵	Jĭdūjingbing	Gēidūkjingbìng
Christian and Missionary Alliance	宣道會	Sywāndàuhwèi	SyùndouHwúi
Christianity n.	基督教	Jĭdūjyàu	Gēidūkgaau
Christmas n.	聖誕節	Shèngdànjyé	Singdaanjit
Christology n.	基督論	Jĭdūlwùn	GēidūkleuHn
church n.	教會	jyàuhwèi;	gaauwúi;
	禮拜堂	lĭhàitáng	láiHbaaıtòHng
-building	教堂	jyàutáng	gaautòHng
-dedication	獻堂典禮	syàntángdyănlĭ	hintòHngdínláiH
-discipline	教會管理法	jyàuhwèigwănlĭfă	gaauwúigúnléiHfaat
-government	教會行政	jyàuhwèisyíngjèng	gaauwúihàHngjing
-history	教會歷史	jyàuhwèilìshř	gaauwúiliHksí
-magazine	教會報	jyàuhwèibàu	gaauwúibou

-members	教友	jyàuyǒu	gaauyáuH
-organization	教會組織	jyàuhwèidzǔjr̄	gaauwúijóujik
-policy	教會政策	jyàuhwèijèngtsè	gaauwúijingchaak
-ritual	禮拜儀式	lǐbàiyishr̀	láiHbaaiyìHsīk
-school	教會學校	jyàuhwèisywésyàu	gaauwúihoHkhaauH
Church of Nazarene	宣聖會	Sywānshènghwèi	Syùnsingwúi
circumcision n.	割禮	gēlǐ	go tláiH
city god	城隍神	chénghwàngshén	sìHngwòHngsàHn
Clement n.	革利免	Gélìmyǎn	GaakleiHmíHn
clergy n.	牧師	mùshr̄	muHksī
clergy house n.	牧師公寓	mùshr̄gūngyù	muHksīgùngyuH
collection n.	献捐	syànjywān	hingyùn
collects n.	祝文	jùwén	jūkmàHn
Comforter n.	保惠師	Bǎuhwèishr̄	BóuwaiHsī
commandment n.	命令	mìnglìng;	miHngliHng;
	誡命	jyèmìng	GaaimiHng
-ten commandments	十誡	shŕjyè	saHpgaai
common prayer book	公禱	gūngdǎushū	gùngtóusyù
communion n.			
-sacrement	聖餐	shèngtsān;	singchāan
-participation	參與	tsānyǔ	chàamyúH
-of saints	聖徒相通	shèngtúsyāngtūng	singtòuHsèungtùng
comparative religion	宗教比較	dzūngjyàubǐjyǎu	jùnggaaubéigaau
condescend to listen	垂聽	chwéitìng	sèuiHting
condescension n.	謙卑	chyānbēi	hìmbèi
confess sins	認罪	rèndzwèi	yiHngjeuiH
confirmation n.	堅振禮	jyānjènlǐ	gìnjanláiH
Confucianism n.	孔教	Kǔngjyàu;	Húnggaau;

	儒教	Rŭjyàu	YùHgaau
Confucius n.	孔子	Kŭngdž	Húngjí
congregation n.	區會	chyūhwèi	kèuiwúi
congregational n.	會眾	hwèijùng	wuiHjung
consecrate			
-v. t. dedicate	奉獻	fèngsyàn;	fuHnghin;
-a. devoted	虔誠	chyánchéng	kìHnsìHng
Constantine n.	康士坦丁	Kāngshìtăndìng	HòngsiIItáandìng
consummation n.	成全	chéngchywán	sìHngchyùHn
contemplation n.	靜觀	jìnggwān	jiHnggùn
contraception n.	避孕法	bìyùnfă	beiHyaHnfaat
convent n.	修女院	syŭmyŭywàn	sàunéuiyún
conversion n.	歸正	gwēijèng;	gwàijìng;
	改宗	găidzūng	góijùng
cornerstone n.	房角石	fángjyăushŕ	fòHnggokseHk
covenant n.	約	ywē	yeuk
-eternal covenant	永約	yŭngywē	wiHngyeuk
-covenant of grace	恩約	ēnywē	yànyeuk
covetousness n.	貪婪	tānlán	tàamlàaHm
Creator n.	創造者	Chwàngdzàujě;	ChongjōuHjé;
	造物的主	Dzàuwùdejŭ	JouHmaHtdìkjyú
crown n.	冠冕	gwānmyăn	gùmmìHn
-corruptible	能壞的冠冕	nénghwàide-gwānmyăn	nàHngwaaiHdìkgùnmiHn
-of life	生命的冠冕	shēngmìngde-gwānmyăn	sàngmiHngdìkgùnmiHn
-of glory	榮耀的冠冕	rúngyàude-gwānmyăn	wìIIngyiuHdìkgùnmiHn
-of righteousness	公義的冠冕	gūngyìdegwānmyăn	gùngyiHdìkgùnmiHn
-of thorns	荊棘冠冕	jīngjìgwānmyăn	gìnggìkgùnmíHn

crucifix n.	十架苦像	shŕjyàkŭsyàng	saHpgafújeuHng
crucifixion n.	十架苦刑	shŕjyàkŭsyíng	saHpgafúyìHng
crucify v. t.	釘十字架	dĭngshŕdżjyà	dèngsaHpjiHga
Crusades n.	十字軍	shŕdżjyūn	saHpjiHgwān
crypt n.	教堂地窖	jyàutángdìjyàu	gaautòHngdeiHgaau (gaautòHngdeiHlòuH)
cult n.	崇拜	chúngbài;	sùHngbaai;
	祭儀	jìyí	jaiyìH
Cumberland Presbyterian Mission	金巴倫長老會	Jīnbālwúnjăng-lăuhwèi	GàmbàlèuHnjéunglóuH
curate n.	副牧師	fùmùshŕ	fumuHksì
custom of the world	世俗	shìsú	saijuHk
cut off from God	與神隔絕	yŭ Shén géjywé	yúH SàHn gaakjyuHt

D

daily vacation Bible school	夏令聖經班	syàlìngShèng-jīngbān	haHliHngSing-gingbāan
Dalai Lama n.	達賴	Dálài	DaaHtlaaiH
Damascus n.	大馬色	Dàmăsè	DaaiHmáHsik
damnation n.	永刑	yŭngsyíng	wìHngyìHng
Daniel n.	但以理	Dànyĭlĭ	DaaHnyĭHléiH
Darwin n.	達爾文	Dáěrwén	DaaHtyĭHmàHn
David n.	大衞	Dàwéi	DaaiHwaiH
Day of Atonement	贖罪節	shúdzwèijyé	suHkjeuiHjit
Day of Judgment	審判日	shĕnpànr̀	sámpunyaHt
day of redemption	得贖的日子	déshúderdz	dāksuHkgeyaHhji
day of salvation	拯救的日子	jĕngjyòuderdz	chìnggaugeyaHtjí
dead faith	死信心	sžsyìnsyĭn	séiseunsàm
Dead Sea n.	死海	Sžhăi	Séihói
deism n.	自然神論	dżránshénlwùn	jiHyìHnsàHnleuHn
deity n.	神明	shénmíng	sàHnmìHng

deliver from evil	脫離兇惡	twōlisyūngè	tyutlèiHhùngngok
demon possession	被鬼附着	bèigwěifùje	beiHgwáifuHjeuHk (gwáiséuHngsàn)
demon worship	拜鬼	bàigwěi	baaigwái
descend into Hades	下陰間	syàyīnjyān	haHyāmgàan
determinism n.	定命論	dìngmìnglwùn	diHngmiHngleuHn
devotional retreat	靈修	língsyōu	lìHngsàu
diaconate n.	執事制	jíshìjì	jāpsiHjai
dialectical materialism	辯証神學	byànjèngshénsywé	biHnjingsàHnhoHk
diocese n.	教區	jyàuchyū	gaaukèui
Dionysius n.	狄尼修	Dínísyōu	DiHknèiHsāu
discretion n.	判斷	pàndwàn;	pundyun;
	辨別	byànbyé	biHnbiHt
discrimination n.	辨別	byànbyé;	biHnbiHt;
	差別待遇	chābyédàiyù	chàbiHtdoiHyuH
disobedience, sons of	背逆之子	bèinìjīdž	buiyiHkjìji
Divinity n.			
-Protest.	上帝	Shàngdì;	SeuHngdai;
	神	Shén;	SàHn;
-Rom. Cath.	天主	Tyānjŭ	Tìnjyú
Divine nature	神性	Shénsyìng	SàHnsing
Divine personality	神格	Shéngé	SàHngaak
divine power	神能	Shénnéng	SàHnnàHng
Dominicans n.	多米尼古派	Dwōmínígŭpài	DòmáiHnèiHgúpaai
Doomsday n.	世界末日	shìjyèmwòr;	saigaaimuHtyaHt;
	審判之日	shěnpànjīr	sámpunjìyaHt
double personality n.	雙重人格	shwangchúngréngé	sèungchùHngyàHngaak
double-minded man	心懷二意	syīnghwáièryì	sàmwàaiHyiHyi
Doxology n.	讚頌	dzànsùng;	jaanjuHng;
	三一頌	sānyìsùng	sāamyātjuHng

E

early church	元 始 教 會	ywánshřjyàuhwèi;	yùHnchígaauwúi
	早 期 教 會	dzăuchǐjyàuhwèi	jóukèiHgaauwúi
earnestly beseech	懇 求	kěnchyóu	hánkàuH
ears become dull	耳 朵 發 沈	ěrdwōfāchén	yíHdéufaatchàHm
Easter n.	復 活 節	fùhwójyé	fuHkwuHtjit
Ebenezer	以 便 以 謝	Yǐbyànyǐsyè	YíHbiHnyíHjeH
ecclesiastical a.	敎 會 的	jyàuhwèide	gaauwúidǐk
-year	敎 會 年 曆	jyàuhwèinyánlǐ	gaauwúinìHnliHk
ecstasy n.	狂 喜	kwángsyǐ;	kòHnghéi;
	恍 惚	fāngfú	fóngfāt
ecumenical a.	普 世 性	pǔshǐsyìng	póusaising
Eden n.	伊 甸 園	Yídyànywán	YìdinyùHn
effect salvation	施 行 拯 救	shīsyíngjěngjyòu	sìhàHngchìnggau
Egypt n.	埃 及	Āiji	ÒikaHp
ego n.	自 我	dzwǒ	jiHngóH
egotism n.	利 己 主 義	lìjǐjǔyì	leiHgéijyúyiH
Elias n.	以 利 亞	Yǐlìyǎ	YíHleiHnga
Elizabeth n.	以 利 沙 伯	Yǐlìshābwó	YíHleiHsàbaak
enter the church	入 敎	rùjyàu	yaHpgaau
enter the narrow gate (LK. 13:23)	進 窄 門	jìnjǎimén	jeunjaakmùHn
Episcopalian n.	聖 公 會	Shènggūnghwèi	Singgùngwúi
epistle n.	書 信	shūsyìn	syùseun
eradication of sin	罪 惡 除 根	dzwèièchúgēn	jeuiHngokchèuiHgàn
eremite n.	隱 士	yǐnshř	yánsiH
Esau n.	以 掃	Yǐsǎu	yíHsou
eschatology n.	末 世 論	mwòshřlwùn	muHtsaileuHn

Esther n.	以斯帖	Yǐsztyē	YíHsìtip
eternal a.	永遠	yǔngywǎn	wiHngyúHn
-glory	永遠的榮耀	yǔngywǎnderúngyàu	wiHngyúHndikwiHngyiuH
-Gospel	永遠的福晉	yǔngywǎndefúyin	wiHngyúHndikfūkyàm
-hope	永生的盼望	yǔngshēugdepànwàng	wiIngsàngdik paanmoIIng
-life	永生	yǔngshēng	wiHngsàng
-redemption	永遠救贖	yǔngywǎnjyòushú	wiHngyúHugausuIIk
-Salvation	永遠得救	yǔngywǎndéjyòu	wiHngyúHndākgau
-truth	永在之眞理	yǔngdʐàijrjēnlǐ	wiHngjoiHjijànléiH
-judgment (Heb. 0.2)	永遠審判	yǔngywǎnshěnpàn	wiHngyúnsámpun
eternally existent	永在	yǔngdʐài	wiHngjoiII
eternity n.	永恆	yǔnghéng	wiHnghàHng
Eucharist n.	感恩;	gǎnēn;	gámyàn;
	聖餐禮	shèngtsānlǐ	singchāanláiH
eugenics n.	優生學	yōushēngsywé	yàusànghoHk
evangelical a.	福晉;	fúyin;	fūkyàm;
	佈道	bùdàu	boudouII
evangelism n.	佈道	bùdàu	boudouH
evangelist n.	佈道家	bùdàujyā	boudouHga
evangelistic band	佈道團	bùdàutwán	boudouIItyùIIn
Eve	夏娃	Syàwá	Hahwà
Evensong n.	晚禱	wǎndǎu	máaHntóu
everlasting a.			
-endless	無窮;	wúchyúng;	mòuHkùHng;
-lasting forever	常存;	chángtswún;	sèuHngchyùHn;
-life	永生;	yǔngshēng;	wiHngsàng;
-bitterness	永苦	yǔngkǔ	wiHngfú

-Covenant	永約	yŭngywē	wíHngyeuk
-destruction	永遠沉淪	yŭngywănchénlwún	wíHngyúHnchàHmlèuHn
-dominion	國存到萬代	gwótswúndàu wàndài	gwokchyùHndou maaHndoiH
-Father	永在的父	yŭngdzàideFù	wíHngjoiHdĭkFuH
-fire	永火	yŭnghwŏ	wíHngfó
-power	永能	yŭngnéng	wíHngnàHng
-punishment	永刑	yŭngsyíng	wíHngyìHng
evil root	惡根	ègēn	ngokgàn
evil spirit	邪靈	syélíng	chèHlìHng
exceeding greatness	何等浩大	hédĕnghàudà	hòHdánghouHdaaiH
exceeding joy	歡歡喜喜	hwēnhwānsyĭsyĭ	fànfùnhéihéi
exorcism n.	驅魔祛鬼	chyūmwóchyègwĕi	kèuimòhipgwái
expiation n.	贖罪	shúdzwèi	suHkjeuiH
Exultation of Christ	基督之升高	Jīdūjīshēnggāu	Gēidūkjisìnggòu
eyes dulled	眼睛昏迷	yănjinghwūnmí	ngáaHnjĭngfànmàiH

F

| faculty of knowing | 知能 | jīnéng | jìnàHng |
| Fa-hsien (Budd.) | 法顯 | Făsyăn | Faathín |

A famous Chinese Buddhist priest who went to India by land in A. D. 399 and returned by sea in A. D. 414 having visited Ceylon and Sumatra on his way home. He spent the rest of his days translating Buddhist Sutras into Chinese.

faith healing	信心醫病	syìnsyìnyìbìng	seunsàmyìbeHng
Fall, the	墮落	dwòlwò	doHloHk
Fall of Man	人類的墜落	rénlèidejwèilwò	yàHnleuiHdĭkjeuiHloH
fall into sin	陷於罪惡	syànyúdzwèiè	haaHmyùjeuiHngok
false prophets	假先知	jyăsyānjĭ	gásìnjì
false tongue	詭詐的舌頭	gwĕijàdeshétou	gwáijadĭksiHttàuH

false witness	假見証	jyăjyànjèng	gáginjing
Family Worship	家庭禮拜	jyātínglĭbài	gàtiHngláiHbaai
fast			
-the break of	開齋	kāijāi	hòijàai
Abba Father	阿爸父	Àbāfù	AbàfuH
Father of light	衆光之父	Jùnggwōngjīfù	JunggwòngjìfuH
Father of spirits	萬靈的父	Wànlingdefù	MaaHnlìHngdikfuH
Feast of Dedication	修殿節	Syōndyànjyé	SàudiHnjit
Feast of Tabernacles	住棚節	Jùpéngjyé	JyuHpàHngjit
Feast of Unleavened Bread	除酵節	Chújyàujyé	ChèuiHhàaujit
fetishism n.	物魅崇拜	wùmeichúngbài	mahItmeiHIsùHIngbaai
feudalism n.	封建制度	fēngjyànjrdù	fùngginjaidouH
field of the heart	心田	syīntyán	sàmtìHn
field of work	工作區	gūngdzwòjyū	gùngjokkèui
fight a good fight	打那美好的仗	dănàmĕihăudejàng	dánáHméiHhóudikjeung
filled with the Holy Spirit	被聖靈充滿	bèiShènglingchūngmăn	beiHSingliHngchùngmúHn
Finnish Missionary Society	芬蘭西差會	Fēnlánsyichāihwèi	FànlàaHnsàichànaiwúi
Fire of the Holy Spirit	聖靈的火	Shènglingdehwŏ	SingliHngdikfó
firmly stand	站立得穩	jànlidéwēn	jaaHmlaHpdākwáu
first place	首位	shŏuwèi	sáuwaiH
first fruits	初熟的果子	chūshúdegwŏdz	chòsuHkdikgwóji
	初結的果子	chūjyēdegwŏdz	chògitdikgwóji
fishers of Men (Mark 1:17)	得人漁夫	dérényúfū	dākyàHnyùHfù
flagellation n.	鞭撻己身	byāntājĭshēn	bìntaatgéisàn
foolishness of the Cross	十字架的愚昧	shŕdżjyàdeyúmèi	saHpjiHgadìkyùHmeiH
Foreign Mission	西差會	Syichāihwèi	Sàichànaiwúi
fortitude n.	堅忍	jyānrĕn;	gìnyáHn;

	剛毅	gāngyì	gòngngaiH
Forty-two Articles	四十二信條	sɜshfèrsyìntyáu	seisaHpyiHseuntìuH
Foundation Stone Ceremony	奠基典禮	dyànjidyǎnlǐ	dingèidínláiH
Four Books	四書	Sɜshū	Seisyù

The four books referred to are the Confucian Analects, the Great Learning, the Doctrine of the Mean, and Mencius.

frankincense n.	乳香	rŭsyāng	yúHhèung
free-will n.	自由意志	dɜyóuyìjɨ;	jiHyàuHyiji;
-offering	自由奉献	dɜyóufèngsyàn	jiHyàuHfuHnghìn
future life n.	來生	láishēng	lòiHsàng

G

Galilee n.	加利利	Jyālìlì	GàleiHleiH
Galileo n.	伽利略	Jyālìlywè	GàleiHleuk
Gandhi n.	甘地	Gāndì	GàmdeiH
Ganges n.	恆河	Hénghé	HàHnghòH
Garden of Eden	伊甸園	Yídyànywán	YìdiHnyùHn
General Thanksgiving	總謝文	dzŭngsyèwén	júngjeHmàHn
genocide n.	集體屠殺	jitɨtúshā	jaaHptáitòuHsaat
genuflection n.	屈一膝	chyūyìsyi	wātyātsāt
Gethsemane n.	客西馬尼	Kèsyimǎní	HaaksàimáHnèiH
Gideon n.	基甸	Jídyàn	GèidiHn
gird the loins	束腰	shùyìu	chūkyìu
give grace	施恩	shrēn	sìyàn
gloria in Excelsis	榮歸主頌	rúnggwēijŭsùng	wìHnggwàijyújuHng
God n.	上帝	Shàngdì;	SeuHngdai;
	神	Shén	SàHn
-R. Cath.	天主	Tyānjŭ	Tìnjyú

God in the Bible

1. Jehovah (Ex. 6:3)	耶和華	Yēhéhwá	YèHwòHwàH
2. I am (Ex. 3:14)	自有的	dzyǒude	jiHyáuHdik
3. Living God (Deut. 5:26)	永生上帝	yǔngsheng Shàngdì	wǐIngsàng SeuHngdai
4. God of Heaven (Ezra 5:11)	天地之上帝	tyāndìjī Shàngdì	tìndeiHjì SeuHngdai
5. God of Hosts (Ps. 80:7)	萬軍之上帝	wànjyūnjī Shàngdì	MaaHngwànjì SeuHngdai
6. Holy One (Ps. 16:10)	聖者	Shèngjě	Singjé
7. Holy One of Israel (Ps. 71:22)	以色列的聖者	Yìsèlyède Shèngjě	YìHsìkliHtdik Singjé
8. Lord of Hosts (Is. 1:24)	萬軍之主	Wànjyūnjī Jǔ	MaaHngwànjì Jyú
9. Lord of Lords (Rev. 17:14)	萬主之主	Wànjǔjī Jǔ	MaaHnjyújì Jyú
10. Mighty God (Ps. 50:1)	大能者上帝	Dànéngjě Shàngdì	DaaiHnàHngjé SeuHngdai
11. Most High (Ps. 7:17)	至高者	Jìgāujě	Jigòujé
12. Most High God (Ps. 57:2)	至高的上帝	Jìgāude Shàngdì	Jigōudìk SeuHngdai
13. Father of Light (Jas. 1:17)	眾光之父	Jùnggwāngjī Fù	Junggwòngjì FuII
14. King of Kings (Rev. 17:14)	萬王之王	wànwángjīwáng	MaaHnwòIHngjìwòHng
25. Father (Matt. 11:25)	父阿	Fù a	FuII a
God be with you	上帝與你同在	Shàngdì yǔ nǐ tíngdzài	ScuHngdai yúH néiH tùHngjoiH
Godchild n.	主內子女	Jǔnèi dznyǔ	JyúnoiH jínéuiH
Goddess of Mercy	觀音	gwānyin	gùnyàm

The most important of the Bodhisattvas in Chinese Buddhism. She has been described as the "Madonna of Asia" as she is much loved by the women of China.

godfather n.	教父	jyàufù	gaaufuH
Godhead	神性	shénsyìng	sàHnsing
godmother n.	教母	jyàumǔ	gaaumóuH

godparents n.	教父教母	jyàufùjyàumŭ	gaaufuHgaaum6uH
gods n.	神明	shénmíng	sàHnmìHng
Goethe n.	歌德	Gēdé	Gōdāk
Golden Rule n.	金科玉律	jinkēyùlyù	gàmfòyuHkleuHt
Golgotha	各各他	Gègètā	Gokgoktà
gospel n.	福音	fúyīn	fūkyàm
gospel van n.	佈道車	bùdàuchē	boudouHchè
grace before meals	謝飯祈禱	syèfànchídǎu	jeHfaaHnkèiHtóu
graft			
–v. t.	接枝	jyējī;	jipjì;
–n.	貪污	tānwū	tàamwù
Grail, the Holy n.	聖杯盤	shèngbēipán	singbūipùHn
graven image	雕刻偶像	dyāukèǒusyàng	dǐuhāakngáuH-jeuHng
great calamity	大災難	dàdzāinàn	daaiHjòinaaHn
Great Ultimate (Taoism)	太極	tàijí	taaigiHk
Great Unity (Confucianism)	大同	dàtúng	daaiHtùHng
Greek Orthodox Church	希臘正教教會	Syīlàjèngjyàu jyàuhwèi	HèilaaHpjinggaau gaauwúi
Gregorian Calendar	貴格利日曆	Gwèigélìrlì	GwaigaakleiHyaHtliHl
growth (spiritual)	長進	jǎngjìn	jéungjeun
guardian Angel	守護天使	shǒuhùtyānshǐ	sáuwuHtìnsi
guest preacher	特請傳道	tèchǐngchwándàu	daHkchéngchyùHndou
guidance n.	引導	yǐndǎu	yáHndouH

H

Hallel n.	讚美詩篇	dzànmĕishīpyān	jaanméiHsipin
hallelujah	哈利路亞	hālìlùyǎ	hāleiHlouHnga
Halloween n.	諸聖日前夕	jūshèngrìchyánsyī	jyùsingyaHtchìHnjiHk

halo n.	榮光圈	rúnggwāngchywān	wìHnggwònghyūn
Harvest Thanksgiving	秋收感恩節	chyōushōugǎnēnjyé	chàusàugámyànjit
Heavenly Father	天父	Tyānfù	TìnfuH
Henotheism n.	大神論	dàshénlwùn	daaiHsàIInleuIIn
Herod n.	希律	Syīlyù	HèileuHt
hexateuch n.	六經	lyòujīng	luHkgìng
hieroglyph n.	象形文字	syàngsyingwéndz̀	jeuHngyìHngmàHnjiH
High Church	高派教會	gāupàijyàuhᵥwèi	gòupaaigaauwúi
high priest	大祭司	dàjìsz̄	daaiHjaisī
Hinduism n.	印度教	Yìndùjyàu	YandouHgaau
Holy Communion	聖餐	shèngtsān	singchāan
Holy place	聖所	shèngawǒ	singsó
Holy Scripture	聖經	Shèngiīng	SīnggÌng
Holy Spirit	聖靈	Shèngling	SinglìHng
Holy temple	聖殿	Shèngdyàn	SingdiHn
Hosanna	和散那	hésànnà	wòHsaannáH
host of heaven (stars)	天上的萬象	tyānshàngdewàn-syàng	tìnseuHngdikmaaHn-jeuHng
host of heaven (angels)	天上萬軍	tyānshàngwànjyūn	tìnseuHngmaaHngwàn
house to house evangelism	逐家佈道	júlyābùdàu	juHkgàboudouH

I

icon n.	圖像	túsyàng	tòuHjeuHng
idealism n.	唯心論	wéisyīnlwùn	wàiHsàmleuHn
ideology n.	觀念學	gwānnyànsywé;	gùnniHmhoHk;
	意識形態	yìshìsyīngtài	yisìkyìHngtaai
idolatry n.	偶像崇拜	ǒusyàngchúnghài	ngáuHjeuHngsùHngbaai
image n.			
-of God	神的形像	Shéndesyíngsyàng;	SàIIndìkyìHngjeuHng;

-graven	雕像	dyāusyàng;	dīujeuHng;
-molten	鑄像	jùsyàng	jyujeuHng
Immaculate Conception	聖靈懷孕	Shènglínghwáiyùn	SinglìHngwàaiHyaHn
Immanuel n.	以馬內利	yǐmǎnèilì	yíHmáHnoiHleiH
immensity n.	廣大無量	gwǎngdàwúlyàng	gwóngdaaiHmòuH-leuHng
immortality n.	靈魂不滅	línghwúnbúmyè	lìHngwaHnbātmiHt
impartiality n.	公平	gūngpíng;	gùngpìHng;
	不偏	bùpyān	bātpìn (m̀pìnsàm)
impeccable a.	無罪	wúdzwèi;	mòuHjeuiH;
	無瑕疵	wúsyátsż	mòuHhàHchì
implication n.	含意	hányì;	hàHmyi;
	含蓄	hánsyù	hàHmchūk
in the name of the Lord	奉主名	fèng Jǔ míng	fuHng Jyú mìHng
incest n.	亂倫	lwànlwún;	lyuHnlèuHn;
	血族相姦	syědzúsyāngjyān	hyutjuHksèunggàan
induction n.	歸納法	gwēinàfǎ;	gwàinaaHpfaat;
	授職儀式	shòujŕyìshŕ	sauHjikyìHsĩk
indulgence n.	贖罪券	shúdzwèijywàn	suHkjeuiHgyun
infallibity, theory of	無謬誤說	wúnyòuwùshwō	mòuHmauHngHsyut
infant baptism	嬰孩受洗	yìngháishòusyǐ	yìnghòiHsauHsái
inferiority complex	自卑感	dżbēigǎn	jiHbèigám
infidel n.	異教徒	yìjyàutú	yiHgaautòuH
inhibition n.	抑制作用	yìjŕdzwòyùng	yìkjaijokyuHng
inner man n.	心靈	syìnlíng;	sàmlìHng;
	內心	nèisyìn;	noiHsàm;
	內己	nèijǐ	noiHgéi
insight n.	洞察	dùngchá;	duHngchaat;
	看破	kànpwò	honpo (táipo)

Introduction to New Testament	新約導論	Syinywēdăulwùn	SànyeukdouHleuHn
Introduction to Old Testament	舊約導論	Jyòuywēdăulwùn	GauHyeukdouHleuHn
investiture n.	授權禮	shòuchywánlĭ	sauHkyùHnláiH
Invitation n.	宣召	sywānjàu	syùnjiuH
invitatory n.	宣召文	sywānjàuwén	syùnjiuHmàHn
riony n.	超理性	chāulĭsyìng;	chìuléiHsing;
	非理性	fēilĭsyìng	fèiléiHsing
Isaiah n.			
-Prot.	以賽亞	Yĭsàiyă;	YíHchoinga;
-R. Cath.	依撒意亞	Yĭsāyìyă	Yìsaatyinga
Islam n.	伊斯蘭教	Yĭszláojyàu	YìsìlàaHngaau
Israel n.	以色列	Yĭsèlyè	YiHsìkliHt

J

Jacob n.	雅各	Yăgè	NgáIIgok
Jacobites n.	雅各教派	Yăgèjyàupài	NgáHgokgaaupaai
Jahweh (Hebrew for God)	雅巍	Yăwèi	NgáHngaiH
Jehovah n.	耶和華	Yēhéhwá	YèHwòHwàH
Jehovah's Witnesses	耶和華見證人	Yēhéhwájyàn-jengrén	YèHwòHwàH ginjingyàHn
Joremiah n.	耶利米	Yēlĭmĭ	YèHleiHmáiH
Jericho n.	耶利哥	Yēlĭgē	YèHleiHgō
Jerusalem n.	耶路撒冷	Yēlùsālěng	YèHlouHsaatláaHng
Jesus n.	耶穌	Yēsū	YèHsōu
Jesus Christ	耶穌基督	Yēsū Jĭdū	YèHsōu Gēidūk
Jesus, in the name of	奉耶穌的名	fèng Yēsūdemíng	fuHng YèHsōudìkmìHng
Jew n.	猶太人	Yóutàirén	YàuHtaaiyàHn

Jesiut n.	耶穌會會員	Yēsūhwèihwèiywán	YèHsōuwúiwuiHyùHn
jingoism n.	主戰論	jŭjànlwùn	jyújinleuHn
Job n.	約伯	Ywēbwó	Yeukbaak
Joel	約珥	Ywēěr	YeukyíH
John	約翰	Ywēhàn	YeukhoHn
John the Baptist	施洗約翰	Shīsyǐ Ywēhàn	Sìsái YeukhoHn
join the church	入教	rùjyàu	yaHpgaau
Jonah n.	約拿	Ywēná	YeuknàH
Jonathan n.	約拿單	Ywēnádān	YeuknàHdāan
Jordan (river)	約但河	Ywēdànhé	YeukdaaHnhòH
Joseph n.	約瑟	Ywēsè	Yeuksāt
Joshua n.	約書亞	Ywēshūyǎ	Yeuksyùa
Jubilate n.	歡呼頌	hwānhūsùng	fùnfùjuHng
jubilee n.	禧年	syǐnyán	héinìHn
Judah n.	猶大	Yóudà	YàuHdaaiH
Judaism n.	猶太教	Yóutàijyàu	YàuHtaaigaau
judgement, Day of	審判日	shěnpànr̀	sámpunyaHt
justification n.	稱義	chēngyì	chìngyiH
justification by faith	因信稱義	yīnsyìnchēngyì	yànseunchìngyiH
just war	義戰	yìjàn	yiHjin
juvenile delinquency	少年罪行	shàunyán-dzwèisyíng	siunìHnjeuiHhàHng

K

kenotic theories	虛己說	syūjǐshwō	hèuigéisyut
King of ages	萬世之王	Wànshr̀jr̄wáng	MaaHnsaijìwòHng
King eternal	永世的君王	Yŭngshr̀de-jyūnwáng	WìHngsaidikgwànwòl
King of glory	榮耀的王	Rúngyàudewáng	WìHngyiuHdikwòHng
King of kings	萬王之王	Wànwángjr̄wáng	MaaHnwòHngjìwòHn

kingdom n.	國	gwó;	gwok;
	國度	gwódù	gwokdouH
-of Heaven	天國	Tyāngwó	Tìngwok
-of God	神的國	Shéndegwó	SàHndìkgwok
Kingship of Christ	基督爲王	Jidūwéiwáng	GēidūkwàiHwòHng
kneelers n.	跪禱者	gwèidăujě;	gwaiHtóujé;
	跪墊	gwèidyàn	gwaiHjin
knowledge of Christ	對基督的認識	dwèi Jidūderènshr	deui GēidūkdìkyiHngsik
knowledge of sin	知罪	jŕdzwèi	jìjeuiII
knowledge of the truth	明白眞道	míngbaijēndàu	mìHngbaaHkjàndouH
Koran n.	可蘭經	Kělànjīng	HólàaItngìng
Kuanyin (Goddess of Mercy)	觀音	gwonyin	gùnyàm

L

Lady, Our	聖母	Shèngmŭ	SingmóuH
laity n.	平信徒	píngsyìntú	pìHngseuntòuH
Lama n.	喇嘛	lămá	lamàH
Lamaism n.	喇嘛教	lămájyàu	lamàHgaau
Lamb of God	神的羔羊	Shénde Gāuyáng	SàIIndik GòuyèuIIng
Lao Tzu	老子	Lăudž	LóuHji

Born about 605 B.C.. The Tao Teh Ching or Bible of the Taoists is ascribed to him but modern scholars deny this. Lao Tzu was one of China's sages.

lapsed, the	背道信徒	bèidàusyìntú	buidouHseuntòuH
Last judgement	最後審判	dzwèihòushénpàn	jeuihauHsámpun
Last Supper	最後晚餐	dzwèihòuwăntsān	jeuihauHmáaHnchāan
Latter-day Saints	末世聖徒	Mwòshŕshèngtù	MulItsaisingtòuH
law-codes n.	法典	fădyăn	faatdín
laxity (moral)	弛緩(道德)	chŕhwăn(dàudé)	chìHwuHn(douHdēk)

lay hands on

  -as a deacon   按手   ànshǒu;   onsáu;

  -do violence   動手   dùngshǒu   duHngsáu

laying the foundation 奠基禮   dyànjilǐ   dingèiláiH

layreader n.   平信徒讀經者   píngsyìntúdújìngjě   pìHngseuntòuHduHk-gìngjé

layman n.

  -laity   平信徒   píngsyìntú;   pìHngseuntòuH;

  -non-expert   外行   wàiháng;   ngoiHhòHng;

  -Budd.   居士   jyūshr̀   gèuisiH

lectern n.   讀經臺   dújìngtái   duHgìngtòiH

Lent n.   大齋期   dàjāichī   daaiHjàaikèiH

Lenten period   預苦期   yùkǔchī   yuHfúkèiH

lesson, Scripture   經訓   Jīngsyùn   Gìngfan

Levite n.   利未人   Lìwèirén   LeiHmeiHyàHn

Lew, Timothy T'ing Fang   劉廷芳   Lyóu Tíng Fāng   LàuH TìHng Fòng

One of the outstanding Christian leaders of China. He holds numerous degrees, has written many books, and is prominent in various Christian Movements in China. Dean of the Yenching School of Religion.

licentiate n.   蒙特許者   méngtèsyǔjě   mùHngdaHkhéuijé

licentiousness n.   淫亂   yínlwàn   yàHmlyuHn

Life of Christ   基督生平   Jīdūshēngpíng   GēidūksàngpìHng

likeness of the Lord   主的樣式   Jǔdeyàngshr̀   JyúdìkyeuHngsìk

litany n.   應答祈禱   yìngdáchídǎu;   yingdaapkèiHtóu;

            總禱文   dzǔngdǎuwén   júngtóumàHn

liturgical service   儀式禮拜   yíshr̀lǐbài   yìHsìkláiHbaai

living bread   生命的糧   shēngmìngdelyáng   sàngmiHngdìklèuHng

living sacrifice   活祭   hwójì   wuHtjai

long for salvation	渴想救恩	kĕsyăngjyòuēn	hotséunggauyàn
look to Jesus	仰望耶穌	yăngwàng Yēsū	yéuHngmoHng YèHsōu
Lord n.	主	Jŭ	Jyú
-the Lord	主宰	Jŭdzăi	Jyújói
Lord, Angel of the	主之使者	Jŭjɪshɪ̆jĕ	Jyújìaijé
Lord God	主神	Jŭ Shén	Jyú SàHn
Lord Jesus	主耶穌	Jŭ Yēsū	Jyú YèHsōu
Lord Holy Spirit	主聖靈	Jŭ Shènglíng	Jyú SinglìHng
Lord of glory	榮耀的主	rúngyàude Jŭ	wìHngyiuIIdĭk Jyú
Lord of Hosts	萬軍之主	Wànjyūnjī Jŭ	MaaHngwànjì Jyú
Lord of lords	萬主之主	Wànjŭjɪjŭ	MaaHnjyújìjyú
Lord of Sabaoth	萬軍之主	Wànjyūnjɪjŭ	MaaHngwànjíjyú
Lord's day	主日	Jŭr	JyúyaHt
Lord's Prayer	主禱文	Jŭdăuwén	JyútóumàHn
Lord's Supper	聖餐	Shèngtsān	Singchāan
Lord's Table	聖桌	shèngjwō	singjeuk
Lot	羅得	Lwódé	LòHdāk
Loving Father	慈愛的父	Tsźàidé Fù	ChìHngoidik FuH
loving kindness	慈恩	tsźén	chìHyàn
low church	低派教會	dɪpàijyàuhwèi	dàipɐɐigaauwúi
Lucifer n.	魔王	Mwówáng	MòwòHng
	路司弗	Lùsźfú	LouHsifāt
Luke n.	路加	Lùjyā	LouHgà

lust n.			
-the lust of the flesh (1 Jn. 2: 16)	肉體的情慾	ròutĭdechíngyù	yuHktáidĭkchìHngyuHk
lustful thoughts	淫念	yínnyàn	yàHmniHm
lying p. a.	說謊	shwòhwăng	syutfòng (góngdaaiHwaH)

M

Macedonia n.

-Prot.	馬其頓	Măchídwùn;	MáHkèiHdeuHn;
-R. Cath.	馬塞道尼	Măsàidàuní	MáHsākdouHnèiH
macrocosm n.	大宇宙	dàyŭjòu	daaiHyúHjauH
Magnificat	聖母頌	Shèngmŭsùng	SingmóuHjuHng
Mammon (riches)	瑪門(財利)	Mămén(tsáilì)	MáHmùHn (chòiHleiH)
Man, the Son of	人子	Réndž	YàHnjí
maniac n.	瘋狂者	fēngkwángjě	fùngkòHngjé
Manichaeism n.	摩尼教	Mwóníjyàu	MòneiHgaau
manna n.	嗎哪	măná	máHnàH
Mariolatry n.	聖母崇拜	Shèngmŭchúngbài	SingmóuHsùHngbaai
Mark n.	馬可	Măkě	MáHhó
Mary n.	馬利亞	Mălĭyă	MáHleiHnga

Mass n.

-R. Cath.	彌撒	mísā;	nèiHsaat;
-Budd.	念經	nyànjīng;	niHmgìng;
-high	大禮彌撒	dàlĭmísā;	daaiHláiHnèiHsaat;
-low	小禮彌撒	syăulĭmísā	síuláiHnèiHsaat
-nuptial	婚禮彌撒	hwūnlĭmísā	fànláiHnèiHsaat
Matthew n.	馬太	Mătài	MáHtaai
matins n.	早禱	dzăudău	jóutóu
Mediator n.	中保	Jūngbău	Jùngbóu

meditate v. i.

in silence	默想	mèsyăng;	maaHkséung;
-as a Buddhist	坐禪	dzwòchán	chóHsìHn

meditation n.

-thought	默想	mèsyăng;	maaHkséung;

-contemplation	深慮	shēnlyù	sàmleuiH
mercy seat n.	恩座	ēndzwò	yànjoH
Messiah n.	彌賽亞	Mísàiyă	NèiHchoinga
Methusalah n.	瑪土撒拉	Mătŭsălā	MáHtóusaatlāai
Micah n.	彌迦	Mijyā	NèiHgà
Milofo n	彌羅佛	Mílwófwó	NèiHlòHfaHt

The messiah of the Buddhisattvas. Also called the 'Laughing Buddha!.

misconception n.	錯誤概念	tswòwùgàinyàn	cho'ngHktoiniHm
missal n.	彌撒經	mísājīng	nèiHsaatgìng
mission year book	年鑑	nyánjyàn	nìHngaam
missionary			
-movement	國外佈道運動	gwówàlbùdàu-yùndùng	gwokngoiHbuudouHwaHnduHng
-training	宣教訓練	sywōnjyàusyùnlyàu	syùngaaufanliHn
-work	宣教事工	sywōnjyàushìgīng	syùngaausiHgùng
missions, board of	差會	chāihwèi	chàaiwúi
missions, principles of	傳道規則	chwándàugwēidzé	chyùHndouHkwāijāk
mitre n.	主教冠	jŭjyàugwān	jyúgaaugùn
mixed marriages	異教聯婚	yìjyàulyánhwūn	yiHgaaulyùHnfàn
	異種通婚	yìjŭngtūnghwūn	yiHjúngtùngfàn
Mohammed n.	穆罕默德	Mùhănmèdé	MuHkhónmaaHkdāk
Mohammedan n.	回教	Hwéijyàu	WùiHgaau
monks and nuns (Buddhist)	僧尼	dzēngní	jàngnèiH
monotheism n.	一神論	yìshénlwùn	yātsàHnleuHn
morganatic marriage	貴賤聯婚	gwjlyán lyánhwūn	gwaijiHnlyùHnfàn
Mormon n.	摩門教	Mwóménjyàu	MòmùHngaau
Morrison, Robert	馬禮遜	Mălisyùn	MáHláiHseun

First Protestant Missionary to China, Sept. 7, 1807.

mortal sin	致死之罪	jìsžjřdzwèi	jiséijìjeuiH
Moses n.	摩西	Mwósyi	Mòsài
Most High, the	至高者	Jìgāujě	Jigòujé
most holy place, the	至聖所	jìshèngswǒ	jisingsó
Mount of Olives	橄欖山	Gǎnlǎnshān	GáamláaHmsàan
myrrh n.	沒藥	mwòyàu	muHtyeuHk

N

nail to the Cross	釘十字架	dìngshŕdžjyà	dèngsaHpjiHga
nail, print of the	釘痕	dìnghén	dènghàHn
name of Jesus, in the	奉耶穌的名	fèng Yēsūdemíng	fuHng YèHsōudikmìHng
Nathaneal n.	拿但業	Nádànyé	NàHdaaHnyiHp
nativism n.	天賦論	tyānfùlwùn	tìnfuleuHn
Nativity n.	耶穌降生	Yēsūjyàngshēng	YèHsōugongsàng

natural a.

-conscience	天良	tyānlyáng;	tìnlèuHng;
-equality	天然平等	tyānránpíngděng;	tìnyìHnpìHngdáng
-Ethics	自然倫理	džránlwúnlǐ;	jiHyìHnleuHnléiH;
-god	自然神	džránshén;	jiHyìHnsàHn;
-religion	自然宗教	džrándzūngjyàu;	jiHyìHnjùnggaau;
-revelation	自然啓示	džránchǐshŕ;	jiHyìHnkáisiH;
-selection	天然淘汰	tyānrántáutài;	tìnyìHntòuHtaai;
-sin	自然罪	džrándzwèi	jiHyìHnjeuiH
naturalism n.	自然論	džránlwùn	jiHyìHnleuHn
Nazareth n.	拿撒勒	Násālē	NàHsaatlaHk
Nebuchadnezzar n.	尼布甲尼撒	Níbùjyǎnísā	NèiHbougaapnèiHsaat
necromancy n.	招魂術	jāuhwúnshù	jiuwàHnseuHt

negation n.

-denial	否認	fŏurèn;	fáuyiHng;
-obliteration	删除	shānchú;	sàanchèuIH;
-annihilation	滅絕	myèjywé	miHtjyuHt
Nehemiah	尼希米	Nísyimǐ	NèiIIhèimáiH
nemesis n.	司命神	szmìngshén	sìmiHngsàHn
neology n.	新義說	syìnyìshwō	sànyiHsyut
new commandment	新命令	syìnmìngling	sànmiIIngliHng
new creation (Gal. 6: 15)	新造的人	syìndzàuderén	sànjouHdìkyàHn
new man (in Christ)	新人	syìnrén	sànyàHn
New Testament	新約	Syìnywē	Sànyeuk
Nicene Creed n.	尼西亞信經	Nísyiyǎsyìnjìng	NèiHsàingaseungìng
nihilism n.	虛無論	Syūwúlwùn	HèuimòulIIeuHn
Nile n.	尼羅河	Nílwóhé	NèiHlòHhòH
Nirvana n.	涅槃	nyèpán	nippùHn
Noah n.	挪亞	Nwóyǎ	NòHnga
nominal Christian	掛名基督徒	gwàmíng Jīdūtú	gwamìHng GēidūktòuH
nominalism n.	唯名論	wéimínglwùn	wàiHmìHngleuHn
Non-being (tacism)	無	wú	mòuH
non-Christian religions	非基督教宗教	fēi-Jīdūjyàu-dzūngjgàu	fèi-Gēidūkgaaujùnggaau
nothingness n.	虛無	syūwú	hèuimòuII

nun n.

-Budd.	尼姑	nígū;	nèiHgū;
-Rom. Cath.	修女	syōunyǔ;	sàunéui;
-Taoist	道姑	dàugū	douHgū
nunnery (Buddhist) n.	菴	ān	àm

O

Obadiah n.	俄巴底亞	Èbādǐyǎ	NgòHbādáinga
obedience to God	順從神	shwùntsúngShén	seuHnchùHngSàHn
oblation n.	祭祀	jìsz̀;	jaigeiH;
	奉献	fèngsyàn	fuHnghin
observe the Sabbath	守安息日	shǒuānsyír̀	sáuōnsikyaHt
obsession n.	着迷	jwómí;	jeuHkmàiH;
	強廹觀念	chyángpwò-gwānnyàn	kèuHngbāakgùnniHm
obtain salvation	得救	déjyòu	dākgau
occultism n.	幽秘主義	yōumìjǔyì	yàubeijyúyiH
offering n.			
-burnt	燔祭	fánjì	fàaHnjai
-drink	奠祭	dyànjì	dinjai
-freewill	甘心祭	gānsyinjì	gàmsàmjai
-guilt	贖愆祭	shúchyānjì	suHkhìnjai
-meal	素祭	sùjì	soujai
-peace	平安祭	píngānjì	pìHngònjai
-sin	贖罪祭	shúdzwèijì	suHkjeuiHjai
-thanks	感恩祭	gǎnēnjì	gámyànjai
-votive	還願祭	hwánywànjì	wàaHnyuHnjai
-whole-burnt	全牲燔祭	chywánshēngfánjì	chyùHnsàngfàaHnjai
-for sacrifice	祭物	jìwù	jaimaHt
offerings n.	供物	gùngwù	gungmaHt
offertory n.	奉献;	fèngsyàn;	fuHnghin;
	捐献	jywānsyàn	gyùnhin
Oh God!	神阿	Shén a!	SàHn a!
Oh Lord!	主阿	Jǔ a!	Jyú a!

oil of gladness	喜樂油	syǐlèyóu	héiloHkyàuH
Olaf n.	阿拉佛	Àlāfú	AlàaifaHt
old man (unconverted)	舊人	jyòurén	gauHyàHn
Old Testament	舊約聖經	Jyòuywē Shèngjīng	GauHyuuk Singging
Olives, Mount of	橄欖山	Gǎnlǎnshān	GáamláaHmsàan
omega n.	俄梅戛	Èméijyá	NgòHmùiHgà
omnipotence n.	全能	chywánnéng;	chyùHnnàHng;
	無所不能	wúswǒbùnéng	mòuHsóbātnàHng
omnipresence n.	全在	chywándzài;	chyùHnjoiH;
	無所不在	wúswǒbúdzài	mòuHsóbātjoiH
omniscience n.	全知	chywánjī;	chyùHnjì;
	無所不知	wúswǒbùjr	mòuHsóbātjì
Omitofu n.	阿彌陀佛	Ànítwófwó	AnèiHtòHfaHt

A popular diety of the Mahayana Pure Land Sect who is supposed to lead his disciples to the Western Paradise. To call on his name is all that is necessary for salvation

Only Begotten Son (Jesus)	獨生子	Dúshēngdž	DuHksàngjí
ontology n.	本體論	běntǐlwùn	búntáileuHn
open a meeting	開會	kāihwèi	hòiwúi
open air meeting	露天聚會	lùtyānjyùhwèi	louHtìnjeuiHwuiH
open heart	坦白	tǎnbái	táanbaaHk
oracle n.	神諭	Shényù;	SàHnyuH;
	聖言	Shèngyán	SìngyìHn
oratorio mentalis (silent prayer)	默禱	mèdǎu	maaHktóu
order of salvation	得救程序	déjyòuchéngsyù	dākgauchìHngjeuiH
order of service	禮拜次序	lǐbàitszsyù	láiHbaaichijeuiH
orders, holy	聖職	shèngjŕ	singjīk
ordinance n.	禮儀	lǐyí	láiHyìH

ordination ceremony	受職禮	shòujŕlĭ	sauHjikláiH
ordination of pastors	按牧禮	ànmùlĭ	onmuHkláiH
original sin	原罪	ywándzwèi	YùHnjeuiH
orthodoxy n.	正統神學	jèngtŭngshénsywé	jingtúngsàHnhoHk

P

pacifism n.	非戰主義	fēijànjŭyì	fèijinjyúyiH
paganism n.	異教	yìjyàu	yiHgaau
Palestine n.	巴勒斯坦	Bālēsztăn	BàlaHksìtáan
Palm Sunday	棕樹日	dzūngshùŕ	jùngsyuHyaHt
panlogism n.	泛理論	fànlĭlwùn	faanléiHleuHn
Panch'an Lama	班禪啦嘛	Bānchánlămá	BàansìHmlamàH

The Panch'an Lama is the highest pontiff of Tibet (after the Dalai Lama) to whom is confided the maintenance of the purity of the religious doctrine.

panpsychism n.	泛靈魂說	fànlínghwúnshwō	faanlìHngwàHnsyut
pantheism n.	泛神論	fànshénlwùn	faansàHnleuHn
papalism n.	教宗主義	jyàudzūngjŭyì;	gaaujùngjyúyiH;
	教皇主義	jyàuhwángjŭyì	gaauwòHngjyúyiH
paranoia n.	妄想症	wàngsyǎngjèng	móHngséungjing
Parent-Teacher Association	家長教師協會	jyājǎngjyàushrìsyéhwèi	gàjéunggaausìhiHpwúi
partake of Communion	領聖餐	lĭngshèngtsān	líHngsingchāan
parochial a.	牧區	mùchyū;	muHkkèui;
	狹隘觀念	syáàigwānnyàn	haaHpaigùnniHm
parson	牧師	mùshŕ	muHksì
particularism n.	特殊論	tèshūlwùn	daHksyùHleuHn
Pascal Lamb	逾越節羔羊	Yúywèjyé Gāuyáng	YùHyuHtjit GòuyèuHn
passion of Christ	基督受難	Jĭdūshòunàn	GēidūksauHnaaHn
Passion Day	受苦日	Shòukŭŕ	SauHfúyaHt

Passion Week	受難週	Shòunànjōu	SauHnaaHnjāu
Passover n.	逾越節	Yúywèjyé	YùHyuHtjit
pastoral a.			
-letters	牧師來信	mùshīláisyìn	muHksìlòiHseun
-sermon	教牧講章	jyàumùjyǎngjūng	gaaumuHkgóngjēung
-theology	教牧學	jyàumùsywé	gaaumuHkhoHk
pastorate n.	教牧職	jyàumùjŕ	gaaumuHkjĭk
Paternalism n.	仁慈專制政治	réntszjwānjŕjéngjr	yàHnchìHjyùnjaijingjiH
patiently bear	包容	bāurúng	bàauyùHng
patriarch n.	族長	dzújǎng;	juHkjéung;
	主教長	jǔjyàujǎng	jyúgaaujéung
patron saint	守護聖徒	shǒuhùshèngtú	sáuwnHsingtòuH
Paul n.	保羅	Bǎulwó	BóulòH
penitence n.	悔罪	hwěidzwèi	fuijcuiH
penitent n.	懺悔人	chànhwěirén	chimfuiyàHn
Pentateuch n.	摩西五經	Mwósyiwǔjīng	MòsàingHgìng
Pentecost n.	五旬節	Wǔsyúnjyé	NǵHchèuHnjit
people of God	神的子民	Shéndedžmín	SàHndìkjímàHn
perdition n.	淪亡	lwúnwńg	lèuHnmòHng
Perfect Man (Taoism)	至人	jìrén	jiyàHn
pericope	聖經選題	Shèngjìngsywǎntí	SinggìngsyúntàiH
pericope texts	三代經題	sāndàijingtí	sàamdoiHgìngtàiH
Period of Classics	經學時代	Jīngsywéshŕdài	GìnghoHksìHdoiH
perpetual adoration	永久崇拜	yǔngjyǒuchúngbài	wíHnggáusùHngbaai
Persia n.	波斯	Bwōsž	Bòsi
person (in Godhead) n.	位格	wéigé	waiHgaak
pew n.	教堂座檯	jyàutángdzwòdèng	gaautòHngjoHdang
phantom n.	幻影	hwànyǐng	waaHnyíng

Pharaoh n.

-Prot.	法老	Fălău;	FaatlóuH;
-R. Cath.	法郎	Făláng	FaatlòHng
Pharisee	法利賽人	Fălìsàirén	FaatleiHchoiyàHn
Philip n.	腓力	Féilì	FèiHliHk
philosophy of religion	宗教哲學	dzūngjyàujésywé	jùnggaaujithoHk
Phonology n.	音韻學	yīnyùnsywé	yàmwáHnhoHk
phrenology n.	骨相學	gŭsyàngsywé	gwātseunghoHk
phylacteries n.	佩經	Pèijing	puigìng
Pilate, Pontius	本丟彼拉多	Bĕndyōubǐlādwō	Búndìubéilāaidō

pilgrim v. i.

-to a sacred place	朝聖	cháushèng;	chìuHsing;
-to Buddhist temple	香客	syāngkè	hēunghaak
pilgrimage n.	朝聖	cháushèng;	chìuHsing;
	進香	jìnsyāng	jeunhēung
Plato n.	柏拉圖	Bwólātú	BaaklàaitòuH
pneumatology n.	靈物學	língwùsywé;	lìHngmaHthoHk;
	聖靈論	Shènglínglwùn	SinglìHngleuHn
polemics n.	論辯	lwùnbyàn;	leuHnbiHn;
	爭論	jēnglwùn	jàngleuHn
pontiff n.	教宗	jyàudzūng;	gaaujùng
	主教	jŭjyàu	jyúgaau
Pope n.	教皇	jyàuhwáng	gaauwòHng
popular religion	民衆宗教	mínjùngdzūngjyàu;	màHnjungjùnggaau;
	一般宗教	yìbāndzūngjyàu	yātbùnjùnggaau
positivism n.	實證論	shíjènglwùn	saHtjingleuHn
possessed by demons	被鬼附着	bèigwĕifùje	beiHgwáifuHjeuHk

Post-Communion	聖餐後段禱文	shèngtsānhòudwàn dǎuwén	singchāanhauHdyuHn tóumàHn
practical theology	實用神學	shíyùngshénsywé	saHtyuHngsàHnhoHk
pragmatism n.	實用主義	shìyùngjǔyì;	saHtyuHngjyúyiH;
	實利主義	shílìjǔyì	saHtleiHjyúyiH
prayer book	祈禱書	chídǎushū	kèiHtóusyù
prayer, silent	默禱	mèdǎu	maaHktóu
prayer, public	公禱	gūngdǎu	gùngtóu
prayer, Lord's	主禱文	Jǔdǎuwén	JyútóumàHn
Prayer meeting	禱告聚會	dǎngàujyùhwèi	tóugoujeuiHwuiH
preach the Gospel	傳福音	chwánfúyìn	chyùlInfūkyàm
preacher n.	傳道人	chwándàurén	chyùHndouHyàHn
precious blood	寶血	bǎusyě	bóuhyut
predestinate v. t.	註定	jùdìng,	jyudiHng;
	命中註定	mìngjūngjùdìng	miHngjùngjyudiHng
predestination n.	命運	mìngyùn	miHngwaHn
prelate n.	教宗	jyàudzūng	gaaujùng
premarital councelling	婚前輔導	hwūnchyánfǔdǎu	fànchìHnfúdouH
presbytery n.	聖品席	shèngpìnsyí;	singbánjiHk;
	中會(長老會)	jūnghwèi (Jǎnglǎuhwèi)	jùngwúi (JéunglóuHwúi)
priest n.			
-Taoist	道士	dàushr̀;	douHsiH;
-Prot.	祭司	jìsž;	jaisì;
-R. Cath.	神父	shénfù;	sàHnfuH;
-Budd.	和尚	héshàng	wòHséung
prodigal son	浪子	làngdž	loHngjí
prophet n.	先知	syānjr̄	sìnjì
-false prophet	假先知	jyǎsyānjr̄	gásìnjì

prophetess n.	女先知	nyǔsyānjr̄	néuiHsìnjì
propitiation n.	挽回祭	wǎnhwéijì	wáaHnwùiHjai
proselyte n.	改宗者	gǎidzūngjě	góijùngjé
Protestant n.	抗議宗	kàngyìdzūng	kongyíHjùng
Providence n.	神	Shén	SàHn
psalmody n.	詩篇	shr̄pyān	sipin
pseudepigrapha n.	偽經	wèijr̄ng	ngaiHgìng
pulpit n.	講壇	jyǎngtán	góngtàaHn
pure heart	清心	chr̄ngsyin	chìngsàm
purgatory n.			
-R. Cath.	煉獄	lyànyù	liHnyuHk
purification n.			
-Jewish	潔淨禮	jyéjìnglǐ	gitjiHngláiH;
-R. Cath.	神酒式	shénjyǒushr̀	sàHnjáusìk
Puritan n.	清教徒	chr̄ngjyàutú	chìnggaautòuH

Q

Quakers n.	貴格派	Gwèigépài	Gwaigaakpaai
Queen of Heaven			
-Budd.	天后	tyānhòu	tìnhauH
quietism n.	寂靜主義	jíjìngjǔyì	jiHkjiHngjyúyiH

R

racialism n.	種族主義	jǔngdzújǔyì	júngjuHkjyúyiH;
	種族成見	jǔngdzúchéngjyàn	júngjuHksìHnggin
rationalism n.	唯理論	wéilǐlwùn	wàiHléiHleuHn
real image	眞像	jēnsyàng	jànjeuHng
realism, philosophic	實體論	shŕtǐlwùn	saHttáileuHn

realism, scholastic	實名論	shímínglwùn	saHtmìIIngleuHn
rebirth n.	重生	chúngshēng	chùHngsàng
receive Jesus	接待耶穌	jyēdài Yēsū	jipdoiH YèHsōu
receive favor	蒙恩	méngēn	mùHngyàn
recession n.	列隊退出	lyèdwèitwèichū	liIItdeuiHteuichēut
reconversion n.	再改宗	dzàigǎidzūng	joigóijùng
re-create v. t.	再造	dzàidzàu	joijouII
Red Cross Society	紅十字會	Húngshídàhwèi	IIùIIugsaHpjiHwúi
Red Sea	紅海	Húnghǎi	IIùIInghói
Redeemer n.	救贖主	Jyòushújǔ	GausuHkjyú
Redeemer Lord	贖罪主	Shúdzwèijǔ	SuHkjeuiHjyú
redemption n.	救贖	jyòushú	gausuHk
Reformation, the	改革運動	gǎigéyùndùng;	góigaakwaHnduIIng,
	宗教改革	dzūngjyàugǎigé	jùnggaaugóigaak
reincarnation n.	再成肉身	dzàichéngròushēn;	joisìIIugyuHksàn;
	再生	dzàishēng	joisàng
relativism n.	相對論	syāngdwèilwùn	sèungdeuileuHn
relevance n.	相關性	syānggwānsyìng	sèunggwàansing
relic n.	聖徒遺物	shèngtúyíwù	singtòuHwàiHmaHt
religion n.	宗教	dzūngjyàu	jùnggaau
-Buddhism	佛教	Fwójyàu	FaIItgaau
-Catholicism	天主教	Tyānjǔjyàu	Tìnjyúgaau
-Christianity	基督教	jidūjyàu	Gēidūkgaau
-Confucianism	孔教	Kǔngjyàu	Húnggaau
-Hinduism	印度教	Yìndùjyàu	YandouHgaau
-Judaism	猶太教	Yóutàijyàu	YàuHtaaigaau
-Lamaism	喇嘛教	Lǎmájyàu	LamàHgaau
-Mohammedanism	回教	Hwéijyàu	WùiHgaau

-Shintoism	日本神道教	Ŕběnshéndàujyàu	YaHtbúnsàHndouHgaau
-Taoism	道教	Dàujyàu	DouHgāau
-Zoroastrianism	波斯教	Bwōszjyàu	Bōsigaau
renunciation n.	否認自己	fŏurèndżjĭ;	fáuyiHngjiHgéi;
	棄絕老我	chìjywélǎuwǒ	heijyuHtlóuHng6H
reredos n.	聖壇飾壁	shèngtánshŕbì	singtàaHnsikbik
restoration n.	復原	fùywán;	fuHkyùHn;
	萬物復興	wànwùfùsyíng	maaHnmaHtfuHkhìng
return good for evil	以惡報善	yĭebàushàn	yíHngokbousiHn
Reverend n.			
-Prot.	牧師	mùshŕ;	muHksĭ;
-R. Cath.	神父	shénfù;	sàHnfuH;
-Budd.	法師	fǎshŕ	faatsĭ
revival meetings	奮興會	fènsyìnghwèi	fáHnhìngwúi
righteous anger	義怒	yìnù	yiHnouH
righteous man	義人	yìrén	yiHyàHn
righteousness	公義	gūngyì	gùngyiH
rite of confirmation	按手禮	ànshŏulĭ	ngonsáuláiH
rites and observances	禮儀	lĭyí	láiHyìH
ritual n.	儀式	yíshŕ	yìHsĭk
robe n.	袍子	páudz	pòuHjí
Rogation Days	特禱日	tèdǎuŕ	daHktóuyaHt
Roman Catholic Church	天主教會	tyānjŭjyàuhwèi	tìnjyúgaauwúi
Roman Empire	羅馬帝國	Lwómǎdìgwó	LòHmáHdaigwok
romanticism n.	浪漫主義	làngmànjŭyì	loHngmaaHnjyúyiH
rosary n.			
-R. Cath.	玫瑰經	méigwèijīng;	mùiHgwaigìng;
-Budd.	念珠	nyànjū	niHmjyū

rubric n.	禮規註解	lǐgwēijùjyě	láiHkwàijyugáai
rule of faith	信仰準則	syìnyǎngjwǔndzé	seunyéuHngjéunjāk
rule, monastic	修道院規律	syōudàuywàn; gwēilyù	sàudouHyúnkwàileuHt

S

Sabbath n.	安息日	Ānsyít	ŌnsìkyaHt
sabbatical year	安息年	ānsyínyán;	ōnsiknìHn;
	休息年	syōusyínyán	yāusìknìHn
sacrament			
-Prot.	聖禮	shènglǐ;	singláiH
-R. Cath.	聖事蹟	shèngshŕjì	singsiHjìk
sacred a.	聖	shèng	sing
duty	神聖義務	shénshèngyìwù	sàHnsìngyiHmouH
-vessel	聖器	shèngchì	singheɪ
sacrifice v. t.	犧牲	syīshēng;	hèɪsàng;
-to a god	献祭	syànjì;	hmjai;
-to one's ancestors	祭祖	jìdzǔ;	jaijóu;
-of things	祭物	jìwù;	jaimaHt;
-n. of animals	犧牲	syīshēng	hèɪsàng
sacrilege n.	褻瀆聖物	syèdúshèngwù;	sitduIIksingmaHt
	竊取聖物	chyèchyǔshèngwù	sitchéuisingmaHt
sacrosanct a.	神聖	shénshèng;	sùHnsing;
	不可侵犯	bùkēchìnfàn	bāthóchàmfaaHɪ
Sadducee			
-Prot.	撒都該	Sādūgāi;	Saatdōugōi;
-R. Cath.	撒杜賽	Sādùsài	SaatdouHchoi
saga n.	古史	gǔshř	gúsí
saint n.	聖徒	shèngtú;	singtòuH;

-day	追思聖徒日	jwēiszshèngtúr;	jèuisisingtòuHyaHt
-worship	聖徒崇拜	shèngtúchúngbài	singtòuHsùHngbaai
sake, for God's	看神面上	kàn Shén myàn-shàng	hon SàHn miHnseuHng
Sakya-muni n.	釋迦牟尼	Shřjyāmóuní	SikgàmàauHnèiH

The name given to the mystic of the Sakya tribe in China.

salvation n.	救恩	jyòuēn	gauyàn
Salvation Army	救世軍	Jyòushřjyūn	Gausaigwān
Samson n.	參孫	Tsānswūn	Chàamsyùn
Samuel n.	撒母耳	Sāmŭĕr	SaatmóuHyíH
sanctification n.	成聖	chéngshèng	sìHngsing
sanctuary n.	聖所	shèngswŏ	singsó
satan n.	撒但	sādàn	saatdaaHn
satanology n.	撒但論	sādànlwùn	saatdaaHnleuHn
satisfaction theory	補罪說	bŭdzwèishwō	bóujeuiHsyut
Saul n.	掃羅	Săulwó	SoulòH
saving faith	得救信心	déjyòusyinsyin	dākgauseunsàm
Savior n.	救主	Jyòujŭ	Gaujyú
-of the world	救世主	Jyòushřjŭ	Gausaijyú
say masses	作彌撒	dzwòmísā	joknèiHsaat (moHngnèiHsaat)
scapegoat n.	替罪羊	tìdzwèiyáng	taijeuiHyèuHng
schism n.	分派	fēnpài;	fànpaai;
	分立	fēnlì	fànlaHp
schizophrenia n.	精神分離症	jingshénfēnlíjèng	jìngsàHnfànlèiHjing
Schikasticism n.	經院學派	jìngywànsywépài	gìngyúnhoHkpaai
School of Forms n.	形名家	syíngmíngjyā	yìHngmìHnggā
science of religion	宗教學	dzūngjyàusywé	jùnggaauhoHk
scriptural exhortation	經訓	jìngsyùn	gìngfan

scriptural passage	經文	jīngwén	gìngmàHn
Scripture n.	聖經	Shèngjīng	Singgìng
seal n.	印	yìn;	yan;
-of baptism	聖洗印記	shèngsyǐyìnjì;	singsáiyangei;
-of confession	告白守秘	gàubáishǒumì;	goubaaHksáubeì;
-of the Spirit	聖靈印記	Shènglíngyìnjì	SinglìIIngyangei
Second Coming	基督復臨	Jīdūfùlín;	GēidūkfuHklàHm;
	基督再來	Jīdūdzàilái	GēidūkjoílòIH
sect n.	教門	jyàumén	gaaumùHn
seeker n.	慕道友	mùdàuyǒu	mouHdouHyáuH
seer n.	先見	syānjyàn	sìngin
self n.	自己	dzìjǐ	jiHgéi
-acceptance	自我肯定	dzìwǒkěndìng;	jiHngóHhángdiHng;
-centredness	自我中心	dzìwǒjūngsyin;	jiHngóHjūngsām;
-defence	自衛	dzìwèi;	jiHwaiH
-denial	捨己	shějǐ;	ségéi;
-destruction	自毀	dzìhwěi;	jiHwái;
	自滅	dzìmyè;	jiHmiHt;
-knowledge	自我認識	dzìwǒrènshì;	jiHngóHyiHngsik;
-respect	自尊	dzìdzwūn;	jiHjyùn;
-righteousness	自以爲義	dzìyǐwéiyì;	jiHyíHwàiHyiH
-sacrifice	捨己爲人	shějǐwèirén;	ségéiwaiHyàHn;
-support	自立自養	dzìlìdzìyǎng;	jiHlaHpjiHyéuHng;
-will	固執己志	gùjŕjǐjì	gujāpgéiji
semi-orthodoxy	半正統神學	bànjèngtŭngshén-sywé	bunjingtúngsàHn-hoHk
sentiment of justice	正義感	jèngyìgǎn	jingyiHgám
septuagesima n.	七旬日	chīsyúnŕ	chātchèuHnyaHt
sermon n.	講道	jyǎngdàu;	góngdouH;

	講章	jyǎngjāng	góngjēung
Sermon of the Mount	登山寶訓	dēngshānbǎusyùn	dàngsànbóufan
serpent, brass	銅蛇	túngshé	tùHngsèH
server n.	陪祭	péijì	pùiHjai
Seven classes of disciples (Buddhist)	七衆	chijùng	chātjung
Sexagesima n.	六旬日	Lyòusyúnr̀	LuHkchèuHnyaHt
sexton n.	守堂人	shǒutángrén	sáutòHngyàHn
Shintoism n.	神道教	shéndàujyàu	sàHndouHgaau
shrine n.	龕	kān;	hàm;
	神龕	shénkān	sàHnhàm
sign n.	異能	yìnéng	yiHnàHng
	神蹟	shénjì	sàHnjìk
Sikhism n.	錫克教	Syíkèjyàu	Sekhāakgaau
silent prayer	默禱	mèdǎu	maaHktóu
simile n.	明喻	míngyù	mìHngyuH
Simon n.	西門	Syimén	SàimùHn
Simon Peter n.	西門彼得	Syimén Bǐdé	SàimùHn Béidāk
simony n.	買賣聖職	mǎimàishèngjr̀	máaiHmaaiHsingjik
sin, actual n.	本罪	běndzwèi	búnjeuiH
Sinai n.	西乃山	Syǐnǎishān	SàináaiHsàan
single text	單一經題	dānyijìngtí	dāanyātgìngtàiH
Siniticism n.	中國宗教觀	Jūnggwódzūngjyàugwān	Jùnggwokjùnggaaugùn
sin-offering n.	贖罪祭	shúdzwèijì	suHkjeuiHjai
sin, original n.	原罪	ywándzwèi	yùHnjeuiH
sins n.	罪行	dzwèisyíng	jeuiHhàHng
smite v. t.	擊打	jídǎ	gìkdá
Socrates n.	蘇格拉底	Sūgélādǐ	SòugaaklàaidáI
Sodom n.	所多瑪	Swǒdwōmǎ	SódòmáH

solipsism n.	唯我論	wéiwǒlwùn	wàiHngóHleuHn
solitude n.	獨居	dújyū;	duHkgèui;
	孤寂	gūjí	gùjiHk
Solomon n.	所羅門	Swǒlwómén	SólòHmùHn
somnambulism n.	夢遊病	mèngyóubìng	muHngyàuHbeHng
Son of Buddha	佛子	fwódž	fnHtjí
Son of man	人子	Réndž	YàHnjí
soteriology n.	救贖論	jyòushúlwùn	gaausuHkleuHn
spiritual a.	屬靈	shǔlíng;	suHklíHng;
	靈性上	língsyìngshàng	lìHngoingseuILng
-blessings	屬靈的福份	shǔlíngdefúfèn	suHklíHngdikfūkfaHn
-gifts	屬靈的恩賜	shǔlíngde ēntsž	suHklíHngdìk yànchi
-life	靈命	língmíng	lìHngmiILng
-meaning	靈意	língyì	lìHngyì
-nature	靈性	língsyìng	lìHngsing
-realm	靈界	língjyè	lìHnggaai
-temple	靈宮	línggūng	lìHnggùng
-unity	心靈合一	syìnlínghéyi	sàmlìHnghaHpyāt
spiritualism n.	唯心論	wéisyinlwùn	wàiHsàmleuHn
spiritually adv.	心靈上	syìnlíngshàng	sàmlìHngseuHng
stained glass	彩畫玻璃	tsǎihwàbwōli	chóiwábōléi
statute n.	律例	lyùlì	leuHtlaiH
steeple n.	禮拜堂尖塔	lǐbàitángjyantǎ	láiHdaaitòHngjìmtaap
stichimetry n.	經節表	jīngjyébyǎu;	gìngjitbíu;
	按意分節	ànyìfēnjyé	onyifànjit
struggle for existence	生存競爭	shēngtswúnjìngjēng	sàngchyùHngingjàng
tumbling block	絆腳石	bànjyǎushí	buHngeukseHk
sub-deacon n.	副會吏	fùhwèilì	fuwuiHleiH

subject-matter n.	題材	títsái	tàiHchòiH
suffragan bishop n.	副主教	fùjŭjyàu	fujyúgaau
suffrages n.	短篇祈禱文	dwǎnpyānchí-dǎuwén	dyúnpìnkèiHtóumàHn
Sunday school n.	主日學	Jŭrsywé	JyúyaHthoHk
super-human	超人	Chāurén	ChìuyàHn
super-world	超然世界	chāuránshìjyè	chìuyìHnsaigaai
survival of the fittest	適者生存	shìjěshēngtswún	sikjésàngchyùHn
symbolics n.	信條學	syìntyáusywé	seuntiuHhoHk
Synagogue n.	會堂	hwèitáng	wuiHtòHng
synod n.			
-Church council	大會	dàhwèi	daaiHwúi
Systematic Theology n'	系統神學	syìtǔngshénsywé	haiHtúngsàHnhoHk

T

tabernacle n.	會幕	hwèimù	wuiHmoHk
Tablet of the Law	法版	fǎbǎn	faatbáan
taboo, tabu n.	禁忌	jìnjì	gamgeiH
T'ai Hsu	太虛法師	Tàisyūfǎshī	Taaihèuifaatsì

The head of Chinese Buddhism today. Renowned Buddhist scholar and lecturer on Buddhism in Europe, Asia, America. Organized the world Buddhist Organization. One of the mo
learned and enlightened Buddhist monks in China who has achieved world renown.

T'ai Shan	泰山	Tàishǎn	Taaisàan

T'ai Shan is the chief of the Five Sacred Mountains of China and is situated north of T'
an in Shantung Province. Sacrifices to Heaven and Earth Were first offered here by the E
peror Wu in 110 B.C.

Taoism n.	道教	dàujyàu	douHgaau
Taoist priest	道士	dàushì	douHsiH

道 德 經   dàudéjǐng   douHdākgǐng

This book is the sacred book of Taoism. It is short but full of meaning and is traditionally ascribed to Laotze.

collector	稅吏	shwèilǐ	seuileiH
Taylor, J. Hudson	戴德生	Dàidéshēng	Daaidāksāng
Temple, Holy n.	聖殿	Shèngdyàn	SingdiHn
Temple, Buddhist n.	佛寺	fwósż	faHtjí
Temple, Taoist n.	道觀	dàugwǎn	douHgùn
Testament. New	新約	Syīnywē	Sànyeuk
Testament. Old	舊約	Jyòuywē	GauHyeuk
testimony meeting	見證會	jyànjènghwèi	ginjingwúi
thanks, give	祝謝	jùsyè	jūkjeH
Thanksgiving Day	感恩節	gǎnēnjyé	gámyànjit
theism n.	有神論	yǒushénlwùn	yáuHsàIInleuHn
theocracy n.	神權政體	shénchywánjèngtǐ	sàHnkyùHnjingtái
theodicy n.	神義論	shényìlwùn	sàHnyiHleuHn
theologia dogmatica	教義神學	jyàuyìshénsywé	gaauyiHsàHnhoIIk
theological seminary	神學院	shénsywéywàn	sàHnhoHkyún
theology n.	神學	shénsywé	sàHnhoHk
theory of relativity	相對論	syāngdwèilwùn	sèungdeuileuHn
theurgy n.	巫術	wūshù;	mòuHseuHt;
	妖術	yāushù	yíuseuHt
thine pro.	祢的	nǐde	néiHdik (néiHge)
thou pro.	祢	nǐ	néiH
Three periods (Buddhism)	三世	sēnshì	sàamsai
thy pro.	祢的	nǐde	néiHdik(néiHge)
tithes n.	什一捐	shíyījywān;	saHpyātgyùn;

	十一奉献	shíyìfèngsyàn	saHpyātfuHnghin
tolerance n.	容忍	rúngrěn	yùHngyán
topical sermon	標題	byāutí	bìutàiH
totemism n.	圖騰教	túténgjyàu	tòuHtàHnggaau
tract n.	單張	dānjāng	dàanjèung
transfiguration n.	改變形像	gǎibyànsyíngsyàng	góibinyìHngjeuHng
transformation n.	變形	byànsyíng	binyìHng
transgress v. t.	違犯	wéifàn;	wàiHfaaHn;
-against the	犯法	fànfǎ	faaHnfaat
trespass v. i.	干犯	gānfàn	gònfaaHn
Trinity n.			
-Prot.	三位一體	Sānwèiyìtǐ	SàamwaiHyāttái
-Budd.	三寶	sānbǎu	sàambóu
-Tao.	三清	sānchíng	sàamchìng
True God	眞神	Jēnshén	JànsàHn
Tu Ti Miao	土地廟	tǔdìmyàu	tóudeiHmíu

The most common country shrines in China where the natives go to burn incense and present their complaints to the Earth God.

turning-point n.	轉捩點	jwǎnlèidyǎn	jyúnleuiHdím
Twelve Causes n. (Nidans)	十二因緣	shíèryīnywán	saHpyiHyànyùHn
type			
-n.	形	syíng	yìHng
-v. i.	預表	yùbyǎu	yuHbíu
typology n.	預表論	yùbyǎulwùn;	yuHbíuleuHn;
	形態學	syíngtàisywé	yìHngtaaihoHk

U

ubiquity n.	遍在	pyàndzài	pinjoiH

uncircumcised a.	未受割禮	wèishòugelĭ	meiHsauHgotláiH
unconscious a.	無意識	wúyìshr̀	mòuHyieilr
unction n.	膏油禮	gāuyóulĭ	gòuyàuIIláiH
ungodly a.	不虔誠	bùchyánchéng	bātkìHnsìHng (m̃kìHnsìHng)
unholy a.	不聖潔	búshèngjyé	bātsinggit (m̃singgit)
universal grace	普恩	pŭen	póuyàn
universal salvation	普世救法	pŭshr̀jyòufă	póusaigaufaat
unleavened bread	無酵餅	wúsyàubĭng	mòuHhāaubéng
unpardonable sin	不赦之罪	búshèjr̆dzwèi	bātsejijeuiH
unrighteousness n.	不義	búyì	bātyiH

V

vainglory n.	虛榮	syūrúng	hòuiwìIIng
vain imaginations	妄想	wàngsyăng	móIIngsáung
Valley of Death	死亡谷	sz̆wánggŭ	séimòHnggūk
Valley of Tears	流淚谷	lyóulèigŭ	làuHleuiHgūk
Vatican Council	梵蒂岡議會	Fándìgāngyìhwèi	FaaHndaigōngyìHwúi
venial sin n.	可恕之罪	kĕshùjr̆dzwèi	hósyujìjeuiH
veracity n.	眞實性	jēnshŕsyìng	jànsaHtsing
verily adv.	確實地	chywèshŕde	kokeaHtdoiII
vespers n.	晚禱	wăndău	máaHntóu
vesper service	晚禱會	wăndăuḷwèi	máaHntóuwúi
vestment n.	禮服	lĭfú;	láiHfuHk
-Budd.	法衣	făyì	faatyì
vestry n.	聖衣所	shèngyìswŏ	singyìsó
vicar n.			
-clergyman	牧師	mùshr̄	muHksī
vicarious atonement	代贖	dàishú	doiHsuHk

vicarious suffering	代替受苦	dàitìshòukŭ	doiHtaisauHfú
view of life	人生觀	rénshēnggwān	yàHnsànggùn
vigil n.	守夜祈禱	shŏuyèchídǎu	sáuyeHkèiHtóu
virgin birth	爲童女所生	wéitúngnyŭswŏ-shēng	wàiHtùHngnéuiHsósàng
vitive gift	還願禮物	hwánywànlĭwù	wàaHnyuHnláiHmaHt

W

wafer bread	聖餅片	shèngbĭngpyàn	singbéngpin
wages of sin	罪的工價	dzwèidegūngjyà	jeuiHdìkgùngga
watch & pray	儆醒禱告	jĭngsyĭngdǎugàu	gíngsìngtóugou
wedding n.	結婚禮	jyéhwūnlĭ	gitfànláiH
Wesley, Charles	衞斯理查理	Wèiszlĭ, Chálĭ	WaiHsìléiH, ChàHléiH
Wesley, Jchn	衞斯理約翰	Wèiszlĭ, Ywēhàn	WaiHsìléiH, YeukhoHn
Whitsunday n.	聖靈降臨節	Shènglíng-jyànglìnjyé	SinglìHng-gonglàHmjit
whole & parts	全部與局部	chywánbùyŭjyúbù	chyùHnbouHyúHguHk-bouH
wholeness n.	完整	wánjěng;	yùHnjíng;
	健全	jyànchywán	giHnchyùHn
wickedness n.	品行不端	pĭnsyíngbùdwān;	bánhaHngbātdyùn;
	不義	búyì	bātyiH
women's rights n.	女權	nyŭchywán	néuiHkyùHn
word of life n.	生命之道	shēngmìngjīdàu	sàngmiHngjìdouH
worship v. t.	崇拜	chúngbài;	sùHngbaai;
-corporate	集體崇拜	jítĭchúngbài;	jaaHptáisùHngbaai;
-individual	個人崇拜	gèrénchúngbài	goyàHnsùHngbaai;
-private	私人崇拜	szrénchúngbài	sìyàHnsùHngbaai
-public	公共崇拜	gūnggùngchúngbài	gùngguHngsùHngbaai
wrath of God	神的震怒	Shéndejènnù	SàHndìkjannouH

| Wu T'ai Shan | 五臺山 | Wŭtáishān | NgHtòiHsàan |

Wu T'ai Shan is one of the Four Hills sacred to Buddhism in China. It is located on a range of mountains near the northeastern border of Shansi Province.

Y

Yahweh n.	耶和華	Yēhéhwá	YèHwòHwàH
yoga n.	瑜咖	yùjyā	yuHgà
Younger Churches	後進教會	hòujìnjyàuhwèi	hauHjeungaauwúi
YMCA	男青年會	Nánchingnyánhwèi	NàaHmchìngnìHnwúi
YWCA	女青年會	Nyúchingnyánhwèi	NéuiHchìngnìHnwúi

Z

Zealot n.	舊銳黨	Fènrwèidǎng	FáHnyeuiHdóng
Zen Buddhism n.	禪宗	Chándzūng	SìHmjūng
Zeus n.	丟斯	Dyōusz̄	Dìusì
Zionism n.	錫安主義	Syíānjǔyì	SekònjyúyiH

THE BOOKS OF THE NEW TESTAMENT

St. Matthew

-Prot.	馬太福音	Mǎtàifúyìn	MáHtaaifūkyàm
-Rom. Cath.	瑪竇福音	Mǎdòufúyìn	MáHdauHfūkyàm

St. Mark

-Prot.	馬可福音	Mǎkěfúyìn	MáHhófūkyàm
-Rom. Cath.	馬爾谷福音	Mǎěrgǔfúyìn	MáHyìHgūkfūkyàm

St. Luke

-Prot.	路加福音	Lùjyāfúyìn	LouHgàfūkyàm
-Rom. Cath.	路加福音	Lùjyāfúyìn	LouHgàfūkyàm

St. John

-Prot.	約翰福音	Ywēhànfúyìn	YeukhoHnfūkyàm
-Rom. Cath.	若望福音	Rwòwàngfúyìn	YeuHkmoHngfūkyàm

The Acts

-Prot.	使徒行傳	Shřtúsyíngjwàn	SitòuHhàHngjyún
-Rom. Cath.	宗徒大事錄	Dzūngtúdàshřlù	JùngtòuHdaaiHsiHluHk

Epistle to Romans

-Prot.	羅書書	Lwómǎshū	LòHmáHsyù
-Rom. Cath.	羅馬書	Lwómǎshū	LòHmáHsyù

I Corinthians

-Prot.	哥林多前書	Gēlíndwōchyánshū	GōlàHmdōchìHnsyù
-Rom. Cath.	格林多前書	Gélíndwōchyánshū	GaaklàHmdōchìHnsyù

II Corinthians

-Prot.	哥林多後書	Gēlíndwōhòushū	GōlàHmdòchìHnsyù
-Rom. Cath.	格林多後書	Gélíndwōhòushū	GaaklàHmdòhauHsyù

Galatians

-Prot.	加拉太書	Jyālātàishū	Gālàaitaaisyù
-Rom. Cath.	迦拉達書	Jyālādáshū	GālàaidaaHtsyǹ

Ephesians

-Prot.	以弗所書	Yǐfúswǒshū	YíHfàtsósyù
-Rom. Cath.	厄弗所書	Èfúswǒshū	Ngāakfātsósyù

Philippians

-Prot.	腓立比書	Féilìbǐshū	FèiHlaHpbéisyù
-Rom. Cath.	斐理伯書	Féilìbwóshū	FèiHléiHbaaksyù

Colossians

-Prot.	歌羅西書	Gēlwósyìshū	GōlòHsáisyù
-Rom. Cath.	哥羅森書	Gēlwóoēnohū	GōlòIIsámsyù

I Thessalonians

-Prot.	帖撒羅尼迦前書	Tyēsālwónìjyā-chyánshū	TipsaatlòHnèiHgà-chiHnsyù
-Rom. Cath.	得撒洛尼前書	Désālwònìchyánshū	DāksaatloknèiHchìHnsyù

II Thessalonians

-Prot.	帖撒羅尼迦後書	Tyēsālwónìjyāhòu-shū	TipsaatlòHnèiHgà-hauHsyù
-Rom. Cath.	得撒洛尼後書	Désālwònìhòushū	DāksaatloknèiHhauHsyù

I Timothy

-Prot.	提摩太前書	Tímwótàichyánshu	TàiHmòtaaichìHnsyù
-Rom. Cath.	弟茂德前書	Dìmàudéchyánshū	DaiHmauHdákchìHnsyù

II Timothy

-Prot.	提摩太後書	Tímwótàihòushū	TàiHmòtaaihauHsyù
-Rom. Cath.	弟茂德後書	Dìmàudéhòushū	DaiIImauIIdūkhauIIsyù

Titus

-Prot.	提多書	Tídwōshū	TàiHdòsyù

-Rom. Cath.	弟鐸書	Dìdwóshū	DaiHdoHksyù

Philemon

-Prot.	腓利門書	Féilìménshū	FèiHleiHmùHnsyù
-Rom. Cath.	費肋孟書	Fèilèmèngshū	FailaHkmaaHngsyù

Epistle to Hebrews

-Prot.	希伯來書	Syìbwóláishū	HèibaaklòiHsyù
-Rom. Cath.	希伯來書	Syìbwóláishū	HèibaaklòiHsyù

Epistle of James

-Prot.	雅各書	Yăgèshū	NgáHgoksyù
-Rom. Cath.	雅各伯書	Yăgèbwóshū	NgáHgokbaaksyù

I Peter

-Prot.	彼得前書	Bǐdéchyánshū	BéidākchìHnsyù
-Rom. Cath.	伯多錄前書	Bwódōlùchyánshū	BaakdòluHkchìHnsyù

II Peter

-Prot.	彼得後書	Bǐdéhòushū	BéidākhauHsyù
-Rom. Cath.	伯多錄後書	Bwódwōlùhòushū	BaakdòluHkhauHsyù

I John

-Prot.	約翰一書	Ywēhànyìshū	YeukhoHnyātsyù
-Rom. Cath.	若望一書	Rwòwàngyìshū	YeuHkmoHngyātsyù

II John

-Prot.	約翰二書	Ywèhánèrshū	YeukhohnyiHsyù
-Rom. Cath.	若望二書	Rwòwàngèrshū	YeuHkmoHngyiHsyù

III John

-Prot.	約翰三書	Ywēhànsānshū	YeukhoHnsàamsyù
-Rom. Cath.	若望三書	Rwòwàngsānshū	YeuHkmoHngsàamsyù

Jude

-Prot.	猶大書	Yóudàshū	YàuHdaaiHsyù

-Rom. Cath.	猶達書	Yóudáshū	YàuHdaaHtsyù

Revelation

-Prot.	啓示錄	Chíshr̀lù	KáiaiHluHk
-Rom. Cath.	若堲默示錄	Rwùwàngmòohr̀lù	YeuIIkmoIIugmaaIIk-siHluHk

THE BOOKS OF THE OLD TESTAMENT

Genesis

-Prot.	創世記	Chwàngshr̀jì	Chongsaigei
-Rom. Cath.	創世記	Chwàngshr̀jì	Chongsaigei

Exodus

-Prot.	出埃及記	Chūāijìjì	Chōutngòikahpgei
-Rom. Cath.	出谷記	Chūgŭjì	Chēutgūkgei

Leviticus

-Prot.	利未記	Lìwèijì	Leihmeihgei
-Rom. Cath.	肋未記	Lèwèijì	LaHkmeiHgei

Numbers

-Prot.	民數記	Mínshùjì	MàHnsougei
-Rom. Cath.	戶藉記	Hùjíjì	wuHjiHkgei

Deuteronomy

-Prot.	申命記	Shēnmìngjì	SànmiIInggei
-Rom. Cath.	申命記	Shēngmìngjì	SànmiHnggei

Joshua

-Prot.	約書亞記	Ywēshūyǎjì	Yeuksyùngagei
-Rom. Cath.	若蘇厄書	Rwòsūèshū	YeuHksòungaaksyù

Judges

-Prot.	士 師 記	Shìshrījì	SiHsìgei
-Rom. Cath.	民 長 記	Mínjăngjì	MàHnjéunggei

Ruth

-Prot.	路 得 記	Lùdéjì	Louhdākgei
-Rom. Cath.	盧 德 傳	Lúdéjwán	LòuHdākjyún

I Samuel

-Prot.	撒 母 耳 記 上	Sāmŭērjìshàng	SaatmóuHyìHgeiseuHng
-Rom. Cath.	撒 慕 爾 紀 上	Sāmùèrjìshàng	SaatmouHyìHgeiseuHng

II Samuel

-Prot.	撒 母 耳 記 下	Sāmŭērjìsyà	SaatmouHyìHgeihaH
-Rom. Cath.	撒 慕 爾 紀 下	Sāmùèrjìsyà	SaatmouHyíHgeihaH

I Kings

-Prot.	列 王 紀 上	Lyèwángjìshàng	LiHtwòHnggeiseuHng
-Rom. Cath.	列 王 紀 上	Lyèwángjìshàng	LiHtwòHnggeiseuHng

II Kings

-Prot.	列 王 紀 下	Lyèwángjìsyà	LiHtwòHnggeihaH
-Rom. Cath.	列 王 紀 下	Lyèwángjìsyà	LiHtwòHnggeihaH

I Chronicles

-Prot.	歷 代 志 上	Lìdàijr̀shàng	LiHkdoiHjiseuHng
-Rom. Cath.	編 年 紀 上	Pyānnyánjìshàng	PìnnìHngeiseuHng

II Chronicles

-Prot.	歷 代 志 下	Lìdàijr̀syà	LihkdoiHjihaH
-Rom. Cath.	編 年 紀 下	Pyānnyánjìsyà	PìnnìHngeihaH

Ezra

-Prot.	以 斯 拉 記	Yǐszlājì	YíHsìlāaigei
-Rom. Cath.	厄 斯 德 拉	Èszdélā	Ngāaksìdāklāai

Nehemiah

-Prot.	尼希米記	nísyǐmǐjì	NèiHhèimáiHgei
-Rom. Cath.	訥赫米雅	Nàhèmǐyǎ	NaaHphaakmáiHngáH

Esther

-Prot.	以斯帖記	Yǐsz̄tyējì	YíHsitipgei
-Rom. Cath.	艾斯德爾傳	Àisz̄déěrjwàn	NgaaiHsdākyíHjyún

Job

-Prot.	約伯記	Ywēbwójì	Yeukbaakgei
-Rom. Cath.	約伯傳	Ywēbwójwàn	Yeukbaakjyún

Psalms

-Prot.	詩篇	Shīpyān	Sipin
-Rom. Cath.	聖詠集	Shèngyǔngjí	SingwiHngjaaHp

Proverbs

-Prot.	箴言	Jēnyán	JàmyìHn
-Rom. Cath.	箴言	Jēnyán	JàmyìHn

Ecclesiastes

-Prot.	傳道書	Chwándàushū	ChyùHndouHsyù
-Rom. Cath.	訓道篇	Syùndàupyān	FandouHpìn

Song of Solomon

-Prot.	雅歌	Yǎgē	NgáHgō
-Rom. Cath.	雅歌	Yǎgē	NgáHgō

Isaiah

-Prot.	以賽亞書	Yǐsàiyǎshū	YìHchoi'ngasyù
-Rom. Cath.	依撒意亞	Yīsāyìyǎ	Yìsaatyi'nga

Jeremiah

-Prot.	耶利米書	Yēlìmǐshū	YèHleiHmáiHsyù
-Rom. Cath.	耶肋米亞	Yēlèmǐyǎ	YèHlaHkmáiHnga

Lamentations

-Prot.	耶利米哀歌	Yēlìmǐáigē	YèhleiHmáiHngòigō
-Rom. Cath.	耶肋米亞哀歌	Yēlèmǐyááigē	YèHlaHkmáiHngangòigō

Ezekiel

-Prot.	以西結書	Yǐsyìjyéshū	YíHsàigitsyù
-Rom. Cath.	厄則克耳	È dzékèěr	NgāākjākhāakyíH

Daniel

-Prot.	但以理書	Dànyǐlǐshū	DaaHnyíHléiHsyù
-Rom. Cath.	達尼爾	Dánǐěr	DaaHtnèiHyíH

Hosea

-Prot.	何西阿書	Hésyìàshū	HòHsàingasyù
-Rom. Cath.	歐瑟亞	Ōusèyǎ	Ngàusātnga

Joel

-Prot.	約珥書	Ywēěrshū	YeukyíHsyù
-Rom. Cath.	岳厄爾	Ywèèěr	NgoHkngāakyíH

Amos

-Prot.	阿摩司書	Àmwósyìshū	Amòsìsyù
-Rom. Cath.	亞毛斯	Yǎmáusz̄	NgamòuHsì

Obadiah

-Prot.	俄巴底亞書	È bādǐyǎshū	NgòHbàdáingasyù
-Rom. Cath.	亞北底亞斯	Yǎběidǐyǎsz̄	Ngabākdáingasì

Jonah

-Prot.	約拿書	Ywēnáshū	YeuknàHsyù
-Rom. Cath.	約納	Ywēnà	YeuknaaHp

Micah

-Prot.	彌迦書	Míjyāshū	NèiHgàsyù
-Rom. Cath.	米該亞	Mǐgāiyǎ	MáiHgòinga⌋

Nahum

-Prot.	那 鴻 書	Náhúngshū	NàHhùHngsyù
-Rom. Cath.	納 鴻	Nàhúng	NaaHphùHng

Habakkuk

-Prot.	哈 巴 谷 書	Hābāgŭshū	Hāpbàgūksyù
-Rom. Cath.	哈 巴 谷	Hābāgŭ	Hāpbāgūk

Zephaniah

-Prot.	西 番 雅 書	Syĩfānyǎshū	SàifàanngáHsyù
-Rom. Cath.	索 福 尼 亞	Swŏfúníyǎ	SokfūknèiHnga

Haggai

-Prot.	哈 該 書	Hāgāishū	Hāpgòisyù
Rom. Cath.	哈 蓋	Hāgài	Hapgoi

Zephaniah

-Prot.	撒 迦 利 亞 書	Sājyālĭyǎshū	SaatgàleiHngasyù
-Rom. Cath.	匝 加 利 亞	Sàjyalĭyǎ	SaatgàleiHnga

Malachi

-Prot.	瑪 拉 基 書	Mălājĭshū	MáHlàaigèisyù
-Rom. Cath.	瑪 拉 基 亞	Mălājĭyǎ	MáHlàaigèinga

CHURCHES IN HONG KONG

American Baptist Mission	美浸信會	Měijìnsyìnhwèi	MéiHjamseunwúi
Anglican Church	聖公會	Shènggūnghwèi	Singgùngwúi
Assemblies of God	神召會	Shénjàuhwèi	SàHnjiuHwúi
Association of Baptists for World Evangelism	萬國宣道浸信會	Wàngwósywāndàu-jìnsyìnhwèi	MaaHngwoksyùndouH-jamseunwúi
Bible Societies	聖經公會	Shèngjīnggūnghwèi	Singgīnggùngwúi
Challenge Bookshop, the	聖書公會	Shèngshūgūnghwèi	Singsyùgùngwúi
China Free Methodist Mission	中華循理會	Jūnghwásyúnlǐhwèi	JùngwaHchèuHnléiHwúi
China Missionary and Evangelistic Association	中國佈道會	Jūnggwóbùdàuhwèi	JùnggwokboudouHwúi
China Peniel Missionary Society, Inc.	便以利會	Byànyǐlìhwèi	BiHnyíHleiHwúi
China Sunday School Association	中國主日學協會	Jūnggwójǔrsywé-syéhwèi	JùnggwokjyúyaHthoHk-hiHpwúi
Chinese Christian Church	中國基督徒會	Jūnggwójidūtúhwèi	JùnggwokgēidūktòuHwúi
Chinese Christian Evangelists' Mission	中國基督徒傳道會	Jūnggwójidūtú-chwándàuhwèi	JùnggwokgēidūktòuH-chyùHndouHwúi
Chinese Christian Literature Council	基督教文藝出版社	Jidūjyàuwényi chūbǎnshè	GēidūkgaaumàHnngaiH-chēutbáanséH
Chinese Christians' Trinity Church	閩南三一堂	Mǐnnánsānyitáng	MáHnnàaHmsāam-yàttòHng
Chinese National Evangelism Commission	中華傳道會	Jūnghwá-chwándàuhwèi	JùngwàHchyùHndouH-wúi
Chinese Reformed Presbyterian Mission	循約長老會	Syúnywējǎnglǎu-hwèi	ChèuHnyēukjéunglóuH-wúi
Chinese Rhenish Church	禮賢會	Lǐsyánhwèi	LáiHyìHnwúi
Christian Children's Fund Inc.	基督教兒童福利會	Jidūjyàu Értúng-fúlihwèi	Gēidūkgaau YìHtùHng-fúkleiHwúi
Christian & Missionary Alliance	宣道會	Sywāndàuhwèi	SyùndouHwúi
Christian Missions in Many Lands	普世基督使命團	Pǔshr Jidū-shrmìngtwán	Póusai Gēidūk simiHngtyùHn

Christian Study Center on Chinese Religion and Culture	基督教中國宗教研究社	Jīdūjyàu Jūnggwó-dzūngjyàu-yánjyòushè	Gēidūkgaau Jùnggwok-jùnggaauyìHngauséH
Church of Christ	基督教會	Jīdūjyàuhwèi	Gēidūkgaauwúi
Church of Christ in China	中華基督教會	Jūnghwájīdū-jyàuhwèi	JùngwàHgēidūkgaauwúi
Conservative Baptist Foreign Mission Society	北美浸信宣道會	Běiměijìnsyìn svwāndàuhwèi	BākméiHjamseun-syìndouHwúi
Cumberland Presbyterian Church South China Mission	金巴崙長老會	Jīnbālwún-jǎnglǎuhwèi	GāmbālèuHn-jéunglóuHwúi
Emmanuel	靈光堂	Línggwāngtáng	LìHnggwòngtòHng
English Methodist Church	英循道會	Yīngsyúndàuhwèi	YìngchèuHndouHwúi
Evangelize China Fellowship Inc.	中國佈道會	Jūnggwóbùdàuhwèi	JùnggwokboudouHwúi
Evangelical Free Church	播道會	Bwòdàuhwèi	BodouHwúi
Evangelical Hakka Church	崇眞會	Chúngjēnhwèi	SùHngjānwúi
Evangelical United Brethren Mission	遵道同寅會	Dzwūndàu-túngyínhwèi	JèundouH tùHngyàHnwúi
Far East Broadcasting Co.	遠東廣播公司	Ywǎndūnggwǎng-bwògūngsz	YúHndūnggwóngbo-gūngsi
Foreign Mission Board of the Southern Baptist Convention	美南浸信會	Měinánjìnsyìnhwèi	MéiHnàaHmjanseunwúi
Foursquare Gospel Church	四方福音會	Sżfāngfúyinhwèi	Seifōngfūkyàmwúi
Free Baptist Mission	自由浸禮差會	Dżyóujìnlǐchāihwèi	JiHyàuHjamláiH-chàaiwúi
Gospel Fellowship Inc.	福音團契	Fúyìntwánchì	FūkyàmtyùIIukai
Grace Evangel Mission	香港傳道會	Syānggǎng-chwándàuhwèi	Hèunggóng-chyùHndouHwúi
Hong Kong Baptist Mission	浸禮會	Jìnlǐhwèi	JamláiHwúi
Hong Kong Chinese Christian Church Union	香港華人基督教聯會	Syānggǎnghwárén-Jīdújyàulyán-hwèi	HèunggóngwàHyàHn GēidūkgaaulyùHnwúi
Hong Kong Christian Council, the	香港基督教協進會	Syānggǎng Jīdū-jyàusyéjinhwèi	Hèunggóng Gēidūkgaau hiHpjeunwúi

Hundred Nations Crusade	萬國浸信會 ¦ 字軍	Wàngwójìnsyìn-hwèishídzjyūn	MaaHngwokjamseunwúi-saHpjiHgwān
Ling liang World-Wide Evangelistic Mission	靈糧世界佈道會	Línglyángshìjyè-bùdàuhwèi	LìHnglèuHngsaigaai-boudouHwúi
Lack Tao Baptist Mission	樂道會	Lèdàuhwèi	LoHkdouHwúi
London Missionary Society	倫敦傳道會	Lwúndwūn-chwándàuhwèi	LèuHndēun-chyùHndouHwúi
Lutheran	信義會	Syìnyìhwèi	SeunyiHwúi
	路德會	Lùdéhwèi	LouHdākwúi
Methodist	循道公會	Syúndàugūnghwèi	ChèuHndouHgùngwúi
	衛理公會	Wèilǐgūnghwèi	WaiHléiHgùngwúi
New Zealand Presbyterian Mission	新西蘭長老會	Syìnsyilán-jǎnglǎuhwèi	SànsàilàaHn jéunglóuHwú
Oriental Boat Mission	福音船	Fúyinchwán	FūkyàmsyùHn
Oriental Missionary Society	遠東宣教會	Ywándùng-sywānjyàuhwèi	YùHnduHng-syùngaauwúi
Overseas Missionary Fellowship	內地會	Nèidìhwèi	NoiHdeiHwúi
Pentecostal Apostolic Church	五旬節會	Wǔsyúnjyéhwèi	NǵHchèuHnjitwúi
Pentecostal Assemblies of Church	加拿大神召會	Jyānádà Shénjàuhwèi	GànàHdaaiH SàHnjiuHwúi
Reformed Church in America	美國歸正教會	Měigwógwēijèng-jyàuhwèi	MéiHgwokgwàijing-gaauwúi
Salvation Army	救世軍	Jyòushìjyūn	Gausaigwān
Scripture Gift Mission	倫敦聖經印贈會	Lwúndwūn Shèng-jing Yìndzèng-hwèi	LèuHndēun Singgìng YanjaHngwúi
Seventh-Day Adventist	安息日會	Ānsyìhwèi	OnsìkyaHtwúi
South East Asia Chinese Sunday School Curriculum Editorial Board	東南亞主日學課程 編輯委員會	Dūngnányǎ Jǔr-sywékèchéng-pyānjì-wěiywán-hwèi	DùngnàaHmnga Jyú-yaHthoHk fochìHngpinchāp-wáiyùHnwúi
Swedish Alliance Mission	瑞典宣道差會	Rwèidyǎn Sywān-dàuchāihwèi	SeuiHdín SyùndouH-chàaiwúi
Swedish Free Mission	瑞典自由差會	Rwèidyǎn Dzyóu-chāihwèi	SeuiHdín JiHyàuH-chāaiwúi

The United Hong Ko-ng Christian Baptist Churches Association	香港浸信聯會	Syūnggǎngjìnsyìn-lyánhwèi	HèunggóngjamseunlyùHnwúi
The United Presbyterian Church in the U. S. A.	美國聯合長老會	Měigwólyánhé-jǎngláuhwèi	MéiHgwoklyǹHnhaHp,jéunglóuHwúi
Union Church	估寧堂	Kūníngtáng	GúnìHngtòHng
United Church of Canada	加拿大聯合教會	Jyānádàlyánhé-jyàuhwèi	GànàHdaaiHlyùHnhaHp,gaauw úi
United Church Board for World Ministries	美國基督教聯合教會	Měigwó Jīdūjyàu-lyánhéjyàuhwèi	MéiHgwok GēidūkgaaulyùHnhaHpgaauwúi
West China Evangelistic Band	華西靈工團	Hwásyī Lìuggūŋgtwán	WàHsài LìHnggùngtyùHn
Y. M. C. A.	基督教青年會	Jīdūjyàu Chīngnyánhwèi	Gēidūkgaau ChìngnìHnwúi
Young Women's Christian Association	基督教女青年會	Jīdūjyàu Nyǔchīng-nyánhwèi	Gēidūkgaau néuiHchìngnìHnwúi

APPENDIX OF SERVICE TERMS

Military Terms

A

AA gun	高射炮	gāushèpàu	gòuseHpaau
absent (AWOL)	無故缺席	wúgúchywēsyí	mòuHgukyutjiHk
accommodation	宿營的地方	sùyíngde dìfang;	sūkyìHngdik deiHfòng;
	住所	jùswǒ	jyuHsó
adjutant	副官	fúgwān	fugùn
advance	前進	chyánjìn	chìHnjeun
advance, to	前進	chyánjìn	chìHnjeun
aerial	天線	tyānsyàn	tìnsin
aim, to	瞄準	myáujwǔn	mìuHjéun
air cover	空中掩護	kūngjūngyǎnhù	hùngjùngyímwuH
air raid	空襲	kūngsyí	hùngjaaHp
air shelter	防空洞	fángkūngdùng	fòHnghùngdúng
air support	空中支援	kūngjūngjīywán	hùngjùngjiwuHn
airborne force	空運部隊	kūngyùnbùdwèi	hùngwaHnbouHdéui
alarm (false)	假警報	jyǎjǐngbàu	gágíngbou
alert, to	警戒	jǐngjyè	gínggaai
all clear	警報解除	jǐngbàu jyěchú	gínbou gáaichèuiH
ambulance	救護車	jyòuhùchē	gauwuHchè
ambush	埋伏	máifú	màaiHfuHk
ambush, to	伏擊	fújí	fuHkgìk
ammunition	彈藥	dànyàu	daaHnyeuHk
ant-tank gun	反坦克車炮	fǎntǎnkèchēpàu;	fáantáanhāakchēpaaū;
	平射炮	píngshèpàu	pìHngseHpaau

anti-tank mine	反坦克車地雷	făntănkèchēdìléi	fáantáanhāakchē-deiHlèuiH
anti-tank missile	反坦克車飛彈	făntănkèchēfēidàn	fáantáanhāakchēfèidáan
approach march	接敵前進	jyēdíchyánjìn	jipdìHkchìHnjeun
arm of service	兵種	bīngjŭng	bingjúng
arms	武器	wŭchì	móuHhei
armed with	裝備	jwāngbèi	jòngbeiH
armour piercing	穿甲	chwānjyă	chyùngaap
armoured	裝甲的	jwāngjyăde	jònggaapdik
armoured car	裝甲車	jwāngjyăchē	jònggaapchè
armoured fighting vehicle	裝甲戰車	jwāngjyăjànchē	jònggaapjinchè
army	陸軍	lùjyūn	luHkgwàn
artillery, light	輕炮兵	chīngpàubīng	hīngpaaubìng
artillery, medium	中型炮兵	jūngsyíngpàubīng	jùngyìHngpaaubìng
artillery, heavy	重炮兵	jùngpàubīng	juHngpaaubìng
assault boat	突擊艇	tùjitĭng	daHtgiktéIIng
assault force	突擊部隊	tùjíbùdwèi	daHtgìkbouHdéui
assault landing	突擊登陸	tùjídēnglù	daHtgikdàngluHk
assault, to take by	攻佔	gūngjàn	gùngjim
assembly area	集中地區	jijūngdìchyū	jaaHpjùngdeiHkèui
atomic weapon	原子武器	ywándzwŭchì	yùHnjínóuHhei
attached to, to be	附屬	fùshŭ	fuHsuHk
attachment	附屬單位	fùshŭdānwèi	fuHsuHkdāanwái
attack	攻擊	gūngjí	gūnggìk
attack, to	攻擊	gūngjí	gūnggìk
automatic rifle	自動步鎗	dzdùngbùchyāng	jiHduHngbouHchēung

B

| backsight | 表尺 | byăuchĭ | biuchek |

badge of rank	證章符號	jèngjāngfúhàu	jingjēungfùHhouH
bandage	綳帶	bēngdài	bàngdáai
bandage, to	裹綳帶	gwŏbēngdài	gwóbàngdáai
barbed wire	鐵絲網	tyĕszwăng	titsìmóHng
barracks	營房	yíngfáng	yìHngfòHng
barrage (fire)	彈幕	dànmwò;	daaHnmoHk;
	火網	hwŏwăng	fómóHng
barrel (gun;rifle)	炮身	pàushēn	paausàn;
	鎗管	chyānggwăn	chēunggún
base	基地	jidì	gèideiH
battalion	營	yíng	yìHng
battery (artillery)	炮兵連	pàubìnglyán	paaubìngliHn
battery (electric)	電池	dyànchí	diHnchìH
battle	戰役	jànyì	jinyiHk
batman	勤務兵	chínwùbìng	kàHnmouHbìng
bayonet	刺刀	tszdāu	chidōu
beach	海灘	hăitān	hóitāan
beachhead	灘頭堡	tāntóubău	tàantàuHbóu
bearing, magnetic	磁方位	tszfāngwèi	chìHfòngwái
belt (clothing; ammunition)	腰帶	yāudài;	yìudáai;
	彈帶	dàndài	daaHndáai
billet	營舍	yíngshè	yìHngse
billet, to	宿營	sùyíng	sūkyìHng
blast	爆炸力	bàujàlì	baaujaliHk
blow up, to (trans; intrans)	炸	jà;	ja;
	炸壞	jàhwài	jawaaiH
bomb	炸彈	jàdàn	jadáan

bomb, to	轟炸	hūngjà	gwàngja
bombard, to	炮擊	pàují	paaugìk
bombardment	炮擊	pànjí	paaugìk
boots	靴子	sywēdz	hèují (chèuHnghèu)
breakdown (mech- anical)	故障	gùjàng	gujeung
bridge	橋樑	chyáulyáng	kìuHlèuHng
bridge, pontoon	浮頭	fúchyáu	fàuHkìuH
bridgehead	橋頭堡	chyáutóubǎu	kìuHtàuHbóu
brigade	旅	lyǔ	léuiH
bullet	子彈	dždàn	jídáan
burst (of shell etc.)	爆炸	bàujà	baauja
burst, to	爆炸	bàujà	baauja
butt (rifle)	鎗托	chyāngtwō	chēungtok

C

camouflage	僞裝	wèijwāng	ngaiHjòng
camouflage, to	僞裝	wèijwāng	ngaiHjòng
camp	營地	yíngdì	yìHngdeiH
camp, to	宿營	sùyíng	sūkyìHng
canteen			
-place	食堂	shŕtáng	siHktòHng
-utensil	飯盒	fànhé	faaHnháp
cap			
-clothing	帽子	màudz;	mouHji (móu);
-ammunition	彈頭帽	dàntóumàu	daahntàuHmóu
captain	上尉	shàngwèi	senHngwai
capture (personnel)	俘擄	fūlǔ	fùlóuH

capture, to	俘擄	fūlŭ	fùlóuH
capture (territory)	佔領	jànlǐng	jimlíHng
car	車	chē	chè
cartridge	藥筒	yàutŭng	yeuHktúng
casualty	死傷	sžshāng	séisèung
casualty clearing station	野戰醫院	yějànyǐywàn	yéHjinyǐyún
cease fire, to	停止射擊 停火	tíngjř shèjǐ; tínghwǒ	tìHngjí seHgǐk; tìHngfó
charge, a (explosive)	炸藥	jàyàu	jayeuHk
civilian clothes	平民衣服 便服	píngmínyǐfú; byànfú	pìHngmàHnyǐfuHk; biHnfuHk
cliff	斷崖 峭壁	dwànyái; chyàubǐ	tyúHnngàaiH; chiubǐk
clip (magazine)	彈夾	dànjyá	daaHngáap
close arrest	禁閉	jìnbǐ	gambai
coast	海岸	hǎiàn	hóingoHn
colonel	上校	shàngsyàu	seuHnggaau
column	縱隊	dzùngdwèi	jùngdeuiH
combined operation	聯合作戰	lyánhédzwòjàn	lyùHnhaHpjokjin
command, to	指揮	jřhwēi	jífài
command post	指揮所	jřhwēiswǒ	jífàisó
commandant	總長	dzǔngjǎng	júngjéung
communicate, to	通知	tūngjř	tùngjì
communications (signals)	通訊	tūngsyìn	tùngseun
(traffic)	交通	jyāutūng	gàautùng
company	連	lyán	lìHn
company commander	連長	lyánjǎng	lìHnjéung

company QMS	連部軍需中士	lyánbùjyūnsyū-jūngshr̀	lìHnbouHgwànsèui; jùngsiH
company SM	連部軍事上士	lyánbùjyūnshr̀-shàngshr̀	lìHnbouHgwànsiH-seuHngsiH
concentrate, to	集中	jíjūng	jaaHpjùng
concentration	集中	jíjūng	jaaHpjùng
compass	羅盤	lwópán	lòHpùHn
concealed	掩蔽的	yǎnbìde	yímbaidïk
concealment	掩蔽	yǎnbì	yímbai
contaminated	着染的	jwórǎnde	jeuHkyíHmdïk
contour	同高線	túnggāusyàn	tùHnggòusin
convoy	護送隊	hùsùngdwèi	wuHsungdeuiH
convoy, to	護航	hùháng	wuHhòHng;
	護送	hùsùng	wuHsung
cookhouse	厨房	chúfáng	chyùHfòng
corporal	下士	syàshr̀	haHsiH
corps	軍團	jyūntwán	gwàntyùHn
court martial	軍事法庭	jyūnshr̀fǎtíng	gwànsiHfaattìHng
cover	掩護	yǎnhù	yímwuH
cover, to take	掩蔽	yǎnbì	yímbai
crest (of hill etc)	山頂	shāndǐng;	sàandéng
	巔峯	dyānfēng	dïnfùng
crew (gun, tank etc)	炮手	pàushǒu	paausáu
crossroads	交叉路	jyāuchālù	gàauchàlouH
cut off the retreat to	切斷退路	chyēdwàntwèilù	chittyúHnteuilouH

damage	損害	swǔnhài	syúnhoiH
damage to	損壞	swǔnhwài	syúnwaaiH
dead	死亡	sžwáng	séimòHng

dead ground	盲地	mángdì	màaHngdeiH
defeat, to	打敗	dǎbài	dábaaiH
defence	防禦	fángyù	fòHngyuH
defend, to	防禦	fángyù	fòHngyuH
defensive	守勢	shǒushr̀	sáusai
demolition	破壞	pwòhwài	powaaiH
depot (stores etc)	倉庫	tsāngkù	chòngfu
depth	深度	shēndù	sàmdouH
detail, to	特派	tèpài	daHkpaai
detention	監禁	jyānjìn	gàamgam
detonator	起爆管	chǐbàugwǎn	héibaaugún
detour	繞道	ràudàu	yíuHdouH
dig in, to	挖掘	wājywé;	waatgwaHt;
	掘壕	jywéháu	gwaHthòuH
disable, to	殘廢	tsánfèi	chàaHnfai
disembark, to (trans; intrans.)	下船	syàchwán	haHsyùHn (loHksyùHn)
dispatch rider	傳令兵	chwánlìngbīng	chyùHnliHngbìng
dispersal area (vehicles)	車輛集散地	chēlyàngjísàndì	chèléungjaaHpsaandeiH
distance (interval)	間隔距離	jyāngéjyùlí	gaangaakkéuiHléiH
ditch	壕溝	háugōu	hòuHgàu (hàangkèuiH)
diversion (of road)	繞道	ràudàu	yíuHdouH
division	師	shī	sì
dressing (wounds)	繃帶	bēngdài	bàngdáai
dressing station	裹傷站	gwǒshāngjàn	gwósèungjaaHm
drill	操練	tsāulyàn	chòuliHn
drill, to	操練	tsāulyàn	chòuliHn
drive, to (vehicle)	駕駛	jyàshr̀;	gasái (jàchè);

	開車	kāichē	hòichè
driver	司機	sžjī	sìgèi
drop, to (eg. by parachute)	空投	kūngtóu	hùngtàuII
dropping zone	空投地帶	kūngtóudìdài	hùngtàuHdeiHdaai
dugout	掩蔽洞	yǎnbìdùng	yímbaiduHng
dump	堆積所	dwēijiswǒ	dēuijìksó
duty, to be on	值班	jífbān	jiHkbāan

E

embark, to (trans; intrans)	上船	shàngchwán	séuHngsyúHn
emplacement	炮座	pàudzwò;	paaujoH;
	炮台	pàutái	paautòiH
enemy (N and adj)	敵人	dirén	diHkyàHn
engine (railway, vehicle, aircraft, launch etc)	發動機	fādùngjī	faatduHnggèi
entrain, to	上火車	shànghwǒchē	séuHngfóchè
equipment	配備	pèibèi	puibeiH
escort (protect)	護送	hùsùng	wuHsung
exercise (training)	演習	yǎnsyí	yínjaaHp
explode, to (trans; intrans)	爆炸	bàujà	baauja
explosion	爆炸	bàujà	baauja
explosive	炸藥	jàyàu	jayeuHk
exposed	暴露的	bàulùde	bouHlouHdik

F

| fall in, to | 集合 | jíhé | jaaHphaHp |
| fall out, to | 解散 | jyěsàn | gáaisaan |

fatigue party	勞作隊	láudzwòdwèi	lòuHjokdéui
ferry	渡船	dùchwán	douHsyùHn
field	田野	tyányě	tìHnyéH
field dressing station	田野裏傷站	tyányěgwǒshāngjàn	tìHnyéHgwósèungjaaHm
field glasses	望遠鏡	wàngywǎnjìng	moHngyúHngeng
field gun	野戰炮	yějànpàu	yéHjinpaau
field of fire	射擊線	shèjísyàn;	seHgǐksin;
	射擊範圍	shèjífànwéi	seHgǐkfaaHnwàiH
field of vision	視線	shr̀syàn	siHsin
fight, to	戰鬥	jàndòu	jindau
fire	火力	hwǒlì	fóliHk
fire, to	射擊	shèjí	seHgǐk
fire, covering	掩護火力	yǎnhùhwǒlì	yímwuHfóliHk
fire, harrassing	擾亂射擊	rǎulwànshèjí	yíuHlyuHnseHgǐk
fire, indirect	間接射擊	jyànjyēshèjí	gaanjipseHgǐk
fire, rapid	急速射擊	jísùshèjí	gāpchūkseHgǐk
fire plan	射擊計劃	shèjíjìhwà	seHgǐkgaiwaaHk
first aid	急救	jíjyòu	gāpgau
flank	側翼	tsèyì	jākyiHk
flash (gun)	閃光	shǎngwāng	sǐmgwòng
fold (of ground)	地皺	dìjòu	deiHjau
force (formation)	部隊	bùdwèi	bouHdeuiH
ford	徒涉場	túshèchǎng	tòuHsipchèuHng
foreground	前地	chyándì	chìHndeiH
foresight	瞄準星	myáujwǔnsyīng	mìuHjéunsǐng
formation	隊形	dwèisyíng	deuiHyìHng
fort	炮台;	pàutái;	paautòiH;
	堡壘	bǎulěi	bóuléuiH

forward area	前方陣地帶	chyánfāngjèndìdài	chìHnfòngjaHndeiHdaai
forward HQ	前方指揮部	chyánfāngjǐrhwēibù	chìHnfòngjífàibouH
forward OP	前進觀測所	chyánjìngwāntsè swǒ	chìHnjeungùnchāaksó
forward slope	前斜面	chyánsyémyàn	chìHnchèHmín
friendly forces (not enemy)	友軍	yǒujyūn	yáuHgwān
front	戰線	jànsyàn;	jinsin
	前線	chyánsyàn	chìHnsin
frontier	國境	gwójìng	gwokgíng
fuel (domestic; ICE)	燃料	ránlyàu	yìHnlíu
fuze	信管	syìngwǎn	seungún

G

garrison	駐軍	jùjyūn	jyugwān
gas	毒氣	dúchì	duHkhei
gas mask	防毒面具	fángdúmyànjyù	fòHngduHkmiHngeuiH
general (ordinary)	普通	pǔtūng	póutùng
general (military rank)	將軍	jyāngjyūn	jēunggwàn
general HQ	總司令部	dzǔngszlìngbù	júngsìliHngbouH
grease	滑機油	hwájiyóu	waaIlkgèiyàuII
grease, to	上油	shàngyóu	séuHngyàuH
greatcoat	大衣	dàyī	daaiHyì (daaiHlōu)
grenade	手溜彈	shǒulyóudàn	sáulàuHdáan
guard, to be on	守衞	shǒuwèi	sáuwaiH
guard, to mount	置衞兵	jìwèibīng	jiwaiHbīng
guerilla	游擊隊	yóujídwèi	yàuHgikdéui
guerilla warfare	游擊戰	yóujijàn	yàuHgikjìn
guide	嚮導	syǎngdǎu	héungdouII

guide, to	指導	jřdǎu	jídouH
gun	炮	pàu	paau
gun carriage	炮架	pàujyà	paaugá

H

H bomb	氫彈	chīngdàn	hìngdáan
H hour	行動開始時刻	syíngdùngkāishř-shřkè	hàHngduHnghòichi-siHhāak
half-track vehicle	半履帶車輛	bànlyǔdàichēlyàng	bunléuiHdaaichèléung
hand to hand fighting	白刃戰	báirènjàn	baaHkyaHnjin
haversack	背包	bèibāu	buibāau
headphones	聽筒	tīngtǔng	tèngtúng
headquarters	司令部	sžlìngbù	sìliHngbouH
high explosive	高度炸藥	gāudùjàyàu	gòudouHjayeuHk
hill	山	shān	sàan
hill (small)	丘	chyōu	yàu
hit, to	命中	mìngjùng	miHngjung
hold out, to	固守	gùshǒu	gusáu
hospital	醫院	yīywàn	yìyún
horizon	地平線	dìpíngsyàn	deiHpìHngsin
howitzer	榴彈炮	lyǎudànpàu	làuHdáanpaau
hut	小房子	syǎufángdz	sìufòHngjí (saifóng)

I

identity disc	名牌	míngpái	mìHngpàaiH
identity documents	身份證	shēnfènjèng	sànfaHnjing
ignition(of explosives)	引火	yǐnhwǒ	yáHnfó
ignition of engines	發火器	fāhwǒchì	faatfóhei

incendiary di,	燒夷彈	shāuyídàn;	sìuyiHdáan;
	燃燒彈	ránshāudàn	yìHnsiudáan
infantry	步兵	bùbīng	bouHbìng
infantryman	步兵兵士	bùbīngbìngshr̀	bouHhìngbìngsiII
information (intelligence)	情報	chíngbàu	chìHngbou
inspection	檢查	jyǎnchá	gímchàH
inspection of troops	檢閱	jyǎnywè	gímyuHt
intercom	內部通話設備	nèibùtūnghwà-shèbèi	noiIIbouHtùngwaH-chitbeiII
interpreter	譯員	yìywán	yiHkyùHn
interrogate, to	訊問	syùnwèn	seunmaHn
interrogation	訊問	syùnwèn	seunmaHn

J

jam, to (machine gun, etc)	有故障	yǒugùjàng	yáuIIgujeung
jam, to (trans radio)	干擾	gānrǎu	gònyíuH
junction (railway; road)	交义點	jyāuchādyǎn	gàauchàdím

K

| killed (casualty) | 死傷 | sz̀shāng | séisèung |
| kit | 兵士行囊 | hīngshr̀syíngnáng | bìngsiHhàHnguóHng |

L

lance corporal	代理下士	dàilǐsyàshr̀	doiIIléiHhaHsiH
landing (from sea)	登陸	dēnglù	dàngluIIk
landing by parachute	着陸	jwólù	jeuHkluHk

landing area	登陸地區	dēnglùdìchyū;	dàngluHkdeiHkèui;
	着陸地區	jwólùdìchyū	jeuHkluHkdeiHkèui
landing craft	登陸艇	dēnglùtǐng	dàngluHktéHng
landing force	登陸部隊	dēnglùbùdwèi;	dàngluHkbouHdeuiH;
	着陸部隊	jwólùbùdwèi	jeuHkluHkbouHdeuiH
landing strip	臨時跑道	línshŕpǎudàu	làHmsìHpáaudouH
latrine	厠所	tsèswǒ	chisó
lay (gun), to	瞄準	myáujwǔn	mìuHjéun
leave n.	休假	syōujyà	yàuga
leave pass	休假證	syōujyàjèng	yàugajing
level crossing	鐵路過道口	tyělùgwòdàukǒu	titlouHgwodouHháu
lieutenant	中尉	jūngwèi	jùngwai
lieutenant colonel	中校	jūngsyàu	jùnggaau
line (front)	前線	chyánsyàn	chìHnsin
line (telephone etc)	電線	dyànsyàn	diHnsin
line of communication	補濟線	bǔjisyàn	bóujaisin
line of fire	射擊線	shèjísyàn	seHgǐksin
line of retreat	退却線	twèichywèsyàn	teuikeuksin
local authorities (civil)	地方當局	dìfāngdāngjyú	deiHfònggdòngguHk
look-out	監視哨	jyānshŕshàu	gàamsiHsaau
lorry	載重汽車	dzàijùngchìchē	joichúHngheichè

M

machine gun	機關鎗	jīgwānchyāng	gèigwàanchēung
magazine (rifle)	彈夾	dànjyá	daaHngáap
main body (troops)	本隊	běndwèi;	búndeuiH;
	主力	jǔlì	jyúliHk

maintenance	修護	syōuhù	sàuwuH
major (rank)	少校	shàusyàu	siugaau
manoeuvre (exercise)	演習	yǎnsyí	yínjaaHp
map	地圖	dìtú	deiHtòuII
map reading	地圖判讀	dìtúpàndú	deiHtòuHpunduHk
map reference	地圖標識	dìtúbyāushr̀	deiHtòuHbìusik
march, to	行軍	syíngjyūn	hàHnggwàn
mark on the map, to	畫在地圖上	hwàdzàidìtúshàng	waaHkjoiHdeiHtòuH-seuHng
mayor (or similar local civil authority)	巿長	shr̀jǎng	síHjéung
mechanised	機械化	jìsyèhwà	gèihaaiHfa
medical officer	軍醫官	jyūnyigwān	gwànyìgùn
medical corps	軍醫部	jyūnyìbù	gwànyìbouH
mess	宿舍	sùshè	sūkse
message	消息	syāusyi	siusik
messenger	傳令兵	chwánlingbīng	chyùHnliHngbìng
military police	憲兵	syànbīng	hinbìng
mine	地雷	dìléi	deiHlèuiH
mine detector	驗雷器	yànléichì	yiHmlèuiHhei
minefield	佈雷區	bùléichyū	boulèuiHkèui
minefield, to lay a	佈雷	bùléi	boulèuiH
minefield, to clear a	掃雷	sǎuléi	soulèuiH
miss, to	沒打中	méidǎjùng	muHtdájung (móuHdájung)
missile	飛彈	fēidàn	fèidáan
missile, guided	導彈	dǎudàn	douHdáan
missile, homing	追蹤飛彈	jwēidzūngfēidàn	jèuijùngfèidáan
missile, ICBM	越洲彈道飛彈	ywèjōudàndàufēidàn	yuHtjàudaaHndouH-fèidáan
(intercontinental ballistic)	洲際飛彈	jōujìfēidàn	jàujaifèidáan

missile, IRBM (intermediate range ballistic)	中程彈導飛彈	jūngchéngdàndǎu-fēidàn	jùngchìHngdaaHndouH-fèidáan
missle, short range ballistic	短程彈導飛彈	dwǎnchéngdàndǎu fēidàn	dyúnchìHngdaaHndouH-fèidáan
missile, AAGW (air to air guided weapon)	空對空導彈	kūngdwèikūngdǎu dàn	hùngdeuihùngdouHdáan
missile, ASGW (air to surface guided weapon)	空對地導彈	kūngdwèididǎudàn	hùngdeuideiHdouHdáan
missile, SAGW (surface to air guided weapon)	地對空導彈	dìdwèikūngdǎudàn	deiHdeuihùngdouHdáan
missile, SSGW (surface to surface guided weapon)	地對地導彈	dìdwèididǎudàn	deiHdeuideiHdouHdáan

N

non-combatant	非戰鬥人員	fēijàndòurénywán	fèijindauyàHnyùHn
non-commissioned officer	軍士	jyūnshr̀	gwànsiH
north, magnetic	北磁極	běitszjí	bākchìHgiHk
north, grid	方格北	fānggébĕi	fònggaakbāk
north, true	眞北	jēnbĕi	jānbāk
nuclear adj.	核子的	hédzde	haHtjídìk

O

objective n.	目標	mùbyāu	muHkbìu
observation	觀測	gwāntsè	gùnchāak
observation post	觀測哨	gwāntsèshàu	gùnchāaksaau
observe, to	觀測	gwāntsè	gùnchāak
observer	觀測家	gwāntsèjyā	gùnchāakgā
obstacle (anti-tank etc)	障礙物	jàngàiwù	jeungngoiHmaHt
occupy, to	佔領	jànlǐng	jimlíHng

offensive adj.	攻勢	gūngshr̀	gùngsai
officer	軍官	jyūngwān	gwàngùn
officer commanding	司令官	sz̀lìnggwān	sìliHnggùn
open country	開擴地	kāikwòdì	hòikwongdeiH
open fire, to	開火	kāihwǒ	hòifó
operation	作戰	dzwòjàn	jokjin
operator (radio telephone etc)	報務員	bàuwùywán	boumouHyùHn
ORs	士兵	shr̀bīng	siHhìng
order n.	命令	mìnglìng	miHngliHng
orderly	勤務兵	chínwùbīng	kàHnmouHbìng
orderly room	勤務室	chínwùshr̀	kàHnmouHsāt
ordance (arm of service)	軍需	jyūnsyū	gwànsèui
out of action (men; material)	失却作用	shrchywèdzwòyùng	satkeukjokyuHng
outflank, to	包抄	bāuchāu	bàauchàau
outpost	前哨	chyánshàu	chìHnsaau

P

parachute	降落傘	jyànglwòsǎn	gongloHksaan
parachute troops	傘兵	sǎnbīng	saanbìng
parade	出操	chūtsāu	chēutchòu
park (vehicle) n.	停車場	tíngchēchǎng	tìHngchèchèuHng
patrol, fighting	戰鬥邏巡隊	jàndòusyúnlwódwèi	jindauchèuHnlòHdéui
patrol, standing	斥候	chr̀hóu	chikhàuH
patrol reconnaissance	偵察巡邏隊	jēnchásyúnlwódwèi	jìngchaatchèuHnlòHdéui
patrol, to	巡邏	syúnlwó	chèuHnlòH
petrol	汽油	chìyóu	heiyàuH
pick (tool)	鶴嘴鋤	háudzwëichú	hoHkjéuichòH

picket	哨兵	shàubīng	saaubìng
pistol	手鎗	shǒuchyāng	sáuchēung
plain	平地	píngdì;	pìHngdeiH;
	平原	píngywán	pìHngyùHn
platoon	排	pái	pàaiH
police (civil)	警察	jǐngchá	gíngchaat
polish, to	擦亮	tsālyàng	chaatleuHng (chaatling)
post (sentry etc)	崗位	gāngwèi	gòngwái
post (sentry etc) to	放哨	fàngshàu	fongsaau
prisoner	俘擄	fūlǔ	fùlóuH
private soldier	兵士	bīngshì	bīngsiH
pull-through	擦鎗管繩	tsāchyānggwǎn shéng	chaatchēunggúnsìHng

Q

| quarter (billet) | 營房 | yíngfáng | yìHngfòHng |

R

radar	雷達	léidá	lèuiHdaaHt
radio	無線電	wúsyàndyàn	mòuHsindiHn
raid	襲擊	syíjí	jaaHkgìk
railway	鐵路	tyělù	titlouH
range (of gun etc)	射程	shèchéng	seHchìHng
range (for firing practice)	靶場	bǎchǎng	báchèuHng
range (mountain)	山脈	shānmài	sàanmaHk
rank (row)	列	lyè	liHt
rank (grade)	階級	jyējí	gāaikǎp

rations	軍糧	jyūnlyáng	gwànlèuHng
rearguard	後衞	hòuwèi	hauHwaiH
receiver (W/T)	收報機	shōubàujī	sàubougèi
recoil	後挫力	hòutswòlì	hauHcholiHk
reconnaissance	偵察	jēnchá	jìngchaat
reconnoitre, to	偵察	jēnchá	jìngchaat
refugee	難民	nànmín	naaHnmàHn
regiment	聯隊	lyándwèi	lyùHndéui
regulation	規則	gwēidzé	kwàijāk
reinforcements	援軍	ywánjyūn	wuHngwàn
relief	換班	hwànbān;	wuHnbàan;
	瓜代	gwādài	gwàdoiH
relieve, to (of duty)	按替	jyētì	jiptai
relieve, (troops in line)	救援	jyòuywán	gauwuHn
rendezvous n.	集合點	jihédyǎn	jaaHphaHpdím
report (account)	報告	bàugàu	bougou
report, to	報告	bàugàu	bougou
resist, to	抵抗	dǐkàng	dáikong
resistance	抵抗	dǐgàng	dáikong
retake, to	收復	shōufù	sàufuHk
retire, to (from service)	退役	twèiyì	teuiyiHk
retire, to	撤退	chètwèi	chitteui
revolver	左輪鎗	dzwǒlwúnchyāng	jóléunchēung
ridge	山脊	shānjí	sàanjek
rifle	步鎗	bùchyāng	bouHchēung
river	河	hé	hòH
road	路	lù	louH
road block	路障	lùjàng	louHjeung

rocket projectile (RP) (also see missile)	火箭彈	hwǒjyàndàn	fójindáan
rocket launcher	火箭筒	hwǒjyàntǔng	fójintùHng
roll-call	點名	dyǎnmíng	dímméng
(one) round (of ammunition)	一發子彈	yìfādždàn;	yātfaatjídáan
	一發炮彈	yìfāpàudàn	yātfaatpaudáan
route	路線	lùsyàn	louHsin
run out of, to (ammunition etc)	缺乏	chywēfá	kyutfaHt

S

safety catch	保險裝置	bǎusyǎnjwāngjr̀	bóuhímjòngji
salute, to	敬禮	jìnglǐ	gingláiH
salvage	救出之財物	jyòuchùjr̄tsáiwù	gauchēutjìchòiHmaHt
sandbag	沙包	shābāu	sàbàau
sapper	工兵	gūngbīng	gūngbìng
scale (of map)	比例尺	bǐlìchǐ	béilaiHchek
scout	斥候	chr̀hóu	chìkhàuH
searchlight	探照燈	tànjàudēng	taamjiudāng
second in command	副指揮官	fùjřhwēigwān	fujífàigùn
second lieutenant	少尉	shàuwèi	siuwai
section	班	bān	bàan
self-propelled	自行的	dz̀syíngde	jiHhàHngdǐk
sentry	步哨	bùshàu	bouHsaau
sergeant	中士	jūngshr̀	jùngsiH
sergeant-major, regimental	准尉	jwǔnwèi	jéunwai
sergeant major, company	上士	shàngshr̀	seuHngsiH
shell	炮彈	pàudàn	paudáan

shell, to	炮擊	pàují	paaugìk
shoot, to	發射	fāshè	faatseH
shot	子彈	dždàn	jídáan
shovel	鏟	chǎn	cháan
signals (arm of service)	通訊部隊	tūngsyìnbùdwèi	tùngseunbouHdeuiH
single file	一路縱隊	yílùdm̀ngdwòi	yatlouHjùngdeuiH
slope, forward	前斜面	chyánsyémyàn	chìHnchèHmiHn
slope, reverse	後斜面	hòusyémyàn	hauHchèHmiHn
sling (rifle)	鎗皮帶	chyāngpídài	chēungpèiHdaai
sniper	狙擊兵	jyùjíbìng	jeuigikbìng
soldier	兵士	bīngshr̀	bìngsiH
source (of information)	來源	láiywán	lòiHyùHn
spare part	零件	língjyàn	liHnggin
sparking plug	火花栓	hwǒhwāshwān	fófachyùHn
spy	間諜	jyàndyé	gaandiHp
squadron	中隊	jūngdwèi	jùngdeuiH
square (of map)	方格	fānggé	fònggaak
staff	參謀	tsānmóu	chàammàuH
staff sergeant	上士	shàngshr̀	seuHngsiH
start point	出發點	chūfādyǎn	chēutfaatdím
station (railway)	火車站	hwǒchējàn	fóchèjaaHm
stores	軍需品	jyūnsyūpǐn	gwànsēuibán
strength (numbers)	兵力	bīnglì	bìngliHk
stretcher	擔架	dānjyà	dàamga
stretcher bearer	擔架兵	dānjyàbīng	dàamgabìng
stripe (badge of rank)	階級章	jyējíjāng	gāaikāpjēung
supplies	補濟品	bǔjìpǐn	bóujaibán
surrender, to	投降	tóusyáng	tàuHhòHng

T

tactics	戰術	jànshù	jinseuHt
take c√ər, to	接收	jyēshōu	jipsàu
tank	坦克車	tǎnkèchē	táanhāakchè
tank trap	坦克壕	tǎnkèháu	táanhāakhòuH
target	目標	mùbyāu	muHkbǐu
tarpaulin	防水布	fángshwěibù	fòHngséuibou
tent	帳篷	jàngpéng	jeungpùHng
terrain	地形	dìsyíng	deiHyìHng
tool	工具	gūngjyù	gùnggeuiH
tool roll	工具套	gūngjyùtàu	gùnggeuiHtou
town major	宿營地司令官	sùyíngdìszlìnggwān	sūkyìHngdeiHsì- liHnggùn
tracer bullet	夷光彈	yígwāngdàn	yìHgwòngdáan
track (route, path)	蹤跡	dzūngjì	jūngjik
track (of tank etc)	履帶	lyǔdài	léuiHdáai
tracked vehicle	履帶車輛	lyǔdàichēlyàng	léuiHdáaichèléung
traffic (vehicles)	交通	jyāutūng	gàautùng
transmitter (W/T)	發報機	fābàujī	faatbougèi
transport	運輸工具	yùnshūgūngjyù	waHnsyùgùnggeuiH
transport, to	輸送	shūsùng	syùsung
treatment (wounded) (Ps. O. W.)	治療	jìlyáu	jiHlìuH
trench	戰壕	jànháu	jinhòuH
trigger	扳機	bǎnjǐ	Ła̧angèi
troops	部隊	bùdwèi	ŁouHdeuiH
troopship	運兵船	yùnbīngchwán	waHnbìngsyùHn
trousers	褲子	kùdz	fuji (fu)

| tunic | 上衣 | shàngyì | seuHngyì (sāam) |
| tyre | 輪胎 | lwúntāi | lèuHntòi |

U

uniform	軍服	jyūnfú	gwànfuHk
unit	單位	dānwèi	dāanwái
unload, to	卸	syè	se (sefo)

V

| valley | 山谷 | shāngǔ | sāangūk |
| visibility | 能見度 | néngjyàndù | nàHnggindouH |

W

waggon	貨車	hwòchē	fochè
war	戰爭	jànjēng	jinjàng
warrant officer	准尉	jwǔnwèi	jéunwai
water point	給水點	jǐshwěidyǎn	kāpséuidím
water supply	給水	jǐshwěi	kāpséui (héiséui)
water, drinking	食水	shfshwěi	siHkséui
water, undrinkable	水	shwěi	séui
wave-length	波長	bwōcháng	bòchèuHng
winch	絞盤	jyǎupán	gáaupùHn
weapon (see also missile)	武器	wǔchì	móuHhei
wire	鐵絲	tyěsž	titsí
wire cutters	鐵絲剪	tyěsžjyǎn	titsíjín
W/T	無線電報	wúsyàndyànbàu	mòuHsindiHnbou

wood (geographical)	樹林	shùlín	syuHlàHm
working party	勞動組	láudùngdzŭ	lòuHduHngjóu
wound	傷	shāng	sèung
wounded	傷者	shāngjě	sèungjé

Z

zero hour	行動開始時刻	syíngdùngkāishǐ-shfkè	hàHngduHnghòichísìH-hāak
zone, dropping	空投地帶	kūngtóudìdài	hùngtàuHdeiHdaai
zone, landing	降落地帶	jyànglwòdìdài	gongloHkdeiHdaai
zone, assembly	集合地帶	jíhédìdài	jaaHphaHpdeiHdaai

WORDS OF COMMAND

about turn!	向後轉！	syànghòujwǎn!	heunghauHjyun
as you were!	歸原位	gwēiywánwèi	gwàiyùHnwái
attention!	立正！	lìjèng!	laHpjing!
cease fire!	停放！	tíngfàng!	tìHngfong!
charge magazine!	裝子彈	jwāngdždàn	jòngjídáan
countersign	口令！	kǒulìng!	háuliHng
dismiss!	解散	jyěsàn	gáaisaan
double march	跑步走	pǎubùdzǒu	páaubouHjáu
eyes front!	向前看！	syàngchyánkàn!	heungchìHnhon!
fall in!	集合！	jíhé!	jaaHphaHp!
fall out	解散	jyěsàn	gáaisaan
fire!	射擊	shèjí	seHgìk
fix bayonets!	上刺刀！	shàngtsżdāu!	séuHngchidōu!
forward march!	開步走！	kāibùdzǒu!	hòibouHjáu!

halt!	立定	lìdìng!	laHpdiHng!
halt or I fire!	站住，要開鎗了！	jànjù, yàu kāi-chyāngle!	jaaHmjyuH,yiuhòi-chēungla
	立定，要開鎗了！	lìdìng, yàu kāi-chyāngle!	laHpdiHng,yiuhòi-chēungla
halt, who goes there?	站住，是誰！	jànjù, shìshéi?	jaaHmjyuH,siHsèuiH?
load!	上膛	shàngtáng	sɤuHngtòHng
mark time!	踏步走	tàbùdzǒu	daaHpbouHjáu
order arms!	鎗放下！	chyāngfàngsyà!	chēungfonghaH!
present arms!	舉鎗！	jyǐchyāng!	gɤuichēung!
quick march!	快步走	kwàibùdzǒu	faaibouHjáu
right dress	向右看齊	syàngyòukànchí!	heungyauIIhonchàiH!
shoulder arms!	托鎗！	twōchyāng!	tokchēung!
stand at ease	稍息	shǎusyí	sáausìk
stand to!	準備	jwǔnbèi	jéunbeiH
unload!	退子彈	twèidždàn	teuijídóɑn

NAVAL TERMS

(Terms that are military as well as naval will usually be found under "Military Terms")

A

AA (anti-aircraft) guns	防空炮	fángkūngpàu;	fòIInghìngpaau;
	高射炮	gāushèpàu	gòuseHpaau
AB (able seaman)	上等水兵	shàngděngshwěi-bing	seuHngdángsɤuibìng;
	二等水兵	èrděngshwěibìng	yiHdángsɤuibìng
abaft	在……後	dzài……hòu	joiH……hauH
abeam (of)	船橫樑上	chwánhénglyáng-shàng;	syùHnwàaHnglèuHng-seuHng

	船正舷	chwánjèngsyán	syùHnjingyùHn
abreast (of)	橫列的	hénglyède	wàaHngliHtdìk
action stations	戰鬥部署	jàndòubùshǔ	jindaubouHchyúH
admiral	海軍上將	hǎijyūnshàngjyàng	hóigwānseuHngjeuŋg
Admiralty, Board of (Mod (Navy))	海軍本部	hǎijyūnběnbù	hóigwānbúnbouH
adrift	漂流的	pyāulyóude	piulàuHdìk
afloat	漂浮的	pyāufúde	piufàuHdìk
aft	在船尾	dzàichwánwěi	joiHsyùHnméiH
ahead	前駛	chyánshř	chìHnsái
ahead. to go	前進	chyánjìn	chìHnjeun
aircraft carrier	航空母艦	hángkūngmǔjyàn	hòHnghùngmóuHlaaHm
alter course	改航路	gǎihánglù	góihòHnglouH
alongside a jetty	靠碼頭	kàumǎtóu	kaaumáHtàuH
alongside another ship	靠舷側	kàusyántsè	kaauyùHnjāk
amidships	在船中部	dzàichwánjūngbù	joiHsyùHnjùngbouH
amidships. wheel!	穩住	wěnjù	wánjyuH
anchor	錨	máu	màauH
anchor, to	撇錨	pyěmáu	pitmàauH (pàaumàauH)
anchorage	停泊所	tíngbwóswǒ;	tìHngpaaksó;
	撇錨地	pyěmáudì	pìtmàauHdeiH pàau-màauHdeiH)
angled deck	航空母艦	hángkūngmǔjyàn;	hòHnghùngmóuHlaaHm
	起飛角度甲板	chǐfēijyǎudùjyǎbǎn	héifèigokdouHgaapbáan
anti-submarine (A/S)	反潛水艦	fǎnchyánshwěijyàn	fáanchìHmséuilaaHm
arresting gear	停機具	tíngjìjyù	tìHnggèigeuiH
arrester wires	停機線	tíngjìsyàn	tìHnggèisin
arrester hook	停機鈎	tíngjìgōu	tìHnggèingàu
artificer, engine room	輪機下級官	lwúnjisyàjígwān	lèuHngèihaHkāpgùn

asdic (sonar)	聲納	shēngnà	sīngnaaHp
ashore, go	岸上	ànshàng	ngoHnseuHng
ashore, run (aground)	擱淺	gēchyǎn	gaakchín
astern	在後	dzàihòu	joiHhauII
astern, go!	退後	twèihòu	teuihauH
awash	興水面齊平	syīngshwěimyàn-chípíng	hīngséuimiHn chàiHpíHng

B

ballast	壓載	yādzài	ngaatjoi
barge, pulled by a tug	駁船	bwóchwán	boksyùHn
barge, royal	御艇	yùtǐng	yuHtéHng
basin	船渠	chwánchyú	syùHnkèuiH
battleship	戰鬥艦	jàndòujyàn	jindaulaaHm
beacon, navigation mark	航標	hángbyāu	hòHngbìu
beam, on the	正橫地	jènghéngdì	jingwàaHngdeiH
bearning, relative	相對方向	syāngdwèifāng-syàng	sèungdeuifòngheung
bearing, true	眞正方向	jēnjèngfāngsyàng	jànjingfòngheung
before	在前	dzàichyán	joiHchìHn
berth (cabin)	臥舖	wòpū	ngoHpòu
binnacle	羅經台	lwójīngtái	lòHgìngtòiH
board, on	船上	chwánshàng	syùHnseuHng
boat	小船	syǎuchwán	síusyùHn (syùHnjái)
bound, for	開往…去的	kāiwǎng…chyùde	hòiwóHng…heuidik
bound, from	從…開來的	tsúng…kāiláide	chùHng…hòilòiHdìk
bow (port, stbd)	左舷船首	dzwǒsyánchwán-shǒu	jóyùHnsyùHnsáu
	右舷船首	yòusyánchwánshǒu	yauHyùHnsyùHnsáu

bows	船頭	chwántóu	syùHntàuH
bridge	指揮台	jǐhwēitái	jífàitòiH
bulkhead	隔牆	géchyáng	gaakchèuHng
buoy (navigational)	浮航標	fúhángbyāu	fàuHhòHngbìu
buoy (mooring)	羈船浮筒	jichwánfútǔng	gèisyùHnfàuHtùHng
buoyancy	漂浮力	pyāufúlì	pìufàuHliHk
	漂浮狀態	pyāufújwàngtài	pìufàuHjoHngtaai

C

cabin	臥艙	wòtsāng	ngoHchòng
cable (anchor)	錨練	máulyàn	màauHliHn
cable ship	電纜船	dyànlǎnchwán	diHnláaHmsyùHn
cadet, naval	海軍學生	hǎijyūnsywéshēng	hóigwànhoHksāang
capsize, to	傾覆下水	chīngfùsyàshwěi	kīngfūkhaHséui
capstan	起錨機	chǐmáuji	héimàauHgèi
captain (rank)	上校	shàngsyàu	seuHnggaau
captain (mode of address)	船長	chwánjǎng	syùHnjéung
cast off (hawsers etc)	解纜	jyělǎn	gáailaaHm
cast off (get under way)	啓錠	chǐdìng	káidiHng
channel	海峽	hǎisyá;	hóihaaHp
	港道	gǎngdàu	góngdouH
chart	海圖	hǎitú	hóitòuH
chief petty officer	士官長	shìgwānjǎng	siHgùnjéung
	上士	shàngshì	seuHngsiH
coaster	延岸航行船	yánànhángsyíng-chwán	yìHnngoHnhòHng-hàHngsyùHn
collision	碰撞	pèngjwàng	pungjoHng
commander (rank)	中校	jūngsyàu	jùnggaau

commander (c of ship)	副長	fùjăng	fujéung
commission	任命	rènmìng	yaHmmiHng
commission, to (ship)	服役	fúyì	fuIIkyiHk
compass	羅經	lwójīng	lóHging
compass card	羅盤	lwópán	lóHpùIIn
complement (men)	規定人數	gwāidìngrénuhù	kWàidiHngyàHnsou
conning tower	潛水艇	chyánshwĕitĭng	chìHmséuitéHng
	指揮台	jĭhwēitái	jífàitòiH
course	航向	hángsyàng	hòHngheung
coxwain (of boat)	舵手	dwòshŏu	tóHsáu
crane	起重機	chĭjùngjī	héichúHnggèi
crew, boats	小艇員	syăutĭngywán	siutéHngyùHn
crew, guns	炮手	pàushŏu	paausáu
crew, ships	船人員	chwánrénywán	oyùIInyàHnyùHn
	水手	shwĕishŏu	séuisáu
cruiser	巡洋艦	syúnyángjyàn	chèuHnyèuHnglaaHm
cutter (motor)	小汽艇	syăuchìtĭng	síuheitéHng

Damage control Dept	損害管制部	swŭnhàigwănjìbù	syúnhoiHgúnjaibouH
dead reckoning	推算位置	twēiswànwèijì	tèuisyunwaiHji
deck	甲板	jyăbăn	gaapbáan
deck-landing (a/c)	在甲板上降落	dzàijyăbănshàng-jyànglwò	joiHgaapbáanseuHng-gongloHk
degaussing (cable)	消磁電纜	syāutsźdyànlăn	siuchìHdiHnláaHm
depot ship	浮動基地	fúdùngjīdì	fàuHduHnggèideiII
depth charge	深水炸彈	shēnshwĕijàdàn	sàmséuijadáan
derrick	起貨桅	chĭhwòwéi	héifongàiH
destroyer	驅逐艦	chyūjújyàn	kèuijuHklaaHm

dinghy	小帆艇	syǎufāntǐng	síufàaHntéHng
dipping asdic	浸入聲納	jìnrùshēngnà	jamyaHpsìngnaaHp
direction finder	無線電測向儀	wúsyàndyàn-tsèsyàngyí	mòuHsindiHn-chaakheungyìH
director, gun	炮火指揮台	pàuhwǒjřhwēitái	paaufójífàitòiH
displacement	排水量	páishwěilyàng	pàaiHséuileuHng
diver, mineclearance	掃雷潛水士	sǎuléichyánshwěi-shř	soulèuiHchìHmséuisiH
dock	船塢	chwánwù	syùHnou
dock, dry	乾船塢	gānchwánwù	gònsyùHnou
dock, floating	浮船塢	fúchwánwù	fàuHsyùHnou
dockyard, naval	海軍船塢	hǎijyūnchwánwù	hóigwānsyùHnou
dockyard, civilian	造船廠	dzàuchwánchǎng	jouHsyùHnchóng
dog watch-first	上暮更	shàngmùgēng	seuHngmouHgàng
dog watch-last	下暮更	syàmùgēng	haHmouHgàng
down stream	在下流頭	dzàisyàlyóutóu	joiHhaHlàuHtàuH
draught (ships)	吃水	chřshwěi	hekséui
dredger	挖泥船	wāníchwán	waatnàiHsyùHn
drift, to	漂流	pyāulyóu	pìulàuH

E

ebb tide	退潮	twèicháu	teuichìuH
echo sounde	回音測探儀	hwéiyìntsètànyí	wùiHyàmchāaktaamyìH
endurance	續航力	syùhánglì	juHkhòHngliHk
engine room	機艙	jìtsāng	gèichòng
ensign (Rank)	海軍少尉	hǎijyūnshàuwèi	hóigwānsiuwai
ensign (flag)	軍艦旗	jyūnjyànchí	gwànlaaHmkèiH
escort	護航	hùháng	wuHhòHng
escort vessel, destroyer	驅逐艦	chyūjújyàn	kèuijuHklaaHm

| evasive steering | 躲避航行 | dwǒbihángsyíng | dóbeiHhòHnghàIIng |
| examination vessel | 檢查船 | jyǎncháchwán | gímchàHsyùHn |

fairlead	導索口	dǎuswǒkǒu	douHsokháu
fairway	港路	gǎnglù	gónglouH
fast patrol boat	快巡邏炮艇	kwàisyúnlwópàutǐng	faaichèuHnlòHpaautéHng
fathom	噚	ɛyún	chàHm
fire, to (gun, rocket, torpedo)	開火	kāihwǒ;	hòifó
	發射	fāshè	faatseH
fire control	炮火指揮	pàuhwǒjǐhwēi	paaufójifài
fishing vessel	捕魚船	bǔyúchwán	bouHyùHɔyùHn
fix	定位	dìngwèi	diHngwái
flag lieutenant	上尉參謀	ɛhàngwèitɛūnmóu	seuIIngwaichàammàuH
flag officer	海軍將官	hǎijyūnjyànggwūn	hóigwànjeunggùn
flagship	旗艦	chíjyàn	kèiHlaaHm
flashing light	閃光燈	shǎngwāngdēng	símgwōngdāng
fleet	海軍艦隊	hǎijyūnjyàngdwèi	hóigwānlaaHmdéui
fleet air arm	艦隊空軍	jyàndwèikūngjyūn	laaHmdéuihūnggwūn
fleet destroyer	艦隊驅逐艦	jyàndwèichyūjújyàn	laaHmdéuikènijuHklaaHm
flight deck	降落甲板	jyànglwǒjyǎbǎn	gongloHkgaapbáan
flood tide	漲潮	jàngcháu	jeungchìuH
flotilla	小艦隊	syǎujyàndwèi	síulaaHmdéui
flush deck	不展低甲板	píngjǎndijyǎbǎn	pìHugjíndàigaapháan
fore, forward adj.	在船頭	dzàichwántóu	joiHsyùHntàuH
	前面的	chyánmyànde	chìHnmiHndik
fore and aft line	縱線	dzùngsyàn	jungsin

forecastle	前甲板	chyánjyăbăn	chìHngaapbáan
foremast (warship, sail)	前桅	chyánwéi	chìHnngàiH
foul (berth)	纏泊地	chánbwódì	chìHnpaakdeiH
foul (anchor)	纏錨	chánmáu	chìHnmàauH
free board	乾舷	gānsyán	gòngyùHn
frigate	護航艦	hùhángjyàn	wuHhòHnglaaHm
	獵犬戰艦	lyèchywănjànjyàn	liHphyúnjinlaaHm
frogman	蛙人	wārén	wàyàHn
furl, to	捲篷	jywănpéng	gyúnpàHng

G

gaff-rigging	斜横	syéhéng	chèHwàaHng
galley (kitchen)	船上廚房	chwánshàngchúfáng	syùHnseuHngchyùHfóng
gangway	舷梯	syántī	yùHntài
gantry	桶架	tŭngjyà	túnggá
great circle sailing	大圈航行法	dàchywānháng-syíngfă	daaiHhyūnhòHnghàHngfaat
guard rail	欄杆	lángān	làaHngòn
guided missile ship	導向飛彈艦	dăusyàngfēidànjyàn	douHheungfèidaaHnlaaHm
gun	炮	pàu	paau
gunwale	舷緣	syánywán	yùHnyùHn
guy	支索	jīswŏ	jìsok
gybe	轉篷	jwănpéng	jyúnpàHng
gyro-compass	電羅經	dyànlwójīng	diHnlòHgìng

H

| halyard, signal | 升降索 | shēngjyàngswŏ | sìnggongsok |
| hard-to-port | 轉舵向在左舷 | jwăndwòsyàngdzài-dzwŏsyán | jyuntòHheungjoiH-jóyùHn |

hatch	艙口	tsāngkŏu	chònghául
haul, to	改變方向	găibyànfāngsyàng	góibinfòngheung
haul down, to	拉下	lāsyà	làaihaH (làailoHklàiH)
hawae pipe	錨鏈孔	máulyànkŭng	màauHlínhúng
hawser (general)	纜	lăn	láaHm
head (torpedo) practice	假的魚雷彈頭	jyădeyúléidàntóu	gádìkyùHlèuiHdáantàuH
head (torpedo) war	魚雷彈頭	yúléidàntóu	yùHlèuiHdáantàuH
headway	船之進行	chwánjrjìnsyíng	syùHnjijeunhàHng
heave, to	拉起	lūchĭ	làaihéi
heave to, to	停船	tíngchwán	tìHngsyùHn
helmsman	舵手	dwòshŏu	tóHзáu
hoist	傳送機	chwánsùngjī	chyùHnsuuggòi
hoist, to	升起來	shēngchĭlái	sìnghéilòih
hold	船艙	chwántsāng	syùHnchōng
Home Fleet	母國艦隊	mŭgwójyàndwèi	móuHgwoklaaHmdéui
home port (Port of registry)	登記港口	dēngjìgăngkŏu	dànggeigónghául
homing torpedo	尋標魚雷	syúnbyāuyúléi	chàHmbìuyùHlèuiH
homing aids (for aircraft)	領航幫助	lĭnghángbāngjù	líHnghòHngbòngjoH
hull	船殼	chwánké	syùHnhok
hydrofoil boat	水翼船	shwěiyìchwán	séuiyiHksyùHn
hydrophone	水中收音機	shwěijūngshōuyīnjī	séuijùngsàuyàmgèi
hydroplane	水平舵	shwěipíngdwò	séuipìHngtóH

I

| intake, snort | 呼吸洞入口 | hūsyídùngrùkŏu | fūkāpduHngyaHphául |
| inshore minesweeper | 近海掃雷艇 | jìnhăisăuléitĭng | gaHnhóisoulèuiHtéHng |

J

jack (flag)	艦首旗	jyànshǒuchí	laaHmsáukèiH
jetty	小碼頭	syǎumǎtóu	síumáHtàuH
jib	艇首三角帆	tǐngshǒusānjyǎufán	téHngsáusàamgokfàaHn
jumper	跨接綫	kwàjyēsyàn	kwājipsin
junior seaman	初級水兵	chūjíshwěibīng	chōkápséuibīng

K

kedge anchor	小錨	syǎumáu	síumàauH
keel	龍骨	lúnggǔ	lùHnggwāt
killer submarine	獵犬潛水艇	lyèchywǎn-chyánshwěitǐng	liHphyúnchìHmséui-téHng
knot (one nm per hour)	海裏速度	hǎilǐsùdù	hóiléuiHchūkdouH
knot (fastening in rope)	結	jyé	git (lit)

L

ladder, accommodation	懸梯	syánti	yùHntài
land, to (aircraft on flying deck)	在飛行甲板上降落	dzàifēisyíng-jyǎbǎnshàng-jyànglwò	joiHfèihàHng-gaapbáanseuHng-gongloHk
land, to (aircraft on water)	在水上降落	dzàishwěishàng-jyànglwò	joiHséuiseuHng-gongloHk
landfall	接近陸地	jyējìnlùdì	jipgaHnluHkdeiH
landing craft	登陸艇	dēnglùtǐng	dàngluHktéHng
landing stage	碼頭	mǎtóu	máHtàuH
landmark	路標	lùbyāu	louHbìu
launch	汽船	chìchwán;	heisyùHn
	汽艇	chìtǐng	heitéHng
launch, to (a ship)	使下水	shǐsyàshwěi	sihaHséui (loHkséui)

launcher, GM	導彈發射器	dǎudànfāshèchì	douHdáanfaatseHhei
launcher, rocket	火箭發射器	hwǒjyànfāshèchì	fójinfaatseHhei
lay, to (gun; mine)	瞄準	myáujwǔn;	mìuHjéun;
	佈雷	bùléi	boulèuiH
lead, (sounding)	測深鐘	tsèshēnjūng	chāaksàmjūng
leading seaman	上等水兵	shàngděngshwěibing	seuHngdángséuibing
leading ship	領先船	lǐngsyānchwán	líHngsìnsyùHn
leeward (of)	下風的	syàfēngde	haHfùngdìk
leeway	風壓	fēngyā	fùngngaat
libertyman	可自由上岸的水兵	kǒdìyóushàngàndeshwěibing	hójìHyàuHséuHngngoHndikséuibing
lieutenant	上尉	shàngwèi	seuHngwai
lieutenant commander	少校	shàusyàu	siugaau
light, navigation	夜航燈	yèhángdēng	ycHhòHngdāng
light, side	側燈	tsèdēng	jūkdāng
lighter	駁船	bwóchwán	boksyùHn
line ahead (abreast)	橫隊	héngdwèi	wàaHngdeuiH
log (book)	航海日記	hánghǎirjì	hòHnghóiyaHtgei
log (instrument)	曳航測程器	yìhángtsèchéngchì	yaiHhòHngchāakchìHnghei
luff, to	駛出上風	shǐchūshàngfēng	sáichēutseuHngfùng

M

mainmast (warship; sail)	主桅	jǔwéi	jyúngàiH
man, to	以人管理的	yǐréngwǎrlíde	yìHyàHngúnléiHdìk
Marines	海軍陸戰隊	hǎijyūnlùjàndwèi	hóigwānluHkjindéui
Marines, Notices to	航行正式通告	hángsyíngjònggshrtunggàu	hòHnghàHngjingsìltūnggouH
mat, collision	塞	sāi	sāk
mess deck	下甲板	syàjyǎbǎn	haHgaapbáan

mile (nautical)	海里	hǎilǐ	hóiléiH
mine layer	佈雷艦	bùléijyàn	boulèuiHlaaHm
minesweeper	掃雷艦	sǎuléijyàn	soulèuiHlaaHm
mizzen mast	後桅	hòuwéi	hauHngàiH
mole	防波堤	fángbwōtí	fòHngbòtàiH
moor,to (2 anchors)	停泊	tíngbwó	tìHngpaak
mooring buoy	羈船浮筒	jichwánfútǔng	gèisyùHnfàuHtùHng
motor boat	汽艇	chìtǐng	heitéHng

N

naval officer	海軍軍官	hǎijyūnjyūngwān	hóigwāngwāngùn
naval vessel	海軍艦艇	hǎijyūnjyàntǐng	hóigwānlaaHmtéHng
naval warfare	海上戰爭	hǎishàngjànjēng	hóiseuHngjinjàng
navigating officer	領航員	lǐnghángywán	líHnghòHngyùHn
navigatien	海航	hǎiháng	hóihòHng;
	航行	hángsyíng	hòHnghàHng
Navy, Royal	皇家海軍	hwángjyāhǎijyūn	wòHnggàhóigwān
neap tides	上，下舷潮	shàng, syàsyáncháu	seuHng, haHyùHnchìuH

O

oar	櫓槳	lǔjyǎng	lóuHjéung
ocean minesweeper	大洋掃雷艦	dàyángsǎuléijyàn	daaiHyèuHngsoulèuiHlaaHm
ocean tug	大洋托船	dàyángtwōchwán	daaiHyèuHngtoksyùHn
oil at sea, to	海上加油	hǎishàngjyāyóu	hóiseuHnggàyàuH
oiler	油船	yóuchwán	yàuHsyùHn
	給油船	gěiyóuchwán	kāpyàuHsyùHn
ordinary seaman	三等水兵	sānděngshwěibǐng	sàamdángséuibǐng
overboard, man!	有人墮海	yǒuréndwòhǎi	yáuHyàHndoHhói

P

passage, on (from A to B)	從A 到B 航行中	tsúng A dàu B hángoyíngjūng	chùHng A dou B hòIIngliàIIngjùng
patrol boat	巡邏艇	syúulwótǐng	chèuHnlòHtéHng
pendant, pennant (flag)	細長三角旗	syìchángsānjyǎuchí	saichèuHngsàamgokkèiH
periscope depth	潛望鏡之深度	chyánwàngjìngjī-shēndù	chìHmmoHnggengjì-sàmdouH
petty officer	下級官	syàjígwān	haHkāpgùn
picket, radar (S/M)	雷達搜索 潛水艦	lèidásǒuswǒ; chyánshwěijyàn	lèuiHdaaHtsáusok; chìHmséuilaaHm
plotting table	定位台	dìngwèitái	diHngwaiHtòiH
port (side)	左舷	dzwǒsyán	jóyùHn
propellor	推進器	tweıjìnchi	tèuijeunhei

Q

quarter (of a ship)	船尾部	chwánwěibù	syùHnméiHbouH
quarters, general	使各就崗位	shǐgèjyòugāngwèi	sígokjauHgōngwái
quarterdeck	後甲板	hòujyǎbǎn	hauIIgaapbáau
quartermaster (in wheelhouse)	舵手	dwòshǒu	tóHsáu

R

radar, AEW	空用防情雷達	kūngyùngfángchíng-léidá	hùngyuIIngfòIIngchìIIng-lèuiHdaaHt
radius of action	續航力	syùhánglì	juHkhòHngliHk
readiness, degree of	準備程度	jwǔnbèichéngdù	jéunbeiHchìHngdouH
rear admiral	海軍少將	hǎijyūnshàujyàng	hóigwānsiujeung
recover, to (torpedoes; mines	收回	shōuhwéi	sàuwùiH
reef (rock)	礁	chyáu	jiu
reef (sail)	索帆（布）	swǒfán (byu)	sokfàaHn (bou)

rigging (general, running, standing)	索具	swǒjyù	sokgeuiHk
right ahead	對直	dwèijŕ	deuijiHk
rope (general berthing)	繩	shéng	síng
rudder	舵	dwò	tóH
rudder, diving (S/M)	作航舵	dzwòhángdwò	jokhòHngtóH
running fix	前進定位法	chyánjìndìngwèifǎ	chìHnjeundiHngwaiH-faat

S

sail	帆	fán	fàaHn
sailor	水手	shwěishǒu	séuisáu
	水兵	shwěibìng	séuibìng
salvage	救難工作	jyòunàngūngdzwò	gaunaaHngùngjok
schooner	斯苦納船	sžkǔnàchwán (transliteration)	sìfúnaaHpsyùHn
scuttle (port)	舷窗	syánchwāng	yúHnchēung
seaworthy	耐波性	nàibwōsyìng	noiHbòsing
shackle-of cable-not used 15 fathoms another cable	十五噚錨鍊	shŕwǔsyúnmáulyàn	saHpngŕHchàHm-màauHliHn
shackle-joining	連接	lyánjyē;	lìHnjip
	連環	lyánhwán	lìHnwàaHn
sheet (rope)	帆絞索	fánjyǎuswǒ	fàaHngáausok
ship	船舶	chwánbwó	syùHnpaak
shrouds	支桅索	jŕwéiswǒ	jìngàiHsok
side (of ship)	船舷	chwánsyán	syùHnyùHn
skiff	小艇	syǎutǐng	siutéHng
snort	通氣管	tūngchìgwǎn	tùngheigún
sonobuoy	聲納浮樑	shēngnàfúlyáng	sìngnaaHpfàuHlèuHng
speed	速力	sùlì	chūkliHk

spring tides MHWS	朔望高潮	shwòwànggāucháu	sokmoHnggòuchìuH
	MLWS	朔望低潮	shwòwàngdīcháu	sokmoHngdàichìuH
stanchion	支柱	jīrjù	jìchyúH
starboard	右舷	yòusyán	yauHyùHn
steer for, to	把舵	bádwò	bátóH
stem	船首樁	chwánshŏujwāng	syùHnsáujùng
stern	船尾	chwánwěi	syùHnméiH
submarine (S/M)	潛水艦	chyánshwěijyàn;	chìHmséuilaaHm;
	潛水艇	chyánshwěitǐng	chìHmséuitéHng
superstructure	上層	shàngtséng	seuHngchàHng
supply officer	供應軍官	gūngyìngjyūngwān	gùngyìnggwàngùn
survey ship	測量船	tsèlyángchwán	chāaklèuHngsyùHn
sweep (M/S) n.	掃雷具	sáuléijyù	soulèuiHgeuiH

T

tackle (rigging)	轆轤	lūlú	lūklòuH
tackle (fishing)	鈎魚用具	dyàuyúyùngjyù;	diuyúyuHnggeuiH;
	捕魚用具	bŭyúyùngjyù	bouHyùHyuHnggeuiH
tampion (of gun)	炮口塞	pàukŏusài	paauháusāk
target(general, practice)	目標	mùbyāu	muHkbīu
task force	特種艦隊	tèjŭngjyàndwèi	daHkjúnglaaHmdéui
tender (mother ship)	母艦	mŭjyàn	móuHlaaHm
tender (stability)	翼側船	yìtsèchwán	yiIIkjāksyùIIn
tide	潮汐	cháusyī	chìuHjiHk
top, fore	中桅	jūngwéi	jùngngàiH
torpedo (see also 'homing')	魚雷	yúléi	yùHlèuiH
torpedo tube	魚雷發射管	yúléifāshègwăn	yùHlèuiHfaatseHgún
tow, to	拖拉	twōlā	tòlàai

track (torpedo)	足跡	dzújì	jūkjìk
track (wake)	船跡	chwánjì	syùHnjìk
trals	試開	shŕkāi	sihòi
tug	拖船	twōchwán	tòsyùHn
turn, to	轉	jwǎn	jyún
turn together, to	一齊轉向	yìchíjwǎnsyàng	yātchàiHjyúnheung
turret	炮塔	pàutǎ	paautaap
twin guns	雙炮管	shwāngpàugwǎn	sèungpaaugún

U

under sail	航行中	hángsyíngjūng	hòHnghàHngjùng
using sail	用帆航行	yùngfánhángsyíng	yuHngfàaHnhòHng·hàHng
under way, to get	開航	kāiháng	hòihòHng
unship, to unload ta take down	卸去	syèchyù	seheui
upder deck	上甲板	shàngjyǎbǎn	séuHnggaapbáan
upstream	溯流	shwòlyóu	soklàuH
uptake (tunnel)	烟喉	yìnhóu	yìnhàuH

V

van	前鋒	chyánfēng	chìHnfùng
'vast'	停住	tíngjù	tìHngjyuH
veer to (cable)	放鬆	fàngsūng	fongsùng
Very light	照明彈	jàumíngdàn	jiumìHngdaaHn
Very light, to fire	發射照明彈	fāshèjàumíngdàn	faatseHjiumìHngdaaHn
vice admiral	海軍中將	hǎijyūnjūngjyàng	hóigwānjùngjeung

W

| watch, men | 守更人 | hǒugēngrén | sáugàngyàHn |

watch, period	值班時間	jíbānshíjyān	jiHkbāansìHgaan
way, head, (stern)	船的前進後退	chwándechyánjīn-hòutwèi	syùHndikchìHnjeun-hauHteui
weigh, to	拔錨	bámáu	baHtmàauH
wheel, steering	舵輪	dwòlwún	tóHlèuHn
wheel, to	轉動	jwǎndùng	jyúnduIng
winch	臥式錨機	wòshìmáujī	ngoIIsikmàauHgèi
wind across	橫風	héngfēng	wàaHngfùng
wind, into	對風	dwèifēng	deuifùng
windward (of)	向上風	syàngshàngfēng	heungseuHngfùng
wiped ships	消滅磁性的船艦	syāumyètszsyíngde-chwánjyàn	siumiHtchìHsingdik-syùHnlaaHm
wreck	失事船	shīshìchwán	sātsiHsyùHn

yacht	遊艇	yóutǐng	yàuHtéHng
yard (rigging)	帆桁	fūnhéng;	fàaHnhàHng
	造船艦所	dzàuchwánjyànswǒ	jouHsyùHnlaaHmsó
yaw, to	偏航	pyānháng	pìnhòHng
yeoman of signals	中士信號水兵	jungshìsyìnhàu-shwěibing	jùngsiHseunhouH séuibmg

| zigzag, to | z字的進行 | Z (zee, zed) eżde-jìnsyíng | Z (zee, zed) jiHdik jeunhàHng |
| zone time | 地方時間 | dìfāngshíjyan | deiHfòngsìHgaan |

AIR FORCE TERMS

(Terms that are military as well as aeronautical will usually be found
under "Military Terms")

A

aerodrome	飛機塲	fēijichǎng	fèigèichèuHng
afterburner	噴射後燃器	pēnshèhòuránchì	panseHhauHyìHnhei
aileron	副翼	fùyì	fuyiHk
air brakes	空氣擎動儀	kūngchìchíngdùngyí	hùngheikìHngduHngyiH
air chief marshal	空軍上將	kūngjyūnshàngjyàng	hùnggwànseuHngjeung
air commodore	空軍准將	kūngjyūnjwǔnjyàng	hùnggwànjéunjeung
air marshal	空軍中將	kūngjyūnjūngjyàng	hùnggwànjùngjeung
air vice marshal	空軍少將	kūngjyūnshàujyàng	hùnggwànsiujeung
aircraft	飛機	fēijī	fèigèi
aircrew	飛行員	fēisyíngywán	fèihàHngyùHn
airman	空軍	kūngjyūn	hùnggwàn
airspeed indicator	空速指示器	kūngsùjřshřchì	hūngchūkjísiHhei
all weather fighter	全天候戰鬥機	chywántyēnhòujàndòuji	chyùHntìnhauHjindaugē
altimeter	高度表	gāudùbyǎu	gòudouHbíu
armament	武裝	wǔjwāng	móuHjōng
artificial horizon	水平綫儀	shwěipíngsyànyí	séuipìHngsinyìH

B

bomb, atomic	原子彈	ywándždàn	yùHnjídáan
bomb, delay action	延期爆炸彈	yánchìbàujàdàn	yìHnkèiHbaaujadáan
bomb high explosive	高度爆炸彈	gāudùbàujàdàn	gòudouHbaaujadáan
bomb, incendiary	燃燒彈	ránshāudàn	yìHnsìudáan

bomb carrier	炸彈架	jàdànjyà	jadaaHngá
bomb-release control	投彈器	tóudànchì	tàuHdaaHnhei
bomber	轟炸機	hūngjàjī	gwànjagèi

C

cannon	小炮	syǎupàu	síupaau
ceiling	上升限度	shàngshēngsyàndù	seuHngsìnghaaHndouH
charter, to	租	dzū	jòu
cockpit	座艙	dzwòtsūng	joHchòng
compass	羅盤	lwópán	lòHpùHn
control column	操縱桿	tsāudzùnggān	chòujunggòn
corporal	下士	syàshì	haHsiH

D

| drop tanks | 可棄的油箱 | kěchìdeyóusyāng | hóheidìkyàuHsèung |

E

| elevators | 升降舵 | shēngjyàngdwò | sìnggongtóH |
| endurance | 續航力 | syùhánglì | juHkhòHngliHk |

F

fighter	戰鬥機	jàndòujī	jindaugèi
fin	直尾翼	jfwěiyì;	jiHkméiHyiHk;
	垂直安定板	chwéijfāndìngbǎn	sèuiHjiHkngòndiHngbáan
flap	襟翼	jìnyì	gamyiHk
flap control lever	襟翼操縱桿	jìnyìtsāudzùnggān	gamyiHkchòujunggòn
flap indicator	襟翼指示器	jìnyìjřshìchì	gamyiHkjìsiHhei
flight lieutenant	空軍上尉	kūngjyūnshàngwèi	hūnggwānseuHngwai

flight sergeant	空軍上士	kūngjyūnshàngshr̀	hūnggwānseuHngsiH
flying officer	空軍中尉	kūngjyūnjūngwèi	hūnggwānjùngwai
four-engined aircraft	四發動機飛機	sz̀fādùngjīfēijī	seifaatduHnggèifèigèi
freight	貨物	hwòwù	fomaHt
fuel tanks	油箱	yóusyāng	yàuHsèung
fuselage	機身	jīshēn	gèisàn

G

ground attack aircraft	地面攻擊機	dìmyàngūngjíjī	deiHmiHngūnggīkgēi
group captain	空軍上校	kūngjyūnshàngsyàu	hūnggwēnseuHnggaau
guided weapon (see under 'guided weapon' and 'missile in Military Terms'	導彈	dǎudàn	douHdáan

H

| helicopter | 直昇機 | jŕshēngjī | jiHksìnggèi |
| hold (of an aircraft) | 飛機貨艙 | fēijīhwòtsāng | fèigèifochōng |

I

| instrument panel | 儀器盤 | yíchìpán | yìHheipùHn |
| instruments | 儀器 | yíchì | yìHhei |

J

jet aircraft	噴射機	pēnshèjī	panseHgèi
jet engine	噴射引擎	pēnshèyǐnchíng	panseHyáHnkìHng
jet pipe	噴射管	pēnshègwǎn	panseHgún
jettison, to	投棄	tóuchì	tàuHhei

K

| kerosene | 煤油 | méiyóu | mùiHyàuH |

L

| land, to | 落地 | lwòdì | loHkdeiH |
| landing ground | 降落場 | jyànglwòchǎng | gongloHkchèuHng |

M

| missile (see 'Military Terms') | 飛彈 | fēidàn | fèidáan |

N

| nose cone | 飛彈頭部 | fēidàntóubù | fèidaaHntàuHbouH |

O

| oil pressure gauge | 油壓表 | yóuyābyǎu | yàuHngaatbíu |
| oil temperature gauge | 油溫度表 | yóuwēudùbyǎu | yàullwàndouHbíu |

P

pilot officer	空軍少尉	kūngjyūnshàuwèi	hūnggwānsiuwai
pitch, coarse	粗螺距	tsūlwójyù	chòulòHkéuiH
pitch, fine	細螺距	syìlwójyù	sailòHkéuiH
propeller	螺旋槳	lwósywánjyǎng	lòHsyùHnjéung
propeller, variable pitch	可變螺距的 螺旋槳	kěbyànlwójyùde lwósywánjyǎng	hóbinlòHkéuiHdik lòHsyùHnjéuug

R

radius of action	活動半徑	hwódùngbànjìng	wuHtduHngbunging
ram jet	動壓噴射引擎	dùngyāpēnshèyǐnchíng	duHngngaatpanseHyáHnkìHng
range (of an aircraft)	飛行航程	fēisyínghángchéng	fèihàHnghòHngchìHng
range (of colours)	色帶	sèdài	sikdáai

rate of climb indicator	上昇率指示器	shàngshēnglyù-jǐrshɪ̀chɪ̀	seuHngsìngleuHtjìsiHhei
rev counter	轉數表	jwǎnshùbyǎu	jyúnsoubíu
rudder	機舵	jɪ̀dwò	gèitóH
runway	跑道	pǎudàu	páudouH

S

sergeant	中士	jūngshɪ̀	jùngsiH
squadron	中隊	jūngdwèi	jùngdeuiH
squadron leader (post)	中隊長	jūngdwèijǎng	jùngdeuiHjéung
squadron learder (rank)	空軍少校	kūngjyūnshàusyàu	hūnggwānsiugaau
stall, to	失速	shɪ̄sù	sātchūk
station	站	jàn	jaaHm

T

tailplane	尾翼	wěiyì	méiHyiHk
tail unit	尾翼的各部份	wěiyìdegèbùfèn	méiHyiHkdìkgokbouH-faHn
take off, to	起飛	chɪ̀fēi	héifèi
throttle	油門	yóumén	yàuHmùHn
transport aircraft	運輸機	yùnshūjì	waHnsyùgèi
turn and bank indicator	傾斜指示器	chɪ̄ngsyéjǐrshɪ̀chɪ̀	kìngchèHjísiHhei
twin-engined aircraft	雙引擎機	shwāngyɪnchɪ́ngjì	sèungyáHnkìHnggèi

U

undercarriage	起落架	chɪ̀lwùjyà	héiloHkgá
undercarriage control lever	起落架操縱桿	chɪ̀lwòjyà-tsāudzùnggān	héiloHkgáchòujunggòn
undercarriage, to lower the	放下起落架	fàngsyàchɪ̀lwòjyà	fonghaHhéiloHkgá

undercarriage, to raise the	收 起 起 落 架	shouchǐchǐlwòjyà	sàuhéihéiloIIkgá
undercarriage retractable	可 伸 縮 的 起 落 架	kěshēnswōde-chǐlwòjyà	hósānsūkdǐkhéiloHkgá

W

warrant officer	空 軍 准 尉	kūngjyunjwūnwèi	hūnggwǎnjéunwai
wing (of an aircraft)	機 翼	jǐyì	gèiyiHk
wing commander (post)	大 隊 長	dàdwèijǎng	daaiHdeuiHjéung
wing commander (rank)	空 軍 中 校	kūngjyūnjūngsyàu	hūnggwǎnjùnggaau
wing load	機 翼 載 重 量	jǐyìdzàijùnglyàng	gèiyiHkjoichúHng-leuHng
wing(2 or 3 squadrons)	大 隊	dàdwèi	daaiHdeuiH
WRAF	英 國 皇 家 女 空 軍	Yīnggwólwángjyū-nyükūngjyūn	YìnggwokwòHnggà-néuiHhūnggwɐn

SIMPLIFIED CHINESE CHARACTERS

A

a

铜〔銅〕

ai

镲〔鑔〕
皑〔皚〕
蔼〔藹〕
霭〔靄〕
*爱〔愛〕
嗳〔噯〕
瑷〔璦〕
嗳〔嗳〕
暧〔曖〕
媛〔嫒〕
碍〔礙〕

an

谙〔諳〕
鹌〔鵪〕
铵〔銨〕

ang

肮〔骯〕

au

鳌〔鰲〕
骜〔驁〕
袄〔襖〕

B

ba

鲅〔鲅〕
钯〔鈀〕
坝〔壩〕
*罢〔罷〕
耙〔耙〕

bai

摆〔擺〕
〔襬〕
败〔敗〕

ban

颁〔頒〕
板〔闆〕
绊〔絆〕
办〔辦〕

bang

帮〔幫〕
绑〔綁〕
谤〔謗〕
镑〔鎊〕

bau

龅〔齙〕
宝〔寶〕
饱〔飽〕
鸨〔鴇〕
报〔報〕
鲍〔鮑〕

bei

惫〔憊〕
辈〔輩〕
*贝〔貝〕
钡〔鋇〕
狈〔狽〕
*备〔備〕
呗〔唄〕

ben

锛〔錛〕
贲〔賁〕

beng

绷〔繃〕
镚〔鏰〕

bi

*笔〔筆〕
铋〔鉍〕
贲〔賁〕
*毕〔畢〕
哔〔嗶〕
筚〔篳〕
跸〔蹕〕

滗〔潷〕
币〔幣〕
闭〔閉〕
毙〔斃〕

bin

*宾〔賓〕
滨〔濱〕
槟〔檳〕
傧〔儐〕
缤〔繽〕
镔〔鑌〕
濒〔瀕〕
鬓〔鬢〕
摈〔擯〕
殡〔殯〕
膑〔臏〕
髌〔髕〕

bing

槟〔檳〕
饼〔餅〕

bu

补〔補〕
钚〔鈈〕

bwo

饽〔餑〕
钵〔缽〕
拨〔撥〕
鹁〔鵓〕
馎〔餺〕
钹〔鈸〕
驳〔駁〕
铂〔鉑〕
卜〔蔔〕

byan

编〔編〕
编〔编〕
*边〔邊〕
笾〔籩〕

贬〔貶〕
辩〔辯〕
辫〔辮〕
变〔變〕

byau

镳〔鑣〕
标〔標〕
骠〔驃〕
镖〔鏢〕
飙〔飆〕
表〔錶〕
鳔〔鰾〕

bye

鳖〔鱉〕
瘪〔癟〕
别〔彆〕

C

cha

馇〔餷〕
锸〔鍤〕
镲〔鑔〕
诧〔詫〕

chai

钗〔釵〕
侪〔儕〕
虿〔蠆〕

chan

搀〔攙〕
掺〔摻〕
缠〔纏〕
禅〔禪〕
蝉〔蟬〕
婵〔嬋〕
谗〔讒〕
馋〔饞〕
*产〔產〕
浐〔滻〕

铲〔鏟〕
蒇〔蕆〕
阐〔闡〕
羼〔羼〕
谄〔諂〕
颤〔顫〕
忏〔懺〕
划〔劃〕

chang

伥〔倀〕
阊〔閶〕
鲳〔鯧〕
*尝〔嘗〕
偿〔償〕
鲿〔鱨〕
*长〔長〕
肠〔腸〕
场〔場〕
厂〔廠〕
怅〔悵〕
畅〔暢〕

chau

钞〔鈔〕

che

*车〔車〕
砗〔硨〕
彻〔徹〕

chen

谌〔諶〕
尘〔塵〕
陈〔陳〕
碜〔磣〕
榇〔櫬〕
衬〔襯〕
谶〔讖〕
称〔稱〕
龀〔齔〕

cheng

柽〔檉〕
蛏〔蟶〕
铛〔鐺〕
赪〔赬〕
称〔稱〕
枨〔棖〕
诚〔誠〕
惩〔懲〕
骋〔騁〕

chi

缇〔緹〕
榿〔榿〕
*齐〔齊〕
蛴〔蠐〕
脐〔臍〕
骑〔騎〕
骐〔騏〕
鳍〔鰭〕
颀〔頎〕
蕲〔蘄〕
启〔啟〕
绮〔綺〕
*岂〔豈〕
碛〔磧〕
*气〔氣〕
讫〔訖〕
荠〔薺〕

ching

靓〔靚〕
轻〔輕〕
氢〔氫〕
倾〔傾〕
晴〔晴〕
请〔請〕
顷〔頃〕
庆〔慶〕

chr

鸱〔鴟〕
迟〔遲〕

驰〔馳〕
*齿〔齒〕
炽〔熾〕
饬〔飭〕

chou

紬〔紬〕
畴〔疇〕
筹〔籌〕
踌〔躊〕
俦〔儔〕
雠〔讎〕
绸〔綢〕
丑〔醜〕

chu

出〔齣〕
蹰〔躕〕
*刍〔芻〕
雏〔雛〕
储〔儲〕
础〔礎〕
处〔處〕
绌〔絀〕
触〔觸〕

chuai

闯〔闖〕

chung

冲〔衝〕
*虫〔蟲〕
宠〔寵〕
铳〔銃〕

chwan

传〔傳〕
钏〔釧〕

chwang

轭〔軛〕
谔〔諤〕
鹗〔鶚〕
鳄〔鱷〕

chwei

锤〔錘〕

绰〔綽〕
龊〔齪〕
辍〔輟〕

chwun

鳍〔鰭〕
鹑〔鶉〕
纯〔純〕
莼〔蒓〕

chyan

骞〔騫〕
谦〔謙〕
悭〔慳〕
牵〔牽〕
*佥〔僉〕
签〔簽〕
〔籤〕
千〔韆〕
*迁〔遷〕
钎〔釺〕
铅〔鉛〕
鸧〔鶬〕
荨〔蕁〕
钳〔鉗〕
钱〔錢〕
钤〔鈐〕
浅〔淺〕
谴〔譴〕
缱〔繾〕
堑〔塹〕
椠〔槧〕
纤〔縴〕

chyang

玱〔瑲〕
枪〔槍〕
锵〔鏘〕
墙〔牆〕
蔷〔薔〕
樯〔檣〕
嫱〔嬙〕
镪〔鏹〕
羟〔羥〕
抢〔搶〕
炝〔熗〕
戗〔戧〕

跄〔蹌〕
呛〔嗆〕

chyau

硗〔磽〕
跷〔蹺〕
锹〔鍬〕
缲〔繰〕
翘〔翹〕
*乔〔喬〕
桥〔橋〕
硚〔礄〕
侨〔僑〕
鞒〔鞽〕
荞〔蕎〕
谯〔譙〕
*壳〔殼〕
窍〔竅〕
诮〔誚〕

chye

锲〔鍥〕
惬〔愜〕
箧〔篋〕
窃〔竊〕

chyou

秋〔鞦〕
鹙〔鶖〕
鳅〔鰍〕
鲔〔鮪〕
巯〔巰〕

chyu

曲〔麯〕
*区〔區〕
驱〔驅〕
岖〔嶇〕
躯〔軀〕
诎〔詘〕
趋〔趨〕
鸲〔鴝〕
龋〔齲〕
觑〔覷〕
阒〔闃〕

chyung

权〔權〕
颧〔顴〕

铨〔銓〕
诠〔詮〕
绻〔綣〕
劝〔勸〕

cui

缞〔縗〕

cuo

鹾〔鹺〕
错〔錯〕
锉〔銼〕

D

da

*达〔達〕
哒〔噠〕
鞑〔韃〕

dai

贷〔貸〕
绐〔紿〕
*带〔帶〕
叇〔靆〕

dan

*单〔單〕
担〔擔〕
殚〔殫〕
箪〔簞〕
郸〔鄲〕
掸〔撣〕
胆〔膽〕
赕〔賧〕
惮〔憚〕
瘅〔癉〕
弹〔彈〕
诞〔誕〕

dang

裆〔襠〕
铛〔鐺〕

*当〔當〕
〔噹〕
*党〔黨〕
谠〔讜〕
挡〔擋〕
档〔檔〕
砀〔碭〕
荡〔蕩〕

dau

魛〔魛〕
祷〔禱〕
岛〔島〕
捣〔搗〕
导〔導〕

de

锝〔鍀〕

deng

灯〔燈〕
镫〔鐙〕
邓〔鄧〕

di

镝〔鏑〕
觌〔覿〕
籴〔糴〕
敌〔敵〕
涤〔滌〕
诋〔詆〕
谛〔諦〕
缔〔締〕
递〔遞〕

ding

钉〔釘〕
顶〔頂〕
订〔訂〕
锭〔錠〕

diu

铥〔銩〕

dou

钭〔鈄〕
斗〔鬥〕

窦〔竇〕

du

读〔讀〕
渎〔瀆〕
椟〔櫝〕
黩〔黷〕
犊〔犢〕
牍〔牘〕
独〔獨〕
赌〔賭〕
笃〔篤〕
镀〔鍍〕

dung

*东〔東〕
鸫〔鶇〕
岽〔崬〕
冬〔鼕〕
*动〔動〕
冻〔凍〕
栋〔棟〕
胨〔腖〕

dwan

*断〔斷〕
锻〔鍛〕
缎〔緞〕
簖〔籪〕

dwei

怼〔懟〕
*对〔對〕
*队〔隊〕

dwo

夺〔奪〕
铎〔鐸〕
驮〔馱〕
堕〔墮〕
饳〔飿〕

dwun

吨〔噸〕
镦〔鐓〕
趸〔躉〕
钝〔鈍〕

顿〔頓〕	赞〔贊〕	镞〔鏃〕	**F**	冯〔馮〕	*冈〔岡〕
	瓒〔瓚〕	诅〔詛〕		缝〔縫〕	刚〔剛〕
dyan		组〔組〕	**fa**	讽〔諷〕	枫〔棡〕
颠〔顛〕	**dzang**		*发〔發〕	凤〔鳳〕	纲〔綱〕
癫〔癲〕	赃〔臟〕	**dzung**	〔髮〕	赗〔賵〕	掆〔摡〕
巅〔巔〕	脏〔臟〕	综〔綜〕	罚〔罰〕		岗〔崗〕
点〔點〕	〔髒〕	枞〔樅〕	阀〔閥〕	**fu**	
淀〔澱〕	驵〔駔〕	总〔總〕		麸〔麩〕	**gau**
垫〔墊〕		纵〔縱〕	**fan**	肤〔膚〕	镐〔鎬〕
电〔電〕	**dzau**		烦〔煩〕	辐〔輻〕	缟〔縞〕
钿〔鈿〕	凿〔鑿〕	**dzwan**	矾〔礬〕	绂〔紱〕	诰〔誥〕
	枣〔棗〕	钻〔鑽〕	钒〔釩〕	绋〔紼〕	锆〔鋯〕
dyau	灶〔竈〕	躜〔躦〕	贩〔販〕	绋〔紼〕	
蜩〔鯛〕		缵〔纘〕	饭〔飯〕	辅〔輔〕	**ge**
铫〔銚〕	**dze**	赚〔賺〕	范〔範〕	抚〔撫〕	鸽〔鴿〕
锦〔錦〕	责〔責〕			赋〔賦〕	搁〔擱〕
窎〔窵〕	赜〔賾〕	**dzwo**	**fang**	赙〔賻〕	镉〔鎘〕
	啧〔嘖〕	凿〔鑿〕	钫〔鈁〕	缚〔縛〕	颌〔頜〕
dye	帻〔幘〕		鲂〔魴〕	讣〔訃〕	阁〔閣〕
谍〔諜〕	箦〔簀〕	**dzwun**	访〔訪〕	复〔復〕	个〔個〕
蝶〔蜨〕	则〔則〕	鳟〔鱒〕	纺〔紡〕	〔複〕	铬〔鉻〕
经〔經〕	铡〔鍘〕			〔覆〕	
迭〔叠〕	泽〔澤〕	**E**	**fel**	鰒〔鰒〕	**gei**
	择〔擇〕		绯〔緋〕	驸〔駙〕	给〔給〕
dz		**e**	鲱〔鯡〕	鲋〔鮒〕	
谘〔諮〕	**dzei**	额〔額〕	飞〔飛〕	负〔負〕	**geng**
资〔資〕	贼〔賊〕	饿〔餓〕	诽〔誹〕	妇〔婦〕	赓〔賡〕
镃〔鎡〕		鹅〔鵝〕	废〔廢〕		鹒〔鶊〕
觜〔鮆〕	**dzeu**	讹〔訛〕	费〔費〕	**G**	鲠〔鯁〕
辎〔輜〕	潲〔籀〕	恶〔惡〕	镄〔鐨〕		绠〔綆〕
锱〔錙〕		〔噁〕		**ga**	
鲻〔鯔〕	**dzeng**	垩〔堊〕	**fen**	钆〔釓〕	**gou**
渍〔漬〕	缯〔繒〕	轭〔軛〕	纷〔紛〕		缑〔緱〕
	赠〔贈〕	谔〔諤〕	坟〔墳〕	**gai**	沟〔溝〕
dza	锃〔鋥〕	鸮〔鶚〕	豮〔豶〕	该〔該〕	钩〔鉤〕
臜〔臢〕		鳄〔鰐〕	粪〔糞〕	赅〔賅〕	觏〔覯〕
杂〔雜〕	**dzou**	锷〔鍔〕	愤〔憤〕	盖〔蓋〕	诟〔詬〕
	诹〔諏〕	饿〔餓〕	偾〔僨〕	钙〔鈣〕	构〔構〕
dzai	鲰〔鯫〕		奋〔奮〕		购〔購〕
载〔載〕	驺〔騶〕	**er**		**gan**	
	邹〔鄒〕	儿〔兒〕	**feng**	干〔乾〕	**gu**
dzan		鸸〔鴯〕	*丰〔豐〕	〔幹〕	钴〔鈷〕
趱〔趲〕	**dzu**	饵〔餌〕	沣〔灃〕	尴〔尷〕	鸪〔鴣〕
攒〔攢〕		铒〔鉺〕	锋〔鋒〕	赶〔趕〕	诂〔詁〕
錾〔鏨〕		*尔〔爾〕	*凤〔鳳〕	赣〔贛〕	钴〔鈷〕
暂〔暫〕		迩〔邇〕	沨〔渢〕	绀〔紺〕	贾〔買〕
		贰〔貳〕	疯〔瘋〕		蛊〔蠱〕
			枫〔楓〕	**gang**	
			砜〔碸〕		

毂〔轂〕	**gwaug**	**he**	讳〔諱〕	**hwun**	钊〔釗〕
愲〔餶〕		诃〔訶〕			赵〔趙〕
鹘〔鶻〕	*广〔廣〕	阂〔閡〕	**hung**	荤〔葷〕	诏〔詔〕
谷〔穀〕	犷〔獷〕	阖〔闔〕		阍〔閽〕	
鹄〔鵠〕		鹖〔鶡〕	轰〔轟〕	浑〔渾〕	**je**
顾〔顧〕	**gwo**	颌〔頜〕	黉〔黌〕	珲〔琿〕	
锢〔錮〕		饸〔餄〕	鸿〔鴻〕	馄〔餛〕	谪〔謫〕
	涡〔渦〕	合〔閤〕	红〔紅〕	诨〔諢〕	辙〔轍〕
gui	埚〔堝〕	纥〔紇〕	荭〔葒〕		鳖〔鱉〕
	锅〔鍋〕	鹤〔鶴〕	讧〔訌〕	**J**	辄〔輒〕
妫〔媯〕	蜗〔蝸〕	贺〔賀〕		**ja**	蛰〔蟄〕
沩〔溈〕	*国〔國〕	吓〔嚇〕	**hwa**		折〔摺〕
规〔規〕	掴〔摑〕			铡〔鍘〕	锗〔鍺〕
鲑〔鮭〕	帼〔幗〕	**heng**	*华〔華〕	闸〔閘〕	这〔這〕
闺〔閨〕	椁〔槨〕		骅〔驊〕	轧〔軋〕	鹧〔鷓〕
*归〔歸〕	腘〔膕〕	鸻〔鴴〕	哗〔嘩〕	鲝〔鮺〕	
*龟〔龜〕	*过〔過〕		铧〔鏵〕	鲊〔鮓〕	**jeu**
轨〔軌〕		**hou**	*画〔畫〕	诈〔詐〕	
匦〔匭〕	**gwun**		婳〔嫿〕		针〔針〕
诡〔詭〕		后〔後〕	划〔劃〕	**jai**	贞〔貞〕
鳜〔鱖〕	辊〔輥〕	鲎〔鱟〕	桦〔樺〕		浈〔湞〕
柜〔櫃〕	绲〔緄〕		话〔話〕	斋〔齋〕	祯〔禎〕
贵〔貴〕	鲧〔鯀〕	**hu**		债〔債〕	桢〔楨〕
刿〔劌〕			**hwai**		侦〔偵〕
桧〔檜〕		轷〔軤〕		**jan**	缜〔縝〕
刽〔劊〕	**H**	壶〔壺〕	怀〔懷〕		诊〔診〕
	ha	胡〔鬍〕	坏〔壞〕	鹯〔鸇〕	轸〔軫〕
		鹕〔鶘〕		鳣〔鱣〕	鸩〔鴆〕
gung	铪〔鉿〕	鹘〔鶻〕	**hwan**	毡〔氈〕	赈〔賑〕
		鹕〔鶦〕		觇〔覘〕	镇〔鎮〕
龚〔龔〕	**hai**	浒〔滸〕	欢〔歡〕	谵〔譫〕	纼〔紖〕
巩〔鞏〕		沪〔滬〕	还〔還〕	斩〔斬〕	阵〔陣〕
贡〔貢〕	还〔還〕	护〔護〕	环〔環〕	崭〔嶄〕	
唝〔嗊〕	骇〔駭〕		缳〔繯〕	盏〔盞〕	**jeng**
		hui	锾〔鍰〕	辗〔輾〕	
gwa	**han**		缓〔緩〕	绽〔綻〕	钲〔鉦〕
		挥〔揮〕	鲩〔鯇〕	颤〔顫〕	征〔徵〕
刮〔颳〕	顸〔頇〕	辉〔輝〕		栈〔棧〕	铮〔錚〕
鸹〔鴰〕	韩〔韓〕	翚〔翬〕	**hwang**	战〔戰〕	症〔癥〕
剐〔剮〕	阚〔闞〕	诙〔詼〕			*郑〔鄭〕
诖〔詿〕	喊〔嘪〕	回〔迴〕	鳇〔鰉〕	**jang**	证〔證〕
	汉〔漢〕	*汇〔匯〕	谎〔謊〕		帧〔幀〕
gwan	颔〔頷〕	〔彙〕		张〔張〕	净〔淨〕
		贿〔賄〕	**hwo**	*长〔長〕	诤〔諍〕
关〔關〕	**hang**	秽〔穢〕		涨〔漲〕	
纶〔綸〕		*会〔會〕	钬〔鈥〕	帐〔帳〕	**ji**
鳏〔鰥〕	绗〔絎〕	烩〔燴〕	伙〔夥〕	账〔賬〕	
观〔觀〕	颃〔頏〕	荟〔薈〕	锪〔鍃〕	胀〔脹〕	斋〔齏〕
倌〔倌〕		绘〔繪〕	获〔獲〕		跻〔躋〕
鹳〔鸛〕	**hau**	诲〔誨〕	〔穫〕	**jau**	击〔擊〕
贯〔貫〕		殨〔殨〕	祸〔禍〕		赍〔賫〕
惯〔慣〕	颢〔顥〕		货〔貨〕		
掼〔摜〕	灏〔灝〕				
	号〔號〕				

缉〔緝〕
积〔積〕
羁〔羈〕
机〔機〕
饥〔饑〕
讥〔譏〕
玑〔璣〕
矶〔磯〕
叽〔嘰〕
鸡〔鷄〕
鹡〔鶺〕
辑〔輯〕
极〔極〕
级〔級〕
挤〔擠〕
给〔給〕
*几〔幾〕
虮〔蟣〕
济〔濟〕
霁〔霽〕
荠〔薺〕
剂〔劑〕
鲚〔鱭〕
际〔際〕
绩〔績〕
计〔計〕
系〔繫〕
骥〔驥〕
觊〔覬〕
蓟〔薊〕
鲫〔鯽〕
记〔記〕
纪〔紀〕
继〔繼〕

jin

谨〔謹〕
馑〔饉〕
觐〔覲〕
紧〔緊〕
锦〔錦〕
仅〔僅〕
劲〔勁〕
*进〔進〕
琎〔璡〕
缙〔縉〕
*尽〔盡〕
〔儘〕
浕〔濜〕

荩〔藎〕
赆〔贐〕
烬〔燼〕

jing

惊〔驚〕
鲸〔鯨〕
鹒〔鶊〕
泾〔涇〕
茎〔莖〕
经〔經〕
颈〔頸〕
刭〔剄〕
镜〔鏡〕
竞〔競〕
痉〔痙〕
劲〔勁〕
胫〔脛〕
径〔徑〕
靓〔靚〕

jou

诌〔謅〕
赒〔賙〕
鸼〔鵃〕
轴〔軸〕
纣〔紂〕
荮〔葤〕
骤〔驟〕
皱〔皺〕
绉〔縐〕
㑇〔偢〕
胄〔冑〕
昼〔晝〕

jr

只〔隻〕
〔祗〕
织〔織〕
职〔職〕
踯〔躑〕
*执〔執〕
絷〔縶〕
纸〔紙〕
挚〔摯〕
贽〔贄〕
鸷〔鷙〕
掷〔擲〕

滞〔滯〕
栉〔櫛〕
轾〔輊〕
致〔緻〕
帜〔幟〕
制〔製〕
*质〔質〕
踬〔躓〕
锧〔鑕〕
骘〔騭〕

ju

诸〔諸〕
槠〔櫧〕
朱〔硃〕
诛〔誅〕
铢〔銖〕
烛〔燭〕
嘱〔囑〕
瞩〔矚〕
贮〔貯〕
驻〔駐〕
铸〔鑄〕
筑〔築〕

jung

终〔終〕
钟〔鐘〕
〔鍾〕
种〔種〕
肿〔腫〕
众〔衆〕

jwa

挝〔撾〕

jwan

*专〔專〕
砖〔磚〕
䏝〔膞〕
颛〔顓〕
转〔轉〕
啭〔囀〕
赚〔賺〕
传〔傳〕
馔〔饌〕

鹃〔鵑〕
镌〔鐫〕
卷〔捲〕
绢〔絹〕

jwang

妆〔妝〕
装〔裝〕
庄〔莊〕
桩〔樁〕
戆〔戇〕
壮〔壯〕
状〔狀〕

jwei

骓〔騅〕
锥〔錐〕
赘〔贅〕
缒〔縋〕
缀〔綴〕
坠〔墜〕

jwo

镯〔鐲〕
浊〔濁〕
诼〔諑〕
锅〔鍋〕

jwun

谆〔諄〕
准〔準〕

jya

家〔傢〕
镓〔鎵〕
*夹〔夾〕
浃〔浹〕
颊〔頰〕
荚〔莢〕
蛱〔蛺〕
铗〔鋏〕
郏〔郟〕
贾〔賈〕
槚〔檟〕
钾〔鉀〕

价〔價〕
驾〔駕〕

jyan

鹣〔鶼〕
鳒〔鰜〕
缣〔縑〕
戋〔戔〕
笺〔箋〕
坚〔堅〕
鲣〔鰹〕
捡〔撿〕
睑〔瞼〕
俭〔儉〕
裥〔襇〕
简〔簡〕
谏〔諫〕
渐〔漸〕
槛〔檻〕
贱〔賤〕
溅〔濺〕
践〔踐〕
钱〔錢〕
*荐〔薦〕
鉴〔鑒〕
*见〔見〕
视〔視〕
舰〔艦〕
剑〔劍〕
键〔鍵〕
涧〔澗〕
锏〔鐧〕

jyang

姜〔薑〕
*将〔將〕
浆〔漿〕
缰〔繮〕
讲〔講〕
桨〔槳〕
奖〔奬〕
蒋〔蔣〕
酱〔醬〕
绛〔絳〕

jyau

胶〔膠〕
鲛〔鮫〕
鹪〔鷦〕
浇〔澆〕
骄〔驕〕
娇〔嬌〕
鹬〔鷸〕
饺〔餃〕
铰〔鉸〕
绞〔絞〕
侥〔僥〕
矫〔矯〕
搅〔攪〕
缴〔繳〕
觉〔覺〕
较〔較〕
轿〔轎〕
挢〔撟〕
峤〔嶠〕

jye

阶〔階〕
疖〔癤〕
讦〔訐〕
洁〔潔〕
诘〔詰〕
撷〔擷〕
颉〔頡〕
结〔結〕
鲒〔鮚〕
*节〔節〕
借〔藉〕
诫〔誡〕

jyou

纠〔糾〕
鸠〔鳩〕
阄〔鬮〕
鹫〔鷲〕
旧〔舊〕

jyu

*车〔車〕
驹〔駒〕
鶋〔鶋〕
锔〔鋦〕

*举〔舉〕	颏〔頦〕	**kwan**	腊〔臘〕	崂〔嶗〕	房〔曆〕
岨〔齟〕	轲〔軻〕		镴〔鑞〕	痨〔癆〕	枥〔櫪〕
榉〔櫸〕	钶〔鈳〕	宽〔寬〕		铹〔鐒〕	苈〔藶〕
讵〔詎〕	颗〔顆〕	髋〔髖〕	**lai**	铑〔铑〕	呖〔嚦〕
惧〔懼〕	*壳〔殼〕			涝〔澇〕	疬〔癧〕
飓〔颶〕	绰〔綽〕	**kwang**	*来〔來〕	唠〔嘮〕	枥〔櫪〕
婴〔嬰〕	克〔剋〕		涞〔淶〕	耢〔耮〕	砺〔礪〕
屦〔屨〕	课〔課〕	绠〔緱〕	莱〔萊〕		蛎〔蠣〕
据〔據〕	骒〔騍〕	绫〔綾〕	崃〔崍〕	**le**	栎〔櫟〕
剧〔劇〕	锞〔錁〕	龄〔齡〕	铼〔錸〕		轹〔轢〕
锯〔鋸〕		铃〔鈴〕	徕〔徠〕	鳓〔鰳〕	隶〔隸〕
	ken	鸰〔鴒〕	赖〔賴〕	*乐〔樂〕	
jywe		*灵〔靈〕	濑〔瀨〕	饹〔餎〕	
	恳〔懇〕	棂〔欞〕	癞〔癩〕		**jin**
觉〔覺〕	垦〔墾〕	领〔領〕	赖〔籟〕	**lei**	
镢〔钁〕			睐〔睞〕		辚〔轔〕
镘〔鏝〕	**keng**	**kwei**	费〔實〕	镭〔鐳〕	鳞〔鱗〕
谲〔譎〕				累〔纍〕	临〔臨〕
诀〔訣〕	铿〔鏗〕	窥〔窺〕	**lan**	缧〔縲〕	邻〔鄰〕
绝〔絕〕		亏〔虧〕		诔〔誄〕	蔺〔藺〕
	kou	岿〔巋〕	兰〔蘭〕	垒〔壘〕	瞒〔蹣〕
K		溃〔潰〕	栏〔欄〕	类〔類〕	赁〔賃〕
	抠〔摳〕	愦〔憒〕	拦〔攔〕		
kai	眍〔瞘〕	愤〔憒〕	阑〔闌〕	**li**	
		赎〔贖〕	澜〔瀾〕		
开〔開〕	**ku**	匮〔匱〕	谰〔讕〕	*离〔離〕	**lyan**
铜〔鐦〕		赍〔賫〕	斓〔斕〕	漓〔灘〕	
恺〔愷〕	库〔庫〕	馈〔饋〕	镧〔鑭〕	篱〔籬〕	帘〔簾〕
垲〔塏〕	裤〔褲〕	赉〔賚〕	褴〔襤〕	缡〔縭〕	镰〔鐮〕
剀〔剴〕	绔〔絝〕		蓝〔藍〕	骊〔驪〕	联〔聯〕
铠〔鎧〕	誉〔譽〕	**kwo**	篮〔籃〕	鹂〔鸝〕	连〔連〕
凯〔凱〕			岚〔嵐〕	缢〔鱺〕	涟〔漣〕
闿〔闓〕	**kua**	鲲〔鯤〕	懒〔懶〕	礼〔禮〕	莲〔蓮〕
错〔鍇〕		锟〔錕〕	宽〔寬〕	逦〔邐〕	鲢〔鰱〕
忾〔愾〕	夸〔誇〕	壸〔壼〕	榄〔欖〕	里〔裏〕	琏〔璉〕
		阃〔閫〕	揽〔攬〕	锂〔鋰〕	奁〔奩〕
kan		困〔睏〕	缆〔纜〕	鲤〔鯉〕	怜〔憐〕
	kwai		烂〔爛〕	鳢〔鱧〕	敛〔斂〕
龛〔龕〕		**kwun**	滥〔濫〕	*丽〔麗〕	蔹〔蘞〕
槛〔檻〕	㧟〔擓〕			俪〔儷〕	脸〔臉〕
	*会〔會〕	阘〔闊〕	**lang**	郦〔酈〕	恋〔戀〕
kang	浍〔澮〕	扩〔擴〕		厉〔厲〕	链〔鏈〕
	哙〔噲〕		锒〔鋃〕	励〔勵〕	炼〔煉〕
钪〔鈧〕	郐〔鄶〕	**L**	阆〔閬〕	砾〔礫〕	练〔練〕
	侩〔儈〕			*历〔歷〕	潋〔瀲〕
kau	脍〔膾〕	**la**	**lau**	〔曆〕	殓〔殮〕
	绘〔繪〕			沥〔瀝〕	裣〔襝〕
铐〔銬〕	狯〔獪〕	蜡〔蠟〕	捞〔撈〕	坜〔壢〕	莶〔薟〕
	块〔塊〕		劳〔勞〕	疬〔癧〕	裢〔褳〕
ke					

ling

鲮〔鯪〕
绫〔綾〕
龄〔齡〕
铃〔鈴〕
鸰〔鴒〕
*灵〔靈〕
棂〔欞〕
领〔領〕

lou

䁖〔瞜〕
*娄〔婁〕
偻〔僂〕
喽〔嘍〕
楼〔樓〕
溇〔漊〕
蒌〔蔞〕
髅〔髏〕
蝼〔螻〕
搂〔摟〕
嵝〔嶁〕
篓〔簍〕
瘘〔瘻〕
镂〔鏤〕

lu

噜〔嚕〕
庐〔廬〕
炉〔爐〕
芦〔蘆〕
*卢〔盧〕
泸〔瀘〕
垆〔壚〕
栌〔櫨〕
颅〔顱〕
鸬〔鸕〕
胪〔臚〕
舻〔艫〕
鲈〔鱸〕
*卤〔鹵〕
〔滷〕
*虏〔虜〕
掳〔擄〕

鲁〔魯〕
橹〔櫓〕
镥〔鑥〕
辘〔轆〕
轳〔轤〕
赂〔賂〕
鹭〔鷺〕
陆〔陸〕
*录〔錄〕
箓〔籙〕
绿〔綠〕
垆〔壚〕
叠〔疊〕

lung;

*龙〔龍〕
泷〔瀧〕
珑〔瓏〕
聋〔聾〕
栊〔櫳〕
昽〔曨〕
笼〔籠〕
茏〔蘢〕
咙〔嚨〕
眬〔矓〕
胧〔朧〕
垄〔壟〕
拢〔攏〕
陇〔隴〕

luan

娈〔孌〕
栾〔欒〕
滦〔灤〕
峦〔巒〕
脔〔臠〕
鸾〔鸞〕
銮〔鑾〕
挛〔攣〕
孪〔孿〕
乱〔亂〕

lwo

骡〔騾〕
胴〔腡〕
*罗〔羅〕

〔囉〕
逻〔邏〕
萝〔蘿〕
锣〔鑼〕
箩〔籮〕
椤〔欏〕
猡〔玀〕
荦〔犖〕
泺〔濼〕
骆〔駱〕
络〔絡〕

lwun

抡〔掄〕
*仑〔侖〕
沦〔淪〕
轮〔輪〕
囵〔圇〕
纶〔綸〕
伦〔倫〕
论〔論〕

lya

俩〔倆〕

lyan

帘〔簾〕
镰〔鐮〕
联〔聯〕
连〔連〕
涟〔漣〕
莲〔蓮〕
鲢〔鰱〕
琏〔璉〕
奁〔奩〕
怜〔憐〕
敛〔斂〕
蔹〔蘞〕
脸〔臉〕
恋〔戀〕
链〔鏈〕
炼〔煉〕
练〔練〕
潋〔瀲〕
殓〔殮〕
裣〔襝〕

裢〔褳〕

lyang

粮〔糧〕
*两〔兩〕
俩〔倆〕
啢〔唡〕
魉〔魎〕
谅〔諒〕
辆〔輛〕

lyau

鹩〔鷯〕
缭〔繚〕
疗〔療〕
辽〔遼〕
了〔瞭〕
钌〔釕〕
镣〔鐐〕

lye

猎〔獵〕
鬣〔鬛〕

lyou

飏〔飀〕
*刘〔劉〕
浏〔瀏〕
骝〔騮〕
镏〔鎦〕
绺〔綹〕
馏〔餾〕
鹨〔鷚〕
陆〔陸〕

lyu

驴〔驢〕
闾〔閭〕
榈〔櫚〕
屡〔屢〕
偻〔僂〕
褛〔褸〕
缕〔縷〕
铝〔鋁〕

*虑〔慮〕
滤〔濾〕
绿〔綠〕

M

m

呒〔嘸〕

ma

妈〔媽〕
*马〔馬〕
蚂〔螞〕
玛〔瑪〕
码〔碼〕
犸〔獁〕
骂〔罵〕
吗〔嗎〕
唛〔嘜〕

mai

*买〔買〕
*麦〔麥〕
*卖〔賣〕
迈〔邁〕
荬〔蕒〕

man

颟〔顢〕
馒〔饅〕
鳗〔鰻〕
蛮〔蠻〕
瞒〔瞞〕
满〔滿〕
螨〔蟎〕
谩〔謾〕
缦〔縵〕
镘〔鏝〕

mang

铓〔鋩〕

mau

锚〔錨〕
铆〔鉚〕
贸〔貿〕

me

么〔麼〕

mea

霉〔黴〕
镅〔鎇〕
鹛〔鶥〕
镁〔鎂〕

men

*门〔門〕
扪〔捫〕
钔〔鍆〕
懑〔懣〕
闷〔悶〕
焖〔燜〕
们〔們〕

meng

蒙〔矇〕
〔濛〕
〔懞〕
锰〔錳〕
梦〔夢〕

mi

迷〔謎〕
祢〔禰〕
弥〔彌〕
〔瀰〕

min

缗〔緡〕
闵〔閔〕
悯〔憫〕

闽[閩]
'黾[黽]
鬓[鬢]

ming

鸣[鳴]
铭[銘]

mou

谋[謀]
缪[繆]

mu

亩[畝]
钼[鉬]

mwo

谟[謨]
馍[饃]
蓦[驀]

myan

绵[綿]
渑[澠]
缅[緬]
面[麵]

myau

鹋[鶓]
缈[緲]
缪[繆]
庙[廟]

mye

灭[滅]
蔑[衊]

N

na

镎[錇]
钠[鈉]

纳[納]

nan

*难[難]

nang

馕[饢]

ne

讷[訥]

nei

馁[餒]

neng

泞[濘]

ni

鲵[鯢]
铌[鈮]
拟[擬]
腻[膩]

niang

酿[釀]

ning

*宁[寧]
柠[檸]
咛[嚀]
狞[獰]
拧[擰]
泞[濘]

nou

挠[撓]
蛲[蟯]
铙[鐃]
恼[惱]
脑[腦]
闹[鬧]

nung

*农[農]
浓[濃]
侬[儂]
脓[膿]
哝[噥]

nwo

傩[儺]
诺[諾]
锘[鍩]

nyan

鲇[鮎]
鲶[鯰]
辇[輦]
撵[攆]

nyau

*鸟[鳥]
茑[蔦]
袅[裊]

nye

*聂[聶]
颞[顳]
嗫[囁]
蹑[躡]
镊[鑷]
啮[嚙]
镍[鎳]

nyou

钮[鈕]
纽[紐]

nyu

钕[釹]

nywe

疟[瘧]

O

ou

*区[區]
讴[謳]
瓯[甌]
鸥[鷗]
殴[毆]
欧[歐]
呕[嘔]
沤[漚]
怄[慪]

P

pan

蹒[蹣]
盘[盤]

pang

螃[螃]
庞[龐]

pei

赔[賠]
锫[錇]
辔[轡]

pen

喷[噴]

peng

鹏[鵬]

pi

纰[紕]
罴[羆]
鲏[鮍]

铍[鈹]
辟[闢]
䴙[鸊]

pin

嫔[嬪]
频[頻]
颦[顰]
贫[貧]

ping

评[評]
苹[蘋]
鲆[鮃]
凭[憑]

pu

铺[鋪]
扑[撲]
仆[僕]
镤[鏷]
谱[譜]
镨[鐠]
朴[樸]

pwo

钋[釙]
颇[頗]
泼[潑]
钹[鈸]
钷[鉕]

pyan

骈[駢]
谝[諞]
骗[騙]

pyau

飘[飄]
缥[縹]
骠[驃]

Q

qin

*亲[親]
钦[欽]
嵚[嶔]
骎[駸]
寝[寢]
锓[鋟]
揿[搇]

que

悫[愨]
鹊[鵲]
阙[闕]
确[確]
阕[闋]

R

rang

让[讓]

rau

桡[橈]
荛[蕘]
饶[饒]
娆[嬈]
扰[擾]
绕[繞]

re

热[熱]

ren

认[認]
任[紝]
纴[紝]
纫[紉]
韧[韌]
紉[紉]

ru 铷〔銣〕 颥〔顬〕 缛〔縟〕 **rung** 荣〔榮〕 蝾〔蠑〕 嵘〔嶸〕 绒〔絨〕 **rwan** 软〔軟〕 **rwei** 锐〔銳〕 **rwun** 闰〔閏〕 润〔潤〕 **S_** **sa** 洒〔灑〕 飒〔颯〕 萨〔薩〕 **sai** 鳃〔鰓〕 赛〔賽〕 **san** 铩〔鎩〕 馓〔饊〕 伞〔傘〕 **sang** 丧〔喪〕 颡〔顙〕 **sau** 骚〔騷〕	缫〔繅〕 扫〔掃〕 **se** 涩〔澀〕 *啬〔嗇〕 穑〔穡〕 铯〔銫〕 **sha** 鲨〔鯊〕 纱〔紗〕 *杀〔殺〕 铩〔鎩〕 **shai** 筛〔篩〕 晒〔曬〕 **shan** 钐〔釤〕 陕〔陝〕 闪〔閃〕 镨〔鐥〕 鳝〔鱔〕 缮〔繕〕 掸〔撣〕 骟〔騸〕 锏〔鐧〕 禅〔禪〕 讪〔訕〕 赡〔贍〕 **shang** 殇〔殤〕 觞〔觴〕 伤〔傷〕 赏〔賞〕 **shau** 烧〔燒〕 绍〔紹〕 **she**	赊〔賒〕 舍〔捨〕 设〔設〕 滠〔灄〕 慑〔懾〕 摄〔攝〕 厍〔厙〕 **shei** 谁〔誰〕 **shen** 绅〔紳〕 *参〔參〕 椮〔槮〕 *审〔審〕 谂〔諗〕 婶〔嬸〕 沈〔瀋〕 谂〔諗〕 肾〔腎〕 渗〔滲〕 掺〔摻〕 **sheng** 声〔聲〕 渑〔澠〕 绳〔繩〕 胜〔勝〕 *圣〔聖〕 **shou** 兽〔獸〕 *寿〔壽〕 绶〔綬〕 **shr** 湿〔濕〕 诗〔詩〕 *师〔師〕 浉〔溮〕 狮〔獅〕 鸤〔鳲〕 实〔實〕 埘〔塒〕 鲥〔鰣〕	识〔識〕 *时〔時〕 蚀〔蝕〕 驶〔駛〕 铈〔鈰〕 视〔視〕 谥〔謚〕 试〔試〕 轼〔軾〕 势〔勢〕 莳〔蒔〕 贳〔貰〕 释〔釋〕 饰〔飾〕 适〔適〕 **shu** 枢〔樞〕 摅〔攄〕 输〔輸〕 纾〔紓〕 书〔書〕 赎〔贖〕 *属〔屬〕 数〔數〕 树〔樹〕 术〔術〕 竖〔豎〕 **shwai** 帅〔帥〕 **shwan** 闩〔閂〕 **shwang** *双〔雙〕 泷〔瀧〕 **shwei** 谁〔誰〕 **shwo** 说〔說〕 硕〔碩〕 烁〔爍〕 铄〔鑠〕	**shwun** 顺〔順〕 **sou** 馊〔餿〕 锼〔鎪〕 飕〔颼〕 薮〔藪〕 擞〔擻〕 **su** 苏〔蘇〕 稣〔穌〕 谡〔謖〕 诉〔訴〕 *肃〔肅〕 **sung** 松〔鬆〕 怂〔慫〕 耸〔聳〕 拟〔擬〕 讼〔訟〕 颂〔頌〕 诵〔誦〕 **swo** 缩〔縮〕 琐〔瑣〕 唢〔嗩〕 锁〔鎖〕 苏〔嗦〕 **swei** 虽〔雖〕 随〔隨〕 绥〔綏〕 岁〔歲〕 谇〔誶〕 **swun** *孙〔孫〕 荪〔蓀〕 狲〔猻〕 损〔損〕 **sya**	虾〔蝦〕 辖〔轄〕 硖〔硤〕 峡〔峽〕 侠〔俠〕 狭〔狹〕 吓〔嚇〕 **syau** 鲜〔鮮〕 纤〔纖〕 跹〔躚〕 锨〔鍁〕 莶〔薟〕 贤〔賢〕 咸〔鹹〕 衔〔銜〕 挦〔撏〕 闲〔閑〕 鹇〔鷴〕 娴〔嫻〕 痫〔癇〕 藓〔蘚〕 蚬〔蜆〕 显〔顯〕 险〔險〕 猃〔獫〕 铣〔銑〕 *献〔獻〕 线〔線〕 现〔現〕 苋〔莧〕 岘〔峴〕 县〔縣〕 宪〔憲〕 馅〔餡〕 **syang** 骧〔驤〕 镶〔鑲〕 *乡〔鄉〕 芗〔薌〕 缃〔緗〕 详〔詳〕 鲞〔鯗〕 响〔響〕 饷〔餉〕

飨〔饗〕	戏〔戲〕	讻〔詾〕	坛〔壇〕	**tou**	**tyun**
向〔嚮〕	饩〔餼〕	词〔詞〕	〔罎〕		
象〔像〕			谭〔譚〕	钯〔鈀〕	*条〔條〕
项〔項〕	**syin**	**sywan**	县〔曇〕	铊〔鉈〕	鲦〔鰷〕
			弹〔彈〕	驼〔駝〕	龆〔齠〕
syau	锌〔鋅〕	轩〔軒〕	钽〔鉭〕	驮〔馱〕	调〔調〕
	诉〔訴〕	谖〔諼〕	叹〔嘆〕	鼍〔鼉〕	粜〔糶〕
哓〔膮〕	衅〔釁〕	暑〔縣〕		椭〔橢〕	
哓〔曉〕		选〔選〕	**tang**	拼〔攤〕	**tye**
销〔銷〕	**sying**	癣〔癬〕		箨〔籜〕	
绡〔綃〕		旋〔鏇〕	镗〔鏜〕		贴〔貼〕
嚣〔囂〕	兴〔興〕	铉〔鉉〕	汤〔湯〕	**tu**	铁〔鐵〕
枭〔梟〕	荥〔滎〕	绚〔絢〕	傥〔儻〕		
骁〔驍〕	钘〔釾〕		镗〔鏜〕	图〔圖〕	**W**
萧〔蕭〕	铏〔鉶〕	**sywe**	烫〔燙〕	涂〔塗〕	
潇〔瀟〕	陉〔陘〕			钍〔釷〕	**wa**
蟏〔蠨〕	饧〔餳〕	学〔學〕	**tau**		
箫〔簫〕		峃〔嶨〕		**tung**	娲〔媧〕
哓〔嘵〕	**syou**	鳕〔鱈〕	涛〔濤〕		洼〔窪〕
啸〔嘯〕		谑〔謔〕	韬〔韜〕	铜〔銅〕	袜〔襪〕
	馐〔饈〕		绦〔縧〕	鲖〔鮦〕	
sye	鸺〔鵂〕	**T**	焘〔燾〕	统〔統〕	**wai**
	绣〔繡〕		讨〔討〕	恸〔慟〕	
颉〔頡〕	锈〔銹〕	**ta**			呙〔喎〕
撷〔擷〕			**te**	**twan**	
缬〔纈〕	**syu**	铊〔鉈〕			**wan**
协〔協〕		鳎〔鰨〕	铽〔鋱〕	抟〔摶〕	
挟〔挾〕	须〔須〕	獭〔獺〕		团〔團〕	弯〔彎〕
胁〔脅〕	〔鬚〕	达〔達〕	**teng**	〔糰〕	湾〔灣〕
谐〔諧〕	谞〔諝〕	挞〔撻〕	誊〔謄〕		纨〔紈〕
*写〔寫〕	许〔許〕	闼〔闥〕	腾〔騰〕	**twei**	顽〔頑〕
亵〔褻〕	诩〔詡〕		滕〔縢〕		绾〔綰〕
泻〔瀉〕	顼〔頊〕	**tai**		颓〔頹〕	*万〔萬〕
绁〔紲〕	续〔續〕		**ti**		
谢〔謝〕	绪〔緒〕	台〔臺〕		**two**	**wang**
		〔檯〕	锑〔銻〕		
syi	**syun**	〔颱〕	䴘〔鷉〕	饦〔飥〕	网〔網〕
		骀〔駘〕	鹈〔鵜〕	驼〔駝〕	辋〔輞〕
牺〔犧〕	勋〔勳〕	鲐〔鮐〕	绨〔綈〕	铊〔鉈〕	
饻〔餏〕	埙〔塤〕	态〔態〕	缇〔緹〕	驮〔馱〕	**wei**
锡〔錫〕	驯〔馴〕	钛〔鈦〕	题〔題〕	鼍〔鼉〕	
袭〔襲〕	询〔詢〕		体〔體〕	椭〔橢〕	*为〔為〕
觋〔覡〕	*寻〔尋〕	**tan**		箨〔籜〕	维〔維〕
习〔習〕	浔〔潯〕		**ting**	箨〔籜〕	潍〔濰〕
镭〔鎘〕	鲟〔鱘〕	滩〔灘〕			*韦〔韋〕
玺〔璽〕	训〔訓〕	瘫〔癱〕	厅〔廳〕	**twun**	违〔違〕
铣〔銑〕	讯〔訊〕	摊〔攤〕	烃〔烴〕		围〔圍〕
系〔係〕	逊〔遜〕	贪〔貪〕	听〔聽〕	饨〔飩〕	涠〔潿〕
〔繫〕		谈〔談〕	颋〔頲〕		帏〔幃〕
细〔細〕	**syung**		铤〔鋌〕	**tyan**	闱〔闈〕
阋〔鬩〕				阗〔闐〕	伪〔偽〕

鲔〔鮪〕
诿〔諉〕
炜〔煒〕
玮〔瑋〕
苇〔葦〕
趄〔䠀〕
伟〔偉〕
纬〔緯〕
硙〔磑〕
谓〔謂〕
卫〔衛〕

wen

鳁〔鰛〕
纹〔紋〕
闻〔聞〕
稳〔穩〕
问〔問〕

wo

涡〔渦〕
窝〔窩〕
莴〔萵〕
蜗〔蝸〕
挝〔撾〕
龌〔齷〕

wu

诬〔誣〕
*乌〔烏〕
呜〔嗚〕
钨〔鎢〕
邬〔鄔〕
*无〔無〕
芜〔蕪〕
怃〔憮〕
庑〔廡〕
鹉〔鵡〕
坞〔塢〕
务〔務〕
雾〔霧〕
骛〔騖〕
鹜〔鶩〕
误〔誤〕

Y

ya

压〔壓〕
鸦〔鴉〕
鸭〔鴨〕
钘〔釾〕
哑〔啞〕
氩〔氬〕
*亚〔亞〕
垭〔埡〕
挜〔掗〕
娅〔婭〕
讶〔訝〕
轧〔軋〕

yan

阏〔閼〕
阉〔閹〕
恹〔懨〕
颜〔顏〕
盐〔鹽〕
*严〔嚴〕
阎〔閻〕
厣〔厴〕
魇〔魘〕
俨〔儼〕
奁〔奩〕
谚〔諺〕
谳〔讞〕
*厌〔厭〕
餍〔饜〕
赝〔贋〕
艳〔艷〕
滟〔灩〕
漱〔灧〕
砚〔硯〕
眈〔眕〕
酽〔釅〕
验〔驗〕

yang

鸯〔鴦〕
炀〔煬〕
疡〔瘍〕
炀〔煬〕

杨〔楊〕
扬〔揚〕
旸〔暘〕
钖〔鍚〕
阳〔陽〕
痒〔癢〕
养〔養〕
样〔樣〕

yau

*尧〔堯〕
峣〔嶢〕
谣〔謠〕
铫〔銚〕
轺〔軺〕
疟〔瘧〕
鹞〔鷂〕
钥〔鑰〕
药〔藥〕

ye

爷〔爺〕
靥〔靨〕
*页〔頁〕
烨〔燁〕
晔〔曄〕
*业〔業〕
邺〔鄴〕
叶〔葉〕
谒〔謁〕

yi

铱〔銥〕
医〔醫〕
鹥〔鷖〕
祎〔禕〕
颐〔頤〕
仪〔儀〕
诒〔詒〕
贻〔貽〕
饴〔飴〕
蚁〔蟻〕
钇〔釔〕
谊〔誼〕
瘗〔瘞〕
镒〔鎰〕

缢〔縊〕
勚〔勩〕
怿〔懌〕
译〔譯〕
驿〔驛〕
峄〔嶧〕
绎〔繹〕
*义〔義〕
议〔議〕
轶〔軼〕
*艺〔藝〕
呓〔囈〕
亿〔億〕
忆〔憶〕
诣〔詣〕
镱〔鐿〕

yin

铟〔銦〕
*阴〔陰〕
荫〔蔭〕
龈〔齦〕
银〔銀〕
饮〔飲〕
*隐〔隱〕
瘾〔癮〕
鲥〔鰤〕

ying

应〔應〕
鹰〔鷹〕
莺〔鶯〕
罂〔罌〕
婴〔嬰〕
璎〔瓔〕
撄〔攖〕
嘤〔嚶〕
鹦〔鸚〕
缨〔纓〕
荧〔熒〕
莹〔瑩〕
茔〔塋〕
萤〔螢〕
萦〔縈〕
营〔營〕
赢〔贏〕
蝇〔蠅〕

瘿〔癭〕
颍〔潁〕
颖〔穎〕

you

忧〔憂〕
优〔優〕
鱿〔魷〕
*犹〔猶〕
莸〔蕕〕
铀〔鈾〕
邮〔郵〕
铕〔銪〕
诱〔誘〕

yu

纡〔紆〕
舆〔輿〕
欤〔歟〕
余〔餘〕
觎〔覦〕
谀〔諛〕
*鱼〔魚〕
渔〔漁〕
歔〔歔〕
卹〔卹〕
*与〔與〕
语〔語〕
龉〔齬〕
伛〔傴〕
屿〔嶼〕
誉〔譽〕
钰〔鈺〕
吁〔籲〕
御〔禦〕
驭〔馭〕
阈〔閾〕
妪〔嫗〕
郁〔鬱〕
谕〔諭〕
鹆〔鵒〕
饫〔飫〕
狱〔獄〕
预〔預〕
滪〔澦〕
蓣〔蕷〕
鹬〔鷸〕

yuan

渊〔淵〕
鸢〔鳶〕
鸳〔鴛〕
鼋〔黿〕
园〔園〕
辕〔轅〕
员〔員〕
圆〔圓〕
缘〔緣〕
橼〔櫞〕
远〔遠〕
愿〔願〕

yun

*云〔雲〕
芸〔蕓〕
纭〔紜〕
涢〔溳〕
郧〔鄖〕
殒〔殞〕
陨〔隕〕
恽〔惲〕
晕〔暈〕
郓〔鄆〕
运〔運〕
酝〔醞〕
韫〔韞〕
缊〔縕〕
蕴〔蘊〕

yung

痈〔癰〕
拥〔擁〕
佣〔傭〕
镛〔鏞〕
鳙〔鱅〕
颙〔顒〕
踊〔踴〕

ywe

约〔約〕
哕〔噦〕
阅〔閱〕
钺〔鉞〕
跃〔躍〕
*乐〔樂〕
钥〔鑰〕

ywo

哟〔喲〕

NAME OF THE MONTHS

1. 正 月； 端月；元月；青陽；二陽；孟陽；睠玉。
2. 二 月； 杏月；如月；中和；花朝。
3. 三 月； 桃月；上巳；寒食。
4. 四 月； 槐月；清和；麥秋。
5. 五 月； 蒲月；榴月；天中；滿月；端陽。
6. 六 月； 荷月；伏月；天貺。
7. 七 月； 桐月；巧月；中元；蘭月。
8. 八 月； 桂月；中秋。
9. 九 月； 菊月；重陽；菊秋。
10. 十 月； 梅月；陽春；小陽春。
11. 十一月； 冬月；仲冬月；長至；葭月。
12. 十二月； 臘月；嘉平；清祀。

THE 24 SOLAR TERMS

Approximate
dates.

February	5	立	春	Spring begins.
,,	19	雨	水	The rains.
March	5	驚	蟄	Insects awaken.
,,	02	春	分	Vernal Equinox.
April	5	清	明	Clear and bright
,,	20	穀	雨	Grain rain.
May	5	立	夏	Summer begins.
,,	21	小	滿	Grain buds.
June	6	芒	種	Grain in ear.
,,	21	夏	至	Summer Solstice.

July	7	小 暑	Slight heat.
,,	23	大 暑	Great heat.
August	7	立 秋	Autumn begins.
,,	23	處 暑	Stopping of heat.
September	8	白 露	White dews.
,,	23	秋 分	Autumnal Equinox.
October	8	寒 露	Cold dews.
,,	23	霜 降	Hoar frost falls.
November	7	立 冬	Winter begins,
,,	22	小 雪	Light snow.
December	7	大 雪	Heavy snow.
,,	21	冬 至	Winter Solstice.
January	6	小 寒	Slight cold.
,,	21	大 寒	Great cold.

SUMMARY OF THE CHINESE DYNASTIES

The Five Rulers.	五帝	B. C.	2852	9	Rulers
Hsia.	夏		2205	17	,,
Shang or Yin	商 or 殷		1766	28	,,
Chou	周		1122	34	,,
Ch'in	秦		255	5	,,
Han	漢，前漢，西漢		206	14	,,
Later Han	後漢，東漢	A. D.	25	12	,,
The Three Kingdoms	三國				
Minor Han	蜀漢		221	2	,,
Wei	魏		220	5	,,
Wu	吳		229	4	,,
Western Chin	西晉		265	4	,,

Eastern Chin	東晉	A,D. 317	11	Rulers
Division between N. & S.	南北朝			
Liu Sung	劉宋	499	9	,,
Ch'i	齊	479	7	,,
Liang	梁	502	6	,,
Ch'en	陳	557	5	,,
Northern Wei	北魏	286	15	,,
Western Wei	西魏	535	3	,,
Eastern Wei	東魏	534	1	,,
Northern Ch'i	北齊	550	7	,,
Northern Chou	北周	557	5	,,
Sui	隋	589	4	,,
T'ang	唐	618	??	,,
The Five Dynasties	五代			
Posterior Liang	後梁	907	2	,,
Posterior T'ang	後唐	923	4	,,
Posterior Chin	後晉	936	2	,,
Posterior Han	後漢	947	2	,,
Posterior Chou	後周	951	3	,,
Sung	宋，北宋	960	9	,,
Southern Sung	南宋	1127	9	..
Yuan or Mongol	元	1280	9	,,
Ming	明	1368	17	,,
Ching or Manchu	清	1644	10	,,
The Republic	中華民國	1912		

THE HUNDRED FAMILY SURNAMES

This is a misnomer, actually there are about 800 Chinese family names which have been derived from the hundred original ones. The author has reduced this number to just over hundred common names.

Arranged Alphabetically in Romanised Mandarin

Chāng	Jèung	張	Hán	HòHn	韓	Kūo	Gok	郭
Chāng	Jèung	章	Háo	Kok	郝	Lài	LaaiH	頓
Chào	JiuH	趙	Hè	HòH	何	Léi	Lèuih	雷
Chén	ChàHn	陳	Hè	HoH	賀	Lí	LàiH	黎
Chèng	JeHng	鄭	Hsìang	HoHng	項	Lí	LéiH	李
Ch'éng	ChìHng	程	Hsǐao	Sìu	蕭	Líang	LèuHng	梁
Chǐa	Gá	賈	Hsìeh	JeH	謝	Lìao	LìuH	廖
Chiāng	Gòng	江	Hsíen	Sín	冼	Lín	LàHm	林
Chǐang	Gèung	姜	Hsíung	HùHng	熊	Líng	LìHng	凌
Chǐang	Jéung	蔣	Hsú	ChèuiH	徐	Líu	LàuH	劉
Chǐen	Gáan	簡	Hsǔ	Héui	許	Lú	LòuH	盧
Ch'íen	ChìHn	錢	Hsùeh	Sit	薛	Lǔ	LóuH	魯
Ch'íh	ChìH	池	Hú	WùH	胡	Lù	LuHk	陸
Chǐn	Gàm	金	Húang	WòHng	黃	Lǚ	LéuiH	呂
Ch'ín	ChèuHn	秦	Húng	HùHng	洪	Lún	LèuHn	倫
Ch'iu	Yàu	邱	Hùo	Fok	霍	Lúng	LùHng	龍
Chōu	Jàu	周	ì(Yi)	YiHk	易	Lúo	LòH	羅
Chū	Jyù	朱	Jèn	YaHm	任	Mǎ	MáH	馬
Ch'ü	Wat	屈	Jǔan	Yún	阮	Mài	MaHk	麥
Chūng	Jùng	鍾	K'ang	Hòng	康	Máo	MòuH	毛
Chúo	Cheuk	卓	Kāo	Gòu	高	Méi	MùiH	梅
Fàn	FaaHn	范	Kú	Guk	谷	Mèng	MaaHng	孟
Fāng	Fòng	方	Kù	Gu	顧	Ōu	Ngàu	歐
Fèi	Fai	費	Kūan	Gwàan	關	P'ān	Pùn	潘
Féng	FùHng	馮	K'ùang	Kong	鄺	P'áng	PòHng	龐
Fù	Fu	傅	K'ǔng	Húng	孔	Pāo	Bàau	包

Pāo	Bàau	鮑	Tèng	DaHng	鄧	Wén	MàHn	文
Pèi	Bui	貝	Tí	DiHk	狄	Wēng	Ung	翁
P'éng	PàHng	彭	Tiao	Dìu	刁	Wū	Wù	鄔
Pĭ	Bāt	畢	T'íen	TìHn	田	Mú	Ngh	吳
P'í	PeiH	皮	Tĭng	Ding	丁	Mŭ	NgII	伍
Pŭ	Būk	卜	Tsài	Choi'	蔡	Mŭ	MóuH	武
Pù	Bou	布	Ts'áo	ChòuH	曹	Yáng	YèuHng	楊
Shā	Sà	沙	Ts'én	SàHm	岑	Yáo	YiuH	姚
Shào	SiuH	邵	Tsēng	Jàng	曾	Yèh	YiHp	葉
Shé	SèH	余	Tsōu	Jàu	鄒	Yĭn	WaHn	尹
Shēn	Sàn	申	Ts'ūi	Chèui	崔	Yú	YàuH	游
Shĕn	Sám	沈	Tù	DouH	杜	Yŭ	Yù	于
Shĭh	Sì	施	T'ú	TòuH	屠	Yù	YuH	俞
Shíh	SeHk	石	Tùan	DyuHn	段	Yú	YùH	余
Shĭh	Sí	史	Tŭng	Dúng	董	Yŭan	YùHn	袁
Sū	Sòu	蘇	T'úng	TùHng	童	Yüèh	NgoHk	岳
Sūn	Syùn	孫	Wàn	MaaHn	萬	Yüèh	LoHk	樂
Sùng	Sung	宋	Wāng	Wòng	汪	Chūké	Jyùgok	諸葛
Tài	Daai	戴	Wáng	WòHng	王	Ōuyáng	NgàuyèuHng	歐陽
T'án	TàaHm	譚	Wĕi	WáiH	韋	Ssūmă	SìmáH	司馬
T'āng	Tòng	湯	Wèi	WaiH	衛	Ssūtú	SìtòuH	司徒
T'áng	TòHng	唐	Wèi	NgaiH	魏	Tūngfāng	Dùngfòng	東方
T'áo	TòuH	陶	Wēn	Wàn	溫			

Chinese Family Tree and Relationships

親屬的稱呼與關係一覽表

第一：父系

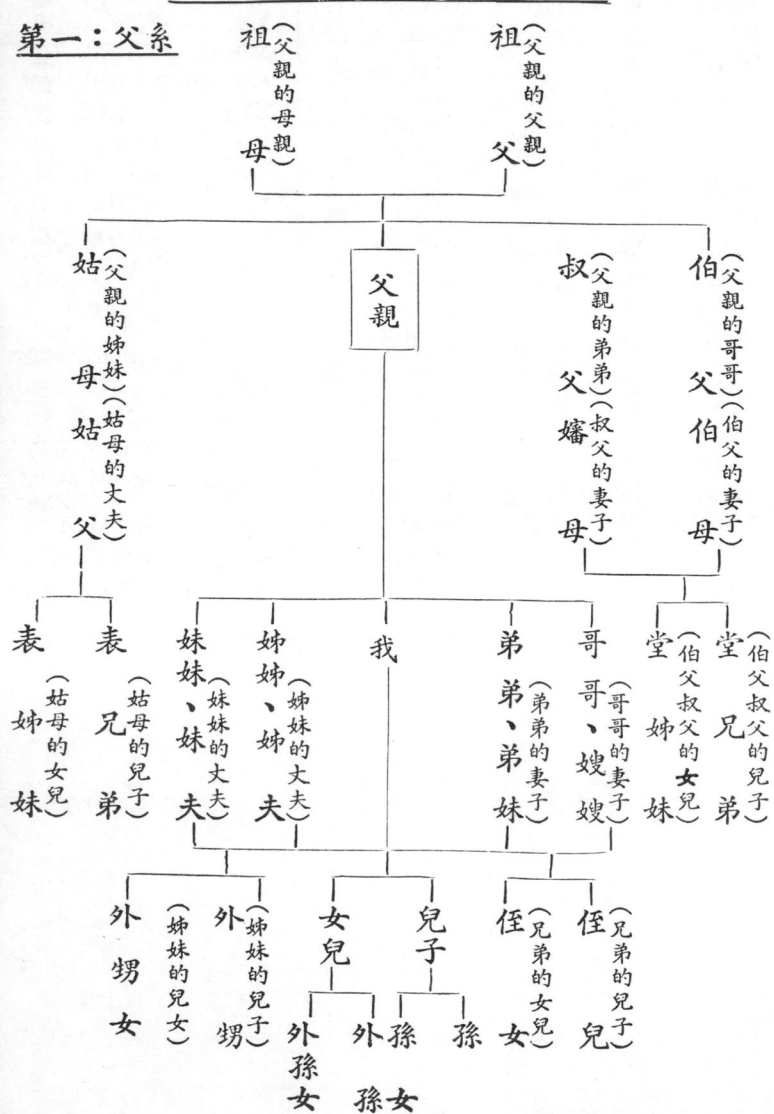

第二：母系

第三：夫妻系

（甲）夫系

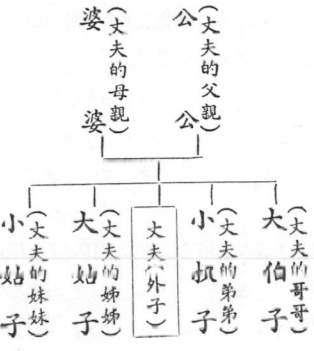

（乙）妻系

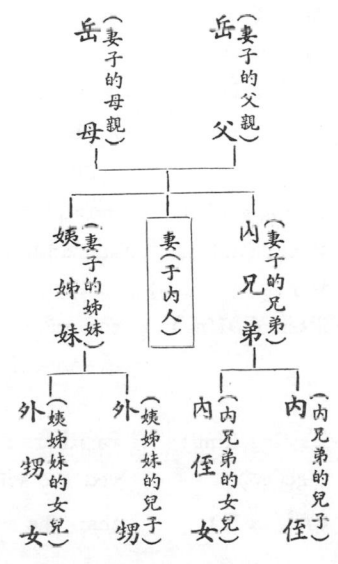

Kinship Terms

Chinese kinship terms ("father, uncle, cousin" and the like) are confusing to speakers of English because in certain cases relative age of speaker and person referred to, or of intermediaries in the relationship, is a factor. Chinese divides the generations of one's family into three categories (輩分 bèifèn, buifaHn), those that preced one's own generation (長輩 jǎngbèi, jéungbui), one's own generation (平輩 píngbèi, pìHngbui), and the succeeding generations. (晚輩 wǎnbèi, máaHnbui).

父fù(fuH)
親chǐn(chàn)
爸bā(bā)
爹dyē(dē)
家jyā(gà)
嚴yán(yìHm)
先syān(sìn)
令lìng(liHng)
尊dzwūn(jyùn)
爺yé(yèH)
母mǔ(móuH)
媽mā(mā)
娘nyáng(nèuHng)
慈tsź(chìH)
雙shwāng(sèung)
堂táng(tòHng)

Parents: "Father" is fùchin (fuHchàn), child-words like "bàba (bàHbā)" are bàba (bàHbā) and dyē (dē), one refers to his own father politely as jyāfù (gàfuH), or jyāyán (gà-yìHm), or, if he is deceased syānfù (sìnfuH) or syānyán (sìnyìHm), the father of the person addressed is politely referred to as lǎutàiyé (lóuHtaaiyèH) or lìngdzwūn (liHngjyùn), "mother" is mǔchin (móuHchàn), child words are mā, māma (màHmā), and nyáng (nèuHng), one refers to his own mother politely as jyāmǔ (gàmóuH), or jyātsź (gàchìH); or, if she is deceased, syānmǔ (sìnmóuH or syāntsz (sìnchìH); the mother of the person addressed is politely referred to as lǎutàitai (lóuHtáai), or lìngtáng (liHngtòHng), the collective terms for parents are fùmǔ (fuHmóuH) and (literary) shwāngchin (sèungchàn)

兄syūng(hìng)
哥gē(gō)
弟dì(daiH)

Brothers and Sister; The fundamental elements involved are syūng (hìng) or gē (gō) for "brother older than the speaker," dì (daiH) for "brother younger

姊 jyě (jé)
妹 mèi (múi)
舍 shè (se)

than the speaker." In referring to a brother or sister one says gēge (gòHgō), dìdi (daiHdái), jyějye (jèHjē) and mèimei (mùiHmúi). In referring politely to one's own brother or sister, when addressing someone outside the family, one may say rather jyāsyūng (gàhìng), shèdì (sedaiH), jyājyě (gājē), and shèmèi (semúi). In referring politely to the brother or sister of the one spoken to, one says often lìngsyūng (liHnghìng), lìngdì (liHngdaiH), lìngjyě (liHngjé), and lìngmèi (liHngmúi), collective terms are dìsyūng (daiHhìng) "brothers" and jyěmèi (jímuiH) "sisters."

The children in a family are sometimes designated serially: dùgō (daaiHgō), èrgē (yiHgū), sāngē (sāamgō) and so on for the older brothers, syǎudì (síudaiH or sailóu) for the youngest brother (or for oneself); dàjyě (daaiHgājē), èrjyě (yiHgājē) and so on for sisters; syǎumèi (saimúi) for the youngest little sister; lǎudà (lóuHdaaiH), lauèr (lóuHyiH), lausān (lóuHsāam) and so on, either naming just the males in order or naming all the children, male and female, in order. Such terms are used generally within the family. (dà' daaiH "big", syǎu, síu or sai "small", lǎu, lóuH "old".)

兒 ér (yìH)
女 nyü (néuiH)
郎 láng (lòHng)
愛 ài (oi)

Children: Parents address their children by name, and refer to them familiarly as wǒmen (ngóHdeiH) lǎudà (lóuH-daaiH) "our oldest son", wǒmen (ngóHdeiH) lǎuèr (lóuHyiH) "our second oldest son" and so on. Very formally, as in correspondence, a parent may refer to sons simply as ér (jái), to daughters simply as nyü (néui). The children of the person addressed are formally referred to as lìngláng(liHnglóng) "your son" and lìngài(liHngoi) "your daughter".

丈jàng(jeuHng)
夫fū(fù)
妻chǐ(chài)
婦fù(fúH)

Husband and Wife: The general rather formal terms are jàngfu(jeuHngfù) and chǐdz(chàijí or taaitáai). At Present reference is often made to any husband or wife with the terms syānsheng (sìnsàang)"mister,sir", and tàitai (taaitáai) "Mrs. madam". An older term which one used in referring to one's own husband wáidz (ngoiHjí) and wife nèirén (noiHyàHn) when speaking to someone outside the family circle. A husband and wife are collectively referred to as fūfù (fùfúH), or fūchǐlyǎ (fùchàiléuHnggo).

爺yé(yèH)
祖dzǔ(jóu)
奶nǎi(náaiH)
外wài(ngoiH)
曾dzēng(jàng)
高gāu(gòu)

Grandparents: Paternal grandfather is called yéye (a-yèH) or dzǔfù (jóufuH), paternal grandmother is called nǎinai (a-màH) or dzǔmǔ (jóumóuH). Maternal grandfather is wàigūng (a-gùng) or wàidzǔfù (ngoiHjóufuH), maternal grand mother is wàipwó (pòHpó) or wàidzǔmǔ (ngoiHjóumóuH). The terms lìng- (liHng-) "your," jyā- (gà-) " my " and syān- (sìn) "my" and syān-(sìn) "my deceased" may be prefixed to dzǔfù (jóufuH) and dzǔmǔ (jóumóuH). Greatgrand father (father's paternal grandfather) is dzēng dzǔfù(jàngjóufuH), and his father is gāudzǔfù (gòujóufuH), their wives are dzēngdzǔmǔ (jàngjóu-móuH), and his father is gāudzǔfù(gòujóufuH), their wives are dzēngdzǔmǔ(jàngjóumóuH) and gāudzǔmǔ (gòujóumóuH).

孫swūn(syūn)

Grandchildren: One's son's sons are swūndz(syūn);

重chúng(chùHng) one's son's daughter's sons are wàiswūn(ngoiHsyūn);.

玄sywán(yùHn) one's daughter's daughters are wàiswūnnyűér (ngoiHsyūnnéui) Greatgrandchildren through the male line are dzēngswun (jàngsyun) or chúngswūn (chùHngsyūn), their sons are sywánswīn (yùHnsyūn). Other greatgrandchildren than those through the male line are called "daughter's male-line grandchildren", "son's female-line grandchildren", and so on.

伯bwó(baak)

叔shū(sūk)

嬸shěn(sám)

姑gū(gū)

夫fū(fù)

舅jyòu(káuH)

姨yí(yï)

Uncles and Aunts: An older brother of one's father is called bwóbwo(a-baak)) or bwófù(baakfuH); if there are several, they are enumerated as dàbwóbwo (daaiHbaak), èrbwóbwo(yiHbaak), and so on Lǎubwó (lóuHbaak) "old uncle" is a term of address to any's father's male friend or the father of one's friend. An aunt who is the wife of one's father's older brother is called bwómǔ(baakmóuH); such aunts are likewise numbered, depending not on their own relative age but on the relative age of their husbands.

A younger brother of one's fathyr is called shūshu (a-sūk) or shūfù(sūkfuH), numbered as èrshū(yiHsūk) and so on.

An aunt who is the wife of one's father's younger brother is called shěnshen (a-sám) or shěnmū (sámmóuH), similarly numbered on the basis of the relative ages of their husband.

An aunt who is one's father's sister (any age) is called gūgu, gūmā (gūmā), or gūmǔ (gùmóuH), numbered dà-(daaiH-), èr(yiH), etc. An uncle who is the husband of such an aunt is called gūfū(gùjeuHng), numbered on the basis of their wives' relative ages, not their own.

An uncle who is one's mother's brother (any age) is called jyðujyou or jyðufù(káuHfú), numbered as are the others. The wife of such an uncle is called jyðumŭ (káHmmóuH), similarly numbered.

An aunt who is one's mother's sister (any age) is called yímŭ (yìHmóuH), with similar numbering; the husband of such an aunt is called yìHjéung).

侄jŕ(jaHt)
甥shēng(sāng)

Nephews and Nieces: Your father's brothers and sisters and your father's brother's wives, call you jŕer (jaHt) if you are male ("nephew"), jŕnyŭ(jaHtnéui) if you are female ("niece").

Your father's sister's husbands, however, will prefix those terms with wài—(ngoiH—).

Your mother's brothers and sister, and their wives and husbands, will call you wàishēng (ngoiHsāang) if you are male, wàishēngnyŭ (ngoiHsāangnéul) if you are female.

堂 táng(tòHng)
叔 shū(sūk)
伯bwó(baak)
表byău(bíu)

Cousins: The children of two brothers may call each other simply by the various terms for "brother" and "sister" (older and younger in each case). When necessary to specify that the relationship is that of cousins, not of brothers and sisters, the term táng-(tòHng-) or shūbwó (sūkbaak) is prefixed.

The children of two sisters or of a brother and sister, but of the same generation, call each other by the terms byăugē (bíugō) "male cousin older than oneself", byăudì(bíudái)"male cousin younger than oneself", byăujyĕ(bíujé) "female cousin older than oneself" byăumèi (bíumúi) "female cousin younger than oneself."

When talking about these cousins, gū- (gù-) is prefixed to specify the child of one's father's sister, and yí-(yĭ-) is prefixed to specify the child of one's mother's sister. Without one of these prefixes, the terms are assumed to refer to children of one's mother's brother.

岳ywè(ngoHk)
丈jàng(jeuHng)
公gūng(gūng)
婆pwó(pòH)
婿syù(sai)
媳)syí(sĭk)
婦fù(fúH)
嫂său(sóu)

伯bwó(baak)
聯襟lyánjǐn
(lìHnkàm)

In-laws: A man calls his father-in-law ywèfù(ngoHk-fuH), and refers to him when speaking to others as "Lăujàngrén (ngoiHfú)", he calls his mother-in-law ywèmŭ (ngoHkmóuH) and refers to her as jàngmŭnyáng (ngoiHmóuH). A woman calls her father-in-law bàba(bàHbā) and refers to him as gūnggung (lóuHyèH): she calls her mother-in-law māma(mùHmā)and refers to her as pwópwo(nàaiHnáai). Notice that a woman calls her husband's parents by the same names he uses.

A man or woman calls his or her sons-in-law and daughters-in-law by name, but refers to a son-in-law as nyŭsyù (néuiHsai) and a daughter-in-law as syífu (sĭkfúH or sànpóuH).

A sister-in-law who is the wife of an elder brother is called săudz or săusau (sóu or a-sóu) numbered dàsău(daaiHsóu), èrsău(yiHsóu), etc.

A sister-in-law who is the wife of a younger brother is called dìmèi(daiHmuiH).

A sister-in-law who is the older sister of one's wife is called dàyídz(yìHmā or yìHmōu); the younger sister of one's wife is syăuyídz(a-yĭ).

A brother-in-law who is the brother of one's wife is called by name or by the terms the wife uses, but the wife's older brother is referred to as nèisyūng (noiHhìng), her younger brother as nèidì (noiHdaiH)

A brother-in-law who is one's older sister's husband is referred to as lyánjìn(lìHnkàm) or, by number, dàyífū (daaiHyìHjéung), èryífū (yiHyìHjéung), etc. He is addressed by personal name.

A wife addresses her husband's brothers and sisters as he does, but older brothers of one's husband may be referred to as dàbāidz (daaiHbaak), and younger brothers as syăushūdz(a-sūk).

The Twelve Branches of Horary Characters

Branches			Corresponding Hours
	Characters	Romanizations	
1.	子	dź jí	11:00- 1:00 A. M.
2.	丑	chŏu cháu	1:00- 3:00 A. M.
3.	寅	yín yàHn	3:00- 5:00 A. M.
4.	卯	mău máu	5:00- 7:00 A. M.
5.	辰	chén sàHn	7:00- 9:00 A. M.
6.	巳	sź jiH	9:00-11:00 A. M.
7.	午	wŭ nǵH	11:00- 1:00 P. M.
8.	未	wèi meiH	1:00- 3:00 P. M.
9.	申	shēn sàn	3:00- 5:00 P. M.
10.	酉	yŏu yáuII	5:00- 7:00 P. M.
11.	戌	syù sēut	7:00- 9:00 P. M.
12.	亥	hài hoiH	9:00-11:00 P. M.

NUMERICAL LIST OF RADICALS

```
    10 20 30 40 50 60 70 80 90 100 110 120 130 140 150 160 170 180 190 200 210
        (3)

0    几 勹 口 宀 巾 彳 方 毋 廾 生  矛  系  肉  艸  谷  辛  阜  音  髟  麻  齊   0
    (1)          (4)              糸  月  廿  㞢      阝         (12)(15)

1    一 入 匕 囗 寸 干 心 旡 比 片  用  矢  缶  臣  虎  豆  辰  隶  頁  門  黃  齒  1
                 卜 旡                  隹                         (16)

2    丨 八 匚 土 小 幺 戈 日 毛 牙  田  石  网  自  虫  豕  辵  隹  風  韋  黍  龍  2
                                  皿冗          辶

3    丶 冂 匸 士 尢 广 戶 曰 氏 牛  疋  示  羊  至  血  豸  邑  雨  飛  高  黑  龜  3
              尣允              示礻          阝  韭             (17)

4    丿 冖 十 夂 尸 廴 手 月 气 犬  疒  内  羽  臼  行  貝  酉  青  食  鬼  黹  龠  4
                 扌   (5)犭                              (11)(13)

5    乙 冫 卜 勹 屮 廾 支 木 水 玄  癶  禾  老  舌  衣  赤  釆  非  首  魚  黽      5
                 氵水      耂      衤          (9)

6    亅 几 卩 夕 山 弋 攴 欠 火 玉  白  穴  而  舛  西  走  里  面  香  鳥  鼎      6
    (2)   日        攵   灬王          (,,)西 (8)      (10)

7    二 凵 厂 大 巛 弓 文 止 爪 瓜  皮  立  耒  舟  見  足  金  革  馬  鹵  鼓      7
              川巛      爪   (6)

8    亠 刀 厶 女 工 彐 斗 歹 父 瓦  皿  竹  耳  臣  角  身  長  韋  骨  鹿  鼠      8
    刂        彐互 歺                          镸             (14)

9    人 力 又 子 己 彡 斤 殳 爻 甘  目  米  聿  色  言  車  門  韭  髙  麥  鼻      9
    亻                     四

    9  19 29 39 49 59 69 79 89 99 109 119 129 139 149 159 169 179 189 199 209
```

ABBREVIATIONS

a. adjective
adv. adverb
Anat. Anatomy
Arch. Architecture
Arith. Arithmetic
Astron. Astronomy
Bib. Bible, Biblical
Biol. Biology
Budd. Buddhist
Chem. Chemistry, Chemical
conj. conjunction
Elec. Electricity
eXam. examination
f. femine, female
fig. figurative, figuratively
Geom. Geometry
govt. government
Gram. Grammar
int. interjection
Math. Mathematics
Mech. Mechanics
Med. Medicine, Medical
Mil. Military
Mus. Music
Myth. Mythology

n. noun
Nav. Naval
N. T. New Testament
O. T. Old Testament
opp. opposed, opposite
P. a. participial adjective
Parl. Parliament, Parliamentary
pert. pertaining
Peotyg. Photography
Phys. Physics, Physical
Plur. plural
P. p. past participle
prep. preposition
Pro. pronoun
Pros. Prosody
Prot. Protestant
Psyceol. Psychology
R, Cath. Roman Catholic
ref. refer
sing. singular
v. verb
v. aux. verb auxilliary
v. i. verb, intransitive
v. t. verb, transitive
w. c. water-closet